Barney Miller and the Files of the Ol' One-Two

Behind the Scenes of the Classic Sitcom

Otto Bruno

Barney Miller and the Files of the Ol' One-Two

© 2022 By Otto Bruno

All Rights Reserved.

No portion of this publication may be reproduced, stored, and/or copied electronically (except for academic use as a source), nor transmitted in any form or by any means without the prior written permission of the publisher and/or author.

Published in the United States of America by:

BearManor Media
1317 Edgewater Dr #110
Orlando FL 32804
bearmanormedia.com

Printed in the United States.

All photos used with permission.

Typesetting and layout by DataSmith Solutions

Cover by DataSmith Solutions

ISBN — 978-1-62933-858-3

For my mom, Adeline Agnello Bruno, and my dad, Otto Bruno, for making it all possible,

For the four D's of Four D Productions, Danny, Donna, David, and Dannel, for making it all necessary,

And for my wife, MaryBeth, for making it all worthwhile.

Contents

Foreword viii
Preface. x

Introduction: Why *Barney Miller*? 1
    Dad 1
    The Human Condition. 2
    Treated the Audience with Respect 4
    Underrated, Under-Appreciated 6

The 1974/1975 Television Season 7
Television Antecedents 9
Danny Arnold, Showrunner. 11
    Ted Flicker 18
    The Danny Arnold–Ted Flicker "Partnership" 19
    Danny's Side of the Story. 22
    How the Film *Detective Story* Inspired Danny Arnold 23
    Danny as Auteur. 26
    Fiercely Independent 29
    Danny's Style. 31
    A Do-or-Die Work Ethic 32
    The Evolution of *Barney Miller's* Shooting Style and the Quad System 34
    Danny at Home 36
    Danny and the Actors. 38
    Danny and the Directors 39

The Players and Their Characters 42
    Hal Linden | Captain Barney Miller 42
    Max Gail | Detective 3rd Grade Stan Wojciehowicz 46
    Abe Vigoda | Detective Sergeant Philip K. Fish 51
    Ron Glass | Detective First Grade Ron Harris 58
    Jack Soo | Detective Sergeant Nick Yemana 61
    Gregory Sierra | Detective Sergeant Chano Amenguale 65
    James Gregory | Inspector Frank D. Luger 67
    Steve Landesberg | Detective Sergeant Arthur P. Dietrich ... 69
    Ron Carey | Officer Carl Levitt 74
    Barbara Barrie | Elizabeth Miller 76
    Florence Stanley | Bernice Fish 77
    Character Development 79

The Writers and the Writing Staff 84
    Chris Hayward 89
    Roland Kibbee 90
    Tony Sheehan 92
    Reinhold Weege 94
    Tom Reeder 96
    Frank Dungan 97
    Jeff Stein 99

Barney Miller and the Female Sex 100
Barney Miller and Real-Life Police Officers 103
Of Its Time and Timeless 107
A Haven for Character Actors 110
    The Cops 112
    The Victims and the Cage Characters 120

The First Pilot: "The Life and Times of Barney Miller" 147
The Second Pilot: "Ramon" 149
Danny Arnold's Guiding Principles 152

Illustrations	154
Episode Guide	201
First Season	201
Second Season (First Full Season)	229
Third Season	281
Fourth Season	324
Fifth Season	368
Sixth Season	415
Seventh Season	460
Eighth Season	504
Epilogue	554
Acknowledgments	557
Partial List of Sources	560
About the Author	563

Foreword

Thanks for the memories, and for a lot I didn't remember, and for a lot I never knew. You're right, it took great writing and a terrific cast (ironically, not one acting Emmy in eight seasons) but mostly an imaginative and courageous producer. Every decision was artistically, not economically, based. We never walked away from a shoot saying, "We'll do better next week."

You plugged into the "funny." As actors we plugged into the "real," and let the "funny" happen. What is amazing is that after forty plus years, it's still relevant and courageous!

It's tragic that Max and I are the only ones left from the regular cast to share in these memories, but I think I can safely predict that forty plus years from now these episodes will be just as relevant and courageous as today, because humans will be just as human, and funny will still be funny.

All the best with the book!!

—**Hal Linden**

"You are obviously a highly intelligent person with a great sense of humor!" Over the years that has become my usual response when people expressed their love for *Barney Miller*, because it has turned out to be true. That conversation often started with the most common first question I would get, "Hey! Where's Barney?"

I've lived longer since the show ended than I had before it began.

Yet here I am writing a foreword to a book, wonderfully researched and written by my now friend Otto Bruno, who was ten when we started on the air and started watching it with his dad. That's another common refrain I've heard over those forty plus years, "I watched it with my dad."

The media landscape has changed immeasurably since those three-network days and yet many younger people keep finding it somewhere and agree with the old timers that it "still holds up." Some even call it a classic.

Otto's straightforward sharing of what he has learned comes from a deep and genuine curiosity and appreciation for collaborative creativity whether it's on the baseball diamond, the music bandstand, or the film and television studio. In this case, the pebble in the pond is *Barney Miller* but the waves that ripple out reflect the humanity that was the centerpiece of Danny Arnold's creation and all of us who were lucky enough to contribute to this special show.

—**Max Gail**

Preface

I learned many valuable lessons while writing this book. One is just how tricky the human memory can be. Not everything that was told to me could be confirmed or backed up by visual evidence within the episodes of the program or by multiple sources. I know that everyone believes the things they remember. Unfortunately, not everything we remember is necessarily true in the most objective way.

The truth is I took on the daunting task of writing about a television show that premiered on the primetime airwaves almost half a century ago. When I began work on the book there were only three remaining weekly cast members who were still around and sadly one of them was already sick and would pass away before we had the chance to speak. The creator and producer of the program had been gone for over a quarter century. What is worse for a researcher/writer, the creator of the show was neither obsessive nor compulsive about keeping memos, records, or journals of his activities. He worked from his gut and while he was a perfectionist by all accounts, he was also a procrastinator, an independent, and a bit eccentric. He left me no paper trail except the scripts of the show.

The layout of how I would tackle the subject changed numerous times. My initial idea was to have a very minimal episode guide. Eventually, that changed so that the guide is now a major component of the book. I also talked to other fans to see what they wanted in a *Barney Miller* book. I have provided most of those things: cast biographies, interview excerpts, photos, personal opinions, and the episode guide.

Ultimately, the most important lesson learned over the course of four years was that the story of *Barney Miller* is the story of Danny Arnold, the show's creator, producer, and show runner. Arnold gave his blood, sweat, and tears to this program for the first five seasons. He essentially put every other aspect of his life on hold to dedicate himself to producing the best show he could turn out every week. He had been in the business for over twenty years by the time he embarked on the odyssey of *Barney Miller*, and he'd had some very respectable successes with shows like *The Real McCoys*, *Bewitched*, *That Girl*, and *My World and Welcome to It*. However, on all of those shows he was essentially working for someone else. He was instrumental in *My World* but Mel Shavelson was the creator and Sheldon Leonard was the guy at the top of the chain of command. He had done a show called *The Wackiest Ship in the Army* in 1965–1966 but it lasted only a single season. *Barney* was, in his mind, his last big chance for immortality and so he put everything on the line and rolled the dice.

There are many with whom I have spoken who are totally convinced that Danny Arnold sacrificed his health for the success of this show. In fact, at the end of the fifth season he was forced by his doctors to step away from the program. He underwent heart bypass surgery and stayed away from the day-to-day operations for two years before returning to the helm in the show's eighth, and final, season.

Each of the main characters was a part of Danny Arnold's personality. Every script, particularly in those first five seasons, no matter who wrote it, had Danny Arnold's stamp on it. He was open to all ideas, but every single idea was given the Danny Arnold treatment before it was used. The show boasted some of the best TV directors around, but Danny had a lot to say about the directing of every episode as well. Some described his style as tyrannical, others respected that he went with his gut and knew what he wanted, and just about everyone described him as a genius.

There's one more thing I learned about Danny Arnold that you won't find in any other sources and that is that Danny Arnold was a tremendous judge of character. I don't mean comedic characters. I don't even mean a terrific judge of talent, although he most certainly was of both. I'm talking about personal character and integrity. I was continually overjoyed to discover that just about every single person who worked for Danny Arnold was/is a mensch. For those not familiar, "mensch" is a Yiddish word that according to Leo Rosten in *The New Joys of Yiddish* means, "1. A human being, 2. An upright, honorable, decent person, 3. Someone of consequence, someone to admire and emulate." The people I interviewed who worked for and with Danny Arnold were to a person, sincere, forthright, charming, kind, generous, and totally down to earth. For a fan of the show for almost fifty years, this was the ultimate rebuttal to the warning, "don't meet your heroes."

Finally, I hope that in the end the contents of this book will reflect the labor of love its creation was for me and the love and devotion of its grateful fan base for all those who helped to make it a television classic.

Introduction: Why Barney Miller?

Over the past few years, as I told people I was writing a book on *Barney Miller*, the most common question I would get is, "Why *Barney Miller*?" In fact, a couple of my interview subjects asked me why I was writing a book about a TV show that was almost fifty years old? Some others, the ones who can't possibly see anything of interest or importance in a television show (you know who these people are) are more direct and shorten their question to the very frank, and slightly patronizing, "Why?"

Soon after I started the research for this book, a friend asked me the question but as I gave him what was apparently a passionate but vague answer, this public relations/branding expert told me, "You need to really determine why *this* show. What made this show so special to you that you felt compelled to write about it?"

It seemed like a simple enough question, one that you would think I had thought about a great deal. In truth, I hadn't examined the specific cause all that closely. Luckily, there was something about the conversation I had with my friend that day that made me really examine exactly "why *Barney Miller*?"

The reality is that I'd been telling people for years the reasons why, long before I ever even contemplated a book about the subject. I loved *Barney Miller* from the moment I first watched its premiere on ABC nearly fifty years ago. In fact, that very first viewing is one of my reasons as to "why *Barney Miller*?"

Dad

I loved my dad—certainly not an unusual or earth-shattering enough reason to write a book—but it does, in its own way, play into the story of why this book came to be. When I was a kid, my dad worked for himself and so he rarely pulled into the driveway before 6 or 6:30 p.m. Most of the other families had

1

finished dinner by that time. Nevertheless, I don't ever remember eating dinner without him. We'd wait for his return and then eat together as a family. Following dinner, my father would retire to the family room. He might read the paper for a little while but soon enough he'd turn on the TV to relax. Like so many fathers of the 1950s, '60s, and '70s, my father liked westerns and detective shows such as *Gunsmoke* and *Kojak* but he also loved to laugh. In fact, he possessed a big, booming, very recognizable laugh.

My father had very little interest in sports, any sport. Years later, looking back on our brief time together, I realized that my interest in television and films came about because it was the one activity we could easily share and enjoy together. My dad took me to a few baseball games when I was a kid but there was never a doubt he was doing it solely for my enjoyment. However, when we went to the movies or sat down on the couch together to watch a TV show or an old movie, well, that was something we could both appreciate.

The first TV show he shared with me was *The Flip Wilson Show*. I remember him reading the paper one morning at breakfast and seeming quite happy that some person named Flip Wilson was getting his own show. When the time came (Thursday night, September 17, 1970, at 8:00 p.m., to be exact), I sat down and watched the new comedy/variety show with him. Soon I had a Flip Wilson/Geraldine talking doll and a t-shirt with "What you see is what you get," inscribed on it. I loved the show as much as, if not even more than, my dad.

Then there was *Barney Miller*. I don't remember this being appointment viewing like *The Flip Wilson Show* had been. Even so, I can clearly remember snuggling on the couch with my dad to watch this new show. He may have seen ads for it on TV before that, but I knew nothing about it. As always, the thing I remember most from that initial viewing was my dad's laughter. When the show ended, we knew we had found another show to watch together. I tell most people that we (my dad and I) watched the first two seasons together but that's not completely true. The last episode of Season Two ran on Thursday, March 18, 1976. My dad died earlier that afternoon at the age of fifty-one from lung cancer. I was twelve years old. He didn't get to see the next six seasons, but I didn't miss a single episode.

The Human Condition

Many years ago, I was channel surfing and accidentally came upon a talk show on the Arts & Entertainment network entitled *Nightcap* with Studs Terkel and

Calvin Trillin. It caught my attention because on this night they were talking with Sid Caesar, Carl Reiner, and Mel Brooks. Being a fan and a student of classic comedy, I was thrilled to happen upon this monumental collection of comedic giants. Of all the fabulous insights and stories that I first heard on this program, the one that stuck in my mind was a story related by Sid Caesar about how, during *Your Show of Shows*' (1950–1954) [more likely Caesar's Hour (1954–1957)] peak of popularity, the legendary comedian received a call from Albert Einstein's secretary saying that Dr. Einstein wanted to meet with Caesar. It took a while for Caesar to be convinced that someone wasn't playing a joke on him, but he eventually realized it was no joke and he nervously made an appointment to meet with the great man. Unfortunately, Einstein died before the two men could ever meet. Soon after Einstein's death, however, Caesar received a call from Robert Oppenheimer, who told Caesar that, "Albert wanted to see you. He figured out the physical equation. He wanted to talk to you about the human equation."

That's an amazing statement and revelation. First, for Albert Einstein to seek you out in order for you to teach him something is obviously a big deal. However, what most impressed me is the two-sided understanding of the power of comedy on and in a society, and the idea that the comedic mind, the court jesters of the world if you will, might have a special insight into the "human equation." Historically, we look to those jesters as the few people brave enough to shout, "The emperor has no clothes." In order to do that, the comedian, critic, satirist, etc. must have an understanding of the human condition. For me, and for Danny Arnold and his *Barney Miller* cast and crew, the basis of the humor and the heart of the 12th Precinct stems from an understanding of, and respect for, the human condition.

The fact that Danny Arnold stocked his 12th Precinct with such a diverse workforce is part of that acknowledgment. When most of us think of the New York City Police Department, particularly the film and television depictions of it from the 1950s through the 1970s, we think of primarily Irish and Italian cops. The *Barney Miller* squad had neither of those two groups represented in its weekly cast. There was an African American, a Latino, a Japanese American, a Polish American, and two Jewish cops when the series began. As the series played out, we met Irish and Italian cops, not to mention gay and female cops, but they were all just seen as part of the tapestry of the department and of the human race.

Prior to *Barney Miller*, *The Andy Griffith Show* (1960–1968) and *Car 54, Where Are You?* (1961–1963) were the two popular sitcoms that revolved around police work. In these shows, the comedy stemmed primarily from funny cops like Barney Fife or Gunther Tooty. In *Barney Miller*, the cops may have been idiosyncratic but that just made them more human. They were real flesh-and-blood characters, not caricatures. No matter what their quirks were, they were very capable police officers. Arnold told his actors, "Imagine you had to ask the police for help. How would you want to be treated?" He wanted them to keep that in mind as they gave life to their characters.

The portrayals of the criminals and victims were a slightly different story. The humor of *Barney Miller* stemmed from the endless parade of fears, prejudices, opinions, and plights of everyday people. Nevertheless, even the most eccentric and kookiest among those who entered the 12th Precinct had a story that, at its core, contained a kernel of truth, a touch of humanity.

Those who worked with Danny Arnold will tell you that he believed that the key to *Barney Miller*'s humor was the idea of "paranoids with proof." In other words, a man or woman would come into the precinct with what initially seemed like a crazy story or complaint but when questioned could actually come up with a legitimate (or semi-legitimate) reason for their fear. If someone in the squad thought the person was nuts or lying, there was usually another member of the group who could relate to or understand that person and would listen and try to quell their fears. The humor came directly from the personalities of the officers and their human responses to the fear, anger, embarrassment, and jealousies of their constituency.

Throughout the eight seasons of the show, Barney is not only the straight man to a precinct full of loonies but he's also a father, a confidant, a teacher, a disciplinarian, a mediator, and a philosopher. He was always there to ensure that humanity and respect were shown to victims and criminals alike.

Treated the Audience with Respect

Creators and writers of TV shows always hope for a hit but it's only when they strike pay dirt with a successful idea that the real work begins. Then they have to figure out how to come up with fresh ideas from week to week and year to year. This is a far more difficult task than it seems. That's how and why so many shows end up "jumping the shark," or coming up with outrageous storylines that don't do justice to the show's history, truth, or characters. In fact, most critics agree that *Barney Miller* was one of the few TV shows that never "jumped the shark."

There haven't been too many shows that come to an end before they are canceled but it does happen. For example, Carl Reiner closed down *The Dick*

Van Dyke Show after five seasons (158 episodes) because it was becoming too hard to come up with fresh ideas. Jackie Gleason pulled the plug on the filmed half-hour sitcom version of *The Honeymooners* (the classic thirty-nine episodes) after only one season claiming the same reason. Danny Arnold would do the same after 171 episodes by ending the show in 1982. It was never canceled. Arnold ended it.

Unfortunately, new storylines aren't the only challenge for long-running sitcom successes. There is also the problem of maintaining strong, intelligent, and fully fleshed out characters throughout the run of the show without allowing featured characters to become caricatures. The longer a program stays on the air, the harder it becomes to maintain a character's integrity. There are a number of excellent shows that remained on the air so long that some of their characters eventually changed from quirky, but recognizably human, characters into cartoonish buffoons.

It's not easy to allow a comedic character to evolve over time without becoming too serious and thus changing into a dramatic character or going so far to the silly side that it becomes a caricature of its former self. Stan Wojciehowicz is an excellent example of a character that certainly evolved and grew over time but was still able to create comedic moments. The origin of the comedy may have changed over time, but the character could still produce laughs without insulting the audience's intelligence. What made *Barney Miller* special is that it never talked down to its audience. The humor could be silly but it was always intelligent.

There were many great sitcoms that came out of the 1970s, shows like *Mary Tyler Moore*, *The Bob Newhart Show*, *Sanford & Son*, *The Odd Couple*, and others. Two of the most influential shows in all of television history began as sitcoms of the 1970s: *All in the Family* and *M*A*S*H*. These were all great shows but, in the case of *All in the Family* and *M*A*S*H*, I have a hard time putting them strictly into the category of comedy. Both of those shows were, without question, terrific shows and I do not dispute their greatness or their impact on our culture. However, they started as comedies and ended up as "dramedies." In fact, I think the word "dramedy" may have even been invented to describe *M*A*S*H*. Depending on the episode, it was hard to tell whether one was watching a comedy or a drama.

Barney Miller was always the one show that could cover serious material while still remaining true to its comedy foundation. There's an old Hollywood quote that says, "If you want to send a message, call Western Union." I'm not saying film or television stories can't have depth or intellect, they can and they should. It's more a case of being true to the origin of the mission. If the mission is to make people laugh then that should be the priority. For *Barney Miller*, it didn't matter whether the stories dealt with nuclear arms, arson, Agent Orange, political asylum, homosexuality, suicide, aging, impotence, homelessness, the American flag, or the American Indian, the comedy was always in sight. There could be very serious and dramatic moments in an episode, but you always knew the writers would deftly return the focus to the comedy. This was a practice first introduced on the television sitcom (as far as we know) by Danny Thomas, who encouraged the "treacle cutter," meaning when there's a serious or dramatic situation always make sure to follow it up with a joke or humorous observation to relieve the tension. Like any artistic pursuit, it was more successful in some shows than others but *Barney Miller* was among the best shows ever in terms of keeping the focus on what was funny at all times. In the long run, the humor keeps the audience interested so they can learn something new, something valuable that they might never have expected in a primetime sitcom.

Underrated, Under-Appreciated

Ultimately, the final and perhaps most important reason for this book is that I have never felt that *Barney Miller* received the critical attention, praise, and immortality that it so richly deserves. The show was nominated for thirty-two Primetime Emmy Awards and won exactly three. Produced by a small independent company, Danny Arnold's Four D Productions, means it never had a big Hollywood corporation behind it to mount aggressive media campaigns to win the awards. Nevertheless, this was not just another good, or even great, show. This is one of the very best shows in the history of the medium. The lack of attention and respect it has received in the decades since its original primetime run has always seemed unjust to me. If nothing else, I wanted to write a book that would celebrate a great moment in TV history.

The 1974/1975 Television Season

The 1970s began with a renaissance of television comedy. In 1970 TV viewers were introduced to *The Odd Couple*, and *The Mary Tyler Moore Show*. The next few seasons would add classics like *All in the Family*, *M*A*S*H**, *Maude*, *The Bob Newhart Show*, and *Happy Days*. By the mid-1970s, the variety shows and westerns of the 1950s and 1960s were giving way to even more situation comedies.

The 1974–1975 television season that saw the introduction of *Barney Miller* was dominated by a gentleman named Norman Lear. Five out of the top ten shows on television that season had Norman Lear's imprint on them: *All in the Family* (#1), *Sanford and Son* (#2), *The Jeffersons* (#4), *Good Times* (#7), and *Maude* (#9). All of Lear's shows reflected a social opinion or significance that proved to be fertile sources of comedy.

In early 1974, sometime between January and March, Danny Arnold and Ted Flicker produced a pilot entitled *The Life and Times of Barney Miller*. In its original incarnation it was intended to be a comedic look at both sides of a cop's life: the mundane daily police procedures of the precinct as well as the home and family to which he returned every night. As comedic police procedurals go, "The Life and Times of Barney Miller" was a much more realistic look at police work than say *The Andy Griffith Show* or *Car 54, Where Are You?*, which aired in the decade prior to *Barney Miller's* debut. However, there was nothing new on the home front, meaning the portion of "The Life and Times of Barney Miller" that pulled back the curtain to reveal life in the Miller household wasn't much different from any of the other domestic comedies of the 1950s or 1960s. Hal Linden says he believes it was the network that was unimpressed with the domestic half of the show and wanted Danny Arnold to put his full focus on the action in the precinct. Arnold, having the comedic mind that he did, would have no doubt figured this out and perhaps recognized the problem at the start right along with the network. Whatever the case, there would be only one other visit to the Miller's kitchen in the entire eight-season run of the show and that occurred in Season One's fourth episode, "Graft."

ABC eventually passed on that first pilot. However, as Danny Arnold recalled in a 1979 interview with Dennis Tardan, "It just so happened that that year, the fall of 1974, the ABC schedule just sort of crumbled to pieces" and, according to Arnold, "that's what gave Barney a life."

The show began with very low ratings. Luckily, there were ABC executives like Michael Eisner and Andy Segal who felt the show had something special and should be supported. Arnold told Tardan, "I absolutely felt . . . that if I could just keep it alive long enough that it would be successful and that people would really grow to love these characters because they were so identifiable, there was so much of everybody in these characters." Ultimately, Arnold's instincts would prove to be correct.

Television Antecedents

In the years preceding *Barney Miller*, there were dozens of cop shows but very few that dealt with crime and punishment in a humorous way. The most well-known is *The Andy Griffith Show* and that is justifiably considered a television classic. As much a small town, rural comedy as a police comedy, *Andy Griffith's* hometown setting of Mayberry was a place where manning the school crosswalk and writing out a jaywalking ticket or two constituted a full day for the local sheriff's office.

The department, such as it was, employed Sheriff Andrew Jackson Taylor, known to his friends as "Andy," and his high-strung Deputy Sheriff Bernard P. Fife, known to one and all as "Barney" or "Barn."

Andy and Barney were as different as night and day. Andy was a widower raising his young son with the housekeeping help of his Aunt Bea. Barney was a swinging bachelor, at least in his own mind. Andy was even-tempered, logical, and an overall calming presence in his community. Barney, well, Barney was not unlike Henny Penny, always ready to assume the sky was falling and spread the news to all who would listen. Andy was a responsible and safe gun owner, hunter, and marksman. Barney accidentally shot more bullets into floors and ceilings than he ever shot at a criminal. Andy ran the town and Barney? Well, Barney was a nut.

However, Barney was a proud nut. He was loyal to his town, his friends, and particularly to his superior officer and best friend, Andy Taylor. Barney was certainly no Sherlock Holmes, but he was honest, willing to work hard, and always had the best interests of his town at heart. There were even occasional instances where Barney was shown to have some real native intelligence.

In the end, most of the laughs were usually at the expense of Barney and some of the other characters in the small town. In the early seasons of *The Andy Griffith Show*, a good portion of the humor was the lack of criminal activity for the office to control. In that way, you couldn't find a more different type of police comedy than a show set in the lower east side of Manhattan. However, in "Andy on Trial" (S. 2/Ep. 29), Barney sums up the philosophy of the Mayberry Sheriff's Office when he testifies in an informal hearing, "You gotta understand, this is a small town. The sheriff is more than just a sheriff, he's a friend. You ask me if Andy runs a taut ship . . . well, no he don't but that's because of something he's been trying to teach me ever since I started working for him and that is that when you're a lawman and you're dealing with people, you do a whole lot better if you go not so much by the book but by the heart." Take away the folksiness of the vernacular and it's a pretty apt description of the 12th Precinct's philosophy as well.

Both forces enjoyed a healthy supply of empathy and interest in their community. In both shows, the police were truly the people's friend in the neighborhood. Both Andy Taylor and Barney Miller taught and provided an example of humanity and honesty when dealing with the public. They could have fun, especially with their underlings but the community, as crazy as it could sometimes be, was sacred.

The TV cop comedy that probably had less in common with *Barney Miller*, despite its setting, was Nat Hiken's *Car 54, Where Are You?* Nat Hiken was, and remains, a respected early television writer/creator/producer of scripted comedy. However, as funny as *Car 54, Where Are You?* could be, it seems much more dated than the other two shows. The location was also New York City but the characters are more cartoonish. Fred Gwynne provides the majority of the humanity in the piece while Joe E. Ross is more of a buffoonish sitcom caricature. It still has its fans after six decades but in this writer's opinion, it's not nearly as funny as Hiken's previous hit show, *You'll Never Get Rich*, a.k.a. *The Phil Silvers Show*, a.k.a. *Sgt. Bilko*, which is one of the funniest sitcoms of all time.

To be fair, I haven't seen every episode of *Car 54* as I have with *The Andy Griffith Show* so I apologize if the reader feels there's more meaning to the show than I can see.

Danny Arnold, Showrunner

He had the Marine in him. He loved to wear leather jackets and he had this big head of reddish-thick hair and a wonderful kind of clown face. He was built, big barrel chest and shoulders. He was very generous. He had a very expansive sense of life, and loved his kids and his wife, Donna. They were almost always there on our shooting nights.

—*Max Gail*

Danny said, "The only reason to do this show is to do the best we can do." There was no network involvement, there was no studio involvement, Danny was an independent. We didn't have a studio executive with a time clock saying, "Gentlemen, gentlemen, we're going into overtime." We didn't have that. Danny said, "As long as it takes to make this the best we can do, that's how long we're going to be."

—*Hal Linden*

"*Barney Miller* is Danny Arnold," meaning the show as a whole, not the character named Barney Miller. Arnold's family, Hal Linden, Max Gail, and others who worked on the show all agreed that each of the main characters in the *Barney Miller* squad room represented a piece of Danny Arnold's personality.

There are show biz professionals who seem to know from the moment of their first conscious thought that they want to be an entertainer while others stumble into it completely by accident. Arnold seems to have fallen somewhere between these two extremes.

Arnold Danny Rothman was born on January 23, 1925, in the South Bronx to immigrants from Romania. According to David Arnold, the eldest of Danny Arnold's two sons, his grandmother was a nurse and his grandfather died when his father was a very young child. Being the only child of a young widow, David says his father felt the pressures and guilt of his Jewish family to essentially be the man of the house. Danny Arnold expressed to his wife and sons his feeling that his mother never really recovered from his father's death.

This less-than-happy atmosphere at home led Arnold to attempt to join the armed forces as soon as the Japanese bombed Pearl Harbor in December of 1941. He was only sixteen at the time and was unable to join. He could join at seventeen but only with a parental signature. Arnold remembered that the day he went to sign up there were long lines to join the Navy and the Army but the line for the Marine Corps was relatively short. As he was expected to be home for dinner by a certain time, he got into the shortest line. It no doubt took some convincing, but Arnold was eventually able to get his mother to sign the papers and, at seventeen years of age, he became a Marine.

David says his father was injured a few times during his service but the last time was serious enough to get him sent back to the States where he wound up in the San Diego Naval Hospital. (Both sons said he won medals for his war service but that it just wasn't something he ever brought up in conversation.) Following his recuperation, Arnold and his service buddies would hitchhike from San Diego to Los Angeles and it was there that he first became exposed to Hollywood and the bustling movie studios of the era. Out of the service and in need of a job, Arnold landed a position as apprentice in the Sound Effects Department at Columbia Pictures.

In a 1987 interview with radio host Bob Claster, Arnold said, "I was sweeping out cutting rooms . . . but I taught myself at night how to cut sound effects for film and that was a time, this was 1944, when the war was still on and many of the technicians were gone." Arnold taught himself how to use the moviolas and sound sync machines and because the studios were so short of qualified technicians, he quickly received opportunities to show his worth.

The Monster and the Ape (1945) was Arnold's first assignment at sound editing a film. It was actually a B-movie serial, the kind that was very popular in the Saturday matinees of the period. Arnold remembered that, "The villain in the piece was a robot who was a man in a cardboard robot suit. So, of course, to create the illusion that he was made out of metal, there were a lot of squeaks and bumps and grinds and bangs as he walked and I had to practically create the character out of sound so it was a fascinating experience." According to Tony Sheehan, Danny told him that he'd also done sound editing on some of the Three Stooges shorts of the 1940s.

Arnold would go on to sound edit some memorable "A" films as well such as *Cover Girl* (1944) and *Tonight and Every Night* (1945). Nevertheless, he told Claster, "after two years of doing that [sound editing] I went back to being an actor. And then eventually got tired of sitting around waiting for an agent to call for a job, decided I would write. Writing proved to be successful. I had no intentions of ever being a writer."

Arnold told Claster, "I went back to being an actor." However, the only acting that we can confirm Danny Arnold did prior to the late 1940s were small parts in the Catskill Mountain resorts as a child. Arnold's mother would take jobs as a nurse in the mountains during the summer season. The mountain stock companies were always looking for kids to fill certain roles and his Uncle Leon, who was an actor, helped the young Arnold get cast in shows. Those small roles, along with his uncle's experiences, whet his appetite for an acting career. However, despite his statement to Claster that "he went back to acting," it does not appear he did any more acting until after his military service and his stint as a Hollywood sound editor.

The first acting credit that we know of was a minor role in a Warner Bros. war movie entitled *Breakthrough* (1950). The question then arises, what was he doing from roughly 1946 to 1950? According to Hal Linden, "Danny was a failed stand-up comic." He played small clubs and bars around Youngstown, OH, and Pittsburgh, PA. It was during this time on the road that he met a young singer and M.C. named Jack Soo. The two became fast friends and many years later, Arnold would cast Soo in a small role in a sitcom called *The Wackiest Ship in the Army* (1965–1966).

However long Arnold may have worked in nightclubs, it does appear that his time in that pursuit was unheralded. At some point, realizing a performing career was not the calling for him, he began to write. He told Claster that the first story he sold was *The Caddy*, a 1953 Paramount picture with Dean Martin and Jerry Lewis. According to Arnold's son David, Danny Arnold met Jerry Lewis sliding into second base during a softball game in a park across the street from 20th Century Fox. Lewis noticed Arnold when he slid into second base wearing blue suede shoes. From that chance meeting, he was cast in small roles in the Martin and Lewis pictures, *Sailor Beware* (1952) and *Jumping Jacks* (1952). At some point, they discovered he had writing talent because he began writing for their appearances on *The Colgate Comedy Hour* as well, where he worked with their chief writers, Norman Lear and Ed Simmons.

The Caddy seems to be the project that propelled Arnold's writing career. In the 1987 interview, Arnold said that after his formative writing years working on comedy, "I decided I wanted to become a serious writer and I would do something that was as far away from the frivolous kind of material that Dean and Jerry were doing so I wrote a heavy mood piece." The film he wrote was a western called *Rebel in Town* (1956) starring John Payne and Ruth Roman. He claimed that film "sort of opened up the business for me." He wrote a few inconsequential films before finishing that portion of his career with a feature entitled *The Lady Takes a Flyer* (1957), with Lana Turner and Jeff Chandler.

From 1957 through to the end of his career in the 1990s, Arnold worked on only one more feature film, *The War Between Men and Women* (1972) starring Jack Lemmon, Barbara Harris, and Jason Robards. Besides that one crossover into film, the remainder of Arnold's career was in the field of television. He wrote everything from comedy to drama to variety television but his strong suit was always comedy.

He worked on a number of variety programs including those for Rosemary Clooney, Dinah Shore, and Tennessee Ernie Ford. The biggest impact of that work came in the form of Donna Arnold, his wife of thirty-four years, whom he met while working on the Ford program. The future Mrs. Arnold was a dancer on Tennessee Ernie's weekly variety show. They were together until Mr. Arnold's death. He had previously been married to starlet Joanne Gilbert but the union lasted just over a year from 1955–1956. Gilbert was the daughter of composer Ray Gilbert, Academy Award-winning songwriter along with Allie Wrubel of the song, "Zip-A-Dee-Doo-Dah."

Following the variety shows, Arnold looked to writing more structured stories. He wrote a couple of episodes for the popular dramatic anthology series, *The Millionaire*. Irv Pincus, creator and producer of the hit series *The Real McCoys*, saw one of Arnold's *Millionaire* programs and asked if he'd be interested in writing a script for *The Real McCoys*. Arnold wrote the script and was amazed when Pincus not only accepted it, but also asked Arnold if he would produce the fifth season of the show. Arnold remembered, "I produced *The Real McCoys* the fifth season it was on the air and directed my first show for them and that was it. From then on I started producing and writing and directing."

He was next hired to be the showrunner for the now classic TV sitcom, *Bewitched*, starring Elizabeth Montgomery, Dick York, and Agnes Moorehead. He also wrote three of the first season's episodes. Once again, in the interview with Claster, Arnold seemed to misremember slightly when he recalled doing the one-season show *The Wackiest Ship in the Army* before working on the first season of *Bewitched*. Regardless, *Bewitched*'s first season ran from 1964–1965 while *The Wackiest Ship in the Army* was on the air from 1965–1966. The reason for the confusion seems to be explained in a 1965 article in *Pageant* by Joseph N. Bell that states, "Producer Danny Arnold appeared with a show called *The Wackiest Ship in the Army* that he wanted Screen Gems to take on. The studio liked the idea, but not for that season, so executive producer Ackerman hired Arnold for *Bewitched*."

Therefore, in a sense, Arnold was correct. His idea for *The Wackiest Ship in the Army* TV show apparently did come before he took on the duties with *Bewitched* but the show itself did not appear on the air until the following season. By that time, his work on *Bewitched* was done. William Asher was not only a producer and director on the *Bewitched* series but also the husband of the show's star, Elizabeth Montgomery. Both Asher and Arnold had reputations for being very strong-willed and so it's not surprising that they parted company after just one season.

The Wackiest Ship in the Army was originally a 1960 movie starring Jack Lemmon and Ricky Nelson but the TV version was created and orchestrated by Arnold. As he remembered it, "The television concept was very different from the film." Arnold tailored the show for his friend, Jack Warden. He was also proud of the fact that he discovered a young actor for the series named Gary Collins. According to David Arnold, both men remained close friends of his dad's up until the time of his death. The show was not your average television comedy in that it was an hour in length and did not include a laugh track, which was highly unusual for a 1960s sitcom.

Unfortunately, *The Wackiest Ship in the Army* only lasted one season. Arnold followed up his first original series with a pilot entitled, *Somewhere in Italy . . . Company B!* That pilot, never picked up as a series, can also be found listed in some sources as *Operation Razzle-Dazzle*.

Arnold's next stop was with a show already in progress. He joined the team running *That Girl* in its second season. The sitcom, starring Marlo Thomas, is now hailed as a feminist precursor to *The Mary Tyler Moore Show* but like *MTM*, the writers and producers of *That Girl* made sure the product was funny before preachy. Creator and producer Bill Persky was friends with Danny Arnold. Persky remembers, "I went over to see him on my way home and he was sitting at his dining room table making model cars because he had nothing to do. We needed someone on *That Girl* and . . . he and Marlo got along so I brought him in as producer of *That Girl*, a show that I had created along with my partner [Sam Denoff]. Within three weeks he wouldn't listen to us but at the same time he was delivering really great stuff." Arnold spent two seasons as producer on *That Girl* before moving on to his next original story idea.

For the 1969–1970 television season, Arnold, along with partners Mel Shavelson and Sheldon Leonard, wrote, produced, and directed *My World and Welcome to It*, starring William Windom. It was an innovative premise for that era mixing both live action and animation in a sitcom format. Based on the works of humorist James Thurber, the show was popular with critics but generated mediocre ratings. In fact, as Arnold told interviewer Claster, "It won the Emmy the night it was canceled."

Not yet ready to give up on Thurber, Arnold and Mel Shavelson, the man who had originally secured the rights from Helen Thurber for her husband's work, joined forces to create a feature film idea based not on Thurber's work but on his life. The film, *The War Between Men and Women* (1972), tells the story of a cartoonist who is slowly going blind and the romantic relationship he is trying to cultivate at the same time. Arnold remembered that, "It opened [at] Radio City Music Hall, it did very well, played for a while and then disappeared. It was too gentle, I think, for the audience at that time."

The early 1970s saw Hollywood turn to the anti-hero, the vigilante, the rogue cop cleaning up the inner cities, to draw the crowds into the theaters. The films of the era reflected a new level of graphic violence not previously seen on the big screen. *The War Between Men and Women*, despite its often biting and sardonic humor, was just too intimate a picture for the times. It was by no means a flop, but it was never going to be titillating enough to grab audiences in the same way *The French Connection* (1971), *Dirty Harry* (1971), or *The Godfather* (1972) could.

Following that brief return to feature films, Arnold immediately put all of his focus back into television development. He worked on possibly two pilots for ABC. The first was "Ann in Blue," which was telecast on August 8, 1974, on a show called *Just for Laughs*, a short series made up of an assortment of unsold pilots. It was a story about female police officers trying to get more meaningful work assignments out of their stodgy captain. Some sources claim that the director was Theodore J. Flicker while the writers included Danny Arnold, Marshall Brickman, Norman Steinberg, and Alan Uger. However, *Unsold Television Pilots 1955–1989* by Lee Goldberg, makes absolutely no mention of Flicker or Arnold in connection with this program. Writer Norman Steinberg says he does believe that Arnold worked on an early version of the script but he never met him or worked with him personally on it. Mary Elaine Monti, one of the actresses in the pilot, also had no recollection of meeting or working with Arnold on this project.

However, on August 22, 1974, two weeks after "Ann in Blue" was telecast, "The Life and Times of Barney Miller" pilot appeared on *Just for Laughs*. Some sources claim this pilot was directed by Theodore J. Flicker as well while the writing credits are assigned to both Arnold and Flicker. The pilot was initially turned down by the network but would resurface in January of 1975 as a project now entirely run and controlled by Danny Arnold with the shortened title of *Barney Miller*. Flicker was never present on the *Barney Miller* set again.

Linden remembers him only from the first pilot while people like Max Gail and Tony Sheehan, who came on board after the initial pilot, never set eyes on Flicker. This did not, however, prevent Flicker from suing Danny Arnold over proceeds from the show. The lawsuit remains a mystery to people like Linden and Sheehan since, with the co-creator credit awarded Flicker, it seems obvious that the show's success must have generated an impressive amount of revenue for Flicker without him having to lift a finger.

Barney Miller's first season (a thirteen-episode run) began in January of 1975 but did not immediately generate big ratings even though the reviews were positive. In fact, the review for the first pilot of the then-entitled *The Life and Times of Barney Miller* was actually more effusive than many of the second pilot's reviews stating, "a good, broadly farcical script and excellent casting soon give the stamp of exceptional TV comedy." However, the reviews of both the August pilot and the remade pilot/series' first episode in January 1975 both note the letdown that occurs when the show's action shifts from the squad room to Barney's home life. Thankfully, critics, network execs, and Danny Arnold were all in agreement over quickly shifting the focus solely to the activities that took place within the walls of the 12th Precinct.

Barney Miller enjoyed an eight-season run on ABC. The show endured the loss of actors Abe Vigoda, who left to star in his own spinoff series [*Fish*], and Jack Soo, who died during the show's fifth season, by adding characters and expanding roles for actors like Steve Landesberg and Ron Carey. Heeding doctor's orders, Arnold stepped away from the day-to-day duties of the show at the end of the fifth season for two years due to a heart ailment. He eventually had quadruple bypass surgery. Tony Sheehan ran the production for those two seasons before Arnold returned to the helm in the show's final season of 1981–1982.

The show spent four of its eight seasons in the top twenty of the Nielsen ratings and was nominated for over thirty Emmy Awards. It was, without question, the most successful and personally satisfying project of Danny Arnold's career. The spinoff (*Fish*) and similarly themed shows (*A.E.S. Hudson Street*) that sprang from *Barney Miller* never captured the energy or appeal of the mother show. Danny Arnold would try one more original program, *Joe Bash*, in 1986 but it was a very dark cop comedy that never really got off the ground and he pulled the plug on that project after just six episodes.

Arnold continued to go to the office and work on the development of potential shows but in his 1987 interview with radio personality Bob Claster, he seemed to know that his time had passed. There was no realistic way he could produce a show in the same manner as *Barney Miller* again. It would not only be financially prohibitive but the networks would never give the same level of independence to a content provider.

In August of 1995, Danny Arnold died at the age of seventy of heart failure. Donna Arnold died of cancer in 2020. Their sons, David and Dannel, live with their families in California.

Ted Flicker

Theodore J. Flicker was born in New Jersey in 1930. He studied for a couple of years at the Royal Academy of Dramatic Art in London before returning to the states and joining the Compass Players in Chicago, the first improvisational theater group in the country. He liked the ideas being pursued by the group but not their execution and so he moved to St. Louis and formed his own branch of the Compass Players. With the help and input of Elaine May, Mike Nichols, and Del Close, he put together a set of formal rules for improvisational theater. The Chicago branch evolved into Second City under the direction of Paul Sills while Nichols and May headed to stardom in New York without Flicker.

Flicker married actress Barbara Joyce Perkins in the 1960s and the two hit the road to Hollywood. He co-wrote the screenplay for a film entitled *The Troublemaker* with Buck Henry in 1964. The film was a moderate success and led to more writing work including the Elvis Presley film, *Spinout* (1966).

In 1967, Flicker got the chance to direct his first feature from a screenplay he wrote entitled *The President's Analyst*. The film starred James Coburn as a doctor hired to be the psychoanalyst for the President of the United States. Once the doctor realizes he "knows too much" about the most powerful man in the world, he panics and starts to run. Ultimately, the satirical comedy poked fun at the FBI, the CIA, and every other American sacred cow that was part of our national culture. News of the film, as well as the screenplay itself, reached J. Edgar Hoover, head of the real FBI, and he was not amused. The film opened to good reviews in December of 1967 but within a few weeks, the studio pulled it out of theaters. Hoover called the White House, the White House called Paramount, and Flicker received a call from his agent telling him his career was all but over.

That was only partially true. The studio system wouldn't touch him for feature films but he had surprisingly little trouble securing work in television. The majority of his work in the 1970s would show up on the small screen in TV movies like *The Last of the Good Guys* (1978) and weekly shows such as *Night Gallery*, *Mod Squad*, and *The Streets of San Francisco*.

In the early 1970s, he and Danny Arnold were teamed up to produce a pilot for ABC set in a police precinct house. As previously stated, the true origin story of their partnership is filled with confusion. All we know for sure is that both men must have worked together on the very first pilot, "The Life and Times of Barney Miller." After that pilot failed to get picked up, Danny Arnold bought out the other investors, went back to work trying to get a second chance with the network and told Flicker his services were no longer required. However, because Flicker's name was on the original pilot as a creator along with Arnold, the Writer's Guild rules stipulated that his name remain on the show after Danny Arnold convinced the network to give it another chance. Therefore, Flicker received residuals as a co-creator for the life of the program creating a lifelong animosity, and a lot of lawsuits, between him and Danny Arnold.

Flicker and his wife eventually took their money, left Hollywood, and moved to New Mexico where Flicker pursued a new career as a sculptor. He eventually built a four-acre sculpture garden on his property. His work was also displayed in art shows and galleries in New Mexico.

Ted Flicker endured numerous surgeries and a variety of health issues before dying in his home after a fall on the night of September 12, 2014.

The Danny Arnold–Ted Flicker "Partnership"

Of course, this was never a partnership in the purest form of the word. Research suggests these two gentlemen never worked together before or after the initial *Barney Miller* pilot. In fact, nearly a half-century after the fact, no one remains from Arnold's family or the *Barney Miller* production staff and stars who can remember anything passing between Danny Arnold and Ted Flicker other than animosity.

In my first interview with Hal Linden, he remembered it as little more than a marriage of convenience. He thought it was Arnold and Flicker's agents who had put them together. He seemed to recall that they both wanted to pitch a police comedy to the network and their agents essentially said, "We'll never sell two and you're both our clients so why don't you guys get together . . . and produce a great one?" Later in my research, I spoke with writer Tom Reeder and writer/producer Tony Sheehan and they seemed to think it was the network that put the two men together. A 1981 book by Sally Bedell (now Sally Bedell Smith), *Up the Tube: Prime-Time in The Silverman Years*, claims that Arnold initially conceived of an idea for a show about a retirement-age

Jewish patrolman in New York City four years prior to producing the first pilot. He brought his idea for a "humanistic cop" to NBC and they turned him down believing "that no ethnic show, especially a Jewish one, could possibly be popular." According to Bedell Smith, "Three years later a William Morris agent put Arnold in touch with another writer, Theodore Flicker, who was trying to develop a drama about a Jewish detective in the San Fernando Valley. They threw out Flicker's drama as unworkable and concentrated on a new comedy about a group of oddball detectives working in an obscure precinct in New York, the sort of place Arnold had seen in his occasional tumbles into trouble as a kid." This version seems to confirm the theory from Hal Linden.

To the best of his recollection, Tony Sheehan remembers Danny Arnold telling him that "Flicker was there during the week of the pilot, which was directed by John Rich, but that Danny did everything, including directing, the writing. And he [Flicker] was there for one week and then he was gone; he was never there for any episodes."

In the interviews I conducted over four years' time, it seemed a unanimous opinion and recollection that Ted Flicker never had anything to do with the day-to-day workings of the show. Everyone, including Arnold's family, Hal Linden, Max Gail, and Sheehan, all agree that Ted Flicker never set foot on the soundstage again after the pilot. That said, there *are* two pilots. The original pilot, "The Life and Times of Barney Miller," lists Theodore J. Flicker, and not John Rich, as the director. However, it should also be noted that the original pilot ends with the statement that the show was a Four D Production and Four D was solely Danny Arnold's production company, the Four D's being Danny, his wife Donna, and their two sons David and Dannel.

Therefore, here is what we know: it was an outside force, either the network or the talent agency, that put Danny Arnold and Ted Flicker together to work on this related idea. The credits of the original pilot indicate Flicker directed, Arnold produced, and the two shared the writing credit. Then again, credits rarely tell the whole story. Hal Linden, Max Gail, and numerous other actors and actresses who worked on the show say that while there were always other directors, Danny Arnold frequently played the role of "de facto" director if he was there. Therefore, we can't assume that Flicker was even the sole director of the first pilot.

"The Life and Times of Barney Miller" was not picked up. According to *Up the Tube*, and confirmed to me by Hal Linden, it was shown during the summer of 1974 and shelved. Linden remembers that it was Danny Arnold who somehow talked the executives at ABC into a very strange deal. Supposedly, the network told Arnold he could have thirteen episodes although ABC only guaranteed a broadcast slot for two more episodes. In any case, once Arnold had a hard commitment for two more episodes, Linden says, "he [Danny Arnold] bought out the deficit financers—whoever put up the money for the first pilot. And then Danny, therefore, became three-quarters owner with Ted Flicker [presumably retaining] twenty-five percent. And I know he [Arnold] mortgaged his house to do that. Yeah, I mean you talk about guts, how about mortgaging your house to get ownership of a dead pilot? That's what he did, basically."

In possible contradiction to Linden's belief that Arnold was encouraged to work on two more episodes with the possibility of thirteen being bought, Bedell Smith writes in her book that, "They [ABC] did ask for four more scripts, however, so Arnold was ready with his show when the fall schedule fell apart and ABC came looking for plugs to fill the holes in January 1975." Nevertheless, Danny Arnold himself told interviewers through the years that ABC made him the offer of two guaranteed episodes that would expand to thirteen if they picked up the show.

Once Danny Arnold owned controlling interest in the show, he apparently cut Flicker loose. The two episodes he shot were not from the original pilot script. Both Hal Linden and Max Gail remember that "Stakeout" was one of the episodes taped but can't remember the second. Whatever it was, the network liked what it saw and gave Arnold the green light for the half season order of thirteen episodes that began in January 1975. For the remainder of the show's run, Flicker would continue to sue Danny Arnold for more profits and Danny Arnold would continue to counter-sue and curse out Ted Flicker whom he felt made millions of dollars for doing absolutely nothing.

Linden also told me, "I had a percentage of profits, and his producer did, and I think eventually Noam Pitlik did, and Flicker sued him saying he had no right to give away any percentage of profit without Flicker's permission . . . he didn't want it diluted by any percentages that Danny had given away. Danny told this story about his first heart attack and he said this is what caused it. The judge in the case specifically kept himself from watching the show because he didn't want to be swayed either way, he didn't want to know anything about the show, he only wanted to know about the contracts. One day the judge came back into court and he said, 'I want you to know that I just had lunch with Judge so-and-so and he tells me he's the biggest fan of your show and that he thinks it's the funniest thing on television.' And Ted Flicker stood up and said, 'Thank you.' And Danny said, 'That's what caused my heart attack!'"

Hal Linden, Tony Sheehan, Shirley Alberti, Perry Krauss, and Danny Arnold's sons all agree that "Ted Flicker" was not a subject you would want to bring up to Danny Arnold. More often than not, at the mere mention of Flicker's name Danny would turn beet red and start swearing.

Unfortunately, the entire Arnold vs. Flicker relationship leaves behind it more questions than answers. Ted Flicker and Danny Arnold were both long gone by the time I began research for this book. Danny Arnold's widow didn't remember any of the details of the lawsuit with Flicker. Arnold's sons were too young to have known any detailed information about this controversy as well. By the time I finally found someone who knew Flicker's widow, he informed me she had just died, therefore robbing me of any information from the Flicker side of the story.

Danny's Side of the Story

In the 1987 interview that Danny Arnold gave to Bob Claster, he makes no mention of Ted Flicker at all. In fact, at one point he tells Claster, "I went back to television and started to work on various projects . . . *Barney Miller* was one of them. Sold the concept to ABC, did the pilot. It didn't get on the air because it seemed, again, to be too different." That's not entirely true. As we know, it did air in August of 1974 on *Just for Laughs*. The August 28, 1974, *Variety* carried a review of the program that states, "This detective comedy opens strongly enough to support reports that ABC-TV has ordered four more episodes, even though it's not on the fall schedule." *Variety* thought the first half in the precinct had "the stamp of exceptional TV comedy" but when the show shifted to Barney's home life, "the contrast is sharply disappointing."

The review also says that the producers already had the order for four more episodes. In Arnold's interview with Claster, he stated his belief that "the only thing that I think got *Barney* on the air was the fact that the 1974–75 season of ABC was such a disaster." In fact, ABC slated only three of the top thirty shows for the season. "They reached down into the bucket for anything they had and my first order for *Barney Miller* was two shows," Arnold said. When Claster questioned the odd number, Arnold clarified his statement saying, "Actually, it was called thirteen shows with the right to cut back to two . . . so I had a two-show order. It was like a network grasping for straws."

The undeniable fact is that whenever the order for thirteen or two or four more shows was made, the original cast had been cut loose and Danny Arnold had to recast the pilot and make it all over again. If he hadn't been forced to make those changes, we might never had been introduced to Ron Harris, Nick Yemana, or Stan Wojciehowicz.

How the Film Detective Story Inspired Danny Arnold

Hal Linden remembers Danny Arnold revealing to him that *Detective Story* (1951) was the inspiration for *Barney Miller*. The influences of Sidney Kingsley's play and William Wyler's film adaptation on Danny Arnold's 12th Precinct are unmistakable. In fact, I would guess that it is no accident that the precinct in *Detective Story* is the 21st while Danny Arnold's squad is the 12th, with just a transposition of the numerals.

Both vehicles spend ninety percent of their storytelling time in the precinct house. Both squad rooms are displayed in the starkest terms; dingy, grungy old offices with furniture that might have been lifted from the curbside. One ironic twist in comparison of the two is that central to the plot of *Detective Story* is Det. Jim McCloud's (Kirk Douglas) home life, which by the last portion of the film spills over into his work environment. This, too, lends credence to the belief that this was Danny Arnold's inspiration because the first pilot, "The Life and Times of Barney Miller," was meant to be just that, an examination of a cop's life both at home and in the squad room and how each affects the other. That idea works better and opens up more possibilities within a drama. Mercifully, that philosophy was abandoned very early on in *Barney Miller*. Miller's home life would only have been a distraction because the focus of the comedy was always going to be found in the precinct among the assorted victims, perpetrators, and "paranoids with proof."

In the first few minutes of *Detective Story* a woman comes into the squad room. Det. Gallagher (Frank Faylen) recognizes her and says, "Oh! Mrs. Ferragut, are those people still bothering you?" She replies, "Worse than ever. Why haven't you given me any protection?" Gallagher tells her he has twelve men guarding her, one of them his own brother. She apologizes but says her neighbors are making atomic bombs "and they blow this atomic vapor right through the wall at me and they have a man watching me from the top of the Empire State Building with radar!" She asks if the President knows about this and Gallagher tells her he just talked with him about it an hour ago. He promises to double the guard on her. While this exchange demonstrates "a paranoid *without* proof," it's a very short walk from Mrs. Ferragut to many of the troubled individuals that came through the 12th. The other difference is that Gallagher plays along with her delusion whereas the members of the 12th Precinct would have deposited such an individual in Bellevue Hospital.

In another storyline, McCloud brings in a young man for stealing $480 from his employer. To McCloud he's just another punk, another rotten thief. Unlike most of the cops in the *Barney Miller* universe, Det. McCloud wants to be the judge, jury, and executioner of the perps he brings in every day. The early Wojo was similar to McCloud in the sense that he was judgmental and tended to view the issues in a very black or white way of thinking. However, Wojo, who would eventually evolve and grow as a person and a cop, never really possesses the anger and violence that Det. Jim McCloud displays.

Eventually, Det. Lou Brody (William Bendix) talks to the young thief, Arthur Kindred (Craig Hill), and learns that he stole the money to make one last attempt to win back his girl. It turns out Kindred returned from the war to discover his girl was now a successful model running with a much more expensive crowd than that with which he could compete. His girl's younger sister comes to the precinct to try to help him and Det. Brody is sympathetic and gets Kindred's boss not to press charges. This, of course, is a very familiar routine in *Barney Miller's* 12th Precinct where the detectives have a heart and can be moved to show empathy for not only the victims but even the occasional "criminal." However, Jim McCloud is not one to show mercy for anyone who has made a mistake. This is his fatal flaw.

We are introduced to McCloud's implacable hatred for the criminal element when attorney Endicott Sims (Warner Anderson) informs precinct leader Lt. Monaghan (Horace McMahon) that his client, Karl Schneider (George Macready), wants to surrender to an outstanding warrant. Monaghan tells the lawyer to talk to Det. McCloud because it's his case but Sims refuses, stating that McCloud is biased and has dealt violently with his client in the past. When asked about the bias, Sims refuses to explain but hints that McCloud knows the reason.

Schneider is a doctor who has lost his license for performing abortions. More than one young mother "in his care" has lost her life and McCloud wants him behind bars. When McCloud walks into Monaghan's office, Sims confronts him.

Sims: For over a year McCloud, you personally have been making my client's life a living nightmare. Why?

McCloud: Because I'm annoyed by criminals that get away with murder. They upset me.

Sims: That's your story.
McCloud: Yeah.

Sims: I've investigated and discovered otherwise.
Monaghan: What are you driving at Sims?
McCloud: What?

Sims: Nothing yet.

Monaghan: I vouch for every man on my squad and that goes for McCloud. Ya got something to say, say it!

Sims: When it serves my purpose, not before. Meanwhile Lieutenant, I'm warning you—not a hand on my client.

When Sims leaves the office, Lt. Monaghan wants to know from McCloud what the barrister was driving at. He doesn't like anyone besmirching the reputation of his squad. As they partake in a heated exchange, Monaghan says to McCloud, "Your moral indignation is beginning to give me a quick pain-in-the-neck." Later in the same conversation he tells McCloud, "You want to be judge and jury too, you can't do it!"

What Sims "has" on McCloud is that his client, Schneider, once performed an abortion on McCloud's wife before she was Mrs. McCloud. Sims assumes that McCloud knows that and that's why he's harassing Schneider. He does not.

In Season One, episode five of *Barney Miller* entitled "The Courtesans," Wojo has rudely treated a suspect brought in for prostitution. Barney invites him into his office.

Barney: Just because we're policemen does not mean we can't be gentlemen. I said policemen, not judge, not jury.

Wojo: Yes sir.

Barney: The citizens of this city, including alleged lawbreakers, are entitled not only to our protection but a certain amount of consideration, a little courtesy.

Wojo: Yes sir.

Barney: Do your job as quickly and as efficiently as you can and skip the moral observations.

Wojo: Okay Barn.

Barney: What happened to yes sir?

The tone of *Detective Story* as compared to *Barney Miller* is entirely different. The film is certainly darker and more tragic but the similarities, for example, between the commanding officers of Lt. Monaghan and Capt. Miller are certainly visible. Both will initially defend their detectives in front of any outsider or accuser but then, in private, they make it perfectly clear to their underlings that they will not stand for insubordination or dirty cops.

Neither Monaghan nor Miller are necessarily averse to bending or loosening the "by the book" rigidity once in a while but in Monaghan's squad the feeling is that violence may be used when necessary to evoke important information whereas in Miller's squad room, the rules may, more often than not, be relaxed as a benefit to the accused or the victim.

While we never see any inappropriate behavior or muscle from the detectives of the 12th Precinct whether in the form of taking bribes or taking punches at criminals, *Barney Miller* acknowledges its tradition and history in the stories of Inspector Frank Luger. The ol' Inspector is fond of such declarations as, "In the old days we used to bust some heads."

The concern about police corruption and graft was particularly acute in the 1970s. The film *Serpico* (1973), starring Al Pacino and based on real life NYC detective Frank Serpico, who refused to fall into line and go on the take like the officers around him, was extremely popular. Frank Serpico's reluctance to corrupt his integrity and his badge almost got him killed and it definitely got him a lucrative book and film deal. The influence of *Serpico* can be seen in the relentless Lt. Scanlon (George Murdock) of Internal Affairs who is ever anxious to find a dirty cop wherever he might be. Scanlon is particularly annoyed by the 12th's "goody two-shoes" reputation and, in turn, Barney's reputation as a real decent guy.

A comedic take on a dark and serious film like *Detective Story* was just the beginning of Danny Arnold's genius in developing the show that would be his greatest television legacy.

The whole *Barney Miller* world is fascinating to examine today in light of all the current controversy surrounding law enforcement practices in the United States. In truth, *Barney Miller* never really referred to a specific racial problem between the police force and people of color. There were suspects and criminals who were African American and Hispanic but there were even more who were Caucasian. Nevertheless, the kind of empathy we saw displayed in the 12th Precinct is very timely. Advocates for change in our current law enforcement crisis are seeking more empathy and more awareness of the mental and social issues that affect the cycle of crime. They may want to look to *Barney Miller* for some textbook explanations of how to treat the public.

Danny as Auteur

> I think sometimes it would be frustrating for producers and directors to work for my dad because they'd be there waiting to do what they got hired to do because he wanted to have his hands in everything. He was there constantly.
>
> *—Dannel Arnold*

The term *auteur* is frequently used in film criticism and analysis but not so much in television. Auteur, the French word for author, is a term that was applied to certain filmmakers in the 1960s by the French New Wave film criticism. The implication is that the filmmaker's personal stamp and influence are so great on the film that he or she is essentially the author of the piece. That being the case, Danny Arnold was the textbook definition of an auteur. Numerous accounts from those who worked with him, and for him, all concur that Arnold had his hand in every aspect of the *Barney Miller* production.

In terms of the writing, Shirley Alberti, Danny's personal assistant for five years, said, "Everything that Reinie [Reinhold Weege] and Tony [Tony Sheehan] wrote had to go through Danny and Danny would drive those writers crazy. They would be working twenty-four hours a day, sometimes more than twenty-four hours!" This is a common memory. Numerous actors and writers have told me that Danny Arnold was always open to creative and funny ideas. However, those who worked for him also remember that Arnold would listen to their idea and then go off, digest it, and rewrite it in his own voice. Amazingly, those whose ideas had been totally rewritten almost to a person agree that once Arnold was finished with it, it was even better and funnier than they'd originally imagined it to be.

Jeff Stein, who along with Frank Dungan and Tony Sheehan, were responsible for most of the last three season's scripts, remembered the trouble he and Dungan had getting used to how Arnold worked. He remembered a specific incident when Arnold was complaining about something they'd written. He was yelling "Why would he do this, why would he say this thing?" Stein explained, "What it really got to was he didn't like a joke we had about olive loaf. Once we took the olive loaf joke out, he said, 'Now it works. Now I see it.'" They hadn't yet figured out the key to Arnold's dynamic with the show. Stein said they finally realized, "Everything is a disaster until he makes a little change or turns a comma into a semi-colon or hyphenates a word or something. It doesn't have to be major, just enough . . . you know, like a dog pissing on a hydrant – that's his and now that it's his, it's fine. We didn't know that and once we realized that, once we cracked the code, things came much easier."

Hal Linden, Max Gail, Arnold's sons, Shirley Alberti, and even Danny himself, all mentioned that every one of the main characters in the ensemble cast represented an aspect of Danny Arnold's personality. Wojo/Max Gail was the youthful idealist always in search of answers, Harris/Ron Glass was the suave and charming guy aspiring to greatness, Nick/Jack Soo was the dry sarcastic wit who just loved to play the horses, and Fish/Abe Vigoda represented his own frustration at growing old. He infused the show with his personal fears, opinions, and hopes. In "The Sighting" (S.4/Ep. 22), one of the characters comes in to complain that her husband has gone crazy and is turning all of the couple's assets into gold. More than one member of the company told me that Danny Arnold encouraged them to buy gold. Danny, like Mr. Brauer in "The Sighting," was paranoid about the monetary system crashing and so he began to buy a lot of gold.

Casting director Harriet Helberg remembered, "It wasn't just the writing for Danny. He directed the shows with the directors there. He produced them, he wrote them. I don't imagine he did line readings with actors but he knew how to work with actors. They loved him." Susan Beavers, a personal assistant to Danny Arnold, laughed when I mentioned a director of a particular episode. Not because she didn't respect the director but because she thought it was funny to think that anyone other than Arnold directed an episode. She laughed as she jokingly (perhaps) said, "Nobody did anything on *Barney Miller* except Danny. Nobody."

Perry L. Krauss, the show's post-production supervisor, said that Arnold would occasionally go down on the set and interrupt a scene that was working quite well. He'd make three or four seemingly minor changes and, inevitably, the scene would work even better. "He took gold and made it platinum," Krauss remembers. "He just had the eyes and the ears and the head for what made it funny."

His friend and fellow writer Ron Friedman worked on a couple of shows but eventually backed away because of the difficulty of dealing with Arnold. "I really enjoyed Danny as a friend," Friedman said. "He was always great to have lunch with, always great to hang out with, and he always wanted me to work/write for him and I always said, 'No, I can't do it Danny, I'm too busy,' because I knew what would happen! And it did. He suddenly went from friend to inquisitor and it was painful. And I didn't need that." Freidman also made the point shared by others that, "He also delighted in coming in after something was written and starting all over again and changing the premise and changing everything." Many times it would make the piece better but again, some believed it was also about his imprint being on everything related to the show. Sheehan said that eventually he and Weege got into the habit of each working on every other week's script. They eventually worked out a system of not handing the script in too early so as to cut down on the possibility of Arnold ripping everything apart and starting over.

Perhaps the most challenging aspect of Arnold's personality for those around him was his tendency to procrastinate. He was not someone who had everything neatly mapped out on paper in terms of what to do and when. He went by instinct. He wouldn't really roll up his sleeves until he was backed up against the wall. It seems as if he needed the adrenaline rush of an impending deadline to bring forth his best work. Once things were "do or die" then he would work and work and wouldn't let it go until it was as near to perfect as he felt it could be. That kind of stress is one thing if your artistic medium is a solitary one like painting. However, Arnold's artistic pursuits were collaborative so one can imagine the level of stress his style caused for those who worked with and for him. He needed others to help him visualize his goal while at the same time having that need to do everything himself.

Arnold's youngest son Dannel said, "My dad was the type of guy who would hire a gardener but mow the lawn for him."

Fiercely Independent

From my earliest interviews with Hal Linden who remembered Danny Arnold as "the gutsiest guy I ever knew" to Nancy Ross Landesberg (Steve's widow) telling me how charming Arnold could be, the impressions of Danny Arnold have been some of the most enjoyable revelations of this entire project. One of the later interviews I did was with Frank Dungan who, along with Jeff Stein and Tony Sheehan, was responsible for most of the storylines of the last three seasons. Sheehan worked with Dungan and Stein during Seasons Six and Seven when Danny Arnold was essentially on medical leave. Sheehan was the showrunner while Dungan and Stein were the story editors so at one point I said to Dungan, "Tony Sheehan was like your Danny Arnold before Danny Arnold returned [for Season Eight]." Dungan quickly corrected me. "You can't compare anybody to Danny Arnold. You can't do that, Otto. Tony was the executive producer, yes, but nobody is Danny Arnold." While his statement elicited the desired laughs, I nevertheless felt it safe to assume that Danny Arnold was a mythic figure to all who knew and worked for him.

Whether Danny Arnold had a charm that bent people to his will, a demeanor that scared the hell out of them, or a self-confident assurance that pissed them off, the result was you either did it his way or he wouldn't do it at all. Bill Persky told me, "He [Danny] was not easy to disagree with and he held onto his opinions extremely intensely. That led him, in a number of situations, to get fired from places where he was doing a good job."

There is no question that the independence Danny Arnold enjoyed on *Barney Miller* would never be possible in today's TV production climate. First of all, in the 1970s networks were not allowed to own their shows. They made deals with production companies and the producers used the network's platform to distribute the product that was the TV show. Once the courts allowed the networks to enter the TV production market it became increasingly more difficult, if not impossible, for a smaller independent production company like Four D Productions (Arnold's company) to crack the network schedule. The creation and success of *Barney Miller* was the result of "a perfect storm" in time, place, and creator.

Hal Linden, Tony Sheehan, and Frank Dungan all mentioned to me instances of the network giving in to Danny Arnold on a certain issue, particularly those having to do with episode content. Linden's favorite example of this had to do with the episode entitled "The Courtesans." It was a first season episode and the network objected to the insinuation that Wojo was going to patronize a prostitute. (See S. 1/Ep. 5 in the episode guide.)

What's even more amazing about Danny Arnold's cockiness in dealing with the network is the fact that the show was never a huge ratings hit. *Barney Miller* never finished a season in the Nielsen's Top Ten. Of the total of eight primetime seasons in which it was an entry, the program finished in the Top Twenty for the middle four seasons. It didn't even make the Top Thirty in the first two or the last two seasons it was on the air. The critics loved the show, however, so it was always seen as a prestige production. Its place on the ABC schedule may have been as a result of the fact that the network held the top spot in the rating's race in the late 1970s due to the creation of "Jiggle TV" and the premieres of shows like *Charlie's Angels* and *The Love Boat*. *Barney Miller* was a counterbalance of class and dignity among the less sophisticated hits of the day.

Tony Sheehan, who was with Danny Arnold and *Barney Miller* longer than any other writer or producer, said, "From early on ABC could have nothing to do with the show. They literally didn't see a script. The only people who could come to the tapings or deal with [us] were Broadcast Standards people, but no ABC executives were allowed to ever contact [us]. When I left the show after Season Seven, I got a call from Tom Werner and Marcy Carsey, who had a production company. They said, 'You don't know us, but we were the ABC executives on your show.' And I said, 'You were? Why didn't you ever call and say hello?' They said, 'Because we were told if we ever tried to contact you about anything about the show—even something on a superficial level—and Danny Arnold found out, he would take the show off the air.' So that basically, ABC—again I don't think they saw scripts and they therefore had no notes—they were simply delivered a final product, so I assume they had to be happy, to some extent, with the final product, because they had no other choice."

Frank Dungan told me, "They [the network] wouldn't dare talk to Danny. As a matter of fact, I remember they were giving us a hard time about something. I forget what it was. It may have been [the storyline about] the sanitation workers in New York being armed. There was something that was bothering the network and we kept arguing with them and we finally said, 'Look, Danny's here, we'll put him on the phone,' and they said, "No, no, it's fine. It's fine.'"

David Arnold, Danny's oldest son, echoed much of what Linden and Sheehan had related to me. I told David Arnold that it sounded to me like his father, after twenty-five years in the business, rolled the dice with everything on the line regarding *Barney Miller*. I asked how and why he could have done such a thing with two young children? David Arnold said, "Well, he knew what he was capable of and he knew that if he were able to do it without [interference] . . . I mean, I'm sure Hal told you some of the stories about executives trying to give him notes and all that stuff and he ended up throwing everyone out. You know, 'I'll shoot you if you come to the stage' kind of stuff." Despite the fact that Danny Arnold told his wife Donna that the show had better work or else they'd be forced to move in with her mother in Van Nuys, David Arnold insists his father knew he'd have a hit if he were left unencumbered by "the suits" at the network. The publication of this book is proof that Danny Arnold's instincts were on the money.

Danny's Style

"He was a genius. He was crazy," remembered his old friend and casting agent Eddie Foy III in an interview with the Archive for American Television in 2003. Memories of Danny Arnold are seldom mild or passive. He was crazy, he was a genius, he was a tyrant, he was the most loyal, he was the most generous. There's very little indifference when people talk about Danny Arnold. Foy claimed "what he brought was total, unabashed freedom. Think free. Think wild. Think funny!"

Arnold smoked large Cuban cigars, rode in limousines, and had a terribly unhealthy diet. He loved pastrami, potato chips, and M&Ms. Nevertheless, he played tennis, swam, and according to Bill Persky, "he was a really great golfer."

Tom Reeder says, "He was larger than life. He was big. He could be very charming, but then, there were those other times when he was pretty intimidating." Bill Persky said, "Danny Arnold was one of the most interesting characters I've ever known. With more knowledge of more subjects—from rare coins to horse racing—I mean he just knew everything."

Persky also mentioned that Arnold always lived above his means. He was a generous and extravagant gift giver. Lori Openden among others said, "Did anyone tell you how he gave Reinie [Reinhold Weege] a car for writing a script overnight?" Everyone who was close to him mentioned his generosity. Nancy Ross Landesberg told me that Danny gave her and Steve a trip to Hawaii when they were married. Shirley Alberti remembers that he gave her a holiday trip to Hawaii as well. He owned a stable of racehorses. In the course of the show's seven-year run, Max Gail bought some property in Malibu. When he told Danny about the purchase, Arnold asked, "You got room for horses there?" Gail answered innocently enough, "Yeah, I suppose I do." Gail said, "Two weeks later some old cowboy pulls up and says, 'I got your horses.' Danny had hired him to pick a couple of good quarter horses and send them out to me."

Danny Arnold lived a life of the quintessential movie version of the Hollywood producer: one of eccentricity, glamour, and style. He was, in every way, a larger-than-life figure.

A Do-or-Die Work Ethic

Hal Linden, Tony Sheehan, and others said that they thought Arnold originally believed that *My World and Welcome to It* would be the critical achievement of his career. In fact, as mentioned earlier, that show did win the Emmy for Outstanding Comedy Series in its first year but was almost immediately cancelled. It's possible that the sting of losing that show made him work that much harder on *Barney Miller* and it may also explain why he wanted Flicker out of the mix so he could finally, after twenty years in the business, be the one solely in charge of a production and, in turn, his own destiny.

Whatever the case, he drove himself into ill health with his lifestyle and his work style. In his 1987 interview with Bob Claster, he mentions how personal *Barney Miller* was to him. He told him, "I had made a calculated decision that I was going to spend a minimum of five years throwing everything else in my life aside, just to do that show. Not many people want to do that. A lot of people thought I was crazy and maybe a lot of them were right. But after that I decided I could no longer work that way so I would have to take and pick my spots. For almost two years, I didn't do anything."

To be totally honest, it wasn't Arnold alone who decided that he needed to step away from the show at the end of that fifth season. He'd pushed himself to the brink. As the show neared the end of its fifth season, Arnold was told by his doctors that he needed to have heart surgery or else risk not living to see a sixth season.

He also put additional stress on himself through his procrastination. Many staff and crew members told me that it wasn't unusual for them to go to the office in the afternoon to meet with Danny and be told he was "at the track" as in the horse races. He would return later in the afternoon and work most nights until at least ten o'clock and then get back to work very early the next morning. Therefore, even with the break to go to the track, he was still working at least twelve to fourteen hours a day often six or seven days a week. The days/nights when they were actually filming, it was not unusual for them to shoot anywhere from twelve to twenty hours straight until they eventually started shooting the show over a span of two days.

As it turned out, by the fifth season he'd trained and groomed two writers that everyone considered "Danny's Golden Boys," Reinhold Weege and Tony Sheehan. However, it was Sheehan he called into his office one day to inform him that he was being forced to walk away from the day-to-day responsibilities of the show for a while. He wanted to know if Sheehan thought he could handle taking over the reins of the show? Tony said, "Sure Danny, Reinie and I can handle it." That's when Arnold dropped the second bombshell and told Sheehan that Weege just signed a development deal with Warner Brothers and would also be leaving. As daunting a task as it was, Sheehan agreed to it and it was probably best that Sheehan took sole control of the show for the next two years. Reinhold Weege, as talented and as funny as he was, was much closer to Danny Arnold in temperament and lifestyle and while it served him well in creating a courtroom version of *Barney Miller* with the hit, *Night Court*, it also sadly led him to an early demise at the age of sixty-two.

Veteran TV director Bruce Bilson told me, "He [Danny Arnold] gave his life to that show. He died not that long afterwards, he worked so hard on it." Bilson directed ten episodes of *Barney* and he recalled, "At one point, and I don't remember what episode, but he just collapsed and was in a room somewhere laying down. And I was shooting the tag and everybody was worried about him." In truth, Arnold died thirteen years after *Barney Miller* went off the air but it is a fact that he did very little following the end of the program's original run. In fact, he made no more than a half dozen hours of television after *Barney Miller* wrapped production in 1982. At the time, Arnold was only fifty-seven years old.

The Evolution of Barney Miller's Shooting Style and the Quad System

> The quad split really comes from his days as an editor and understanding timing, and editing, angles, and capturing those little nuances, either a word or an actor's face and how something works or doesn't work if you cut too early or too late. Those are the things he impressed on me if I wanted to follow his footsteps and end up directing or whatever. The base of it was all in the editing.
>
> —*David Arnold*

There was one battle Danny lost and that was at the very beginning of the production. The original pilot, "The Life and Times of Barney Miller," was shot on film, as a movie would be shot. Everyone knows that film is better than tape. It looks better, it holds up better through the years. This fact was significantly more important in 1975 before digitized imagery. However, film was also more expensive than videotape. For its part of the bargain, ABC was not willing to spend the money on film, so Danny was forced to use videotape. He wasn't happy about it but he moved forward.

When it came to writing, Danny was in charge. However, his penchant for both procrastination and perfectionism led to the fact that full scripts were rarely completed even in draft form on the first day of the workweek. On more than one occasion, the principals would meet for a table reading on Monday morning that consisted of a one- or two-page synopsis. Sometimes, it might be a full first scene or even a first act but rarely a full script. Naturally, this made casting a challenge and video blocking the camera movements all but impossible. Cast and crew alike agree that they would often begin shooting without a fully completed script. Most likely, this is a major factor in why Danny Arnold moved away from using the live studio audience. In the beginning, they would shoot the show in front of a live studio audience and then release the audience and the cast and crew would stick around to get "pick-ups," which normally mean close-ups or different angles that may have been missed in the initial taping. However, as time went on, Danny Arnold and his writers would come up with a better ending or a better scene after the audience had left and so they started to do minor, then major, rewrites and reshoot.

Soon, Danny started to cancel the live studio audiences, sometimes quite close to the scheduled taping. The office that controlled the ticketing and seating of those audiences told him that he couldn't do that. It was bad public relations. People who expected to see the show and were then told at the last minute that they would not be able to watch the taping were not happy. Eventually, Danny Arnold just stopped shooting in front of the live studio audience and began shooting the show somewhat in the manner of the way a motion picture would be shot except that the show was shot in sequence and on tape. Most films are shot out of sequence. Today, shows like this are called single camera shows but Danny shot with four cameras not counting the fifth camera he used to shoot the bank of four camera monitors that would assist him later on in the editing room. His little creation was called "the quad system" and is used regularly today.

Here's the explanation Danny Arnold gave to interviewer Bob Claster in 1987. "I had done the pilot in front of an audience. [I] would have continued to do so except that . . . it was a technological problem that forced me to do it without an audience . . . to maintain the quality of the show I knew I had to eventually do it without an audience because it had to be shot like a film. It couldn't be shot like a play, in the old system of switch feed as the show is being shot because there were too many extremely sensitive . . . relationships and moments that required fine editing and very careful shooting." The switch feed system he mentions had a director in a booth somewhere up off the floor watching a bank of monitors that showed the different coverage being shot on each camera by the individual cameramen. The director would then essentially edit the show while it was being performed by snapping directions to a board operator to "Switch to Camera Two" and then "Switch to Camera Three." The shots that the director called for were the shots that made up the program. That was how the majority of sitcoms were shot in the 1970s.

Barney Miller was different. Arnold explained to Claster, "I couldn't put the cameras down front . . . the way they were used to doing broad strokes situation comedy in those days. Big jokes and big characters. These were very small, very intimate moments that had to be covered very carefully. I couldn't go on film, the network insisted that I go on tape and there was no technological method, in those days, to edit. You couldn't put four cameras, as you did on film, on four moviolas and have that complete facility of rocking back and forth, frame by frame, and be able to pick the exact frame you wanted to make a cut in. While you could start four rolls of tape at a common number and roll them forward, you couldn't stop and go back and forth, I mean, tape stretched. It didn't have sprocket holes, you know, so there was no way to do it." However, Danny Arnold was not one to be told he couldn't do something. As the old saying goes, "Necessity is the mother of invention."

Arnold explained, "I put together a system whereby the four isolated cameras were all fed into four monitors and the four monitors were filmed by a fifth camera, so that all four frames could be moved frame by frame in synchronous movement. [This was the famous Quad System] So the control that I got was through this system but it dictated the very careful editing, very careful shooting, very careful playing, of a show that was very different and it helped *Barney* to maintain the quality that it had."

Susan Beavers, one of Danny Arnold's Production Assistants who went on to a very successful career as a TV writer and producer, told me, "Danny showed the network that he could end up making shooting on tape just as expensive as shooting on film."

Actor James Cromwell opined, "Danny's thing was, 'I don't want an audience. I don't need an audience. The audience is the people who watch it at home. I know what's funny and . . . if it needs a laugh track, I'll put that in. What I want is performance.' And people gave very nice performances, easy, comfortable. I mean, they were all absolutely perfect people and I loved every minute of it."

Basically, Danny Arnold wanted and achieved the intimacy of a stage play without the technological intrusion of the multiple cameras and pre-blocking. Most sitcoms that were shot in the traditional three or four camera style with live directing/editing would have to rehearse the script for a day or two and then spend another day or two blocking out the moves in advance so everyone knew where each camera was going to go in each scene. Danny Arnold rarely had scripts done ahead of time so the lack of audience and the quad-system of editing allowed him to make changes up until the last minute. The crew and the cast would work on one scene at a time. Once it was complete, then they'd move on to the next scene.

It should also be noted that one of Danny Arnold's oldest friends, and earliest employers, was Jerry Lewis. Arnold wrote for Martin and Lewis on television and in the movies and was no doubt on movie sets watching Lewis work in those early years. When Jerry Lewis began directing some of his own films in the 1960s, he supposedly came up with the idea for the Video Assist, the practice of mounting a video camera next to or very near to the film camera so the director could get an idea of what the processed film would look like on screen. This was long before you could instantly see a scene you just shot using a digital camera.

Danny at Home

> We were always, always on the set, every week. It really was the only time we really got to spend time with him during the *Barney* years. My dad

wanted to see us but he had an incredible responsibility to keep *Barney*, at the beginning, on the air. That's what fed us. I remember my dad telling a story that he came home after *Barney*, the first show, and it wasn't the success that it was later on and he was like, "We may have to sell the kids! We don't have any money, it's all in the show."

—*David Arnold, oldest son of Danny Arnold, who worked with his dad on Joe Bash*

I didn't look at him as "Hey, it's Danny Arnold, the producer of . . ." just that's my dad and he does what he does and I'm a kid doing what I'm doing.

—*Dannel Arnold, youngest son of Danny Arnold*

The impression I received from talking to Donna Arnold for this book was that Danny was not a man to share his work issues at home. Donna was unable to tell me much of anything about how Danny hit upon the idea for *Barney Miller*, how he ended up with Ted Flicker as a partner, or the resulting relationship and feud with Ted Flicker other than the fact that it ended badly.

David and Dannel have great love and respect for their father but they made it a point to say that their father never played the nepotism game with them when it came to show business. Both said they had to earn whatever they could in the industry because Danny was very sensitive about the possibility of people thinking they only got where they were through his favoritism. As it turned out, both sons experimented with show business but ultimately went in a different direction. In a fascinating twist of events, both of Danny Arnold's sons ended up with successful careers in law enforcement.

Donna believes that her sons' pursuit of law enforcement as a career was directly related to *Barney Miller* and the cops who served as technical consultants on the series. While her sons agree that there is some truth to that theory, it was also the policemen they met in their own backyard who influenced their careers as well. It seems that at some point there was a story written in one of the trade papers about certain industry writers and for some reason they put Arnold's address in the story. He was not at all pleased and since his sons were young at the time and he was often away from home working, he was spooked by the breach in his privacy and his [family's] potential security. As a result, Danny Arnold hired off-duty police to patrol around his home and the boys have fond memories of hanging out with those officers, talking to them, learning from them.

Many people connected with the show say that Danny Arnold essentially lived at the studio in the first few years of the show. According to Donna Arnold, Danny didn't completely leave home but it was close. She remembers that he would get up somewhere between 3 or 4 a.m. and take a swim in the family's swimming pool. She was afraid of him being in the water without anyone around so she would get up and sit by the pool while he got his early morning exercise. He would then get dressed, have a cup of coffee, and be off to work by around 5 a.m. at which point she would go back to bed. If it wasn't a night when they were shooting the show, he'd return home around 10 or 11 p.m., have something to eat, watch the news, and go to bed.

That leaves essentially no time with his children, which is why the boys were often brought down to the studio to spend time around the show and their father. If they hadn't done that, they might never have seen him. Thankfully, both sons have nothing but fond memories of those days hanging around the set with the cast and crew that helped their dad create a television classic.

Danny and the Actors

> My dad never really supported my efforts of being an actor. I remember him saying to me one time, "You know how lucky you are that you decided not to be an actor."
>
> *—Dannel Arnold*

> He told me if you take a five-pound bag of salt and that represents all the actors in the world and then take a thimble and you pour out that salt on top of the thimble, the thimble represents all the jobs available to actors.
>
> *—David Arnold*

There are more than enough accounts of how intimidating Danny Arnold could be but the actors who did the show all remember Arnold as being supportive, encouraging, and dare I say, nurturing? Mari Gorman, who portrayed Bruno Bender's wife Naomi, remembered Danny Arnold, saying, "Oh, he was fabulous. He loved doing what he was doing and he was very generous with his laughter and his appreciation for anything you did that he liked." Peggy Pope, who appeared in six *Barney Miller* episodes, wrote in her autobiography that, "Danny Arnold was an actor's guardian angel. Danny would stand close by and act silently with the actor. He also laughed so quietly that the mike couldn't pick it up, but the actor could. This gave us a 'live audience'—a gift that makes for a better performance."

That's not to say he couldn't be intimidating. Ray Stewart who played Daryll Driscoll on the show remembers, "I walked into Danny Arnold's office and he was at this big desk and it's pretty intimidating to go in and read. I didn't read for the casting director, I read for Danny alone in his office . . . and he's a rather imposing man. He's kind of scary looking but on the wall behind his desk was this banner that was like six feet wide and four feet tall with four big letters on it: H-E-L-P. This huge sign that said 'help.' Instead of trying to scare me, he was pleading for help. It made me laugh. It relaxed me. We chatted and I don't think I read anything but, he hired me."

Those close to Arnold believed that his early experiences as an actor gave him a special appreciation and understanding of the challenges of the work. He was also smart enough to understand that really good acting could and would elevate his writing. "He would find an actor who got how to play the stuff that we were doing which was to play it as realistically as possible," recalls Max Gail. "We used a lot of wonderful actors who had done a lot of Broadway and stuff like that. They were strong characters . . . they weren't just doing jokes."

At the same time, it wasn't easy being an actor on *Barney Miller*. Casting director Lori Openden remarked, "It was really hard for them to work the schedule where you had no script all week and then you stayed up until five in the morning shooting. You know, it was hard. It's one thing for all of us, we're not on camera, but they were on camera having to be funny and have high energy. It was not easy."

Danny and the Directors

As noted previously, while there were many fine directors who were credited through the years as having directed *Barney Miller*, almost everyone with whom I spoke either stated or hinted at the fact that Danny Arnold always had his hand in the show's direction as well.

Over the course of the show's eight seasons, only three men are credited with directing ten or more episodes: Bruce Bilson (10), Danny Arnold (13), and Noam Pitlik (102). There were nine different directors, including Flicker with the original pilot, who are credited with directing just a single episode. Among the remaining eleven, one was an editor, Homer Powell (2), that Arnold let try his hand at directing, another was a writer, David Swift (3), who occasionally directed, two were stars of the show, Hal Linden (3) and Max Gail (5), and one was the show's writer/producer, Tony Sheehan (2). Alex March (4) was a prolific director who worked on shows such as *Naked City*, *Ben Casey*, and *Quincy, M.E.* and Lee Bernhardi (8) went on to direct multiple episodes of *Fish*, *What's Happening*, and *Webster*.

Bruce Bilson was really the only *Barney Miller* director who was somewhat "outside the *Barney Miller*" inner circle to direct a substantial number of episodes. Arnold obviously trusted Bilson and Bilson apparently tolerated Arnold's need for involvement on all levels. Bilson had good reason to be secure in his abilities. By the time he got behind the cameras to direct *Barney*, he'd been a full-time television director for over ten years helming such comedy classics as *Hogan's Heroes*, *Love, American Style*, and *The Odd Couple*. Mr. Bilson won his only Emmy Award in 1968 for Outstanding Directorial Achievement in Comedy for his work on *Get Smart*.

Noam Pitlik

If there is a single director most associated with *Barney Miller*, it's Noam Pitlik. In his more than twenty years of directing television, Pitlik helmed over 250 episodes of various television sitcoms and more than a half dozen TV movies. He also appeared as an actor in hundreds of episodes of primetime television programs. In a broadcasting career that spanned nearly half a century, Noam Pitlik was nominated for two Emmy Awards and Four Director's Guild of America Awards. He won one Emmy and one DGA prize, for directing two different *Barney Miller* episodes, one in 1979 and another in 1981.

Pitlik was born in 1932 and began acting in live television at WCAU-TV in Philadelphia in the 1950s. He made his off-Broadway debut in *The Threepenny Opera* in 1957. He moved to California in the early 1960s and began to appear in both films and television as a reliable character actor. He made occasional forays into films such as *The Fortune Cookie* (1966), *Fitzwilly* (1967), and *The Front Page* (1974), but his work in primetime TV shows of the 1960s and 1970s was ubiquitous. He was cast in numerous episodes of *Ben Casey*, *The Fugitive*, *Hogan's Heroes*, *Bewitched*, and *The F.B.I.*, as well as recurring roles on *Sanford and Son* (1972–1977) and *The Bob Newhart Show* (1972–1978).

Pitlik's first directing credits came in 1973, on the *New Dick Van Dyke Show* (1971–1974), a program created by Carl Reiner. He started directing *Barney Miller* episodes in the show's first season and continued to direct during every season of the program except the last. While it's been established that Arnold had his hand in every facet of the production, Tony Sheehan said that Pitlik really began to shine in Seasons Six and Seven when Arnold was forced to step away from the day-to-day operations of the show. Sheehan said "Pitlik's expertise was invaluable during those two seasons." He would eventually direct 102 episodes of *Barney Miller*, a little over 70 percent of the entire series. He went on to helm multiple episodes of *Taxi*, *One Day at a Time*, *Mr. Belvedere*, and *Wings*.

Every actor with whom I spoke remembered Noam Pitlik as a very warm and wonderful director. As an actor himself, he had the ability to make the ensemble comfortable and confident.

Pitlik died of lung cancer in 1999. His *Los Angeles Times* obituary described him as "a director whose booming laugh, bear hugs and belief that television is a collaborative effort endeared him to actors and crew members."

The Players and Their Characters

Hal Linden

Hal Linden started his long career in show business as a reed man, doubling as a vocalist, in Swing and Dixieland jazz bands. From there he moved into musical comedy and appeared in a number of Broadway shows including *Bells Are Ringing*, *Wildcat*, and *Illya Darling* before winning the coveted Tony Award in 1971 for the musical *The Rothschilds*. When Danny Arnold tapped him to be the lead in a comedy pilot set in a gritty squad room of the New York Police Department, he'd made no more than a half dozen prior appearances on network television.

The character Linden played in *The Rothschilds*, a patriarch named Mayer Rothschild, was far removed from Barney Miller, at least on the surface. "[*The*] *Rothschilds* were heavily characterized characters," Linden said. "I wasn't playing me, I was playing a real character, a beard, I got to be in my eighties. I mean it was an epic role."

Once *Barney Miller* had been in production for a while and Danny Arnold and Hal Linden became friends, Linden asked how and why he got the part. He knew for a fact that he was not the network's choice but Danny's choice. According to Linden, Danny Arnold told him "I wanted to give the character [of Barney Miller] a Talmudic sense of justice—a Talmudic sense of justice—the concept that there but for the grace of God goes all of us on the other side of the desk from the arresting officer."

Hal Linden was born Harold Lipshitz on March 20, 1931, in the Bronx, New York. According to a 1975 *TV Guide* article, he grew up with a somewhat confused identity. He was a Dodgers' fan living in the home borough of the Yankees. He played stickball and saxophone. He once recalled that, "Even in the worst of times, . . . my parents gave me music lessons." His older brother and cousins all played instruments so he was expected to be a musician. He went to New York's High School of Music and Art. He began to play in bands at various churches on Friday nights and synagogues on Saturday nights. One of the popular big bands of the day was led by a man named Sammy Kaye and the band's motto was "Swing and Sway with Sammy Kaye." The young man instinctively knew that "Swing and Sway with Harold Lipshitz" didn't have a very melodic ring to it so one day as he was driving into Linden, New Jersey, he decided to take the town's name as his own and soon became Harold "Hal" Linden.

He graduated from CCNY in June of 1952 with a degree in Business but in the July 19, 1975, *TV Guide* article by Arnold Hano, Linden remembers that his brief stint as a delivery boy was "the only honest work I ever did." Instead, he actually landed a job with Sammy Kaye and immediately went on the road as a member of his band. He recalled his days on the road for a publication called *In the Know* in 1976 saying, "When I was with Sammy [Kaye] we made a tour in which we played a different town every night, we did a hundred consecutive one-nighters in 102 days. I think we had two days off the whole trip. When we weren't playing we were in the bus on the way to the next town." Life in a big band was tough but the young musician nevertheless had dreams of someday leading his own group.

The dream was put on hold when Linden was drafted into the Army in October of 1952 and was placed in an army band. On occasion, he was loaned out to the Special Services branch and it was there he got his first taste of acting in front of an audience. It proved to be a valuable experience. When his time in the service was completed he began acting in summer stock and off-Broadway productions. He continued to play music as well, landing stints with the bands of Bobby Sherwood and Boyd Raeburn.

He met his future wife, Frances Martin, in a Hyannis stock company production and they were married in 1958. His new wife helped him get an audition for a show she was in called *Bells Are Ringing*. Linden was hired as Sidney Chaplin's understudy in the Broadway hit and when Chaplin left the show, he took over the lead male role of Jeff Moss.

Bells Are Ringing afforded him the opportunity to play against legendary comedienne Judy Holliday. His memories of Holliday are a mixture of happy and sad. "Judy was one of the brightest women I have ever known, and she was a killer at Scrabble. But she never came to terms with her dumb-blonde image. I learned a lot about my craft from her, and just by watching her." Holliday, a heavy smoker, died of cancer in 1965, just a few weeks short of her forty-fourth birthday.

The next ten years were a struggle with Broadway and Off-Broadway parts here and there. To make money to support his growing family, he did voiceover work on dozens of commercials as well as dubbing numerous foreign films. He also worked industrial trade shows dancing around cars. Sometimes there was no work at all and he collected unemployment. "Once I appeared in an off-Broadway production. I had to take a cut in pay to go to work," Linden recalled.

In the fall of 1965, he got the job of Louis Jourdan's understudy in *On a Clear Day You Can See Forever*. When Jourdan left the production, Linden naturally assumed his big chance was at hand. It was not. The part went to an actor named John Cullum. "That was the low psychological moment of my career, not getting that job," Linden remembered. "I couldn't even quit in a huff. I needed the job as a standby."

He continued with voiceovers and singing commercials until he landed the lead in the 1970 Broadway musical, *The Rothschilds*. On March 28, 1971, at the 25th Tony Awards, Hal Linden took home the honors for Best Performance by a Leading Actor in a Musical. The days of working as an understudy or dancing through industrial shows were over for Linden.

The Rothschilds closed in January of 1972 and Linden made appearances on a couple of TV series and starred in a made-for-TV movie that doubled as a pilot for a potential hour-long detective show entitled *Mr. Inside/Mr. Outside*, co-starring Tony LoBianco. Unfortunately for Linden, but fortunately for future *Barney Miller* fans, the movie was not picked up to be a series.

It was not long after that failed movie pilot that Danny Arnold's office called Linden and brought him back to Los Angeles in early 1974 to film the pilot for *The Life and Times of Barney Miller*. As we know, the original pilot wasn't picked up but Danny Arnold coaxed the network into letting him try again with a slightly altered concept. When production on the show resumed, nearly a year had passed and the only actors still available to film the new episodes were Linden and Abe Vigoda but Linden wasn't sure he wanted to go back to LA for a show that *might* make the schedule. He had an offer to do another Broadway play that, even if it wasn't a success, meant months of work between rehearsals and previews. Linden said he was notoriously slow to make up his mind. Finally, the Broadway producer called and said they needed to know his decision by close of business Friday.

"There I was sitting in my manager's office on Friday, [and] he says, 'I've got to give her an answer, what do you say?' And . . . I'll never forget it because I was quite cavalier about it. I said, 'Ah, listen, we've done Broadway, let's try television.' It was that cavalier a choice and we decided to go out and we did two new episodes and that was picked up and we went into production."

Linden spent eight years playing the most famous role of his life as Barney Miller on the ABC sitcom of the same name. He was nominated for a Primetime Emmy Award for Outstanding Lead Actor in a Comedy Series for all seven of the full seasons of *Barney Miller* but never won the prize. He did, however, eventually take home three Daytime Emmy Awards: two for Special Classification of Outstanding Individual Achievement as Host of a series of five-minute educational spots called *FYI: For Your Information* and another for his role in a 1984 *CBS Schoolbreak Special* entitled "The Writing on The Wall."

He lost his wife of fifty-two years, Frances, in 2010 but the years following *Barney Miller* have been busy and full for Hal Linden. He starred in three more series: *Blacke's Magic* (1986), *Jack's Place* (1992–1993), and *The Boys Are Back* (1994–1995), but none lasted more than a season and a half. Nevertheless, he has remained in demand on many popular TV shows including *The Golden Girls*, *The Nanny*, *Touched by an Angel*, *Will & Grace*, *Law & Order*, and many more. He continues to sing and perform his music at various cabaret venues around the United States and has even put together a one-man show that spotlights his years on *Barney Miller*. When interviewed for this book, he was in rehearsals for a Los Angeles production of *The Fantastiks*. The review from *Broadway World: Los Angeles* gushed, he "is a National Treasure, milking every bit of humor, but never going over the top." The same review went on to say, he "still has the stuff that has made him one of our finest comedic actors."

Toughest Job of Them All

In the setting of one of the funniest and most intelligently written sitcoms of all time, Hal Linden had the toughest job of anyone in the room—that of the straight man. Comedy professionals will often talk about the challenges of the straight man and just how important that role is in carrying out the material to its funniest conclusion. Many of the actors, writers, and crew of *Barney Miller* agreed that Hal Linden held the show together with his performance.

When I told Tony Sheehan that Linden and I had discussed the fact that the show, in general, had no jokes because it was more of a character comedy, Sheehan agreed but with reservations. "You would laugh at his [Linden] reactions, at his exasperation, at his anger, at his sarcasm. Even though he wasn't doing the jokes, it was funnier that way," Sheehan said. "Essentially, Linden's role was in reacting as opposed to acting."

"Anyway, we had jokes," Sheehan insisted, "but it wasn't people exchanging jokes, it was people in the middle of conflict saying funny things. You'd find yourself laughing along the way of a conversation as opposed to 'here comes the next joke, here comes the next joke.'"

Captain Barney Miller

Bernard J. Miller is a Captain in the New York City Police Department. His badge number is 233451. Due to conflicting answers from Miller, the best we can speculate is that he started on the force sometime between 1957 and 1960. He was passed over for Deputy Inspector in 1975, 1978, and 1980. He was finally promoted to D.I. in 1982.

He is married to his wife Elizabeth, with whom he has two children, Rachel, born approximately 1958, and a son David, born approximately 1963. Rachel attended Julliard and moved out of the house at the age of seventeen. Years later, David expressed the desire to move out at the same age.

Miller is left-handed, roughly 6' 1" tall and in his forties with salt-and-pepper hair and a moustache. He has a tattoo under his left arm that he got when he was fifteen years old in honor of V.E. Day. Knowing that, we also know he was born in 1930 or 1931. The tattoo is of the letters VE with a rose under it. He doesn't like to go to parties but nevertheless seems to have strong interpersonal skills.

As a boss he is supportive but strict. He will always defend his men but in return he expects them to be honest with him and thoughtful in their actions. He is passionate, patient, and fair but he does have a temper if pushed too far.

Max Gail

Max Gail has portrayed many eccentric, passionate, activist characters in his fifty-year-long acting career. These multifaceted roles reflect a very real side of the off-screen Max Gail. He is a humanist who respects the rights of all and has dedicated his life to a variety of social causes, many of which work to achieve more respect for the Indigenous populations of America. That's why it's all the more surprising to learn that his paternal grandmother's family, the Trowbridges, were part of the Blue Book of Michigan society. While Gail admits he "had no real connection to the high society part of his family," it did, as a teenager, get him invited to a slew of debutante parties where he was treated to "good food, great bands, and lots of pretty girls."

Maxwell Trowbridge Gail Jr. and his twin sister are just one of three pairs of twins born to Mary Elizabeth (née Scanlon) and Maxwell Trowbridge Gail. The couple produced seven children in a matter of six years. Gail's dad had been a piano player in a big band in Detroit. He was particularly adept at booking the group's gigs and eventually opened a talent agency that specialized in booking bands and musical acts. He also took over an office supply booth owned by his uncle in the Motor City's Penobscot Building and grew it into a successful office supply store. His mom was an actress who attended the American Academy of the Arts and once swam in *Billy Rose's Aquacade*. The large family more or less put an end to his mom's professional career. As he remembered it, "my folks were both wonderful, energetic, talented in their ways. They made a commitment to raising us all. There were no radio shrinks at the time—people just soldiered through by drinking, smoking, having a good attitude."

Max Gail received his Bachelor's Degree from Williams College in Massachusetts and returned to the Midwest and his home state when he enrolled at the University of Michigan for a Master's in Business Administration. It was during his graduate years that he took a course in acting. Gail remembers, "It was called Theory of Acting. I thought, well, that probably means we watch movies and write papers." He soon learned just what an acting course was and a whole new world of self-discovery opened to him. He had played piano since childhood but acting had never been an interest for him until he stumbled onto this class.

He graduated with an MBA in 1969 and followed a girlfriend to California. The relationship didn't last but he ended up in San Francisco and began to play piano in small bars to earn cash. He saw an ad in a local paper casting for understudies for a production of *One Flew Over the Cuckoo's Nest*. The ad was a mistake because it was supposed to be an ad looking for someone to run the concession stand. Regardless, they let him read and his talents and his sturdy build helped him win the part of understudy for the character of Chief Bromden.

He continued to apply for jobs in corporate America although he was slowly beginning to realize that the prospect of spending his days behind a desk was not what he wanted. He'd just lost a regular gig playing piano at the Hyatt House when he got a call from the theater. The actor playing the Chief had a physical altercation with another cast member and was removed from the show. The producers wanted Gail right away. He remembers, "I showed up, and they took me in and showed me where my marks were and I went on and did the play and I ended up doing it for two years."

In the two years working in *One Flew Over the Cuckoo's Nest*, Max Gail met many actors who became lifelong friends such as Ron O'Neal, William Devane, Raul Julia, Michael Moriarty, and Robert Walden. In fact, Walden introduced him to The Actor's Studio and his connections began to pay off with small parts in *Dirty Harry* (1971) and *The Organization* (1971). At the end of the play's run, Gail decided to try his luck in Hollywood with the hope that he could spend two or three years in LA and make enough money to move back to San Francisco. He was finding himself as an actor, but stardom was never his ultimate goal.

Gail moved to Los Angeles and began to get small roles on weekly series television. He was particularly successful landing cop shows like *Cannon* and *Get Christie Love!* but as he told me, "I really did not have any interest being a TV cop . . . some of the things that I was probably obviously right for physically and all." The producers of *One Flew Over the Cuckoo's Nest* had repeatedly offered him a place in the New York production. He initially turned down the offers but soon he decided, "You know before I take off for Hawaii or wherever I'm going next in life, I would like to explore New York."

It was around this time that Max Gail was starting to become aware of the American Indian movement and got involved in the challenges faced by the Indigenous tribes of the United States. Following his time in New York, he returned to Los Angeles to read for a part in a film. He didn't get the part but was able to get a good deal on some property in Malibu and took residence on the beach. He began to jog on a daily basis and as he ran, he began to put rhymes together in his head. He found somebody who had a piano and began to write some original music. Looking back at that time now, he says, "It was about opening up this creative voice for me, something that really means something to me." The new energy and confidence resulted in him starting to get more roles. He even remembers getting a turndown from a producer saying, "You know, we're so embarrassed. The network wants us to hire this blue-eyed blond guy but we just want to tell you that your reading was fantastic."

It was during this period of creative bliss that Gail met with Danny Arnold for the first time. Arnold informed Gail that they had done a pilot for a show that was turned down but that he'd bought out his partner and got another deal with ABC to do two more shows. Arnold told Gail that the actor he wanted was currently in New York directing a play (Charles Haid, who later co-starred in *Hill Street Blues*) and although he didn't think Gail was anything like the character, if he wanted to read for the part he could. Gail auditioned and Arnold told him, "You're very good. You showed me there's a different way to do it." He was offered the part and so Hawaii, and any other adventures, would have to wait.

From the first, Gail was concerned about signing any long-term deals. He was too naive at the time to even know how rare an eight-season run would be for any network show. He spent the next eight seasons as Detective Stan Wojciehowicz ("You spell it just like it sounds"), or Wojo, as his fellow officers at the 12th Precinct called him. He took the character of Wojo from a young cop who saw justice in very black and white terms to one of the 12th's most compassionate officers who was always in search of the truth, no matter how uncomfortable the results might be. As the years passed, the compassion of Max Gail very clearly shone through in the character of Stan Wojciehowicz.

Gail remembers, "I didn't have the craft that Hal [Linden] and Ron Glass and others had. I didn't have that sort of theater craft. So, I was the one who was always, 'Wait a minute. Does this make any sense? And does this and this?' And I think it forced us into something that made the scene more real and funnier . . . and I think Stanislavsky's thing . . . you don't do it by acting broadly, you gotta believe it . . . was probably my biggest contribution and I was the one who was more often the one that would be saying that I don't think we have this scene yet, I don't think we've figured out something yet and in time, it went from me being a nuisance to me being a valuable nuisance, in a sense."

In his time on *Barney Miller*, Max Gail became friends with numerous American Indian leaders, artists, and activists including John Trudell, Floyd Westerman, and Buffy Sainte-Marie, as they made music together and worked diligently in activist roles to preserve the dignity and the rights of America's Indigenous people.

In the years since *Barney Miller*, he has worked steadily on stage and in both film and television. He has co-starred in some critically acclaimed series like *Whiz Kids*, *Sons and Daughters*, and *Review*. Unfortunately, like his friend and former co-star Hal Linden, none of the series lasted more than a season. He has, however, done guest spots on series such as *Chicago Hope*, *Judging Amy*, *NCIS*, *Psych*, and *Mad Men* as well as appearing in independent films like *The Frontier* (2014) and big budget Hollywood prestige pictures like *42* (2013).

In 2018 he joined the cast of the popular ABC soap opera *General Hospital*. In the show he portrayed Mike Corbin, a man struggling with a diagnosis of Alzheimer's, who tries to reconcile with his son before it's too late. Gail's performance was widely praised and led to two Daytime Emmy Awards for Best Supporting Actor in a Drama Series. It also led to his joining the cause to raise awareness of this dreaded disease.

Max was first married shortly after the end of *Barney Miller*'s run but sadly, his wife died a few years later from cancer after welcoming a daughter. He later remarried and is currently amicably separated from his second wife and engaged to another wonderful lady. His relationships have gifted him with a beautiful group of children and grandchildren for which he is constantly grateful.

Max Gail is a true artist and humanitarian. He is a writer, a musician, an actor, and an activist. He brings both a gentility of spirit and a passionate commitment to all that he does.

Detective 3rd Grade Stan Wojciehowicz

A native of Buffalo, New York, Stanley Thaddeus Wojciehowicz weighed eleven and a half pounds at birth and has at least one brother. He also has an incredibly strong constitution. Through the years he was poisoned with arsenic, suffocated in a tunnel collapse, bit by both a rat and a dog, and lived through it all.

He led a pretty healthy lifestyle. He took vitamins, jogged daily, and took part in a lot of "physical activity." In fact, when poisoned the doctors told him "a man with an ordinary constitution would have cashed it in." Apparently, Wojo had built up a tolerance for arsenic because of all the fruits and vegetables he ate.

His mother must have also had an amazing physical constitution since he once said she was dead and then on two later occasions he was worrying about buying her gifts. All we can assume is she either came back to life or he was thinking of buying her a gift and sending it to the cemetery.

As strong as his physical constitution was, he was, as his mother always said, "high-strung" and we see a great deal of evidence of that over seven and a half years. He's afraid of flying in planes, he faints whenever he gets an inoculation or shot, and he has a persecution complex. It certainly seems that he is the youngest member of the detective squad but what he lacks in experience, he makes up for in passion.

Punctuality was not his strong suit. He was often late for work. The two primary reasons were he had slept somewhere other than in his own bed or he made an arrest on the way to work. He had a few other bad habits like chewing his gum with his mouth open.

Whatever shortcomings he may have had, he was a good friend with a big heart. He was a Vietnam veteran and even though he had no medical training like some in the squad, he delivered two babies in his time. He once said that Phil Fish was "the closest thing I've had to a father since I've been in New York." Surely, this was not true since all visual evidence suggests his relationship with Barney was far more paternalistic than his relationship with Fish.

In terms of hobbies, he plays the flute, handball, and enjoys watching sports on television. He was also an amateur manualist. His favorite tie tack is a pair of tiny handcuffs. His prized possession is a baseball signed by the New York Yankees and New York Giants from the 1936 World Series.

Wojo began the series as one of the more one-dimensional characters. He was a reactionary that viewed most issues in simplistic "right or wrong" terms with little room for subtlety or circumstance. As time goes on, however, Wojo becomes less judgmental in certain cases while his dedication to "the underdog" grows. As he matures, he's less concerned with going "by the book" than he is with helping the people who always seem to get the short end of the stick, the poor, the homeless, and the independent spirits.

Stan Wojciehowicz, though never discussed within a storyline, appears to wear a hairpiece, or does he? Tony Sheehan said, "One time Max said to me, 'Hey Tony, why don't we do a story where you reveal that Wojciehowicz wears a hairpiece?' And I said, 'Well, Max, Wojo isn't bald, *you're* bald!' (laughs). Well, in my mind his character was not bald, he's not wearing a hairpiece, only Max did. I think maybe Max wanted to work without a hairpiece."

That may be true. Max Gail usually chooses to go au naturel for his roles. Being the gracious man that he is, I felt comfortable asking Gail whose decision it was that he wear a hairpiece on the show. He told me that it didn't really matter to him but George Spiro Dibie, the Lighting Director/Director of Photography asked him to do it to avoid the lights reflecting off his forehead. Gail said he's glad he went with the toupee as opposed to some of the actors of his era who opted for hair plugs. According to Gail, as the person's hairline continued to recede, they'd end up with a bald head and a row of hair plugs in front making for some rather odd comb overs.

Abe Vigoda

There were few people in the entire world beyond the reach of his immediate family who had ever heard of Abe Vigoda prior to his small but pivotal role in the cinematic classic, *The Godfather* (1972). He had worked mainly in the theater before he was thrust into the national spotlight by his role in Francis Ford Coppola's Oscar winning film. That spotlight brought him to the attention of the *Barney Miller* producers and inevitably led to his portrayal of Det. Sgt. Philip K. Fish of the 12th Precinct.

Abraham Charles Vigoda was born in New York City on February 24, 1921, to Samuel Vigoda, a tailor, and Lena Moses Vigoda. Both of his parents were Jewish immigrants from Russia. His mother was concerned he wouldn't be able to support a family as an actor but his father encouraged him to pursue whatever kind of work he desired.

He told interviewers that he knew he wanted to be an actor since he was six years old, when he was cast in a school play entitled *Candlelight*. Needing one more boy to portray a fifty-year-old man in the play, Vigoda's teacher asked for volunteers. Vigoda and a number of his classmates raised their hands. She chose Vigoda because she told him, "Abe, you look old." In an interview with his grandson from 1995, he said "I've been playing old roles ever since, older than I am so that's how it started, at the age of six years old."

Growing up he joined a number of small theater groups to gain experience. He referred to it as "something I had to do; it was like a calling." The experience of being on the stage gave him confidence. He didn't formally study acting until he got out of the Army and studied the dramatic arts at Lincoln Center in New York City under the GI Bill.

In addition to his work with a variety of theater groups, he remembered starting on live television with Jimmy Durante in the *Four Star Revue* in 1951. Nevertheless, his work in front of the cameras was sporadic throughout the 1950s and 1960s. Abe Vigoda was essentially unknown until, at the age of fifty, he took on the role of Tessio in the *The Godfather*. Once the film became a national phenomenon, winning the Academy Award as Best Picture of 1972, Abe Vigoda became a familiar face to fans and casting agents.

Vigoda began to book guest shots on some of the more popular episodic programs on network television like *Kojak*, *Mannix*, *The Rockford Files*, and *Hawaii Five-O*. Not surprisingly, *The Godfather* landed him a slew of offers but it also typecast him as an organized crime figure.

Vigoda, despite his hangdog looks, was actually a well-conditioned athlete. He jogged regularly and was a competitive handball player. In a featurette called *Inside the 12th* for the Shout! Factory DVD release of *Barney Miller: The Complete Series,* Vigoda recalled that his agent contacted him one day right as he finished jogging and wanted him to hurry straight to an audition for a new show. He didn't want him to go home or change, just head straight to the audition. Hal Linden believes that Danny Arnold was initially interested in Vigoda for the part of Sgt. Grimaldi, the character that eventually became Nick Yemana. No doubt because of Vigoda's success in *The Godfather*, Arnold assumed he'd be good to play the Italian cop. However, once he saw him, he switched gears and began to tell Vigoda about Phil Fish, the "oldest cop in the precinct." Vigoda remembers Arnold telling him he looked tired. "Of course I'm tired," Vigoda told him, "I jogged five miles this morning, I'm exhausted." The next comment was the clincher. Arnold told Vigoda, "Yeah, yeah, tell me, you look like you have hemorrhoids?" Vigoda shot back, "What are you, a doctor or a producer?"

No one would have ever guessed when *Barney Miller* finally made it to the air that Abe Vigoda would be the breakout star. Nevertheless, the sardonic, sarcastic, and exhausted Phil Fish struck a chord with audiences. By the middle of *Barney Miller*'s third season on the air (1976–1977) Vigoda was given his own spinoff entitled, *Fish* (1977–1978). He left *Barney Miller* in the fall of 1977 when Phil Fish retired from the NYPD. Unfortunately, the spinoff was canceled following its second season.

His final noteworthy role after Tessio and Fish came about in the spring of 1982. When *Barney Miller* finished its eight-season run in March of 1982, the show held a big cast party after the series wrapped. There was a reporter covering the event for *People* magazine. Vigoda wasn't there because he was working on a play in Canada. The reporter wrote in the article that Vigoda was dead. The sad-faced actor took it in stride and even posed with the *People* magazine cover while sitting in a casket for the cover of *Variety*. In the end, he may have become more famous for not being dead than he ever was as Tessio or Fish.

He spent the next thirty years playing off the image of not being dead on TV, in movies, and with Late Night hosts David Letterman and Conan O'Brien. A website appeared on the Internet that people could track every day to see if Abe Vigoda was still alive. He appeared in commercials that used his age, look, and build as a punch line. The last thirty years of Vigoda's career may have not been filled with the highest quality roles but he was busier than ever.

To the disappointment of millions, Abe Vigoda really died on January 26, 2016, at the age of ninety-four. He was finally gone but fondly remembered by audiences and peers across America.

Too Much of a Good Thing

The fact that Danny Arnold cast Abe Vigoda for the part of Detective Fish was an inspired stroke of genius. No one knew Abe Vigoda in 1974 for anything other than Tessio, a Capo in the Corleone Crime Family. However, once Arnold saw that one-of-a-kind Vigoda face, he switched course and came up with the character of Fish.

In addition to his other talents, Danny Arnold had a type of radar for great, offbeat character actors. Lori Openden, one of the show's casting directors, told me, "He taught me what to look for in comedic actors. He could spot an actor that was right for the part that was in his head. And sometimes the actors helped him write the characters." In the case of Abe Vigoda and Phil Fish, it was a match made in heaven.

Let's assume the character of Phil Fish was an inspiration Danny Arnold had upon auditioning Abe Vigoda. He writes this curmudgeonly, aging, Jewish cop with every physical ailment under the sun. He's the "old man" in the squad room. Absolutely no one could have predicted that the character of Fish would be the audience favorite at the end of the show's first season. Vigoda presented a sort of elderly hero to American primetime audiences. He was a person who was well qualified in his job despite the ravages of time and yet, the inflexibility of bureaucracy was forcing him to give up the one thing he knew and understood best: police work.

But Vigoda's success as Fish was the beginning of Danny Arnold's headaches. More than a few individuals close to the production said that prior to the beginning of Season Two, Vigoda suggested to Danny Arnold that he change the name of the show to *Barney and Fish*. Needless to say, Arnold did not embrace that idea. Arnold's youngest son Dannel told me that as much as his dad loved character actors, he had far less patience with stars.

Both Hal Linden and Max Gail talk of Abe Vigoda with respect and appreciation but Linden has described him in interviews as "unique" while Max told me that, "Abe had his own way of working." The main issue seemed to be that Linden was an actor who approached material in a very organized fashion. Dino Natali, who played Officer Zatteli, said, "Hal Linden had a photographic memory. He knew the whole script the second day, the whole script." According to Gail, Vigoda came at the material from more of the Method acting style. He would take his time and try to find his inner motivation. Linden's reaction to that way of working is unclear but "the Method" was not a philosophy that Danny Arnold embraced.

Max Gail likes to tell the story of "Snow Job," the show's third episode. In the story actor Ron Feinberg is arrested as a flasher. At one point, he asks to be allowed to go to the men's room. After a prolonged absence, the lights dim and we hear a yell from the bathroom. When they break in, they discover he's tried to kill himself by sticking his finger in a light socket and his foot in the toilet. Fish then delivers the line, "I didn't know he was that tall." Gail recalls that there was some discussion as to how to play the scene because at that point in the story it is presumed the man is dead. Vigoda says, "We should play it with a loose hat." Gail recalls watching Danny Arnold and Hal Linden as they glanced at each other with a "what the hell is he talking about?" look between them.

By the middle of the second season, the Fish character was more popular than ever and a spinoff was inevitable. From the very beginning of the series, the character of Fish was identified as a cop who was nearing a reluctant retirement. *Variety*, dated December 10, 1975, reviews what it identifies as the "Fish & Bernice" spinoff pilot which was the *Barney Miller* episode entitled "Fish" (S.2/Ep.12). This is the same episode that introduces us to Steve Landesberg's character of Arthur Dietrich. At the time the episode was filmed, Florence Stanley was working on a show called *Joe & Sons* and was replaced by Doris Belack. The rest of the cast involved in the spinoff were to be Emily Levine as Fish's school teacher daughter, Darryl Seman, as one of her students, and Landesberg. It's unclear from the article whether Landesberg was supposed to pull double duty or leave *Barney* for *Fish*. In the end, it was a moot point because this version of the *Fish* spinoff was not favorably reviewed as *Variety* observed, "What evolved was a funny enough *Miller* episode that still didn't suggest the makings of a successful series in its present form."

In the first episode of Season Three we are introduced to the character of Jilly Pappalardo, a wayward youth who attaches herself to Mr. Fish. A few episodes later we meet her friend Victor Kreutzer and when they cross paths with Bernice Fish, she quickly decides that they deserve a loving home instead of being sent to a group home and we have ourselves a spinoff. Fish and Bernice will host a group home for wayward youth.

By the time production got underway there were "difficulties brewing" between Arnold and Vigoda. Susan Beavers, one of Arnold's Assistants, told me, "Danny made up a whole new corporation to [produce] *Fish* . . . he didn't want *Fish* under Four D Productions." He created a company called Mimus. When I mentioned to Beavers that I got the impression that perhaps Danny Arnold's heart wasn't in *Fish*, she replied confidently, "Oh, it was not. He hated that show. No, he didn't want to do that show."

The creation of the new production company for *Fish* may say as much about the deterioration within the Arnold/Vigoda relationship as anything from that time. When Gregory Sierra left *Barney Miller*, there is reason to believe that his relationship with Danny Arnold was also strained. However, when his new Danny Arnold created show, *A.E.S. Hudson Street*, was made, it was done under Four D Productions.

The first episode of *Fish* aired on February 5, 1977. There were six remaining episodes in the *Barney Miller* season but Vigoda would only appear in two of them. The premiere episode of *Fish* garnered a surprisingly good review in *Variety* that stated, "Danny Arnold's *Fish* spinoff . . . made its debut as an ABC-TV entry with a mirthful episode that suggested the Abe Vigoda-starrer has a future—despite its present burden of being placed in opposition to the CBS comedy block on Saturdays." There's no doubt the initial placement on Saturday night was anything but helpful. To make matters worse, the network ran the first eleven episodes from February through April and then aired the twelfth episode in June and the thirteenth in August. It's unlikely that Arnold had any power over network decisions but it certainly seems like a disinterested programming strategy on the part of the network.

When the show returned in the fall, it was placed onto the Thursday night schedule after *Welcome Back, Kotter* and before *Barney Miller*. By that time, the strained relations between Danny Arnold and Abe Vigoda had been aired out in the trade papers. In *Variety*, Wednesday, June 29, 1977, there was a headline that read, "Vigoda Takes CBS Role as Arnold Fumes." The story states that Vigoda, who had previously been expelled from the cast of an NBC mini-series called *79 Park Avenue* due to Danny Arnold's protests that it conflicted with production dates on *Barney Miller* and *Fish,* was now working on a CBS TV movie called *The Comedy Company*. It wasn't expected to be a problem because its shooting schedule finished before he was due back to film the two-part season premiere of *Barney* entitled "Goodbye Mr. Fish."

When *Variety* reached out to Arnold for a comment, he told them that he was never informed of Vigoda's plan to do the TV movie but didn't care as long as it didn't interfere with his other commitments. However, when pressed, he left no doubt as to how he felt about the situation or Vigoda. "Every one of my actors on every other show has done other jobs, including Vigoda," Arnold stated. "His quote that I vetoed an attempt for him to do a Dean Martin Roast is a blatant lie, and in actual fact what happened was he told me about the roast. It came up on a shooting day, and I tried to explain to him that he could not go away when we were shooting a show . . . He went to Las Vegas (to do the roast) and did not show up for a shooting call. The man just breached his contract for the second time and left me hanging on a shooting date." Vigoda claimed that Arnold had given him permission to do the roast and then withdrew it even though, according to Vigoda, it did not conflict with shooting schedules. Who was right or wasn't right isn't really important. The point is the relationship between the two men seems to have been in tatters.

Michael Druxman, Vigoda's long-time publicist and friend, said that when *Fish* began production, he landed Vigoda an interview with a columnist at *Variety*. According to Druxman, the day the story ran, he received a phone call from Danny Arnold. "You will never do any publicity on Abe Vigoda without my approval first," the angry producer told him. Taken aback, Druxman replied, "'Well, you know, I don't work for you. I work for Abe Vigoda and . . . it's up to him.' He says, 'You want to lose him as a client?' And I said, 'Well, that's up to Abe' and he hung up on me."

Druxman summed up the relationship of Arnold and Vigoda saying, "They were always at war . . . but they were together because they needed each other."

Susan Beavers remembers a *Barney Miller* episode that featured Florence Stanley as Bernice. During an initial reading of the script, or what there was of a script, there's a line where Bernice says, "Fish" and Fish snaps back at her with, "Bernice!" The stage direction in the script was "(Fish snaps) 'Bernice!'" Vigoda misunderstood or else didn't read the stage direction carefully and when they came to the line, he snapped his fingers and then says, "Bernice." Beavers told me, "It was like that kind of a thing where everyone in the room managed to catch everyone else's eye at the same moment. It was so funny."

A less humorous production tale of Vigoda and Stanley has to do with work on an early *Fish* episode. Tom Reeder, who wrote two of the first five *Fish* episodes that were shot, remembered that, "He [Vigoda] would do things that made her [Stanley] nuts." Reeder described the opening scene of a show where Stanley was having some sort of problem with the kids. "And then Fish walks in," Reeder recalls, "and the studio audience applauded and instead of just holding which is what an actor should do in those circumstances, Abe broke character, turned to the audience, and went, 'ta-daaa,' which got a huge laugh, and Florence was so annoyed at that, that she stalked off the stage."

In the end, it's hard to pinpoint exactly what went wrong with *Fish*. It wasn't funny. It was exactly the kind of domestic sitcom format that *Barney Miller* veered away from because it was just not that interesting. Vigoda excelled as a supporting character but not as a lead. The show had some solid writers, some whom had written for *Barney*, but it just didn't work.

After it failed, there was speculation Vigoda might return to *Barney* on a regular basis but that was never going to happen. Too many bridges had been burned. After much haggling over money, Vigoda did return to *Barney Miller* one last time, three years after *Fish* went off the air. When his character is asked about the group home, he says the city cut off the funding and took back the kids. Thus ended the chapter on Fish and Bernice outside of the precinct.

For Vigoda, the post-*Barney* years were busy but not necessarily filled with the highest quality parts. Michael Druxman said that Vigoda felt, "Danny put out the word and kind of had him blacklisted." There is no proof to back up the allegation but Vigoda's feelings were what they were. The actor's 1986–1987 run on Broadway in *Arsenic and Old Lace* was, in Druxman's opinion, the best thing the actor did in the post-*Barney Miller* years.

Vigoda and Arnold were both very strong personalities. Druxman said that Vigoda struggled for so long in small parts and Off-Broadway theater that when he became a star all of a sudden at the age of fifty, "I think to a certain extent, it went to his head. He had toiled so hard and so long without any attention . . . but I loved the guy. He was a good friend for over thirty years."

Detective Sergeant Philip K. Fish

Phil Fish is the squad's resident curmudgeon. We are never told his exact age but in terms of mandatory retirement ages, we can assume his is roughly fifty-eight or fifty-nine when we first meet him. Therefore, it's all the more impressive that a man could accumulate so many health issues in such a short time and still remain on the force. According to Fish, he suffers from paranoid depression, sore back, sore neck, and sore legs, hot flashes, gout, forgetfulness, menopause, kidney stones, bad feet, gall bladder problems, a compressed disc, hernia, obesity, and hemorrhoids. His bad feet may explain why he keeps a pair of slippers under his desk.

He lives in Brooklyn with his wife, Bernice. They were married on February 12th in either 1939 or 1940. We know that deep down Fish loves Bernice but sometimes it is hard to tell. In addition to once suggesting they take separate vacations, he insults her cooking, her appearance, and apparently keeps a secret bank account from her in Hamilton Bank on 11th Avenue and Stuyvesant. On top of all that, he's only been home four times for lunch between April 12, 1945, and December 4, 1975.

If his record as a husband is less than stellar, his record as a New York policeman is to be envied. In the course of his career, he's received three Commendations 1950, 1957, 1962, and a Medal of Valor "for conspicuous bravery and total disregard for his personal safety in coming to the aid of his fellow officers." That doesn't mean he's always happy in his work. On the occasions when he has threatened to quit, he goes to the park and throws stale bread at the pigeons.

He claims to be a vain man but he also freely admits that he can't carry a tune and he has false teeth. To round out this vibrant personality, he speaks a little Japanese, he doesn't like lime Jell-O, and he drinks only in the privacy of his home, "where it's necessary."

Ron Glass

When Ron Glass broke into television in the early 1970s there were still relatively few roles for African American men that were fully developed characters as opposed to stereotypical caricatures. Through Danny Arnold's brilliant writing and Glass's sensitive and realistic acting style, they combined to make Det. Sgt. Ron Harris one of the first in a line of increasingly progressive portrayals of black men on American television.

Ronald Earle Glass was born in Evansville, Indiana, to Lethia and Crump Glass in July of 1945. He was the youngest of five children and although his parents divorced when he was still a baby, he was coddled and encouraged by his mother and four older siblings and raised to believe he was special.

His mother was a strong-willed woman who cleaned people's houses for a living but according to Glass in a 1978 *TV Guide* profile, "her life was her children—and her church." Despite her Baptist faith, she sent her kids to a parochial school in the belief that they would be provided a better education. She herself went back to school as her children grew up to obtain her own high school degree at the age of thirty-nine.

His mother and one of his older brothers were his main role models. Glass told *TV Guide* that, "My mother's sense of dignity, of ethics, of pride, set the tone of my childhood." He began as a Liberal Arts student at the University of Evansville when he was convinced to try out for the school play. It was about slavery and they were desperate for black actors. He said, "Sure, I'll try anything once," and just like that, he found his calling.

He eventually earned his Bachelor of Arts in both Drama and Literature while winning awards for his acting. Following college, he was offered training and a job at the prestigious Guthrie Theatre in Minneapolis, Minnesota. There he honed his craft as he worked through the plays of Shakespeare, Shaw, and other classics of the theater.

When he arrived in Hollywood, he experienced a strange form of prejudice. He was too educated to fit Hollywood's usual portrayal of African American men. Glass told *TV Guide*, "My English was so good that my agent told me I'd never work." In fact, the agent eventually dropped him because he wasn't bringing in enough money. In an effort to go beyond his Shakespearean training, Glass took a job at an answering service to learn to talk more like everyday people.

It wasn't long before Glass was cast in a memorable episode of TV's hottest property, *All in the Family*. The producer, Norman Lear, obviously liked what he saw from Glass because he also hired him for *Maude*, *Good Times*, and *Sanford and Son*, all of which were created by his company. Glass said, "I got to be known as Norman Lear's repertory actor." That was quite a badge of honor in the landscape of 1970s television.

Danny Arnold spotted Glass on an episode of *Maude* and sent for him because he thought he'd be right for a part in his new sitcom. According to Arnold, "I knew I wanted him as Harris before I met him." Glass recalled that they just talked and laughed at the very informal first meeting. When he arrived home, he learned from his new agent that Danny Arnold offered him a regular role on a new weekly sitcom. Believe it or not, Glass wasn't particularly thrilled at the prospect. He wanted to do more serious roles. Thankfully, he relented and became one of only four actors who were part of the *Barney Miller* storyline from beginning to end. After Hal Linden and Max Gail, Glass appeared in more *Barney Miller* episodes than any other actor. [James Gregory was the other actor who was in the entire run of the series.]

In an interview with David Levin for the website *Pop Goes the Culture*, Glass remembered that his character started out as just a black guy in the room. According to Glass, however, "Danny and the writers . . . they were so bright and so sensitive and so alert. They started to perceive things about that black actor who was that black character who was on the show and . . . we ended up with a totally well-rounded, totally wonderful character to play, but it didn't necessarily start out that way."

Following *Barney Miller*, Glass co-starred in a failed attempt at an *Odd Couple* remake with Demond Wilson. Glass worked on TV throughout the 1980s and 1990s. He was a regular cast member on three more shows in the 1990s that didn't last more than a year, *Rhythm & Blues* (1992–1993), *Mr. Rhodes* (1996–1997), and *Teen Angel* (1997–1998). He was part of yet another one season flop in the 2002–2003 season called *Firefly*. The sci-fi story set five hundred years into the future, however, has found a cult following in the years after its initial run and there are many fans who now know Ron Glass as Shepherd Derrial Book, a preacher of the future. *Firefly* even introduced Glass to the world of fan conventions and he was amazed at the loyal following that the one season show garnered from its audience.

In the 1990s, he made a name for himself in voice-acting circles when his voice became familiar to a new generation of viewers who grew up watching the popular Nickelodeon cartoons, *Rugrats* (1990–2006) and *All Grown Up!* (2003–2008). Glass voiced the character of Randy Carmichael.

In his interview with Levin, he happily recalled the *Barney Miller* experience and his co-workers, saying, "It was an extraordinary group of guys and headed by somebody [Danny Arnold] who will never be replaced. He was just magnificent. Magnificent guy." The cast didn't stay closely in touch but they remained friends. Nancy Landesberg, Steve's widow, remembered how kind and sensitive both Glass and Max Gail had been to her and their daughter Elizabeth when her husband got sick. "They were so wonderful," she said.

Ron Glass was a practicing Buddhist and though he never married, he enjoyed the loyalty and love of numerous friends within the acting community and beyond who mourned his loss in November of 2016 when he died at the age of seventy-one.

Detective First Grade Ron Harris

We don't know Harris's origins. In fact, all we really know about his childhood is that his mother sculpted Spam into the form of a turkey for Thanksgiving and when he resorted to stealing, he stole books. That literary interest would serve him well in the years to come. He also spent time protesting the Vietnam War before serving two years in the United States Coast Guard.

He knows what he likes and it's all more than he can afford to spend. He has expensive tastes but he doesn't let that stop him. He wears fine tailored clothing, buys fine wine, goes to expensive restaurants, etc. Naturally, as a man who always believed he was going to be wealthy, he identifies as a Republican. He's also a smoker and he carries a pearl handled revolver.

Harris always expressed the desire to be a writer. His first published work was in a magazine named *Sir Gent: Entertainment for the Sophisticated Male*. The story submitted was entitled "John and Mary." However, after editorial got finished with it, the new title was "John and Mary and Harry and Frank." Titles were constantly changing for Harris. His first book was to be called *A Week in the Life of a New York City Detective*. He later either changed the title or the subject of the book or both and the manuscript he sold was called *Precinct Diaries*. As it turned out, the publisher changed that title to *Blood on the Badge*.

Once his literary ship came in, there was no stopping the spending. He invested in stocks, bonds, art, gold, and diamonds. He threw fancy dinner parties. He was becoming a literary star until, the lawsuit. Attorney Arnold Ripner sued him for defamation of character and wiped out all of Harris's hard-earned royalties.

Harris struggled to regain his literary footing after the lawsuit and eventually did sign a profitable contract for a second book. When last we see Sgt. Harris we're not quite sure whether he's actually going to accept his transfer to Flushing Meadow, Queens, or retire and devote himself full time to writing.

Jack Soo

Jack Soo played dozens of nightclubs in the 1940s and 1950s as he was pursuing a career in show business. However, none had quite the meaning in his life as Charlie Low's Forbidden City. A famous Asian American nightclub in San

Francisco's Chinatown, Forbidden City served as the basis for the club in the Rodgers & Hammerstein Broadway musical, and subsequent film, *The Flower Drum Song*. The owner, Charlie Low, was known for giving his performers nicknames like "The Chinese Frank Sinatra," "The Chinese Sophie Tucker," etc. Hal Linden claims that Jack Soo had been known as "The Chinese Bing Crosby." In the documentary *You Don't Know Jack: The Jack Soo Story*, his childhood friend Sachi Kajiwara remembers listening to him sing when she was a kid. "He loved to imitate Bing Crosby and other singers who were popular at the time."

Soo was actually born Goro Suzuki on October 28, 1917. His parents were living in Oakland, CA, but they wanted their first child to be born in Japan so they made plans to visit there but Jack came into the world on the ship before they actually made it back to Japan. His father was a tailor and his mom a seamstress. They ran a tailor shop in Oakland. The Japanese were restricted to where they could live in Oakland. Segregated as they were, there was nevertheless no real community like Chinatown so they found "community" in the Oakland Japanese Methodist Church.

In the documentary, Soo's daughter Jayne Soo Carelly recalled her father's love of sports. During his high school years, he played basketball, football, and baseball but his true love was baseball. *Barney Miller* co-star Steve Landesberg remembered Jack telling him that he'd played against Joe DiMaggio at Oakland Tech High School. As a seventeen-year-old high school student, he also won an award for a speech given at the Japanese American Citizens League entitled, "Why I'm Proud to Be an American."

That pride turned to confusion and panic on December 7, 1941, when the Japanese bombed Pearl Harbor. In February of 1942, the Japanese people of San Francisco were taken by bus and placed into the Tanforan Assembly Center Internment Camp. There, Goro Suzuki somehow had the courage to take it upon himself to host and emcee talent shows and impromptu entertainments for the camp's detainees. He organized the young people to do theater work. He got permission to let them take the kids out of camp to practice at one of the local high schools. No one was supposed to leave the camp, but he got approval from the administration.

His group was eventually moved to a camp called Topaz. It was while at Topaz that some were allowed to leave if they could prove they had a job offer. He had difficulty getting out because he was considered a Japanese-born citizen by the fact that he was born on the ship heading to Japan. He was, therefore, an alien and not a naturally born American citizen. Those who knew him and grew up with him and lived in the camps with him believed this was how and why he changed his name to Jack Soo. He wanted people to believe he was Chinese, far more acceptable during World War II when China was still a US ally. He eventually got a release from the camp and worked for military intelligence.

He met his wife Jean Zdelar in Ohio in the 1940s. She had done some modeling work and he was working as a singer. She was of Croatian ancestry. It was an unusual match, particularly for 1945, but the couple remained together for over thirty years until his death. The union produced three children: Jaynie, Jimmy, and Ricky.

Following the war, he began working in nightclubs in the Midwest around Cleveland and Akron, OH. One of Soo's friends believes that he was even doing some radio work until it was learned that he was not born in this country. All who knew Goro Suzuki/Jack Soo remember him as a man who showed no bitterness at the injustice of being thrown into an internment camp at the age of twenty-four when just a few years earlier he'd won a contest with his essay entitled "Why I'm Proud to Be an American."

In the late 1940s, while Soo was still known for, and booked as, a singer, he began to introduce comedy into his act. He even teamed up with a young comic named Joey Bishop for a year or two starting in 1949. He suffered through some lean years but his marriage was strong and his wife was supportive and so he continued to plug away until he caught the most important break of his career with *The Flower Drum Song*. Rodgers and Hammerstein deserve some credit for wanting to stage a musical about Asians with mostly Asian actors. It was not unusual in the 1950s or 1960s to have Caucasian actors and actresses take the roles and "play Chinese" or "play Japanese." Soo had no Broadway experience but was the Master of Ceremonies at Forbidden City in San Francisco. When Rodgers and Hammerstein were having trouble finding Asian actors to fill all their roles they went to the source, the original Forbidden City nightclub. It was there that Soo was spotted by Gene Kelly and offered a role in the Broadway show. He played Frankie Wing and understudied Larry Blyden's role of Sammy Fong. A year after the show opened, Blyden left and Soo replaced him in the meatier role of Sammy Fong that he then reprised in the 1961 film adaptation.

According to George Takei in the documentary *You Don't Know Jack*, when Soo got the role in *Flower Drum Song* on Broadway he sensed that it would make a huge impact on his career and he decided he wanted to use his real name. The producers had to turn him down because the story was a Chinese American story set in San Francisco's Chinatown district. Two of the female leads, Myoshi Umeki and Pat Suzuki, were Japanese and they needed as many Chinese names in the cast as possible for credibility.

He may have been thwarted in his attempt to lose the Soo moniker but he was essentially correct about the influence of *Flower Drum Song* on his career. It opened up television and films for him and he was even signed to co-star with James Franciscus in the 1964–1965 television series, *Valentine's Day*. He racked up other credits on the small screen on shows such as *The Jack Benny Program, Julia, The Jimmy Stewart Show, The Odd Couple* and *M*A*S*H*, to name just a few. He also worked in films with screen giants like Dean Martin, John Wayne, and Bette Davis.

Late in 1974 he received a call from an old friend he'd met decades earlier while working the nightclub circuit in the Midwest, Danny Arnold. The producer had thought of him for a role on his new ABC television series and, as the old saying goes, the rest is history. Today, all *Barney Miller* fans remember Jack Soo fondly for his dry wit and his character's bad coffee. Sadly, Soo didn't get to enjoy the entire eight-season run of the show. He was diagnosed with cancer in 1978 and died in January of 1979 in the middle of the show's fifth season. Instead of immediately writing him out of the show, Danny Arnold and the cast paid tribute to Soo by coming out of character for the final episode of the season and fondly sharing personal memories of their beloved colleague.

Detective Sergeant Nick Yemana

Nick Yemana was born in Omaha, Nebraska, but he does speak Japanese. He claims to have no family and yet we know that he has at least two uncles, one who was head of a garment union in Japan and another who ran a schmatte (Yiddish term meaning, "cheap, shoddy, junk") business in Hawaii. Since most of us have parents, I suppose we can assume he had parents as well.

In addition to his life of crime solving, Nick was a passionate and dedicated gambler. Horse racing was his favorite sport to bet on but he just loved the excitement of the risk that gambling presented. We know that, at the very least, he also bet on football—think Alcorn State—and politics—think the 1976 Presidential election. His lucky number is 1232.

His love of animals extended to his life at work. He enjoyed watching the ants play on the ice in the bathroom sink and he became friendly with one of the office cockroaches. He had a cat once but it ran away from home.

Nick was the second in command after Fish retired but for whatever reason, he somehow ended up in charge of the coffee and the filing system. The squad's constant complaints about the quality of his coffee made him consider abandoning that job on more than one occasion.

Personally, he was a smoker, he was adept at using office supplies for chopsticks, and although he hadn't been to church in years, he still had a certain respect for men of the cloth. He also had a healthy fear of werewolves.

Gregory Sierra

Sierra was one of the busiest character actors in Hollywood during the last thirty years of the twentieth century. He garnered hundreds of TV credits and appeared in major motion pictures including *Papillon* (1973), *Towering Inferno* (1974), and *Hot Shots! Part Deux* (1993).

Born in New York City in 1937, he was of Puerto Rican descent and was raised by his aunt and grandmother. He once told a writer, "When I was a baby we were a typical Puerto Rican family. Everybody lived together—grandmother, grandfather, aunt, two uncles, mother, father . . . gradually everyone went their [own] way." In the same interview he said, "I never really had a father," and remembered his childhood saying, "it wasn't one of the happiest of times for me." As a kid, the only thing he seemed to enjoy was hockey. "I played with a Long Island team for awhile," he said. "This was roller hockey. They had rinks where you played."

He grew up in a rough neighborhood and had to contend with the gang violence around him. Sierra attended a high school called Cathedral College that was actually a prep school for priests. By the time he reached high school, however, he'd lost interest in academics. His aunt and grandmother eventually let him quit and he joined the Air Force.

Following the service, he accompanied a friend to an acting class and was encouraged to participate. The teacher told him he had potential and so Sierra began to study acting. Spanish had been his first language but he also discovered a facility for accents and dialects and it helped him to get small parts on television starting in 1969.

Sierra landed a recurring role on the NBC hit show *Sanford and Son* in November of 1972 as Julio, a Puerto Rican neighbor who moves in next door to Fred Sanford's junkyard in Watts. He appeared in a dozen episodes of the show until landing the role of Chano Amenguale on *Barney Miller* in 1975. He stayed with the show for only thirty-five episodes, the first two seasons. It's possible that he only took the part because ABC had promised him his own series and asked him to be part of *Barney Miller* while they found a suitable vehicle for him. According to interviews with other actors who knew Sierra, it sounds like he wanted to break away from "the stereotypical Puerto Rican character" and was afraid of being typecast. He was eventually given the lead in another Danny Arnold sitcom called *A.E.S. Hudson Street* that ran for only five episodes in the spring of 1978. It was a funny show but the network didn't give it much of a chance.

His time on *Barney Miller* was marked by contradictions and complexities. Multiple sources confirm that he resented playing the typical hot-blooded Latino character. Nevertheless, in a 1976 interview in a book entitled *TV Talk 2: Exploring TV Territory*, he said, "I think *Barney Miller* is much more real than any other cop show. The people in the show have real problems. Kojak never worries. Everything is always under control on that show. You never see the frustrations of police work or the kind of joking that goes on among real policemen. Those are the kinds of things we show on *Barney Miller*." In addition to all of that, his second wife Susan committed suicide during his *Barney Miller/A.E.S. Hudson Street* years. They were separated at the time of her death but in a 1978 interview, Sierra said, "We had been together six years, and her death leaves me feeling guilty as well as feeling the grief."

After leaving Danny Arnold's production family, Sierra joined the final season of *Soap* as a South American revolutionary named Carlos "El Puerco" Valdez to great comic effect. In 1984, he had a chance for a regular role on *Miami Vice* but opted out after four episodes because he didn't want to live in Miami. Nevertheless, Sierra acted steadily in television throughout the 1980s and 1990s. He did very little on film or TV in the twenty-first century.

The author reached out to Mr. Sierra for an interview but never received a reply. Unfortunately, the reason may very well have been Mr. Sierra's failing health. Gregory Sierra died in January of 2021. His obituaries noted that he'd endured a long battle with cancer. There was an outpouring of praise for his work by fans and colleagues. His widow, Helene Tabor, said, "He was still receiving fan mail in the days since his death."

Detective Sergeant Chano Amenguale

Chano is 6' 1", 170 pounds with brown eyes, black hair, and a slightly receding hairline. His career as an officer was a dangerous one. He once suffered a broken arm in the line of duty when a fellow officer pushed him out of the way of a bullet. Shortly after that, he was forced to kill two bank robbers who were holding hostages in a bank.

Ultimately, since he only served at the 12th for two seasons, we know less about Chano than any of the others. We know that he was a bottle baby, that he can produce a dynamite British accent, and that he has a brother-in-law that is in the country illegally.

James Gregory

James Gregory as Inspector Frank Luger was an old school example of the New York City Police Department whose character played off the newer, more enlightened, approach of Barney and his men to great comic effect. Gregory was often cast as authority figures throughout a busy fifty-year career in theater, films, and television.

Born on December 23, 1911, in the Bronx, James Gregory was raised in New Rochelle, New York. He began acting in high school and was elected president of the drama club. He was also captain of the golf team and his skills on the links landed him a job as a caddy with a member of a Wall Street brokerage firm. After high school, he was hired as a runner on Wall Street and spent five years in the world of stocks and big business before turning his amateur status and interest in the theater into an actual vocation. He began as a director in summer stock and soon joined Actor's Equity as a performer as well. He made his Broadway debut in November of 1939 in the stage drama, *Key Largo*. He performed in a number of Broadway flops before landing a role in the more successful *Dream Girl* (1945–46).

In *Comical Co-Stars of Television* by Robert Pegg, Gregory told the author, "An actor's life is hard and it was hard back then. I trouped around all over Broadway like many other young actors before I landed my first professional job in *Key Largo*."

In 1947, Gregory worked as the Assistant Stage Manager on Arthur's Miller's *All My Sons* while understudying various cast members. He took on the same role for Miller's *Death of a Salesman* from 1949 to 1950 and eventually replaced Arthur Kennedy in the role of Biff. With the exception of three years of military service during World War II, Gregory spent over a dozen years on the stage before venturing into the new medium of live television in the 1950s. From the start he was cast in the roles of police officers, military personnel, and even priests. If the casting department needed an authority figure, Gregory was the man. He told Pegg, "I once appeared live in five different productions in a ten-day period."

Gregory's early law enforcement roles included an uncredited role in his first film *The Naked City* (1948) and television programs *Police Story* (1952) and *The Man behind the Badge* (1953–1954). At the same time, he was playing a cop on radio in a show entitled *The Twenty-First Precinct* (1953–1956). It seems providential that he worked on a show set in the 21st Precinct. Simply reverse the numbers and you get the 12th Precinct, that rundown little Greenwich Village precinct that Inspector Frank Luger oversaw during the 1970s and 1980s. However, Gregory's greatest brush with foreshadowing his *Barney Miller* role came when he played real life police officer Barney Ruditsky fighting the rackets in New York during the Roaring Twenties in a show called *The Lawless Years* (1959–1961). Ruditsky, who was ever present on *The Lawless Years* set as a consultant was also friends with *Barney Miller* creator Danny Arnold. According to multiple sources, Arnold named the lead character of his police sitcom after his old friend.

Most of the TV actors of the 1950s came from the theater because so much of the work was live and film actors weren't used to memorizing an entire script. Movie actors thought of television as a step down when, in reality, it was more taxing work than your typical studio production. Gregory, being a consummate character actor, found it a little more accessible to break into films while working on television. One of his first major film roles came in 1962 in the classic Frank Sinatra film, *The Manchurian Candidate*. Gregory remembered that, "my character was actually the title character. He was the one that Angela Lansbury and the communists from Manchuria were promoting to be President." He went on to numerous substantial roles in films like *Captain Newman, M.D.* (1963), *The Sons of Katie Elder* (1965), *The Love God* (1969), and *Beneath the Planet of the Apes* (1970). Many fans will also remember him as MacDonald, the chief to Dean Martin's parodied James Bond character, Matt Helm, in a series of four films made for Columbia Pictures between 1966 and 1968.

Gregory would not admit to having any favorite roles or jobs throughout his career. Instead, Gregory told Pegg, "I like a job. For an actor, the most important thing is the next job. You don't go into it expecting to like anything. You may like some jobs more than others. But the thing is the job. The work. That's what you do."

All those jobs playing military and police officers certainly seemed to have contributed to his spin on the character of Frank Luger. Gregory claimed there was no connection between the Luger character and Barney Ruditsky; however, he did say, "the real Barney Ruditsky was a very down-to-earth New York detective and there was no shillyshallying with him. He had a sense of humor but he was not a comedian . . . nor was Luger." It certainly sounds like Luger and Ruditsky were kindred spirits.

Gregory was briefly missing from *Barney Miller* during the fall of 1979 while he was starring in his own sitcom called *Detective School* about a weather-beaten private investigator who opens up a school for young wannabe Sam Spades. It didn't work and was shut down after twelve episodes after which Gregory happily returned to the 12th Precinct. Following the end of *Barney*

Miller, Gregory did very little work. His last TV appearance seems to have been a guest spot in an episode of *Mr. Belvedere*, a show that was created by *Barney Miller* writers Frank Dungan and Jeff Stein. He and his wife of over fifty years retired to Arizona where Gregory died in 2002 at the age of ninety.

Inspector Frank D. Luger

Frank Luger is by far one of the more sentimental characters in the 12th Precinct. No one cries more than the Ol' Inspector. The tears are most often inspired by his reminiscing about his old partners Foster, Kleiner, and Brown. However, sometimes it's just the building itself that touches his heart. Like many old timers, he's not real open to change. He once told Barney in reference to the squad room, "Do me one favor, will ya? Don't ever paint this place."

He was old school when it came to policing styles. He believed in roughing up the suspects to get whatever was needed for an arrest or a conviction. He thought Barney was too nice, too empathetic. We know that before he became what seemed to be "a roving inspector," he walked a beat on Eighth Avenue and worked at the 93rd Precinct in Brooklyn in 1947.

He has trouble with names but that may be because he wasn't the world's greatest listener. He preferred to be the storyteller. He also loved to sing and often broke into song. He enjoyed Charlotte Russes and as far as social activities go, we can only confirm that he saw *Pal Joey* on Broadway and attended at least one game of the 1936 World Series.

He was a frugal man. He owned a Dumont TV set for almost twenty years after the company ceased manufacturing sets. He revealed to Barney that his estate was worth in excess of $230,000.

Concerned about living out his final days alone, he enlists Barney's help to get him a mail order bride. Prior to this romantic endeavor, he seemed to have a special affinity for cashiers and waitresses from the Bensonhurst section of Brooklyn. He eventually marries Perlita Avilar, a young and attractive Filipino whom he affectionately calls his "Filly from Manilly" or "Sweet Leilani." The last we heard; he was going to retire on May 5, 1982.

Steve Landesberg

Steve Landesberg, along with Ron Carey, holds the distinction as having entered the *Barney Miller* universe as a criminal first before transitioning to his permanent role as Det. Sgt. Arthur Dietrich. There seemed to be absolutely no subject on which Dietrich was not an expert. Originally, he astounded his co-workers with his vast storehouse of knowledge until he began to annoy them with it. Finally, they settled into a routine of just looking to Dietrich to explain something they didn't understand.

Landesberg, once again just like Carey, was a standup comedian before coming to *Barney Miller*. He was a very successful and respected standup in the 1970s but he seems to have been overshadowed historically by contemporaries like David Brenner, Robert Klein, and Richard Pryor. Brenner and Max Gail, among others, called him "a comic's comic."

He was born in the Bronx in November of 1936 to Jewish immigrant parents from Poland. His dad owned a grocery store called Abe's Dairy in the Bronx and his mom was a milliner. Until his death in December of 2010, no one seemed to know his exact age because he either refused to give it or gave out misleading information. His daughter Elizabeth explained that her dad started in show biz late and so he was afraid of giving his true age for fear casting directors would be wary of a forty-year-old "newcomer."

Ironically for someone who would play such a learned character as Dietrich, he was an uninterested student. According to a 1977 *TV Guide* profile on him, "he dropped out of more classes (both scholarly and dramatic) than just about any other graduate of DeWitt Clinton High School." He held a variety of jobs before drifting into show biz. His widow, Nancy Ross Landesberg, told me he sold girdles and bras in a department store, he worked in the credit department of a hotel, and "He was a mailman. He was a terrible mailman. One time he was getting mail out of the mailbox down there [by the river] and it flew everywhere and he was like, 'Well, I can't. I just can't.' And so that was it. And that's why I always said to him, people are still waiting for important mail they never got."

Finally, he read a piece in the *New York Post* about an open audition for *The Tonight Show* at Greenwich Village's Bitter End nightclub. He decided to give it a try and although he didn't get picked for *The Tonight Show*, the audience liked him and he discovered that he liked performing.

By 1969 he was working on routines at the Improvisation nightclub and meeting other comedians who would remain friends like Brenner, Jimmie Walker, and Rodney Dangerfield. In the early 1970s he formed a comedy troupe called The New York Stickball Company along with Alan Uger, Martin Braverman, and Emily Levine. Friends like Peter Boyle, Robert Klein, and Brenner directed some of the group's shows. The group toured for about a year and a half and appeared once on *The Ed Sullivan Show*.

In 1971, he finally earned a spot on *The Tonight Show*. He'd worked on a German Professor character that Carson found "slightly wacko" and he was booked on the show four times from December of 1971 through April of 1972. That led to his being hired for the summer replacement series, *Dean Martin Presents: The Bobby Darin Amusement Company*. Landesberg told *TV Guide* that he apparently came on a little too strong for Darin's tastes. However, he must have pleased someone on the *Dean Martin Show* team because he began to get booked on Martin's variety show and occasional roasts.

Finally, in 1974, Danny Arnold spotted Landesberg on the show *Paul Sand in Friends and Lovers* where he used his German accent to comic effect. According to the TV Guide article, "Danny Arnold watched him one night, remarked, 'Too bad this guy's German, 'cause he's good,' and upon learning of Landesberg's true origins, coaxed him into *Barney*." He was initially cast as a fraudulent priest in the premiere episode of Season Two's, "Doomsday." Just a few months later, Arnold introduced him as Arthur Dietrich, the officer who would eventually take the place of retirement bound Phil Fish. Landesberg would remain with the show until the end of its run in 1982.

Actress Diana Canova, one of the stars of another hit ABC sitcom of the 1970s, *Soap*, dated Landesberg in the 1970s while he was doing *Barney Miller*. She said, "Steve was such a unique talent and Danny knew what to do with Steve. Danny saw that talent and capitalized on it. Steve adored Danny." Nancy Landesberg confirmed that, telling me, "He had so much respect for Danny Arnold, Danny was a good friend. We used to have dinner with he and his wife [Donna] and Steve would go to Danny for advice. If Danny said, 'Don't do it,' he wouldn't do it."

Landesberg once said that his biggest regret was that his father never got to see his success on *Barney Miller*. "He never thought I was very funny and was always against my going into show business until I started doing more and more TV," Landesberg said. "He was retired in Miami Beach by then and he loved it."

In the years following *Barney*, he continued to do stand up and appeared regularly on the talk show circuit, eventually garnering over forty trips to *The Tonight Show Starring Johnny Carson* as well as numerous appearances on *The Mike Douglas Show*, *Hollywood Squares*, and *Late Night with David Letterman*. He also lent his talents to numerous commercials and one campaign in particular generated the ultimate windfall for him.

In 1986 he shot a spot for Ryder Trucks. At the end of the shoot, one of the producers of the commercial teased him about his New York accent and he teased her right back. They met again when he flew to Atlanta to shoot another spot. A telephone romance ensued. In a year's time, he and Nancy Ross were married and within a year of their marriage they welcomed their daughter

Elizabeth. Both mother and daughter stressed what a wonderful husband and father Landesberg was.

He was fifty years old when he married and settled down. On her talk show, Dr. Ruth Westheimer once asked him why he'd waited so long to get married? His reply was short and simple. "I'd never met my wife before," Landesberg said with a smile.

Entertainer Geoffrey Mark who was a friend of Landesberg's told me they both used to attend dinners of Yarmy's Army, a group of comedians and friends who came together to support their friend actor Dick Yarmy when he was diagnosed with cancer. Following Yarmy's death, the group continued to gather once a month for dinner to swap stories and share some laughs. Following the birth of his daughter Landesberg's attendance dwindled. When Mark called him one day to remind him about the dinner and encourage him to attend, Landesberg told him, "I've got this beautiful baby at home. Why would I want to go sit with a bunch of old Jews and hear the same old stories?" He did, however, continue to participate in the shows the group routinely did to raise money for charities but his attendance at the dinners was rare. Domestic life agreed with him.

In 1998 he relocated the family to Los Angeles from New York for a part in a show called *Conrad Bloom*. It only lasted half a season but he was back where the action was and his TV and film career enjoyed a bit of a renaissance in the 2000s with appearances on *That '70s Show* and *Everybody Hates Chris*. He also became a regular on the series, *Head Case* (2007–2009).

Nevertheless, those who knew Landesberg best described him as the ultimate New Yorker. He grew up in the shadow of Yankee Stadium and was a big baseball and Yankee fan. He enjoyed walking the streets of the city. His wife and daughter told me that when he got the part on *Barney Miller*, he went to Greenwich Village and walked into a police precinct house to soak up the atmosphere and meet some of the people who worked there. This resulted in a lifelong friendship with a detective named Sal Mazzola who subsequently introduced Landesberg to Sonny Grosso, one of the police officers whose story was the basis for *The French Connection* (1971), who also became a close family friend.

As for the old *Barney Miller* cast, he was very close with his fellow standup Ron Carey. Nancy Landesberg said that although he didn't necessarily hang out with Max (Gail) and Ron (Glass) they always stayed in touch. When Landesberg was diagnosed with cancer, Nancy let Gail and Harris know (Carey was already deceased) and she remembers, "they were so wonderful with me and EB." Following his death, Gail, Brenner, and Geoffrey Mark all helped Nancy Landesberg organize a Memorial Service at a theater in Los Angeles where he was eulogized by his friends and fellow comics Jimmy Walker, Richard Lewis, Tom Dreesen, and numerous others.

In the years since his death in 2010, Landesberg's daughter Elizabeth has become a successful documentary filmmaker and traveled the world for her work. In 2020, she premiered a documentary short entitled *On the Road & Other Places*, utilizing tapes of her dad's old talk show appearances, family videos, and her father's notebooks. Her mother believes Elizabeth could be a working standup like her dad but for now, she's sticking with the cinematic side of the business.

Steve Landesberg is greatly missed by his wife and daughter more than a decade after his last bow but the memories of him are happy ones. A friend of Elizabeth's was trying standup in college and asked her dad for some advice. Landesberg told them, "If you're getting up there and you have a good time, then you can't lose." Elizabeth says, "That was his motto in life, to have a good time with whatever you're doing."

Detective Sergeant Arthur P. Dietrich

Arthur Dietrich was born on October 23, 1947, at St. Mary's Hospital in Allentown, Pennsylvania. All we really know about Dietrich's parents are his mother is French and would like him to send her a current photo. By the time he got to the 12th Precinct his father was dead. We don't know a lot about his childhood except he didn't have a lot of friends. He did, however, have an ant farm.

He identifies as an Atheist and he doesn't believe he has a soul, religious or otherwise. Nevertheless, he is a deep philosophical thinker. We know that by his late teens "the writings of Schopenhauer and Kant began to dominate [his] epistemological outlook almost to the point of excluding the consideration of any other viewpoint with the exception of certain aphorisms of Nietzsche." He's also an admirer of Goethe and pretzels.

Dietrich is a well-rounded thinker and as such had difficulty choosing and committing to a career. He once considered being an actor and in college played the role of Nick the bartender in Saroyan's play, *The Time of Your Life*. He spent time in Medical School and Law School before he joined the police force. He's a touch typist and knows at least three languages: English, German, and at least one of the American Indian languages although he does not identify which tribe or nation.

He joined the New York City Police Department on November 2, 1973. He was at the 33rd Precinct before being sent to the 12th when the 33rd was closed down due to financial cutbacks.

In terms of his personal life, when he first joined the squad he told them he'd never been married. Later on we learn that he was married at seventeen to his law school sweetheart. It was a short-lived union. He also had a torrid affair in college with a woman named Cynthia Reese. He once lived with co-worker Ron Harris for a short time and it should be noted that he once saved the life of Ron Harris in the line of duty.

Dietrich's sensitive gastrointestinal issues included an avoidance of Chinese food because MSG gave him a headache and Italian food because it was too starchy for him. The only other insight in Arthur Dietrich's personality is that he does a fabulous impression of Gregory Peck.

Ron Carey

Ron Carey played the diminutive but omni-present Officer Carl Levitt, one of the very few regular cast members who were uniformed police officers as opposed to plainclothes detectives.

Carey was born Ronald Cicenia in 1935, the youngest of two boys in a large Italian extended family in Newark, New Jersey. His father worked as a singing waiter before finishing his career as a member of the New Jersey Parks Department.

He earned a Bachelor's Degree from Seton Hall University in 1956 and briefly contemplated entering the priesthood. In what seems a natural alternative, he left his theological studies behind and instead turned to standup comedy with a decidedly Roman Catholic flavor. Carey's widow Sharon said his parents were not particularly crazy about him pursuing a career in show business. She said his mother was supportive but his dad was very strict and concerned that he wouldn't be able to support himself in the entertainment industry.

Bill Persky and Sam Denoff, who wrote and produced *The Dick Van Dyke Show* and went on to create *That Girl*, wrote much of Carey's early material. Bill Persky said, "He was a very religious kid and he was very troubled, a lot of emotional stuff. And he would only take jobs where he could hear WNEW on the radio because that's where we [Persky and Denoff] worked. He needed the support that represented. That was safety to him."

He met his future wife, Sharon Boyeronus, a nurse, while working at the Improv comedy club. She remembers that he was doing standup at the time as well as working as a waiter. When I asked her if, as I'd been told by so many, Ron Carey was really as religious as it seemed or was he just in it for the comedy? Sharon Carey told me, "He was always religious, very religious . . . but conflicted."

In a 1981 *TV Guide* article, Carey explained that he got caught up in religious scrupulosity. He defined it as, "You go to confession, the priest tells you to do five Our Fathers and five Hail Marys as penance; you do sixty of each." The same article mentions that Carey gave credit to one of his teachers, a priest, and his older brother in helping him deal with his anxiety-based depression. Nevertheless, at the time of the article, he was actually separated from his wife. The couple did eventually reconcile and were together until Carey's death.

Carey spent a decade or more in New York doing standup and commercials before any episodic television opportunities came to him. He became friendly with Joe Bologna, Art Metrano, and Rudy Deluca who were comics and writers. He initially went to Hollywood for two sitcoms that ultimately failed, *The Corner Bar* (1973) and *The Montefuscos* (1975). He stayed in Hollywood for the one sitcom that did not fail, *Barney Miller*.

Danny Arnold spotted him on *The Montefuscos* and he was hired for a guest spot on the last episode of the second season as a tunneling jewelry store robber named Angelo "The Mole" Molinari. According to Carey, "At the end of 'The Mole' episode, Danny came up to me and said, 'Say, what are you doing next year?'" Carey told him, "Anything you want!" Uniformed officer Carl Levitt was introduced in the third episode of Season Three and remained a part of the 12th Precinct until the end of the show's eight-season run. He also became part of Mel Brooks's stock company of comedic actors working in three of the director's films: *Silent Movie* (1976), *High Anxiety* (1977), and *History of the World: Part I* (1981). In addition, he's brilliantly funny in the one and only film ever directed by Mel Brooks's wife, Academy Award winning actress Anne Bancroft, *Fatso* (1980), as Frankie aka "Junior" DiNapoli.

In the years following *Barney Miller*, Carey got cast as Father Vincent Paglia in another short-lived sitcom called *Have Faith* (1989). Carey's friend, actor Sal Viscuso, told me that he remembered that Carey had a chapel in his home and he believed that he was conflicted about not having become a priest.

Everyone interviewed for this book whether they were a secretary, a casting director, an actor, or a director, remarked about what a sweet and funny man Ron Carey was. He is the one guy remembered for keeping everyone "up" on set, making jokes, bringing in baked goods, etc. Viscuso, who worked with Carey numerous times throughout their careers, remembered Ron Carey saying, "He took care of me like the brother I never had. Ronnie really cared about the people around him." Longtime co-star Steve Landesberg once described Carey as "the most giving of performers. Ron's very quick to tell people what a great job they've done. He's very lovable . . ."

Ron Carey died in January of 2007 of a stroke at the age of 71. The actor was survived by his wife, Sharon, and his brother, James Cicenia.

Officer Carl Levitt

Carl Levitt is a Capricorn from New Jersey. He is self-conscious about his height and is convinced it's holding back his progress with the police department. He is, to be exact, 5' 6¼" tall.

He has a deaf sister and as such is fluent in American Sign Language. He routinely pirouettes as he leaves the squad room. He's a fashion trendsetter having appeared for plain clothes duty at various times in checkered jackets, a denim ensemble, and a powder puff blue tuxedo. He once used narcotics to work overtime and he also wears lifts in his shoes.

Sgt. Harris nicknames him "L'il Levitt," Inspector Luger regularly calls him "Levine," and he gets on Captain Miller's nerves with his constant inquiries into his career advancement.

Barbara Barrie

Born Barbara Ann Berman in Chicago, Illinois, she earned a Bachelor of Fine Arts degree in Drama from University of Texas at Austin in 1952. She followed a boyfriend to New York after college and although she had flourished in theater during college, she never gave it a serious thought as a future career. Nevertheless, she soon found stage work in Western New York regional theaters in Corning and Rochester. Barrie's Broadway debut came in October of 1955 in a play called *The Wooden Dish* starring Louis Calhern and John Randolph.

By the mid-fifties, Barrie made her first television appearance on *Kraft Television Theatre* and soon appeared on many popular live TV dramas of the day. She worked on critically acclaimed programs such as *The Twilight Zone*, *Naked City*, *The Defenders*, and *The Alfred Hitchcock Hour*. Her first job as a series regular came in 1973 on *Diana* starring Diana Rigg. She was soon cast as Elizabeth Miller in the second *Barney Miller* pilot that premiered in January of 1975.

Barrie's role in the show was an ill-fated one. The original idea was to switch back and forth between Captain Miller's home life and his work life. Unfortunately for her, the home life portion of the show was quickly abandoned.

The relationship between Elizabeth and Barney Miller was one filled with humor, zest, and sexual energy but by the second season, the producers and writers were having difficulty coming up with reasons for Mrs. Miller to stop by the precinct. Barbara Barrie wanted her character to find a career but Danny

Arnold didn't want to put his energies in that direction. By the third season Barbara Barrie's name was gone from the opening credits. She would make only two more appearances in the series, one in Season Four and one in Season Five. Like so many others, she insisted Danny Arnold was a comedic genius but also admits that her departure from the show was less than a happy one.

In addition to her television work, Barrie was nominated for the New York Film Critics Award and won the Cannes Film Festival Award for Best Actress for her role in *One Potato, Two Potato* (1964), and received an Academy Award nomination for 1979's *Breaking Away*. She also received an Independent Spirit Award for her role *Judy Berlin* (1999).

Ultimately, she always returned to the small screen for opportunities like portraying Mamie Eisenhower in *Backstairs at the White House* (1979). She made guest appearances on popular primetime hits like *MacMillan and Wife*, *The Mary Tyler Moore Show*, and *Family Ties*. In 1980 she recreated her film role in the short-lived *Breaking Away* TV series and later co-starred for four seasons on the Brooke Shields' sitcom *Suddenly Susan* (1996–2000).

Barbara Barrie is a cancer survivor and since the 1990s has been outspoken about the importance of early detection for all cancers. She was married to actor, singer, director, and producer Jay Harnick for forty-two years before his death in 2007 and is the sister-in-law of Tony Award-winning lyricist, Sheldon Harnick.

Elizabeth Miller

Barney's wife Elizabeth, also known as "Liz," was never a big fan of her husband's profession or New York City. Her windows have bars over them and her front door has numerous locks. On more than one occasion, she suggests Barney quit his job so they can move out of New York. She's so upset by his job that she attends group therapy for the wives of police officers.

She is a homemaker but as the kids grow older she gets a job as a social worker. She must have had a mind for figures as well because she's the person who does the couple's income taxes.

All we know about her family is that she has a brother in Philadelphia.

Florence Stanley

Born Florence Schwartz in Chicago in 1924, Florence Stanley was a prolific and highly regarded performer who achieved success on stage, film, and television in a career that spanned more than half a century.

Stanley graduated from Northwestern University and then traveled to Germany as a Civilian Actress Technician in the US Army Special Services unit just after WWII. She performed in and directed a number of musical productions in Europe. She returned to the States and performed at the Cherry Lane Theatre in Irwin Shaw's *Bury the Dead* where she met her future husband Martin Newman.

She appeared in numerous live TV productions in New York in the 1950s. In 1964 she co-starred with Lee Grant in the New York Shakespeare Festival's production of *Electra* as the title character's vengeful mother Clytemnestra. In 1966, she replaced Bea Arthur as Yente in the Broadway musical *Fiddler on the Roof*. After more than 2,000 performances, she left *Fiddler* to take a role in Mike Nichol's production of *The Prisoner of Second Avenue*. She later reprised her role of Pearl in the film version of Simon's play.

In 1967 Stanley landed her first motion picture role in *Up the Down Staircase* with Sandy Dennis. She soon garnered other small parts in films like *Day of the Dolphin* (1973) and *The Fortune* (1975). Nevertheless, it was television that would make Stanley a recognizable character actress in the 1970s.

She made his first appearances as Bernice in two episodes of *Barney Miller's* first (half) season, "The Stakeout" (S.1/Ep.6) and "Hair" (S.1/Ep.12). However, in April of 1975 she co-starred in the pilot of a sitcom called *Joe and Sons*. The pilot got picked up and the show premiered in September of 1975 but only lasted half a season. Following the failure of *Joe and Sons*, Stanley returned to *Barney Miller* as the sweet albeit much maligned Bernice Fish. She would continue that role for the two seasons of the spinoff *Fish*. Her time on *Barney Miller* and *Fish* may have been relatively short but her ability to draw out both laughter from the audience while adding a sense of poignancy to her portrayal made her a sought-after TV actress.

A decade after *Fish*, Stanley landed a co-starring role in the sitcom *My Two Dads* with Paul Reiser. The show lasted three full seasons on NBC. In the 1990s, she enjoyed recurring roles on the shows *Nurses*, *Dinosaurs*, and *The Simple Life*.

Stanley died in October of 2003 after suffering complications from a stroke.

Bernice Fish

Bernice is the long-suffering spouse of Phil Fish. She can occasionally be a little paranoid and jealous but she is ultimately a loving and supportive wife. She is a full-time homemaker and the one time she did try to get a job, she was turned away for lack of experience. This made Fish happy as his male insecurities didn't want her to work.

All we really know about Bernice besides the fact that she loves children and is a loyal partner to Fish, is that she has a mother who lives in Poughkeepsie and, according to Fish, she gets "turned on" by the smell of wet corduroy.

Character Development

How much do the characters change over the course of the series? In large part, it depends on just how long their characters are on the show. In the case of a character like Chano, he changes very little because he didn't really have time to grow or change. The initial pickup was just a half season and so the second season was actually the first full season. Chano was a hot-blooded Latino when he started and a hot-blooded Latino when he finished although he did get the opportunity to show his emotional depth at the end of the first season when he's forced to kill the bank robbery suspects who are holding hostages.

Apparently, one of the reasons that Sierra left *Barney Miller* was he didn't care for the stereotypical character he was playing. Numerous people, including Hal Linden and Tony Sheehan, confirmed that he didn't like to rely on the Puerto Rican outbursts in his character's native tongue that became a hallmark of the Amenguale character. Danny Arnold thought it was a great opportunity for laughs but Sierra wanted to stretch his acting muscles more. When you look at the one-dimensional character of Stan Wojciehowicz at the start of the series compared to the complex character that Gail had forged by the end of the series, there's reason to believe that Sierra may have been given similar opportunities to explore his character's possibilities had he stuck around a little longer.

The next to leave was Abe Vigoda, a.k.a. Phil Fish. The character of Sergeant Fish changes very slightly but he does become a little less harsh as he moves towards retirement at the beginning of the fourth season. Don't misunderstand, he retains his status as the precinct curmudgeon up to the very end but as we're introduced to Bernice and then his eventual wards, Jilly Pappalardo and Victor Kreutzer, played respectively by Denise Miller and John Cassisi, there is revealed a hidden warmth under the crusty exterior of the wizened Fish.

The next to go was Jack Soo and as we know, his departure was not premeditated as Sierra's and Vigoda's were. Not long before Soo died, we began to see some rumblings of change and growth in Nick Yemana as he stood up for himself and began to demand a little more respect from Captain Miller and his fellow officers. The fact is, everyone always loved Nick but whether it was his gambling or bad coffee, he was never taken quite as seriously as everyone else and he began to resent it. It's interesting to think what may have become of Yemana's character had Soo lived through the end of the series. The fact that he was incredibly funny is unquestionable but I think had he been given more time, he would have surprised viewers and critics alike with the depth of his acting talents.

There are three characters who logged in long careers at the 12th and while they certainly grew during their time on the job, their basic personalities seemed to change less than some of the others. James Gregory as Inspector Frank Luger spanned the entire eight seasons of the program although he was never a weekly regular. He appeared forty-nine times over the course of the series. He was always the old cranky cop but in a different way than Sgt. Fish. In the case of Luger, he was an authority figure although we never quite figured out how he got to his advanced position. The only assumption that can be made is that he was appointed by the kind of good old guys he forever championed when he talked about the toughness of his old squad, Foster, Kleiner, and Brownie. Luger's affinity for old-fashioned police intimidation tactics remained with him up until the end but he slowly learned and began to accept that the world and the department were changing. No matter what his bluster and political incorrectness may have been, he always showed himself to be dedicated and appreciative of the men in his command. When he has his heart episode, he thanks and salutes his men as he's being wheeled out of the room on a gurney. It may have seemed sappy but Luger was totally sincere in his feelings of warmth and pride for his men. In his biggest sign of growth, near the end of the series run, Luger admits his fear of ending his life alone. His resulting marriage, as unromantic as its initiation may have been, shows a true step towards the future instead of his usual habit of looking back.

Arthur Dietrich, as brilliantly portrayed by Steve Landesberg, was another character that showed small, baby steps of growth and change over his six full seasons on the show. When he entered, he basically knew every bit of esoteric trivia there was to know in the world. When he left, he still knew every bit of esoteric trivia. He was deadpanned and sarcastic at the beginning and he was deadpanned and sarcastic at the end. Dietrich's growth, if any, comes from a certain social maturity gained at the 12th Precinct. If nothing else, he learned about commitment and perseverance. We learn in the course of his service that he had tried various careers prior to police work but never saw anything through to the end. He even attempted to quit the police force during his time at the 12th but his fellow officers and friends wouldn't allow him to give up on them or himself. Arthur Dietrich's main area of growth while being a member of Barney Miller's squad may have been the initiation and retention of true friendships for the first time in his life.

Then there's Carl Levitt, played by the wonderful Ron Carey. Levitt grows the way all the characters grew in the sense that he started as an archetype and then was given flesh and bone as we learned intimate details of his life such as the fact that he knew sign language because he had a hearing-impaired sister. He's the brunt of many jokes about his height and status until he blows up at both his fellow officers and Captain Miller and they slowly realize this guy is more than just a wannabe in a uniform. Like Luger, we think of him as a joke but there are numerous examples that show him to be a capable and courageous cop as in the time he saved the little boy from the scaffolding on the building of a closed construction site. Levitt's changes are subtle but, in the end,, he wins the respect of all who worked with him and watched his struggle to achieve through the years.

And finally, there are the three characters who change the most fundamentally over the course of the show and it should come as no surprise that they are the three characters who appeared in more episodes than everyone else. Hal Linden as titular lead character Barney Miller was actually the only character that appeared in every episode of the show. It's only right. After all, the show is named after him.

I think it's fair to say that Miller's character changes a noticeable amount from the first show to the very last but it doesn't seem that way because the transformation is slow, subtle, and natural. In retrospect, it's generally accepted that Barney Miller was the straight man who could, and did, set up the laugh lines for not only his men but for the hordes of victims and criminals with whom he would interact for eight seasons. However, in the earlier episodes, Miller is actually getting his share of laugh lines within the format of the scripts. Whether it was just in the mind of actor Hal Linden or if his awareness and acceptance was made known to the writers and thereby affected the writers, the major change for the actor came in the landmark "Hash" episode in the third season. Linden was perplexed that everyone "got an aria" to play except him. Danny Arnold explained to him that Miller needed to remain sober to create the template for humor. If no one in the squad were straight, there'd be nothing with which to compare the bizarre behavior of the other officers. Every great comedic situation needs a straight man or woman, as the case may be. It's not so much that Linden's character became the official or unofficial straight man after this episode but that Linden finally understood and accepted that role in large part due to this episode.

As the years went on, Miller's life changed dramatically—his marriage faltered but regained stability, he went to jail for his principles, he lost patience with his underlings and his superiors and he displayed both anger and insecurity when it came to his own career advancement or the lack thereof. By the end of the series, Barney Miller was still the symbol of Talmudic justice that Danny Arnold had envisioned and found in *Rothschild's* star Hal Linden but he was also somewhat of a harder man. He was always fair, always compassionate, but by the last days of the 12th, the incessant bureaucracy and the lunacy of the human race had changed him. He was older, wiser, and more experienced. His sense of justice remained intact but with it was the realization that it came with a price.

The transformation of the character of Ron Harris was one that I had remembered as being more jarring, more abrupt until I watched the series all the way through again. It was, in fact, consistent and believable considering the experiences of the dapper detective. Harris's sartorial splendor is with the character from the beginning. However, his style of speech is much looser and more colloquial at the start of the series than it is at the end. In the early days, Harris's streetwise lingo and slang is just a part of who he is but by the end, his use of that same style of speech is a reversion to his former self. It's normally used to make a point or to mock the prejudice or ignorance of someone else.

The quest for fame through writing is revealed early on and while it reflects a need to express oneself, his literary pursuits absolutely reveal a desire for fame, for respect, and for status. In fact, Captain Miller will later question Harris's literary motivations after he's lost all the material wealth he gained with the success of his novel in a lawsuit. Harris's quest for status is also tied up in his internal struggle about race and prejudice and inequality. His pride in his heritage is more sardonic and worldly in the early shows and the shift in his attitude seems to emerge after the success of Alex Haley's *Roots* became a cultural watershed for an enlightened racial awareness in America. While the idea of "Black Pride" had existed for a long time before *Roots*, the book and especially the TV miniseries, made respect for Black Heritage more mainstream.

Harris's character changes throughout the series, sometimes within the same show, but throughout the entire series he's consistently a person who displays integrity, intelligence, and sensitivity. He is, in fact, both mercurial and consistent.

And finally, there is Wojo. This is the character that changes most of all in the *Barney Miller* universe. At the start, Wojo is the green, hyperactive, judgmental kid in the squad. His sense of right and wrong is very matter-of-fact like that of a child's with no subtlety or gradations. It's unlikely that the writers had a definite idea or goal as to how much Wojo would grow over the course of the series. However, the intent for him to grow is clear in the earliest episodes by revealing the father-son dynamic in Wojo's relationship with Captain Miller. This relationship will be key in many of the storylines throughout the course of the series.

One of the more memorable aspects of Wojo's character includes his reaction to, and relationships with, prostitutes. His is a very judgmental view of prostitution and the women who practice it, particularly those with whom he crosses paths in his work. However, as much as he continues to disapprove of it, by the end of the series, even he realizes that he has his own personal hang-ups because he continues to be drawn to these women. In the end, The audience, and Wojo himself, are left to ponder whether it's a weakness of his character, a desire to save these women, or merely just a personal turn-on?

The other interesting aspect of Wojo's transformation concerns his relationship to the Vietnam War, his service, and society's feelings toward the war. In the beginning, Wojo tries not to flaunt his Marine background or appear to be too much of a hawk but he was clearly proud of his service. As time moves on, you get the feeling that his pride remains but that his reasons for serving may have had more to do with his belief that it was his duty than it was with his support of the cause. Finally, in the "Agent Orange" episode, Wojo can't help but reveal a sense of betrayal. He doesn't want to be ashamed of his service and yet he realizes that his country and his government lied to him. He's not only worried about his future health but he's also angry at being used by a military complex that never really cared about him.

Wojo starts the show as a tough guy, a "guy's guy," fearless and sure of himself. By the end, he's not quite so sure of anything. He can still be a reactionary but now he's a reactionary for justice. He's almost always on the side of the underdog by the end of the series. Instead of taking any truths for granted, he's become the precinct questioner. He's the guy who researches everything he doesn't know or understand. He realizes that life is made up of a vast palette of colors instead of the black and white view he held at the beginning. He's not superhuman but he is more fully human.

The Writers and the Writing Staff

Any play, film, or television program is only as good as its writers. In the case of *Barney Miller*, I'm reminded of a line from the film *My Favorite Year* (1982). Bill Macy, as the head writer of a comedy variety show in the 1950s, is standing up for something he's written and says, "First comes the word and the word was funny!" The greatness of *Barney Miller* comes from the fact that regardless of the weightiness of the subject matter, the emotional depth, or the controversial topic, the scripts were always funny. Always.

Earlier shows like *Make Room for Daddy* or *The Andy Griffith Show* would often mix emotion with humor but it was more clearly delineated. There might be a very emotional exchange between Danny Williams and one of his children and it would just warm the cockles of your heart. Then, to remind you that you were still watching a sitcom, Danny Thomas's writers would insert what he'd call "a treacle cutter"—a funny remark to jar the audience back from the brink of cloying sentimentality. However, with a *Barney Miller* script, the humor was more seamlessly interwoven within the emotion of the moment. It is not an easy trick to pull off but they consistently succeeded in doing it.

The quality of the writing on *Barney Miller* not only elevated it to the highest echelon of TV excellence when it was on primetime television but has also kept it relevant almost half a century since its debut. Numerous *Barney Miller* staffers told me that Danny Arnold put his stamp on every script during his years as the showrunner. Nevertheless, he did not write every word. He needed talented writers to help him. The struggle to find those writers and to put out a quality show every week is a revealing element of the *Barney Miller* history.

We've already discussed the Arnold/Flicker feud so we'll skip past the idea of ever truly knowing who came up with the original tenets of the story. Once the show was given the green light for broadcast, it seems that Danny Arnold alone carried the bulk of the load for those first thirteen episodes that aired starting in January 1975. His main contributors for that first half season were a mixture of friends, older and more experienced writers that he'd known in the business for many years, and a few well-chosen rookies.

Aside from Arnold, the two writers with the most dominant presence for that first season were Chris Hayward and Roland Kibbee. Interestingly enough, Hayward is credited with contributions to ten of those first thirteen episodes. Kibbee on the other hand has no writing credits until Season Three but later contributors Tony Sheehan and Tom Reeder maintain that Kibbee always had a presence in Danny Arnold's office and inner circle.

Sheehan and Reeder both said that Arnold hired a lot of his old cronies in those early years. In that first season you'll find the names Jerry Davis, Richard Baer, and Howard Leeds in the credits, all men who worked with Arnold on earlier shows such as *The Tennessee Ernie Ford Show*, *Bewitched*, and *That Girl*. In addition, there were seasoned veterans like Ron Friedman, Lila Garrett, Howard Albrecht, and Sol Weinstein who made contributions as well.

Tom Reeder, who penned over a dozen *Barney Miller* episodes, suggested that Danny's demanding personality led to a lot of young writers working for him who "didn't know any better." Some of those young writers in Season One included Steve Gordon who went on to write the Oscar-nominated screenplay for *Arthur* (1981) and Jerry Ross who went on to contribute scripts to a number of hit shows including *The Cosby Show*, *Murder, She Wrote*, and *The Fresh Prince of Bel-Air*. It was no secret to anyone that Danny Arnold was, as Reeder put it, "a real taskmaster."

There were those who ultimately didn't end up working for Danny Arnold but still had their Danny Arnold stories. Ken Levine, who along with his writing partner David Isaacs, penned numerous episodes of classics like *M*A*S*H*, *Cheers*, and *Frasier*, wrote a very funny remembrance on his blog entitled *. . . by Ken Levine* about writing a spec script for *Barney Miller*. First Arnold loved their writing. When they came in to pitch their ides, he hated everything but one germ of an idea. They revised it and he loved it again until he didn't anymore and dropped it. Either way, he paid them for a first draft and a revision but Levine considered himself lucky to get out of there with his sanity intact.

Tony Sheehan, whose first credits came in Season Two said, "Danny had very strong opinions on how he wanted things done and he second-guessed a lot of people. That didn't go down very well." Sheehan told me, "I came on I guess about episode fifteen? They had done the first thirteen episodes with freelance writers and Danny and Chris Hayward had written every script themselves." What he probably should have said was rewritten. Friedman told me, "He [Arnold] was impossible to work for because you couldn't read his mind and he had a fertile mind and he was always changing things to fit what his ideal was."

What's fascinating is that as challenging as it seems Danny Arnold could be to work for, he nevertheless engendered some very devoted employees through the years. He could be difficult but he was also loyal and generous to those who stuck with him.

Tony Sheehan said that not only was Danny Arnold a perfectionist but he was also a procrastinator. Naturally, that combination caused stress and anxiety among the company. First of all, there was the horse racing. Arnold owned a stable of horses and this led to his frequent disappearances in the middle of the day. Shelley Zellman, one of the few female writers to ever work on *Barney*, told me, "He [Danny] went to the track a lot. He had this chauffeur, a short guy who would sit in the office all day long and read the racing form in case Danny wanted to take off and go to the track."

"The script wasn't ready, ever," Tony Sheehan said. Then when Arnold *was* ready to work, Sheehan recalled, "Danny would go and tear a story apart and I'd go, 'What are you doing that for, Danny?' . . . and he'd be right, but still that wreaked havoc with the process."

The three young writers who made the biggest impact in those first five seasons were Sheehan, Reeder, and Reinhold Weege. All three made substantial contributions to the writing. Reeder may well have been an even more integral part of the company if it weren't for his agent. He contributed four scripts in Season Two. He told me, "Then, before Season Three began, I was offered a story editor job and before I knew about it, my agent had turned it down because he knew what a stressful place to work it was . . . and so he made what was then known as a multiple deal that guaranteed me 'X' number of scripts a year. But every year Danny would try to get me to come on board and Stu Robertson [Reeder's agent] would say no."

As it turned out, Sheehan and Weege would become Arnold's two most valued Lieutenants in the Writer's Room. Harriet Helberg, Casting Director for Season Five, recalled Sheehan and Weege as "Danny's golden boys." Helberg said, "They were perfectly suited for Danny. They were both brilliant writers. They both loved to wait until the last minute to write and do it." Shirley Alberti, Arnold's Special Assistant for the first four years of the production, remembers, "that everything Reinie and Tony wrote had to go through Danny and Danny would drive those writers crazy. They would be working twenty-four hours a day—sometimes more than twenty-four hours!"

To be fair, Arnold was working himself hard as well. Reeder remembered a time when, "We were in Chris Hayward's office and I was pitching and Danny was sitting on the couch and he had a cigar in his mouth. I was pitching away and Chris was nodding and then he gestured over toward Danny and I looked over and Danny had fallen asleep with his lit cigar in his mouth. Chris gestured that we should leave the office to continue somewhere else. We got up and we were almost out the door and Danny jerked awake and said, 'You assholes were gonna leave me here with a lit cigar in my mouth!' Danny was just there all the time in those early years."

Reeder went on to tell me, "This was a Danny Arnold that some of the later writers probably didn't see . . . but when he was on he could pitch out [weave a story], he'd be pitching out a story and playing all the characters and coming up with these great lines of dialogue. I would be trying to take notes as fast as I could because I knew, sooner or later, it was gonna go in the script anyway."

As the process got a little more organized, the writers, whether it was a freelancer on assignment or staff writers like Zellman and Dalton, would submit their scripts to Weege or Sheehan. As Shelley Zellman recalled, "We would write an episode then it would go to Reinhold Weege or Tony Sheehan because they were his right-hand men. They alternated each week [doing the rewrites] and then it would go to Danny. Everything, every episode went through [Danny]."

At the end of Season Five, Arnold informed Tony Sheehan that he was leaving due to health concerns and Weege was leaving for a deal at Warner Brothers. For the next two seasons, Tony Sheehan was in the driver's seat. He hired Frank Dungan and Jeff Stein as his chief lieutenants and later they would bring on Nat Mauldin and Jordan Moffet for additional help. Sheehan remembered that when Danny Arnold was in charge, his perfectionism would often dictate shooting fifteen or twenty takes for a certain shot or scene. "When he [Arnold] left, we were able to do it a little smoother for two years," Sheehan recalled, "although I worked every day, literally from June until late February you worked every day . . . including Christmas and New Year's."

It took a little while for Sheehan to learn how to be in charge just as it took time for Dungan and Stein to find their roles in the process. Jeff Stein said, "Tony was the most even-tempered person in the world. Just really smart, really focused . . . he'd be in his office writing and writing and writing.

"Remember, Frank and I, we have no credits, we're baby writers. We're not expected to run a show . . . or even expected to be any good. At one point, we're sitting in the office . . . we've only been there a week or so and we thought, 'Well, should we go in there and see what he is doing?' So we go in and say, 'Hey, what are you working on?' And for some reason, the three of us just clicked. I mean we sat there and started pitching, 'Well how about this? How about that?' Next thing you know, we're writing all the scripts together, the three of us in the same room and we wrote two seasons like that."

Sheehan had been credited as a producer since sometime in the fourth season. Once Dungan and Stein became his main writers, it apparently didn't take long for them to prove their worth. By the middle of the sixth season they began to be listed as story editors in addition to whatever story or writing credits they earned on various episodes. The trio proved to be a winning combination.

In addition to running the show in those seasons, Sheehan prepared Dungan and Stein for more than just a writing career. Frank Dungan told me, "The other thing Tony did, and I really give him credit for this, . . . he not only groomed us as writers but he made sure we were in casting, he made sure we went to editing. He made sure we were down on the stage dealing with the actors, so when we went in [to run the show] we had done all of that. If you're an executive producer on a comedy, especially if you've got a limited staff, you're responsible for the budget, casting, editing, you gotta be involved . . . so he made sure we were exposed to every facet of the show."

By the end of Season Seven, Danny Arnold was trying to decide what to do with the show. Sheehan was burned out and wanted to leave. According to Sheehan, Arnold said in front of the cast and crew, "Well, if you leave the show, I'm going to take it off the air." Sheehan remembered, "the actors looked at me like, 'Oh, you're going to take away our paychecks just as we're getting to the big-time money?'" Two things happened to convince Arnold to do one more season. Sheehan convinced him to talk to Dungan and Stein and assured Arnold that they could handle the duties of the showrunner. Also, Ted Flicker saw rumors in the trade papers that Arnold was thinking of ending the show and threatened to start yet another lawsuit because he claimed Arnold was voluntarily and unnecessarily diminishing the profits of the show.

As Season Eight dawned, Sheehan was gone, Noam Pitlik had left, and Danny returned. Nevertheless, it wasn't the same. As Dungan said, "The continuity was shot." They had twenty-two episodes to write for a season and that meant about sixty-six stories.

Dungan recalled Arnold walking into the office one day holding one of their scripts out away from his body like a piece of dead fish. "Fellas, we got trouble," Arnold said. The writers asked him what the problem was. Arnold told them he'd read the script and it didn't work. "I'm gonna have to call your agent," Arnold said. "We'll probably have to shut down." Naturally, they were concerned and pressed him to tell them the problem. Arnold said, "This joke on page seventeen doesn't work." They asked him if he had a line. He told them he did and showed them his joke. Dungan said, "That's great. That's funny. We'll change it. And we'd love to get your humor. I mean, this is your show. We'd love to hear your jokes and your attitudes and that sort of thing.' Danny says, 'Really? All right, well go ahead.'

"That night we're there at about eleven o'clock at night. The door opens and it's Danny and he says, 'You guys need anything?' We said, 'No, we're good, Danny.' He replies, 'Okay. All right. You're doing a fine job.' Same day."

It was Arnold and Dungan and Stein for all of Season Eight until the end. Arnold decided to absolutely end the show after that season regardless of Flicker's lawsuit threats. Dungan and Stein found a way to make it work with Danny Arnold but it was never as comfortable a working relationship for them as it had been with Tony Sheehan. When they reached the end of the season and were looking for a way to wrap up the series, Sheehan was asked to come back and help and together, Arnold, Sheehan, Dungan, and Stein wrote the 12th Precinct's last chapter in three parts.

Chris Hayward

> Chris had a way of not minding it when Danny [Arnold] was impossible. He was able to hook on and stay focused.
>
> *—Ron Friedman*

Chris Hayward was born in 1925 in Bayonne, New Jersey. He was a self-taught singer and composer who quit high school to pursue a musical career but soon determined that his stage fright was an insurmountable obstacle to stardom. A night class in screenwriting encouraged him to pursue a different career path.

His first big break came writing stories at Jay Ward Productions for *Crusader Rabbit*. Soon he became one of Ward's most dependable writers for a show called *Rocky and His Friends* which became much more famous in syndication as *The Bullwinkle Show*. Hayward worked on all storylines within the show including "Fractured Fairy Tales" and "Peabody's Improbable History" but became well-known as the creator of "The Adventures of Dudley Do-Right." Unfortunately, not everyone loved Dudley Do-Right as much as American children did. The dimwitted Canadian Mountie was deemed so harmful to national esteem that the program was not shown on Canadian television for a number of years. In 1988, reminiscing about his early years with Jay Ward,

Hayward told the *Los Angeles Times*, "The pay was low and the insecurity great. Jay felt the writers should pay him. His theory was, 'Never show a profit or else you'll have to pay people.'"

In 1964, Hayward and his writing partner Allan Burns came up with a concept for a program about a family of monsters to be done as an animated series. The idea was then given to two other writers who developed it as a live action series. He and Burns were eventually awarded "creator" credit by the Writers Guild of America for *The Munsters* (1964–1966) TV show.

Following their years in animation, he and Burns created the famous, or more accurately, infamous sitcom, *My Mother the Car*, starring comedian Jerry Van Dyke. The show is remembered today for being one of the silliest bombs in TV history but the fact remains, it is remembered. Next came the critically acclaimed but commercially unsuccessful *He & She* (1967–68), starring Richard Benjamin and his real-life wife, Paula Prentiss.

Burns and Hayward went their separate ways after *He & She* and Hayward spent a couple of seasons writing for the hit show *Get Smart*. He wrote pilots and a few other sitcom episodes before joining Danny Arnold's team on *Barney Miller* in 1975.

Chris Hayward was an important player in getting *Barney Miller* off the ground. In fact, Hayward's name is on over thirty episodes as co-writer of the teleplay or story in the show's first three seasons. He doesn't show up in the credits after Season Three but his relationship with Arnold continued because he's given development and/or creator credit on three more Danny Arnold programs: *A.E.S. Hudson Street* (1977–1978), *Fish* (1977–1978), and *Joe Bash* (1986).

Hayward was nominated for three Primetime Emmy Awards and three Writers Guild of America prizes and won an Emmy in 1968 with co-writer Allan Burns for *He & She*. Chris Hayward died of cancer in 2006.

Roland Kibbee

> I think he [Roland Kibbee] was our Danny handler. I'm pretty sure we went into Kibbee's office once and he had a board and he had all these script titles and Jeff and I sit down and we look up at this board and it's like one through twenty-two. [Laughing] We said, "Kibbee, what the fuck is this?" And he said, "Pay no attention to that. That's for Danny." We said, "But we don't have all those stories." Kibbee just says, "I know it, I know it, I know it."
>
> —*Frank Dungan*

> He [Danny Arnold] brought in Kibbee to be a buffer between [him] and us. He didn't trust us, so Kibbee's the guy he brought in to supervise us.
>
> —*Jeff Stein*

Roland Kibbee was born in Monongahela, Pennsylvania, in February of 1914. He was the "old man" of the *Barney Miller* writing staff when the show began in 1975. His comedy pedigree was impressive. In his fifty-year career he worked with TV producing powerhouses such as Nat Hiken, Norman Lear, and Danny Arnold. In his book, *Even This I Get to Experience*, Norman Lear singled out Kibbee as one of his most influential comedy teachers. Lear wrote, "I learned from Kib that just about anything can be improved, and that reaching for perfection, not necessarily achieving it, was worth the effort. He couldn't tolerate a false note . . ." Sounds like Danny Arnold learned a lot from Kibbee as well."

Kibbee began his career in radio working as a staff writer for Fred Allen. He went on to write what many Marx Brothers fans regard as the last watchable Marx Brothers film, *A Night in Casablanca* (1946). He also wrote the screenplays for six Burt Lancaster films. At some point in the mid-1950s, it is believed that Kibbee was blacklisted. By the late 1950s, he was back to work although there is no evidence that he testified to anyone about his background.

He started writing for television with *The Tennessee Ernie Ford Show* in late 1957. That is where he met Lear and, most likely, Danny Arnold. He and Lear created a western called *The Deputy* that ran for two seasons from 1959 to 1961. He was head writer on the first *Bob Newhart Show* (1961–1962). It was an hour-long variety series that won the Emmy for Outstanding Program Achievement in the Field of Humor in its first season on the air and was then canceled.

Kibbee created two more shows in the 1960s, the unsuccessful *Bob Cummings Show* (1961–1962), which lasted just a single season, and the more popular spy adventure, *To Catch a Thief* (1968–1970) with Robert Wagner. He also won his second Emmy, as part of the writing team on the TV mystery series *Columbo*, in 1974.

The exact origin of Kibbee's relationship to Danny Arnold is unknown although, as cited above, it's reasonable to assume that the two met on the writing staff of *The Tennessee Ernie Ford Show* in the late 1950s. As previously stated, Danny had a lot of his old cronies who'd been radio and/or early television writers surrounding him. Tony Sheehan believes his most active involvement was during the last season, however, starting in Season Six Kibbee is listed as Executive Producer. This was also the first season that Danny Arnold was not overseeing day-to-day operations due to his health. Tony Sheehan was the showrunner for Seasons Six and Seven so Kibbee was there perhaps as Arnold's eyes and ears.

Roland Kibbee was also given the task of being showrunner for the short-lived *A.E.S. Hudson Street*, the Gregory Sierra show that lasted only five or six episodes in 1978.

Roland Kibbee died at the age of seventy just two years after *Barney Miller* went off the air. Everyone who worked with him on the show remembers him with great warmth and fondness.

Tony Sheehan

> To know Tony is to love him. He's a great guy. He's a phenomenal writer—great at just breaking story or finding problems in story and that sort of thing.
>
> —*Frank Dungan*

Tony Sheehan and Reinhold Weege were Danny Arnold's two protégés whose careers grew out of *Barney Miller*. Weege has been gone for many years so I was thrilled to have the opportunity to interview Tony Sheehan and discuss his memories of Danny Arnold and the history of the show. The story of how Sheehan actually came to write for *Barney Miller* is so casual and random that it's hard to believe.

Tony Sheehan grew up on the edge of "the business" as his father was an Assistant Director on shows like *The Mary Tyler Moore Show* and *The Bob Newhart Show*. However, despite his father's background Sheehan never told his parents that he was trying to be a writer. Instead, he would write unsolicited spec scripts and send them off to various shows. Most of the time, the scripts would be sent back to him with a note explaining that the producers were unable or unwilling to read scripts that had not come through an agent. When he finally did get an answer it was from none other than Larry Gelbart. Sheehan had sent in a *M*A*S*H* script (incorrectly identifying the show's location in the title, "The Outcast of the 4099" instead of 4077) and Gelbart responded. He felt Sheehan had potential but as it turned out, Gelbart left *M*A*S*H* shortly thereafter. However, when he departed he contacted his friend Danny Arnold, who was desperate for writers for his new show. Gelbart recommended Sheehan to Arnold and he was almost immediately hired for *Barney*. "I was hired to be the lowest of the low, a staff writer, and I got there and after a few days I discovered I was the only person on staff," Sheehan recalled. "It was like, you're invited to a dinner party and there's only one other person there."

Interestingly, once he arrived, he discovered he had another connection to *Barney Miller*. At the age of eighteen, while he was still in college, he'd sent a script to *Get Smart*. The producer, Chris Hayward, wrote him back saying, "Hey, we liked the script. Come on in if we get picked up for another season." *Get Smart* got canceled but Chris Hayward ended up as Danny Arnold's writing partner in the formative years of *Barney Miller*.

On his first freelance assignment, Sheehan remembers he handed it in and there was a quick turnaround because they were always under the gun in terms of schedule. Sheehan said, "I got the finished copy of what Danny and Chris Hayward had rewritten of my script and they had rewritten half of [it]. I thought I was in such trouble, thinking maybe they wouldn't pay me or maybe they'll ask for some of their money back. I go into the office and I find out I'm a hero. No one had ever gotten a joke into the script and I had gotten in half of a script—it was still there!" Sheehan recalled, "I learned the hard way that everything I thought about the way things worked didn't work that way and I learned it in the moment." However, to be fair, Sheehan later told me that once he left *Barney Miller*, he quickly discovered that no one worked the way Danny Arnold did on *Barney*.

Sheehan's first *Barney Miller* credit was the sixth episode of the second season, "The Arsonist." He and Reinhold Weege became indispensable to Danny Arnold in the early years of the show. As they neared the end of Season Five, Arnold approached Sheehan and dropped the bombshell that he and Weege were both leaving and Sheehan would be the showrunner for Season Six. Sheehan, who'd done nothing but write for four years, would now be expected to deal with the actors, the cameras, the editing, everything. Danny asked him if he thought he could handle it? Sheehan said, "Sure, Danny."

Sheehan became the showrunner for Seasons Six and Seven and hired Frank Dungan and Jeff Stein as his primary writing staff. When Arnold returned for Season Eight, Sheehan left but was asked to return by Arnold to help them with the show's ending trilogy.

In 1985, Sheehan joined the staff of *Mr. Belvedere*, a show created by his protégés and friends, Dungan and Stein. Throughout the six seasons of the series, he did a little bit of everything: he wrote, directed, and produced. He has continued to write and produce a variety of sitcoms throughout the years since *Barney*. He created a show called *Sister Kate* that lasted only one season in 1989–1990 but he has also contributed his talents to shows such as *Ned and Stacey, Something So Right*, and *Dharma & Greg*. In the twenty-first century, he has served as Executive Producer on the Kevin James's sitcoms, *The King of Queens* and *Kevin Can Wait*.

When I interviewed Tony Sheehan in 2017, he was particularly proud of the fact that he kept such a low profile over the years that it was nearly impossible to find a photograph of him. As you will see, I finally found one.

Reinhold Weege

> Reinhold Weege, right? We pictured like some college professor in a plaid coat with patches on the elbows or smoking a pipe surrounded by leather-bound books, pensively thinking, like on the back of a book cover. That's the kind of person we *thought* was writing that stuff. Little did we know that it was basically a 400-pound truck driver.
>
> —*Jeff Stein*

Reinhold Weege, along with Sheehan, were, as Harriet Helberg described them, Danny Arnold's "golden boys." Weege came on board in 1976 and his first credit was for the second season's, "Fear of Flying." By Season Four he was listed as a Story Editor and by Season Five, he was a Producer. It was his work on *Barney Miller* that then got him a development deal with Warner Brothers.

Weege was born in 1949 in Chicago, Illinois. He played football at Prospect High School when an injury forced him off the team. As a result, he joined the theater department and played the part of Cromwell in his senior year production of *A Man for All Seasons*. The play's cast included future TV star Bruce Boxleitner and Shelley Pierce, who would eventually become Weege's wife.

Following high school, Weege attended De Paul University and was studying at Second City Improv when he was drafted. Following the service, he graduated from Harper College with a degree in journalism. He wrote a story that got picked up and published by the *Daily News* and that was all the encouragement his writing career needed.

In short order, he sold his couch, "the only asset my wife and I had," and moved to Hollywood. He wrote three scripts for three different situation comedies to show agents. One of the agents signed him and his career began. His first big break came with an assignment for *Barney Miller*. He was the perfect employee for Danny Arnold in that he, too, was a procrastinator as well as an incredibly witty writer. He also became known for his great ad-libs on the set. Weege would have a hand in writing some classic *Barney Miller* episodes including "Werewolf," "The Indian," and "The Harris Incident." His script for "Good-Bye, Mr. Fish," was nominated for both the Humanitas Prize and the Writers Guild of America Award.

Dungan and Stein, although they ended up working for and with Tony Sheehan, acknowledge that it was Weege who mentored them in the *Barney Miller* world. He was eccentric but supportive. Dungan told me, "Now you've got to picture Reinie's office. It was basically pitch black and he had a green banker's light on. I think he had English blackout curtains in his office to keep it dark. Every now and then we'd see smoke come out from behind that lamp. Do you remember the scene in Papillon when the guy (Anthony Zerbe) with leprosy offers the cigar to Steve McQueen? He kind of leans in and out of the shadows? That was Reinie."

At the end of the fifth season, Weege departed to develop his own shows at Warner Brothers Television. His first attempt, a sitcom called *Park Place*, lasted only five episodes. However, he hit pay dirt in January of 1984 with a midseason replacement show entitled *Night Court*, about a late-night courtroom and the cast of zanies that come through the door as both victims and criminals. Sound familiar? There can be no doubt that *Night Court* has its roots in the *Barney Miller* model but Weege's creation was more slapstick and surreal than Arnold's precinct predecessor. The show lasted nine seasons and earned over thirty Emmy nominations. Weege left after six seasons and never helmed another TV project of note.

Many of those who knew Weege acknowledged that he did not give the proper attention to his health. He was usually both overweight and overworked. Jeff Stein said, "But he loved the way he looked. He was this multimillionaire from *Night Court* and he loved the way people would just dismiss him. He'd walk into a bank or an investment place and they'd say, 'Deliveries in the rear.' Then he'd say, 'Oh, I got this half-million dollar check I want to do something with, you want to help me with that?' He got a big kick out of that. He was living the blue-collar, Chicagoan, fantasy life – he had Bulls tickets, Black Hawks tickets, . . . he had all this stuff that Joe Six Pack dreams about when he dares to dream."

Weege and his wife eventually divorced. Just around the time the divorce was finalized, he died at the age of sixty-two in 2012. Stein said, "He had a great funeral though. It's the only funeral I've ever been to where they gave you a bobble head of the deceased." Weege's wife put the send-off together with Weege's two daughters. They brought in the *Night Court* set and had a huge bar with all the various candies Weege loved. Even so, as Stein remembered, "Everybody was very sad . . . all that money and you die anyway."

At the time of his death, actor John Larroquette, who'd won four Emmys for his portrayal of Dan Fielding on *Night Court*, tweeted, "In life there are those who impact us with such force everything changes. Reinhold Weege was that in mine. May he truly rest in peace."

In 1998 Weege told the *Hollywood Reporter*, "My specialty is being funny and substantial at the same time. I want people to watch a half hour and give a damn about it afterward." He left a rich legacy of substantially funny television.

Tom Reeder

Tom Reeder is a native of Redlands, California. He was in a few plays in high school and that sparked his interest in acting. Following graduation, he enrolled in a summer program at the Pasadena Playhouse where, according to him, he was lucky enough to discover he didn't have any real acting talent. He went to Junior College in San Bernardino where he met a professor who encouraged him to write. Reeder told him he thought he would be a sports announcer because he could make more money. His teacher told him, "you can make more money running a whorehouse but I think you have writing talent."

That planted the seed that changed the arc of his life and career. He transferred to USC and graduated from there in 1969. In a few short months, he married, reported for active duty in the Army and was released upon the condition of signing up for the Reserves.

During his time at USC, he got a job as an usher as CBS. Following his active duty in the military, he landed a job at an ad agency and that led to a job in the promo department at CBS. When his boss at CBS left for ABC, he took Reeder with him. Once at ABC, he began to write spec scripts including one for *Barney Miller*. Chris Hayward read it and although he didn't buy that script, he encouraged Reeder and told him that he thought he could write for the show.

Reeder's first credit came in Season Two for the episode, "Discovery." He would be credited with a dozen episodes over four seasons. His relationship with Danny Arnold, however, was less than comfortable. Reeder said Danny Arnold was the only producer he worked for who challenged him on writing credits. Reeder said, "Danny always just routinely submitted scripts to the Writers Guild for arbitration. Every other show I've ever worked on, if a writer has done a good job and turned in a solid draft, it's just understood that part of your job [as the showrunner] is punching up . . . 'let's fix this joke, we can shorten this scene,' stuff like that. It's rare that shows are submitted for arbitration. Danny, every episode, I wrote fourteen and I lost one arbitration."

Tony Sheehan said he never had this problem and never heard complaints from others but Ron Friedman said he wouldn't be surprised if Arnold challenged credits. Reeder himself said he felt it had something to do with the constant legal struggle over rights and credits that he was in with Ted Flicker. That sounds plausible since the Arnold/Flicker court battles raged on for years.

Ironically, in the two seasons that Danny Arnold was not running the show, Reeder never wrote an episode and then came back in Season Eight, when Arnold returned, and wrote "Possession" with his old pal Roland Kibbee. Reeder's absence in the sixth and seventh seasons is, no doubt, related to the fact that he was writing and producing the show *Benson* with Robert Guillaume. It was a valuable experience for Reeder because it convinced him he never wanted to be a producer again although years later he did serve as a Consulting Producer for a short time on *Cosby*.

In the long run, Reeder enjoyed a long and successful career as a freelancer and worked for a number of years on the sitcoms *Dave* and *Frasier* as a Creative Consultant. He also recognizes the valuable role that Danny Arnold ultimately played in his career. "He gave me a chance . . . so I started out on a good show. I didn't start out on something I had to apologize for later and that was huge in getting my career started." Prior to the Covid-19 pandemic he was happily retired traveling around the United States and the world with his wife.

Frank Dungan

Frank Dungan was a Vietnam Vet from Philadelphia when he came out to Los Angeles in 1976. He wanted to be an advertising writer but was having no luck. He was working two part-time jobs and decided to go to the Comedy Store one night for some diversion. After the show he asked the manager if comedians ever bought jokes? The manager told him, "Well, if they got any fucking money [they do]." He soon returned to the club and started peddling jokes to the various comedians who worked and hung out there. He sold his first jokes to Elayne Boosler. As he remembered it, "I made twenty bucks or something and I'm in show business!"

Eventually, he was hired by Jimmy Walker to write jokes for him. Dungan described Walker as an angel. "Jimmy had joke meetings," Dungan recalled.

"If he believed in comedy people, he backed them." It was at one of these joke meetings that Dungan met his future writing partner, Jeff Stein. He remembers they had a veteran's connection because Stein had recently been discharged from the Air Force. Standing outside of the club talking, they both agreed that the only TV show they would be interested in writing for was *Barney Miller*. They had a casual acquaintance with standup comedian Steve Landesberg from seeing him in the club. When they approached him and told him they wanted to write for the show he said, "You write a spec script, I'll give it to the producer because they're dying over there. They got two writers. Nobody can write the show."

They wrote a script and true to his word Landesberg took it and gave it to someone on the show. Weeks went by before they received a call from Reinhold Weege who told him that their script sucked. He then said, "I can't tell you to write another one. The Guild would go after me, but if you write another one, I'll read it." That was all the encouragement they needed. After months of pitching and meetings, they got an assignment and as soon as they got hired regularly, their mentor, Reinhold Weege, left the show for a deal at Warner Brothers.

Little did Dungan and Stein ever realize when they started out at the Comedy Store that they would end up being the two predominant writers for one of the best shows on television within a couple of years. It was Dungan and Stein who, along with Tony Sheehan, wrote most of the scripts for Seasons Six and Seven. Sheehan left at the beginning of Season Eight, but Dungan and Stein remained. It was a challenging adjustment for them to work with just Danny Arnold above them, but they managed and along with Arnold and Sheehan they wrote the last chapter of the 12th Precinct's story.

The writing team followed up their *Barney Miller* success by creating a sitcom based on the classic *Mr. Belvedere* movies that starred Clifton Webb. In the series, Christopher Hewitt took on the role of the title character with Bob Uecker and Ilene Graf playing the parents of the household Belvedere runs. The show was quite popular and ran for six seasons. Following *Belvedere*, and another show they created together called *Sister Kate*, the two men branched out on their own but remain close friends.

In 1996, Dungan was one of the creators of a cable sitcom called *Campus Cops*. It was in the style of the Naked Gun movies that were popular at the time with Leslie Nielson. The show had some devoted fans but only lasted a season. He also wrote some freelance episodes for *Coach*, *Smart Guy*, and *So Little Time*. These days he continues to write and occasionally entertains himself by coming up with current ideas/issues that would make a good *Barney Miller* story.

Jeff Stein

Jeff Stein was working in the warehouse of a record company when he got laid off. He wasn't too upset since he really wanted to get into writing. The problem was he didn't know anyone "in the business," as they say. Then he came upon an article in the *Los Angeles Times* about amateur night at the Comedy Store and he thought, "Well jokes, shit. I'll start writing jokes . . . it doesn't seem like a lot of work." He started writing jokes and at his first amateur night, he went up on stage and read the jokes he'd written off a yellow legal pad. "I mean, I had no stage presence whatsoever . . . the worst," he remembered. However, once he left the stage the comedians told him how awful his delivery was but how good the jokes were. Jimmy Walker heard him one night and offered to buy some of his jokes. A few days later Helen Kushnick [Walker's manager] called and told him Walker wanted to sign Stein to his management company as a comic. Stein's reply was, "What? No, I don't want to be a comic. I'm terrible at it." Instead, they hired him to be one of Walker's writers.

As previously stated, it was at one of the Jimmy Walker joke meetings where he met Frank Dungan and the two soon became writing partners. Stein confirmed that it was indeed Steve Landesberg who helped them get their foot in the door at *Barney Miller* but it wasn't quite that easy. As Stein recalls, "For Frank and I to write that first *Barney*, get it to them, have a meeting, have them finally read it, call us, have Reinie talk to us about it, have us go be disappointed, then shake it off and say, 'I think the guy left the door open and told us to write again. We better write another one.' I mean that had to happen over the course of at least a year."

Persistence paid off and starting in Season Six they were officially on board at *Barney Miller* where they would remain through the end of the show's run three years later. They had never written a TV show before *Barney Miller* so it's not unfair to say they started at the top.

Stein has worked primarily as a freelancer since then and his most recent credit was on an episode of the *Ned and Stacey* reboot.

Barney Miller and the Female Sex

There is a sense of camaraderie evoked by the men of the 12th Precinct that the female characters were never able to fully infiltrate. Despite Fish's frequent wife jokes directed at the ever-patient Bernice, there is certainly a respect for women but in a very post–World War II, twentieth century style. It's not a respect of total equality but certainly one that is slowly, if not altogether willingly, giving way to the changing roles of women in society. June Gable, who portrayed Det. Maria Battista in the second season said, "you could see the timbre and genre of the show by looking at it. It was not a woman's show, it was definitely a men's bromance kind of show."

Danny Arnold and his team made efforts to incorporate female cops into the storyline but it never took hold. There were at least three attempts to bring a female cop into the day-to-day team at the 12th Precinct as well as some undercover cops and some uniformed female officers. There were also female roles depicting doctors, lawyers, therapists, and historians. However, it is true there were certainly as many, if not more, roles that portrayed housewives or prostitutes.

Arnold did employ a few female writers but again it was a very low percentage of the overall group. One of the female writers, Shelley Zellman, told me, "It was a very male-oriented show." Nevertheless, when she and her writing partner, Wally Dalton, submitted a spec script they were quickly hired to follow through with their idea. When the show they wrote actually made it to air, Arnold offered them a position as staff writers. They accepted and contributed to over a half dozen episodes in the show's fifth season. At the same time, Zellman admitted that in those days female writers often teamed with male partners to have a better chance at having their scripts read by producers.

All the women I interviewed for this book remember Danny Arnold as charming and brilliant but there's no mistake that the female characters of the 12th Precinct were never quite on an equal footing with the men. As out of place as the inequities of this portrayal is in today's environment, the truth is, *Barney Miller's* storylines and characters are very reflective of the times. Police work was still a male-dominated career track in the 1970s as women were just beginning their struggle to infiltrate the ranks and level the playing field in law enforcement. In that sense, the struggles of Officers Wentworth (Linda Lavin), Battista (June Gable), and Licori (Mari Gorman) are totally realistic and authentic for the time.

The show was not initially intended to be such a male-dominated project. As previously stated, both pilots showed Barney Miller's life at home contrasted with his life at work. However, when critics and viewers alike revealed their indifference to the domestic side of the story, the show quickly shifted focus and became a workplace comedy. The ratings for the show's first half season (it was a January 1975, mid-season replacement) are some of the lowest in its eight-season run. The one real casualty in this shift was Barbara Barrie's character Elizabeth Miller, Barney's wife. In the first two seasons, she is given star billing in the opening credits of the show. However, in the second season, she doesn't appear in an episode again after "Happy New Year," broadcast in January. She isn't in any Season Three episodes at all and returns for one episode in the fourth season and one in the fifth season and then never again. Oddly enough, she doesn't even appear in the series-ending trilogy.

Speaking of that trilogy, none of the female cops who served at the 12th came back to say goodbye either. Linda Lavin was shown in a quick flashback as were Abe Vigoda, Gregory Sierra, and Jack Soo but that was it. It would have been totally natural and a nice touch to have some of the old officers back but it was not to be.

It's interesting to note that when Bill Persky and Sam Denoff hired Arnold to produce their series *That Girl* in the show's second season (1967-68), Arnold hired a female writer, Ruth Brooks Flippen, to add a female voice to the writers' room. Flippen had previously worked on the *Gidget* franchise for both film and television. Following *That Girl* she wrote for *My World and Welcome To It*, the show Arnold worked on prior to *Barney Miller* but it appears she never worked on *Barney*. Nevertheless, it seems that there were definitely times when Danny Arnold felt a female voice was needed and, at those times, he went out and hired a female writer.

Veteran TV writer Lila Garrett is credited with the first season episode "Graft" but according to Tony Sheehan, she and Danny had a falling out. He didn't know the circumstances that caused the parting of ways, only that Danny did not have fond memories of her. In addition to the aforementioned

Shelley Zellman, he also hired at least two other female writers for the *Miller* series, Judith Anne Nielsen and Sybil Adelman. The vast majority of the show's writers were men and combined with the lack of female writers, and the lack of sustainable female characters in the *Barney Miller* universe, that might confirm that Arnold himself thought of *Barney Miller* as primarily a guy's show.

Barney Miller and Real-Life Police Officers

One of the more intriguing reasons to watch *Barney Miller* is that, through the years, real-life police detectives have cited the show as being the most realistic depiction of police work on television. It seems incredible at first thought but makes total sense when you hear police officers and former police officers explain their feelings about the show. The first person to drive this point home to me was actor Dennis Farina. I stumbled onto an old talk show on YouTube called *Dinner for Five* hosted by filmmaker Jon Favreau in which he and four guests would sit around the table at a restaurant, eat dinner, and talk. The episode I came across featured Jon Livingston, Faizon Love, Gina Gershon, and Dennis Farina. At one point, the conversation turned to the fact that Farina had spent nineteen years as a Chicago police officer before becoming an actor. Naturally, he was asked what was the best police film ever made and he answered, "The best police movie ever made—there were two of them—*The French Connection* [1971] and there was a movie that followed that called *The Seven-Ups* [1973]. And I think the best television show about policemen, believe it or not, *Barney Miller*. Because, it was in that setting, you know they were in that precinct house and you know . . . usually your days, you kind of just go along, . . ." Farina went on to say that his biggest complaint about most police films and series was the fact that they so rarely showed the humor the officers shared to help them get through the day. *Barney Miller* was exactly that—it showed the men, and occasional women, having a little fun, sometimes at the expense of a criminal or victim and sometimes at the expense of a fellow officer but it never really offended. The humanity of all the characters was so central to the heart of the show that they could be funny and have fun without trivializing the serious aspects of the job and the culture.

In the March 21, 1981, issue of *TV Guide* there was an article written by Lt. John J. Yuknes entitled "A Cop's-Eye View of *Barney Miller*." In it, Yuknes describes what we think is a scene from the show before revealing that he's describing his own squad room as leader of the detectives of the 6th Precinct on West 10th Street in Manhattan. Yuknes writes, "I'm a fan of the show, and so are most of my men. I think that Barney Miller is a good cop. He presents a positive image of what a police officer can be. I also think that the show's writers are right on target much of the time when they show how the detectives on the series react to situations."

The fact that he points out that "Barney Miller is a good cop" is a substantial observation. This is a sitcom but the level of the writing and the acting and the subject matter always lifted it to a higher plain. You rarely hear people talk about the impact the show may have had on the public's perception of the police or its potentially positive influence on law enforcement recruitment. Quite honestly, movies like *Dirty Harry (1971), The French Connection* (1971), *The Seven-Ups* (1973), *Serpico* (1973), *Freebie and the Bean* (1974), and *The Choirboys* (1977), all of which hit movie screens Between 1971 – 1977, didn't do much for the reputation of America's law enforcement agencies. *Barney Miller*, on the other hand, presented a picture of idiosyncratic individuals with human flaws and weaknesses who took their job seriously and always tried at least to carry themselves with a certain amount of dignity.

In the same *TV Guide* article from 1981, Yuknes went on to say, "I think police officers like *Barney Miller* because it's deeper than most television sitcoms. It's more like a slice of life. Not that it is 100 percent accurate, but it illustrates some of what goes on in a squad room. The way the detectives work together, or sometimes get mad at each other. The black humor that crops up from time to time. The fact that sometimes cops use unorthodox methods."

It should be noted that Danny Arnold almost always had a real-life cop or former cop in the studio with the cast and crew to advise and make suggestions or corrections. For a long time, that person was Lieutenant Paul Glanzman. Tom Reeder, who wrote over a dozen episodes, recalled that the writers were encouraged to call Glanzman with any technical questions. Reeder said, "So if you were doing an episode about, let's say, somebody was carrying a gun and he didn't have a permit, you could call Glanzman and ask, 'What are the criteria for getting a permit to carry a gun in New York?' Or, you know, 'How would you handle this kind of case? What would the official charges be called if you were bringing in such-and-such a case?' He was good and [accessible] with us. That kind of attention to detail was probably another factor as to why, as Reeder noted, "A lot of New York City cops really enjoyed [the show]."

In 2005, as the TV series *NYPD Blue* was ending its twelve-year-run on ABC, Detective Lucas Miller of the New York Police Department wrote an op-ed article about the program for the March 5, 2005, issue of the *New York Times*. In his appreciation piece about the show, however, he took the time to write, "Many police officers maintain that the most realistic police show in the history of television was the sitcom *Barney Miller*, far more so than that father of reality TV, *Cops*. The action was mostly off-screen, the squad room was the only set, and the guys were a motley bunch of character actors who were in no danger of being picked for the N.Y.P.D. pin-up calendar. But they worked hard, made jokes, got hurt and answered to their straight-man commander."

"For real detectives," Miller continued, "most of the action does happen off-screen, and we spend a lot of time back in the squad room writing reports about it. Like Barney Miller's squad, we crack jokes at one another, at the cases that come in, and at the crazy suspect locked in the holding cell six feet from the new guy's desk. Life really is more like *Barney Miller* than *NYPD Blue*, but our jokes aren't nearly as funny."

Thomas Vinciguerra also wrote about the series in the *New York Times* on October 28, 2011, as the complete series was released on DVD by Shout! Factory. Vinciguerra observed that, "*Barney Miller* rewrote the rules of cop shows and sitcoms alike. Its principals weren't heroes; they were jaded lifers contending with assorted wackos, . . ." Most importantly, he identifies writer Joseph Wambaugh as an early fan of the show. "He [Wambaugh] began tuning in shortly after stepping down as a Los Angeles Police Department detective sergeant, to write full time . . . 'I was uncertain if I could make it without the badge,' Wambaugh said. 'But I could turn on *Barney Miller*. It filled a void for me. I could have gone onto that set, sat down and gone to work.'"

Writer Frank Dungan recalled returning years ago to his hometown of Philadelphia and going out to a series of bars with an old friend. On the last stop of the night, his friend, who'd had a few drinks, started pressing Dungan to tell the strangers situated around the bar what he did for a living. Dungan assumed his friend had had too much to drink and begged off but then the patrons got curious and they started pressing him to find out what he did. Finally, Dungan told them, "I write for *Barney Miller*. 'What! What! So where were you on the force?' I said, I was never on the force. And [one of the guys] asks, 'Well, how do you know this stuff?' And now he's calling all these cops over and all they want to do is talk about *Barney Miller* and the rotating door of you bringing in the perps and they go back out, the endless paperwork, the bureaucracy. In their minds, that's what Barney captured."

Dungan's friend had brought him into a police hangout and, as Dungan recalls, the patrons "could not believe that none of us [Jeff, Tony, and I] had anything to do with any police force. *Barney* was their favorite show. Hands down.

Years after the series went off the air, Hal Linden, Max Gail, Abe Vigoda, Steve Landesberg, all of them stated that former cops would come up to them and tell them how much they appreciated the show. In fact, in a coincidence of life imitating art that Dennis Farina would have appreciated, Steve Landesberg became close friends with Sonny Grosso, the real-life New York City cop whose exploits inspired films like *The French Connection* (1971) and *The Seven-Ups* (1973).

Of Its Time and Timeless

Generally speaking, because they're (usually) a one-shot deal, movies tend to be more timeless in nature than television shows. For example, if you're making one ninety-minute movie, your story is tightly controlled. Prior to filming, you've mapped out the storyline as well as the time period in which it's set. The production itself usually has a timeline ranging anywhere from six months to two years for completion. Television is a different beast. On TV, unless you're making a period piece like *Dr. Quinn, Medicine Woman* or *The Wonder Years*, the clothes, the social references, often even the dialogue, is reflective of the era in which it's produced. You may be writing and filming the show for one year or ten years and therefore you have no idea how well certain aspects of the production will hold up. If you fill your scripts with current events and pop cultural references, chances are the shows will not hold up as well. If you write with a certain sense of timelessness to the situations, as they tended to do on *The Andy Griffith Show* and *The Dick Van Dyke Show*, you have a chance to create a show that will stay popular and relevant for multiple generations.

None of these issues are controlled by simple black and white rules. For example, social attitudes regarding the roles of husbands and wives are vastly different today than they were in the early 1950s when *I Love Lucy* hit the airwaves. Let's be honest, the paternalistic attitude that Ricky displays towards Lucy is hard to swallow in modern times regardless of the fact that Lucy's actions are often by design, juvenile enough to merit such disrespectful treatment. However you look at it, the dynamics of that domestic situation are antiquated and yet it's still a popular show. Why? I believe it's because slapstick comedy, which is the primary comedic engine of the show, is timeless. The social attitudes don't hold up but the natural reaction to masterfully performed slapstick comedy remains.

There are other shows that are totally out of step with the sea change of cultural mores that have taken place over the past sixty years and yet people still watch these shows. A program like *Leave It to Beaver*, *Father Knows Best*, or *Hazel* are all relics of the past but in those cases, that actually contributes to their continued popularity. As the TV generation ages, they long to look back with rose-colored glasses to what they perceive as the simpler days of their youth. TV shows of the period, particularly sitcoms, tended to present the most idyllic view of the "The American Family" in the 1950s. Fans watch those shows today as if they're watching old home movies of their happy childhood. Never mind that they are usually whitewashed depictions of middle class, Protestant characters living in a world without racial injustice, economic strife, or educational disparities.

Barney Miller came along twenty-five years into television's history and straddled the line on all sorts of cultural fronts on a weekly basis for seven years. Watching the show today, we can't help but notice Nick and Wojo's wide neckties and Ron Harris's Afro hairstyle. There are considerable references made to the dire economic situation of New York City in the 1970s throughout the early seasons of the show. Combine all those elements with the fact that many of the storylines were taken right from the headlines of the day by the show's writers and you have a show that is very reflective of its era. And yet, it doesn't seem as out of touch and antiquated as shows like *The Brady Bunch* or *Diff'rent Strokes* do today. There are, no doubt, two reasons for this: one is simple, the other a little more nuanced.

The simple answer to why *Barney* reflects a timeless quality of excellence comes from the writing. *Barney Miller* enjoyed some of the best writing in the history of the television sitcom. Great writing usually stands the test of time. What makes one piece of writing smarter than another? In my opinion, if you start from a point of truth and proceed with honesty and intelligence, showing a respect for your audience, then that usually results in great writing and stories that audiences will want to return to again and again.

As I re-watched these shows for the tenth, twelfth, fifteenth times, I was really amazed by two things. First, no matter how many times I've seen an episode, I still laugh at the comedy. I can't help it. You know how you know when something is truly funny? When you're watching it alone and you laugh out loud. Laughter tends to come more freely when you watch with a crowd. You elicit one another's laughter. If you're alone and you laugh without even thinking about it, *that's* funny! *Barney Miller* accomplishes that feat for me to this day.

In terms of the more nuanced answer, that brings us back again to the fact that at its core, this is a show about the Human Condition. It's totally about the relationships of human beings, one to the other. However, instead of strictly the romantic comedy angle which even in the most popular shows like *Cheers*, *Moonlighting*, and *Friends*, got incredibly tiresome after a certain number of trips back to that all too familiar well, this was a show about *all* relationships. It had stories about husbands and wives, siblings, co-workers, artists and capitalists, rich and poor, ugly and beautiful, gay and straight, black and white, and the list goes on and on in as many different variations as you can discover within the human family. *Barney Miller* wasn't afraid to observe and examine any type of human relationship. That's what makes it special and that's also what makes it timeless.

A Haven for Character Actors

> We called them cage characters . . . the people who were going to wind up in the cage. Some of those guys, by the way, were to Danny's credit . . . guys who had been blacklisted during the McCarthy era. In fact, Roland Kibbee had been in that situation. I want to give him credit for making a conscious decision to hire some of those guys. I'm pretty sure Phil Leeds was one of them. I think Jeff Corey may have been [he was]. There were several of those guys and to Danny's credit . . . they had to be good but he helped restore some people's careers.
>
> —*Tom Reeder*

As I grow a little older, it seems to me that everyone on TV is in their twenties with perfect teeth, perfect bodies, and full heads of thick, luxurious hair. That's okay, actors like that have been around forever. They used to be called "leading ladies" or "leading men." Today they're just called "the cast" of whatever film or show you're watching. However, years ago Hollywood seemed to make films and TV shows with all kinds of characters inhabiting the scene. In some cases they were there to make the star look good, in other cases they added comic relief, and sometimes they were there just to creep us out! It was much more obvious who the leading players were and who the supporting players, or "character actors," were. The character players were bald, hairy, fat, skinny, short, or tall, they had uneven teeth, some limped, and some were cockeyed. Today I'm not sure I should even say or write half the words in the preceding sentence. Whatever the case, they represented an eclectic and more realistic cross section of humanity.

I have always loved the great character actors and actresses of the big and the small screen. From the classic movie players like Beulah Bondi, Barton MacLane, Spring Byington, and Allen Jenkins to those characters on the TV shows of my youth like Jack Riley, Jane Dulo, Roscoe Lee Brown, and Vito

Scotti—all of these people made everything they appeared in better, brighter, funnier, more poignant. There may have never been a better show to present character actors/actresses in their best light than *Barney Miller*. This show was extra-special because even the stars were great character actors. Some may have enjoyed leading man/lady looks but they were still able to disappear into their character. Add to that the amazing performances of the victims and the criminals who came through the 12th Precinct's squad room doors and you have a unique moment in history. All of these characters left an indelible mark on our collective television conscious. I loved them all and, for me, they were the hot fudge in the *Barney Miller* sundae.

Barney Miller may have shot in Hollywood but Harriet Helberg, casting person for the show's fifth season, said, "Danny Arnold [had] a terrific, tremendous appreciation of great New York character actors." However, working for the procrastinator/perfectionist that Danny Arnold was, it could be challenging to cast a weekly show. Helberg would draw up a list of actors at the beginning of the week and submit it to Danny and wait for him to look it over and that sometimes didn't happen until Wednesday. In addition, they were constantly rewriting the script, assuming they even had one on Monday morning. Helberg remembers, "I would have actors show up on the set to audition for Danny. Sometimes they would add parts, sometimes they would cut parts. Sometimes they just didn't have the material until they were taping."

It was an incredibly chaotic way to work and yet, somehow, Arnold did just that—he made it work. The show may have never cracked the top ten but it was a highly respected production and actors loved to have it on their résumé. Many of the people with whom I spoke talked of it as "Danny Arnold's troupe of players." That may be why Arnold liked to hire stage actors, it was like a summer stock experience where you get little time to rehearse and are always changing characters.

Max Gail and I were talking one day about all the great character actors who appeared on the show over the years. I asked him about some of my favorites, what was it about those people, particularly the ones Danny Arnold hired over and over again, that made us feel so connected to them? Max felt the best were "People who would come in and not just try to play the jokes, not just go for the funny. You know, some of them were Broadway comic actors and actresses that were funny and at the same time they had that sense of deeper character and playing the moment and stuff like that so they weren't just gags, you know? And when somebody came in and did that, then Danny would find a way to bring them back because that was the key to the show I think, you know, not trying to play to the punch lines."

As Gail remembers it, "That was one of the really wonderful things of doing that show as much as the friendships with the guys and the feeling that we were all in it together, was watching these wonderful people coming in and work. You know the guest performers, they were a real character with a heartbeat and we were there to support them as much as they were there to support us, whereas in a lot of other shows it really is about the regulars. Most people that come in are there to deliver a pizza and make a joke."

The Cops

The profiles below were assembled from interviews with the author except in the cases of Linda Lavin and Michael Lembeck. George Murdock is deceased so his information was gathered from previously written sources and Dick O'Neill's bio was taken from a note written to the author by Mr. O'Neill's widow, Jackie.

June Gable as Det. Maria Battista

June Gable's character of Maria Battista was another short-lived female cop within the 12th Precinct. As she told me, she was brought in as a kind of combination of Gregory Sierra and Linda Lavin, both of whom left the show after the second season. It's hard to tell how good she would have been because she only did two episodes but she was very funny. Unfortunately, the fact that she was such a good actress is related to how and why her tenure was so short.

Gable recalled, "When I replaced Rita Moreno in *The Ritz*, everybody thought I was Latina. Danny Arnold . . . came with his casting agent . . . to see me do *The Ritz*. He hired me to come out and to do this recurring role of Detective Battista. He never asked me, 'Are you Spanish?' He just assumed it!"

As they were filming the first episode, Arnold asked her to throw in a little Spanish. She told him, "'I don't know it. I'm going to have to get a coach . . . then I'll throw in some Puerto Rican or Spanish phrases.' He was appalled. I remember he was eating this huge corned beef and pastrami sandwich, you know, with pickles and potato chips all stuffed in his mouth at once. I thought it was all going to come out.

"He says, 'Wait a minute. Aren't you Puerto Rican? Aren't you Spanish?' No, No, I'm not. To make things even worse, there was a group called HOLA and that group was fighting for Latino roles going to Latinos. So with that pressure on him . . . for hiring me to play a Latina when I was clearly not . . . the contract was canceled."

The bright side of the story is that June Gable had a successful career before and after her two episodes of *Barney Miller*. Prior to *Barney*, she was nominated for a Tony Award for Best Featured Actress in a Musical for her work in 1974's *Candide*. She did *Comedy of Errors* for Joe Papp at the New York Shakespeare Festival as well as the successful run replacing Moreno in *The Ritz*. In the 1990s and beyond, she had recurring roles on successful TV shows like *Dream On* and *Friends*.

Gable also became a yoga therapist and a homeopathist. She traveled and spent time in India. Through the years she's been an actor, a writer, a caregiver, a painter, and an activist. She even designed and built a log cabin home. She is truly a Renaissance woman.

Mari Gorman as Roberta Kerlin, Officer Rosslyn "Roz" Licori, and Naomi Bender

Mari Gorman is a native New Yorker whose family moved to Milwaukee, Wisconsin, for the last two years of her high school experience. She loved Wisconsin but returned to New York as soon as she had the chance because she wanted to be an actress. Her first love was live theater and she spent over a decade treading the boards. Her big break came when she was cast in Lanford Wilson's off-Broadway play, *Hot L Baltimore*. She was so well received in the play that she won both a Theatre World Award and a Drama Desk Award for her portrayal of Jackie.

Her success in the play led to a recurring role in the soap opera *Edge of Night* and a part in the Joe Sargent-directed feature *The Taking of Pelham One Two Three* (1974). She moved to Los Angeles in 1977 and spent twenty-two years working primarily in television with the occasional foray into films.

Her first role on *Barney Miller* came in 1977 as a housewife who attempts prostitution to get her husband's attention. She was terrific in the role and Danny Arnold would ask her back five more times over the course of the show's run. In turn, she loved the experience, saying, "*Barney Miller* was the only really great, artistic or collaborative experience I had working in anything out there. The ensemble and the feeling that Danny Arnold created, the excitement, it was not like anything else. It spoiled me because it was one of the earliest things I did and nothing ever was even remotely as fun. We had all these wonderful character actors and people relished watching each other do these things and the writing was marvelous. It was just a great, great show."

Gorman's next *Barney* assignments were as Detective Roz Licori. She appeared in a three-episode arc as the third female detective introduced into the 12th Precinct after Linda Lavin and June Gable. She remembers "they did put me on some kind of a hold when I did those shows to not take another series and they gave me a bunch of money. It seemed like a fortune to me at the time because I was from the theater." Unfortunately, as was always the case within the *Barney Miller* universe, the female cop didn't catch on. Gorman remembers, "I think they were trying with the Roz Licori character, . . . to create something but they weren't quite sure what direction to go." Tony Sheehan confirmed that the female detective was always a challenging stumbling block for the writers. As time went on and the dynamic between the men had become so strong and well-defined, it became increasingly difficult to add new characters.

Her last two appearances on the show came in the show's final season when she returned in the recurring role of Bruno Bender's wife, Naomi. As always, she was terrifically funny although some of the writing for those episodes would not be done today as there are hints of spousal abuse in her character's reactions to her husband. Nevertheless, she was asked to be in the series' final episode in 1982. "I was so honored by that, I really, really was," Gorman said.

During her years in Hollywood, she worked on shows for some of the industry's most important writers and producers including Norman Lear, Garry Marshall, and Gary David Goldberg. She even worked again for Tony Sheehan, Frank Dungan, and Jeff Stein on *Mr. Belvedere*. Eventually, however, she longed to return to New York and the world of live theater. She moved back to the city in 1999 and went back to school. She wrote a book entitled *Strokes of Existence*, and even started her own theater company called Glass Beads Theatre Ensemble. Mari Gorman, like so many of the *Barney Miller* alumni, is kind, sensitive, and very talented.

Milt Kogan as Officer Kogan

This child of immigrants has led a fascinating life indeed. Born in Philadelphia and raised in Camden, New Jersey, Milt Kogan was the star of his high school basketball team and that talent along with his six-foot, six-inch frame led him to Cornell University. An injury in his second year nixed any aspirations of a professional basketball career and instead he went on to medical school in Philadelphia and then Los Angeles for his internship.

Once in Tinseltown, a friend encouraged him to join an acting class to meet young starlets. In an interview with Jim Suva for a *Rockford Files* reunion (Kogan was in three episodes), he told Suva, "My first acting class was with an extremely erudite acting teacher, Jeff Corey, and his assistant, Lenny Nimoy." The class was filled with actors and dancers who were out in Hollywood filming a movie version of *West Side Story*. Kogan remembered, "[They] were so passionate, that I became show biz hooked immediately."

He fell in love with acting and at the same time earned his medical degree. According to an August 25, 1975, *People Magazine* article, Kogan borrowed $1,000 from his dad to try acting full time for six months. After an uneventful six months, he went to work in a friend's private practice. Once he finally started to land some acting jobs, he was unwilling to give up medicine so he did both simultaneously. He told *People*, "I'm a doctor who's also an actor. I couldn't give up one or the other."

He landed his role on *Barney Miller* through an audition and when Danny chose him for the role, he changed the character's name to Kogan because he liked the young actor's surname.

Milt Kogan, doctor and actor, has nothing but fond memories of Arnold and the show. "Danny Arnold was one of the funniest men I have ever met in my life. He would come up with these things . . . if you were an actor in the show, how could you keep a straight face? He was just an amazing, amazing guy . . . that's the biggest thing about *Barney Miller* is the incredible talent of Danny Arnold."

These days Milt Kogan is a farmer in Oceanside, California. He seems to have a well of inexhaustible energy because he's still acting and keeping up his medical skills as well.

Linda Lavin as Detective Janice Wentworth

Linda Lavin was born into a musical family in Portland, Maine in 1937. Her mother was an opera singer and Lavin sang, danced, and studied acting from an early age. Following her graduation from the College of William and Mary she worked with the Compass Players and then relocated to New York City where she appeared in numerous Off-Broadway productions.

A Family Affair in 1962 was Lavin's Broadway debut. Her first taste of stardom came in 1966 with a leading role in *It's A Bird . . . It's A Plane . . . It's Superman*, a musical directed by Harold Prince with music by Adams and Strouse. In 1969, she co-starred in Neil Simon's play *Last of the Red Hot Lovers* and earned her first of an eventual six Tony Award nominations.

In the early 1970s she married actor Ron Liebman and the couple moved to Los Angeles. Lavin soon began appearing in weekly TV series such as *The Great American Dream Machine*, *Rhoda*, and *Harry O*. Lavin was introduced as Det. Wentworth in the Season One episode of *Barney Miller* entitled "Ms. Cop" and then disappeared until returning for four episodes in the second season. The character of Det. Sgt. Janice Wentworth may have been a high-strung, emotional female but she was clearly a very capable police officer as well.

Following Season Two of *Barney Miller*, Lavin was offered the lead in her own sitcom, *Alice*, a TV adaptation of Martin Scorsese's 1974 film *Alice Doesn't Live Here Anymore*. This ignited her career as the sitcom went on to enjoy nine successful seasons on CBS while earning numerous Emmy and Golden Globe nominations. In addition to acting, *Alice* offered her the opportunity to try her hand behind the camera as she directed at least ten episodes of the popular series.

After an absence of almost fifteen years, she returned to the Broadway stage in November of 1986 in Neil Simon's *Broadway Bound*. Her second Simon play earned her yet another Tony nomination. This time she won the coveted award for Best Performance by a Leading Actress in a Play. In fact, the last thirty years have been filled with stage successes including plays such as *The Sisters Rosensweig*, *The Diary of Anne Frank*, and *The Tale of the Allergist's Wife*. Her work in *Death Defying Acts* and *The Lyons* both earned her Obie Awards.

Throughout her busy acting career, she has continued to honor her calling as a vocalist with a popular cabaret act. She works frequently with the talented pianist Billy Stritch and has released at least two CDs in recent years, *Possibilities* and *Love Notes*.

George Murdock as Lt. Ben Scanlon and Master Sgt. J. R. Reville

George Murdock's depiction of Lieutenant Ben Scanlon has got to be considered one of the most memorable of all the characters who ever passed through the 12th Precinct. He played every scene with a deadly seriousness that translated into pure comedy gold. Scanlon was as miserable a human being as Barney was a good one.

A native of Salina, Kansas, Murdoch's film and television career spanned an amazing six decades. He appeared in numerous feature films but never achieved much notoriety for his film work until 1989 when he appeared as God in *Star Trek V: The Final Frontier*. He's best remembered by *Trek* fans for striking down Captain Kirk with a lightning bolt when the captain asks, "What does God need with a starship?"

He also spent time in Off-Broadway and Broadway productions before moving to Los Angeles and becoming one of the original members of the Melrose Theater and starring in *Lester Sims Retires Tomorrow*. Additional theater work included productions at South Coast Repertory, the Los Angeles Theatre Center, and the Odyssey Theatre.

Murdoch's greatest contribution came in the medium of television. His small screen roles extend all the way back to *The Twilight Zone* and *The Untouchables* and continue through *Ironside*, *Gunsmoke*, and *Battlestar Galactica*. His twelve *Barney Miller* assignments are more than any other actor that was not considered a series regular. In fact, he has more appearances than series regular Barbara Barrie who played Liz Miller. Barrie was credited in thirty-six episodes but only appeared in eleven. Max Gail remembered Murdock fondly, telling me, "George came at it with just a huge amount of enthusiasm. He loved playing that part. He loved all those moves and everything. He just devoured it. His enthusiasm for playing that part was a great lesson for me."

In the years following his work on the Danny Arnold sitcom, Murdock co-starred in a sitcom called *What a Country* (1986–1987) and played recurring roles on *The X-Files*, *Law & Order*, and *Judging Amy*. He worked four episodes of *Night Court* for *Barney Miller* alum Reinhold Weege and even appeared in a memorable episode of *Seinfeld* as Testikov, a famous Russian novelist.

Throughout his career, his deep, commanding voice with his craggy character actor's face put him on track to play either authority figures like policemen and judges, or darker, more malevolent characters. When he was once asked if he objected to being typecast his response was, "Getting the job is important. Who cares where it comes from?"

George Murdock died of cancer on April 30, 2012, leaving behind a legacy of over 200 roles for fans to remember him by.

Dino Natali as Officer Zatelli

Dino Natali was born in the North Beach Italian Neighborhood of San Francisco. He started his career with the musical-comedy group, the Vagabonds. He and the group literally traveled the world as an opening act for some of the biggest names in entertainment. Equally adept at music (he was a bassist) and comedy, he forged working relationships and lasting friendships with entertainers such as Lucille Ball, Carol Burnett, Dean Martin, Harvey Korman, Ann-Margret, and Tony Bennett, to name just a few.

He made appearances on television on *The Danny Kaye Show*, *The Lucy Show*, and *Kojak* before landing the recurring role of Officer Zatelli on *Barney Miller*. His first appearance came in 1978 and although we'd seen openly gay characters by this time on *Soap*, *All in the Family*, and *Barney Miller*, it was still an important step forward to show a gay cop. The character himself was not in the least bit effeminate and it is understood that he is very capable in his job. It was a subtle but very progressive character and storyline.

Natali has fond memories of the show as well as of Danny Arnold. In discussing Arnold's penchant for shooting into the wee small hours of the morning, Natali said Arnold didn't want to start shooting on Thursday and then have the actor go home and have a personal or family problem takeover their attention so that when they came in the following day to finish filming, the previous night's feeling would be lost. That's why, according to Natali, once they started filming they didn't stop until the show was done. "And that's the key to doing it with feeling, with passion, with love. He was sensational."

Natali also worked on *Joe Bash*, Danny Arnold's last original project for television that only lasted for six episodes in the spring of 1986. Natali says, "We were all looking for a long show. In all honesty, the reviews came out, they were sensational. The public didn't dig it . . . they thought it was kind of dark."

As for the effervescent Natali, he's still going strong as he nears the end of his seventh decade in show business. In recent years, he's appeared in cabarets with singer Elizabeth Holmes and has traveled with and promoted a vocalist named Pasquale Esposito in a show filmed for PBS entitled, "The Legend of Enrico Caruso."

Dick O'Neill as Detective Kelly

Born in New York City, O'Neill, like so many *Barney Miller* actors, spent his early years honing his skills in live theater. He appeared on Broadway in *The Unsinkable Molly Brown*, *Skyscraper*, and *Promises, Promises*. He also appeared in a show called *Tough to Get Help* that opened and closed on the same night in 1972. One of his co-stars in that flop was an actor named Abe Vigoda.

In New York, he and his friend Hal Linden lived in the same apartment building. Hal Linden recalls, "Dick and I were 'unemployment buddies' as well as good friends. We would walk our dogs together and on Thursdays [we'd walk] to the Unemployment Office to sign for our checks." When the two actors married their wives, the couples socialized and remained good friends. In 1974, another friend and co-star, Walter Matthau, asked O'Neill if he'd like to play a part in Billy Wilder's cinematic remake of *The Front Page*. Matthau recommended O'Neill and the character actor moved his family to California and began a whole new life in films and television.

O'Neill's widow Jackie said, "He was like a kid at Christmas when his agent would call with an audition. If he landed the job he was a stickler for being at the studio early and knowing his lines." He may be best remembered today for his five seasons as Detective Cagney's father, Charlie, on the popular police drama *Cagney & Lacey* (1982–1988). He loved working on that show and was proud of how well the actors worked together as a cast.

On *Barney Miller* he played the obnoxious and bigoted Detective/Patrolman Kelly who could always be depended upon to say the wrong thing to anyone at any time and not really care. Jackie O'Neill wrote me, "The cast was like a well-oiled machine . . . they blended together perfectly. I remember Noam Pitlik was one of his favorite directors and he thought Danny Arnold was a gentleman and a genius. The show was a perfect example of ensemble acting and Dick always came home happy after a day on that set. Lots of jokes, laughter, and good work at the end of the day."

Dick O'Neill was proud to be a character actor and he was one of the very best of his generation. He believed laughter to be the best medicine for whatever ails you and he shared a lot of laughter and joy through his acting.

O'Neill died of heart failure in 1998 at the age of seventy.

Foster, Kleiner, and Brown

We don't ever meet Foster, Kleiner, or Brown but we felt like we knew them thanks to the endless reminiscences of their ol' pal, Frank Luger. However, one area remained somewhat murky. Exactly how did Foster, Kleiner, and Brownie meet their end?

In "The Sniper" (S. 2/Ep. 16), Luger says, "Foster died of pneumonia suckin' for air, Kleiner, three strokes like that—he lay there like a carrot. Brown, he's up there in that happy house up in New Hampshire. They're feeding him tapioca three times a day on a spoon."

In "Quarantine: Part 2" (S. 3/Ep. 3), Luger's story changes substantially when he says, "Foster—Blew him up in his car. Nothing left of him. Kleiner—Gunned down over on 13th Street. Not a bad way to go. Brownie—I wouldn't want to go like ol' Brownie though, huh? That vein blew out in his head. There he is up in that nursing home in Vermont laying there stretched out like a carrot (begins to tear up)."

The ol' Inspector doesn't bring the subject up again until Season Five and then he only covers Brownie and Foster and doesn't mention Kleiner at all. In "The Radical" (S. 5/Ep. 10), Luger mentions he went to visit Brownie up at the nursing home. According to Luger, his old pal was "Laying in bed all day long looking like so much summer squash." A couple of months later, in "Graveyard Shift" (S. 5/Ep. 21), Luger specifies that Foster was killed when "they (he doesn't specify who 'they' are) shoved six sticks of dynamite under the front seat of his Packard in the middle of Sixth Avenue. Boom! Yecch. Even had his seatbelt fastened, Barney. Didn't help a bit."

On October 4, 1979, in "The Brother" (S. 6/Ep. 4), Brownie dies in his nursing home in Vermont. It's at this time that Luger first mentions to Barney that he's in his will. He tells him "it's nothing to sneeze at" and then follows up with the revelation that it includes some Studebaker stock. That might be why Barney was taken aback a couple of years later when he discovers just how much Luger has squirreled away over the years. Finally, in "The Slave" (S. 6/Ep. 5), Luger says goodbye to his old pal at Brownie's sparsely attended funeral.

The Victims and the Cage Characters

All the profiles in this section were taken from interviews with the author for this book with the exception of Candice Azzara, Lou Cutell, and Sal Viscuso, which were taken from previous interviews with the author for magazine profiles of the actors.

Candice Azzara as Miss LaMotta, Miss Lambert, and Audrey McManus

Candice Azzara, or Candy to her friends, was born into a colorful Italian American family from Brooklyn. She loved art and wanted to study painting but her parents wanted her to marry and raise a family. She married her high school sweetheart and while he was in the Army, she joined a local theater group. Her marriage didn't last long but her interest in acting grew. Everywhere she went, she was told that she was "naturally gifted" but she wanted to *learn* her craft and credits Eleanora Duse and Giulietta Masina as important theatrical influences.

In 1968 she began her association with Joe Bologna and Renee Taylor, appearing in the original company of their acclaimed Broadway play, *Lovers and Other Strangers*. She would work with them again in a film written by the couple entitled *Made for Each Other* (1971) and a short-lived TV series called *Calucci's Department* (1973).

Her agent convinced her to move to Los Angeles after *Calucci's Department* and her naiveté worked to her advantage as she wrote cards to people asking about job opportunities. Through her unique networking style she was cast in the film *Hearts of the West* (1975) and soon the opportunities began to pour in. She's appeared in over 400 commercials while also landing recurring roles on shows such as *Rhoda*, *Soap*, *Who's the Boss?*, and *Caroline in the City*.

She appeared in three different episodes of *Barney Miller* and considered it a special treat because it gave her the opportunity to work with the person she describes as her best friend in the business, the late Ron Carey. They knew each other as teenagers and worked together in *Lovers and Other Strangers*, *Made for Each Other* and *Fatso* (1980). Each of her roles on *Barney Miller* was unique and tremendously funny. The soft-spoken innocence of whatever character she portrays never outshines the character's native intelligence.

She's worked with everyone from Walter Matthau and Carl Reiner to Shelley Winters and Ernest Borgnine. She has continued to work steadily in the twenty-first century with roles in feature films including *Catch Me if You Can* (2002), *Ocean's Twelve* (2004), and *Little Boy* (2015) and on TV in *ER*, *Joan of Arcadia*, and *Rizzoli & Isles*. In a career that has spanned over half a century, Azzara has done it all and most recently, she's turned her talents to writing. In 2018, she and Michael Conley co-authored a book of stories entitled, *God, Please Give Me Patience . . . and Hurry!*

Diana Canova as Stephanie Wolf

Diana Canova came from a show biz family. Her mother Judy Canova performed in nightclubs and vaudeville with her siblings before moving on to the Ziegfeld Follies and success in radio and films. Diana Canova inherited the family's musical genes and considered using her voice for opera before falling in love with musical theater. Spotted by an agent in a high school production of *Hello Dolly*, Canova had her SAG card by the time she was nineteen and worked on an *Ozzie and Harriet* redux called *Ozzie's Girls* (1973).

Her vocal talent originally got her noticed but her natural comedic timing soon got her numerous jobs on shows like *Happy Days*, *Chico and the Man*, and the feature film, *The First Nudie Musical* (1976).

One day her agent sent her to audition for a part in what he described as "one of the funniest scripts I've ever read." She auditioned and went home without thinking too much of it. As soon as she walked into her apartment, she got a call asking her to go right back to the studio and read again for network chief Fred Silverman. He liked what he saw and she was immediately given the role of Corinne Tate on the new ABC sitcom, *Soap*. Her natural girl-next-door demeanor won her the role of a lifetime playing a young woman who was a mixture of innocence and promiscuity.

In her one *Barney Miller* appearance, she played a graduate student earning money for school by working as an exotic dancer. In a case of art imitating life, Dietrich's character becomes smitten with her. At the time, the two actors were dating. From *Soap* she went on to star in two short-lived, sitcoms, *I'm a Big Girl Now* (1980–1981) and *Throb* (1986–1988). Canova sang the theme songs for both programs but her musical career never really took off. Canova told me, "Trying to have a pop career back then was difficult if you were on TV. I performed all the time on variety shows, but as far as recording, I was a person on *Soap* so it didn't really matter how good a musician I was because I was going to be Corinne."

It wasn't until she married and left Hollywood in the 1980s that she was able to find true joy through her music. Her singing teacher encouraged her to teach in addition to her own singing. She now says, "It's the longest gig I've ever had and I really love teaching."

Canova has been happily married for over thirty years to Elliot Scheiner, a Grammy Award-winning music producer and the founder and owner of the Bristol Blues, a minor league baseball team in the Futures Collegiate Baseball League. The couple has two grown sons, one working in baseball and the other in music.

Oliver Clark as Fur Thief, Charles Yusick, Vern Bidell, Dr. Richard P. Gesslin, DDS, Eugene Corbett, and Carl Ebling

Oliver Clark was born Richard Mardirosian in Buffalo, New York in 1939. His parents were Armenian and Greek immigrants and his brother Tom Mardirosian is also a successful actor. He graduated from the University of Buffalo and became a high school English teacher.

He got involved with theater in college and acted in some community theater plays while teaching but he soon felt that he wanted to pursue acting full time. He moved to New York and changed his name. At the time, *Oliver* was the biggest show on Broadway and he coupled that with a simple last name. Years later when he told colleagues how he took his name from the Lionel Bart musical, his friend Charles Nelson Reilly said, "You're lucky the big hit in town wasn't *Fanny*."

His first role on Broadway was in a play by Brecht entitled *The Evitable Rise of Arturo Ui* that closed after a few days. Clark then spent six months as Louis XVI in *Ben Franklin in Paris* opposite Robert Preston. In 1966 he co-starred in Woody Allen's first Broadway play *Don't Drink the Water* and after a run of almost 600 performances, he made the move to California at the prodding of a friend.

His good friend, David Birney, had just landed a TV series called *Bridget Loves Bernie*. Birney called Clark and said, "Why don't you come to California [with me]. I'll introduce you to my agent. You can live free of charge because they're giving me a house, a car, . . . I'm going to be on the set five or six days a week. You can drive me to the studio and then use the car to go to auditions for yourself." That began three decades of work in some of the most iconic TV shows in history: *The Rockford Files, Cannon, M*A*S*H, Night Court, The Jeffersons, The Golden Girls* and many more. He also had recurring roles on *The Bob Newhart Show, Mary Hartman, Mary Hartman, St. Elsewhere* and *Murder One*.

Danny Arnold used him in six different roles on *Barney Miller*. "Danny seemed to like me because I got my laughs," remembered Clark. "I'll never forget that particular show where I was a dentist. There was a line that was written with the character talking out loud to himself saying 'Well, I've had such a career as a dentist and now all of it down the drain.' And I remember thinking, 'I'm gonna change that without letting him know,' and I said, 'Here I am . . . all of it down the spit sink.' Danny went crazy he was so happy with that . . . so, he allowed for a little ad-lib and the spit sink line was a lot funnier than down the drain."

Oliver Clark is now semi-retired and has returned to his beloved New York.

David Clennon as Bodhisattva, Jeffrey Stevens, Justice Dept. Counsel Chester Monahan, Howard Speer, and Howard Weckler

David Clennon's roots are in the same hometown as the legendary Jack Benny (Waukegan, Illinois) but he was raised just up the New York Central line from Broadway in Bronxville, New York. His dad was an accountant and his mom was a housewife who loved Broadway musicals. Clennon never gave a thought to an acting career until his favorite professor of Literature at Notre Dame told his class after having read the play *Hamlet* that "What we've been looking at are just words on a page but it's a play, not a book, so you should all go see it." The university was mounting the play and a friend suggested to Clennon that they should try out for the relatively minor roles of the two gravediggers. Clennon initially balked but eventually gave in only to discover that his friend backed out. Once at tryouts, he felt obligated to stay and because the roles of the gravediggers were already cast he was asked to try out for the part of Guildenstern, a character he describes as just about [one of] the most thankless parts in all of Shakespeare. He was surprised to get the part without any experience or training but he recalls, "I did it and then I got the bug and wanted to keep on doing it."

He went to drama school after Notre Dame and was soon working off-Broadway in productions like Sam Shepard's *The Unseen Hand*. In 1977, he appeared on Broadway in Chekhov's *The Cherry Orchard*.

Clennon's career in front of the cameras began in 1973 on the television show, *The Paper Chase*. In a few short years, he was appearing in such major Hollywood films as *Coming Home* (1978), *Being There* (1979), *Hide in Plain Sight* (1980), and John Carpenter's cult classic, *The Thing* (1982). The majority of his work in the '70s and '80s was in feature films but he always maintained a presence on the small screen as well. In those early years of his career, some of his very best TV work came on *Barney Miller*. He made five appearances on the show as five different characters. He has very fond memories of working within that company of actors who he described as "truly down to earth, not pretentious, . . . just doing their work." If forced to pick one role, he admitted that "I loved the guy in 'Homeless' because he wanted to help people but he just didn't have the authority to do it and he couldn't control the situation."

His career has been a long and productive one. He's been a part of numerous Oscar-nominated and winning films including *Missing* (1982), *The Right Stuff* (1983), and *Syriana* (2005). His best remembered role is probably that of Miles Drentell in the popular 1990s drama, *thirtysomething*. He has continued to shine into the new millennium with roles on shows such as *Grey's Anatomy*, *Boston Legal*, *Weeds*, and *House of Cards*.

James Cromwell as Sgt. Wilkerson, Neil Spencer, Jason Parrish, and Dr. Edmund Danworth

James Cromwell grew up surrounded by the film business. The second child of actress Kay Johnson and prominent film director John Cromwell, he was born in Los Angeles in January 1940. His mother was a New York stage actress before coming to Hollywood and working in films with directors C. B. DeMille, Frank Capra, and Cromwell, her future husband. His father was the respected director of film classics *Of Human Bondage* (1934), *The Prisoner of Zenda* (1937), and *Since You Went Away* (1944).

The young James Cromwell, known to his friends as Jamie, honed his craft in live theater for years before returning to Hollywood in 1974. His first TV audition was for *All in the Family* and he landed the job that very same day. The role was that of the legendary Stretch Cunningham, the funniest man on the loading dock where Archie Bunker worked. In a timespan of just a few years he worked on other Norman Lear shows including *Mary Hartman, Mary Hartman*, *Hot L Baltimore*, and *Maude*, in addition to other big hits like *M*A*S*H*, *Three's Company*, and *Little House on the Prairie*.

The actor landed his first role on *Barney Miller* in the winter of 1977 during the show's third season. He remembers enjoying the opportunity to work with Danny Arnold and the ensemble cast. Cromwell said, "I felt especially like an equal, like a peer, like I had something to offer and that what I did made a difference." He ended playing four very different roles on the show during its eight-season run and expressed admiration for Arnold and the entire cast.

His first feature films were Neil Simon's *Murder by Death* (1976) and *The Cheap Detective* (1978). An Academy Award nomination for Best Supporting Actor in the 1995 film *Babe* was a career milestone that led to five years of consistent film work including Oscar-nominated films *L.A. Confidential* (1997), *The Green Mile* (1999), and *Space Cowboys* (2000).

Cromwell is a passionate activist for a variety of social causes including animal rights, environmental protection, and civil rights. He has gone to jail on more than one occasion fighting for the issues he believes in.

In the new millennium, Cromwell has continued to assert his talent in a variety of projects including *Angels in America* (2003), *Six Feet Under* (2001–2005), and *The Artist* (2011). Right before the pandemic shutdown of 2020, he was starring on Broadway in *Grand Horizons*. He has acted with his son, John Cromwell, in three different film projects including *American Horror Story* making for three generations of Cromwells in the acting profession.

Lou Cutell as Jerome Grodin and Mr. Roselle

Lou Cutell, the proud son of Sicilian immigrants, has had a long and successful career as a character actor. Raised by his mom and maternal grandparents after his dad's premature passing, Lou Cutell attended Glendale Community College before moving on to UCLA where he was classmates with Carol Burnett and James Dean. Even with that stiff competition, Cutell won the Best Acting Award his first year at UCLA and worked in many school productions. At the urging of his mother, he also earned a teaching certificate and taught for a short while after graduation but he always knew acting would be the center of his life.

Following a stint in the Army, Cutell moved to New York and worked in a variety of industrial shows before moving up to Off-Broadway and eventually Broadway productions. By the mid-1960s, he was landing guest spots on television programs such as *The Dick Van Dyke Show* and *The Wild, Wild West*. He appeared in multiple episodes of *The Bob Newhart Show*, *Alice*, *Mad About You*, and, of course, *Barney Miller*.

In the 1990s, Cutell turned his talents to writing and adapted a couple of foreign-language based plays that he then performed hundreds of times on the stage. The plays were Nino Martoglio's *L'Aria del Continente* retitled *The Sicil-*

ian Bachelor and a play from a young Brazilian named Joao Machado called *Viagra Falls*.

The new millennium found him in roles on *Curb Your Enthusiasm*, *How I Met Your Mother*, and *Grey's Anatomy*.

Rosanna DeSoto as Miss del Fuego, Elena Elezando, and Teresa Tasco

Rosanna DeSoto, one of nine children, was the first American-born child of parents from Michoacán, Mexico.

DeSoto attended San Jose State College majoring in drama and Spanish. She studied during the day and spent her evenings performing with the Light Opera Company. She moved to Los Angeles after college and began her acting career in the Improvisational Theatre at the Los Angeles Music Center. She also did a stint at the New York Shakespeare Festival and soon began booking supporting parts on television shows.

Barney Miller was the first sitcom DeSoto worked on and she has nothing but fond memories of creator Danny Arnold. "He was just magnificent. He hired me right on the spot," DeSoto said. "He [was] the greatest audience because his measure was 'If you can make me laugh, you can make anybody laugh.'"

Arnold liked her so much that he cast her in his show *A.E.S. Hudson Street* in 1978. Unfortunately, only five episodes were broadcast before the network pulled the plug. All together she did four episodes of *Barney*, *A.E.S. Hudson Street* and when Danny produced his final show in 1986, *Joe Bash*, he cast DeSoto in that as well. He obviously respected her work and the feeling was mutual. "He was original. His take, his humor, was not something that was canned. It was alive. Danny was a people person . . . he was a sponge. He was very vital that way and passionate . . . he kept you engaged, he kept you hooked."

Following her years working with Arnold, DeSoto continued in television on shows like *Miami Vice*, *Melrose Place*, and *Murder, She Wrote* while also landing roles in some choice films including *About Last Night* (1986), *La Bamba* (1987), and *Face of the Enemy* (1989). In 1988 she won the Independent Spirit Award for Best Supporting Actress for her role in *Stand and Deliver*. She even became a permanent part of the Star Trek universe when she was cast in *Star Trek VI: The Undiscovered Country* (1991) as Azetbur.

These days she has moved to the East Coast to be closer to her children and continues to remain active in community service and public speaking.

Alex Henteloff as Arnold Ripner and Mr. Polanski

Alex Henteloff was born in Los Angeles in 1942. Drawn to the theater, one of Henteloff's teachers at John Marshall High School suggested he go to Los Angeles City College because he heard their theater department worked everybody very hard and he told Henteloff, "You can see if you just enjoy it or if you can put in the work."

Following college he went east and did some summer stock at the Cape May Playhouse in New Jersey and some theater work in New York before returning to Los Angeles and the L.A. Youth Theater. Not long after his return home, he landed his first part on network television in an episode of *I, Spy*.

The 1970s proved to be a fertile period for network sitcoms and network detective shows and Henteloff made the rounds of both genres. At one time or another, the actor worked on *Ironside, McCloud, M*A*S*H, Mannix, Baretta, The Streets of San Francisco, Soap, Barnaby Jones, Night Court*, and the list goes on and on. In 1975, he was cast as Arnold Ripner, a shyster lawyer, in *Barney Miller's* second episode of the series, "Experience." He remembers wearing a trench coat to the audition because the character made him think of Walter Matthau's "Whiplash Willie" Gingrich in *The Fortune Cookie* (1966). Henteloff returned in Season Two as Harold Polanski, a forger, before returning once every season except the fifth as the slimy Mr. Ripner. Hentleoff remembered his appearances on the show fondly saying, "They got terrific people on that show. I was so proud to be on their team. I really was."

Henteloff settled in as a very active network guest star and continued to work on various shows throughout the 1980s like *Alf, Family Ties, Simon & Simon*, and *St. Elsewhere*. Throughout his busy TV career, he always returned to live theater whenever he had the opportunity. He was a founding member of a theater troupe called The Company of Angels.

He and his wife Judy have been married for over fifty years. They have one daughter and four grandchildren.

Bruce Kirby as Lt. Rossmore, Franklin Claymore, and Frank Rossman

Bruce Kirby was born Bruno Giovanni Quidaciolu in 1928 in Greenwich Village. As far as Kirby's son John knows, his dad was the first to change the family name realizing that "Quiodaciolu" was not marquee friendly.

He studied with Lee Strasberg for nine years on a scholarship. He served as an M.C. at the famous Bon Soir club while doubling as a utility man in the acts of artists like Mae Barnes, Tiger Haynes, and others.

His work at the Bon Soir led to a long working relationship with theatrical impresario Julius Monk at cabarets such as Upstairs at the Downstairs and Plaza Nine at the Plaza Hotel. There he made lifelong friends of artists Alice Ghostley and Kaye Ballard. In the early years he also did industrial musical shows including one for Rambler with a young Hal Linden and their friendship would be rekindled throughout the years including on *Barney Miller*.

In the summer, he took his wife Lucille and their two sons with him as he toured in Summer Stock productions of *Gypsy*, *The Sound of Music* and *Bye Birdie*, a show that started a long-time professional relationship with Van Johnson. These summer plays also served as the earliest theatrical roles for his sons Bruno and John Kirby, both of whom became professional actors. Bruno played the Young Clemenza in *The Godfather Part Two* and John is a highly respected acting teacher.

He moved his family to California in the late 1960s at the urging of friends Alice Ghostly and her husband, actor Felice Orlandi. He quickly began booking roles on TV staples like *I Dream of Jeannie*, *Hogan's Heroes*, and *Bonanza*. He was in the pilot episode of Rod Gallery's *Night Gallery* starring Joan Crawford and directed by a newcomer named Steven Spielberg.

From the late 1960s onward, it was hard to find a busier character actor than Bruce Kirby. In addition to the numerous guest appearances on television, he also enjoyed recurring roles in *Kojak*, *Holmes and Yoyo*, *Hunter*, *Anything But Love*, *L.A. Law*, and *Columbo*. The keys to his success and his style were, as son John recalls, "He was constantly working at his craft. He really loved investigating material and he never stopped working out no matter how busy he was in film and TV. He just always played the truth . . . he was funny and very real and very touching."

Bruce Kirby died at the age of ninety-five in January 2021.

A Martinez as Claudio Ortez and Joseph Montoya

Born Adolpho Martinez III in 1948, the oldest of six children, some of his fondest childhood memories are of his family piling into the car for a trip to the local Drive-In movie theater. The larger-than-life screen images made a distinct impression on the young man.

He headed to UCLA with thoughts of a potential law career but his roommate was a Theater major and Martinez was soon won over by the creative nature of that course of study. By chance, a casting agent from American International Pictures sat in on one of his classes and that led to him being cast in a film about racial tensions at a high school entitled *The Young Animals* (1968).

Following that first film, Martinez soon racked up numerous weekly television credits usually playing Hispanic or Indigenous youths on shows such as *Ironside*, *Adam-12*, *Mannix*, and *Bonanza*. Within just three years of his first film appearance, he was cast in *The Cowboys* (1972) with veterans John Wayne and Roscoe Lee Browne. He admits that the success of the film and the headiness of working with screen legends including Bruce Dern and Colleen Dewhurst gave him the idea that films were the only acceptable jobs for him to consider. When work became scarce, he decided that TV wasn't so bad after all.

It was daytime TV rather than feature films that brought him worldwide recognition. Since 1984 he has appeared in over 1700 hours of daytime dramas including *Santa Barbara*, *General Hospital*, *One Life to Live*, and *The Days of Our Lives*. Martinez won a Daytime Emmy in 1990 for his work on *Santa Barbara*.

He guested on *Barney Miller* in 1979 and 1981 and developed a lifelong friendship with actor Max Gail. In both episodes he played small time crooks who discover that their crimes got them in over their head in situations they don't completely understand.

In recent years, A Martinez has continued to work steadily in both feature films and episodic television including stints on *Days of Our Lives* and films such as *Christmas on the Range* (2019) and *Ambulance* (2022). He's particularly proud of the critically acclaimed *Longmire*, a modern western set in Wyoming that filmed from 2012–2017. He writes and performs music and is a lifelong baseball fan. After fifty years in the acting profession, he continues to ride high in the saddle.

Joanna Miles as Eleanor Driscoll

Joanna Miles was born to expatriate American abstract painter Jeanne Miles and French painter-museum curator Johannes Schiefer in 1940. Escaping the Nazis, her family fled France in 1941 and relocated to America.

Her first love was theater but she began working in television soap operas in the 1960s to make ends meet. She was accepted into the prestigious Actor's Studio in New York where she remains a lifelong member. In 1973 she landed the role of Laura Wingfield in a TV production of *The Glass Menagerie* costarring Michael Moriarty and the legendary Katherine Hepburn. Miles loved working with Hepburn, saying, "It was wonderful. She [Hepburn] was very strict, very serious about what it was we were doing." In the end, both Miles and Moriarty won Emmys for their performances.

Miles remembers her one and only appearance on *Barney Miller* with great fondness. Her role as the ex-wife of Marty's friend Mr. Driscoll included a good bit of drama and comedy. "I remember at the time I wanted the job so much because it was a comedy and it was one that I really liked." What she didn't expect was the *Barney Miller* style of production. "We shot the first half of the show and then they decided they didn't like the second half so they started rewriting it. Of course, I had to relearn it and that was a little scary. I had never had that happen to me that I'm halfway through something and then they suddenly say, 'well, we're going to rewrite it.' I had no idea, you know. When you go into shows like that and you're not a regular . . . you don't know what they're used to doing and you sort of keep your mouth shut and try to do a good job and don't complain."

In 1990, Miles founded the Playwrights Group in Los Angeles and served as its Artistic Director for nine years. An ex-New Yorker, she lives in California with her husband, producer and novelist Michael Brandman. In recent years, she has focused her energies more on the theater than in film or television.

Allan Miller as Dr. Gregory Bickman, Nelson Haskell, Williams Collins (Justice Dept.), and Father Clement

Miller is a renowned character actor and acting teacher who was featured on dozens of iconic television shows of the 1970s and 1980s. The Brooklyn-born actor began his career by chance while in the Army in Japan in 1946. As a way to spend time in Tokyo, he answered an ad in the *Stars and Stripes* for "actors wanted" and was hired. He was immediately drawn to the camaraderie of the acting troupe. When he got out of the Army, a friend took him to an acting class in New York and he decided to use his GI Bill money for classes at the Dramatic Workshop.

Soon he was working steadily off-Broadway and in a variety of the soap operas that were then shot in New York. He joined the Actor's Studio and made such an impression on Lee Strasberg that he was given the chance to teach. He became a renowned teacher and has worked with actors such as Meryl Streep, Barbra Streisand, Lily Tomlin, and Dustin Hoffman.

He moved to the West Coast in 1974 and spent a few months struggling for work before being called to Universal for a possible role on *Kojak*. He made an impression on the casting director Milt Hamerman with an impromptu audition and from that meeting he got the role on Kojak and then "went to the *Rockford Files* to *Get Christie Love!* and about five other shows at Universal."

Miller's first interaction with Danny Arnold was as a recurring character on the Gregory Sierra sitcom *A.E.S. Hudson Street*. The show lasted only a half-dozen episodes but it introduced Miller to many of the men and women of Danny Arnold's stock company of character actors like Ray Stewart, Ralph Manza, and Rosanna DeSoto. His first *Barney Miller* came a year after *Hudson Street*. He was on the show four times from 1979 to 1981 and played everything from a psychiatrist to a government agent to a priest. Like so many others, he has very fond memories of the *Barney Miller* experience. "The great thing about *Barney Miller* was you'd read it over, the writers were there with the actors, you'd discuss it, talk about it, and then try it again," Miller recalled. "We were always hoping to get it as fully fleshed and three-dimensional as we could. It was just a wonderful group of people to try things out with. It was my favorite half-hour show to be on."

He later went on to recurring roles in such shows as *Soap*, *Nero Wolfe*, *Knot's Landing*, and *Archie Bunker's Place*. Through it all, he continued to remain active in live theater as an actor, director, and acting teacher. His last known role was in the HBO show *Silicon Valley* in 2017 at the age of eighty-eight. His has been a long, eclectic, and influential career in the dramatic arts.

James Murtaugh as Ron Giles, Vincent Bondell, and Joseph Saxon

James Murtaugh was born in Chicago and began doing plays in high school and college. When it was time to decide on a career, he chose acting with the thought in mind, "I may not be rich but at least I'll be happy."

His early professional experiences came with the Milwaukee Repertory Company, the Barter Theater in Virginia, and then as an Actor-In-Residence at Vassar College. Up to this point, his schooling had kept him from being drafted and sent to Vietnam. He had just passed his physical and was about to be drafted when some activist priests broke into the draft board in Milwaukee and stole all the A-1 records (no computers then) and destroyed them. Murtaugh never heard from the draft board again and he was free to pursue his dreams of an acting career.

He was now in New York and began to go out on auditions. He got a play and then met a guy who could write and together they wrote and performed standup comedy. A friend from Vassar brought a producer down to the city who worked for Young & Rubicon Advertising Agency. He got commercial work from that connection and after getting married, he won a role in the traveling company of *That Championship Season* and the play brought him out to Hollywood. Ironically, he didn't really want to take the play but he was newly married and it was a steady paycheck.

Once in Hollywood, he got an agent and soon was getting booked on shows like *Ironside*, *The Rockford Files*, and *Police Woman*. He worked on three *Barney Miller* episodes in the last two seasons of the show including an appearance in the trilogy that wrapped up the program's storyline. The funniest of his portrayals was as Vincent Bondell, a Peace Corps recruiter who gets a little violent when all the young college students pass up his recruitment booth for higher paying opportunities.

Murtaugh has enjoyed a long and steady career with roles in feature films such as *All the President's Men* (1976), *The Howling* (1981), *Blue Thunder* (1983), and *Everybody's Fine* (2009). He's worked with directors Joe Dante, Spike Lee, and Alan J. Pakula. TV credits extend from the 1970s to the present with guest shots on *Alice*, *Spenser for Hire*, *NYPD Blue*, and into the new millennium on *The Sopranos*, *30 Rock*, and *Law and Order*.

Jenny O'Hara as Teresa Schnable and Sgt. Holly Scofield.

Ms. O'Hara could have been included in the officer's section above for her role as Sgt. Holly Scofield but her turn as Teresa Schnable was such a tour de force that I've included her in this section instead. In my opinion, the Schnable characterization is one of the most poignant in the entire run of the show.

Jenny O'Hara grew up in a talented family (her brother is a singer/songwriter and her sister is a singer/actress) with a mother who encouraged her children's interests and talents in the arts. She and her sister Jill both opened within a month of one another on Broadway in starring roles – Jill in *Promises, Promises* (December 1968) and Jenny in *Fig Leaves Are Falling* (January 1969). *Fig Leaves* failed to find an audience but she actually ended up replacing her sister Jill in *Promises, Promises* in 1970.

O'Hara grew up in the Northeast where her mom put together a children's theater and her dad was a traveling salesman. Her mom eventually went back to school and earned a teaching degree. In high school she was active in all the theater productions. She began at Carnegie Tech in Theater but never finished her degree because she began getting acting jobs.

Her career began Summer Stock and soon after she started taking acting lessons with John Elmer and then Lee Strasberg in New York. Throughout the 1960s and into the 1970s she worked in the theater, soap operas, and commercials before moving to Los Angeles in the mid-seventies with her boyfriend Stefan Gierasch. It was through Gierasch that she met Danny Arnold and earned a role on *Barney Miller*. She remembers Arnold's as a work experience unlike any other. "Rewrites were coming down like raindrops, which was interesting," she said. "I'd never done anything like that in my life. It was fascinating but man, it was exhausting." On returning home from a late night of shooting *Barney*, she recalled getting pulled over by cops for not making a complete stop at a stop sign. When the police officer learned she was a guest that week on *Barney Miller*, he let her go with a warning.

She and Gierasch eventually split up but remained good friends. Her TV career flourished in California and she married actor/writer Nick Ullett in 1986 and they have two children. In the new millennium, she has enjoyed recurring roles on *King of Queens*, *The Mindy Project* and *Transparent*.

Stuart Pankin as Donald, Anthony Moreau, and Alex Fleischer

Born in Philadelphia, Stuart Pankin entered Dickinson College with the idea of studying Psychology. However, his life and direction changed forever when he tried out as a freshman for the school's production of *Our Town* and was bitten by the acting bug. With the support and encouragement of his parents, he went on to study Drama as a Graduate Student at Columbia and spent almost ten years learning and honing his craft in various Off-Broadway and Broadway productions. He spent two years with Joseph Papp's Shakespeare Festival and performed in the first New York City production of *Joseph and the Amazing Technicolor Dreamcoat* at the Brooklyn Academy of Music.

He was brought to Hollywood in 1977 for what he described to me as, "Aaron Spelling's first and last attempt at hour long comedy" with a show called *The San Pedro Beach Bums*. The show lasted for only ten episodes but it got him seen by casting agents. He soon started getting parts on shows like *B.J. and the Bear*, *Benson*, and *Barney Miller*. He appeared three times on *Barney* with his last appearance as a postman who only occasionally delivers the mail being the most memorable role.

Pankin's big break came with an early HBO comedy show entitled *Not Necessarily the News* in 1983. Despite a relatively small audience in those early cable days, the show is well remembered and can, in its way, be seen as something of a precursor to shows like *The Daily Show* or *Full Frontal with Samantha Bee*. His work on the show earned him four Cable ACE Award nominations for "Actor in a Comedy Series." He took home the prize in 1987.

Stuart Pankin's resume is nothing short of astonishing with guest roles and appearances on everything from *Trapper John, M.D.* to *The Golden Girls*, and *Night Court* to *Knots Landing*. In the 1990s, he became an icon to an entirely new generation of TV viewers as the voice of Earl Sinclair on ABC's strange but popular program, *Dinosaurs*. The stars of the show were animatronic dinosaurs created by Jim Henson for Walt Disney Company and voiced by accomplished actors. That success led to a string of voice-over jobs on numerous animated series including *Aladdin, Duckman, The Angry Beavers,* and *As Told by Ginger*. The new millennium brought roles on hit shows like *Curb Your Enthusiasm, Boston Legal*, and *Desperate Housewives*.

Joe Regalbuto as Peter Rankin and Officer Earl Slatic, Sanitation Police

Joe Regalbuto achieved TV immortality as the hilariously funny investigative journalist Frank Fontana on *Murphy Brown* (1988–1998, 2018) and is, in fact, one of only three actors to have appeared in every single episode of that series, the other two being Faith Ford and Candice Bergen.

Born in Brooklyn, Regalbuto's father was a Sicilian immigrant who worked as a union plasterer and his mother was a homemaker. He saw a production of *Brigadoon* as a kid and that led him to a career in acting. Self-described as a so-so student, Regalbuto felt that dramatics was something that he could concentrate on. He went to the American Academy of Dramatic Arts and NYU's Tisch School of the Arts.

In his years at NYU, he performed in numerous Off-Broadway productions. Following graduation he worked in regional theaters in Seattle and Cincinnati and then worked an entire season at the prestigious Guthrie Theater in Minneapolis. He also worked Joseph Papp's Shakespeare Festival in New York with actors like Meryl Streep, John Cazale, and Sam Waterson. It was in New York that he was hired and then flown out to California to work in a sitcom called *The Associates* from the creative team of James Brooks, Stan Daniels, and Charlie Hauck. The show only lasted half a season but Regalbuto got noticed.

It wasn't long after *The Associates* that Regalbuto won his first part on *Barney Miller* in the episode entitled, "Agent Orange." His second role was that of a Sanitation officer, aka "a garbage cop," who gets a little carried away with his power. Regalbuto says, "I mean who wouldn't want to, you know, play a part where he's firing warning shots because you're throwing down Snickers wrappers? I mean come on. I still think of that. That's just hilarious."

In the mid-eighties Regalbuto landed recurring roles on *Street Hawk*, *Knots Landing*, and *Magnum P.I.* before landing *Murphy Brown*. By the end of the decade, he was not only acting but started a new concurrent career directing television and live theater. Since that time he has helmed over 200 episodes of television including *Friends*, *Veronica's Closet*, and, of course, *Murphy Brown*.

These days Regalbuto has a production company called Pesto Productions and continues to develop projects.

Lavelle Roby as Miss Duquette

Lavelle Roby never thought of a career in acting because as she told me, "I'm from Mississippi and that's not a job." Nevertheless, she loved the theater. "I studied speech and drama as a minor, . . . I always participated in acting but never thought of it for anything other than my pleasure," she recalled.

She originally traveled to California to take summer school classes at UCLA. She quickly went to work once she discovered how expensive it was to live in California but continued to take acting and modeling classes. Her first national TV job was a role on *Get Smart*. Roby recalled, "One by one, step by step, I just started to work. At a certain point, I just stopped being embarrassed to say that I was an actress and made a decision that this is what I wanted to do.

In 1968 she heard that Russ Meyer was casting for a new film and asked her agent to get her an audition. The agent told her that Meyer would never hire her because he only hired buxom actresses. She not only got the part but was also, according to Ms. Roby, the first African American actress he'd ever hired and "the first woman that he had ever auditioned who didn't have to show her breasts." That first film was called *Finder Keepers, Lovers Weepers* (1968). She later appeared in *Beyond the Valley of the Dolls* (1970) that was also directed by Meyers.

In the early 1970s she went to Europe to film a movie and stayed on in Europe for a couple of years before returning to the states. *Barney Miller* was the first television job she landed upon her return. She appeared in two separate episodes of the show as one of the neighborhood's "Ladies of the Evening," well known by the squad at the 12th. Roby remembers, "Danny Arnold was an amazing man and it was an amazing group of people."

In Europe she'd discovered Buddhism and she and Ron Glass eventually became close friends through their Buddhism. They worked together in leadership positions in SGI, an international Nichiren Buddhist movement founded in 1975. Ms. Roby told the author that she was as close to Glass as her own biological brother.

In the end, Lavelle Roby loved the path she chose working on classic shows like *Ironside*, *Barnaby Jones*, and *Equal Justice* as well as films such as *The Laughing Policeman* (1973), and *Love at First Bite* (1979). She also did a lot of print work as a model and remains active and ready for the next challenge.

Ray Stewart as Daryl Driscoll

Ray Stewart was born and raised deep in the heart of Texas just twenty miles north of the Mexican border. He can't remember a time when he didn't want to be a performer. At the age of four, he memorized the song "Lullaby of Broadway" and would perform it for anyone who was willing to listen.

He attended the University of Texas at Austin and studied radio and television, primarily because his parents couldn't take the idea of someone studying drama seriously. After graduation he worked at a local television station before being drafted. Following his military service, Rip Torn, who was a friend from college, introduced him to Sanford Meisner, one of the legendary acting teachers in New York. Stewart auditioned for him and was accepted into the Neighborhood Playhouse.

Upon graduation from the Neighborhood Playhouse, Stewart toiled for years in local, regional, and summer stock theater productions before landing a spot with a Second City troupe in Greenwich Village. When he was finally offered a part on Broadway, Rip Torn lent him the $150 to join Actor's Equity.

Stewart worked in five Broadway productions before he moved to California in 1974. He quickly booked guest spots on *Cannon*, *The Bob Newhart Show*, and *The Rookies*, playing everything from a congressman to a hit man. When he received a call about a role on *Barney Miller*, he wasn't familiar with the show. The agent told him, "But it's a gay character." Stewart pondered the information and asked if it was funny. When the agent said it was, Stewart told him, "Well, I don't care what it is as long as it's funny." In the long run, his role as Daryl Driscoll would be both a blessing and a curse. "The first time the people in the business really noticed me, I think, was the *Barney Miller*. That put me on the map, and after that, I would be called up for interior decorators, beauticians, curators of a museum, very aesthete kind of people."

Like Jack DeLeon, the actor who played his gay friend Marty Morrison, Stewart would be forever typecast. "It really, really limited my TV work," he said. At the same time, he has no regrets. "I don't think we've gotten enough credit for . . . how far ahead of our time we were, you know? Back in '75, '76, we were playing these sympathetic gay characters. Even though it pretty much ended my television career, I've never regretted the experience. If that had been the last show I ever did in my life, I wouldn't complain. I was so proud of the work we did and so proud of the show and to be a part of it was a thrill. I've never, ever regretted it."

Following his TV career, Ray Stewart continued to do a lot of theater work and even did some teaching. Twenty years ago, he moved back to his native Texas and continued his work in regional theater.

Todd Susman as Andrew Siegel, Edward Yakel, and Neil Hackett

Todd Susman is an actor who does not like to talk about himself but if he was, he'd certainly have a lot to discuss. Susman has enjoyed a long and successful career.

He was born and raised in the suburbs of St. Louis. He had no specific desire to enter show business but he did do some folk singing in his youth. He finally studied acting during his junior and senior years of college, "for lack of wanting to do anything else."

Following college, he moved to Los Angeles and roomed with a friend who was an aspiring screenwriter. They collaborated on a couple of scripts but to no avail. He eventually began auditioning for acting jobs and his first theatrical production, the lead in Murray Schisgal's *Jimmy Shine*, got him his very first agent.

Susman was soon getting booked regularly on some of the most memorable sitcoms of the 1970s including *Love, American Style*, *Room 222*, and *M*A*S*H*. He and fellow *Barney Miller* alum Sal Viscuso both were the voice of the PA Announcer on *M*A*S*H* at different times during the run of the TV classic. He worked both drama and comedy but really made his mark in television comedy with recurring roles on *Fresno*, *Empty Nest*, *Grace Under Fire*, and a hilarious turn as Officer Shifflet on the long-running CBS sitcom, *Newhart* (1982–1990).

His agent sent him to audition for *Barney Miller* in 1978 and he landed the role of Andrew Siegel, heir to the Siegel Department Store, in the hour-long episode that kicked off *Barney Miller's* fifth season entitled, "Kidnapping." He remembers Tony Sheehan, Danny Arnold, and all the regulars as very nice people. Susman says, "*Barney Miller* wasn't topical, per se, but it was revealing, innovative in terms of its quirky depiction of human behavior."

The new millennium has kept the actor busy with theater, film, and television projects as well as being a sought-after voiceover artist for numerous commercials. He is now in his sixth decade as a professional actor.

Ken Tigar as Fletcher, Stefan Kopechne, Elliot Porter, Jesus Christ, and Philip Pollock

Ken Tigar is a lifelong New Englander. He was born in Chelsea, Massachusetts and was the first in his family to go to college eventually earning a Ph. D. in German Literature from Harvard and attending the University of Göttingen as a Fulbright Scholar. He fully intended to become a professor of German Literature but fate had other plans.

He remembers seeing Eva Le Gallienne's production of *Alice in Wonderland* as well as Jean Arthur and Boris Karloff in *Peter Pan* on stage as a child and those shows sparked his interest in theater. He did his first play at the age of twelve for an organization called The Boston Children's Theater. He was hooked. He continued to act in plays in junior high, high school, and college but never with the intention of pursuing it as a career. It was just a hobby that he enjoyed.

He followed an old girlfriend to Vienna after college and landed a part in a local Viennese Theater Company. His fluency in German allowed him to stay in the part for the entire season. When he returned to the states, he began to pursue acting as a career. He did a variety of theater work and as soon as he landed a few small roles on TV and films, he became a rather ubiquitous presence in episodic television. He appeared on every popular show one can imagine including, *The Waltons*, *The Rockford Files*, *Cheers*, *Hill Street Blues*, *Night Court*, *Dallas*, and the list goes on and on. Tigar once told me, "I've never made a lot of money but I've always made a living. Never had to drive a taxi, never had to wait tables."

Tigar's *Barney Miller* evolution is interesting because his first role was that of an innocuous little man who gets mugged by a little old lady in a Season Two episode called, "Massage Parlor." Tigar said, "For some reason they liked me and the next year, I got a phone call and they offered 'The Werewolf' to me. I didn't have to audition. They started to write for me. How they got me from being beaten up by a little old lady to the werewolf, I don't know." It was a stretch but it worked and Tigar was brilliantly funny as a man who believes he's a werewolf. It's probably the best-remembered show in the entire run of the series after "Hash." Tigar would end up appearing in six different episodes and remembers *Barney Miller* as, "one of the best written shows I ever did."

All in all, Ken Tigar's life has been an exemplary one of "a working actor." Even now in his sixth decade in the theatrical arts he continues to work in films, television, and live theater.

Sal Viscuso as Brenner, Thomas Vitella, Joseph Beatty, and Victor Renaldi

Sal Viscuso is not just an actor. He is a force of nature. Inspired to become an actor after watching Ivan Dixon in a *CBS Playhouse* presentation of "The Final War of Olly Winter," he graduated from the NYU School of the Arts with his MFA and worked in live theater before moving to Hollywood in 1975 to co-star in a Perksy-Denoff sitcom called *The Montefuscos*. The show lasted only nine episodes but he soon landed roles on *M*A*S*H* and *Barney Miller* and a fortuitous meeting with Mel Brooks and Anne Bancroft at Carl Reiner's house led to movie roles in films like *The World's Greatest Lover* (1977), *Fatso* (1980), and *Spaceballs* (1987).

The big break came in 1977 when he was cast in the part of Father Timothy Flotsky on the popular but controversial sitcom, *Soap*. He remembers the experience as a creative environment filled with young, talented actors who were all hungry for work, experience, and stardom. Viscuso was in the middle of one of the show's most sensitive storylines—a priest who's in love with his childhood sweetheart and struggles with whether or not to leave the priesthood for her. Unfortunately, after a couple of years, the show had so many different plotlines going at once that Viscuso grew frustrated by how little work was coming his way. When he asked for more to do, the producers bought out his contract. "I was an actor. I wanted to act," he says of his decision. "I didn't care about the money, I wanted to act."

There was no shortage of work for Viscuso following *Soap*. He was featured in episodes of *Cagney and Lacey*, *Family Ties*, and *Spenser for Hire*. His sense of humor made him an ideal guest on shows like *Mike Douglas*, *The Tonight Show*, and *Dinah!* He was a favorite on games shows like *The 25,000 Pyramid* as well.

He particularly loved working on *Barney Miller*. Danny Arnold liked his energy and, along with Tony Sheehan, wrote a specific role for him in a Season Three episode called "Fire 77," as an escapee from Riker's Island who, despite his criminal past, seems quite dedicated to his duty to attend Sunday Mass. The actor loved appearing on the ensemble show and has fond memories of the cast, particularly his friend Ron Carey who he describes as "a sweet, funny man." Viscuso remembers Danny Arnold as "a father figure" and "a brilliant guy."

The twenty-first century saw the screwball ethnic character actor, who was always full of frantic energy and fun, turn to more serious roles on television in *Law & Order: Special Victims Unit*, *ER*, and *Scandal* as well as critically acclaimed performances in stage productions of *The Elephant Man*, *Glengarry*

Glen Ross, and *A Steady Rain*. He also happens to be a talented painter who has worked at his art for over twenty years and has exhibited his work in galleries.

All the Rest

This group of actors frequently visited the 12th Precinct as well but, unfortunately, moved on to that big stage in the sky before I had the opportunity to interview them. I have gathered what information I could about them through various print and Internet sources and quotes from other interview subjects.

Stanley Brock as Arnie, Burgess, and Bruno Bender

Stanley Brock appeared in nine different *Barney Miller* episodes. His first two appearances were as two separate characters. In the Season Four premiere, "Good-Bye Mr. Fish: Part 1," he shows up for the first time as Bruno Bender, a local shop owner. He would ultimately appear seven times as Bender, *Barney Miller's* answer to Archie Bunker. He wasn't as outwardly racist as Bunker but he was definitely politically incorrect and abrasive. However, in his second-to-last appearance as Bruno Bender, he gave us a slight reason to hope that he might be loveable if you dug down deep enough. Even so, you would have to dig *really* deep.

Brock was New York born and bred and began his show biz career in the Borscht Belt resorts of the Catskill Mountains. He also worked at a refrigeration and air conditioning company where he would try out new material on his fellow office workers. As he sharpened his skills he eventually played numerous comedy clubs in and around Manhattan as a standup comedian.

In the mid-1970s he moved to Los Angeles and quickly earned small character parts on shows such as *Police Woman*, *Phyllis*, and *The Rockford Files*. He always seemed at his best when he was playing slightly larcenous characters. He's wonderful in Barry Levinson's 1987 film, *Tin Men*. He's also remembered by fans for a three-year run on the soap opera *Days of Our Lives* as a private detective named Howie Hoffstedder and in the short-lived 1986 sitcom, *He's the Mayor*.

For *Barney Miller* fans, Brock will always be the cigar-chomping Bruno Bender. Max Gail remembers that, "He was that guy and I think that Danny [Arnold] figured out a way to use that." Arnold loved the New York characters and found marvelous ways to seamlessly integrate them into the program. Thanks to actors like Stanley Brock, you always felt the 12th Precinct was a real place and if you went into Greenwich Village you could find it and walk right in.

Like many *Barney Miller* alumni, Brock went on to appear in multiple episodes of Reinhold Weege's *Night Court*. Sadly, Brock died at the relatively young age of fifty-nine in 1991.

Don Calfa as Mr. DiLucca, Angelo Dodi, Leon Bidell, Calvin Kendall, Gilbert Lesco, Arthur Thompson, and Edward Pratken

Hal Linden remembers Don Calfa as the quintessential *Barney Miller* actor. He did, after all, make seven appearances as seven different characters over the course of eight seasons. That would have been impressive enough but even more of an accomplishment is how memorable those performances were.

Calfa was born in Brooklyn in 1939 and dropped out of high school to pursue his interest in acting. He worked for years in Off-Broadway productions until 1965 when he made it to Broadway with *Mating Dance*. He made his film debut in *No More Excuses* (1968) by independent filmmaker Robert Downey Sr. In his long film career he worked with such celebrated directors as Mark Rydell, Peter Bogdanovich, and Martin Scorsese.

His biographies all mention *Weekend at Bernie's* (1989) and *Return of the Living Dead* (1985) as his most memorable roles but long before those cult classics, he was one of Danny Arnold's treasured stock company of New York character actors. He was able to play copycat criminal Angelo Dodi and habitual criminal Leon Bidell with manic comedic energy and later return as lobotomized ex-criminal Gilbert Lesco or homeless man Eddie Pratken and just tear your heart out with his innocence and vulnerability. Calfa's portrayals were some of the most memorable depictions of the human condition in the history of the series.

Don Calfa went on to work in *Park Place* and *Night Court*, both shows created by *Barney Miller* alum Reinhold Weege and also appeared in an episode of Hal Linden's short-lived crime drama *Blacke's Magic*. Calfa died on December 1, 2016, two days shy of his 77th birthday.

Jack DeLeon as Marty Morrison

Jack DeLeon changed his name after seven years of *Barney Miller* to Christopher Weeks because he felt he'd become typecast as either a gay actor or an actor who could only play a gay character. There's no doubt that typecasting is a way of life in Hollywood but back in the early 1980s, there weren't enough roles for openly gay characters to keep an actor working steadily as that character type.

There is little to be found about DeLeon's early years. His roots were as a Catskills comic. He worked the famous Borscht Belt for many years but he never had an act that set himself apart from the rest of the comics of his time. He worked cabarets and lounges in Las Vegas and his *Barney Miller* co-star, Ray Stewart, who played Daryl Driscoll to DeLeon's Marty Morrison, said that "He [DeLeon] did a dynamite Cagney impression. Drop dead Cagney . . . he was perfect!"

He recorded at least two comedy albums and some of his earliest and most consistent work throughout his career was as a voiceover artist. For over twenty years, he provided voices on cartoon shows such as *The Fantastic Four*, *Emergency +4*, and *DuckTales*. He also voiced Sergeant Samuel McPherson in the 1977 Dr. Seuss special, *Halloween Is Grinch Night* and Dwalin in the 1977 animated version of *The Hobbit*.

For better or for worse, Marty Morrison was the defining role of DeLeon's career. Regardless of the typecasting problems it caused the actor, the fact is it was a groundbreaking role. Billy Crystal's role as Jody Dallas on *Soap* is often discussed as the first openly gay character on television but that's not possible as Marty preceded him by almost two years.

In addition to his work on *Barney Miller*, DeLeon landed roles on multiple shows of the era including *Get Smart*, *That Girl*, *Starsky and Hutch*, and *Sanford and Son*. DeLeon/Weeks died in 2006 at the age of eighty-one in Los Angeles.

John Dullaghan as Jackson, Sylvester White, Harold Durrell, Milt Loftus, and Ray Brewer

John Dullaghan appeared in ten episodes of *Barney Miller*. Four of the ten were all different one-and-done characters. The last six were as a bum turned Salvation Army worker named Ray Brewer. Of the six Brewer episodes, four of those were both ends of a two-part episode. I gave special mention to Ray Brewer in the episode guide saying that it was obvious that he was a character who "always wanted to belong to a group, to *the* group." He may have been what in the parlance of the day was called a bum but he had a very gentle and endearing quality about him. When I asked Max Gail about the actor who played Ray, he remembered him as, "a really earnest person and actor. His feelings about the integrity you bring to the process included not taking it too far, being understated, trying to be real." Gail went on to say, "He's a great example of Danny's greatest gift and that was to take something into the character and meld it with the characteristics and qualities of the actor who was to play the part."

That is an insightful and sensitive assessment. Imagine then, my surprise when I discovered that prior to Dullaghan's successful 1975–1995 run on a variety of primetime television shows, he'd been known as something of a "soft porn vet" in the late '60s and very early '70s starring in such productions as *Ego Trip* (1969), *Sex and the Single Vampire* (1970), and *Adultery for Fun & Profit* (1971). He also had roles in some R-rated horror/exploitation films. In his defense, it seems clear that he used that segment of the industry to get by until more respectable and lucrative jobs came along. As soon as Dullaghan started getting spots on shows like *Kojak*, *Cannon*, and *The Rockford Files* in the mid-1970s, he never looked back.

In addition to Dullaghan's multiple appearances on *Barney*, he had recurring roles in *Battlestar Galactica* and *B.J. and the Bear*. He also took to the stage and performed in over sixty productions including *Major Barbara* at the Mark Taper Forum in New York. A native of Brooklyn, Dullaghan died in California in 2009.

Phil Leeds as Arthur Bloom, Lou Hector, Harry Kruger, Horace Chandler, Gilbert Letier, Louis Nash, and Brent LaMear

Phil Leeds was born in New York City and raised in the Bronx. He began his career in the 1930s as a comedian and served in an Army Special Service Unit in World War II entertaining the troops. Upon leaving the service, he began to work nightclubs in New York like The Blue Angel and The Village Vanguard.

In the 1950s, he appeared in numerous Broadway shows including *Can-Can* (1953–1955), *The Matchmaker* (1955–1957), and *Romanoff and Juliet* (1957–1958). It should be noted that he was hurt by the McCarthy and HUAC witch hunts and was blacklisted for a time. In those dark days, live theater was one of the few places an actor could usually find work.

Once the curse of the blacklist was lifted, Leeds became a ubiquitous presence in both film and television. His feature credits included films like *Rosemary's Baby* (1968) and *Beaches* (1988) although TV was where you'd find him most often, appearing on *The Dick Van Dyke Show*, *The Odd Couple*, *All in the Family*, and *Night Court* as well as recurring roles on *The Larry Sanders Show*, *Everybody Loves Raymond*, and *Ally McBeal*.

He played seven different characters on *Barney Miller*, everything from a talent agent with a historically unfunny standup client to a phony but efficient policeman. His unique appearance was often part of the joke but his delivery and timing are what made him special. Max Gail remembers, "He had a very piercing visage and energy. He had a confidence about him." It was his attitude combined with that look that made him special.

In describing himself, he once said, "I'm not pretty, but I'm warm and feisty." In spite of his less than matinee-idol looks, Leeds went on to have an extraordinary show biz career of over half a century. In the tradition of so many great character players, you may not always remember the name but you never forget the face of Phil Leeds.

The prolific actor died in 1998 at the age of eighty-two.

Ralph Manza as Anthony Barelli, Eddie Blake, and Leon Roth

Ralph Manza was born in 1921 in San Francisco and studied pre-med at UC Berkeley before entering the US Army in World War II as a medic. He was assigned to a troupe of entertainers and there discovered his true love and talent for acting.

Manza's foothold in entertainment came through the new medium of television. The actor started showing up regularly on the small screen in the early 1950s. In nearly five decades of television work, he appeared on numerous classic shows such as *Dragnet, Perry Mason, The Twilight Zone, Get Smart,* and *Soap.* He held recurring roles on *The D.A.'s Man, Banacek,* and *Newhart.* Manza's film work was less prolific than his television résumé but he made numerous, usually uncredited, appearances in films like *That Touch of Mink* (1962), *Blazing Saddles* (1974) and *Dave* (1993).

Manza played four different characters in *Barney Miller.* His very first appearance was as an aging mobster named Anthony Barelli in "Protection," chauffeur Eddie Blake in "Kidnapping Parts 1 & 2," and, of course, the recurring Mr. Roth, the blind shoplifter, one of the 12th precinct's most indelible characters. Max Gail had fond memories of Manza saying, "Ralph was wonderful. He was another one who just had a great appetite for the humor, not just getting his laugh . . . but he loved the whole humor of the situation." Referring to Manza's characterization of Leon Roth, Gail said, "He played blindness for real and he did it very well so you know it wasn't a blind joke but it was funny."

The actor worked into his late seventies and was, in fact, filming a Budweiser television commercial when he suffered a heart attack in January of 2000. He died three weeks later from complications related to that attack.

Jack Somack as Mr. Cotterman

Jack Somack had a short but busy acting career. He was born in Chicago in 1918 and trained as a Chemical Engineer. He appeared for many years in amateur productions but his first known professional work came in a 1966 Off Broadway production of Arthur Miller's *A View from the Bridge*.

In 1969 he was cast in a commercial for Alka Seltzer and became known as the man who got heartburn eating that "spicy meata-ball." The commercial proved controversial and memorable, getting pulled from the air after protests from various Italian American groups. Nevertheless, it raised Somack's exposure and soon got him cast in small independent features and TV series.

Norman Lear hired him in 1972 for an appearance on *All in the Family* and eventually he worked on two other Lear productions, *Sanford and Son* and *The Jeffersons*. He quickly became a regular presence on network television and he even went back to Broadway briefly to play in Neil Simon's *The Prisoner of Second Avenue*.

Somack's first appearance on *Barney Miller* came in the Season Two episode "The Arsonist" (1975). He would make a total of five appearances as the lovable but robbery-prone Mr. Kotterman from Season Two until Season Six. In what has to be considered the worst miscalculation in *Barney Miller* history, the writers killed him off in Season Six much to the dismay of the show's loyal audience.

Unfortunately, Somack died of a heart attack in 1983 while rehearsing a guest role in the sitcom *Benson*. Somack, whose career had started so late, made an all-too-early exit at 64.

Philip Sterling as Mr. Buckholz, Noel Cadey, Mitchell Warner, Judge Philip Gibson, Frank Rolling-FBI, and Howard Spangler

Philip Sterling was another one of those actors who did it all: radio, theater, television, and films. The son of a Philadelphia lawyer, he was born in New York City and graduated from the University of Pennsylvania and the Wharton School of Business. He made his Broadway debut in 1955 in Cole Porter's *Silk Stockings* and he played Dwight D. Eisenhower in *An Evening with Richard Nixon and . . .* but his longest run on Broadway came as Jack in Neil Simon's Tony-nominated *Broadway Bound*. Sterling was with the play from its debut in December of 1986 through September of 1988.

The actor enjoyed half a century of work on radio and in film and television starting in the late 1940s. He played primarily professional men, often authority figures such as doctors, lawyers, judges, and politicians. In the early days of television, Sterling appeared on live shows such as *Studio One in Hollywood*, *Kraft Theatre*, and *Stage 13*. In the 1970s, he worked on numerous shows including *Harry-O*, *The Rockford Files*, and, of course, *Barney Miller*.

Danny Arnold always seemed to cast him as a man in the middle of a nervous breakdown or dangerously close to one. Sterling had an incredible ability to simultaneously make you laugh and tear your heart out. Whether portraying Mr. Buckholtz, a suicidal man hiding from the Bellevue attendants under Chano's desk or Howard Spangler, a bitter, disillusioned ex-hostage who wants to return to his South American captors, his performances were some of the most moving of any guest star.

Max Gail remembered Sterling as a man who "had his own great kind of sophistication and dignity about him, [a] sense of himself without being hung up on ego. He really found that connection with those characters inside. What great dignity he had."

Sterling was also the first president of the Screen Actors Guild Foundation and an accomplished jazz and classical pianist. He died in 1998 at the age of seventy-six.

The First Pilot: "The Life and Times of Barney Miller"

The first pilot, entitled "The Life and Times of Barney Miller," was shot on January 18, 1974, and featured Hal Linden as Captain Barney Miller and Abe Vigoda as Detective Fish. Veteran character actor Val Bisoglio appeared as Sgt. Grimaldi, a detective with a penchant for gambling, and Charles Haid played a young, trigger-happy cop named Kazinski. There was also an African American detective named Wilson played by former NFL player Rod Perry.

"The Life and Times of Barney Miller" opens in the squad room of the 12th Precinct. A young mugging suspect named Ramon asks to be taken to the bathroom where he separates Fish from his service revolver. The next few minutes are a standoff between Ramon and his hostages, the men of the 12th. It's a solid opening scene that introduces us to Barney Miller's humane philosophy and his belief in treating everyone with fairness and respect, not exactly your typical stereotype of a big city cop. He convinces Ramon to give him the gun in exchange for a business card of one Stanley Mankowitz, an up-and-coming Public Defender who just happens to "keep company" with his daughter.

The second half of the show is set in Barney's apartment at the end of his eventful workday. His son sneaks up on him with a toy gun, his teenage daughter wants to move to her own apartment to be closer to school, and his wife Elizabeth clearly does not like the fact that Barney is one of New York's finest.

In this early version of Elizabeth Miller (Abby Dalton), we see that Liz is constantly on the lookout for a way to get Barney to leave the force. On this particular evening she has invited her Uncle Charlie, a NYC alderman, over to dinner to discuss a business proposition with Barney. When he realizes the deal is co-ownership of what is clearly slum housing, Barney declines and Liz must reluctantly agree.

Unfortunately, as soon as that issue is resolved in walks Stanley Mankowitz to pick up Rachel for a night out and to thank Captain Miller, the hero, for sending him a client. The story of the day's exciting standoff, which Barney had purposely neglected to tell Liz, is out of the bag before Barney can muzzle Stanley. Naturally, Liz and Rachel are quite upset. Rachel and Stanley depart and Barney suggests that Uncle Charlie should probably come for dinner on Friday night. As he leaves, Uncle Charlie, played by veteran character actor Henry Beckman, in a line foreshadowing the character of Frank Luger, says, "Barney, you are a decent, moral, upstanding man of integrity but, if Elizabeth loves you, that's all right with me."

Barney tries to make Liz laugh through her tears as he explains what happened in the squad room that day was a once-in-a-lifetime occurrence that means he's now safe for the duration of his career of ever being held at gunpoint in the squad room by a desperate criminal again. (As it turned out, that was not true. See S. 4/Ep. 20 and S. 6/Ep. 20.) Liz vows that she will not stop searching for a way to get Barney off the force before his scheduled retirement.

The epilogue returns us to the squad room where Stanley Mankowitz brings Barney a thank you gift from his client Ramon—a list of the pushers and dealers in the neighborhood. Suddenly, Fish, Kazinski, and the boys come running in with shotguns drawn to tell Barney of a "10-30 in progress." Just as Barney checks his revolver for bullets and tells the men to "mount up," Liz walks into the squad room to surprise Barney and take him out to lunch.

From the opening moments of the program, we know this is no ordinary sitcom. Barney goes out of his way to treat the suspect, Ramon, with honesty and compassion. True, he's trying to convince a drug addict with a gun pointed at everyone in the room to surrender his weapon but even after the standoff ends in his favor Miller stays true to his character and follows up on the promises made under duress.

The Second Pilot: "Ramon"

At first glance the "second pilot," shot on December 20, 1974, would seem to be identical to the first but there are both subtle and not-so-subtle differences between the two shows. The original "The Life and Times of Barney Miller" pilot opened in the squad room. The second "Ramon" opened with a whole new scene in the Miller home. Liz (now played by Barbara Barrie) is listening to the horrible daily news on the radio as she opens her curtains to reveal the ominous bars on her apartment house windows. As soon as Barney enters, she tells him that she doesn't think he should go to work today. Instead, she thinks he should resign from the police force and move to Montana to raise chickens.

The first five minutes of the program are essentially Liz trying to guilt Barney into quitting his job. The only other plot point revealed in this opening scene is when Rachel tells her parents she's going out with Stanley Mankowitz that night to celebrate the printing of his first business card. She gives one to Barney who reads aloud, "Stanley M. Mankowitz, Attorney at Law, Public Defender's Office," and then after remarking about the impressive, raised letters on the card, deposits it in his shirt pocket.

The next scene is almost identical to the opening scene of "The Life and Time of Barney Miller." In fact, the standoff in the squad room uses substantial portions of identical dialogue to that which was used in the same scene in the original pilot.

The third and final scene on the DVD version from Shout! Factory takes place back in the Miller's apartment with Stanley Mankowitz coming to pick up Rachel and spilling the beans about the excitement at the 12th Precinct that morning. Unlike "The Life and Time of Barney Miller," this program makes no mention of an Uncle Charlie.

Strangely, the Season One disc in the Shout! Factory release doesn't include the epilogue to "Ramon." Instead, you have to go to the Bonus Features section on the very last disc to see the original epilogue to the second pilot. It's an important scene too because in it, we see Sgt. Harris dressed as a woman bringing in a man who offered him a hundred dollars. As the series rolls out, each man will have to work "mugging duty" where they don a dress and a wig to entice what must be some seriously nearsighted muggers in the park after dark. However, in the series, part of the gag was that Harris did everything he could to avoid the duty because it meant he'd have to shave off his moustache. In this pilot, we discover he was not only the first one to pull this assignment but also that he did it *with* his moustache still on!

The "Ramon" episode is basically the same as the original pilot except for some minor rewriting and restructuring of how the story is told. This second pilot essentially breaks up the material in act two of "The Life and Time of Barney Miller" pilot into two separate scenes. The most important differences between the two programs are the personnel and the music.

In the original pilot, Val Bisoglio plays the gambler in the room, identified only as Sgt. Grimaldi. In "Ramon," Jack Soo now takes on the role of the squad's inveterate gambler, Sgt. Nick Yemana. In an interview with Hal Linden, the show's star remembers that in the interim between the initial pilot and the shooting of the series, Bisoglio had appeared in a film entitled, *Linda Lovelace for President* (1975). It was apparently nothing more than a film made to capitalize on the celebrity of Linda Lovelace who had starred in the infamous 1972 porn film, *Deep Throat*. Not X-rated or even sensual, *Linda Lovelace for President* is nothing more than a cheaply done camp comedy. Nevertheless, Linden believes that Bisoglio's appearance in the film made producers and the network wary of making him a regular on the show. It was a time of rampant censorship battles and possibly Danny Arnold and/or the network didn't want to give Middle America an excuse to complain. Bisoglio would appear, however, in a guest shot in the Season Two episode entitled, "You Dirty Rat."

In "The Life and Time of Barney Miller," Charles Haid plays a young cop named Kazinski. However, by the time the second pilot was shot, Haid was directing a play in New York City. Given the choice of flying back to Hollywood to shoot another pilot for a show that had already been turned down once by the network or remain with his play in New York, Haid chose to stay in New York. The part of Kazinski was given a little more meat and given to a young actor named Max Gail. The new part also came with a new name, Det. 3rd Grade Stanley Wojciehowicz. The name, in and of itself, would become a recurring joke to which the young officer would always reply, "Wojciehowicz. You spell it just like it sounds."

Two years later, Charles Haid was cast in the part of another Polish police officer, Sgt. Paul Shonski, in a police drama starring Judd Hirsch entitled

Delvecchio. The show lasted only one season but Haid's luck finally changed when instead of playing a Polish police officer he took on the role of southern-born cop Andy Renko on the streets of the big city in the hit series *Hill Street Blues*.

Finally, the other major cast change was in the role of Elizabeth Miller. In the original pilot, Abby Dalton played Barney's wife, Liz. For the second pilot the part was given to veteran actress Barbara Barrie. Hal Linden doesn't remember now why Dalton wasn't there for the second pilot unless she was working on another project. IMDb lists that Dalton did appear on a new Andy Griffith vehicle entitled *Adams of Eagle Lake* in 1975 that lasted only two episodes.

The other major difference between the two pilots is music. "The Life and Times of Barney Miller" has a very traditional 1960s sitcom theme song. It had no lyrics, but its melody and instrumentation were a much more family oriented, almost Disney-like tune. The second pilot, however, replaced the original theme song with a very hip baseline intro and funky jazz-fusion style music written by Jack Elliott and Allyn Ferguson that clearly ushers in a new show and a new style of sophisticated situation comedy. Ultimately, it became one of the more memorable theme songs in the history of television.

Danny Arnold's Guiding Principles

There are some founding principles or attributes that run throughout the eight-season run of *Barney Miller*. They are described here so that you will better be able to recognize them as you view the various episodes that were produced.

The Look of the Show

The fact that *Barney Miller* had a very distinctive "look" to it that was quite different compared to other sitcoms of the era was not a coincidence. Danny Arnold, along with Director of Photography George Spiro Dibie, had a very specific vision of what the precinct house should look like. They wanted that dingy, run-down look. In fact, as the series went on, the building, its advanced age, and its history became more and more of a character in the story, culminating in the storyline of the show's final three episodes.

The Mundanity of Police Work

More than once in this first season, an allusion will be made to the fact that police work is often more exciting and action-packed on TV and in the movies than it is in real life. This idea runs beneath the surface of every episode. This is, no doubt, the reason that so many real-life police officers felt that *Barney Miller* was the most realistic portrayal of cops to be found on TV.

Paranoids with Proof

"Paranoids with proof" was a popular Danny Arnold term when it came to humor and *Barney Miller*. Numerous people, including Hal Linden, Max Gail, and writer/producer Frank Dungan, all mentioned this phrase to me. Dungan wrote, "A philosophy of Danny's was 'There's nothing scarier than a paranoid with proof.' That's why, no matter the story—Agent Orange, the government experimenting with chemicals on the NY subway system in the '50s, some imminent economic collapse driving a man to convert all his money to gold, etc.—the arrested party would always produce the article detailing the specifics that drove their actions out of fear and/or frustration." By "the article," he meant an article from a newspaper, magazine, or academic journal. In cases where this was not possible, a victim or suspect would rant or rave about their motivations. If and when the officers scoffed at the explanation, Sgt. Dietrich was almost always available to back up their story with his vast storehouse of knowledge.

Illustrations

Our introduction to the "Talmudic justice" of *Barney Miller* in "Ramon" (1975).

Just before the *Barney Miller* pilot, Hal Linden co-starred in a dramatic police pilot/made-for-TV movie with Tony LoBianco entitled *Mr. Inside/Mr. Outside*. Fortunately, for future *Barney Miller* fans, the show did not get picked up, leaving Linden open for the next opportunity.

George Maharis and Jack Soo in a 1969 made-for-TV movie called *Monk*. It was a pilot for a possible detective show with Maharis but the show was panned and never got off the ground.

James Gregory was the most seasoned veteran of the *Miller* cast. He was, in fact, the actual *Manchurian Candidate* (1962) in the iconic Sinatra thriller.

The initial 12th Precinct squad of detectives. Clockwise from lower left: Phil Fish (Abe Vigoda), Nick Yemana (Jack Soo), Stan "Wojo" Wojciehowicz (Max Gail), Chano Amenguale (Gregory Sierra), Ron Harris (Ron Glass), Barney Miller (Hal Linden) (1975).

Elizabeth Miller (Barbara Barrie) and Barney in "The Social Worker" (1975).

Fish, Wojo, and Barney try to decipher a message.

Sometimes Nick was too calm for Barney.

Arthur Dietrich (Steve Landesberg), Harris, and Barney check out the soap opera listings for *Endless Tomorrows* in "The Judge" (1979).

Illustrations • 161

Lance Peterson (Charles Frank), Det. Janice Wentworth (Linda Lavin), and Barney in the show's take on the movie *Midnight Cowboy* in "Massage Parlor" (1976).

Dietrich and Barney help Edna Relkie (Brett Somers) get out the vote in "The Election" (1976).

Danny Rizzo (Michael Tucci) informs Captain Miller and Officer Levitt (Ron Carey) of his unlawful imprisonment in "The People's Court" (1980).

You win some, you lose some. The 12th's squad room as of October 1977 with Yemana, Dietrich, Harris, Capt. Miller, Inspector Frank Luger (James Gregory), Wojo, and Levitt.

Illustrations • **163**

Marty Morrison (Jack DeLeon) and Darryl Driscoll (Ray Stewart) try to enlist Barney's help in "The Child Stealers" (1980).

Mr. Driscoll, his ex-wife Eleanor (Joanna Miles), and Capt. Miller try to work out some child custody issues in "The Child Stealers" (1980).

Officer Zatelli (Dino Natali) is telling Barney things he doesn't really want to know in "Inquisition" (1979).

Calvin J. Kendall (Don Calfa) tries to explain to Levitt, Barney, and Wojo why an arrest at this time is not convenient for him in "Identity" (1979).

Stephanie Wolf (Diana Canova) and Dietrich discuss anthropology in "Strip Joint" (1979).

Mr. Kotterman (Jack Somack) tells Levitt the story about how he's been robbed again in "Identity" (1979).

Harris signaling to Barney that Mr. Baskin (Kip King) has been a bit overstressed at work in "Identity" (1979).

Alfred Royce (Leonard Frey), the self-proclaimed "people's candidate" for President introduces himself to Dietrich in "Vanished: Part 2" (1980)

Joseph Beatty (Sal Viscuso) and Acting Detective Levitt in "The Photographer" (1979).

Indentured servant William Nu (Sumant) meets Inspector Luger while Dietrich stands back and enjoys the conversation in "The Slave" (1979).

Harris, Levitt, Barney, and Wojo along with prisoner Arthur Duncan (J. J. Barry) and civilian Carl Bernie (Norman Bartold) enjoy the premiere of *Four Women*, a pornographic masterpiece by Det. Harris in "Movie—Part 2" (1981).

Dr. Glick (Allan Miller) and Mrs. Hollis (Queenie Smith) in *A.E.S. Hudson Street*, a show that was loaded with *Barney Miller* alumni.

Dr. Antonio Menzies (Gregory Sierra) from the short-lived Danny Arnold production *A.E.S. Hudson Street* (1978). Sierra left *Barney Miller* a season before Vigoda did, but he got his own show a year after Vigoda got *Fish*.

Wojo takes Jesus (Ken Tigar) to Bellevue while his soon-to-be disciple, Joseph Beatty (Sal Viscuso), looks on in "The Photographer" (1979).

The cast of characters from *Fish* (1977). Diane Pulaski (Sarah Natoli), Mike Faroni (Len Bari), Jilly Papalardo (Denise Miller), Loomis (Todd Bridges), Phil Fish (Abe Vigoda), Bernice Fish (Florence Stanley), Victor Kreutzer (John Cassisi), and Charlie Harrison (Barry Gordon). This spinoff lasted longer than *A.E.S. Hudson Street* but was still less than successful.

The spinoff that didn't spin. Nancy (Darlene Parks) and Wojo in "Wojo's Girl: Part 2" (1979).

Barney, Fish, and Harris try to get Mr. Wittenour (Jack Kruschen) to tell them where's he's buried his friend Leonard in "Burial" (1977).

A dapper Nick Yemana and Capt. Miller holding down the precinct (ca. 1977).

Fish contemplating his various aches and pains.

Wojo and his beloved baseball from the 1936 World Series.

Harris looking up to his pal Dietrich. Courtesy of Nancy Ross Landesberg.

Captain Miller with his next in command, Phil Fish.

Harris, Wojo, Levitt, Dietrich, and Barney in "Uniform Days" (1980).

Pet store owner Mr. Tragash (Martin Garner) doesn't want any trouble from Barney or Wojo in "The Bird" (1979).

Dietrich and Inspector Luger in "Dietrich's Arrest" (1980).

A happy Jack Soo as Nick Yemana.

Max Gail as Wojo, making a point.

Levitt and the old double salute.

An unusually happy Arthur Dietrich. Courtesy of Nancy Ross Landesberg.

Barney taking a call.

A group photo of the gang at the ol' one-two from 1982. Standing: Ron Carey, Max Gail, James Gregory, and Steve Landesberg. Seated: Ron Glass and Hal Linden.

Liz Miller and husband Barney contemplate the possibility of their first Christmas apart in "Toy" (1978). Courtesy of David and Dannel Arnold.

The almost-too-attractive Sgt. Harris ready for mugging duty. Dietrich and Barney are impressed in "The Search" (1978). Courtesy of David and Dannel Arnold.

Officer Zatelli (Dino Natali) faces his, and everyone's, worst nightmare, Lt. Scanlon (George Murdock) in "Movie – Part 1" (1981). Courtesy of David and Dannel Arnold.

A portion of the cast rehearsing "Blizzard" (1977). From left: Ron Glass (seated), Hal Linden, Jack Soo, Lou Cutell, Max Gail, and Alex Henteloff. Courtesy of Peter Manera Manse.

A more expansive rehearsal shot with Lou Cutell, Hal Linden, Danny Arnold, Alex Henteloff, and the back of an unknown production staffer. Courtesy of Peter Manera Manse.

Ken Tigar and Max Gail have a little fun rehearsing "Werewolf" (1976). Courtesy of Kenneth Tigar.

The real class clown, Ron Carey. (1978). Courtesy of David and Dannel Arnold.

Yemana, Harris, and Dietrich trying to figure out what it's all about in the squad room. Courtesy of David and Dannel Arnold.

Harris, Inspector Luger, and Dietrich discussing the old days? Courtesy of David and Dannel Arnold.

Hal Linden reading script revisions at Barney's desk. Courtesy of Peter Manera Manse.

Even when not in character, Jack Soo was taking care of the coffee station. Courtesy of Peter Manera Manse.

Steve Landesberg and Max Gail getting a little punch drunk, perhaps? That's actor Kip King behind them. Courtesy of David and Dannel Arnold.

Writers Tom Reeder and Bob Colleary. Courtesy of Tom Reeder.

Above: Stein & Dungan. Below: Dungan & Stein. Whatever the order, Frank Dungan and Jeff Stein made a great writing team for *Barney Miller*. Courtesy of Frank Dungan.

Danny Arnold (center) with his "Golden Boys" Reinhold Weege (left) and Tony Sheehan (right) (1977).

Danny Arnold and his titular star, Hal Linden (1978).

Danny and Ron Glass in a serious rehearsal moment. Courtesy of David and Dannel Arnold.

Danny in a rehearsal with two-time guest actor Peter Jurasik. Courtesy of David and Dannel Arnold.

Danny rehearsing with Alex Henteloff, aka the great shyster lawyer, Arnold Ripner. Courtesy of Peter Manera Manse.

A deservedly exhausted Danny Arnold. Courtesy of David and Dannel Arnold.

Danny, Jack, and Hal enjoying a more lighthearted rehearsal moment (photo combo).
Courtesy of David and Dannel Arnold.

View from the cage. On left is Jack Soo, next, to the right, is guest actor Lewis Charles holding court. Courtesy of Peter Manera Manse.

Danny Arnold's famed Quad System bank of monitors just off the set, with unidentified crew member in foreground. Courtesy of Peter Manera Manse.

A Barney Miller party! Max Gail, Hal Linden, James Gregory, Ron Glass, Ron Carey (with cake), Steve Landesberg, and Jack Soo (ca. 1978). Courtesy of Nancy Ross Landesberg.

Ken Tigar (Mr. Kopechne) and author.

Max Gail, Hal Linden, and the author at the 2019 Chiller Convention in Parsippany, New Jersey.

The man behind it all. Danny enjoying the proceedings. Courtesy of Peter Manera Manse.

Danny with his ever-present cigar. Courtesy of Peter Manera Manse.

Episode Guide

Notes: In the credits for writers there are a variety of terms used through the years: story, teleplay, written by, etc. Most of the writers with whom I spoke said that it was, more often than not, a collaborative process but that Danny Arnold almost always had something to contribute or change before the scenes went before the cameras. There is more about "credits" in the section devoted to the show's writers. Since every episode gives Danny Arnold and Theodore J. Flicker a "created by" credit, it is not listed with the credit information for each separate episode.

One other note: There are many classic "Barney Miller" jokes referenced in the episode guide. If your favorite isn't included, it doesn't mean I didn't appreciate it. It is simply that I wanted to leave more goodies for people to discover when they go back and watch this TV classic once again or for the first time.

First Season

This first season was, really, just a half season. Like so many classic scripted shows, the first season is always experimental. It's not unusual for the actors to take that first season to "find" the characters. In this case, it took a little longer since that first season was only thirteen episodes. The characters that seemed to find their center fairly quickly were Fish, Nick, and to a lesser extent, Barney. In the case of Chano, he was only present for two seasons so we will never know just how he might have evolved, although his character was rather consistent in those first two seasons. Undoubtedly, the two characters that changed and grew the most over the course of the series are Harris and Wojo. In the case of both characters, this initial season offered some uncomfortable moments and traits that faded out as the series progressed. Think gum chewing and speech patterns. That said, Arnold, the writers, and the actors should be commended for how all the characters were allowed to grow in a realistic way without ever devolving into caricatures as happens so often in long-running shows, particularly sitcoms. All in all, the first season was certainly a sign of the great things to come.

Season 1, Episode 1: "Ramon."
Original Airdate: January 22, 1975.
Writers: Theodore J. Flicker and Danny Arnold.
Director: Bill Davis.
Cast of Characters: Hal Linden (Barney Miller), Barbara Barrie (Elizabeth Miller), Abe Vigoda (Det. Philip K. Fish), Max Gail (Det. Stanley T. Wojciehowicz), Gregory Sierra (Det. Chano Amenguale), Jack Soo (Det. Nick Yemana), Ron Glass (Det. Ronald N. Harris), Chu Chu Maleve (Ramon Santos), Anne Wyndham (Rachel Miller), Mike Moore (Stanley Mankowitz), Michael Tessier (Davey Miller), Buddy Lester (Harry the bookie), John Hawker (Radio announcer—voice only).

The Rundown

A young Puerto Rican junkie overtakes Fish, gets his gun, and proceeds to hold the squad hostage. Barney, in the first of his many opportunities to shine as the Solomon of the squad room, quietly reasons with the young man to turn over the gun by promising him a good attorney in the person of his daughter's boyfriend, Stanley, who works for the Public Defender's office. The secondary plot point concerns Barney's trouble at home with his wife Liz's feelings toward his dangerous job.

Out of Step

In this first episode, and for much of the first season, Harris's speech reflects more of a 1960s/1970s ghetto vibe. Some might even say it harkens back to an *Amos & Andy* type inflection: "I'm a policeman, baby. I goes where I'se needed." Mercifully, this persona gradually fades away as a far more sophisticated Ron Harris emerges.

Wojo is another character that will evolve as the series progresses and change significantly. In this pilot episode, Wojo appears as a loud, crude, hotdog cop. His early character could be interpreted as what was known in those days as a

Foreshadowing

Gregory Sierra's Chano Amenguale loses his temper in Spanish with the young Puerto Rican mugger they've arrested and tells the kid that he's an embarrassment. He tells the suspect that every time he [Chano] comes upon a crime in progress, he feels the need to address the situation using a British accent because he's so embarrassed that one of his own people is involved in a crime and thereby perpetuating a stereotype. Ironically, Sierra didn't like his character's use of angry Spanish for comic effect. He didn't want to be just "the Puerto Rican cop" but that's what Arnold hired him for and thought added to the humor of the room. Sierra would leave after the second season and while this isn't the only reason he left, it was apparently a contributing factor.

For the Record

Barney: You really hate that I'm a cop?
Elizabeth: Yes.

Season 1, Episode 2: "The Experience."
Original Airdate: January 30, 1975.
Writer: Steve Gordon.
Director: Danny Arnold.
Cast of Characters: Max Gail (Wojo), Jack Soo (Yemana), Hal Linden (Barney), Rod Perry (Det. Wilson), Abe Vigoda (Fish), Jack DeLeon (Marty Morrison), Alex Henteloff (Arnold Ripner), Jane Dulo (Purse Owner), Ray Sharkey (Hold-up man), Noam Pitlik (Man with briefcase), Milt Kogan (Officer Kogan).

The Rundown

Fish and Detective Wilson (Rod Perry) run down a robbery suspect on the neighborhood streets but Fish can't keep up with the pursuit. When Wilson and the suspect arrive at the precinct minutes before Fish, the squad's elder statesman gets to thinking he should retire immediately so he doesn't compromise the safety of his fellow officers. The secondary plot concerns a mysterious bomber that's been targeting public buildings around the city.

Missing Persons

The precinct bomber is played by Noam Pitlik in his only onscreen *Barney Miller* appearance. He is credited with directing 102 *Barney Miller* episodes, more than all the rest of the series' twenty-two directors combined.

Between the Moon and New York City

Steve Gordon, the credited writer of this episode, is best known for his screenplay of the hit Dudley Moore movie, *Arthur* (1981). He was also the creator of the funny, but short-lived, sitcom *The Practice* (1976-1977), starring Danny Thomas as a curmudgeonly family physician.

For the Record

This episode also features dialogue between Fish and Det. Wilson, an African American, that you won't hear for long on *Barney Miller* and the kind you would never hear on television today.

>**Det. Wilson:** (to Fish) You're out of shape, baby.
>**Fish:** "Baby" your Aunt Jemima—What am I, a lion hunter? My people were all in the restaurant business!

>**Season 1, Episode 3:** "The Snow Job."
>**Original Airdate:** February 6, 1975.
>**Writers:** Ron Friedman, Danny Arnold, and Chris Hayward.
>**Director:** Richard Kinon.
>**Cast of Characters:** Ron Glass (Harris), Jack Soo (Yemana), Hal Linden (Barney), Gregory Sierra (Chano), Abe Vigoda (Fish), Max Gail (Wojo), Ron Feinberg (Lyle W. Farber, Attorney at Law), Richard Stahl (Mr. Gross—Siegel's Dept. Store accountant), Reid Cruickshanks (Bellevue attendant #1), Paul Lichtman (Charlie—Bellevue attendant with oxygen), Jeffrey Kramer (Stick-up man), Ted Noose (Pete).

The Rundown

The city is in the middle of a snowstorm and Siegel's Department Store, fearing a robbery, asks the men of the 12th hold on to their receipts until Monday when the banks open up again. Barney appears less than thrilled by this responsibility but Wojo has already told Siegel's they would keep the money for them. In a secondary storyline, Chano arrests Mr. Farber, a flasher, for public exposure. Mr. Farber attempts suicide and Barney saves his life using CPR.

The Lineup

Richard Stahl, who plays Siegel's accountant, was one of the most recognizable character actors in TV comedy during the 1970s and 1980s. His dry, often sarcastic delivery led him into a rewarding career as a comic foil for everyone from Bob Newhart to Peter Falk to Jack Klugman and Tony Randall. He appeared in no less than nine episodes of *The Odd Couple* (1970–1975). In each case, he played a different character. The idea of casting an actor in completely different character roles over the life of a series was a practice that would be utilized by Danny Arnold on *Barney Miller* throughout its run. Stahl himself would appear in two future *Miller* episodes, "The Indian" (1979) and "Obituary" (1982).

Misdemeanor

After Mr. Farber is "put in the cage," Barney says, "Call Bellevue. Tell them we have a prune danish to go." The Bellevue humor eventually becomes Harris's specialty and one that Barney will generally frown upon.

Animal Lover

Nick enters the room and says to Harris, "Hey, you want to see something funny? Come in the toilet."

Nick is highly entertained by the fact that the building's cold temperature has frozen the water in the bathroom sink and the ants are slipping and sliding all over the place. As we will see in the future, Nick has an affinity for squad room pests.

Fraudulent Testimony

In this episode, the combination to the safe is said to be, "one left, two right, three left, four right" except in the previous episode, "The Experience," we hear Fish say out loud as he's unlocking the safe, "seven left, eleven right . . ." and then he finishes the rest without saying the numbers out loud. It's likely after the bomb blew up in the safe, they replaced the lock with a very uncreative combination in case of future bombs.

In a true continuity error, when Wojo brings in the box full of Siegel's receipts at the beginning of the episode, it's filled right to the top. When they finish counting and putting the receipts back in the same box at the end of the episode, the box is only half full.

Just the Facts

$216,487—the exact amount of Siegel's receipts.

Expert Testimony

This episode marks the first time that Barney will be considered for the promotion to Deputy Inspector. Like Wojo and the sergeant's exam, it will take a few times before Barney finally gets the recognition he deserves. Barney, trying to downplay the situation, tells Fish he knows he hasn't a chance to get it.

Barney: There are five precinct captains who've got more time on the force than I do—there's Cook, Leeds, Stevenson, Rourke, and Burns.
Fish: And Carmichael. (Fish leaves Barney's office and closes door.)
Barney: (alone at his desk) Carmichael, who's Carmichael? Of course, with a set up like that, you just knew Carmichael would get it.

For the Record

Barney: His heart stopped and I had to hit him in the chest with my fist.
Paramedic: Yeah, I think you saved his life. And I *know* you broke his ribs.

Season 1, Episode 4: "Graft."
Original Airdate: February 13, 1975.
Writers: Danny Arnold and Chris Hayward (teleplay). Lila Garrett and Sanford Krinski (story).
Director: Noam Pitlik.
Cast of Characters: Gregory Sierra (Chano), Max Gail (Wojo), Abe Vigoda (Fish), Jack Soo (Yemana), Hal Linden (Barney), Dick O'Neill (Kelly), Buddy Lester (Harry the bookie).

The Rundown

A former member of the 12th, Det. Kelly, is now a member of Internal Affairs and has come snooping around his old precinct looking for officers taking graft.

The Lineup

This episode marks Buddy Lester's second (third, if you count the first failed pilot, "The Life and Times of Barney Miller") and last appearance as Harry the bookie. He does show up again in the Season Three episode, "Abduction," but for some unknown reason he has changed his name to Sidney the bookie. Perhaps he was trying to hide from people to whom he owed past due winnings?

Lester had a long and successful nightclub career. He was friendly with the Rat Pack and worked with them on the nightclub stage as well as appearing in *Ocean's Eleven* (1960) and *Sergeants 3* (1962). Following his films with Frank and Dean, he went on to appear in five different Jerry Lewis–directed movies including *The Nutty Professor* (1963).

It should also be noted that Lester was something of a pioneer. In May of 1950, NBC produced the very first late-night television show called *Broadway Open House* (1950–1952). Hosting duties were split with Morey Amsterdam who hosted the program on Monday and Wednesday nights while Lester hosted it on Tuesday, Thursday, and Friday. Naturally, they began to compete with one another to the detriment of Amsterdam who was let go in November 1950. Lester hung around until the middle of 1951 when he left on his own accord supposedly because he was jealous of Dagmar, a buxom blond with no discernible talent who had become quite popular with the late-night audience. The show itself went off the air entirely just weeks later but it is generally considered the precursor to NBC's iconic *Tonight Show* franchise and therefore the precursor to late-night shows in general.

Lester never appeared in another *Barney Miller* episode again after 1977. However, he did previously work for Danny Arnold multiple times on both *That Girl* (1966–1971) and My *World and Welcome to It* (1969–1970).

Probable Cause

Liz informs Barney that they're having filet mignon for dinner. When he inquires how they can afford such an extravagant meal, she explains to him that the butcher gave it to her for $1.98 per pound.

Liz:	The secret is in knowing a butcher who is crazy about the way you walk. He gives me special considerations.
Barney:	I've watched you walk. I've never given you any special consideration.
Liz:	You don't think I walk for you the way I walk for a butcher.

Fraud

At the beginning of the scene, according to their dialogue, Barney was coming home "from" dinner but soon it becomes obvious that Barney has come home "for" dinner.

Potential Infractions

Kelly's witch-hunt gets Barney and the boys paranoid about things like complimentary newspapers and discounted meat. Each member of the squad stews over what terrible sins they may have committed that Kelly could discover to the detriment of the precinct.

Barney:	Cheap meat and free trips.
Nick:	His face. "Kelly's always had a thing about Orientals being on the police force. He says we screw up the look of the St. Patrick's Day Parade."
Fish:	Cheated on his income tax nine or ten years ago. Went to a police convention and took the deductions for Bernice although he didn't take Bernice. IRS found out and they disallowed it.
Chano:	Has a brother-in-law living in NYC who's an illegal immigrant from Argentina.
Wojo:	Three years ago when Wojo took the test for Detective 3rd Grade, he wrote some answers on his shirt.

Just the Facts

Barney keeps his bullets in a locked cupboard above the fireplace and his gun in a separate cupboard above the entrance to the kitchen.

Damning Testimony

At one point, tempers flare in the squad room as Wojo reprimands Yemana for his constant gambling, insinuating that things like that are what has put Kelly on their trail. When Wojo tells Yemana, "Go fry a noodle," Nick speaks for us all when he deadpans, "That's beneath you."

For the Record

Kelly comes back to the 12th as a patrolman. He followed the corruption right up to the top—the Commissioner's Office . . . and got busted back to patrolman for his trouble. In this case, that must make Kelly "the paranoid with proof."

Season 1, Episode 5:	"The Courtesans."
Original Airdate:	February 20, 1975.
Writers:	Jerome L. Davis, Chris Hayward, Danny Arnold, and Sybil Adelman (teleplay). Sanford Krinski and Jerome L. Davis (story).
Director:	Noam Pitlik.
Cast of Characters:	Gregory Sierra (Chano), Jack Soo (Yemana), Abe Vigoda (Fish), Ron Glass (Harris), Max Gail (Wojo), Nancy Dussault (Linda Fuller), Audrey Christie (Rose), Naomi Stevens (Donna's mother), Lavelle Roby (Miss Duquette), Rosanna DeSoto [as Rosana Soto] (Miss del Fuego), Shannon Christie (Donna).

The Rundown

The boys bring in some ladies of the evening on a routine bust that is done every month or so. This episode introduces us to Wojo's issue with members of the world's oldest profession. He is repulsed by them professionally but attracted to them personally. In this episode, he focuses on a new girl, Linda (Nancy Dussault), from Appleton, Wisconsin. He wants to reform her and then he decides he wants to date her. She isn't interested in either offer. The secondary plot has Barney's daughter wanting to move into her own apartment.

A Rosy Background

Audrey Christie appears in this episode as Rose, the madam of the local club. Christie, like so many of the guest stars who will pop up in future seasons of *Barney Miller*, had an extensive background on the legitimate stage appearing in the original production of *The Women* on Broadway in 1936. Her filmed performances were primarily in television although she did appear in some A-list motion pictures such as *Keeper of the Flame* (1942), *Deadline-U.S.A.* (1952), and *Splendor in the Grass* (1961).

Precedent Setting

According to Hal Linden, this episode was integral to the overall success of the show. At the time this episode was produced, the television industry was under scrutiny from Washington, DC, over the amount of violence and sex on television. This particular episode premiered on February 20, 1975. By the fall of 1975, the industry created "The Family Hour," between 8 and 9 p.m., when certain adult themes, language, etc., would not be tolerated. The Family Hour proved to be a huge controversy within the TV community and producers like Norman Lear, Danny Arnold, and others eventually sued the networks over what they considered to be arbitrary censorship. Looking at the timeline of events, it's worth wondering if the *Barney Miller* "Courtesans" episode didn't help to expedite the network's creation of the Family Hour.

The network was uneasy with the subject matter and was haggling over dialogue with Danny Arnold. The tipping point came at the end of the episode when Wojo asks Barney to lend him fifty bucks until payday. The script clearly insinuates that Wojo intends to use the money to spend time with Linda the prostitute.

At this point, Hal Linden will tell the rest of the story:

> Okay, so now we're doing the last scene in the show . . . the relationship between Wojo and I was kind of like father and son. He tells me how devastated he is and I give him my Sears Roebuck psychology that Barney had, that you can't control anybody else's life, you can only control your own behavior and how you react to it, how you deal with it. And he says, "Yeah, I guess so, Barney." Then he's just about to exit the door when he turns around and says, "Barney, can you lend me fifty bucks until payday?"
>
> Okay, now the entire show is built up to reach for that line. Well, the network says, "You can't say that." And Danny says—and again, this is all secondhand 'cause all this happened between Danny and the network but he did tell us about it, that's how I know about it—the network says, "Well, that means he's going to go with the hooker." And Danny says, "That's very astute of you." And they said, "Well, you can't say that."
>
> So now we're downstairs shooting that show and we get to the last scene. Director picks up the phone, calls up Danny. He's in the office arguing

with the censor. This was first year? Maybe the second year? [It was actually the fifth episode broadcast in Season One. There is no confirmation as to when it was filmed.] The director picked up the phone and asked, "Danny, we're up to that scene, what's the last line?" Danny says, "Shoot it" and hangs up the phone, turns to the censor and says, "I'm shooting the show the way I wrote it. It's your option to put it on or not put it on. If you don't put it on, I'm not gonna shoot any more shows."

Now this was a show—it was not a top ten show! It was the first season. I'm telling you this 'cause I think Danny Arnold was the most gutsy guy I ever knew in my life. Talk about mortgaging your home for a dead pilot. Here was a guy who had a show on the air and he told them, "this is the way I'm doing it, you can do whatever you want with it, but if you don't put it on, I'm not making any more." Walking away from a show, you know, it was insane! You know what the network did? They released it as X-rated.

But they put it on . . . X-rated. Now I need to tell you that, just that information getting out that it was X-rated, we had the biggest viewing audience that we had all year. It made the show. We took a real leap [in the ratings] like from 58th place to 30th place, something like that.

The episode in question, "The Courtesans," debuted on February 20, 1975. I was unable to find any reference to an X-rated *Barney Miller* episode in *Variety*, the industry trade paper, in the days leading up to, or immediately following, the broadcast of "The Courtesans." However, months later, the November 19, 1975, edition of the industry publication does contain an article with the sub-headline, "Prostie on 'Barney'—With Disclaimer." That article refers to "Horse Thief" (S. 2/Ep. 10), which premiered on November 20, 1975, and dealt with a man who gets beat up by a prostitute in his hotel room.

By the fall of 1975, The Family Hour was fully implemented and despite warnings from the network, Arnold wrote another prostitute into a script and so the network reluctantly ran it but with the aforementioned disclaimer. (See S. 2/Ep. 10)

Coroner's Report

Wojo reveals in this episode that his mother is dead when he says, "My mother must be spinning in her grave."

For the Record

This episode provides our first glimpse of the literary Sgt. Harris when he gives a very erudite, academic, and verbose review of a porno flick that he and Yemana checked out for a police report. He's standing behind Yemana dictating his review while Yemana types. Nick then reads the report to Barney.

Nick: *A Man and a Woman and Another Man* is a dirty film.
Harris: Hey man, what happened to everything I just told you?
Nick: Oh. I thought you were on the phone.

Season 1, Episode 6: "The Stakeout."
Original Airdate: February 27, 1975.
Writer: Danny Arnold.
Director: John Rich.
Cast of Characters: Abe Vigoda (Fish) Hal Linden (Barney), Max Gail (Wojo), Marjorie Bennett (Mrs. Richline), Eddie Barth (Detective DeLuca), Lou Jacobi (Harry Tannenbaum), Vic Tayback (Mr. Stavochek), Brett Somers (Mrs. Stavochek), Florence Stanley (Bernice Fish), Jo Jo Malone (Brandy), Lucille Meredith (Prospective tenant), Peter Carew (Prospective tenant).

The Rundown

The men of the 12th conduct a stakeout near the docks in the hope of capturing a group that is smuggling in drugs. Barney asks the landlord of the apartment they are using to please keep their presence under his hat. In a very short time, the entire building and neighborhood know about the stakeout. Liz is redoing the bathroom and kitchen and keeps calling Barney for his input. Meanwhile, Fish is fighting with Bernice and doesn't go home when his shift ends, prompting her to come look for him.

The Lineup

The landlords of the building the men are using as their base for the stakeout are the Stavocheks played by Vic Tayback and Brett Somers. When Mrs. Stavochek hears that Wojo is Polish, she begins speaking to him in Polish and he answers back fluently in the mother tongue.

This episode marks the single appearance of Vic Tayback. He would go on to co-star in the popular and long-running CBS sitcom *Alice* (1976–1985) as the gruff but lovable Mel Sharples, owner and cook at Mel's Diner. Tayback had originated the role in the 1974 Martin Scorsese film, *Alice Doesn't Live Here Anymore*. The long-running series starred former *Barney Miller* alum Linda Lavin as the title character.

Brett Somers was primarily a stage actress who often appeared in guest spots on episodic television. She was married to actor Jack Klugman for over twenty years and made numerous appearances on *The Odd Couple* as his ex-wife Blanche. In 1973, Klugman appeared on a new game show called *Match Game* (1973–1982). He suggested to the producers that his wife would be a good fit for their celebrity panel. The suggestion led to Somers's most memorable job in show business. From 1973 to 1982 Brett Somers became a household name as she appeared in over 1,600 episodes of *Match Game*. She and fellow thespian Charles Nelson Reilly became unofficial comedy partners on the popular game show.

Repeat Offenders

This episode introduces us to the first delicatessen owner with whom the boys of the 12th interact, "Tannenbaum of Tannenbaum's Fine Liquors and Delicatessen." The great Lou Jacobi appears as Tannenbaum and tells the men that he's one of their best customers. He's been robbed thirty-six times in the last fourteen years. Tannenbaum is a predecessor to Mr. Kotterman of Kotterman's Liquors played by Jack Somack who would appear on six different *Barney Miller* episodes between 1975 and 1980.

It's somewhat surprising that Jacobi, the definitive New York actor, appears in just this one episode of *Barney Miller*. However, he was an actor who appeared just as often in films as he did on television so perhaps his absence owed more to scheduling than anything else. In the years that *Barney Miller* was on the air Jacobi had parts in a wide variety of features including *Next Stop, Greenwich Village* (1976), *Arthur* (1981), and his tour de force as Uncle Morty in *My Favorite Year* (1982).

Missing Persons

Barney (talking to Det. DeLuca) says, "All right, who've we got on this week? Wilson's on vacation, Yemana's with the D.A.'s office. That leaves you, me, Wojciehowicz and Fish." Det. DeLuca (Eddie Barth) never appears again in another *Barney Miller* episode. He would be the first of many "one and done" officers at the 12th Precinct before the series concluded in 1982. A case could be made for Rod Perry as Sgt. Wilson getting the distinction of the first "one and done" officer of the 12th since he made only one appearance in a regular season *Barney Miller* episode. However, he did appear as Wilson in the original pilot so I'm counting that as two appearances.

Months later Barney mentions Wilson, DeLuca, and Feldman as three officers who are laid off at the beginning of the Season Two episode, "The Layoff" (S. 2/Ep. 3).

First Show?

Hal Linden and Max Gail both feel this is one of the two shows they shot when the network gave Danny Arnold the tentative approval for two more shows after the original pilot was turned down. As previously cited, neither Harris nor Chano are mentioned when Barney discusses the manpower with Eddie Barth's character, DeLuca. That could be because Harris and Chano didn't exist yet. There's also reason to believe that this may have been the very first episode shot after Arnold convinced the network to give the show another chance because Tony Sheehan thought that John Rich had directed the pilot. John Rich only directed one episode and it was this one. This episode also lists Danny Arnold as the sole writer, perhaps because he hadn't yet enlisted the help of Roland Kibbee or Chris Hayward although Hayward is listed as a producer. This episode was broadcast sixth in the first season but the evidence suggests it may have been shot first.

For the Record

We learn in this episode that Bernice and Fish have been married for thirty-six years and that coffee without cream makes Fish nauseous.

Season 1, Episode 7: "The Bureaucrat."
Original Airdate: March 6, 1975.
Writers: Richard Baer, Chris Hayward, and Danny Arnold.
Director: Bob Finkel.
Cast of Characters: Hal Linden (Barney), Jack Soo (Nick), Abe Vigoda (Fish), Max Gail (Wojo), Gregory Sierra (Chano), David Wayne (E. J. Heiss), Milton Seltzer (Murray Grossman), Claudio Martinez (Manolo Reyes), Elliot Reid (Wayne Boley), Milt Kogan (Officer Kogan).

The Rundown

A drunk is hauled in on a disorderly conduct charge and is brought up to Barney's office because he is a government official. Secondary plot concerns Wojo finding a dead fly in one of his sandwiches ordered from Grossman's Delicatessen. He reports it to the Health Department and they padlock the deli until improvements are made. The squad is not happy with Wojo because Murray Grossman is the only guy who delivers.

The Lineup

David Wayne, who plays Mr. Heiss, was one of the great character actors in the history of Hollywood films. He provided memorable turns in classics such as Adam's Rib (1940), *How to Marry a Millionaire* (1953), and *The Three Faces of Eve* (1957). He showed up even more frequently on television in the latter half of his career on shows like *The Twilight Zone* (1959–1964; "The Escape Clause"), *Batman* (1966–1968; as the Mad Hatter), and *The Streets of San Francisco* (1972–1977; "In the Midst of Strangers"). He even pulled down co-starring roles, as in the one-year run of *Ellery Queen* (1975–1976) on NBC playing Ellery's dad, Inspector Richard Queen, and as Dr. Amos Weatherby on the TV series *House Calls* (1979–1982).

Milt Kogan and Hal Linden have a difficult time stifling their laughs when Wayne first comes into the squad room and delivers his inebriated pronouncement of who he is. Just in case you don't remember, he is the head of "The Bureau of Federal Regional Development and Planning for Underprivileged Suburban Areas, Parks, Mines, and Indians."

Job Opening

Fish brings a cup of coffee to Mr. Heiss and says, "I just made this fresh, Mr. Heiss," indicating that Nick Yemana was not yet established as the squad's unofficial coffee maker.

Thanks for Your Support

In addition to David Wayne, there are two more recognizable character actors in this episode, Elliot Reid and Milton Selzer. This will be the one and only appearance in the series for both men. Elliot Reid's career stretched all the way back to films of the 1940s but he might be best remembered as Prof. Shelby Ashton, the rival of Fred MacMurray's Prof. Ned Brainard for the affections of

Nancy Olson, in the Disney film classics, *The Absent-Minded Professor* (1961) and its sequel, *Son of Flubber* (1963). As for Selzer, he had a long list of credits stretching over five decades including working for Danny Arnold on four separate series: *The Wackiest Ship in the Army* (1965–1966), *That Girl*, *My World and Welcome to It*, and *Barney Miller*.

Sports Fan

Claudio Martinez plays Manolo Reyes, the twelve-year-old who robs Chano's apartment. When Chano brings him in he's wearing a #81 Minnesota Vikings jersey. The number belonged to Hall of Famer Carl Eller.

Season 1, Episode 8:	"Ms. Cop."
Original Airdate:	March 13, 1975.
Writers:	Chris Hayward and Danny Arnold.
Director:	Noam Pitlik.
Cast of Characters:	Jack Soo (Yemana), Gregory Sierra (Chano), Abe Vigoda (Fish), Hal Linden (Barney), Linda Lavin (Det. Janice Wentworth), Howard Platt (Charles Hackman), Wynn Irwin (Horace Percival Schmidt a.k.a. Earl Schmidt).

The Rundown

This marks Linda Lavin's first appearance as Det. Janice Wentworth and the struggles she faces to be accepted as a female detective in an all-male squad room. She returns in Season Two as a semi-regular, appearing in four episodes. The secondary plot has Chano working on a case involving a chronic prank phone-caller.

The Lineup

Wynn Irwin appears as Earl Schmidt in this episode. The rubbery-faced character actor showed up in a number of iconic shows of the '70s including *The Mary Tyler Moore Show* (1970–1977), *All in the Family* (1971–1979), and *Charlie's Angels* (1976–1981). He also co-starred in the 1973–1974 sitcom *Lotsa Luck* with Dom Deluise and another *Barney Miller* alum, Beverly Sanders. The show, created by Carl Reiner, Bill Persky, and Sam Denoff, was the story of a single New York City bus driver living with his mother, his sister, and her lazy, out of work husband played by Irwin. Considering the talent involved, it should have been a fabulously funny and successful show. Unfortunately, It was not particularly funny and it was definitely not successful as it was canceled after the first season.

Missing Persons

There is no Wojo or Harris in this episode. They're at Narcotics and won't be back until the end of the week.

MO (Modus Operandi)

One of the things that made *Barney Miller* special was its unorthodox portrayal, at least by television's standards, of police work. Rather than the shoot-'em-up, heroic portrayal of good guys vs. bad guys, *Barney Miller* highlighted the fact that police work consisted of far more boring paperwork than heretofore portrayed on the big or small screens. There are two prophetic pronouncements in this episode that seem to explain the unique perspective of the *Barney Miller* creators.

> **Wentworth:** I hate filling out forms. I thought when you did plainclothes, you did more than fill out forms.
>
> **Chano:** Oh yeah, we do a lot of heroic stuff around here. But if we didn't fill out forms, no one would ever know about it.

A short while later, Wentworth is alone in the squad room and the rest of the gang is out on an armed robbery call. Barney's wife, Liz, comes in to find Wentworth typing. Wentworth makes a snide remark about her filing and typing work. Liz then makes what seems like an inside joke by the writers/producers of the show.

> **Liz Miller:** If people knew that detective work was ninety percent paperwork, they'd never watch television.

Art Imitating Life?

It seems fair to make comparisons to the struggles of the squad to accept a woman in their ranks and the struggle of the producers and cast to do the same. Linda Lavin's Wentworth may have been the first female cop introduced into the culture of the 12th Precinct but she wouldn't be the last. At the same time, none of the female cops/actresses were ever successful at establishing a foothold with Danny Arnold's team. Max Gail certainly enjoyed working with Linda Lavin and the chemistry they shared in Season Two is evident but Danny Arnold dragged his feet in signing her for Season Three and she jumped at the opportunity offered her at CBS. The result was a successful nine-year run on her own sitcom *Alice* that brought her two Golden Globe victories and one Emmy nomination.

Physically Fit

Her first arrest made Wentworth so "high" from the thrill of the hunt that while Fish took the elevator and she took the stairs, she still beat him to the fifth floor.

Let's Eat

This is the episode where Nick Yemana uses a pencil as a chopstick and ends up eating the eraser.

Just the Facts

A "10-30" is an armed robbery.

For the Record

> **Fish:** (speaking to Bernice over the phone) Of course I still love you. What else have I got to do?

Season 1, Episode 9: "The Vigilante."
Original Airdate: March 20, 1975.
Writers: Danny Arnold and Chris Hayward (teleplay). Howard Albrecht and Sol Weinstein (story).
Director: Noam Pitlik.
Cast of Characters: Abe Vigoda (Fish), Hal Linden (Barney), Max Gail (Wojo), Gregory Sierra (Chano), Gabe Dell (Al Shreiber), Tito Vandis (Jacinto Escobar), Marla Gibbs (Mrs. McBee), Lee de Broux (Charlie), Nick Holt (Thief).

The Rundown

The 12th Precinct has a vigilante who is beating up muggers before the police can get to the scene of the crime and Wojo arrests a cross-dresser for what is explained to the suspect as an unclassified misdemeanor. According to Barney, an unclassified misdemeanor is a law that states "a person is not allowed to wear a disguise in public."

The Lineup

Titos Vandis (Jacinto Escobar) was a Greek character actor who can be found in dozens of episodic series throughout the 1970s. He often appeared, quite logically, as a Greek immigrant although he could also be found playing Italians, Eastern Europeans, and, as in this episode, a Latino. He would return in two more *Barney Miller* episodes, "The Ghost," and "The Librarian." His other credits include *The Odd Couple*, *M*A*S*H* (1972–1983), and multiple episodes of *Baretta* (1975-1978). Born and raised in Greece, he began his career in the 1950s in his native country before coming to America in the mid-1960s. He worked steadily in Hollywood until the late 1980s when he returned to his native Greece to finish his career. He died in 2003 in Athens.

By the time Marla Gibbs shows up as Mrs. McBee in this episode of *Barney Miller*, she'd been seen for a couple of months on the CBS midseason replacement, *The Jeffersons* (1975–1985). She would gain fame and security as Florence Johnston, the sarcastic maid who was always happy to put George Jefferson (Sherman Helmsley) in his place. She continued in a spinoff of the Florence Johnston character called *Checking In* (1981) but it lasted only four episodes. She would later star in the successful sitcom, *227*, from 1985–1990.

Statute of Limitations

Arresting a person for cross-dressing (unclassified misdemeanor) seems like a flimsy charge, especially since it would have to be a charge made specifically against a man for putting on a dress because by 1975 women were routinely dressing in pants and t-shirts. Surely, Mr. Shreiber would have more precedent today to sue for harassment than when this episode was produced.

Most *Barney Miller* episodes hold up quite well, which is rather surprising given the changing nature of cultural mores and judicial precedents. This one does not. Sadly, the continued relevance of many of the show's other storylines reflect either a lack of progress on society's part or some prophetic nature of Danny Arnold's vision.

The cross-dresser, Mr. Schreiber, explains to Barney that he was just out for a walk. He wasn't hurting anybody.

Barney: The point is the law prohibits anyone for attempting to conceal his identity.
Shreiber: I'm not hiding anything. I told him [Wojo] my name. I live at 575 E. 3rd Street. I've been a truck driver for twenty-three years.
Wojo: You drive a truck?
Shreiber: Yes.
Wojo: A little truck.

Schreiber goes on to tell them that he drove a tank during World War II, Third Division, United States Marine Corps, South Pacific, Silver Star, Two Purple Hearts. Relevant or not and harassment or not, Wojo's treatment of Al Shreiber seems patronizing even for 1975.

Quite a Rap Sheet

Gabe Dell, who plays Al Schreiber in this episode, first appeared on film at the age of seventeen as one of the original Dead End Kids in the 1937 Samuel Goldwyn film *Dead End* featuring Humphrey Bogart. Starting in the late 1950s, he gained notoriety as a member of Steve Allen's troupe of comedic sketch players on Allen's various television programs.

For the Record

This episode marks the first appearance of Inspector Frank Luger and the first mention of Inspector Luger's old Racket Squad that worked out of the 12th Precinct made up of Luger, Foster, Kleiner, and Brown (eventually to be referred to by Luger as "Brownie").

Luger is introduced as an old-school cop who believes in kicking butt and knocking heads together to get results. He chastises Barney for his patient, open, kindhearted style.

Luger: (to Barney) You're getting the worst reputation in town, Barney. People like you!

Season 1, Episode 10: "The Guest."
Original Airdate: March 27, 1975.

Writers:	Danny Arnold, Chris Hayward, and William Taub.
Director:	Noam Pitlik.
Cast of Characters:	Abe Vigoda (Fish), Jack Soo (Yemana), Max Gail (Wojo), Gregory Sierra Chano), Hal Linden (Barney), Ron Glass (Harris), Herb Edelman (Alan Schuster), Jack DeLeon (Marty Morrison), Ed McCready (Telephone Repairman), Milt Kogan (Officer Kogan), Len Ross (Phony policeman).

The Rundown

The 12th Precinct plays host to an accountant who is a star witness in a trial against the mob. Mr. Schuster is convinced that he is not safe anywhere, even in police custody. A secondary plot concerns Chano trying to raise money from his fellow officers to make a purchase in a drug case he's been working on.

Cost of Crime

Chano is working undercover to try to bring down a narcotics ring. Unfortunately, the Narcotics Division doesn't have any money he can use and he needs $3,500 to make the buy. He collects the following amounts from his fellow officers: Fish—$325, Wojo—$524, Yemana—$373, Harris—$475, Barney—$813. He kicks in $950 of his own and takes $40 from petty cash.

When he makes his bust, he finds out he's tangled up in an FBI sting. They confiscate all the money and the squad is understandably upset. Barney tries to calm everyone down assuring them they'll all get their money back "in about six months."

More Than An Accountant

Herb Edelman who portrays Mr. Shuster was a terrific comic actor active in theater, film, and television. He appeared in films such as *In Like Flint* (1967), *I Love You Alice B. Toklas* (1968), and Danny Arnold's and Mel Shavelson's *The War Between Men and Women* (1972). He co-starred in the sitcom *The Good Guys* (1968-1970) with Bob Denver and appeared as a recurring character in numerous shows including *Nine to Five* (1982-1983), *St. Elsewhere* (1982-1988), and *The Golden Girls* (1985-1992).

Priors

Mr. Schuster spends his entire time in custody listing off the ways in which the mob rubbed out other witnesses in the trial for which he is now the key witness:

> "They got Friedman in a laundry mat; snuck up behind him and pushed him into a dryer. They threw in seven quarters. The coroner said two would have been enough to kill him."
>
> "Friedman's secretary drowned in the ocean, a beautiful swimmer."
>
> "Steinmetz, a vice-president, took a two-week vacation . . . and that was a year ago."
>
> "Burnside, the bagman, poison in his toothpaste. They found him in the bathroom with a swollen tongue."
>
> "Kleinerman, the auditor, stashed in a hotel in Chicago. Scrambled eggs. He was dead before he could put his fork down. Police found someone had injected poison into the eggshell with a hypodermic needle."

Paranoid with Proof

Considering the above information, Mr. Schuster is the "paranoid with proof" in this episode. He is most definitely paranoid that the mob is going to kill him and despite the reassurances from the officers of the 12th, the facts regarding the previous witnesses are on his side. To further strengthen his case, the lunches the squad room orders come laced with arsenic.

In the end, they use the poisoned sandwiches to their advantage and leak a story to the newspapers that Shuster was killed, thereby taking the heat off their star witness who was still very much alive.

First but Not the Last

This episode marks the first brush with death for one of the 12th's finest. Wojo eats poisoned food intended for the mob witness the men are trying to protect. When Harris returns from the hospital, Barney asks him how Wojo is. Harris tells him, "Sick as a dog but he's gonna be okay. Doctor said a dude with an ordinary constitution would've cashed it in."

The Last Word

Schuster: (to Nick) Very funny, very funny. I didn't know Orientals had a sense of humor.

Nick: Are you kidding? We invented gunpowder!

Season 1, Episode 11: The Escape Artist."
Original Airdate: April 10, 1975.
Writers: Howard Leeds, Danny Arnold, and Chris Hayward.
Director: Noam Pitlik.
Cast of Characters: Jack Soo (Yemana), Ron Glass (Harris), Abe Vigoda (Fish), Gregory Sierra (Chano), Max Gail (Wojo), Hal Linden (Barney), Roscoe Lee Browne (Charlie Evans Jeffers), Danny Dayton (Harry the snitch), Leonard Frey (Roland Gusick), Judson Pratt (Lt. Faraday), Reid Cruikshanks (Bellevue attendant).

The Rundown

The 12th Precinct hosts a charming and philosophical convict who has escaped from five different prisons when a local stool pigeon tells Barney that Charlie Jeffers (Roscoe Lee Browne) is hiding out in his precinct. Secondary plot concerns a man who has fashioned a homemade set of wings and wants to jump off a NYC roof to test his creation. Finally, and most significant in terms of the future of the show, Det. Harris begins work on a novel.

By the Book

The story of Ron Harris, novelist, is one that will continue throughout the series. This is not exactly the book that ultimately gets published but it grows out of this seed of an idea. This book is entitled, *A Week in the Life of a New York City Detective.* In his pursuit of storylines for his book, Harris becomes fascinated with Charlie Jeffers, the aging escape artist convict played by Roscoe Lee Browne. Every epigram or bit of philosophy spouted by Mr. Jeffers elicits a response from Harris along the lines of, "That's beautiful, man." When someone comments on his treasure trove of insights, Jeffers responds, "The years force a certain amount of wisdom upon you whether you like it or not."

The precedent for Ron Harris came in the person of Joseph Wambaugh, who published his first work of fiction based on his experiences in the Los Angeles Police Department, *The Choirboys*, in 1971. Just like Wambaugh, Harris would continue to work on the force after his first novel was published. Wambaugh went on to a prolific career as a best-selling author. As for Harris, he suffered from a spell of writer's block after the success of his initial foray into publishing before breaking through with a second book contract. We don't know the extent of his ultimate success because the show ended.

Unjust Reward

Roscoe Lee Browne was an African American character actor known for his rich baritone voice and his regal bearing. He was nominated for an Emmy for Outstanding Single Performance by a Supporting Actor in Comedy or Drama Series, as Charlie Jeffers, but lost to Gordon Jackson in *Upstairs, Downstairs* (1971–1975). It was a ridiculous category in that it mixed the competition between comedy and drama. All of the other four nominees had appeared in dramatic shows. The categories have changed over the years with some improvement and there are now awards for Outstanding Guest Actor and Actress in a Comedy Series as well as equivalent awards for Drama Series.

Bupkis

The true philosopher in the episode, however, turns out to be Mr. Gusick, the man who dares to fly. His first exchange with Barney:

> **Mr. Gusick:** Death has never been a deterrent. Obscurity is more terrifying than death, Captain Miller. Accomplishment's what's important. If I die in an attempt to accomplish something, who's the sufferer?
>
> **Barney:** Self-destruction happens to be against the law in this state, Mr. Gusick.
>
> **Mr. Gusick:** Archaic bupkis!! If I fall from valor, it's my business.

Both Barney and Fish are Jewish and yet we hear very little Yiddish in the course of the series. Thankfully, Mr. Gusick was there to give us a little lesson in language and culture. Of course, the gentleman who portrayed Mr. Gusick, actor Leonard Frey, had some serious Jewish credentials. He played Motel the tailor in the 1971 film adaptation of the Broadway musical hit, *Fiddler on the Roof*.

For the record, according to the online Yiddish Slang Dictionary, "bubkes" or "bupkis" is considered a vulgar word, meaning goat or horse droppings. It may also be related to a Polish word for beans, "bobik."

Repeat Offender

As we near the end of the first season (technically, half-season) Wojo continues to patronize the suspects he cannot understand and/or considers eccentric. Gusick responds to Wojo's smugness, saying, "We're finished as a culture, do you know that? Where courage is a sickness and imagination is a crime, culture is dead. The minute we start spitting on pioneers, we've had it."

He may not be paranoid but in Mr. Gusick we have another character that society considers deranged or delusional and yet taps into feelings many of us have lurking under our traditional exteriors.

Barney the Humanitarian

The men from Bellevue come to pick up Mr. Gusick. When Mr. Gusick asks for his wings, the attendant tells him he won't need them. Barney intercedes.

> **Barney:** Wojo, give him his wings. We're here to enforce the law, not shatter a man's visions.

Season 1, Episode 12: "Hair."
Original Airdate: April 17, 1975.
Writers: Ron Pearlman, Danny Arnold, and Chris Hayward (teleplay). Jerry Ross (story).
Director: Allen Baron.
Cast of Characters: Hal Linden (Barney), Max Gail (Wojo), Jack Soo (Yemana), Ron Glass (Harris), Gregory Sierra (Chano), Abe Vigoda (Fish), Michael Lembeck (Detective Paul Gardino), Charles Fleischer (Floyd), Henry Beckman (Lyman Cooper), Florence Stanley (Bernice).

The Rundown

Det. Paul Gardino gets transferred from Narcotics to the 12th Precinct. He is, depending on how you look at it, an obvious rip-off or homage to Al Pacino's character in the feature film, *Serpico*. He resents having to shave his beard and immediately asks for a transfer back to Narcotics. Secondary plot concerns Bernice's ongoing insecurity over Fish's love for her particularly after he visits a massage parlor.

The Lineup

Michael Lembeck who plays Gardino is the son of comedic actor Harvey Lembeck, best known as Cpl. Rocco Barbella in *The Phil Silvers Show*, a.k.a. *Sgt. Bilko* (1955–1959). Papa Lembeck was also featured in *Stalag 17* (1953) and appeared in numerous *Beach Party* movies as the comically inept motorcycle gang leader, Erich Von Zipper.

The younger Lembeck began his career as an actor in the late 1960s and is best recognized for his roles as Tommy Ricardo, the son of Peter Falk's Vince Ricardo, in *The In-Laws* (1979), and as Max Horvath, Julie's husband, on the long-running CBS sitcom, *One Day at a Time* (1975–1984). By the late 1980s, however, he changed focus and began to pursue a directing career. Since that time, he has helmed hundreds of TV episodes and directed such feature films as *The Santa Clause 2* (2002), and *Tooth Fairy* (2010). He and his sister Helaine Lembeck continue to run the Harvey Lembeck Comedy Workshop, the longest running Comedy Workshop in Los Angeles, started by their dad in the 1960s.

Charles Fleischer appears as Floyd, in what was just his third appearance on TV. He soon became a recurring character (Carvelli) on another ABC sitcom, *Welcome Back, Kotter* (1975–1979). He continued to act and do stand-up comedy for another decade before his voiceover talents made him a celebrity as the title character in 1988's blockbuster live action/animation hit, *Who Framed Roger Rabbit?*

Finally, Henry Beckman returns in his one and only appearance since playing Liz Miller's Uncle Charlie in the original pilot, "The Life and Times of Barney Miller." Beckman's familiar mug can be found in hundreds of TV shows through the years including *McHale's Navy* (1962–1966), *Peyton Place* (1964–1969), and *The X-Files* (1993–2002).

Statistics

In the Semi-Annual Pistol Range qualifications Wojo finished first, Chano was third. Yemana barely squeaked by although he blamed it on his eyelids and Fish did not qualify. He claimed it was cold so he wore gloves.

Wojo's results are surprising since in the first episode, "Ramon," Barney insinuates that Wojo wasn't the greatest shot.

Ladies' Day

When Elizabeth drops in with Bernice, the latter watches as Chano locks up a young suspect he picked up for being stoned and in possession of marijuana.

Bernice: (to the suspect) You've got your whole life ahead of you. Whaddaya need that for?
Stoned suspect: 'Cause I got my whole life ahead of me.

For the Record

This episode reveals that many of the detectives of the 12th apparently have lucky charms and superstitions.

- Wojo wears his Marine dog tags for luck.
- Harris wears an antique slave bracelet that belonged to his great-grandfather.
- Chano has a good luck tattoo.

And finally:

Fish: I got lucky teeth.
Nick: How come they're lucky?
Fish: My dentist died before they were half paid for.

Season 1, Episode 13: "The Hero."
Original Airdate: May 1, 1975.
Writers: Danny Arnold and Chris Hayward.
Director: Noam Pitlik.
Cast of Characters: Hal Linden (Barney), Jack Soo (Yemana), Abe Vigoda (Fish), Gregory Sierra (Chano), Ron Glass (Harris), Max Gail (Wojo), James Gregory (Inspector Luger), Barbara Barrie (Liz Miller), Todd Bridges (Truman Jackson), Cal Gibson (Mayflower / Richard).

The Rundown

Chano is forced to kill two bank robbers who were holding hostages and then deal with the emotional ramifications of his actions. Barney does his best to support Chano and convince him that he had no choice. The secondary plot involves Barney's wife Liz making a Citizen's Arrest—on an eight-year-old boy.

The Lineup

Child actor Todd Bridges makes his first appearance on primetime TV with his role as pickpocket Truman Jackson. Bridges would become one of the kids (Loomis) living in the group home with Det. Fish and his wife Bernice when the *Barney Miller* spinoff *Fish* (1977–1978) premiered in January 1977. The spinoff didn't last more than a season and a half but Bridges rebounded nicely with an eight-season run as Willis Jackson on *Diff'rent Strokes* (1978–1986), the protective older brother of Arnold Jackson (Gary Coleman). Surely, you must remember Arnold's famous catchphrase, "What you talkin' 'bout, Willis?" directed to his straightforward older brother.

That's the Job

Chano has understandably been upset by the day's events. As usual, Luger comes in saying all the wrong things and tells Chano he'll probably get a medal for killing the two bank robbers. The remark only upsets Chano more.

Later in the episode, Barney visits Chano's apartment to check on how he's doing. He doesn't sugarcoat what has happened he just says that's our job. Once Barney leaves, Chano breaks down into tears.

Not By the Book

This was a fitting final episode to the "first season" of *Barney Miller* that was really just half a season consisting of thirteen episodes. The unusual nature of this sitcom is exemplified in a scene between Nick and Barney following Chano's interaction at the bank with the two robbers. Nick asks Barney if he's ever had to do what Chano did today, that is, kill a perp in the commission of a crime. Barney tells him no, but he's come close. Nick remarks that he was always secure knowing that he couldn't hit the side of a barn.

Once again, this conversation presents a very different picture from the cop shows and feature films of the day that regularly depicted shootouts and hostage situations. The 1974–1975 television season alone featured such programs as *Kojak* (1973–1978), *S.W.A.T.* (1975–1976), *Baretta*, *The Streets of San Francisco*, and *Police Woman* (1974–1978), to name a few, all of which regularly featured shootouts and violent altercations with criminals.

Later in the episode the writers make another nod to this discrepancy when Chano tells Barney that the movie he went to see to get his mind off of the events of the day was *Dirty Harry* (1971), not only a story filled with the kind of violence Chano was trying to forget but exactly the kind of cop story that *Barney Miller* was not.

The exchange between Barney and Chano illustrates how *Barney Miller* was able to deal with serious issues in a very realistic, non-preachy way, make an impactful point, and still remain funny. Many of the socially conscious shows of the 1970s, important as they were to the culture and TV history, lost their understanding of how to do that and all too often fell into the trap of maudlin proselytizing.

The Last Word

Nick: (to Barney) You know, I went to a cop show last night and saw them kill a couple dozen guys—didn't bother them at all.

Barney: That's 'cause they didn't have to be there when the lights went up.

Second Season (First Full Season)

The second season was the first full season of the show. In the very first episode we're introduced to Steve Landesberg in the role of a criminal suspect, Father Paul, a sketchy priest. Danny Arnold must have really liked Landesberg because he was brought back just eleven episodes later and introduced to audiences as Arthur Dietrich, an officer transferred to the 12th from the closing 33rd Precinct. He will eventually fill the desk of the retiring Phil Fish.

Season 2, Episode 1:	"Doomsday."
Original Airdate:	September 11, 1975.
Writers:	Danny Arnold, Chris Hayward, and Arne Sultan.
Director:	Noam Pitlik.
Cast of Characters:	Jack Soo (Yemana), Ron Glass (Harris), Hal Linden (Barney), Abe Vigoda (Fish), Max Gail (Wojo), Gregory Sierra (Chano), William Windom (George Webber), Steve Landesberg (Father Paul), J. J. Barry (Plumber).

The Rundown

Mr. Webber has rigged himself to be a human bomb with dynamite attached to a vest that he is wearing. He spends most of the episode with his finger on the detonation button. He wants warrants issued for the Mayor, City Council, and the Governor of New York for dereliction of duty in solving the problems of society. Secondary plot involves Wojo bringing in Father Paul because he is a "phony priest." Wojo gets angry with "a guy making a con out of religion." Fr. Paul was selling bibles in exchange for donations to his church, "The Church of the Street."

Wisdom of Solomon

Barney was essentially the father-confessor and mediator of the 12th Precinct. For the most part, he exhibited the patience of Job and the wisdom of Solomon. Nevertheless, true to the realism of *Barney Miller*, we will also see the humanity and the frailties of Barney's character along the way as well. "Doomsday," however, reveals Captain Miller as the compassionate friend to the friendless. Just as he did in "Ramon," he talks in a calming and reassuring manner to a fellow human in distress. The episode succeeds in creating real tension and suspense in Barney's interaction with Mr. Webber. As a half-hour primetime sitcom on ABC in 1975 we know we're not going to see anyone blowing themselves up but, at the same time, the scene works fabulously well because we can all identify with Mr. Webber's frustration and exhaustion. Sadly, forty years after this episode originally aired we are still dealing with many of the same problems.

At the end, Barney is in his office grappling with these huge issues and recites the laundry list of problems to Fish, who merely replies, "But we can't do anything about it." While a true activist would disagree with Fish's resignation towards the ills of society, the more important point is that in this twenty-four-minute situation comedy, unlike most shows of its kind, there are no easy answers at the end of the program. Fish's lack of an easy answer makes the scene and the episode all the more relatable.

Previous Record

William Windom makes his first guest appearance on *Barney Miller* in this episode as Mr. Webber. By 1975, Windom and Danny Arnold were well acquainted. Windom had starred in Arnold's sitcom, *My World and Welcome to It* based on the cartoons of humorist James Thurber. The show was a critical success, winning Emmys for "Outstanding Comedy Series" as well as one for Windom for "Outstanding Continued Performance by an Actor in a Leading Role in a Comedy Series." Unfortunately, despite the show's strong showing at the 1970 Emmy Awards, the series was canceled by NBC.

Following the cancellation of the series, Windom got permission from the Thurber estate and did two different Thurber one-man shows all across the country for the next twenty years to rave reviews. He thought of himself as a "traveling professor of Thurber" and took his script almost verbatim from the author's essays and stories, most of which were originally printed in *New Yorker* magazine.

Windom, or rather Windom's voice, would make one more appearance on *Barney Miller* in Season Seven's two-part episode, "Contempt."

Disperse the Crowd

This second season premiere episode is somewhat rare as you hear the applause from a live studio audience as all the major players make their initial entrance in the show. This was a common practice on sitcoms of the late 1970s and through the 1980s. Watching it here, you can understand why Danny Arnold eventually lost the live studio audience as it impedes the timing of the comedy.

For the Record

This episode marks the first appearance of stand up Steve Landesberg as Father Paul. Less than three months later, he returns as Det. Sgt. Arthur Dietrich.

The Last Word

Barney asks Mr. Webber what blowing himself up will accomplish.

Mr. Webber: Just maybe someone would pay attention to me. I am sick and tired of being lied to and robbed and poisoned.
Fish: That's the wrong way, Mr. Webber. First, try a divorce.

Season 2, Episode 2: "The Social Worker."
Original Airdate: September 18, 1975.
Writers: Danny Arnold, Chris Hayward, and Arne Sultan.
Director: Noam Pitlik.
Cast of Characters: Max Gail (Wojo), Abe Vigoda (Fish), Hal Linden (Barney), Ron Glass (Harris), Gregory Sierra (Chano), James Gregory (Inspector Luger), Art Metrano (Det. Mike Lovatelli), Alex Henteloff (Harold Polanski), Herbie Faye (Nathan Levine).

The Rundown

Wojo bags a bagman, Nathan Levine (Herbie Faye). Harris is looking for a forger who's written thirteen bad checks totaling $374.30. According to Harris, "He's crooked but he's not greedy." Barney's wife, Liz, has a new job as a social worker and Barney is nervous about her next case, which sends her to a rough part of the Bronx. Inspector Luger is itching to get his hands on Wojo's signed baseball from the 1936 World Series.

One and Done

Art Metrano is introduced in this episode as Det. Mike Lovatelli. We will never see him again after this episode. Metrano was arguably one of the funniest men never to have an act. That's not exactly true. He did have an act but the act was based on his lack of an act. In other words, it was an act about "nothing" and this was long before anyone ever heard of a guy named Jerry Seinfeld. Appearing as "The Amazing Metrano," he would dash onto the stage while humming the music to an old standard written by songwriter Kay Swift called *Fine and Dandy*. Ostensibly he was a magician but his tricks weren't exactly tricks. They were merely silly movements made to appear as magic tricks. The whole concept was so clever and hilariously funny that it cannot adequately be described in words.

In 2007, Art Metrano brought a lawsuit against the producers of the TV show *Family Guy* (1999–) for stealing his act. In an animated film, Stewie Griffin claiming that Jesus's powers may have been overstated goes back in time and shows Jesus doing Metrano's act. Claiming copyright infringement, Metrano sued for $2 million. The producers settled with him out of court.

Impersonating an Officer (Of the Court)

Alex Henteloff plays the part of Harold Polanski, a master forger. He previously appeared in "Experience" (S. 1/Ep. 2), as ambulance-chasing attorney Arnold Ripner. Apparently, the writers and producers must not have envisioned him as a recurring character when this episode was cast. Either that, or Danny Arnold just didn't care. As we will see time and again during the run of the show, when Arnold found an actor he liked, he would not hesitate to use him over and over again in different roles. Henteloff would go on to appear in five more episodes through the end of the series but always as Arnold Ripner.

Peculiarities

The wonderful Herbie Faye appears as Nathan Levine, a bagman for the numbers racket. He informs Wojo that, "There are thirty-two Nathan Levines in the greater New York area." For the first, and only, time in the series we learn that one of the questions on an arrest report is "Peculiarities?" This man's "peculiarity" is that he sleeps in the nude. Inspector Luger says that sleeping in the nude isn't a peculiarity. "Peculiarities is if a man goes around collecting women's shoes, something in that line. He may be a bagman but he ain't a weird bagman."

Something to Do

Barbara Barrie as Liz Miller was desperate for something to do by the start of the second season. It was all well and good that the show that was originally supposed to feature Barney Miller's work and home life was quickly changed to focus on the precinct action but it left Liz Miller precious little to do outside of an occasional visit to the squad room. Barrie pushed Arnold to give Liz Miller a career. She suggested Liz go out and get a job working in the Emergency Room of a local hospital but Danny Arnold said no. Her persistence is no doubt what led to this episode where she starts a new career as a Social Worker. According to Barrie, Danny Arnold was just never comfortable or interested with incorporating a storyline of Liz working into the show. That's why, after this episode, Liz's social worker career is never mentioned again. (See the chapter *"Barney Miller* and the Female Sex" for more about the Liz Miller conundrum.)

For the Record

Luger lusts after the signed baseball from the 1936 World Series that Wojo uses as a paperweight. Luger reads the signatures: Carl Hubbell, Lou Gehrig, Mel Ott, Red Ruffing, Lefty Gomez, "Twinkle Toes" Selkirk. Understandably, Wojo doesn't want to give it up. Luger is disgusted that his underling won't part with the ball. In fact, he more or less threatens Wojo when he tells him it's good to have friends higher up in the department.

Soon Harris and Chano enter with Mr. Polanski, their forger. Polanski considers himself an artist. When he was a kid he used to dream about signing the Declaration of Independence and in his words, "now I can."

When Luger returns and continues to pressure Wojo about the ball, he eventually relents and tells the Inspector he wants him to have it. No charge. Luger is touched. Once again, in amazement, Luger reads the signatures on the ball, "Carl Hubbell, Lou Gehrig, John Hancock . . . was he with the Giants?"

Wojo: No, he was one of the original Yankees.
Luger: Oh, yeah, yeah . . . utility infielder, right?

Wojo cleverly had Mr. Polanski sign another ball with all the same signatures . . . almost.

Final Words

Fish returns from a doctor's appointment and claims to have menopause. "I caught it from Bernice."

Season 2, Episode 3: "The Layoff."
Original Airdate: September 25, 1975.
Writers: Danny Arnold, Chris Hayward, and Arne Sultan.
Director: Noam Pitlik.
Cast of Characters: Max Gail (Wojo), Abe Vigoda (Fish), Ron Glass (Harris), Hal Linden (Barney), Jack Soo (Yemana), Gregory Sierra (Chano), Bob Dishy (Mr. Shine), Candice Azzara (Miss Dorothy Lamotta), Oliver Clark (Charlie, the fur thief), Sandra Deel (Ethel Gorman), Milt Kogan (Kogan).

The Rundown

Layoffs are plaguing the NYC Police Department and the 12th is not immune. Wojo, Harris, and Chano get laid off. An ex-stockbroker is arrested for purse snatching and a manicurist is brought in for stabbing a client who got too fresh. With a fur thief already in custody, it made for a full house with a short staff.

Cut the Fat

In the end, the city receives a loan from Connecticut so the police department is able to go back on full power. That may be true but it doesn't change the fact that we never again see detectives Wilson (S. 1/Ep. 2), DeLuca (S. 1/Ep. 6), or Lovatelli (S. 2/Ep. 2).

Sign of the Times

This is just one of many episodes of *Barney Miller* that deal with, or mention, the many financial problems that were plaguing the city of New York during the 1970s.

My Cop, the Doctor

In "The Layoff," as Harris is leaving the squad room and Kogan is coming in with Miss Lamotta (Candy Azzara), Harris says, "Man, I should have been a doctor." Kogan replies laconically, "Yeah, me too." The inside joke is that in real life, Milt Kogan was actually a licensed medical doctor. For many years he simultaneously practiced medicine while working as an actor.

He's No Gunslinger

In keeping with the atypical nature of your average police show of the time, please note Nick Yemana's reluctance to get into the action. He's already expressed his discomfort with firearms at the end of Season One, "The Hero" (S. 1/Ep. 13), when Chano is forced to kill two armed robbers. Here, Harris, Chano, and Wojo have already been relieved of duty when a call comes in about four men with guns holding up a grocery store. When Barney tells Nick that it's him, Fish, and Barney, Nick responds rather incredulously, "Just us older guys?"

Immediately, the laid off men tell Barney to pretend that he forgot to tell them about the layoff and let them go out on the call to help him. Barney tells them they're not even on salary, "Who's going to pay you?" Nick chimes in, "I will."

For the Record

When *Barney Miller* began its run on ABC, no one expected Phil Fish (Abe Vigoda) to be the breakout star but that's the way it turned out. Everyone loved Fish. This was 1975 and the country was still reeling from Vietnam and Watergate and the cynicism, sarcasm, and discontented jokes coming out of the precinct's resident senior citizen turned out to be an irresistibly winning combination.

Frank Dungan, who along with writing partner Jeff Stein, wrote for the show during seasons six, seven, and eight, told me, "We both missed Fish and Nick and would have loved to have written [for] those characters." Fish was so well defined so fast that the best lines always seemed to go to him. Once again, he got to deliver the funniest line in this episode.

> **Phil Fish:** (Speaking of the layoff) It can't last long. This city can't survive without cops. This isn't Blue Water, Wisconsin . . . This is New York! We're living in a, in a fear-ridden, crime-filled, freaked-out disaster area . . . so, uh . . . cheer up!

Season 2, Episode 4: "Ambush."
Original Airdate: October 2, 1975.
Writers: Danny Arnold, Chris Hayward, and Arne Sultan.
Director: Noam Pitlik.
Cast of Characters: Max Gail (Wojo), Abe Vigoda (Fish), Hal Linden (Barney), Gregory Sierra (Chano), Ron Glass (Harris), David Doyle (Emil Ditka), Dick O'Neill (Det. Kelly), Milt Kogan (Kogan).

The Rundown

Someone is making phony distress calls in order to get the police to a destination where they can then be ambushed. The secondary plot concerns Barney being pursued by a fictional Florida town to take the position as Police Chief of their sleepy little hamlet.

Previous Service

Wojo's stint in the Marines will be mentioned throughout the *Barney Miller* run, but in this episode we also learn that Harris once served in the US Coast Guard. He was "stationed" in the Legal Department.

Turn the Other Cheek

Nick Yemana gets shot in the cheek. No, not that one—the posterior one. After Barney talks to Nick, he relays the message to the squad that "Nick sends his love and he says in lieu of flowers, he'll take a rubber donut." Det. Kelly (Dick O'Neill) is sent to the 12th (or as he calls it, The United Nations) as a temporary replacement for Yemana.

Color Blind?

When Kelly comes in to report for duty his sport coat repeatedly changes color within the scene from green to brown.

Law Enforcement History

When Wojo tells Kelly about Nick being ambushed, Kelly waxes poetic on the cinematic history of law enforcement and how it affects their image. "Back in the old days we used to be George Murphy, Phil Regan, Pat O'Brien," Kelly says with a smile. Then he remembers, "Nowadays we're Al Pacino, Richard Roundtree. No wonder we're getting ambushed."

Hey Mel!

When Harris expresses interest in the Florida job if Barney turns it down, Kelly, master of the politically incorrect says, "*You* in Florida? You gotta be kidding me." Harris quickly responds with, "Why not man, they must have seen *Blazing Saddles* (1974) by now." He's referring to Mel Brooks' blockbuster feature film comedy that features a black sheriff in the old west.

Known Perpetrators

David Doyle who portrays gun enthusiast Emil Ditka (like Emil Sitka of Three Stooges fame) was a busy character actor from the 1960s–1990s. The height of his popularity would occur in the 1970s when shortly after this *Barney Miller* appearance, he took a role in a pilot about three beautiful female detectives entitled *Charlie's Angels*. He spent the next five seasons as Bosley in the popular ABC "T & A" police drama. In the 1990s he turned to voice work and finished his prolific career as the voice of Grandpa Lou Pickles on the popular children's animated series, *Rugrats* (1990–2006). He died in 1997 at the age of sixty-seven.

Mr. Ditka is brought in for questioning after he was spotted on a roof cleaning his gun. When asked why he was cleaning his gun on the roof, he replies, "I like to be in full view of the local youth. Just another way of saying, 'Emil Ditka's got a gun.'"

Life on the Streets

The ambush incidents initiate a search for "cop haters." When another call comes in and Chano recognizes the voice as the person who made the call that resulted in Nick's ambush, they rush out to get their man. They capture the ambusher and as they're putting their suspect into the squad car, spectators from the adjacent apartment building throw garbage on them. This leads to the Harris quip, "I'll tell you one thing. I am *totally* disenchanted."

An Offer He Can Refuse

When Barney turns down the job offer from the small Florida town, he recommends Fish. Following Fish's phone conversation with the Florida police department he reveals to Barney some new evidence he's gathered.

Fish: Did they tell you why they need a new chief of police?
Barney: The old Chief passed away.
Fish: He died of boredom. He was sitting behind a desk one day, in his office, when a guy who was bored came in and shot him.

Season 2, Episode 5: "Heat Wave."
Original Airdate: October 9, 1975.
Writers: Danny Arnold and Chris Hayward (teleplay). Danny Arnold, Chris Hayward, and Arne Sultan (story).
Director: Noam Pitlik.
Cast of Characters: Abe Vigoda (Fish), Max Gail (Wojo), Hal Linden (Barney), Ron Glass (Harris), Gregory Sierra (Chano), Linda Lavin (Det. Janice Wentworth), Janet Ward (Mrs. Boyle), Gloria Calomee (Det. Bailey), Peter Elbling (Fresh Talker), Paul Lichtman (Beckman), Angelo Gnazzo (Mugger).

The Rundown

Det. Janice Wentworth (Linda Lavin) is back. In this episode, the detectives are going out on mugging detail in pairs. We are introduced to another female, Det. Bailey (Gloria Calomee), who successfully worked the detail with Chano. Sadly, as happens so often in *Barney Miller*, we will never see Det. Bailey again. Wentworth and Wojo go out on mugging detail together and an assailant pushes Wentworth aside to get to Wojo. The mugger gets away but Wojo says he'll know him when he sees him "because I marked him."

Barney: You shot him?
Wojo: I bit him in the neck.

This is Linda Lavin's second appearance as Wentworth and we begin to see the romantic sparks fly between her and Wojo.

Grace Under Pressure

New York is experiencing a heat wave. Presumably, the insulation in the building that houses the 12th Precinct has been eaten away over the years by the cockroaches and rats and therefore it's very hot in the summer and freezing cold in the winter. As this episode opens, all the detectives are sweating profusely—all but one.

Wojo: (to Harris) How can you sit there wearing a tie and not sweating?
Harris: Willpower.

Makeup!

Just watching this episode will have you reaching for a towel and/or a bag of ice. With the exception of Harris, most of the actors have been made up to exude that hot, sticky, humid look that comes with an oppressive New York City heat wave. Linda Lavin, Max Gail, and Peter Elbling all look like they walked through a sprinkler on the way in for their scene together.

A Sad Sign of the Times

A wife comes in to complain that her husband beat her up. She complains about what an animal he is but only the female officer, Wentworth, shares the woman's outrage. Fish, the man who takes her statement, is more or less indifferent.

Mrs. Boyle: Listen, whaddaya think of a man who hits his wife?
Fish: (long pause) You only hurt the one you love.

She then spends the better part of the episode deciding whether or not to actually prefer charges against him. Many victims are naturally afraid to prefer charges against their abusers. The attitudes expressed by men like Fish certainly don't make it any easier. In essence, this episode illustrates that women hadn't completely learned to stand up for their rights yet and it shows us why. In fact, it was so unusual that the woman originally walks out without signing the complaint, the officers make a little joke, and we assume that's the end of the scene. Suddenly, she walks back into the squad room, signs the complaint, and walks out.

In the post–"Me Too" era, this seems to be the obvious course of action and yet at the time, this was no doubt quite a progressive storyline. In Season Four, we will be faced with another controversial episode entitled "Rape" about a woman contemplating a charge of rape against her husband. These are challenging episodes to watch forty to fifty years after the original run of the show. The times and the attitudes have changed and hopefully, in cases such as these, for the better.

Introducing

Paul Lichtman makes his second of five *Barney Miller* appearances in this episode and his first as Beckman, the superintendent of the building. He appeared in the Season One "Snow Job," as an ambulance attendant but here he gets a name and a character that will recur three more times. He started in show business later in life after having gone to law school and working for the IRS. He entered the entertainment field as a writer, penning episodes for *All in the Family*, *Happy Days* (1974-1984), and *The Bob Newhart Show* (1972-1978) before he turned to acting. In the years following *Barney Miller*, he got involved in film financing, production, and distribution.

Change of Uniform

This is also the first episode in which we learn of Harris's reluctance to go out on the mugging detail. He doesn't mind dressing as a woman but he can't bear to shave off his moustache. At the end of the episode, Harris bribes Wojo with cash to take his turn in the rotation. It's a deal that works for both because Wojo wants to be with Wentworth.

Just the Facts

- Even in this early episode, Harris was already spending $30 for a shirt.
- In the last scene, Harris states that it is 110 degrees outside.

The Last Word

Fish: "You'll never open that window. They nailed it down in 1932. On the day this building was condemned."

Season 2, Episode 6: "The Arsonist."
Original Airdate: October 16, 1975.
Writer: Tony Sheehan.
Director: Noam Pitlik.
Cast of Characters: Max Gail (Wojo), Gregory Sierra (Chano), Abe Vigoda (Fish), Ron Glass (Harris), Hal Linden (Barney), Roger Bowen (Francis Lindquist), Jack Somack (Mr. Cotterman), Leonard Stone (Louis Lindquist), Steve Franken (Edward Foreman).

The Rundown

The 12th is on the lookout for an arsonist who is targeting their neighborhood. In the meantime, Chano brings in a suspect who has assaulted a vending machine with a deadly weapon.

The Lineup

This is the first appearance of Jack Somack as Mr. Cotterman, owner of a liquor store, who is chronically getting robbed. This time they took $214 in cash and three bottles of Scotch, "Thank God, they were on special." He would appear in five different episodes as Cotterman from 1975–1980, ending in the two-part episode, "Homicide."

Somack was an active character actor on TV from the late 1960s until his death at the age of sixty-four in 1983. He landed guest spots on such iconic TV shows as *Kojak*, *Laverne and Shirley* (1976–1983), and *The Rockford Files* (1974–1980). He is, however, best remembered for his role in a commercial for Alka-Seltzer where he uttered (repeatedly) the famous and infamous line "Mama mia, that's a spicy meat-a-ball!" The commercial drew so much ire from Italian American organizations that it was eventually pulled off the air.

Roger Bowen makes his one and only *Barney Miller* appearance in this episode as Mr. Lindquist, a man who is repeatedly cheated out of his money/candy by a machine at the Lexington Avenue subway station. He finally has enough and snaps.

Chano: If the machine kept cheating you why didn't you go someplace else?
Lindquist: Principle. I wanted that machine to give me a Butterfinger. It wouldn't so . . .
Chano: So you shot it.
Lindquist: I even gave it another chance. I put in 20¢ and I got back zip. So I let it have six, right in the coin slot.

When Mr. Lindquist expresses frustration upon having to leave a message on his lawyer's answering machine, Chano observes that he really does hate machinery. Lindquist confirms this fact prompting Fish to say, "There's a stamp machine on Sixth Avenue I'd like to put a contract out on."

Bowen was a brilliantly funny actor who is probably best remembered by audiences today for his portrayal of Lt. Col. Henry Blake in the film version of *M*A*S*H* (1970). He, too, died rather young in 1996 at the age of sixty-three.

Repeat Offenses

Wojo displays his judgmental side when he says to Barney, "Not much of a witness, Barn—she's a hooker." Barney answers, "Hookers have been known to see." Wojo also displays little patience for Harris's beliefs in psychology and modern police techniques when trying to pin down an arsonist.

Wanted

Steve Franken portrays the arsonist with mother issues. Franken was a prolific character actor who appeared in dozens of iconic television shows of the 1960s and 1970s including *Petticoat Junction* (1963–1970), *The Patty Duke Show* (1963–1966), *Adam-12* (1968–1975), and *Love, American Style* (1969–1974). He was probably best known for his multiple appearances on *Bewitched* (1966–1971) as a variety of oddball characters as well as for his recurring role as Chatsworth Osborne, Jr. on *The Many Loves of Dobie Gillis* (1960–1963).

Legal Counsel

Louis Lindquist, lawyer: You don't break the law, Francis. You find a way to take it out on somebody else.

Season 2, Episode 7: "Grand Hotel."
Original Airdate: October 23, 1975.
Writers: Danny Arnold, Chris Hayward, and Arne Sultan (teleplay). Danny Arnold and Chris Hayward (story).
Director: Noam Pitlik.
Cast of Characters: Gregory Sierra (Chano), Abe Vigoda (Fish), Max Gail (Wojo), Hal Linden (Barney), Linda Lavin (Det. Janice Wentworth), Robert Mandan (Charlie Huntsinger), Adam Arkin (Howard Smith), Queenie Smith (Wilson the Maid), Beatrice Colen (Miss Hearthstone), Arnold Soboloff (Lenny "The Confessor" Kelso), Joe Medalis (Bellhop).

The Rundown

The Hotel Greenwich has had six robberies in four days. Wojo and Wentworth are sent to the hotel undercover to check in as husband and wife and try and catch the very professional culprits. Their new assignment only heightens the sexual tension that exists between the two officers.

Repeat Offender (Sort of)

The show opens with Wentworth bursting into the squad room with a suspect in handcuffs. The act of arresting people tends to get Wentworth's adrenaline flowing so intensely that she relates the whys and wherefores of "her collar" to the rest of the squad at the top of her lungs. In this case, once her tirade is complete, Barney greets the suspect as an old friend. It turns out she has brought in Leonard Kelso, better known to the New York City Police Department as "Lenny the Confessor." Barney informs Wentworth that Mr. Kelso has previously confessed to the Brink's Armored Car Robbery in Massachusetts, the Getty Kidnapping, the murder of Albert Anastasia, and the sinking of the Andrea Doria. Chano reads the scorecard from Lenny's file, "twenty-four confessions, no convictions."

Just the Facts

- Wojo's family never took a vacation when he was a kid. His father thought vacations were slothful. Wojo remembers, "He used to have us all out working on Easter Sunday. He'd say, 'If the Lord can get up and move a rock, so can you.'"

Impersonating an Officer

Charlie Hunsinger (Robert Mandan), the Greenwich Hotel's house detective, brings Howard Smith (Adam Arkin) into the 12th and wants him arrested for 3rd degree rape because he checked into the hotel with a minor, Howard's seventeen-year-old girlfriend/fiancee.

Robert Mandan is best known to TV viewers as Chester Tate on the ABC sitcom *Soap* (1977–1981) that would premiere on the network less than two years after this episode of *Barney Miller* first appeared. The two shows would eventually occupy back-to-back sound stages on the ABC lot. Both shows offered a bonanza of character roles and many actors and actresses appeared at one time or another on both programs.

Veteran character actress Queenie Smith also appears in this episode as the tidy hotel housekeeper who really knows how to clean up. Smith's credentials stretch all the way back to her days as a supporting player in Hollywood films of the 1930s, '40s, and 50s, alongside such stars as Irene Dunne, Henry Fonda and Claudette Colbert. By the 1960s and 1970s, she became a familiar face on TV sitcoms including *That Girl*, *The Odd Couple*, and *Maude* (1972–1978), to name but a few. She would appear on *Barney Miller* one more time in the oft-remembered episode, "Werewolf."

Just Another Pretty Face

Miss Hearthstone is played by Beatrice Colen who was a familiar face on TV sitcoms in the 1970s. She's best remembered as Marsha Simms, the waitress on wheels at Arnold's Drive-In during the first three seasons of *Happy Days* (1974–1984). She also had a recurring role on *Wonder Woman* along with appearances on other TV classics such as *The Odd Couple*, *The Rockford Files*, and *All in the Family*. It turns out she had comedy in her genes. Her grandfather was the great American playwright George S. Kaufman. Sadly, her career was cut short by fatal lung cancer that claimed her in 1999 at the age of fifty-one.

Season 2, Episode 8: "Discovery."
Original Airdate: October 30, 1975.
Writers: Tom Reeder, Danny Arnold, and Chris Hayward.
Director: Lee Bernhardi.
Cast of Characters: Gregory Sierra (Chano), Ron Glass (Harris), Jack Soo (Yemana), Abe Vigoda (Fish), Hal Linden (Barney), Max Gail (Wojo), Jack DeLeon (Marty Morrison), Philip Sterling (Mr. Buckholtz), Ray Stewart (Darryl Driscoll), Paul Jenkins (Det. Sgt. Forbes), Johnny LaMotta (Bellevue hospital attendant).

The Rundown

When Fish doesn't receive his paycheck he learns the department's computers have him listed as "deceased." Harris and Chano bring in a despondent man who tried to commit suicide and Marty (Jack DeLeon) and his friend Mr. Driscoll (Ray Stewart) inform Capt. Miller that there's a cop in the 12th going around shaking down members of the local homosexual community.

Precedent Setting

When Barney hands out the week's paychecks, there is none for Fish. When Fish calls the Payroll Department of the NYC Police Department they inform him that Philip K. Fish is deceased. He relays the information to Barney who says, "It's probably a mistake." Fish pauses before he replies, "I wonder."

This episode of *Barney Miller* was filmed and premiered seven years before *People* magazine erroneously published premature reports of Abe Vigoda's death. Vigoda took the error in good humor. In a photo that ran in *Variety*, he posed sitting up in a coffin holding the *People* magazine. Regardless, people on the street and in the business continued to think he was dead. He made numerous appearances on the late-night shows of both David Letterman and Conan O'Brien, often playing off the idea of his dead/undead nature.

Paranoid Without Proof

Sgt. Wojciehowicz has a difficult time understanding and accepting the lifestyle choices of Marty and Mr. Driscoll. He's clearly worried that homosexuality could be something contagious as he asks Barney, "How do you think guys get like that?" It's a scene that seems silly by today's standards of awareness but in 1975 was slightly more believable due to the public's ignorance and paranoia. Even though Barney's answer is also one we wouldn't back up today, he is, as always, far more sensitive to the feelings of others than Wojo is in these early episodes.

My favorite response was from Yemana who was in the middle of Barney and Wojo's conversation and when Wojo looks to him for his input he states simply, "I don't care. It's none of my business."

A Cup of Color

Barney remarks to Nick that his coffee seems to be a funny color. Nick answers matter-of-factly, "It's maroon."

> **Barney:** How'd it get to be maroon?
> **Nick:** It's the color spectrum. You mix brown coffee with yellow water and you got maroon.

This is both an early example of dropping the responsibility of the coffee into Nick's lap and also of Nick's ability to explain away something so as to make even the most ridiculous seem logical. Yemana's strength in this area will be more fully utilized when he tries to instruct the others on the navigation of his unorthodox filing system.

Quite a Revelation

Marty has been criticized for being somewhat of a caricature of a gay man of the time. However, in this episode Marty displays empathy for a fellow human being that is quite separate from his homosexuality. He tries to comfort a man who has attempted suicide.

Marty Morrison:	I wanted to be John Wayne until I was seventeen. And then one day I didn't anymore. I just wanted to die.
Mr. Buckholtz:	Well, what made you change your mind?
Marty:	Well, I was standing on the railing of the Brooklyn Bridge and this car came by and they had the radio on and Doris Day was singing "Que Sera, Sera." And I thought, "You know, she's right."
Buckholtz:	There's nothing wrong with me. I'm a perfectly normal man.
Marty:	Well, if you want to settle for that, it's all right by me.

The Last Word

Mr. Driscoll:	(to Fish) You know you look exactly like Boris Karloff.
Fish:	That's because we're both dead.

This humorous exchange also proved to be prophetic because more than a decade later Vigoda would play the role of Jonathan Brewster in a revival of the play *Arsenic and Old Lace* on Broadway from 1986–1987. Boris Karloff originated the role of Jonathan Brewster for over three years in the play's first run on Broadway from 1941 to 1944. One of the running jokes in the play by Joseph Kesselring is that due to some botched plastic surgery, Jonathan looks like movie monster Boris Karloff.

Season 2, Episode 9:	"You Dirty Rat."
Original Airdate:	November 13, 1975.
Writers:	Arne Sultan, Chris Hayward, and Danny Arnold (teleplay). Arne Sultan (story).
Director:	Noam Pitlik.
Cast of Characters:	Max Gail (Wojo), Hal Linden (Barney), Ron Glass (Harris), Jack Soo (Yemana), Gregory Sierra (Chano), Abe Vigoda (Fish), Ned Glass (Becker the exterminator), J. Pat O'Malley (Mr. Holliman), Franklin Ajaye (Wendell Frazier), Val Bisoglio (Det. Delvecchio).

The Rundown

Chano, Nick, and Fish lose a drug suspect in a chase but he drops a box filled with twenty kilos of marijuana. Unfortunately, when Narcotics sends an officer to the 12th to collect the evidence, two kilos are missing. Fish passes out in the Evidence Room and it's discovered he has a kidney stone. Harris and Wojo bring in a vagrant who spent the weekend in Siegel's Department Store and Wojo is bitten by a rat in the evidence closet.

A Busy Guy

Val Bisoglio plays Det. Delvecchio in this episode. Bisoglio portrayed Sgt. Grimaldi in the original pilot, "The Life and Times of Barney Miller." This was Bisoglio's only other appearance on *Barney Miller* despite, or perhaps because of, being such an otherwise busy character actor. He was a regular presence on episodic television during the 1960s and 1970s in shows like *M*A*S*H*, *Ironside* (1967–1975), and *All in the Family*, before landing a regular role on *Quincy M.E.* (1976–1983) as the owner/bartender of Quincy's (Jack Klugman) favorite after hours hangout, Danny's.

The Kindness of Strangers

J. Pat O'Malley's three appearances on *Barney Miller* easily earn him the title of the most charming and likeable "bad guy" ever on the show. In this, his first appearance, he plays Mr. Holliman, an old man on a fixed income who falls asleep in Seigel's Department Store and spends the weekend. He will play a frugal counterfeiter and a harmless rainmaker in his other two Miller appearances and, for the most part, is always treated with kindness and respect by the men of the 12th. After all, they can spot a benign "criminal" when they see one.

In a career that spanned more than forty years, O'Malley appeared in dozens of classic films and television shows. His gentle Irish brogue must have been a favorite of Walt Disney's as he voiced characters in no less than half a dozen Walt Disney cartoons and features. O'Malley's film credits include classics like *Lassie Come Home* (1943), *Witness for the Prosecution* (1957), and *Hello, Dolly!* (1969), but his legacy on television is astounding with roles on *Maverick* (1957–1962), *Perry Mason* (1957–1966), *The Dick Van Dyke Show* (1961–1966), *The Twilight Zone*, *Hogan's Heroes* (1965–1971), *Bonanza* (1959–1973),—and that's just scratching the surface of this actor's extraordinary career.

Color of Grass

Franklyn Ajaye, who plays Frazier the car thief, was a popular stand-up comic of the 1970s but also made periodic appearances in shows like *The Chico and the Man* (1974–1978), and *The New Odd Couple* (1982–1983). From 1974 to 1990 he appeared almost twenty times on *The Tonight Show Starring Johnny Carson* (1962–1992). In the 2000s, he was a recurring character on the popular series *Deadwood* (2004-2006).

Motto of the 12th Precinct

When the men brought in the box of marijuana they confiscated from their botched stakeout there were twenty bags (kilos) of grass. However, when they get the word that an officer from the narcotics division is coming to pick up the evidence and they retrieve the box from the evidence closet, there are only eighteen bags. Panicked, they search high and low for the missing product. They know none of them took it but where did it go?

Delvecchio from Narcotics arrives and he's very easygoing about their missing grass. He plays it as though he assumes they just took a little for themselves off the top. The more they try to convince him that they're not dirty cops, the more he tells them not to worry about it. Eventually, the mystery is cleared up when it's discovered that the rogue rat stole and gnawed his way into the missing bags.

In the ensuing years, there will be others who have a hard time believing that these cops could actually be totally honest. Nevertheless, Barney's words to Delvecchio will ring true for the rest of the series as a motto of the 12th Precinct, "That's not the way we operate around here. We do everything by the book, according to regulations, above board."

Now That's a Stool Pigeon!

Frazier (Franklin Ajaye) returns to the 12th to sell them some information. Barney and Harris tell him they might be interested but no money until they hear what it is he's got for them. He then tells them, "Fish passed his stone." At this point, they both start to pull out some "long green" to give him. The question is, how and why would a first-time car thief know that Fish passed his stone? This was a rare moment of totally unrealistic humor in a *Barney Miller* script. It was a convenient joke for the tag but it's inconsistent with the reality of the story.

Season 2, Episode 10: "Horse Thief."
Original Airdate: November 20, 1975.
Writer: Tony Sheehan.
Director: Noam Pitlik.
Cast of Characters: Gregory Sierra (Chano), Hal Linden (Barney), Ron Glass (Harris), Jack Soo (Yemana), Max Gail (Wojo), Abe Vigoda (Fish), Ron Masak (Officer Shriker), Jack Dodson (Mr. Franklin), Liam Dunn (Fuzzo), Bruce Solomon (The flag salesman), Judy Cassmore (Tracy Gifford).

The Rundown

This episode aired on November 20, 1975, and yet it's focused on Bicentennial activities and celebrations. Mr. Fuzzo, the proprietor of a Hansom cab, has had his horse stolen. Chano brings in Mr. Franklin, a guest at the Greenwich Hotel, who has clearly been assaulted but insists that he fell and hit his head. Wojo brings in a street vendor selling uniquely American novelty gifts for the Bicentennial.

Sign of the Times

In what must be one of the more ironic offenses in the history of the show, Wojo brings in a street vendor, played by Bruce Solomon, for selling novelties with the image of the American flag on them. As a proud American and former marine, he is naturally offended by the disrespectful treatment of the flag. However, Barney informs him that the Supreme Court recently handed down a decision saying that such things were not illegal. That must have been quite a profitable decision as it's difficult to walk ten feet in modern day America without seeing an American flag emblazoned on t-shirts, lunch coolers, bathing suits, lapel pins, etc. Wojo would be shocked!

In his zeal to find a reason to charge the disrespectful vendor, Wojo tells Barney he's at least going to check the guy's record to see if he has any prior offenses. In the meantime, Wojo won't allow the guy to sit down because he has a big patch of the flag sewn on the seat of his pants. When Wojo runs a background check, he is doubly shocked to discover that the flag salesman, like Wojo, is a veteran of the US Marine Corps.

Overall, this is one of the more dated episodes. In addition to the Bicentennial talk and the sanctity of the American flag, there's also a dated reference to the long-running series of commercials that veteran actor Karl Malden made for American Express Traveler's Checks in which the tag line was "Don't leave home without them." Nick Yemana was apparently a fan as he mentioned Malden and the commercials on more than one occasion.

Life on the Streets

Liam Dunn who plays Fuzzo the Hansom cab driver was a ubiquitous character actor of the 1970s. Dunn seems to have been born old. It appears that most of his work prior to the late 1960s was in theater although a biography of Warren Beatty identifies Dunn as having been a casting director in the 1950s. He was virtually unknown to film and TV audiences for the first fifty years of his life before capturing everyone's attention in a short but hilariously funny scene in the 1972 feature *What's Up Doc* (1972) as a harried judge trying to sort through a collection of loonies. Mel Brooks spotted him and gave him the role of Rev. Johnson in the classic *Blazing Saddles* (1974). Suddenly, he was a hot commodity. In 1973 alone, he appeared in at least thirteen TV series, three made-for-TV movies, four feature films, and a network pilot.

Sadly, Dunn was diagnosed with emphysema and died in 1976 at the age of fifty-nine. From 1970 to 1976, Dunn racked up over seventy credits, an astounding burst of productivity for any actor. His talents, timing, and face made him a natural for the *Barney Miller* style of comedy. Had it not been for his early departure, I have little doubt he would have been one of Danny Arnold's "repeat offenders."

Last Known Address

Mr. Franklin is played by actor Jack Dodson who is best remembered by TV fans as Howard Sprague, the County Clerk in Mayberry, North Carolina on *The Andy Griffith Show* (1960–1968). The residents of Mayberry would be shocked to hear that he'd been assaulted in a hotel room in the big city. They would have been more than shocked to learn that the person who claims to have committed the assault was a prostitute who was angry over not receiving her compensation.

Repeat Offense

It's late in the game but, in a moment of frustration, we hear a little ghetto slang from Sgt. Harris in this episode. He's come from a riot in one of the parks and describes to Barney the mayor's difficulty in exiting the chaotic scene. "His limousine ran out of gas, he didn't have no money, and wouldn't nobody give him none."

Cleaning Up the Files

Veteran character actor Ron Masak also makes his one and only *Barney Miller* appearance in this episode as Shriker of the Mounted Division. Masak's career extends over six decades. He spent the better part of seven seasons in the role of Sheriff Mort Metzger on the CBS mystery *Murder, She Wrote* (1984–1996) with Angela Lansbury.

One for the Ages

Mr. Fuzzo tells Fish that driving the Hansom Cab is a wonderful job for a man once he reaches retirement age. When Fish asks Fuzzo how he knows how old he is, Fuzzo gives him an easy equation to use when calculating a man's age. "You takes a guy's height then you multiply it by the number of times he goes to the bathroom every day."

The Last Word

>
> **Fish:** Mr. Fuzzo, how much can a man make driving people around the park?
> **Fuzzo:** You mean reported income?
> **Fish:** That much, huh?

Season 2, Episode 11: "Rain."
Original Airdate: November 27, 1975.
Writers: Tony Sheehan (teleplay). Danny Arnold and Chris Hayward (story).
Director: Noam Pitlik.
Cast of Characters: Hal Linden (Barney), Max Gail (Wojo), Jack Soo (Yemana), Gregory Sierra (Chano), Abe Vigoda (Fish), Ron Glass (Harris), Sidney Miller (Jackie Ace), Phil Leeds (Arthur Bloom), Stanley Brock (Gardino—club owner), Joe Perry (Building inspector), Paul Lichtman (Beckman).

The Rundown

The unrelenting rain has the squad room under siege by a number of leaks that threaten to collapse the roof. The rain also sows the seeds of depression within the squad, spreading from Wojo to Nick to Harris to Chano and finally Barney. Fish, being chronically dour, is relatively unscathed by the meteorological misery. A fight breaks out in a nightclub over the comic stylings of a less than hip stand-up comedian.

That Should Be a Crime

Sidney Miller plays Jackie Ace, a lounge comic with a penchant for historic humor. Some of his hot material includes Bicentennial impressions, vignettes of our nation's founders, like this impersonation of James Monroe—"Is there a doctrine in the house?" or John Hancock signing the Declaration of Independence—"Wait a minute, don't I get to read this first?"

In an acting career that spanned six decades Miller worked with everyone from Jimmy Cagney to Spencer Tracy to Lucille Ball and Jerry Lewis. He had meaty roles in classics like *Boys Town* (1938) to small guest shots in TV shows like *Get Smart* (1965–1970). He was also a prolific TV director in the 1950s and 1960s. One of the shows he directed was *The Real McCoys* (1957-1963), produced by a young guy named Danny Arnold.

First Offense

Stanley Brock makes his first of nine appearances on *Barney Miller* as a nightclub owner named Gardino. He'll make one more appearance later in this same season as a barber before he returns in Season Four in the first of his seven episodes in the role of Bruno Bender, *Barney Miller*'s version of Archie Bunker.

Phil Leeds also makes the first of what will be a total of seven visits to the 12th Precinct, each as a different character.

Grace Under Pressure

The melancholy caused by the rain effects everyone in the squad differently. Wojo becomes homesick, Nick's coffee tastes even worse than usual, Harris feels like a failure because he's not yet retired in a tropical paradise on the proceeds from a bestselling novel, and Chano feels that the work they're doing as cops is meaningless.

Once part of the ceiling actually falls in on the squad, the normally calm, cool, and collected Barney snaps and launches into a rant against the building and the department. When he apologizes to everyone, they assure him that they were all depressed. He was just the first person to demonstrate his frustration at the top of his lungs.

Fear Under Pressure

Susan Beavers, one of Danny Arnold's assistants, remembers that it took them a while to figure out how to get the leaking effects for the rain coming through the ceiling and roof. Beavers told me, "They ran plastic tubes across the set . . . and they had holes. It would drip but they'd melt [because of the hot lights] and every so often it would burn. When they would break or pop, there was water and . . . everybody on the cameras and booms would jump off of them. Nobody wanted to be sitting on [or near] electrical equipment when the tubes popped."

An Umbrella of Monetary Protection

Nick is reading an article that claims the weather is controlled by the Rockefeller family to bring about one world government. In response to Wojo's doubt, Nick asks, "Ever see Rocky with an umbrella? He don't need one. It don't rain on him."

The "Rocky" to whom Yemana refers is the late Nelson Rockefeller, Governor of New York State from 1959 to 1973. At the time this episode was filmed and subsequently aired, Rockefeller was serving as Vice President of the United States under Gerald Ford.

Building Lore

According to Beckman the Superintendent, the 12th is housed in a bad building. (No kidding!) It created a big scandal when it was built in 1932. "They put sand in the cement, water in the plaster, they used rotten wood for the frames. Everybody went to jail." Barney responds, "Ironic, isn't it?

Just the Facts

- Ron Glass is absent from the next three episodes in a row. He doesn't show up again until "Happy New Year." There is nothing listed on IMDb to suggest he was working on another show or film. In total, he will be absent from four episodes this season while Jack Soo will be missing from five. Perhaps their contracts did not yet have them signed to a full season?

The Last Word

Nick: What you gotta do is develop an oriental philosophy. Like my grandfather used to say, "Many things look bleak at the moment of occurrence . . . but at least we ain't got locusts."

Season 2, Episode 12: "Fish."
Original Airdate: December 4, 1975.
Writers: Danny Arnold, Chris Hayward, and Herbert Baker.
Director: Noam Pitlik.
Cast of Characters: Hal Linden (Barney), Abe Vigoda (Fish) Gregory Sierra (Chano) Jack Soo (Yemana), Max Gail (Wojo), Steve Landesberg (Arthur Dietrich), Doris Belack (Bernice Fish), Emily Levine (Beverly Fish), Darryl Seamen (Biff Waltoon).

The Rundown

This episode introduces serious discussion about Fish's impending retirement. Due to the city's financial troubles, police precincts are getting shut down and the 12th receives a new transfer from the newly defunct 33rd Precinct.

How Old Is He?

We learn that Fish went through the academy in 1937 so he is probably in his late 50s or early 60s. He will retire (and leave the show) in a little less than two years. The department is pushing Barney to encourage Fish to take leave until retirement or go on restricted duty. Fish gets depressed as he feels the only life he's ever known is slipping away from him. When the squad receives a transfer from the 33rd Precinct in the person of young Arthur Dietrich, Barney assigns him to work with Fish, saying, "If you're going to learn, learn from the best." Fish sees this as even more pressure to leave.

Short of Cash

This episode returns to a subject that will be referenced throughout the series—the ailing finances of the city of New York and how that affects essential services such as the NYPD. In this episode, the 33rd Precinct gets shut down. Half of the officers are laid off and the rest are re-assigned. When Chano states that he can't understand how the greatest city in the world could be going bankrupt, Nick gives his simple explanation, "It's the Off-Track Betting. The losers are all in New York. The winners are all in New Jersey."

Impersonating an Officer?

Steve Landesberg had only just appeared in the Season Two premiere of *Barney Miller*, "Doomsday," on September 11, 1975, portraying a con man posing as a priest who Wojo arrested for selling stolen bibles. This, his first appearance as Arthur Dietrich, premiered less than three months later on December 4, 1975.

It's interesting to note that although Dietrich was introduced into the squad room in episode twelve of Season Two, he doesn't show up in another episode until almost a year later in episode four of Season Three. He must have had a lot of vacation time accumulated from the 33rd.

Not as a Stranger

Dietrich's uncanny impersonation of Gregory Peck, "Go away, Beverly is busy," comes about because Fish's daughter Beverly fears her ex-boyfriend may have followed her home. The actress who played Beverly is Emily Levine who was a member of the New York Stickball Company, an improvisational comedy troupe that included Steve Landesberg, in the early 1970s. According to a 2015 interview with Levine, this episode was supposed to be the pilot for the *Fish* spinoff. Landesberg recommended her for the role of Fish's daughter. In the ensuing fourteen months before *Fish* actually premiered, the entire concept of the show was changed and so she never ended up being a part of the final spinoff project. There was, in fact, no daughter Beverly in *Fish* at all. Levine, however, did go on to write for shows such as *Angie* (1979–1980), *Designing Women* (1986–1993), and *Love and War* (1992–1995).

Years later, Levine actually met and got to know Gregory Peck and his wife Veronique. At the time, Peck's daughter Cecelia was working on an acting career and he told Levine that he had every tape of every performance his daughter ever did, even auditions. Levine told him she saw an audition Cecelia did for a show Levine worked on and Peck didn't have it so she sent him a copy.

When he called over a week later to thank Levine, she answered the phone and heard a man say, "Emily. This is Greg Peck" and she immediately assumed it was her pal, Steve Landesberg.

Bigamy?

If Dietrich's quick change from crook to cop isn't confusing, how about the fact that Bernice Fish is not the same woman we've already seen in two previous episodes? Florence Stanley appeared as the much-talked-about Bernice Fish in two different Season One episodes, "The Stakeout" and "Hair." However, Season One of *Barney Miller* was only half a season running from January 1975 until May of 1975 with a total of thirteen episodes. In the 1975–1976 TV season, Florence Stanley was cast in a sitcom with Richard Castellano entitled *Joe and Sons* and so in this episode Bernice is played by actress Doris Belack. It's interesting to note that Belack portrays Bernice in a more traditional Jewish mother style. Her attitude and inflection are quite different from that of Stanley. Belack was a prolific character actress, showing up in feature films like *Tootsie* (1982) and *What About Bob* (1991) as well as TV shows like *The Golden Girls* and *Law and Order* (1990–2010).

Joe and Sons lasted only fourteen episodes before being canceled by CBS. Florence Stanley returned as Bernice Fish in the Season Three episode, "Recluse" and remained the only Bernice Fish that fans would see through her final appearance on *Barney Miller* in Season Four's "Good-Bye, Mr. Fish: Part 2" on September 22, 1977. She would, however, continue to portray the character until May of 1978 when ABC canceled the short-lived spinoff, *Fish*.

The Last Word

Dietrich: You have any idea where he went?
Bernice: He went to the park. He always goes there when he quits. He feeds the pigeons.
Dietrich: I can't imagine him feeding the pigeons.
Bernice: Well, actually, he buys day old bread and throws it at them.

Season 2, Episode 13: "Hot Dogs."
Original Airdate: December 11, 1975.
Writers: Tony Sheehan (teleplay). Chris Hayward, Danny Arnold, and Arne Sultan (story).
Director: Lee Bernhardi.

Cast of Characters: Max Gail (Wojo), Abe Vigoda (Fish), Hal Linden (Barney), Gregory Sierra (Chano), Jack Soo (Yemana), James Gregory (Inspector Luger), Jonelle Allen (Officer Turner), Nellie Bellflower (Officer Carney), David L. Lander (David Gordon), Howard Honig (Mr. Victor).

The Rundown

As progressive as the men of the 12th Precinct could be, they always seemed to have trouble with women police officers. No female officer ever seemed to stay at the 12th for more than a few episodes. In this story, we discover two uniformed lady cops trying to make points by making arrests in their free time. The secondary storyline concerns Mr. Victor who comes in to report that his wife is missing.

Probable Cause

Officers Turner (Jonelle Allen) and Carney (Nellie Bellflower) make a collar in their off hours on a case to which they have not been assigned and in the process botch a potential case that Chano has been working on. Officer Turner says, "We just thought a narcotics bust would make someone at Division sit up and take notice." Barney assures her, "Someone from Division is on their way down here to notice you in person."

The person sent from Division Headquarters turns out to be Inspector Luger who responds with the opinion, "two women police officers . . . it's enough to make your skin crawl."

As always, the women don't fare too well in the *Barney Miller* universe but they are able to bring up issues and subject matter relevant to the struggles they faced. It had to be an uphill battle for any female to break into the ranks of the old boys' club structures like police departments and fire departments of the 1970s. They don't succeed as often as women today would like but, more than likely, they are an accurate depiction of the times. If nothing else, Arnold can be given credit for putting the conversation out there in numerous storylines throughout the course of the series.

Political Science

Chano is upset that his collar was ruined by the two female "Hot Dogs." He comes into the squad room ranting in Spanish and then says, "When people lose faith in government, it gives way to anarchy." Turning to Nick he says, "You know what anarchy is?" Nick replies, "Yeah. That's when everyone runs around doing whatever they feel like doing. Like the Jets."

Scene of the Crime

David Lander, as the low-level drug dealer brought in by the ambitious policewomen, says to Fish, "You look awfully old to be a cop." Fish replies, "It's the light in here."

That was no joke. The Lighting Director was George Spiro Dibie. In his interview for The Archive of American Television, Dibie said, "We came in and I lit it like it was a squad room. I was in New York and I looked at it and boy, dingy, dirty, smelly, all that. And we did that. We made the whole thing dirty green—although I didn't like green because when you go close it reflects green on you, but we didn't care, that's the squad room. And we shot it and I made it very gutsy and grainy."

Never on a Monday

Mr. Victor's (Howard Honig) wife has been gone for less than twenty-four hours but he thinks she may have been taken by force because she never would have gone out on a Monday. "It's our special night." The audience laughs as they assume Mr. Victor is alluding to sex. Then he continues, ". . . *Rhoda* (1974–1978), *Phyllis* (1975–1977), *All in the Family*, *Maude*. I mean she wouldn't have missed those unless she was taken away by force." In an added layer of humor and irony, only Danny Arnold would publicly name, and thereby promote, shows on a rival network. While all four CBS shows listed above did indeed finish the 1975–1976 primetime season in the Top Ten and were solidly set in the national consciousness, ABC could not have been too thrilled with his choices. He could have at least plugged ABC's Tuesday night lineup that offered the choices of *Happy Days*, *Welcome Back, Kotter*, *The Rookies* (1972–1976), and *Marcus Welby, M.D* (1969–1976).

The Human Touch

This episode gives us numerous examples of the compassion we come to know and expect from Capt. Miller. He fights for a more lenient treatment of the female officers, he lets the low-level pusher out on a warning, and once he discovers Mr. Victor's trouble may be more than just a missing persons case (the photo of his missing wife is actually a photo of 1930s film star Jean Harlow), he has a sensitive heart-to-heart and recommends him to a doctor. This is the side of Barney that Luger refers to derisively as "the human touch." As Barney settles in to talk to Mr. Victor, Luger departs but before he does he turns back to Barney and says, "Sucker!"

No Show

When they finally send Mr. Victor on his way, Wojo turns to the room and says, "They're all cracking up out there." Nick responds, "Let's hope they don't bring it in here." Yet that was the whole basis for the show, wasn't it? The parade of people who were being put to the test by the world around them is what fueled all the stories. Without the Mr. Victors, there'd be no 12th Precinct and there'd be no show.

So Hard to Forget

In what may be the most frightening image of the series, we are led to believe in this episode that Fish and Bernice are still sexually active.

Season 2, Episode 14:	"Protection."
Original Airdate:	December 18, 1975.
Writers:	Tom Reeder (teleplay). Danny Arnold, Chris Hayward, and Tom Reeder (story).
Director:	Noam Pitlik.
Cast of Characters:	Abe Vigoda (Fish), Ron Glass (Harris), Jack Soo (Yemana), Hal Linden (Barney), Gregory Sierra (Chano), Max Gail (Wojo), James Gregory (Inspector Frank Luger), Jack Somack (Mr. Cotterman), Ralph Manza (Anthony Barelli), Ray Sharkey (David Salas).

The Rundown

Word is out on the street that the next precinct to close due to the city's financial concerns is going to be the 12th. The possibility of a departing police presence has the storeowners in the neighborhood turning to a protection racket. In an attempt to learn more about the rackets, Wojo brings in a local syndicate leader who hasn't been active in the business since the 1940s.

An Offer He Can Refuse

Ralph Manza pays his first visit to the 12th Precinct as Anthony Borelli, an elderly Italian gentleman who was the head of the syndicate in 1942. Wojo believes that they "can lay the whole protection racket in his lap." Barney, Fish, and Inspector Luger try to explain to Wojo that Borelli hasn't been active for decades but since he's brought him in, Barney allows Wojo the chance to question him. All Wojo can get from Borelli, who is deeply confused by Wojciehowicz's name, is that he works in his garden growing zucchini, carrots, tomatoes.

This is another episode where Linden is caught laughing. As Mr. Borelli gets up to leave, he asks Wojo what his name is? When Wojo says "Wojciehowicz," Mr. Borelli says, "What?" Wojo's responds with his standard, "Just like it sounds," line followed by the spelling. This leaves Mr. Borelli even more confused. There is no doubt that Manza's Italian ancestry helped inform his characterization as he not only voiced a perfect accent but as Wojo shows him the door, Borelli leaves talking to himself in his native tongue and we can see Barney and Nick laughing in the background.

That Old Gang of Mine

Luger comes in to break the news that the precinct is being closed. The feds won't bail the city out. The sentimental Luger takes the photo of he, Foster, Kleiner, and Brownie off the wall and starts singing "That Old Gang of Mine" which brings him to tears.

This episode references the famous speech by then-President Gerald R. Ford that inspired the *New York Daily News* headline, "Ford to City: Drop Dead." That particular speech was given on October 29, 1975, and this episode aired December 18, 1975, making this one of many examples of Danny Arnold and his writers finding ideas for shows in the daily papers.

Out of the Mouths of Babes

All the talk of precincts closing, a city short on funds, and crime in the streets being handled with vigilante justice leads to gallows humor from the veterans like Yemana and Fish while it stirs the emotional idealism of the younger cops like Chano and Wojo. The cynical gallows humor by the way is one of the traits that real-life police officers often cited when praising the realism of *Barney Miller*.

The ethnic diversity of the 12th Precinct is a frequently discussed feature of the show but the dichotomy of old vs. young was also an ongoing plot point in the *Barney Miller* universe. Typical of Danny Arnold's honesty, realism, and wisdom, there was never a clear-cut winner. Both sides were shown to have their strengths and their weaknesses.

Looking back a couple episodes, this battle may have been best expressed in "Fish" (S. 2/Ep. 12) when Nick asks Dietrich, "How many guys they lay off at the 3-3 [33rd Precinct]?" Dietrich tells him, "Oh there was about twenty-six uniforms and nine detectives." Fish then pipes in and asks, "What about the older cops, the better cops?" Dietrich responds sincerely without intended disrespect, "Well, I'm afraid we've lost some of the older cops but then we've lost some of the better ones too."

Sad But True to Form

In this episode, Luger casually, and without any actual interest, says, "How's the family, Nick?" Nick replies, "I ain't got a family." The lack of family for the men of the 12th was an intentional decision on the part of the producers and writers. Ironic since the original idea of the show was supposed to explore Captain Miller's life at home and at work. However, once the decision was made that the freshest and funniest material was derived from the interaction with the victims and the perps at the precinct, the idea for a home life for anyone was essentially taken off the table.

Hal Linden told me that they would occasionally get ideas from outside writers suggesting stories like Barney's brother comes to visit but it was almost always immediately dismissed. They knew that their most fertile ground for material was the workplace not the home. It's no accident that less than ten percent of the episodes ever showed us any location outside of the precinct house.

As for Nick, he actually does mention his grandfather when he wants to recall a wise old saying and we also learn along the way that he has a couple of uncles. Wojo has a mother who is sometimes dead and sometimes not. Levitt has a deaf sister. However, for the most part, we hear very little about the men's families with the exception of Barney and Fish and it's probably just as well.

Just the Facts

Questions the kids may ask you:

- *Who's Jimmie Walker?* In the context of *this* episode, he was the playboy mayor of New York City in the 1920s. Bob Hope starred

in a biopic about Walker in 1957 entitled *Beau James*. However, for Baby Boomers he was a stand-up comic who was featured in the Norman Lear sitcom, *Good Times* (1974–1979).
- *What's the London Blitz?* It refers to a massive bombing campaign that the Nazis inflicted upon the United Kingdom in the early years of World War II.
- *Who's Jimmy Hoffa and why did he need to be found?* Hoffa was the controversial leader of the Teamsters Union. He disappeared in 1975 and it has long been believed he was killed by Organized Crime.

Season 2, Episode 15: "Happy New Year."
Original Airdate: January 8, 1976.
Writers: Danny Arnold, Chris Hayward, and Arne Sultan.
Director: Bruce Bilson.
Cast of Characters: Ron Glass (Harris), Jack Soo (Yemana), Max Gail (Wojo), Gregory Sierra (Chano), Hal Linden (Barney), Abe Vigoda (Fish), Edith Diaz (Pregnant Shoplifter), Joseph Bova (Michael D. Crowley), John Dullaghan (Jackson the pickpocket).

The Rundown

It's New Year's Eve and the 12th is turned into a makeshift maternity ward as a shoplifting suspect goes into labor. Fish answers a call to the site of a possible suicide by a man who is threatening to jump off a building unless there is peace in the Middle East before midnight. A drunk gets his pocket picked and needs to sober up before he can press charges.

New Year's Resolution

Yemana announces to Harris that his resolution for 1976 is to stop making the coffee for the squad room. He's sick and tired of the snide comments like "Hey Nick, you might be a cop but your coffee's a crime." When Barney, who has yet to learn of Nick's resolution, has his first cup of the night and says, "Good coffee tonight, Nick," Yemana deadpans, "You're too late."

Repeat Offenders

John Dullaghan makes his first *Barney Miller* appearance in this episode as Jackson the pickpocket. He would be one of the most frequent character actors called into duty by Danny Arnold, appearing in ten half-hour programs. Two of those ten were two-parters so he technically appeared in eight storylines. However, he only appeared as five different characters because his fifth appearance, "Open House," introduces us to a homeless man named Ray Brewer. The character of Ray Brewer would eventually end up as part of four different episodes including the show's very last, "Landmark: Part 3" (1982).

John LaMotta, who appeared in three separate episodes of the show as an ambulance attendant of some sort or another, is in this episode as a paramedic sporting a full beard but is not credited. LaMotta, the nephew of former middleweight boxing champ Jake LaMotta, was best known for his role as Trevor Ochmonek in the 1980s sitcom, *Alf* (1986–1990).

For the Record

Liz Miller stops into the precinct to drop off some goodies for the guys before she heads over to ring in the New Year with Bernice Fish. However, while Liz's usual MO is to arrive at the 12th at the most inopportune times, this particular evening it proves to be a blessing. When it comes time to deliver the baby of a shoplifting suspect, it's assumed that Liz is the only one present who has actually experienced childbirth. However, as the moment of the baby's delivery draws near, Wojo reveals to Barney that he once delivered a baby in Vietnam. Therefore, when the big moment arrives the attending "midwives" at the birth are Wojo, Liz Miller, and Chano, as interpreter for the Spanish-speaking mother.

The Human Condition

Barney Miller was special because, first and foremost, it was about "the human condition." It's not about the good guys fighting the bad guys, it's always about trying to restore sanity through understanding, tolerance, compassion, and when the situation calls for it, the law. The "Happy New Year" episode is one of the best examples of the shared humanity of the 12th Precinct. They deliver a woman's baby, as cops have been known to do, but when the baby is born they celebrate the birth as though it is one of their own. In the world of *Barney Miller*, it truly *is* one of their own because of the constant reinforcement within the series of a shared humanity.

That shared humanity is further highlighted by Fish's dedication to his jumper on the Mercantile Building. Fish tries to contact Henry Kissinger and the Israeli Consulate to share the man's concerns and requests. He really tries to help his fellow human being in pain. He acts cynical and sarcastic but it's obvious that he truly cares particularly when he arrives back at the 12th and Barney announces, with great joy, the birth of the baby. Noting Fish's defeated look he approaches his colleague and asks, "How'd you do?" Fish responds with, "You win one, you lose one." It's a somber moment of the reality of victory and defeat intertwined in the human experience.

Don't Make a Federal Case

When Chano and Barney ask Wojo what she shoplifted, he explains that it was just baby stuff like diapers, talcum powder, etc. When Chano said he'd be willing to pay for it, Wojo explains that he and Nick already offered but the clerk at the drugstore wanted to make a federal case out of it. Once again, this shows the empathy of the men of the 12th.

Last Name First

The young mother tells Chano in Spanish to thank everyone and to tell Wojo that she wants to name her new baby son after him. When she asks, "Como se llama?" Chano replies, "Wojciehowicz." Naturally, Wojo offers his usual advice, "You spell it just like it sounds." Ultimately, he tells Liz, "Tell her Stan's all right."

> **Season 2, Episode 16:** "The Sniper."
> **Original Airdate:** January 22, 1976.
> **Writers:** Tom Reeder, Danny Arnold, and Chris Hayward.
> **Director:** Lee Bernhardi.
> **Cast of Characters:** Ron Glass (Harris), Gregory Sierra (Chano), Abe Vigoda (Fish), Hal Linden (Barney), Max Gail (Wojo), Charlotte Rae (Mrs. Rebecca Sobel), Sully Boyar (Mr. Stewart Sobel), Jay Robinson (Morton Hackler).

The Rundown

A sniper in the neighborhood takes a shot at Wojo and Inspector Luger. A man comes in to report that his wife has purchased a one-way ticket to Saturn from a slick con man.

One and Done

Veteran character actress Charlotte Rae makes her one and only *Barney Miller* appearance in this episode as Mrs. Sobel, a woman coming to terms with middle age. She may have been fresh off the failed ABC sitcom *Hot L Baltimore* (1975) but her biggest TV success was still ahead as Edna Garrett in *Different Strokes* and *The Facts of Life* (1979–1988). It should be noted that Charlotte Rae was also a semi-regular on *Car 54, Where Are You?* (1961–1963), the most notable sitcom set within a big city police force before *Barney Miller*.

Sully Boyar, who played Rae's husband in this episode, had just been seen as Mulvaney the bank manager in the feature film *Dog Day Afternoon* (1975) with Al Pacino and John Casale. Unfortunately, this would be his only appearance on the show.

For the Record

The 12th Precinct was known for its racial and cultural diversity. This progressive practice in casting stands out even more because it was rarely played for self-congratulatory pats on the back. As a rule, it was just a bunch of capable human beings doing a difficult job. Naturally, there were individuals who would make unwelcome remarks like Detective/Patrolman Kelly or Lt. Scanlon, but most of the time it was treated as nothing unusual. In this episode, however, Harris makes a rare crack that calls attention to the diversity of the squad room.

Following the sniper's shot at Wojo, the detectives receive a visit from Inspector Luger who subtly insinuates his disappointment in Wojo and the squad that they weren't able to immediately apprehend a suspect. Wojo takes offense and feels Luger is accusing him of being a coward. When he leaves, Mr. Sobol who has witnessed the fireworks apologizes to the men for being in the way. Barney tells Mr. Sobol not to worry, it happens all the time.

Chano: Absolutely, Mr. Sobol. You see we policemen work under a great deal of pressure and to relieve the tension, we insult each other a lot but it doesn't mean anything.

Harris: That's why you see so many different ethnic types around, you know, it gives us a lot of ammunition.

The Right to Remain Stifled

Hal Linden's occasional difficulty stifling a laugh has been noted. In this episode, we see an even rarer instance of Abe Vigoda trying not to laugh at Sully

Boyar as Mr. Sobol. When Fish returns from the bathroom, Mr. Sobol continues to explain his problem with his wife and he pulls up a chair beside Fish at his desk. Boyar (Mr. Sobol) pulls his chair a little closer to Fish every few seconds. Finally, Vigoda (Fish) places his hand over his mouth and turns away. It could be Boyar improvised the bit moving the chair. Otherwise, Vigoda, like the rest of us, was just reacting to how funny the show was!

Way Out

Jay Robinson is hilarious as Morton Hackler, a man selling junkets to Saturn. He would appear one more time on the show but it would have to wait until the final season, "The Tontine." He also made an appearance in Danny Arnold's short-lived *A.E.S. Hudson Street* (1978). His screen debut was in 1953 as a very campy Caligula in Twentieth Century Fox's *The Robe*.

Season 2, Episode 17: "Fear of Flying."
Original Airdate: January 29, 1976.
Writer: Reinhold Weege.
Director: Lee Bernhardi.
Cast of Characters: Jack Soo (Yemana), Abe Vigoda (Fish), Gregory Sierra (Chano), Hal Linden (Barney), Ron Glass (Harris), Max Gail (Wojo), Valerie Curtin (Gloria Cooney), Jack Riley (Frederick Clooney), Charles Murphy (Eugene Woolen).

The Rundown

Wojo has to accompany a prisoner to Cleveland for extradition. Unfortunately, he is deathly afraid of flying. The prisoner is a bigamist with one wife in New York City and one in Cleveland. His NYC wife shows up at the squad room and downs a bottle of sleeping pills. The third storyline is about an honest citizen who finds an envelope with $3,500 and turns it in.

First-Time Offender

This appears to be the first episode penned by Reinhold Weege who would be credited with writing the teleplay or the story for more than thirty episodes. He would go on to create another successful sitcom, this one for NBC, in the form of *Night Court* (1984–1992).

Repeat Offender

Jack Riley shows up in his first *Barney Miller* episode as the bigamist, Frederick Clooney. He returns in Season Five's, "The Counterfeiter," this time as the enraged husband of a plastic surgeon's patient.

Riley, a native of Cleveland, started out on radio and eventually moved to California to write for his former radio cohort, Tim Conway. He eventually turned to acting and appeared in important movies like *Catch-22* (1970) and *McCabe and Mrs. Miller* (1971). However, he found his home in the sitcom world of the '70s with appearances on *Mary Tyler Moore*, *M*A*S*H*, and *Happy Days*. He found lasting fame, however, starting in 1972 when he was hired to play Elliot Karlin, the paranoid and prickly patient to psychiatrist Dr. Robert Hartley, on *The Bob Newhart Show*. In the 1990s, Riley enjoyed the second major break of his career when he was hired to be the voice of Stu Pickles on the popular and long-running children's animated shows, *The Rugrats* and *All Grown Up* (2003-2008).

The Final Curtin

This episode featured the one and only appearance of actress Valerie Curtin, cousin to SNL's Jane Curtin. In addition to her acting credits in films such as *Alice Doesn't Live Here Anymore* (1974) and *All the President's Men* (1976), she's also talented writer. Curtin and then husband Barry Levinson wrote the screenplays for . . . *And Justice for All* (1975) and the semi-autobiographical *Best Friends* (1982) starring Burt Reynolds and Goldie Hawn.

Precedent Setting

The squad is absolutely stunned when Mr. Woolen (Charles Murphy) turns in the package he found on the street containing $3,500 and no other identification or clues as to its owner. Harris tells him if he ever decides to go into politics, he's got Harris's vote for President. Later on, Barney is also impressed but apparently not as much as Harris since he only offers his vote for Mayor. The subtle beauty of the *Barney Miller* humor and writing is displayed through Mr. Woolen's realization of the squad room's reaction to his good deed. You get the feeling that as soon as he turns in the money and sees their reaction, he begins to question and regret his decision. On the upside, he's told that if no one claims the money in thirty days, it's his. He then comes back thirty minutes later to see if anyone has claimed it.

Verbal Commitment

Barney Miller was a show that constantly reminded audiences that it's not necessarily what you say but how you say it. The majority of the humor came from characters' attitudes. The longer the show went on and the better we got to know the characters, the easier it was to laugh at any line that reinforced our humorous view of that character. In this episode, Fish gets a big laugh merely by announcing, "I gotta go to the bathroom!" On the surface, it's not a funny line. However, within the context of the scene, our familiarity with his character, and the delivery of the line, it's extremely funny.

Grace Under Pressure

To help alleviate Wojo's horror at the prospect of flying to Cleveland, Harris gives him a book to take along on the plane. The book is Erica Jong's *Fear of Flying*, a huge bestseller in the 1970s, about a woman's sexual awakening and independence. The title of the book led Wojo to think it was a self-help book.

Missing Property

In this episode, Wojo's signed baseball from the 1936 World Series is missing from its usual perch on his desk. Perhaps Inspector Luger figured out Wojo fooled him with a counterfeit ball (S. 2/ Ep. 2) and he stole the original?

Best Part of the Job

This episode features a three-minute scene in Barney's office between Wojo and his Captain. Max Gail told me that some of his favorite scenes throughout the course of the series were when he and Hal Linden had the opportunity to work out a long scenario like this one. The office conversations were the rock upon which their father-son dynamic was built. Through the years, Linden has often mentioned to interviewers his love of rehearsing and working out scenes with his fellow actors so no doubt he enjoyed these opportunities as well. There would be many opportunities for these tête-à-têtes in Barney's office over the eight seasons—some would be humorous, some would be filled with anger, and many would be filled with an intimate exchange of ideas, fears, and hopes. Barney's office became a safe space for his men to vent and visit when they needed his calm and reasoned advice.

Sign of the Times

The city of Cleveland is subject to an array of jokes in this episode. In the 1970s, the city was often referred to as "The Mistake on the Lake."

That's the Job

Wojo: They oughta throw the book at him. The guy's got no respect for the law, no respect for women—and I gotta chauffeur him all around the country.
Barney: Wojo, that's part of the job.
Harris: Boredom is the rest of it.
Barney: If you guys wanted romance and excitement, you should've joined the Navy. Being a cop is, uh, . . . going to Cleveland.

The Eternal Question

Why does Wojo have two pairs of sweat socks in a metal index card container?

Season 2, Episode 18: "Block Party."
Original Airdate: February 12, 1976.
Writer: Tom Reeder.
Director: Noam Pitlik.
Cast of Characters: Gregory Sierra (Chano), Ron Glass (Harris), Jack Soo (Yemana), Abe Vigoda (Fish), Hal Linden (Barney), Max Gail (Wojo), Linda Lavin (Det. Janice Wentworth), George Murdock (Lt. Ben Scanlon), Larry Bishop (Hurley), Stanley Brock (Burgess the barber).

The Rundown

Harris is struggling to come up with a subject for his column in the Police Department newsletter, *The Sentinel of Truth*. Chano and Wentworth are assigned crowd control at a block party for a local union organizer. Wojo and Wentworth are now in a relationship and they're not fooling anyone. A man sits naked in a laundromat waiting for his clothes to clean and dry. A barber comes in looking for a gun permit.

Closing In

Actor Stanley Brock shows up for the second time at the 12th Precinct, this time as Mr. Burgess, a local tonsorial specialist. He is looking to purchase a gun to protect himself and his establishment. The next time he comes into the 12th he will enter as Bruno Bender, a local business owner advocating vigilante justice "to aid the local police." Bruno will become a regular visitor to the precinct for the rest of the series.

Sign of the Times

The fact that the issue of gun control is brought up in this 1976 episode is either a testimony to how prophetic Danny Arnold and his writers were or just how little progress we've made in this arena after half a century. More than likely, it's a little bit of both. Knowing as we do how much Danny Arnold and his writers scoured the newspapers for story ideas, this is proof that gun control was already part of the national conversation in the 1970s.

Sons of Rats in Cages

The 12th was known to have infestations of cockroaches and rats but in this episode, Larry Bishop, son of Rat Pack comedian Joey Bishop, ends up in "the cage" as he plays the man from the laundromat who hates how clothes feel on his body. He won't be the only person who turns up in the 12th through the years who's more comfortable in the buff than fully clothed.

For the Record

George Murdock makes his first appearance as Lt. Scanlon; however, in this episode, he is the commanding officer at Manhattan South. Oddly enough, unlike Steve Landesberg and Ron Carey who started out as perps and then got chosen for their long running characters, Sgt. Arthur Dietrich and Officer Carl Levitt, Murdock starts as Scanlon then plays one other separate character in Season Three, Episode Twenty, "Group Home," before returning and remaining as Scanlon. In this way, it is similar to Alex Henteloff's trajectory on the show.

On the Front Burner

This episode keeps the challenges of being a female cop in the spotlight when Wentworth saves a man's life from a possible assassin and Lt. Scanlon of Manhattan South, who was in charge of the detail she and Chano were working, tries to cut her out of any of the credit. She is patronizingly dismissed by Scanlon and his officers simply because she's a woman. As he does so often with his officers, Barney tells them to take the high road and not to let it bother them. Once he's behind closed doors he fights for the respect and recognition he feels his men, and in this case, women, deserve.

Priors

At the end of the episode, Harris saves the day by getting Wentworth her proper credit on an arrest through something he writes for the department newsletter. She is so overjoyed and thankful for his help that she throws her arms around him and kisses him on the lips. Today, thankfully, that doesn't mean much. However, this is 1976 and just eight years previous to this show, there was a controversy over "interracial contact" when Petula Clark touched Harry Belafonte's arm in a variety special on NBC. A few months after that, NBC expressed concern about a scripted kiss between Lt. Uhura and Captain Kirk in *Star Trek*. They ordered the crew to shoot the scene two different ways, one with the kiss and one without the kiss. According to actress Nichelle Nichol (in her autobiography *Beyond Uhura*) the actors repeatedly flubbed their lines in the version without the kiss and essentially forced the network's hand to use the episode with the kiss.

This issue of interracial kissing on television was a topic of discussion for a few years in the 1960s and early 1970s. Happily, this *Barney Miller* episode went right to the heart of that issue, it was done matter-of-factly and, as far as I can determine, caused no problems in the media.

Season 2, Episode 19: "Massage Parlor."
Original Airdate: February 19, 1976.
Writer: Tony Sheehan.
Director: Dennis Steinmetz.
Cast of Characters: Hal Linden (Barney), Ron Glass (Harris), Jack Soo (Yemana), Gregory Sierra (Chano), Linda Lavin (Wentworth), Max Gail (Wojo), Abe Vigoda (Fish), Florence Halop (Ms. Mabel Kleiner), Meg Wylie (Mrs. Oppenheimer), Kenneth Tigar (Fletcher), Charles Frank (Lance Peterson), Opal Euard (Mrs. Krause), Janet Ruff (Mrs. Mary Dexter).

The Rundown

The local merchants association complains about a massage parlor in the neighborhood and Barney sends each officer in to see if they get propositioned. Finally, Wentworth volunteers and gets a "Midnight Cowboy" to take the bait. A mild-mannered gentleman gets mugged and tells the officers that the assailant was an old lady.

First Time Offender

Chano doubts that an old lady could have inflicted that kind of punishment on a young man. He thinks it could be a man dressed as a woman. Barney wants them to look into both possibilities. When Barney follows up and asks about the "man dressed as a woman theory," Wojo and Harris tell him they found three possibilities but they're all accounted for. "One of 'em's in Joliet, one of 'em's waiting on trial over at the tombs, and uh, one's in Copenhagen." Back in the dark ages of the 1970s, one had to go to Europe if you wanted to get a sex change operation or, at the very least, get it done discreetly.

Kenneth Tigar plays the mugging victim in this his first *Barney Miller* appearance. Ironically, this is the most boring character he will ever be given on the show. He will rise to *Barney Miller* royalty in Season Three when he portrays (for the first of two times) Stefan Kopechne, a man who believes he is a victim of lycanthropy, in the appropriately entitled "Werewolf." In future episodes he will play a psychic, a man who is being harassed by a ghost, and Jesus Christ himself until he finally returns for a final time as Stefan Kopechne. When Mr. Kopechne returns, he's grappling with a possession by the devil.

Fraud

The officers of the 12th each have a different reason and/or explanation why they feel they didn't get propositioned at the massage parlor.

Chano: I think the girl knew I was a cop. She never got below my shoulders.

Harris: Man, you know, I think what my problem was, was that nobody could believe that I would have to go to a place like that. I just don't look desperate enough!

Wojo: Second the lady touched me, I started to giggle. I'm not even ticklish, can you figure that?

Fish: I couldn't get anyone to do anything to me, for *any* amount of money.

A Developing Situation

Wojo remains a rather unenlightened male in this episode. First of all, he's uncomfortable having Wentworth buy him dinner because he didn't want people to think he was "a kept man." He then exhibits his sexism regarding Wentworth not only wanting to go out on the massage assignment but succeeding where all the others failed. As mentioned, the character of Wojo will slowly develop and evolve over the eight seasons to become a more sensitive, fully human character. Nevertheless, his attitudes towards women in this episode are what we would now consider archaic.

The Usual Suspects

Just as Det. Gardeno (Michael Lembeck) in the Season One episode "Hair" is reminiscent of the popular movie character Frank Serpico, so our male masseuse in "Massage Parlor," Lance Peterson (Charles Frank), bears a striking resemblance to Joe Buck (Jon Voight), in the 1969 film, *Midnight Cowboy*. That film, by the way, remains the only movie with an "X" rating to win the Academy Award for Best Picture.

Racial Unrest

The beauty of the 1970s is that, thanks in large part to Norman Lear's creation of Archie Bunker, racial tensions were brought out into the open for us to examine and discuss. *Barney Miller* did one particularly serious episode about this situation in Season Five called, "The Harris Incident." However, in this particular episode the issue is dealt with in a more subtle and humorous fashion. Harris brings in three old ladies for a lineup to see if Mr. Fletcher can identify his assailant. He's introducing them to Chano and when he gets to the third lady, this exchange occurs:

Harris:	And this is Mrs. Mabel Kleiner. Don't turn your back on Kleiner.
Chano:	(leading her to a seat) Mrs. Kleiner, if you'd be so kind ...
Mrs. Kleiner:	Take your clumsy paws off me ... ya lousy bull!
Chano:	(to Harris) Bull?
Harris:	Uh yeah, I believe that was a term used for police officers sometime around the Civil War.
Mrs. Kleiner:	(to Harris) You want to hear another term from the Civil War?
Harris:	Careful!

By the end of the episode she seems more like just a crotchety old lady from another time rather than a Civil War era racist. As soon as she sits at Nick's desk, she says to Nick, "Hey boy . . . How about some coffee?" Nick replies with, "For you? Sure." Since everyone hated the squad room's coffee, we can safely assume Mrs. Kleiner got what she deserved.

False Identity

When Harris originally brings in the three old-lady suspects they are, in order, Mrs. Mary Dexter, Mrs. Eunice Smith, and Mrs. Mabel Kleiner. However, when Chano tricks the assailant to tip her identity he says, "Your black belt is showing Mrs. Dexter." The only problem is that the Mrs. Dexter to whom he refers was originally introduced to us as Mrs. Eunice Smith. A continuity error such as this was probably understandable considering the famously long hours the *Barney Miller* crew put in shooting each episode. The earlier scene may have been shot at 9 p.m. while the latter might not have been put on tape until 3 a.m. or later.

Season 2, Episode 20:	"The Psychiatrist."
Original Airdate:	February 26, 1976.
Writers:	Tony Sheehan, Danny Arnold, and Chris Hayward (teleplay). Gregory Teifer (story).
Director:	Noam Pitlik.
Cast of Characters:	Jack Soo (Yemana), Gregory Sierra (Chano), Ron Glass (Harris), Max Gail (Wojo), Hal Linden (Barney), Abe Vigoda (Fish), Fred Sadoff (Dr. Esterhazy), Martin Garner (Mr. Frumkus), Neil J. Schwartz (Lawrence Speigelgas), Madison Mason (Joseph Petrano).

The Rundown

Wojo brings in a purse-snatcher who later claims Wojo verbally and physically threatened him. Internal Affairs is called to look into the incident. Mr. Frumpkis is brought in for knocking over newsstands in front of his place of business because he objects to the filth that is being sold. The insurance company raises rates on Fish's life insurance policy.

Two-Timer

In the preceding episode, Mr. Frumpkis was referenced but never seen. He was on the phone at the beginning of the episode complaining, on behalf of the Second Avenue Merchant's Association, about the massage parlor in the neighborhood. In this episode, we actually get to meet Mr. Frumpkis when he's arrested for continuing his campaign to clean up the streets of New York, this time by destroying a newsstand selling pornographic material in front of his business, Frumpkis Fine Foods. Martin Garner plays Frumpkis in the first of an eventual five different *Barney Miller* roles.

Fred Sadoff makes his first *Barney Miller* appearance as a psychiatrist, Dr. Paul Nathan Esterhazy. Sadoff will appear in five more episodes over the remaining run of the show.

To Each His Own

Wojo is accused by a purse-snatcher of coercion, intimidation, and threatening the well-being of a suspect so the department sends Wojo to a psychiatrist for a mental evaluation. The shrink, Dr. Esterhazy, decides that Wojo is unfit for active duty and comes into the 12th Precinct to administer Rorschach tests to all the men in the squad. Naturally, each member sees something different in the little ink blots.

Wojo: Can't tell nothin' from a bunch of dirty spots that look like nothin'.
Chano: Birds and flowers.
Harris: I saw a few countries—France and Spain and Madagascar.
Fish: An enlarged heart.
Nick: An elephant wearing a hat.
Barney: To each his own—that's the name of that test.

In the end, Barney's passionate defense of his men and his common sense expose some of the doctor's own insecurities and phobias and gets his squad a seal of approval.

Unsung Leader

In a series full of eccentric and sometimes hilarious characters, Hal Linden spent the vast majority of his 171 episodes as the straight man for the entire squad room and all the victims and suspects that made their way through the 12th over the years. As is always the case, the straight man's role is a thankless job. The better the straight man, the less he stands out, and the more easily his difficult but ultimately crucial role is overlooked. There's a scene in "The Psychiatrist" where Barney is talking to someone from headquarters about Wojo being put on suspension. It's a simple and easily forgotten scene. Even so, it's a perfect example of Linden's committed connection to his character. There is no artifice, no scene chewing, just a commanding officer fighting for his men. Linden's commitment to the reality of the character made all of those around him shine. Without Linden being believable as the necessary sane voice in the chaos of the room, none of the humor would have hit the mark as solidly as it did, week in and week out.

Specializing in Harassment

Inspector Luger comes in to tell Wojo how proud he is of him for getting such an intimidating reputation. Wojo isn't quite as happy since all it got him was a suspension. Luger tells Wojo, "In time you'll find out that harassment is a skill like anything else."

Now That's Dark!

George Spiro Dibie, the show's Director of Photography, made the conscious decision along with Danny Arnold to make the squad room as visually dirty, dingy, and dull as was possible. In this episode, however, even the pornographic newspapers that Mr. Frumpkis was dumping in the street have covers so dark and dirty that you can barely read what's on the front. It begs the question was that done for the TV audiences so that there was no possibility of showing a controversial image on camera or did the set designers just spray a little too much dulling spray on the newspapers? Only their set dressers know for sure!

Check the Board

Speaking of George Spiro Dibie, if you look closely at the chalkboard where the men sign in, you will see the name Det. G. S. Dibie under the name Det. Shuman in this episode. Shirley Alberti, Danny Arnold's assistant for the first four seasons, told me that it was a common practice for various members of the crew to put their name or those of other crew members on the Detective's sign-in board. Therefore, if you keep a close eye on the board over time you'll see names like Alberti, Sheehan, etc.

The Last Word

The exchange between Inspector Luger and Dr. Esterhazy is one of actor James Gregory's shining comedic moments.

Inspector Luger: (to Dr. Esterhazy) "I want you to know that my men continuously conduct themselves in a legal and orderly manner especially when dealing with the public, most of whom are freaks anyway."

Season 2, Episode 21: "The Kid."
Original Airdate: March 4, 1976.
Writers: Tony Sheehan, Chris Hayward, and Danny Arnold.
Director: Stan Lathan.
Cast of Characters: Hal Linden (Barney), Gregory Sierra (Chano), Jack Soo (Yemana) Max Gail (Wojo), Arny Freeman (Victor Newell), Charles Murphy (Eugene Woolen), Angelina Estrada (Mrs. Trujillo), Jose Flores (Claudio Trujillo).

The Rundown

Fish brings in a young pickpocket who tried to pinch his wallet on the subway. The waiting period is over and Mr. Murphy returns to collect the $3,500 he found on the streets and turned in last month. Chano and Wojo bring in a subject whose hearing loss prompted him to hold up a store for a pair of hearing aids.

Right to Remain Silent

Wojo is trying to read Mr. Newell (Arny Freeman) his Miranda rights. Unfortunately, Mr. Newell is so hard of hearing that he can't quite grasp what Wojo is trying to tell him. In frustration, Wojo just keeps yelling louder and louder to try to penetrate Mr. Newell's hearing loss. Unfortunately, he's driving the other guys crazy until Barney suggests Wojo use the evidence (the stolen hearing aid) to help him communicate with the suspect.

Hopalong Miller

In the last two episodes of Season Two, Barney is shown with a big cast on his right foot. The subject of his broken foot is cause for curiosity on Wojo's part and some unintentional humor on Fish's part as he asks Barney if the cast is making his foot itch? It didn't until Fish mentioned it.

Barney's broken foot is a minor plot line that adds to the realism of the show. The injury was indeed real. Hal Linden had actually broken his heel bone playing tennis and so the writers were forced to incorporate it into the story.

Subtle Touch of Humanity

Barney Miller seemed to balance the goodness and generosity of humanity with the selfish, mean-spirited leanings of the species as well. Some shows through the years have found it difficult showing the kinder side of our nature without getting a bit sentimental and heavy-handed in promoting positive lessons. *Barney Miller* was always funny first and then maybe, just maybe, they'd sneak in a valuable lesson. In this episode we witness Mr. Woolen's natural desire to get his money before someone else claims it. When he finally does get it, Barney gently cajoles him into considering giving some of his money to Mr. Newell so he can purchase a pair of much needed hearing aids. Mr. Woolen ends up getting such a rush of joy from giving money to someone who's in need that he then wants to do it again.

As the Solomon of Greenwich Village, there are countless examples of Barney mediating disputes but there are also those times when Barney uses his gentle talents of persuasion to move someone to "do the right thing." This is one of those times. In this case, it wasn't difficult as Mr. Woolen was a good guy to start.

The Last Word

Nick: Mr. Woolen, my grandfather used to say to me, "The anticipation of one's dreams is greater than the realization of one's ambitions . . . unless one blows it altogether."

Season 2, Episode 22: "The Mole."
Original Airdate: March 18, 1976.
Writers: Reinhold Weege, Chris Hayward, and Danny Arnold.
Director: Mark Warren.
Cast of Characters: Jack Soo (Yemana), Ron Glass (Harris), Gregory Sierra (Chano), Hal Linda (Barney), Max Gail

(Wojo), Abe Vigoda (Fish), Dean Santoro (Philip Schroeder), Ron Carey (Angelo Molinari a.k.a. The Mole), Severn Darden (Randolph Cook), Richard Ramos (Dr. Alvin Crain).

The Rundown

A doctor and an insurance salesman get in an altercation over premiums. Wojo and Harris get called out on a jewelry store heist. Fish is stressed out about his need for an operation to alleviate his hemorrhoid problem. Wojo has to decide whether or not to take the sergeant's exam for the third time. Finally, "a bum," who's looking for a nice place to sleep comes in claiming vagrancy.

Missing Person

This is the last episode of Season Two and is therefore the last appearance of Gregory Sierra in the role of Sgt. Chano Amenguale. Sierra would eventually show up in his own Danny Arnold sitcom called *A.E.S. Hudson Street* about an Emergency Services clinic in a poor NYC neighborhood. Unfortunately, the show, which was described by some as "*Barney Miller* in a hospital," failed to catch on and lasted only five episodes. Of the eleven actors/actresses who appeared in more than one episode of *A.E.S. Hudson Street*, nine of them appeared, at least once, on *Barney Miller*.

Long List of Priors

Severn Darden who plays Randolph "Randy" Cook in this episode was famous for being one of the original members of The Compass Players and then Second City in Chicago. Born to wealth and position in New Orleans, he became known for his eccentric behavior (wearing formal clothes with sneakers) and his wildly inspired improvisational comedy. One of his most heralded performances is in the film, *The President's Analyst*, a satirical film comedy written and directed by *Barney Miller* co-creator, Ted Flicker.

Fish's Medical History

Fish has never had an operation. In fact, he's never even had his tonsils out. He not only needs a hemorrhoid operation but this episode clearly reveals that he also moves his lips when he reads.

Animal Control

This episode marks the first appearance of Ron Carey as jewelry store thief Angelo Molinari. The thief, known professionally as "The Mole," leads the officers on a merry chase through the sewers of New York. When they bring in the suspect, their smell clears the room of all the detectives.

Mr. Molinari later claims he hurt his leg when he slipped over an alligator in the sewer. According to "The Mole," "Jewish kids bring them back from Miami and then flush 'em down the toilets."

It should be noted that the future Carl Levitt portrays an Italian American in this first *Barney Miller* appearance. As the character wrestles with himself over his line of work and the lack of a future in it, his gesticulations and attitude mark him as the typical New York Italian on TV and in the movies in the 1970s. Ron Carey, whose real name was Ronald Joseph Cicenia, was, in fact, a nice Italian boy from New Jersey.

Clothes Horse

After chasing "The Mole" through the sewers, Harris submits a requisition form to the Finance Office to get paid for his ruined clothing ensemble. Barney reads his list, "One custom tailored sport jacket, $165; one pair custom tailored slacks, $55; one custom tailored shirt, $30 for a total of $250."

Harris remarks, "Yeah, I'm going to eat the tie and the socks."

This all begs the question, where did Harris get the money to wear such expensive outfits as a member of the NYPD in 1976? It's no wonder Lt. Scanlon of Internal Affairs was always snooping around the 12th Precinct.

Not in Front of Fish. Please!

Chano and Nick bring in two gentlemen who are charging each other with assault. It's the old story—an insurance agent and a doctor walk into a bar and come to blows over malpractice insurance. Unfortunately, their continued fighting inside the squad room doesn't help quell Fish's anxiety over his upcoming operation.

Dr. Crain: He spit an olive in my face.
Mr. Schroeder: I didn't spit. I coughed.
Dr. Crain: Listen to that. As if a trained physician can't tell the difference between a spit and a cough.

Mr. Schroeder:	Yeah, well all that training doesn't seem to screen out the hacks and butchers that pass themselves off as doctors.
Fish:	Oh, God!

Who's in Charge?

Noam Pitlik is credited with directing more than 100 episodes of *Barney Miller*, far more than any other individual. However, Max Gail and Hal Linden remember that Danny Arnold often directed when he was around whether he was credited or not. As the years went by, the collaborators in front of, and behind, the cameras had worked together so long that they didn't need a lot of direction.

The director credited for this episode is Mark Warren who was an African American director best known for the feature film *Come Back, Charlestown Blue* (1972) and directing multiple episodes of *Rowan & Martin's Laugh In* (1969–1972) and *What's Happening!!* (1976–1979). However, there's a subtle error in a scene where Nick answers the phone. He tells the person calling that "Yeah, he's here." He then presses the button for hold so Fish can pick it up but says, "Okay" into the receiver after he's put the call on hold.

Hero Worship

In this episode, Wojo notes a nice turn that Barney does very matter-of-factly for a bum and later praises him for it. Barney, the humble guy he is thanks him and then makes a little joke that Wojo doesn't immediately recognize as a joke. It's an interesting little scene in that it doesn't necessarily serve a purpose in this episode but it does continue to lay the foundation of Wojo's feelings toward Barney as a father figure.

The Last Word

Chano asks Nick how much money he would have if he never bet the horses? Nick's guess is five or six thousand. "If I'd never bet a loser, I'd have about $3 million. Tough choice, ain't it?"

Third Season

We were introduced to Steve Landesberg's Sgt. Arthur Dietrich in Season Two but the character starts to become a more familiar face in Season Three although he's still not considered a regular member of the cast as witnessed by the fact that he is not included in the opening credits. In those episodes where he's featured, his name shows up in the closing credits along with those of the other guest stars in that particular episode.

This season will introduce us to Jilly Papalardo and her friend, Victor Kreutzer. They live at a group home for orphaned children. Jilly attaches herself to Fish and she and her story will provide the producers with the basis for the *Fish* spinoff in the coming year.

The show really hit its stride in Season Three and includes two of the most memorable episodes in the history of the program: "Werewolf" (S. 3/Ep. 6) and "Hash" (S. 3/Ep. 11).

Season 3, Episode 1:	"Evacuation."
Original Airdate:	September 23, 1976.
Writers:	Danny Arnold (teleplay). Chris Hayward and Danny Arnold (story).
Director:	Noam Pitlik.
Cast of Characters:	Hal Linden (Barney), Ron Glass (Harris), Abe Vigoda (Fish), Max Gail (Wojo), Jack Soo (Yemana), Kenneth Mars (Officer Callahan), Paul Lichtman (Beckman), Joe Petrullo (Krevey), Denise Miller (Jilly Papalardo), James Gregory (Inspector Frank Luger).

The Rundown

Heavy rains are hitting the city as Hurricane Dottie moves up the Eastern seaboard. Wojo is Public Information Officer for the week and is alarmed when he learns that there is no plan in place to evacuate the population of NYC in case of an emergency. His concern starts a chain of gossip leading to panic within the force. It's basically a modern-day retelling of "Henny Penny and the Falling Sky." The B story involves a young woman who is brought in after trying to pawn some stolen goods at a local pawnshop.

Missing Person

Harris tells Barney at the beginning of the episode that Dietrich is in court. In fact, he doesn't show up until episode four of this third season and ultimately appears in only nine of the third season's total of twenty-two episodes.

Never Quite Made It

According to Miles B. Lawrence of the National Hurricane Center in an April 1977 abstract, "Dottie began spectacularly and ended ignominiously." That's another way of saying the fourth storm of the 1976 tropical storm/hurricane season never officially made it to "Hurricane" status. It was, in the end, Tropical Storm Dottie and was active from August 17–21, 1976.

First Time Offender

This episode introduces us to Jilly Papalardo (Denise Miller), a juvenile delinquent who lives in a group home. Fish finds the child distasteful and the idea of a group home, "disgusting." When Harris explains to Barney that there are people who the city pays to live with the kids, Fish remarks, "Some people will do anything for money."

One and Only

This episode marks the only appearance of Kenneth Mars, a great comedic character actor, best known for his role as Franz Liebkind in Mel Brooks's classic film, *The Producers*. He worked in dozens of TV shows and films for over forty years and was also a prolific voice actor in numerous cartoons. I first saw Kenneth Mars in the 1972 Peter Bogdanovich screwball comedy, *What's Up Doc?*, in which he was brilliantly funny as Hugh Simon, an egotistical geology professor. It's curious that Danny Arnold didn't tap Mars more than once for *Barney Miller*. He would have been a great resource for the type of character-driven comedy at which Arnold excelled.

We are also introduced to a uniformed officer of the 12th named Krevey in this episode, played by actor Joe Petrullo. We never see Krevey again following this episode. He must have been transferred.

Human Nature and the Human Condition

This is a perfect example of the comedy that appealed to Danny Arnold. In "Evacuation," he provides a simple insight into human nature—how a rumor can get blown out of proportion from the tiny bit of information that started it—and turns it into hilarious and insightful circumstances. As the old saying goes, "It's funny because it's true!"

It's also one of the first episodes to demonstrate the development of Wojo's character from the gum-chomping, narrow-minded rookie of the first two seasons into the more passionate, curious, and relentless Wojo who evolves over the run of the series. Wojo is not trying to set off a panic with his questions about an evacuation plan. He's genuinely concerned for his city. He's just trying to do his job as best he can.

Did They Reopen?

Callahan calls Wojo looking for another copy of the gray book manual, *Procedures in the Event of Civil Disasters*. Wojo tells him he doesn't have another copy. He suggests Callahan try either Manhattan South or the 33rd Precinct. There's only one problem, the city closed the 33rd Precinct, remember? Dietrich came to the 12th when the 33rd was shut down.

> **Barney:** Wojo, Wojo, you're going to have to learn to live with one irrevocable fact and that is, that if anything happens, there is no way to get 11 million people out of this city in a hurry.
> **Wojo:** Then what are we gonna do?
> **Barney:** We just have to hope that mankind never gets to that point in their relationships where they'll allow something to happen. And we have to do everything we can to prevent it.
> **Wojo:** Okay. (pause) What'll we do?
> **Barney:** Wojo, you're making me crazy. (Freeze frame—cue music).

Annoying or not, Wojo has a point and through all of the humor and sarcasm and irreverence, so did Danny Arnold. There was always a point. Oh, and by the way, we still haven't figured out what to do.

Season 3, Episode 2:	"Quarantine: Part One."
Original Airdate:	September 30, 1976.
Writer:	Tony Sheehan.
Director:	Lee Bernhardi.
Cast of Characters:	Jack Soo (Yemana), Ron Glass (Harris), Abe Vigoda (Fish), Hal Linden (Barney), Max Gail (Wojo), Jack DeLeon (Marty Morrison), Ray Stewart (Darryl Driscoll), Paula Shaw (Paula Capshaw), Arthur Peterson (Dr. Freedman), David Darlow (Philip Dupree), James Gregory (Inspector Frank Luger).

The Rundown

Wojo brings a guy in for trying to rip off a warehouse by the river. When the suspect passes out, a doctor quarantines the 12th Precinct until he can confirm whether the man has chicken pox or smallpox. Guests for the overnight stay include Marty (Jack DeLeon) and Mr. Driscoll (Ray Stewart), who came in hoping to use Barney as a reference for Marty's petition to leave the state while still on parole so they can move to California where they'll be more readily accepted; Paula Capshaw (Paula Shaw), a working woman of the streets who was being processed when the infected man was brought in; and Inspector Luger (James Gregory), who ignored the "Quarantine" sign on the door, walked into the squad room and got stuck for the night.

Military Protocol

Arthur Peterson makes his one and only *Barney Miller* appearance as Dr. Freedman. A year later, he would be a regular cast member on the ABC series *Soap*. He played Jessica Tate's and Mary Campbell's father, a senile World War II veteran who was referred to by almost all who knew him as "The Major."

Homophobia, Part One

Inspector Luger displays the homophobia in this episode we normally relate to Wojo. In this episode, however, while Wojo is still uncomfortable around Marty and Mr. Driscoll, he's too busy alarming the troops about the potential dangers of smallpox so Luger picks up his mantle of homophobic paranoia. It must be understood that while the basic idea put forth in this episode and others is that homosexuality is an "unnatural" behavior, the show is, after all, almost fifty years old. In 1976, those antiquated ideas and explanations still ruled the conversation about such things. What's more striking is that there is throughout the *Barney Miller* timeline, particularly from Barney himself, a level of respect for these individuals that was rarely shown in films or on network television at the time.

Too Much Information

As the series progressed, Wojo developed an insatiable curiosity. It often led to trouble or panic as it did in the previous episode, "Evacuation." In "Quarantine: Part One," Wojo finds a dictionary and despite Barney's attempts to prevent him from reading the definition of smallpox aloud, he plunges right in, reading: "an acute, highly contagious, sometimes fatal, disease caused by a virus and characterized by an inflammatory fever and the eruption of deep-seated pustules that leave permanent scars."

Barney: (sardonically) Thank you.
Wojo: Wait 'til you hear what pustules are . . .
Barney: That won't be necessary.

Season 3, Episode 3: "Quarantine: Part Two."
Original Airdate: October 7, 1976.
Writers: Tony Sheehan and Danny Arnold.
Director: Noam Pitlik.
Cast of Characters: Jack Soo (Yemana), Max Gail (Wojo), Ron Glass (Harris), Hal Linden (Barney), Abe Vigoda (Fish), Ron Carey (Officer Carl Levitt), Jack DeLeon (Marty Morrison), James Gregory (Inspector Frank Luger), Paula Shaw (Paula Capshaw), Ray Stewart (Darryl Driscoll).

The Rundown

Still under quarantine, the men of the 12th and their guests spend a hot, uncomfortable but enlightening night in the squad room together. Luger learns a little about acceptance, or at least tolerance, and the detectives take a peek into the inner recesses of Sgt. Harris's subconscious.

Constructive Suggestion

At the end of part one, Barney surveys the gloomy group and encourages them that while they're all stuck there, to try to do something constructive with their time instead of just moping. Mr. Driscoll takes the suggestion and Part II opens as he has cleaned all the coffee mugs and made a fresh pot of coffee about which Wojo declares, "this coffee ain't bad." When Nick wonders why the cups look different, Mr. Driscoll says he scrubbed off all the mold and mildew. Nick admits, "I thought it was a pattern."

Homophobia, Part Two

Never one to disappoint, Wojo displays his paranoia when handing out cot assignments and places Marty on one side of the room and Mr. Driscoll on the other side. When voices rise, Barney intercedes and says in that understanding way of Barney's, "Wojo, let them be as comfortable as they can, wherever they can. They're our guests."

Introducing Carl Levitt

This episode marks the debut of the tenacious Officer Carl Levitt. At the end of Season Two, character actor and former stand-up comedian Ron Carey played Angelo "The Mole" Molinari, a jewelry store thief who led Harris and Wojo on a not-so-merry chase through the NYC sewer system. In "Quarantine, Part Two," Carey returns to the set as Carl Levitt, a uniformed officer from downstairs. He will soon be seen delivering the mail, manpower reports, and bail tickets to the squad room. He essentially fills the role once held by Officer Kogan (Milt Kogan). In the seasons to come he will move up the ladder and fill in for sick or absent detectives in his ever-passionate quest to achieve the rank of detective. As far as he can tell, the number one reason he hasn't yet made detective is because he's too short.

As Levitt returns downstairs, he interacts briefly with Mr. Driscoll. After Driscoll walks away, Levitt asks Marty how tall Driscoll is. Marty, in his singularly effeminate way, responds, "Six foot three and three quarters." Levitt looks knowingly at Harris and says, "See, when you're that tall they overlook anything!"

A Million Ways to Die

Wojo in his panic starts contemplating the fragility of life.

Nick says, "I remember what my great grandfather said right before he died: 'Although one may conspire to delay the moment of one's death . . .'" and then stops. Impatiently waiting for the rest of the statement, Wojo asks Nick what he said. Nick informs him, "That's as far as he got."

Luger says he doesn't care how he goes as long as he's not rotting away in some hospital hooked up to a machine. He graphically displays that if need be, he'll blow his brains out before being put on life support.

Harris Rants

As Sgt. Harris sleeps, some of his subconscious pet peeves boil up to the surface. Among his fevered rants are:

"Get out of that bathroom, man"

"Rotten coffee. Racin' forms and la-zzyyyy!!"

"Human relations, plffft. Lock all them crazy mothers up! Hey, Barney, don't give me none of that old psychology, man. Compassionate turkey!"

"Royalties, stocks, bonds, big gold bars, oh God, I want to *be* somebody!!!"

The Last Word

The episode's "Lady of the Evening," Miss Capshaw, thanks all for their consideration and as she leaves says, "Never have I spent so much time with so many for so little."

No Way Around It

This two-part episode is one of the more problematic scripts of the series when measured against today's standards of sexism and homophobia. There are remarks about men and women that would not be accepted by audiences in 2021 America. It may make some cringe but don't lose sight of the forest for the trees. Those were the prevailing attitudes at that point in history. In many ways the show was socially progressive, in other ways not so much. Thankfully, things have improved for the better in these subject areas and how they're depicted on TV.

Season 3, Episode 4:	"Bus Stop."
Original Airdate:	October 14, 1976.
Writers:	Tony Sheehan, Danny Arnold, Reinhold Weege, and Jerry Ross (teleplay). Reinhold Weege, Chris Hayward, and Danny Arnold (story).
Director:	Noam Pitlik.
Cast of Characters:	Jack Soo (Yemana), Steve Landesberg (Det. Sgt. Arthur Dietrich), Ron Glass (Harris), Hal Linden (Barney), Max Gail (Wojo), Candice Azzara (Miss Lambert), Philip Bruns (Harry Cranston), Joe George (Mr. Strand, the bus driver), Sal Viscuso (Brenner), Florence Halop (Mrs. Pierce), Howard Honig (Mr. Quentin).

The Rundown

The victims and perpetrator of a hijacked bus bring a variety of complaints, mysteries, and stories into the 12th. Dietrich is trying to find his place within the squad without ruffling any feathers. Fish struggles with some old ailments and Wojo fails the sergeant's exam again.

Do You Know the Way to the 12th?

The episode opens with Nick speaking on the phone to a woman telling her, "We're right around the corner from McDougall Alley. You'll recognize it by the blue and white cars out front. And the expired meters. And no tickets on the windshield." In terms of Greenwich Village geography that means the 12th Precinct is located somewhere in the two blocks bordered on the west by Sixth Avenue, the east by Fifth Avenue, the North by West Eighth Street and to the south by Waverly Place and Washington Square North.

The Outsider

This is the first time we've seen Sgt. Dietrich since he was introduced in "Fish" (S. 2/ Ep. 12). He's very conscious of his outsider status and he's also a little odd. When he shows concern for Barney holding his chest, he pulls a pamphlet out of his briefcase that's titled, *Are You Courting a Coronary?* He tells Barney, "That's good reading."

First Offender

Character actor Sal Viscuso makes his first of four *Barney Miller* appearances in "Bus Stop." The following fall of 1977 Viscuso won the recurring role of Father Timothy Flotsky on the ABC comedy *Soap* (1977-1981). Since Father Tim didn't show up in every episode of *Soap*, Viscuso was able to occasionally take assignments on other hit shows like *M*A*S*H*, *Fantasy Island* (1977-1984), and *Barney Miller*.

Known Associates

Candice Azzara and Sal Viscuso shared a lot of screen time in the late 1970s and early 1980s. These two wonderful character actors worked together on television in *Barney Miller*, *Soap*, *The Montefuscos* (1975), and on the feature films *The World's Greatest Lover* (1977) and *Fatso* (1980). There's also the additional *Barney Miller* connection through Ron Carey who also worked with Azzara and Viscuso in *The Montefuscos* and *Fatso*. All three actors were friends off camera. To this day, Azzara and Viscuso speak lovingly of their departed friend, Ron Carey.

Father Figure

As the commanding officer, Barney always did whatever he could to support and encourage his men. However, there was something special between Wojo and Barney, the father-son dynamic that didn't exist in Barney's other inter-office relationships. In "Bus Stop," Barney must convince Wojo to continue taking and trying to pass the sergeant's exam. Wojo infers he's going to just give up and be the best Detective 3rd Grade there is. It should be noted, however, that in the season-ending episode the previous March, Wojo is trying to decide whether to take the sergeant's exam again for a third time. Yet in this fourth episode of the third season, Wojo claims he has failed the exam four times. That means he would have had to take two exams in a relatively short period of time. Whatever the case, Max Gail is brilliantly effective in his scene in Barney's office as he is practically in tears when Harris interrupts their conversation to call Barney out into the squad room. By this time, Gail was really starting to inhabit Wojo's character and it made his performances far more compelling and convincing.

Barney makes an impassioned plea to the victims of the bus hijacking to tell them that without their help in pressing charges, the justice system is toothless. If nothing else, Barney's passion inspires Wojo to keep on trying for that sergeant's badge.

When Barney sends Wojo to the hospital to get some statements from the bus-jacking accident victims Wojo turns to him and says, "Hey Barn, I like your style." Barney smiles and replies, "I never had it as a third grade."

Donut Lovers and Proud of It

The last scene of this episode has Fish and Nick eating a couple of donuts from a box on Nick's desk. Dietrich is telling them how bad doughnuts are for them as he tries to explain the risks of fat and cholesterol. The two veteran cops stare blankly at Dietrich as they just keeping chomping away at their donuts without any fear of repercussions.

This was a perfect example of *Barney Miller* humor. Both Abe Vigoda and Jack Soo were masters of the deadpan. Without saying a word, they create a hilarious scene that speaks volumes.

The Last Word

Barney quotes Shakespeare near the very end of the episode saying, "Conscience doth make cowards of us all." This will not be the last time Captain

Miller will quote the immortal bard. This particular quote comes from *Hamlet*, act 3, scene 1.

Season 3, Episode 5: "The Election."
Original Airdate: October 21, 1976.
Writer: Tom Reeder.
Director: Lee Bernhardi.
Cast of Characters: Jack Soo (Yemana), Hal Linden (Barney), Max Gail (Wojo), Steve Landesberg (Det. Sgt. Arthur Dietrich), Ron Glass (Harris), Brett Somers (Edna Relke), Richard Venture (Charles Relke), Gilbert Green (Crippen), James Gregory (Inspector Luger).

The Rundown

Wojo comes in energized with the enthusiasm of Election Day. Harris brings in a well-dressed, seemingly affluent gentleman for shoplifting women's underwear at Siegel's Department Store. A husband locks his wife in the bathroom in an attempt to prevent her from voting.

Nearest of Kin

With the exception of Fish and Barney, the men of the 12th were notoriously detached from emotional entanglements. We rarely hear the men talk of relatives or serious girlfriends but in this episode Nick reveals, "my uncle has a schmatta business in Honolulu." The revelation of actual family nearly overshadows Nick's use of the Yiddish word, schmatta, which means a business that sells low quality goods or junk.

Repeat Offender

The lovely Brett Somers makes her second and last appearance in this episode as Edna Relke, a woman locked in her bathroom by her husband to prevent her from voting Republican. Her husband is upset because he reads, he follows the issues and so, he votes Democratic. His wife, on the other hand, is going to vote Republican just to cancel out his vote! When it comes right down to it, she really has no idea how she should vote and ends up badgering just about everyone in the squad room, asking them to tell her for whom she should vote.

Curious and Curiouser

Wojo is very curious to know who everyone is voting for but Barney has to remind him the privacy of the ballot box is sacred. Wojo would have loved the era of social media. Not only do you know who everyone supports politically but you get dozens of photos of their food preferences too!

Nick's Criminal Coffee

Nick asks Mrs. Relke if she would like some more coffee to which she replies, "I can't drink coffee. Do you have any more of this?" holding up a cup of Nick's coffee that someone had originally given her.

Tallying the Trivia

The election discussed in this episode is the 1976 Presidential election between former Georgia Governor Jimmy Carter and Incumbent Republican President Gerald Ford. Carter won the popular vote by 1.7 million votes and took the election with 297 electoral votes to 240. Ford served as President for two and a half years although he had never been elected to the office. He was Richard Nixon's second Vice President and ascended to the Presidency following Nixon's resignation on August 9, 1974.

You can also hear the announcer at one point say, "We'll be going back to Harry Reasoner." *Barney Miller* was an ABC network show and Harry Reasoner was, at the time, an ABC News employee.

History Lesson

Luger: We haven't had a candidate like Jake Scofield since the days of a, heh, did you ever hear of Tammany Hall?
Wojo: Yeah, they were a bunch of crooks.
Luger: Where did you get that?
Wojo: I learned it in school.
Luger: School. Blech! Consider the source!

The Last Word

It's not often I agree with Inspector Luger about anything but this episode proved that there's a first time for everything.

Barney: Well, Inspector, the public must be served.
Luger: Yeah. Damn shame, ain't it.

Season 3, Episode 6: "Werewolf."
Original Airdate: October 28, 1976.
Writers: Tony Sheehan, Reinhold Weege, Danny Arnold, and Seymour Blicker (teleplay). Seymour Blicker and Tony Sheehan (story).
Director: Noam Pitlik.
Cast of Characters: Jack Soo (Yemana), Abe Vigoda (Fish), Max Gail (Wojo), Ron Glass (Harris), Hal Linden (Barney), Kenneth Tigar (Stefan Kopechne), Janet MacLachlan (Miss Jackson), Queenie Smith (Mrs. Fuller), Jon Lormer (Mr. Fuller).

The Rundown

The Swine Flu has wiped out half the plainclothes officers in the city, leaving the detectives tired and edgy. The city sends a nurse from the Board of Health to administer Swine Flu vaccination shots to the squad. We meet an elderly couple on vacation that gets robbed by their cab driver and the squad is introduced to Mr. Stefan Kopechne. He's a nice enough guy but it just so happens he's a werewolf.

A Cooperative Psychopath

Vital stats: Stefan Kopechne (Ken Tigar), shipping clerk, b. September 13, 1943 (full moon). Stefan Kopechne will return in Season Eight, Episode Four, "Possession," in which Mr. Kopechne comes in possessed by a demon. In "Werewolf," Mr. Kopechne is convinced that he's under a Romanian curse handed down by his great-grandfather who came from the Carpathian Mountains. He calls the station alerting them to stop him. Unfortunately, like Larry Talbot (Lon Chaney Jr./*The Wolf Man*, 1941), he had trouble getting anyone to believe him.

A Literate Captain

Wojo is starting to get a little spooked by Mr. Kopechne and his claims of being a werewolf. He looks to Barney for assurance that Kopechne is just plain nuts but instead, Barney drops some Shakespeare on him when he smiles and says, "More things in heaven and earth, Wojo." The full quote is "There are more things in heaven and earth, Horatio, than are dreamt of in your philosophy." It comes from Hamlet (act 1, scene 5, lines 167–68), Hamlet to Horatio.

This is Barney's second quote from Shakespeare in a span of three episodes.

Runner Up

This is probably the second most famous episode in the series behind the "Hash" episode later on in this same season. Tigar's howls and Jack Soo's responses to those howls are legendary. Danny Arnold was obviously impressed with Tigar. This was his second *Barney Miller* guest shot and he would be invited back four more times for a total of six appearances.

Nick's Favorite TV Detective

Once again, Nick references Karl Malden and his American Express Traveler's Cheques commercials that were widely run on network TV at the time. The first three seasons that *Barney Miller* was on the air, Karl Malden was starring as Detective Mike Stone in *The Streets of San Francisco*. Not only was *Streets of San Francisco* also an ABC show but it played on the same night, Thursday, directly after *Barney Miller* on most network stations around the country.

An Old Cowhand

Jon Lormer makes his one and only *Barney Miller* appearance as Mr. Fuller. Lormer enjoyed a busy TV career. He was often cast in Western dramas such as *Bonanza*, *Gunsmoke*, and *The Big Valley* (1965–1969). Outside of horse operas he also made a dozen appearances on *Perry Mason* almost always as a coroner or autopsy surgeon.

Grandpa Strikes Again

The men are exhausted from all the overtime and to make matters worse they run out of coffee. Wojo wonders how they're going to stay awake without any coffee. Nick says, "My grandfather told me an old Oriental trick for staying awake if you had to. You convince yourself that if you fall asleep, you die. Thinking about it keeps you awake." Harris wonders about the natural extension of that practice. What happens then if you want to sleep and can't because you're filled with anxiety thinking about death? Nick's guess is, "I think that's what opium dens are for."

Achilles' Heel

Mr. Kopechne tells Barney that the moon drives him crazy. Barney tells him that everyone has something that affects him or her in a strange way. For Barney, it's the accordion.

From the Werewolf's Mouth

The first time I met Ken Tigar was in September of 2011 and I naturally asked him about *Barney* and specifically about the role that he's probably best remembered for by fans of the show, Stefan Kopechne, the man who sincerely believes he's a werewolf. Here are some of the insights and memories of that episode from Tigar himself:

> That was the second one that I did. They liked me and I got a phone call and they offered the werewolf role to me. I didn't have to audition. How they got me from being beaten up by a little old lady [Tigar's first Barney Miller role, "Massage Parlor, S. 2/Ep. 19] to the werewolf, I don't know.
>
> Danny Arnold . . . was one of the only geniuses I ever met out in LA. He was a great man. And he was so creative . . . and he was a real control freak to a great extent. I mean he and Hal Linden were fighting about the character of Barney into year seven. I mean Hal would do things and Danny would say, "What are you doing?" He'd say, "Well, this is the way he'd do it." And Danny would say, "Barney would never do something like that!"
>
> When I got there to do "The Werewolf," they had only finished writing the first half of the script . . . so we sat around the table and read the first half of the script. Now, if you go back and look at that film, I'm not in the first half of the script. But they told me what they had in mind . . . they weren't going to do any makeup but they wanted me to do the transformation into the werewolf. It was not that long after Ionesco's play *Rhinoceros* had appeared. They said, "You know, it's like what Zero Mostel did in *Rhinoceros* where he turns into a rhinoceros on stage but there's no makeup." I thought, "Oh God, what do I do now?" I learned in Children's theater way back when I was a teenager, one of my very first big roles, God, I must have been about fourteen, was playing the Cowardly Lion from *The Wizard of Oz* and you know, it's big, it's big acting. It's acting for kids and so in a way, I was able

to take some of that and, you know, make faces for the camera. That's basically what it is.

The Last Word

Nick: He really is a werewolf, Barn. Look, he's got hair growing out of his face!
Barney: That's a beard! Haven't ever seen one?
Nick: Not in my family.

Season 3, Episode 7: "The Recluse."
Original Airdate: November 11, 1976.
Writers: Reinhold Weege and Danny Arnold (teleplay). Chris Hayward and Reinhold Weege (story).
Director: Bruce Bilson.
Cast of Characters: Jack Soo (Yemana), Ron Glass (Harris), Hal Linden (Barney), Max Gail (Wojo), Abe Vigoda (Fish), Florence Stanley (Bernice Fish), Ivor Francis (Mr. Unger), Arnold Soboloff (Graham Roberts), John Cassisi (Victor Kreutzer), Denise Miller (Jilly Papalardo).

The Rundown

Wojo brings in a man for disturbing the peace. He was kneeling in traffic on Hudson Street predicting the end of the world. Wojo and Harris get sent to pick up a man who refuses to serve jury duty and has barricaded himself in his home. Fish is dealing with the pre-retirement blues, and Jilly Pappalardo returns with a friend.

Child Services

Jilly Pappalardo (Denise Miller) wants a loan from Mr. Fish. The group home didn't work out so she's back in Children's Center. She and her friend, Victor Kreutzer (John Cassisi), want to go west and start a whole new life.

Fish's immediate reaction is to ask, "What did he do?" Victor yells, "I didn't do nothing! I just came in with her. Ask the colored guy."

Harris and Wojo are talking to Nick around his desk. Nick answers Victor, saying, "I wasn't paying attention." Victor says, "Not you, him" (pointing to Harris). Nick says, "He's black. I'm colored. Everybody else is blank."

Sign of the Times

Mr. Roberts (Arnold Soboloff) is desperately trying to inform people that the world is coming to an end at 5:30 p.m. that evening. He's treated as a psych case and sent to Bellevue. In 1976 you were clearly crazy if you were predicting the immediate end of life on earth. Since that time, if we locked up every person or group, religious or otherwise, who has predicted the imminent end of days there might be more people locked up than there would be those who were free.

This was Arnold Soboloff's second and last appearance on *Barney Miller*. He also appeared as Lenny the Confessor in "Grand Hotel" (S. 2/Ep. 7). Soboloff was a busy New York stage actor who found work on television periodically throughout the 1960s and 1970s, including a non-credited guest spot on Nat Hiken's *Car 54, Where Are You*. He also appeared in two Mel Brooks's movies and the only feature film Anne Bancroft directed, *Fatso* (1980). We may have seen more of him in the *Barney Miller* universe had he not dropped dead of a heart attack at the young age of forty-eight in 1979 after having just completed a stage performance on Broadway.

Jews Love Chinese Food

Fish tells Bernice he doesn't like Japanese restaurants because the food's raw and you have to sit like an Indian. He doesn't like Mexican food either. He asks Nick to suggest a good Chinese restaurant to which Nick offers, "Yamamoto's."

This is a rare example of Nick reacting negatively to a stereotypical comment about the Japanese and exacting a little revenge. The name Yamamoto is quite clearly Japanese, not Chinese. As a detective, you would think Fish would know that.

The further joke is that Jack Soo had changed his name after the war so he could pass as Chinese instead of Japanese. It's no accident that his character on the show was Japanese. It was a way for Soo to reassert his pride in his ancestry.

Are We Still at War?

Mr. Unger (Ivor Francis) hasn't left his apartment in thirty-five years. He hasn't heard a thing since Pearl Harbor. When he sees Nick he says, "I just assumed we won," to which Nick replies, "We did."

Laying the Ground Work

When Bernice comes to pick up Fish for dinner, she learns of the existence of Jilly and Victor. She's heartbroken that the system has discarded them. She begs Fish to let them come to dinner with them. In just a few months, Phil and Bernice Fish will be the host parents in a group home that will house Jilly and Victor among others in Abe Vigoda's spinoff series, *Fish*.

Progress

Nick: Care for some coffee, Mr. Unger?
Unger: Huh? Coffee? Oh! I'd almost forgot it existed. I ran out in 1944.
Nick: Then you're in for a treat.
Unger: It's funny. I don't remember it tasting like this.
Nick: Progress, Mr. Unger.

Season 3, Episode 8: "Noninvolvement."
Original Airdate: November 18, 1976.
Writers: Reinhold Weege (teleplay). Chris Hayward, Danny Arnold, and Reinhold Weege (story).
Director: Bruce Bilson.
Cast of Characters: Hal Linden (Barney), Jack Soo (Yemana), Abe Vigoda (Fish), Ron Glass (Harris), Alex Henteloff (Arnold Ripner), Ron Feinberg (Lyle W. Farber), Oliver Clark (Charles Yusick), Lucille Meredith (Mrs. Hanson), June Gable (Det. Maria Battista), Mike Kellin (Al Mitchell).

The Rundown

Fish is outraged by the investments being made by the Police Pension Fund. He has one year until retirement and his anxiety is building over his financial future. There's also a new female detective in the 12th, Detective 3rd Grade Maria Battista. The main storyline has to do with Wojo's arrest of a man who took no action as he watched a woman get her purse snatched on the street.

Doesn't Translate

Battista, like all of the female cops who passed through the 12th Precinct, did not last long—only two episodes to be exact. In this case, it was for a very specific reason: she wasn't actually a Latina. Danny Arnold saw June Gable in the Broadway play *The Ritz* where she had taken over the part originally played by Rita Moreno and hired her for the recurring role of Maria Battista, a cross between Gregory Sierra and Linda Lavin, both of whom had just left the show. Arnold just assumed she was Latina but Gable was actually Eastern European in heritage. At the time, groups like HOLA (Hispanic Organization of Latin Actors) began demanding that Latino roles went to actual Latinos. Arnold was feeling pressure from HOLA and similar groups and felt compelled to cancel her contract.

The position of a group like HOLA is certainly understandable and possibly even justified, however, it also leads to a question very much in debate these days: If you're an "actor" are you only allowed to act certain parts? Isn't the actor's job to become something or someone that he or she is not?

In any case, it's a shame as far as Det. Battista is concerned because she was a very funny addition to the 12th Precinct.

The Negotiator

Barney would often negotiate settlements between accusers in a case of mutual assault like a bar fight or some such altercation. However, in this episode, he needs to do some quick thinking to save Wojo and the city from a false arrest lawsuit. The settlement negotiations are some of Barney's best work although this time, rather than using his sense of justice or patented *Barney Miller* compassion, he reverts to good, old-fashioned bluffing.

One and Done

Mike Kellin appears as Al Mitchell, the man thrown in jail by Wojo for "doing nothing." Kellin was a very dependable blue-collar type character actor throughout the 1950s, 1960s, and 1970s. His first film was the 1950 Martin and Lewis feature, *At War with the Army*. Interestingly, Danny Arnold's first screenplay was the 1953 Martin and Lewis picture, *The Caddy*.

Arnold and Kellin worked together prior to *Barney Miller* on the first series created by Arnold, *The Wackiest Ship in the Army*. Kellin was a regular in the role of CPO Willie Miller. He was also the only actor to have appeared in the movie of the same name upon which the series was based, a 1960 film that starred Jack Lemmon and Ricky Nelson.

In "Noninvolvement," his quintessential New York character belies the actor's origins in Hartford, CT. Kellin was a graduate of Boston College and a respected stage actor with a long list of Broadway and Off-Broadway credits.

Mitchell's (Kellin) protest over his false arrest is one of my favorite outbursts of the entire series.

Al Mitchell: What did I do wrong, huh? I witnessed a crime. Is that a crime to witness a crime?
Barney: Certainly not.
Al Mitchell: Ask the lady with the coffee (the purse-snatching victim). What happened, huh? I saw this guy snatch your purse. Am I right, lady with the coffee?
Lady with the coffee: You coulda helped me.
Al Mitchell: I coulda helped but I didn't gotta!

Triumphant Return?

Mr. Lyle Farber returns to help out a fellow flasher. Interestingly, he has the same coat from "Snow Job" (S. 1/Ep. 3), a coat that he supposedly gifted to Barney at the end of that episode.

Season 3, Episode 9: "Power Failure."
Original Airdate: December 9, 1976.
Writers: Tony Sheehan and Danny Arnold (teleplay). Reinhold Weege, Danny Arnold, and Tony Sheehan (story).
Director: Noam Pitlik.
Cast of Characters: Steve Landesberg (Dietrich), Jack Soo (Yemana), Hal Linden (Barney), Abe Vigoda (Fish), Max Gail (Wojo), Stefan Gierasch (Charles Foster Keller / Lenny / Neal), Arny Freeman (Mr. Rosten), Susan Brown (Dr. Fitzgerald), Paul Lichtman (Beckman).

The Rundown

Wojo arrests a man for beating up his bookie. The suspect, Charles Foster Keller (Stefan Gierasch), informs Wojo that it was not he who beat up the bookie but his other personality, Lenny. Wojo doesn't believe in split personalities but Dietrich, of course, tries to explain split personalities to Barney and Wojo. In addition, there's a blackout covering twenty-five square blocks of Manhattan.

Everybody's Doin' It

This particular episode with a suspect who has multiple personalities premiered just less than four weeks after the highly publicized miniseries, *Sybil*, in which Sally Field plays a young woman with sixteen different personalities. One of this episode's multiple personalities is named Charles Foster Keller which is too similar to Charles Foster Kane of *Citizen Kane* (1941) fame to be a coincidence.

On another plain of popular culture, Charles Ernest Keller, better known as Charlie "King Kong" Keller, was an outfielder for the New York Yankees and Detroit Tigers from 1939–1952. Keller missed one year to war service in 1944 but was part of three championship Yankee teams in 1939, 1941, and 1943.

Everyone's Human

Susan Brown as Dr. Fitzgerald flirts with Barney in his office and although he's obviously somewhat attracted to her, he's also very married. At one point, he apologizes that he doesn't seduce well. She then smiles and asks, "Do you seduce at all?" His reply is, "So far, I've only lusted in my heart." The line brings a laugh that might confuse viewers today because it essentially paraphrases a statement Governor Jimmy Carter made in a *Playboy* magazine interview when he was candidate for President in 1976.

Cool as a Cucumber and Twice as Funny

Wojo and Nick are checking stores in the neighborhood during the blackout to try to prevent looting. The owner of a jewelry store, not knowing they are cops, takes a shot and just misses Nick, grazing his sideburns. When the storeowner tries to apologize to Nick he tells him not to worry about it.

> **Mr. Rosten:** Oh officer, I'm so sorry. I really didn't mean to do it. I think it was just a reflex action. I was in the infantry in World War II.
> **Nick:** (looks at Wojo) Sometimes I wish I was Chinese.

Triple Threat

Stefan Gierasch, who plays three different personalities stuck in one body in this episode, was a prolific actor who worked in films and television for over fifty years. He enjoyed roles in some high-profile Hollywood films including

The Hustler (1961), *What's Up Doc?* (1972), *Jeremiah Johnson* (1972), *High Plains Drifter* (1973), and *Carrie* (1976) as well as numerous TV shows from the 1950s through the 1990s. He was also a regular on Danny Arnold's short-lived *A.E.S. Hudson Street*.

In addition, Gierasch had a long list of Broadway credits stretching from the 1940s through the 1980s including the role of Herr Zeller in the long-running *The Sound of Music* (1959–1963). He died in 2014 at the age of eighty-eight.

Season 3, Episode 10:	"Christmas Story."
Original Airdate:	December 23, 1976.
Writers:	Reinhold Weege and Tony Sheehan.
Director:	Bruce Bilson.
Cast of Characters:	Hal Linden (Barney), Abe Vigoda (Fish), Ron Glass (Harris), Max Gail (Wojo), Jack Soo (Yemana), James Gregory (Inspector Frank Luger), Nobu McCarthy (Miss Dorothy Murakami), Jay Gerber (Mr. Craig), John Morgan Evans (Mugger).

The Rundown

It's Christmas Eve at the 12th and Harris is filling out a complaint from Miss Murakami, a victim of a purse-snatching. When Nick arrives in the office, he's attracted to Miss Murakami and asks her for a date after the shift ends. Wojo buys presents for the squad despite the agreement not to exchange gifts with one another. Santa Claus gets mugged in front of Siegel's Department Store.

Color Blind

Wojo flips out when Nick brings in a blue tree for them to decorate in the office. Truthfully, it always looked two-tone to me with touches of both blue and green but Wojo and Barney didn't seem to think so. Blue or green, it was inarguably one of the ugliest trees you ever saw, especially once the men finished decorating it with pink bulbs, gold garland, and silver tinsel.

Orphans

It wasn't bad enough that Wojo overreacted to Nick's choice of a Christmas tree but then he had to go and ruin Nick's enthusiasm about his date with Miss Murakami (Nobu McCarthy) by telling him she was a prostitute.

When Nick originally asked her for the date, she demurred, but then he tells her, "You know, it's nice to be among your own on a holiday." With that line, she agrees to come back and meet him when his shift ends at midnight. It was a poignant moment because these were two people on opposite sides of the law who were both lonely and without a family on a holiday that celebrates family.

There is some iciness between the characters when she returns to the squad room after Wojo's revelation to Nick about her occupation. Nevertheless, all's well that ends well when Miss Murakami and Nick declare that they are "off duty" and leave to spend Christmas Eve together.

It also seems odd that Wojo, of all people, would be concerned about Nick dating a hooker. After all, it was already something of an established fact that Wojo himself had a penchant for ladies of the evening.

We Can All Relate

When Harris and Fish answer a call at Siegel's about Santa Claus getting robbed, they end up arresting Mr. Craig (Jay Gerber) for breaking a display window. It seems Mr. Craig was unable to put together the Zoom-A-Go-Round that he had bought there. He tried to go back to the store to get help but they had just closed and wouldn't let him in. It's both hilariously funny and relatable to all of us who've ever had kids and couldn't get that complicated toy together on Christmas Eve.

The Last Word

The men had supposedly agreed that they weren't going to exchange Christmas gifts. Nevertheless, Wojo comes in filled with the Christmas spirit claiming he never agreed to the deal and hands out gifts to the guys much to everyone's chagrin. This innocent gesture of good will activates the guilt gene in the others. For example, when Harris goes out he stops into an all-night drugstore and quickly picks up gifts for the squad. He presents it to the gang in a big brown paper bag and has them dig their hands in to pick out a gift.

> **Harris:** Merry Christmas Wojo!
> **Wojo:** **Thanks** Harris but uh, ya didn't have to get me a present just 'cause I got you a present.
> **Harris:** That wasn't it.
> **Wojo:** Sure it was.
> **Harris:** No.

Wojo: Yes.
Harris: Look, Merry Christmas, will ya'?

As far as I'm concerned, "Look, Merry Christmas, will ya'?" is one of the great lines in the annals of American entertainment and the history of holiday celebrations.

The Numbers Are Off

When Mr. Craig doesn't want to pay Siegel's for the display window he broke in return for having the charges dropped, Harris says, "Hey man, pay the man $2." Hard to believe that even in 1976 a display window for a department store could possibly cost only $2.

At the end as Fish hands out gifts to Barney, Wojo, and Harris (Nick had already left on his date), Barney says, "I seem to be the only one who didn't get anything for anybody." Not totally true because we didn't see Nick pass out any gifts to anyone either unless he'd done it during a commercial break.

Season 3, Episode 11: "Hash."
Original Airdate: December 30, 1976.
Writer: Tom Reeder.
Director: Noam Pitlik.
Cast of Characters: Jack Soo (Yemana), Abe Vigoda (Fish), Hal Linden (Barney), Max Gail (Wojo), Ron Glass (Harris), Ed Peck (Officer Frank Slater), Walter Janovitz [Janowitz] (Janusz Makowski), George Perina (Zbigniew Psczola), Michael Tucci (Fred), Ron Carey (Officer Carl Levitt).

The Rundown

Wojo brings in some homemade brownies compliments of Gloria, his new girlfriend, and the squad ends up getting baked by the goodies. Nick and Harris check out a report about two men having a duel with sabers in Washington Square. An old acquaintance of Fish's from the academy shows interest in Bernice.

Quintessential Barney

This is probably the most famous episode in the history of the show as all the members of the squad, with the exception of Captain Miller, end up higher than a kite from the hash brownies that Wojo unwittingly brings into the office.

A Pot By Any Other Name

Tom Reeder, the lead writer of this episode, said, "The episode was originally called 'Pot.' Then somebody, probably either Tony or Reinie, when I turned that draft in said, 'You know, for it to act this quickly and have the effects be this strong, it should be hashish. It would have a more profound effect.' So that's how it changed from 'Pot' to 'Hash.'"

Reeder told Ken Levine, another fine television writer, (*M*A*S*H*, *Frasier* (1993-2004), etc.), that he seems to remember the germ of the idea for this episode came from Roland Kibbee and that Reinhold Weege also added to the dialogue.

Dueling Poles

The men in the park dueling with sabers turn out to be a Polish actor and a Polish theater critic. Once again, Wojo's fluency in the language is needed to translate.

Walter Janovitz portrays the actor, Janusz Makowski, in the first of five *Barney* appearances. Janovitz was born in Austria-Hungary in 1913 in an area that is now part of the Czech Republic. His accent worked well to add some flavor to the proceedings. There were numerous foreign characters that came through the 12th Precinct over the years that helped remind the audience the detectives were, after all, operating in the melting pot of the United States.

Janovitz appeared in numerous TV shows of the 1960s. He may be best remembered for the more than one dozen guest spots on *Hogan's Heroes*. He also made two very memorable appearances on *The Odd Couple* with Tony Randall and Jack Klugman in the early 1970s.

Medicinals

Poor Fish, all he can say when he learns about the contents of the brownies is, "First time in twenty years I felt really good, and it has to be illegal."

The Singing Sergeant

As a rule, the 12th Precinct's most frequent crooner is Inspector Luger. However, in this episode, Nick Yemana steals the show with a heartfelt rendition of

"Almost Like Being in Love." In fact, it's his singing that initially alerts Barney that something's not quite right and, with a little help from the hip Harris, leads to the discovery of the hashish brownies.

As mentioned earlier, in the 1940s, Jack Soo was a singer who was sometimes billed as "The Chinese Bing Crosby" in nightclubs and theaters. In 1961, Jack Soo won the role of a lifetime as Sammy Fong in the film version of the Rodgers and Hammerstein Broadway musical, *The Flower Drum Song*.

Defining Moment

In the author's interviews with Hal Linden, the actor described this episode as a clarifying moment in the development of his character of Barney Miller:

> Once we read the script and everybody has—it wasn't comedy—everybody had an aria and everybody reacted to the hash in a different way, you know what I mean? And I was the only one who didn't have an aria, so I said to Danny, "Hey, everybody's got their great dramatic scene and here I don't have. . . ." and he gave me a quick lesson in comedy right there. He said, "I have to have somebody to compare them to." And I said, "Of course, that's my function."
>
> I was the anchor that you could compare the odd behavior to. That's what made it odd, that there was somebody being solid and doing his job all the time. And I came to terms with that very quickly. In one line, he gave me the whole concept of what my function was in that comedy and how comedy works. "I had to have someone to compare them to."

Virtuoso Performance

While Linden states that everyone has an aria in this episode except Barney, the standout performance belongs to Jack Soo's Nick Yemana. If this is the most quotable of all *Barney Miller* episodes, and I believe it is, it's Nick Yemana's quips and stream-of-consciousness (semi-consciousness?) ramblings that stick with us to this day. All I'll say is, "Mooshy-Mooshy." Beyond that, I'm going to refrain from writing out all the great lines and just encourage the reader to go back and watch this episode again. It never gets old.

Brace Yourself

For those who feel Phil Fish doesn't appreciate his wife Bernice enough, you may be surprised by the passion and feelings he expresses in this episode when another man challenges him for her affections.

Season 3, Episode 12: "Smog Alert."
Original Airdate: January 6, 1977.
Writers: Reinhold Weege (teleplay). Chris Hayward and Danny Arnold (story).
Director: Bruce Bilson.
Cast of Characters: Hal Linden (Barney), Jack Soo (Yemana), Max Gail (Wojo), Ron Glass (Harris), Abe Vigoda (Fish), Lee Kessler (Renee Pettit), Alan Haufrect (Antoine McCarthy), June Gable (Det. Maria Battista), Ron Carey (Officer Carl Levitt).

The Rundown

A first-aid smog alert is declared by the City of New York, Battista arrests a vulgar graffiti artist, and Fish collapses after he talks a jumper off the Brooklyn Bridge.

Survival of the Fittest

When Barney asks Nick what the smell is in the office, Nick tells him it's the smog. Barney finds that hard to believe since they're indoors. Nick explains that it comes through the holes in the wall that the cockroaches made. Barney asks, "Don't tell me we got cockroaches again?" Nick reassures him, "Not anymore, the rats ate them."

Reach for the Top

In another early visit from Officer Levitt, we are provided with the kind of paranoia and complaining that made him a less than respected colleague in the early years. In this case, he's upset at the fact that the force would promote a five-foot tall woman to detective while there are still a lot of good men who haven't been promoted due to their size. He has his own childish, but harmless, way of making Battista pay for the slight.

A Real Go-Getter

We learn from Barney that Battista has made more arrests that week than the rest of the squad combined. When she comes in that morning she's seething over some filthy graffiti she read in the ladies' room of the 14th Street subway station. She wrote it down for evidence (no cell phones). When Yemana reads it he opines, "It's too complicated to be obscene." Harris adds, "It's got everything but a plot." Naturally, we don't get to hear what was written.

A Message to Garcia

The graffiti artist (Alan Haufrect) steals the chalk from the squad room's chalkboard and writes a message to Miss Pettit (Lee Kessler), the attempted suicide, on the wall of the cell she will inhabit after him. She is a lonely, frustrated, self-loathing woman who is energized by the message she discovers written to her. The laughter elicited from her facial and physical reaction to the message comes strictly from the viewer's imagination as we never actually see the text on the cell wall; however, we do know that the graffiti artist leaves her his phone number because she's repeating it to herself as Harris leads her away to Bellevue.

Season 3, Episode 13: "Community Relations."
Original Airdate: January 13, 1977.
Writers: Tony Sheehan, Larry Balmagia, and Dennis Koenig (teleplay). Winston Moss and Tony Sheehan (story).
Director: Noam Pitlik.
Cast of Characters: Jack Soo (Yemana), Ron Glass (Harris), Abe Vigoda (Fish), Hal Linden (Barney), Max Gail (Wojo), David Tress (Frank Pisano), Joseph Perry (Leonard K. Hauser), Ralph Manza (Leon Roth), Judson Morgan (Philip Lukeather).

The Rundown

Harris and Nick make a bet to see who can give up his bad habit first, Harris with his smoking or Nick with his gambling. Siegel's Department Store calls in a complaint about an unusual shoplifting suspect. Wojo is in danger of losing a case in court due to his extreme nerves when speaking in front of people. The hyper-tense Assistant District Attorney only aggravates the situation and a bossy, rude slumlord comes in to demand the eviction of a tenant.

Introductions All Around

In this episode, we're introduced to the blind but incredibly resourceful Leon Roth, played by Ralph Manza. The diminutive character actor was first seen in the previous season's "Protection" episode as retired racketeer, Anthony Barelli. Following his appearance here as Mr. Roth, he will next be seen as Eddie Blake, a chauffeur in the Season Five premiere one-hour episode "Kidnapping," before reappearing as Mr. Roth in one episode a year during the final three seasons of the show.

Prior to his work on *Barney Miller*, Manza was best known as George Peppard's chauffeur, Jay Drury, on the mystery program, *Banacek* (1972–1974). Following his appearances on *Barney Miller*, he would become a recurring character on Bob Newhart's second hit series, *Newhart* (1982–1990) as Bud, the floor manager at a local TV station. Danny Arnold obviously liked Manza because he also cast him in his short-lived sitcom, *A.E.S. Hudson Street*.

When Barney asks Mr. Roth exactly how he, a blind man, presumed he could get away with shoplifting, Roth answers, "No one expects a blind man to steal. I was counting on the element of surprise." Nick says, "I was surprised."

One and Done

David Tress makes his one and only appearance in this episode as the memorably high-strung Assistant District Attorney (ADA), Frank Pisano. Tress is hilarious as he frets over Wojo's ineptitude as a witness and goes on the attack when he meets slumlord Leonard K. Hauser played by familiar character actor, Joseph Perry. Tress makes such an impression as Pisano that it's too bad Danny Arnold didn't bring him back as a recurring character.

Self-Awareness

ADA Pisano is questioning all the suspects Barney's men are bringing into the squad room—blind people, dispossessed veterans? Barney apologizes saying, "I'm sorry. We attract an appealing class of criminal around here." You can't argue with that observation. The officers of the 12th always brought in the most interesting, and often sympathetic, criminals in the annals of crime fighting.

The Last Word

Mr. Roth shows off how heightened his other senses are when talking to Nick and Harris and he perfectly identifies Harris's character just by talking and listening to him. Nick gets curious and asks him, "How do I feel?"

Mr. Roth: You? Well, you're cool and collected. Got a lot of personal discipline. You're very, very intelligent. Either that or you're Japanese.

Season 3, Episode 14: "The Rand Report."
Original Airdate: January 20, 1977.
Writers: Reinhold Weege (teleplay). Roland Kibbee and Reinhold Weege (story).
Director: Noam Pitlik.
Cast of Characters: Max Gail (Wojo), Hal Linden (Barney), Steve Landesberg (Dietrich), Jack Soo (Yemana), Ron Glass (Harris), Ron Carey (Levitt), Abe Vigoda (Fish), James Gregory (Inspector Frank Luger), Martin Garner (Steven Himmel), Anna Berger (Georgia Himmel), John William Evans (Mark Swykirk).

The Rundown

The Rand Corporation, a California Think Tank, publishes a report saying that as a rule beat cops do most of the day-to-day police work while detectives spend more time polishing their image. The story breaks in *Newsweek* magazine and causes unrest in the department. A jealous and worried husband is brought in when he is disrupting emergency efforts to free his wife and a purse-snatcher who are stuck together on an elevator. Fish is working undercover at an old age home where the residents are being robbed.

Uniforms Only

The Rand Report causes the NYC Police Department to react by requiring all Third Grade Detectives and below to work as a uniformed officer one week per month. At the 12th, that applies only to Det. Wojciehowicz. When informed of the new policy, Wojo quits and walks out. Levitt comes looking for him because he's due to report on his squad. Barney asks Levitt to give Wojo some time to cool off. We're given an insight into the out-of-office friendships when Harris mentions that he went by Wojo's apartment the night before but Wojo wasn't home.

Eyes of the Beholder

Martin Garner makes his second of five *Barney Miller* appearances. Each role is a different character. Here he plays the hysterical husband, Mr. Himmel, who is worried about his "sex goddess" wife being trapped inside a stuck elevator with a purse-snatcher who he assumes is also a sex maniac. When the fire department finally frees Mrs. Himmel, played by Anna Berger, and Mark, played by John William Evans, we discover that Mrs. Berger, although attractive for a woman in her fifties is certainly no Rita Hayworth. Mrs. Himmel's jealous husband gets even more paranoid when his wife tells him that absolutely nothing happened and then adds, "Mark was a perfect gentleman." She's coy with her husband and then, when he walks away mumbling she turns to Dietrich, smiles, and says, "You have to keep a little mystery in your marriage."

Film Criticism

Naturally, Inspector Luger is less than impressed with the fact that, "some eggheads out in California come up with a lousy report, the whole police department goes crazy. Probably like them actors out in Hollywood, Barney, you know, a bunch of tutti-fruttis, you know what I mean? Except for 'the Duke,' of course." The Duke was a reference to Western star John Wayne who always played "a man's man" in his long and storied career on the Silver Screen. For the record, James Gregory played the bad guy, Morgan Hastings, opposite John Wayne, in the movie, *The Sons of Katie Elder* (1964).

Really Petty Larceny

Fish discovers that the thieves at the nursing home are all the residents. They rob from one another at night for a little fun and excitement. When he discovers the truth, they wind up giggling at him. It sent chills up Fish's spine.

Season 3, Episode 15: "Fire '77."
Original Airdate: January 27, 1977.
Writer: Tony Sheehan.
Director: Bruce Bilson.
Cast of Characters: Steve Landesberg (Dietrich), Abe Vigoda (Fish), Hal Linden (Barney), Jack Soo (Yemana), Max Gail (Wojo), Ron Glass (Harris), Howard Platt (Lawrence Weiskoff), K Callan (Gwen Baxter), Sal Viscuso (Thomas Vitella), Russell Shannon (Fireman).

The Rundown

Harris and Wojo bring in a thief caught robbing the poor boxes in St. Mark's Cathedral. A man and a woman make a suicide pact and both fail to follow through on their agreement. Harris is dabbling in the stock market.

Kinky Perps

The two suicide "teammates" played by Howard Platt and K Callan seem turned on by the idea of killing themselves which leads Dietrich to give the psychiatric background for such an obsession. He even consults with the doctors at Bellevue when he drops the couple off at the hospital. This is one of many consultations that Dietrich will have with medical personnel during the run of the program.

Good Catholic Boys

This is Sal Viscuso's favorite of the four episodes in which he appeared. His character, Thomas Vitella, insists that no matter what the circumstances, he's still a good Catholic. Once he sees Wojo's name he asks him just how often he goes to Mass.

When they check him for priors, it's discovered that Vitella is AWOL from Riker's Island. He'd gone out on a work furlough and never returned. Vitella then sets fire to the squad room's bathroom with the idea of creating a diversion so he could escape. It didn't work but he did destroy the bathroom. On the bright side, Miller tells him he doesn't have to worry about going back to Riker's because he'll probably get sent to Elmira or Attica now. Vitella takes this as good news. "I hear they have a nice chapel up in Attica. And a great mass!"

Ironically, in a few short months, Viscuso would be cast as Father Timothy Flotsky in the new ABC sitcom *Soap*. Like Mr. Vitella, Father Tim would prove to be less than a paragon of Catholic obedience and fidelity.

Should Be Against the Law

Nick is making Shabu Shabu for his lunch on a hotplate in the squad room. Wojo says it smells like garbage. Nick replies, "Garbage? Are you kidding? This is a Japanese delicacy—fish heads, cabbage leaves, cucumber rind, celery tops, . . . come to think of it, that *is* garbage."

Repeat Customer

Howard Platt is featured in this episode as Lawrence Weiskoff. He had previously appeared in "Ms. Cop" (S. 1/Ep. 8). He will return to appear in three more episodes in three different roles. Platt was a familiar sitcom actor of the 1970s but was best-known for his role in *Sanford and Son* (1972–1977) as one of the neighborhood cops, Officer "Hoppy" Hopkins. He was the super square white dude who was partnered with the more relatable black cop, Officer "Smitty" Smith, portrayed by Hal Williams. Prior to Hoppy Hopkins, Officer Smith's first partner was Officer "Swanny" Swanhauser. In a bit of coincidental *Barney Miller* trivia, Noam Pitlik, who would go on to direct over 100 *Barney Miller* episodes, portrayed Officer Swanhauser.

Season 3, Episode 16:	"Abduction."
Original Airdate:	February 3, 1977.
Writers:	Tony Sheehan, Reinhold Weege, and Tom Reeder (teleplay). Tom Reeder (story).
Director:	Bruce Bilson.
Cast of Characters:	Hal Linden (Barney), Abe Vigoda (Fish), Max Gail (Wojo), Jack Soo (Yemana), Ron Glass (Harris), Florence Stanley (Bernice Fish), Rod Colbin (Joe Wheaton), Vivi Janiss (Lois Wheaton), David Clennon (Bodhisattva), Jane Alice Brandon (Barbara Lynn Wheaton / Praknamurti), Buddy Lester (Sidney the bookie).

The Rundown

Harris gets his first piece of fiction published but is disappointed by the outcome. A middle-aged couple from Rhode Island travel to New York in search of their daughter. Bernice Fish wants to get a job and Nick has a gambling windfall.

Some Sort of Religious Cult

The Wheatons are upset that their daughter has left home and been brainwashed by a goofy cult. However, at twenty-two, she's free to make her own decisions. They abduct her from the restaurant and the men of the 12th must get her back and mediate the family strife.

This marks the first of five appearances by actor David Clennon. He portrays Bodhisattva, the business savvy owner of The Light of the East Temple and Herbarium and a dead look-a-like for Jesus Christ. In three out of the four remaining *Barney Miller* guest shots, Clennon will play a bureaucrat of some sort or another but he is hilarious in this role as a very hip, but pragmatic, cult leader and restaurateur.

Clennon relished the opportunities that Danny Arnold gave him with the various characters he portrayed on the show. When I told him that this was my favorite of his portrayals, he remarked, "Jesus Christ with a subtle New York accent. I had forgotten about the accent and then I think it was four episodes later, they bring me in to play a very straitlaced Southerner. I didn't realize that those two episodes came so close together, but you know, you will never see anything like that on television today where they give an actor a chance to do that. You know, one a very calm and confident businessman who happens to look like Jesus Christ and the other one, a very jittery kind of uptight Southern gentleman, who's in way over his head."

What Are the Odds?

When Sidney the Bookie is giving his statement to Fish, Bodhisattva walks in looking like he just emerged from forty days in the desert. Sydney and Fish exchange a glance and Sidney says, "I'll give you 75–1 it ain't."

Don't Fence Me In

Rod Colbin, as Mr. Wheaton, makes his first of seven appearances in this episode. Each time he walked into the squad room he was a different character. In addition to his acting talents, Colbin was a fencing master and instructor for many years.

Impersonating a Productive Member of Society

In one of the more insulting storylines for modern audiences to swallow, Fish is opposed to his wife getting a job. Bernice, however, wants to help out and feel productive. He commands her (yikes!) not to go to the job interview and she says, "Fish, I can't live my whole life through you. I'm growing. I'm changing."

Unfortunately, when she makes inquiries at an employment agency, she's told that she's unskilled, has no experience, and is too old. Fish tells her, "Forget it. Look on the bright side." Unfortunately, he doesn't identify exactly what the bright side is to that ringing refusal of validation.

Impersonating a Magazine

Harris is thrilled to have his first story, "John and Mary Ann," published in a men's magazine called *Sir Gent*, complete with centerfold and all. Unfortunately, when his advanced copy arrives from the publisher, the title has been changed to "John and Maryann and Harry and Frank" and he discovers he's been extensively edited and rewritten. He's disgusted when he discovers the new title of his piece. "Oh man, I wrote a beautiful story about a man and a woman—who the hell are Harry and Frank?"

Season 3, Episode 17: "Sex Surrogate."
Original Airdate: February 10, 1977.
Writers: Tony Sheehan, Larry Balmagia, and Dennis Koenig (teleplay). Jerry Ross and Tony Sheehan (story).
Director: Noam Pitlik.
Cast of Characters: Hal Linden (Barney), Jack Soo (Yemana), Ron Glass (Harris), Abe Vigoda (Fish), Max Gail (Wojo), Ron Carey (Levitt), Billy Barty (Mr. Resnick), Doris Roberts (Louise Kaufmann), Marilyn Sokol (Dr. Lorraine Dooley), Eugene Elman (Mr. Kaufmann).

The Rundown

Wojo and Fish are called to a shooting on Sixth Street. The shooting leads to an investigation of a sex clinic. Harris discovers that a string of robberies carried out by what he thought was a juvenile is actually the work of a little person. Levitt is considering leaving the force due to his belief that his lack of height is holding him back.

A Rose By Any Other Name

Doris Roberts as Mrs. Louise Kaufmann shoots her husband because she believes he's visiting a house of prostitution. Eugene Elman (Mr. Kaufmann) claims it's a misunderstanding. He was seeing a doctor, not a prostitute. Wojo discovers the place is called The New York Institute of Sexual Dysfunction. Naturally, Wojo's take is that if a woman is "working with a man in that subject area" and being paid, it's prostitution. Barney's more wary of the ambiguities of the situation.

The lady who runs the clinic is Dr. Lorraine Dooley played by Marilyn Sokol. She's not being charged with a crime but she's brought in for questioning. The role and work of sexual therapists was not yet universally understood. When she wants to know how long she will be held, Barney begs her indulgence. "We are," Barney explains to her, "entering a sensitive area here. I mean the services of a surrogate come uncomfortably close to the legal definition of prostitution." As Harris walks into the squad room and hears her explaining what she does to Barney, he asks Nick who that is. Nick replies, "My new doctor."

Auspicious Beginning

This marks Doris Roberts' first of four *Barney Miller* appearances. The next three will be as a recurring character, Harriet Brauer, who routinely has problems with her husband played by actor Peter Hobbs. Roberts gained iconic TV status twenty years later as Marie Barone, the overbearing Italian mother, on the long-running sitcom *Everybody Loves Raymond* (1996–2005).

As for Marilyn Sokol who plays the sex therapist, she spent over a decade voicing various characters on *Sesame Street* (1969–present). She's also enjoyed a very long, varied, and successful stage career.

Short People

Proving that size really doesn't matter, the legendary Billy Barty plays the role of a thief in this episode. Harris twice refers to him as a midget and Barty corrects him, telling him, "I'm a little person." This was an important issue to Barty who would often stress the distinction when appearing on talk shows. He founded an organization called The Little People of America in 1957 to support people like himself who were born with dwarfism.

When Levitt brings up the mail, Barty says, "You guys, you got it made." Levitt asks, "You talking to me?" Barty responds with, "All you tall guys. You oughta try getting somewhere from down here." Barty's appearance makes Levitt realize that size, like most things, is relative.

Season 3, Episode 18: "Moonlighting."
Original Airdate: February 17, 1977.
Writer: Reinhold Weege (written by).
Director: Noam Pitlik.

Cast of Characters: Jack Soo (Yemana), Max Gail (Wojo), Hal Linden (Barney), Steve Landesberg (Det. Sgt. Arthur Dietrich), Ron Glass (Harris), John Dullaghan (Sylvester White), George Pentecost (Rev. Albert Carrey), Cal Gibson (Del Mitchell), Jan Stuart Schwartz (Tom Fields).

The Rundown

A priest is running a thrift shop stocked with stolen merchandise. A mentally challenged young man is being used as an unknowing pawn by a racketeer and Harris takes a second job as Captain of Security at a condo called the Kingman Arms.

Thou Shall Not Fence

The aptly named George Pentecost plays Reverend Albert Carrey, a man of the cloth who has been running a thrift shop to help raise funds for his economically struggling church. He's purchased lots of cheap merchandise without asking, or wanting to know, where it came from.

When Barney asks Nick to bring the Reverend down for pictures and prints he begs off, explaining, "I haven't gone to church in years, there might be repercussions." Barney then turns to Dietrich who says he doesn't mind. Dietrich turns to Barney and asks the eternal question, "Do you believe in God?" Barney replies, "Well, I've always felt there was something up there, out there . . ."

Dietrich says he doesn't believe and gives what he feels is the more likely scientific explanation. Barney then asks him what if he's wrong and someday he finds himself in an afterlife having to explain his lack of faith, what will he say? Dietrich's deeply intellectual response is, "Whoops?"

Positive ID

This episode is a solid example of the writers really starting to hone in on the character of Arthur Dietrich. Landesberg shines in this episode as we see all the facets of his developing character: humility, intellectualism, affinity for corny humor and puns, sarcasm, and deadpan delivery. The attitudes and the humor of the Dietrich character are as fresh and as funny today as when the show originally aired.

Don't Panic

Barney uses the word "retarded" in this episode to describe a young man with developmental challenges. This word is no longer accepted in society and that's great but the fact is it was quite commonly used forty-plus years ago when describing individuals with mental challenges so don't panic. This is just another one of those anachronisms you'll have to chalk up to a different historical epoch.

Season 3, Episode 19: "Asylum."
Original Airdate: February 24, 1977.
Writers: Roland Kibbee, Danny Arnold, Reinhold Weege, and Tony Sheehan (teleplay). Roland Kibbee (story).
Director(s): Danny Arnold, Alex March.
Cast of Characters: Jack Soo (Yemana), Hal Linden (Barney), Ron Glass (Harris), Steve Landesberg (Dietrich), Max Gail (Wojo), Jack DeLeon (Marty Morrison), David Clennon (Jeffrey Stevens), Michael Panaieff (Andre Bulganov), Ion Teodorescu (Fyoder Jininski), Louis Zito (Uniformed cop).

The Rundown

Marty gets caught with a small amount of marijuana shortly before his probation period is over. Wojo gets the 12th Precinct entangled in international politics when he grants political asylum to a Soviet citizen and the drama being played out in the squad room inspires Harris to write a story.

Statute of Limitations

The idea of Marty getting caught with less than half an ounce of marijuana being any kind of serious police issue is now a dated one in twenty-first century America where numerous states have legalized marijuana.

International Politics 101

The end of the Cold War should have rendered the controversy of a Russian seeking asylum in the United States as obsolete, as well. However, politics seems to be one of those subject areas where "the more things change, the more they stay the same." Tensions remain between the two nations and continued controversies surrounding immigration and asylum for endangered populations are, sadly, still a major news story here and around the world.

Repeat Offender

As a matter of course, Danny Arnold had no qualms about using character actors repeatedly in different roles. In most cases, however, an actor usually wasn't seen in different roles more than once a season. In this episode, however, David Clennon shows up just three weeks after his first *Barney Miller* appearance in "Abduction." In this case, it wasn't a problem because in "Abduction" his character bore a remarkable resemblance to Jesus Christ with a beard, long hair, and a long flowing white robe. In "Asylum," he plays a very clean-cut young man with a southern drawl and a new job with the State Department. This episode premiered just a few weeks after James Earl "Jimmy" Carter was inaugurated as the 39th President of the United States. There was much humor and political commentary made at the time about Carter's roots as a Georgia peanut farmer. When Clennon's character, Jeffrey Stevens, with his deep Southern drawl, informs Barney that he just started the job last week with the new administration, Barney says, "Ah yes. As a matter of fact, now that you mention it, I do detect a slight accent." Stevens's reply is, "We no longer have accents, *you* do!"

It All Sounds Very Silly

The scene in Barney's office between Captain Miller and Stevens of the US State Department is a mixture of satire and farce that *Barney Miller* executed so well. The show often exposed and poked fun at the ludicrous red tape and bureaucracy all citizens have to deal with on a daily basis in our society.

When Barney asks Stevens if he is going to grant Mr. Jininski asylum or not, Stevens tells him, "Oh, I can't give anyone asylum. The only person who can formally grant asylum is the District Director of Immigration." Naturally, Barney asks him, "Then why are you here?"

Stevens: It's my job.
Barney: To do what?
Stevens: I don't know! I'm new!

Who Is That Man?

The myth of Dietrich really starts to take hold in this episode. As Stevens of the State Department is leaving, Dietrich asks him if he's going to be seeing the President anytime soon. Stevens say that he's flying down to Washington the next day.

Dietrich: Do me a favor, will ya? Tell him Arthur says "Hey."
Stevens: Arthur who?
Dietrich: He'll know. (He smiles and walks back to his desk.)
Stevens: (asks Nick) Who is that man?
Nick: (looks at Dietrich and in typical deadpan fashion) We're not sure.

Stevens starts to walk out the door and then turns back and gives a long suspicious look at Dietrich. There will be other intimations throughout the series that Dietrich may have connections that would boggle the imagination.

Season 3, Episode 20: "Group Home."
Original Airdate: March 10, 1977.
Writers: Danny Arnold and Tony Sheehan (teleplay). Larry Balmagia and Dennis Koenig (story).
Director: Lee Bernhardi.
Cast of Characters: Hal Linden (Barney), Jack Soo (Yemana), Max Gail (Wojo), Abe Vigoda (Fish), Ron Glass (Harris), Florence Stanley (Bernice Fish), George Murdock (Master Sgt. J. R. Reville), James Cromwell (Sgt. Wilkinson), Don Calfa (Mr. DiLucca), Phil Leeds (Lou Hector), John Cassisi (Victor Kreutzer), Denise Miller (Jilly Papalardo).

The Rundown

An Army recruiting officer reports a bomb threat from a volunteer who was turned away and a sketch artist is called in to identify the suspect. Fish is preparing for a mugging detail while Bernice visits the 12th with Victor and Jilly. Harris, inspired by the TV series, *Roots*, is disappointed with the results a genealogy service provides him about his family history.

Identity Crisis

George Murdock made his first *Barney Miller* appearance in the Season Two episode entitled "Block Party" as Lt. Ben Scanlon of the Manhattan South division. In this episode, however, he shows up as Master Sgt. J. R. Reville, who's Army recruiting office has been threatened by a bomber. Most of the humor in his storyline is directed towards his mistrust of working with Sgt. Yemana, a Japanese American. At one point, Reville says, "It don't make sense. I mean why would anyone want to blow up a United States military installation?" Nick deadpans, "Nostalgia?"

Murdock would visit the 12th Precinct another ten times in the ensuing years as Lt. Scanlon only he left Manhattan South and went to work in Internal Affairs. Once transferred to IA, Murdock as Scanlon was allowed, and no doubt encouraged, to unleash the most unappealing facets of the character's personality. Scanlon essentially embodies "the anti-Barney," if you will. Where Barney is patient, Scanlon jumps to conclusions. Where Barney treats others with the respect that he would like to receive from them, Scanlon likes to make people squirm with fear and discomfort.

Halloween Horror

One of the least sought-after assignments in the 12th was mugging detail because it required the officer to dress as a woman and take a nighttime stroll in the park in order to fool a mugger into thinking they were attacking a vulnerable female. It had to be pretty dark for a mugger to mistake these guys as women. The only officer who ever looked good in a dress was Harris who, ironically, avoided the detail longer than anyone else because he didn't want to shave off his moustache. As unappealing as Wojo and Dietrich were in a dress, there was something downright disturbing about Fish's makeover. Think of Boris Karloff in drag. The only thing funnier than Abe Vigoda in drag was the genuine interest he inspired from Phil Leeds as Lou Hector, the man who tries to pick up Fish in the park. Leeds's earnestness as Hector never falls into any kind of joke at the expense of homosexuality. In fact, it's more likely that Mr. Hector is not only extremely lonely but has his own, rather unique, taste in women.

The Usual Suspect

Don Calfa makes his first of seven *Barney Miller* appearances as Mr. DiLucca in this episode. The bug-eyed character actor was a favorite of Danny Arnold's and the cast. His oddball characterizations were the perfect embodiments of the 12th Precinct's gentle lunacy.

In this episode Calfa plays one of Danny Arnold's famous "paranoids with proof" who is convinced his decades-old cough is a result of the US Government's use of the New York subway system to test germ warfare. He seems like a nut and yet he does have an article detailing the government's unethical use of the subway system.

No Kunta Kinte

Inspired by the recent TV miniseries, *Roots*, Sgt. Harris pays a genealogy company $35 to research his ancestry. He is woefully disappointed when, rather than divulging any African royalty in his past, they discover that his great-great grandfather owned a liquor store in Cleveland.

The Last Word

> **Fish:** You have no sense of humor, Bernice. That's one of the reasons I married you.

Season 3, Episode 21: "Strike: Part 1."
Original Airdate: March 24, 1977.
Writers: Reinhold Weege (teleplay). Larry Balmagia and Dennis Koenig (story).
Director: Jeremiah Morris.
Cast of Characters: Hal Linden (Barney), Max Gail (Wojo), Steve Landesberg (Dietrich), Jack Soo (Yemana), Ron Glass (Harris), Peter Hobbs (Charlie Prevette), Peggy Pope (Lana Lane), Ron Carey (Levitt), James Gregory (Inspector Luger).

The Rundown

The NYC Police Department has been hit with a severe case of "the Blue Flu" as officers are calling in sick in anticipation of a full-fledged strike over working conditions, the hours they've been putting in, and the pay. Amidst the chaos, a lady gets robbed by a man she meets through computer dating while another man tries to rob a liquor store to take advantage of the police department strike.

Roller Coaster of Emotions

Inspector Luger visits the 12th early in the morning and expresses his disgust for the young punks who want to strike for better working conditions, or as he calls it, "stinko-pinko talk." He believes that Barney's men have a special loyalty to their captain and because of that, will report to work. When Wojo walks in the door, Luger is overjoyed and feels vindicated. Unfortunately, when he later learns that the men have "walked off" the job in the middle of the day, it's all he can do to prevent himself from getting physically ill. His graphic description of his gastrointestinal tumult does little to alleviate Barney's stressful situation.

Shop Talk

Dietrich and Yemana are forced to "Sit In" while they wait for Wojo and Harris to return from a call so they need to just sit and not work. Dietrich tries to initiate some small talk and asks Nick about labor strife in Japan. Nick reveals that he has an uncle who is head of one of the garment unions in Japan. He says to Dietrich, "I guess you could call him a rabble rouser." Dietrich replies, "Or a rabor reader." When Nick gives him a frown, Dietrich uncomfortably replies, "You know, ethnic humor. It's part of our heritage."

It's an uncomfortable moment for the two characters but the fact of the matter is, Dietrich is correct. Ethnic humor has indeed been a part of our heritage. It was a popular style of humor in the Vaudeville era and ethnic and/or dialect humor was still being employed on television in the 1970s and 1980s on shows such as, *All in the Family, Taxi, Saturday Night Live, Perfect Strangers, Soap, Night Court,* etc. In fact, Danny Arnold's desire for Chano Amenguale to get angry and spew out his frustration in rapid-fire Spanish is an example of using the character's ethnicity towards humorous ends. As for this scene, we already know Dietrich well enough to realize he has no prejudice. His comment, no doubt, had more to do with his love of puns and language than with any kind of racist feelings. That is why it surprises both the viewers and Nick Yemana.

A Rare Achiever

Peter Hobbs makes his first *Barney Miller* appearance in this episode at Charlie Prevette, a cynical crank who tries to take advantage of the Police Strike to rob a liquor store. Prevette's opinion is, "I hate scabs worse than I do the bosses!" Hobbs will eventually portray three characters in five storylines. He will portray

Philip Brauer in three of those stories and in each one Doris Roberts will join him as his wife, Harriet Brauer.

Hobbs was a solid working actor for nearly five decades on stage, film, and television. As an example of his talent and respect within the industry, Hobbs worked on *The Dick Van Dyke Show*, *The Andy Griffith Show*, *All in the Family*, *The Odd Couple*, *The Mary Tyler Moore Show*, *M*A*S*H*, *The Rockford Files*, and, of course, *Barney Miller*. All of these programs maintained the highest standards of quality in television entertainment. There are not many actors who performed in so many legitimate classics.

Inspector Luger: You know when the going gets rough you can always depend on the Polackish people.

Season 3, Episode 22:	"Strike: Part 2."
Original Airdate:	March 31, 1977.
Writers:	Tony Sheehan, Danny Arnold, Reinhold Weege (teleplay). Larry Balmagia and Dennis Koenig (story).
Director:	Danny Arnold.
Cast of Characters:	Hal Linden (Barney), Jack Soo (Yemana), Ron Glass (Harris), Steve Landesberg (Dietrich), Max Gail (Wojo), Peter Hobbs (Charlie Prevette), Peggy Pope (Lana Lane), Joe George (John Blomquist), Ron Carey (Levitt), James Gregory (Inspector Luger).

The Rundown

Barney continues to struggle with manpower problems as his crew consists of Luger, Levitt, and himself. Robbing victim, Lana Lane, tries to offer support to the cause and to Barney. Luger lets his suspect fill out his own arrest report.

Backstory

At the opening of "Strike: Part 2," we are privy to scenes that supposedly were from the preceding show except the scenes and dialogue shown were not part of the original episode. For example, there's a scene in Barney's office where he tells his superiors over the phone that Sgt. Fish is legitimately ill. We were never shown that in Part One. All we knew was that Bernice had called in sick for Fish.

It's worth noting that Abe Vigoda's spinoff, *Fish*, premiered on the ABC network as a midseason entry on February 5, 1977. That means that by the end of Season Three, Abe Vigoda was splitting his time between the sets of both *Barney Miller* and *Fish* and explains why he is missing from four of the last five episodes of Season Three. The "Strike" two-parter finished Season Three and another two-parter, "Goodbye Mr. Fish," kicked off Season Four as Fish retires from the NYPD. Vigoda would make two more subsequent visits to *Barney Miller* following Fish's retirement, one in Season Four and one in Season Seven.

Try Me

Peggy Pope as the sex-starved Miss Lane is anxious to lend a hand to Captain Miller in his time of need. She accidentally slipped in the previous episode that she is a virgin. Once we know that, nearly everything she says is either sexual or seems to have a sexual connotation to it.

Emotions Run Wild

When the squad returns to work, Dietrich suggests the group, as a whole, openly express their feelings and clear the air. Wojo feels "we walked out on Barney." Harris says they walked out on the bureaucracy, not Barney. Barney respects their decisions but points out that he was the one who paid the price more than the bureaucrats. Harris makes sure that Barney knows that no matter what happened, it was not a reflection of the level of respect that they have for Barney. In turn, Barney lets his men know that he thinks they're "a wonderful group of officers and I feel it's a privilege to serve with you."

It's an unusually serious and emotional moment in the series and so it is only right that within seconds of Barney's praise of his men, Nick exclaims, "Hold it! I have a few things I'm bugged about." Naturally, the conversation very quickly gets around to Nick's coffee.

Fourth Season

This is a significant season in the makeup of the 12th Precinct. Fish retires in the Season Four two-part premiere and as he departs, Sgt. Arthur Dietrich and Officer Carl Levitt become regulars on the show. This season also marks the one, and only, season that James Gregory, who plays Inspector Luger, will be included in the opening credits. It's also safe to say that by Season Four the show was no longer being shot in front of a live studio audience.

By Season Four, Danny's quad split [discussed earlier in the book] would have been in full use. Arnold grew tired of going back and forth from the set to the booth. He kept this quad split setup off set but down on the floor with the actors so that he and they could immediately see how a certain shot looked.

Season 4, Episode 1: "Good-Bye, Mr. Fish: Part 1."
Original Airdate: September 15, 1977.
Writers: Reinhold Weege and Danny Arnold.
Director: Danny Arnold.
Cast of Characters: Ron Carey (Levitt), Ron Glass (Harris), Max Gail (Wojo), Steve Landesberg (Dietrich), Hal Linden (Barney), Arny Freeman (Mr. Rosten), Jack Somack (Mr. Cotterman), Stanley Brock (Bruno Bender), Gregory V. Karliss (Harold Stimple).

The Rundown

Fish fails to show up on time on his last day of work and the squad grows worried. A local merchant encourages vigilantism by offering rewards for the capture and/or killing of local criminals. Two local merchants accidentally kill a thief robbing one of their stores.

Every Precinct's Got One

This episode introduces us to the inimitable Bruno Bender as played by character actor Stanley Brock. Bruno will remain an annoying presence in the 12th up until the final episode of the series. In fact, he will appear in one episode every year from here on out until Season Eight when he makes two separate appearances. Not unlike Archie Bunker, Bruno Bender is a rather small-minded reactionary who loves his guns and assorted weaponry. In keeping with Bunker's continuing evolution, Bender will also occasionally display a more humane side that only serves to make the character more fully fleshed-out and realistic.

Not Like on TV

The shock, shame, and remorse displayed by Mr. Freeman and Mr. Cotterman when they learn of the death of the robbery suspect in this episode is very real and very raw. It harkens back to the last episode of Season One, "The Hero," where Chano is forced to kill two men holding hostages in a bank. At the time,

Nick Yemana and Barney were discussing how people get killed in the movies (and on TV) all the time and the characters don't think twice about it. In real life, it's not quite that simple. Just another example of what made *Barney* special.

Season 4, Episode 2: Good-Bye, Mr. Fish: Part 2."
Original Airdate: September 22, 1977.
Writer: Reinhold Weege.
Director: Danny Arnold.
Cast of Characters: Hal Linden (Barney), Max Gail (Wojo), Steve Landesberg (Dietrich), James Gregory (Inspector Luger), Ron Glass (Harris), Jack Soo (Yemana), Larry Gelman (Edward Sellers), Timothy Jerome (Harold Sanders), Florence Stanley (Bernice Fish), and Special Guest Star, Abe Vigoda (Philip K. Fish).

The Rundown

As the day wears on, concern grows in the precinct over Fish's absence. Bernice comes to the station looking for him and Inspector Luger says all the wrong things. Once Fish shows up, he refuses to accept the idea that this is his last day. A man is brought in for pulling down security cameras in the supermarket.

Paranoid with Proof

This episode's "paranoid with proof" is Edward Sellers as played by the incomparable Larry Gelman. Mr. Sellers is horrified by the fact that "they're watching us" and making us "get the operation" to become clones. Once in the cage, he tries to talk to Nick in a very high-pitched voice because, as he explains, clones can't speak in that tone, only real humans can. At the end, when Dietrich attempts to get him out of the cage to bring him downstairs for the trip to Bellevue, Mr. Sellers panics, insisting that Bellevue is where they do the operation. Dietrich pauses and then speaks to Sellers in a high, squeaky voice, assuring him that it's okay. Once Sellers hears Dietrich's tone, he relaxes and lets Dietrich escort him downstairs.

In any other cop show, and maybe even in an actual police station, they might carry the perp out in a straitjacket, kicking and screaming, but not in Barney Miller's 12th. The key is to always do what you can to allow everyone, victim and criminal alike, the respect and dignity that is due them as human beings.

Earlier in the episode, shortly after Mr. Sellers is brought in, Harris tells Barney, "I'll call the Twinkie-mobile." Barney admonishes Harris about his unflattering euphemisms. However, in a rare use of that same vernacular, when he is trying to get Fish to accept the reality of retirement, Barney asks Fish if he wants to end up like that Twinkie out there. It's one of the rare times that we'll ever hear Barney use that slang.

Tour de Force

In his last day on the job as a series regular Abe Vigoda displays his full range of acting skills in this emotional farewell. Fish has walked the floor all night long and then walks to work from Brooklyn to Greenwich Village in the morning. He's not ready to retire but that doesn't matter. The system is not built to deal with individuals. In this world, you reach a certain age and you're obsolete. This underlying message pairs well with Mr. Sellers's paranoia about a *1984* existence where Big Brother is not only watching but also replacing the fallible humans with infallible clones.

Barney's empathy shines through as he and Fish have a heart to heart in his office. He is empathetic but also realistic and decisive. Fish is unwilling to accept his fate but Barney tells him sternly yet, dare I say, lovingly, that the curtain is coming down on this act of his life. He tries to reason that this ending is only the ending to a chapter, not to the entire story. There is more life yet to be lived, just not as a NYC police officer. The concern, the understanding, the connection between these two longtime friends who have seen so many difficult days together is one of the most touching scenes in the entire run of the series.

The Gift

The entire precinct pitched in to purchase a farewell gift for Fish but it was Wojo who was put in charge of choosing it. In a joke that doesn't land as well today as it did in 1977 when NYC was in dire financial straits, Fish opens the envelope to discover that Wojo has purchased a NYC Municipal Bond. Everyone is aghast. Wojo innocently points out that the bond is worth $1,000 when it matures to which Fish shoots back, "*If* it matures!" Then he looks closer and exclaims, "In 1997? (pauses)I would have been 83."

Ironically, Abe Vigoda would be seventy-six years old in 1997 and would live another nineteen years, passing away in 2016 at the age of ninety-four! He outlived three fellow cast members in the scene who were younger than him:

Florence Stanley (1924–2003), Ron Carey (1935–2007), and Steve Landesberg (1936–2010). James Gregory (1911–2002) and Jack Soo (1917–1979) both predeceased him but they were older than Vigoda.

This episode confirms that Vigoda was playing a character seven years older than the actor. However, Barney mentions that forced retirement is sixty-three and yet Luger is still in place and will be until the end of the run, five years later. Are we to believe that Luger was younger than Fish by at least five years? Or was there a different rule for administrative jobs?

One Final Injustice

Vigoda was nominated for an Emmy for the performance but lost out to Ricardo Montalban!

Season 4, Episode 3: "Bugs."
Original Airdate: September 29, 1977.
Writers: Larry Balmagia and Dennis Koenig.
Director: David Swift.
Cast of Characters: Max Gail (Wojo), Steve Landesberg (Dietrich), Hal Linden (Barney), Ron Glass (Harris), Jack Soo (Yemana), Mari Gorman (Roberta Kerlin), Robert Costanzo (Bill Kerlin), Paula Shaw (Paula Capshaw), Sammy Smith (Keller, exterminator), Lavelle Roby (Miss Duquette).

The Rundown

While spraying for an infestation of cockroaches, an exterminator discovers some bugs of a different kind that sets off a chain reaction of precinct paranoia. A suburban housewife tries to put some excitement back into her life by trying her hand at prostitution.

A Roach Man

In another example of Nick's affection for office pets (remember his fun with the ants in the bathroom sink?), he expresses regret that they have to kill all the cockroaches. According to Nick, "That's about as close as I've ever come to having a pet."

Internal Affairs

When the exterminator accidentally discovers electronic listening devices in the squad room and Barney's office, the boys naturally assume that they are being targeted by Internal Affairs in some kind of sting operation. This happens occasionally throughout the series and Barney always needs to remind his men that they have nothing to hide.

New York City in the 1970s was not only beset by financial problems and political turmoil but was also the decade of Frank Serpico and his disclosure about the rampant corruption within the NYC Police Department. This historical reality colors these particular episodes and was, no doubt, the inspiration for the long-running obsession of Lt. Scanlon to find a bad apple in the barrel of the 12th Precinct.

Political Mention

As the boys start to search for more microphone bugs, Barney thinks they're overreacting. Harris says, "It's like 1984!" To which Nick adds, "1942."

Nick's comment is particularly poignant because as a Japanese American, Goro Suzuki (not yet known as Jack Soo) had been put in an internment camp in 1942 following the start of World War II. It's hard to believe Nick's comment is just a coincidence as opposed to a political statement on what happened to Japanese Americans and therefore, to Jack Soo himself. Soo was the one actor on the show that Danny Arnold knew better than anyone else so he certainly knew of Soo's history.

First Time Visit

Mari Gorman makes the first of what will be six appearances on *Barney Miller*. Like Landesberg and Carey, although she starts as a criminal of sorts, her next three appearances are as Rosslyn Licori, a police officer assigned to the 12th. Unfortunately, like most policewomen assigned to the squad, she doesn't last long as a part of the 12th Precinct's "boy's club." In her last two appearances, she will be cast in another memorable role as that of the unfortunate spouse of Bruno Bender.

Gorman is hilarious in this auspicious debut as a neglected Connecticut housewife willing to do anything to reignite her husband's interest and passion. Compassionate Barney eventually gets her to open up when he spots a picture of her family in her wallet. She's the mother of four children: Billy Jr (aged thirteen), Tracy (eleven), and eighteen-month-old twins. When Barney guesses that this is the first time she's ever tried this, she sighs and replies, "You can go crazy in Connecticut, you know?"

Paranoia Will Destroy-Ya

By the way, it's eventually discovered that the listening devices are old and not in working order so the boys are relieved . . . for the time being. Once again, however, we've seen a great example of Danny Arnold's belief in the humor of paranoia.

Season 4, Episode 4: "Corporation."
Original Airdate: October 6, 1977.
Writers: Lee H. Grant, Tony Sheehan, and Danny Arnold (teleplay). Lee H. Grant (story).
Director: Hal Linden.
Cast of Characters: Ron Glass (Harris), Hal Linden (Barney), Steve Landesberg (Dietrich), Jack Soo (Yemana), Max Gail (Wojo), David Dukes (Brad Laneer), Fran Ryan (Mrs. Hirsch, homeless woman), Vernon Weddle (Alvin Trager, the hawk).

The Rundown

A corporate lawyer comes in to file a complaint about a rash of vandalism being perpetrated on his company by a corporate avenger self-named The Hawk. Wojo brings in a Bag Lady who's been the victim of a mugging.

Like a Mother to Me

Wojo finds it difficult sending Mrs Hirsch the bag lady, played by Fran Ryan, back out on the streets. Barney argues that he must respect her right to live her life as she chooses. Ultimately, Wojo says he feels as though helping her would make up for the pain he caused his own mother. When Barney tells him that we all have the same feeling about growing up, Wojo reveals that he's talking about the physical pain he caused his mother. He was eleven and a half pounds at birth and his mother endured thirteen hours of labor.

For her part, Mrs. Hirsch doesn't necessarily think of him as a son. With a twinkle in her eye, she asks Wojo if he'd like to go to Bermuda with her next winter?

42 Across

Actor Vernon Weddle, as Alvin Trager, The Hawk, is a window washer at MacMillan Chemicals and gets brought in for spray-painting a letter on various windows of the building, described by Nick as "a giant, filthy crossword puzzle." Mr. Trager's logical response is, "People love word games."

Trager is this episode's "paranoid with proof." He says that one of the chemicals they're manufacturing made the men who were working on it in the manufacturing plants sterile. He may come across as a raving lunatic but history has certainly validated many of his claims.

> **Trager:** Every living thing you see is covered with filth and stinks of contamination!

In retrospect, it may not be funny but it's certainly true.

Captain of the Ship

This was the first of three episodes directed by Hal Linden. Max Gail was the only other cast member to direct any episodes during the run of the series.

Season 4, Episode 5: "Burial."
Original Airdate: October 20, 1977.
Writer: Michael Russnow.
Director: Danny Arnold.
Cast of Characters: Hal Linden (Barney), Ron Glass (Harris), Max Gail (Wojo), Steve Landesberg (Dietrich), Jack Soo (Yemana), Abe Vigoda (Fish), Jack Kruschen (Julius Wittenow), Sy Kramer (Nelson Hubbard).

The Rundown

Fish makes his first post-retirement visit to the 12th and is itching to get back in the saddle and help out when he realizes Barney is short-handed. A body is stolen from a mortuary and the squad has to figure out where the deceased's best friend has buried his body. It's a simple but marvelously acted episode with only one crime that is then perfectly integrated with the secondary storyline of Fish's boredom with retirement.

Subtle but Brilliant

The magic of *Barney Miller* was the absolute believability of the men of the 12th. The show's format was one that allowed, and occasionally even called for, over-the-top scene chewing by victims and suspects alike. However, the cops within the squad, while quirky, were never caricatures. Every actor's portrayal of their character's foibles and eccentricities rang with the truth of authenticity. It is a testament to the talents of this stellar group of actors.

There's a subtle brilliance in Wojo painfully explaining to Barney why he can't bring himself to go to the funeral parlor. He tells Barney that his grandmother died when he was six and his parents told him she was asleep. Barney tries to reassure him, telling Wojo, "Not unusual." Wojo replies, "I tried to wake her up." Barney immediately just assigns another officer to visit the funeral parlor rather than continue down this road with Wojo. It's simple, the timing is spot on, and it makes an otherwise mundane exchange absolutely hilarious.

The Undertaker Blues

Sy Kramer as the harried undertaker, Mr. Hubbard, steals the comic glory in this episode. He's a bundle of nerves and complaints due to his stressful occupation. His most disturbing complaint comes when he says to Barney, "Business is bad enough. I mean, with all the modern medical techniques, pretty soon people are liable to live 'til they're a hundred. And then where will I be?"

Kramer played a good number of small character parts throughout the late seventies, particularly on TV detective shows like *Kojak* and *Starsky and Hutch* (1975–1979). He also appeared in one episode of Danny Arnold's short-lived cop comedy/drama *Joe Bash* in 1986. Kramer died at the relatively young age of fifty-eight in 1992.

Another Great Résumé

Jack Kruschen was another character actor with a long list of credits that spread out over nearly half a century. Canadian-born Kruschen's long career was primarily in the medium of television but he made some memorable appearances in films such as *The Apartment* (1960), *Cape Fear* (1962), and the infamous *Under the Rainbow* (1981). His TV work included dozens of guest shots on network television programs including *Dragnet* (1951–1959), *The Rifleman* (1958–1963), and *Ironside*. He also appeared in the original 1962 Broadway production of *I Can Get It for You Wholesale* with a nineteen-year-old Barbra Streisand.

The Last Word

> **Julius Wittenow:** Never trust a man who can't get a squirrel to eat out of his hand.

Season 4, Episode 6: "Copy Cat."
Original Airdate: October 27, 1977.
Writers: Douglas Wyman and Tony Sheehan.
Director: Jeremiah Morris.
Cast of Characters: Jack Soo (Yemana), Steve Landesberg (Dietrich), Hal Linden (Barney), Ron Glass (Harris), Max Gail (Wojo), Don Calfa (Angelo Dodi), John Dullaghan (Harold Durrell), Don Sherman (Mr. Boston), Norman Bartold (Roy Jenkins).

The Rundown

Wojo finally passes the sergeant's exam but is disenchanted when he realizes that not much has changed with the day-to-day mundanity of his cop's life. Harris is having difficulty finding a new apartment. Nick is on the trail of a copycat criminal who is getting ideas from television shows.

Fifth Time's a Charm

It took Wojo five times before he passed the sergeant's exam. Now that he's a sergeant he's disappointed that so little has changed. He still has to fill out reports, do filing, answer the phone, etc. However, Barney speaks for all of us when he asks Wojo, "What did you expect to happen? That all of a sudden all the paperwork, all the tedium was miraculously going to disappear?" One of the constant themes of *Barney Miller* is that real life police work is nothing like the shoot-'em-up action that movies and television portray as a cop's life.

Copycat Crimes

Don Sherman as Mr. Boston comes in to report an attempted robbery at his coffee shop. He tells Nick that the M.O. used by the culprit was the same as he saw on a TV cop show a couple of nights earlier. Barney says the crime reported by Mr. Boston is the fifth copycat crime in the last two weeks. Nick explains, "There's a lot of good things on. It's a new season."

Nick's explains to Mr. Boston why he can't watch TV cop shows.

Nick:	I can't enjoy them because being a cop myself I spot the mistakes and inaccuracies and the fantastic things that in real life never happen.
Mr. Boston:	On the show they caught him.
Nick:	Good example.

Meta Danger

Nick searches through the *TV Guide* to try to get a lead on the copycat criminal's next job. The issue Nick's reading has a cover art portrait of Donny and Marie Osmond done by Richard Amsel from the Oct. 8-14, 1977 edition. The cover story was about Marie's new image (she was just about to turn eighteen) that included hard-hitting reportage detailing how Bob Mackie would now be designing Marie's gowns and Arnie Kogen, one of Dean Martin's old writers, would now be penning her show's comedy sketches.

As for schedules, it was the week ABC broadcast the fifth episode of their shocking new show, *Soap*. In fact, below the listing for *Soap* the *TV Guide* printed a disclaimer that read, "Pre-empts regular programming. ABC plans to make an announcement that this episode may not be suitable for all family members." The storyline in question has to do with Corrinne, played by the lovely Diana Canova, trying to seduce a priest, Father Tim Flotsky, played by *Barney* alum Sal Viscuso. Luckily, there was no *Barney Miller* episode broadcast that week or else Yemana might have thought he'd slipped into the Twilight Zone.

A Part of the Family

While actors like Don Calfa and Phil Leeds are remembered for the number of times they appeared on the show as different characters, it's John Dullaghan who appeared on *Barney Miller* more times than anyone else who was not a member of law enforcement or Barney's wife, Elizabeth. Dullaghan played four separate characters before appearing as Ray Brewer, the persona he would maintain through his last six appearances on the program right up to, and including, the series finale, "Landmark: Part 3." In this episode he plays a recovering alcoholic who has fallen off the wagon. He tried to hold up a liquor store using his finger as a gun. Unfortunately, he forgot to put his finger in his coat pocket before he made his attempt.

The aforementioned Calfa makes his second visit to the 12th as the copycat criminal Angelo Dodi who's damaged his hearing by riding on top of a speeding subway train. His character is portrayed as a whimsical criminal looking to share in the magic that is television, saying, "I just wanted a little of the adventure and excitement that they always have on TV."

We're introduced to another *Barney Miller* frequent flier in this episode in the person of Norman Bartold. This is his first of five appearances on the show and he always plays a guy who's ultra-calm, ultra-cool, ultra-dull. Oh, and ultra-funny.

Just the Facts

- Harris deals with "Unfair housing practices," not because he's black but because he's a cop. They won't rent to anyone who doesn't have a steady job.

The Last Word

In another example of the meta-fictional nature of this episode, Dodi says to Dietrich, "You don't look like cops. You don't act like the cops I seen on TV."

Dietrich: Mr. Dodi, television has created a false image of policemen. Portraying them as colorful, infallible super beings when actually we're just average people. Pretty much like everybody else.
Dodi: (sadly) Ohhh.
Dietrich: (with sass) And that's the name of *that* tune.

(Dietrich borrows a line from Robert Blake who, at the time, was playing the flashy, hip police detective Tony Baretta on the popular ABC drama, *Baretta* (1975–1978).

Season 4, Episode 7: "Blizzard."
Original Airdate: November 3, 1977.
Writer: Tony Sheehan.
Director: Danny Arnold.
Cast of Characters: Steve Landesberg (Dietrich), Hal Linden (Barney), Jack Soo (Yemana), Max Gail (Wojo), Ron Glass (Harris), Alex Henteloff (Arnold Ripner), Lou Cutell (Jerome Grodin), Tom Henschel (Eugene LaSalle), Lewis Charles (Leo Lujak), Louis Quinn (EMS Man), John David McCall (EMS Man), Al Berry (Coroner's pickup man), Trent Dolan (Coroner's pickup man).

The Rundown

In the middle of a city snowstorm, Wojo runs down a culprit who was rolling drunks. The suspect then dies in the middle of questioning. Dietrich and Harris bring in a man harassing pedestrians while warning them of a coming new Ice Age. Harris considers incorporating himself while ambulance chaser Arnold Ripner is searching for a lawsuit.

R. N. Harris, Inc.

Harris is planning to incorporate himself in anticipation of his eventual wealth as an author. He informs Barney that he has a number of manuscripts and screenplays out, presumably to producers and publishers.

This proposed incorporation is one of the first things Harris does that tends to indicate he is setting himself above his co-workers. These incidents escalate when Harris actually does get a book published and his attitude begins to generate resentment from the members of the squad.

Ultimately, Arnold Ripner talks Harris out of incorporating, telling him that it's more trouble and cost than it's worth to him in his current situation. Years later, Ripner actually does sue Ron Harris, author. Had Harris incorporated at this time and stayed incorporated he might have better protected himself against the infamous ambulance chaser.

All Dressed Up and No One to Sue

Lujak, played by Lewis Charles, is a mugging suspect who dies of a heart attack during questioning. As luck would have it, Alex Henteloff's infamous Arnold Ripner, the shyster lawyer, turns out to be Lujak's attorney. As always, Arnold smells a lawsuit. Eventually, Barney and Wojo realize that because the client is dead and he had no next of kin, there's actually not anyone on whose behalf Arnold can sue!

Secrets of the Orient

When Nick offers Barney a cup of ginseng tea, it's approached as a strange and exotic "Oriental herb." Today it's common in vitamin supplements, teas, facial creams, and candies.

Oh, and we don't say "Oriental" anymore either.

The Big Freeze

Lou Cutell's character Jerome Grodin warns of the next Ice Age. He stresses the change of the climate, the cooling of the oceans. Sadly and ironically, just the opposite came true. For example, according to the Grodin character, the perimeter of the polar ice cap was increasing by forty-six feet per year. In reality, the amount of polar ice has been consistently decreasing now since the 1980s.

Tribute or Typo?

Why is Fish's name still on the blackboard? He retired over a month ago.

The Last Word

Ripner: Dietrich, I want to talk to you. I want you tell me everything you know.
Dietrich: Sure, how much time ya got?

Season 4, Episode 8: "Chase."
Original Airdate: November 17, 1977.
Writers: Tom Reeder, Reinhold Weege, and Danny Arnold.
Director: Jeremiah Morris.
Cast of Characters: Hal Linden (Barney), Jack Soo (Yemana), Max Gail (Wojo), Ron Glass (Harris), Steve Landesberg (Dietrich), George Murdock (Lt. Ben Scanlon), Luis Avalos (Antonio Mione), George Loros (Glynn / Sgt. Michael P. Hunt), Joey Aresco (Bando), Mews Small as "Marya Small" (Sheila Rosen).

The Rundown

Harris and Dietrich bring in a heroin dealer who turns out to be a spy for Internal Affairs. A cab driver and his fare come into the precinct to report their cab being stolen. Turns out that the culprit is Wojo who commandeered it to chase a man who robbed a liquor store.

The Most Beautiful of All the Romance Languages

Luis Avalos plays Antonio Mione, the cab driver, who regales us with his passionate rage in Spanish. If you think of Detective Chano Amenguale, Detective

Maria Battista, and this character played by Avalos, it seems hard to dispute that Danny Arnold loved a Spanish accent. I think it's probably something native to our English language ears that a romance language tirade, particularly Spanish or Italian, contains not only the spark of passion but a sense of inherent humor as well.

Avalos was part of the group of actors including Rita Moreno, Judy Graubart, and Morgan Freeman that appeared in the popular educational children's program *The Electric Company* (1971–1977).

Les Miserables

It's both reasonable and fun to think of Lt. Scanlon as the Inspector Javert (*Les Miserables*, publ. 1862) of the *Barney Miller* universe. He is fanatically committed to finding a chink in the armor of the honest men of the 12th Precinct. Through the years, he's constantly sniffing out every minor infraction, only to come up short of the damning evidence he's desperate to find.

Shining Example

This episode contains one of the series' best scenes with Barney and his nemesis from Internal Affairs. Scanlon is desperate to get Barney to admit that it's at least possible for Barney to do something wrong and Barney refuses to give him the satisfaction. All the men turned down Scanlon's man when he offered them bribes. Scanlon also reveals in this confrontation that he spent sixteen years on the Vice Squad and proudly proclaims that he has "the respect of every hooker and deviant between Times Square and the Village."

Left Out

Nick Yemana reveals to Dietrich that in all his years as a cop, he's never once been offered a bribe. When Dietrich asks if that bothers him, Nick tells him, "Well, I wouldn't take the money but sometimes it's just nice to be asked."

A Face for the Mug Book

Character actor George Loros plays Scanlon's undercover man, Sgt. Michael P. Hunt. Loros was a familiar face on 1970s television, particularly on various detective shows such as *Kojak*, *Starsky and Hutch*, and *The Rockford Files*. As a character actor, he was invariably cast as a criminal or a cop. Since the

1990s, Loros has been busy as an acting teacher while appearing on stage in a variety of productions, including playing Duke Mantee in an Off-Broadway production of *The Petrified Forest*. In the 2000s, he returned to the small screen with a recurring role in the popular *Sopranos* (1999–2007) on HBO and as part of that cast won a SAG Award for Performance by an Ensemble in a Drama Series.

Glutton for Punishment

Wojo is going to Sid's for sandwiches and asks Barney if he wants anything. Barney asks him, "Isn't that the place on Tenth that the Board of Health closed down?" Wojo tells him they opened up again. "You want to take a chance?" Barney declines. However, we can assume from this exchange that Wojo is quite the culinary adventurist. After all, it was he who once found a dead fly in his sandwich from Grossman's Delicatessen (S.1/E.7) and then weeks later almost died of food poisoning when the mob intercepted a deli order in an attempt to kill an important witness (S.1/E.10). His appetite was apparently bigger than his fear of walking into that big deli in the sky.

Season 4, Episode 9: "Thanksgiving Story."
Original Airdate: November 24, 1977.
Writer: Reinhold Weege.
Director: David Swift.
Cast of Characters: Hal Linden (Barney), Jack Soo (Yemana), Max Gail (Wojo), Ron Glass (Wojo), Steve Landesberg (Dietrich), Ian Wolfe (Rudolf Biederman), George Skaff (Dr. Engels), Anita Dangler (Ana Rada), Tom Lacy (Ed Gerrity), Susan Davis (Nurse Krewson), Ted Schwartz (Dukane), Charles Lucia as "Chip Lucia" (Kenny Brewster), Kip King (Paul Powell).

The Rundown

A man stabs his unemployed brother-in-law over a turkey drumstick. Three patients wander off from a private mental hospital. Nick tries to run down college football scores while Inspector Luger is searching for an invitation to holiday dinner.

The Morning Line

Nick's underdog pick for his Thanksgiving football game is Alcorn State. Unfortunately, he has a difficult time finding anyone who's heard of the team, let alone has a score. Barney asks Nick, rather incredulously, "They play even on Thanksgiving?" Strange since Thanksgiving football was already a tradition. Apparently, Barney wasn't much of a football fan.

Different Neighborhoods

When Harris and Dietrich bring in a man who stabbed his brother-in-law over a turkey drumstick, Barney wonders out loud, "Whatever happened to old fashioned Thanksgiving? You know, family and friends, your mother made a big roast turkey, stuffing, cranberries . . ." Harris, staring off into space, interjects, "Spam." Taken aback, Barney just says, "Sorry." Harris continues, "She formed that stuff into little drumsticks."

It's a very understated moment that calls attention to what must have been two very different economic backgrounds. The insularity of the *Barney Miller* universe is such that we rarely hear anything about the childhoods or the families of the men of the 12th Precinct. Therefore, when someone *does* let a morsel slip, it's even more compelling.

Happy Thanksgiving

The inspector comes in ostensibly to wish everyone a Happy Thanksgiving. In truth, he's there angling for an invitation to Thanksgiving dinner with Barney. His other choice is to go visit ol' Brownie in the nursing home. When Barney says, "I'm sure he'd appreciate that," Luger says to Barney, "Appreciate it? Barney, he can't tell the difference between me and a lamp. He just lays there like a sack full of Jell-O. He gurgles every now and then."

Luger's also a little miffed when he extends the "Happy Thanksgiving" greeting to Dietrich and doesn't receive a similar sentiment back. Dietrich tells him that as an agnostic, he doesn't adhere to the custom because of his uncertainty over whom to thank specifically.

Luger: I mean saying "Happy Thanksgiving" is just the same as saying, "Hey, good morning, hiya buddy!"
Dietrich: That's true.
Luger: So? Happy Thanksgiving!
Dietrich: Hiya, buddy!

Paranoid with Proof

In this episode, our "paranoid with proof" is Dukane as portrayed by actor Ted Schwartz. Dukane is one of the three "escapees" from the mental hospital. When he panics or feels threatened, he strips off all his clothes and goes naked. As he's leaving he yells, "I don't care what anybody says, it's healthier to live without clothing!" Dietrich replies, "You're right," confirming Dukane's belief.

Dukane: You agree?
Dietrich: Studies have shown that as a group nudists are less frustrated than people who wear clothes. Their blood pressure is lower and in general their outlook is much better.
Dukane: Then why do you wear clothing?
Dietrich: Gotta wear a badge.

Season 4, Episode 10: "Tunnel."
Original Airdate: December 1, 1977.
Writers: Michael Russnow and Tony Sheehan (teleplay). Michael Russnow (story).
Director: David Swift.
Cast of Characters: Jack Soo (Yemana), Max Gail (Wojo), Hal Linden (Barney), Ron Glass (Harris), Steve Landesberg (Dietrich), Jay Gerber (Howard Gabriel), J. J. Barry (Leroy Kreutzer), Leonard Stone (Burton Shaw).

The Rundown

The phones seem strangely silent until it's discovered that they are out of order. A teacher snaps and has a breakdown in front of the student body. Wojo dies in a tunnel collapse, temporarily. Nick discovers the hunch bet of a lifetime and Harris is still looking for a place to live.

Welcome Back

Jay Gerber plays Howard Gabriel, a History teacher at Harding High School who's been pushed over the edge by his students. Barney is somewhat shocked when Nick shows him the contents of Gabriel's briefcase: handcuffs, mace, and a blackjack. Gabriel explains to Barney, "That's the first rule of teaching—get their respect."

Gabriel mocks the then-popular show, *Welcome Back Kotter*, telling Barney, "If I told them jokes like he did they'd cut my heart out with their little pencils!" He was referring, of course, to comedian Gabe Kaplan, who played the title character Gabe Kotter who returns to his former high school to teach the most unteachable group of students. He wangles his way into their hearts with old jokes and a Groucho Marx impersonation. At the time, *Kotter* ran at 8 p.m. Thursday nights on ABC preceding *Barney Miller*, which came on at 9 p.m. For the 1977–1978 TV season, *Welcome Back, Kotter* finished twenty-sixth in the Nielsen ratings while *Barney Miller* finished seventeenth.

Leonard Stone as Burton Shaw, Vice Principal of Harding High School, comes in to retrieve Gabriel but the teacher refuses to go back. Shaw shrugs off Gabriel's mental breakdown telling Barney, "You want crazy? Mrs. Slade—She taught Sex Education. She showed an animated VD film narrated by a little cricket. The kids tore that room apart! She's in a rest home upstate now."

Déjà Vu All Over Again

J. J. Barry as the tunneling thief Leroy Kreutzer is very reminiscent of Angelo "The Mole" Molinari portrayed by Ron Carey in the Season Two finale, "The Mole" about a guy tunneling into a jewelry store in order to rob it. Once in custody both "The Mole" and Barry's character, Kreutzer, complain about how challenging their business has become what with the cost of materials, rents, alarms, wardrobe, etc.

Unsolved Mysteries

Wojo gets caught in a tunnel collapse chasing the would-be jewelry store robber. Barney tells the squad that when they pulled him out of the debris he had no heartbeat, no pulse. He's originally sent to the hospital for observation but shows up a short time later, telling Barney he feels good. The men are thrilled to see their friend "back from the dead." In a very poignant little moment, Nick is on the verge of tears when he sees Wojo.

Nick asks Wojo if he felt anything when he was "gone." Before Wojo can answer, Dietrich says, "No. After death there's a void. There's a complete cessation of all feeling." Wojo begs to differ, telling Nick, "Yeah, I felt something. It was kinda pleasant. I felt real warm and uh I think I might've heard these voices." Dietrich immediately interjects, "Sure, you were laying on the phone line."

A Sign from God

Nick discovers the hunch bet of a lifetime in the morning racing form. Running in the first race at Belmont is a horse named "Pick Me Nick." It's 30–1 on the morning line.

At the end of the episode Dietrich's certainty of nothingness has Wojo questioning what comes after this life. Barney begs off saying it's not his area of expertise. Nick says to Dietrich, "You mean to tell me that you don't believe that there is something up there that plans everything for all of us?" Dietrich replies, "If you're talking about a personal interested being who's directing our lives and destinies, I'd have to say no." Nick tells Dietrich he doesn't happen to agree with him. Just then the phone rings and Nick answers it. When he gets off the phone, he announces to the squad that "Pick Me Nick" won and he made four hundred bucks. He then says with certainty, referring to their existential debate, "I guess that settles that."

Season 4, Episode 11:	"Atomic Bomb."
Original Airdate:	December 15, 1977.
Writers:	Tom Reeder and Reinhold Weege.
Director:	Noam Pitlik.
Cast of Characters:	Steve Landesberg (Dietrich), Max Gail (Wojo), Jack Soo (Yemana), Hal Linden (Barney), Ron Glass (Harris), Phil Leeds (Harry Kruger), Stephen Pearlman (Sgt. Kavanaugh), Karl Bruck (Dr. Reinhold Bauer), John Getz (William McKuen), Helen Verbit (Evelyn Kruger), Al Ruscio (Mr. Seldes), Will Seltzer (James Thayer), Rod Colbin (Mr. Swanson of Metropolitan New York Cryonic Society).

The Rundown

An apartment superintendent is concerned about a young man doing experiments in his room. A hysterical wife comes in concerned about her husband who wants to spend all their money to cryogenically freeze himself.

The Deep Freeze

Evelyn Kruger, played by Helen Verbit, comes into the precinct in hysterics over the fact that her husband wants to freeze himself for a hundred years and come back when the world and medical technology have advanced to a better state.

In 1977, cryogenics was a generally unknown phenomenon in mainstream society. The American Cryogenic Society began in 1969 and started selling the idea of freezing people in the 1970s. There is a company called Alcor whose most recent statistics state that as of 2020 more than 1,300 people have signed up to be preserved when they die. There is a yearly membership fee and the actual cost of freezing once a member dies ranges from approximately $88,000 (for just a head) to over $200,000 (for the entire body). Baseball fans will recall all too well the very public battle that Ted Williams's children had over the question of freezing their dad's head.

The questions set forth by Mrs. Kruger are the logical reasons against freezing. "What would we do there? Everyone we know would be gone."

Just A "C" Student

Will Selzter is the college student, James Thayer, whose "creative" activities are brought into question. They retrieve a device from his apartment but have no idea what it is. Steven Pearlman as Sgt. Kavanaugh of the bomb squad is certain, however, that it's not a bomb. Thayer assures them it is indeed a bomb. "It just lacks the fissionable material to make it operational." Even as Barney realizes the young man is talking about an atomic bomb he thinks, or perhaps hopes, it's just a model, not an actual bomb per se. Thayer assures him, "A smaller version but a practical working model. About 2 kiloton I would judge." He explains that it's part of his Master's thesis. He wanted to do something a little different.

Mr. Know-It-All

Following the long discussion trying to determine whether or not the project that Thayer has produced is, in fact, an atomic device or not, Dietrich walks in from the other room to ask Barney an unrelated question. As soon as he spots the device on Nick's desk he says, "Where the hell didya get the atomic bomb?"

Unusual Circumstances

This is a different type of *Barney Miller* episode in that Danny Arnold and the writers Reinhold Weege and Tom Reeder take a very definite stance within the storyline against nuclear arms. This episode premiered in the years between the Strategic Arms Limitation Treaties between the United States and Russia that were signed in 1972 and 1979.

Karl Buck plays the physicist, Dr. Reinhold Bauer, from the Atomic Energy Commission. At one point he says to Thayer, "My dear boy, can you imagine how things would be if we had developed this first?" Thayer looks at him puzzled and says, "We did." Bauer in his thick German accent says, "Huh? Oh, sure, sure, *now* we did but before, we didn't."

Thayer tells Bauer that he believes as scientists they have a responsibility to proceed with progress and technology in a cautious manner for the sake of mankind. Bauer disagrees. He believes as scientists they are meant to explore and create and what mankind does with their discoveries is not their responsibility. In a moment of proselytizing worthy of a late run episode of *M*A*S*H*, Bauer says to Nick in disgust, "Look at that boy, he's going to waste a brilliant mind. Passing up the chance of a lifetime." Nick quietly says to him, "Yeah. Maybe he's giving us one."

Generally speaking, the program was apolitical. It certainly satirized bureaucracy but if it can be accused of promoting any kind of philosophy at all it would probably be humanism.

Anachronism

Barney: Can we get you a cup of coffee?
Mrs. Kruger: I can't drink coffee. I got a gall bladder I wouldn't wish on Marshal Tito.

Marshal Tito was the dictator of Yugoslavia for almost three decades from the 1950s until 1980. Mel Brooks loves to tell the story about shooting his film *The Twelve Chairs* in Yugoslavia in the mid-1960s. As a Soviet bloc country, travel was restricted and according to Brooks they couldn't go anywhere because "Tito had the car."

Season 4, Episode 12: "The Bank."
Original Airdate: January 5, 1978.
Writer: Tony Sheehan.
Director: Noam Pitlik.
Cast of Characters: Hal Linden (Barney), Steve Landesberg (Dietrich), Jack Soo (Yemana), Max Gail (Wojo), Ron Glass (Harris), Sandy Sprung (Helen Bateman), Peter Jurasik (Philip Hamel), Jodie Mann (Arlene Hamel), John LaMotta (Moving van driver).

The Rundown

Detective Harris finds himself without a place to live while all of his possessions are loaded in a moving van with no place to go. A disgruntled customer breaks up a sperm bank when he discovers they have lost/destroyed his, um, deposit. Harris blows up at Inspector Luger when he uses the phrase "shuffling off."

Reconciliation Can Hurt

Harris is about to move into a new apartment when he arrives at his new place and learns the couple from whom he is subletting, Harold and Lois Nemmings, has decided not to break up and to keep their apartment. He arrives at the precinct with his possessions in tow and a moving van full of his stuff. According to his calculations, just having the van standing by is costing him 95¢ a minute!

Another Area of Expertise

Not surprisingly, Wojo is disgusted by what he considers the unnatural idea of a sperm bank. Even less surprising is that when it comes to the subject of sperm banks Dietrich has the advantage over his fellow officers. When Dietrich begins to speak on the subject, Barney says, "I have a sinking feeling that we have just entered another of your areas of interest and expertise." It displays an early frustration in Barney over Dietrich's vast storehouse of knowledge. If Barney is growing annoyed at Dietrich now, how's he going to handle the next three and a half years?

Barney's frustration with Dietrich is mild compared to his partner across the desk, Ron Harris. Their relationship will be made even more complex starting with this episode when Harris is forced to move in with Dietrich until he can find another apartment.

Shuffle Off to Greenwich Village

Inspector Luger is genuinely concerned when he offends Harris with the phrase, "Before you shuffle off." He is aghast that they could think he is a racist although that term is never used. This unfortunate incident also reveals Luger's insecurity and self-awareness. He begins to display his paranoia over the possibility that everyone finds him to be dull or boring.

In the second half of the episode, Luger apologizes to Harris and he truly means it. He does great until he tries to get Harris to do what he thinks is a hip handshake, indicative of the type used by black men at the time. The exchange is at once uncomfortable, sweet, and hilarious.

This is a wonderful episode for James Gregory as he shows off not only the depth of feelings within Luger but also the scope of his own acting talent.

Self Control

Kudos to Jodie Mann who plays Mrs. Hamel in this episode, the wife of the man whose sperm was accidentally destroyed. She cries, nonstop, throughout her entire time onscreen until the very last moments when Dietrich reveals to her and Mr. Hamel the potential solution of artificial insemination. Mann wrote me, "Originally I wasn't supposed to cry . . . that wasn't in the script. When I finally started, I cried from about 3 p.m. until 4 a.m. the next day! You can only imagine the headache I had for the next two days."

For the Record

Inspector Luger makes a comment to Barney in which he admits to being "no Herb Shriner." Long forgotten now, Shriner was a humorist on radio and then early television. He and his wife died in 1970 in an automobile accident. He was fifty-one years old. His son, Wil Shriner, is also a talented comedian, actor, and television director.

Season 4, Episode 13: "The Ghost."
Original Airdate: January 12, 1978.
Writer: Reinhold Weege.
Director: Lee Bernhardi.
Cast of Characters: Jack Soo (Yemana), Hal Linden (Barney), Max Gail (Wojo), Ron Glass (Harris), Steve Landesberg (Dietrich), Nehemiah Persoff (Carl Simms), Tito Vandis (Dimitrios Stefanos), Kenneth Tigar (Elliot Porter), Caroline McWilliams (Tricia Morgan).

The Rundown

Nick investigates complaints about a pornographic bakery while Harris discovers the difficulties of living with Arthur Dietrich. A wife-for-hire wants her husband to leave her alone. The men investigate a call about a man destroying his apartment but when they arrive the suspect in question swears it wasn't him, it was a ghost.

Cut the Calories

According to Nick, the woman who called in complaining about the pornographic bakery was particularly offended by a pair of strawberry cupcakes. As far as we know, the baked goods that Nick purchased for evidence was a loaf of rye bread with poppy seeds and at least one cookie.

Casper by Any Other Name

Naturally, Wojo is skeptical about the existence of Mr. Porter's (Ken Tigar) ghost. He patronizingly refers to the spirit as Casper but as we will subsequently learn, the ghost's name is Julius. He's been in Mr. Porter's family for years. He died in the Revolutionary War—shot for treason.

Poor Ken Tigar got a lot of physical workouts in that cage between his appearances as a werewolf, a man obsessed by the devil, and Mr. Porter's harassment from Julius.

Occupation: None

Caroline McWilliams, the attractive young actress that plays Tricia Morgan in this episode, would join the cast of *Soap* on ABC just a few months after this episode aired. She hadn't done a lot of TV work before *Barney Miller* and, according to Diana Canova who played Corinne on *Soap*, the two shows shot very near one another on the ABC Television Center lot on Prospect Avenue so it's entirely possible that one of *Soap's* producers or casting agents saw her on the *Barney Miller* set and grabbed her for their show.

In the show, Wojo suggests she get a regular job, "be a secretary, something legit." Ironically, when she joined the second season of *Soap* as the recurring character, Sally, she played the sexy, smitten secretary in Burt's construction office.

A year after her stint on *Soap*, she landed a weekly role in the *Soap* spinoff, *Benson* (1979–1986), and spent two years as Marcy Hill. This time she was secretary to Governor Eugene X. Gatling, played by James Noble.

In real life, McWilliams was married to actor Michael Keaton from 1982 to 1990 with whom she had a son, Sean. Sadly, she died in 2010 at the age of sixty-four from cancer.

Tito Vandis makes his second of three appearances, this time as a Mr. Stefanos, the man who marries Ms. Morgan so he can stay in America. The immigration officer, Mr. Simms, is portrayed by legendary character actor Nehemiah Persoff who is making his first of three appearances on *Barney Miller*.

God Complex

Even in the 1970s, a job in the Immigration Department was a difficult one. Mr. Simms, US Immigration, is a man under a lot of stress. He says to Barney, "Do you know what it's like to look into their pathetic, hopeful faces and to say, 'You stay, you go. You live, you die.' Do you know what it's like dealing with 290,000 huddled masses yearning to be free? Oh sure! 'Give me your tired and your poor.' Big talk from a statue!"

The Last Word

Mr. Simms: Look, they beat the system. They got around the law.
Mr. Stefanos: It's the American way, no?

Season 4, Episode 14: "Appendicitis."
Original Airdate: January 19, 1978.
Writer: Tony Sheehan.
Director: Noam Pitlik.
Cast of Characters: Max Gail (Wojo), Jack Soo (Yemana), Steve Landesberg (Dietrich), Ron Glass (Harris), Hal Linden (Barney), Ron Carey (Levitt), Jack Bernardi (Abel Kleiner), Michael Durrell (Howard Altman), Jade McCall (Ambulance attendant), Jerry D'Emilio (Ambulance attendant), Norman Klar (Victor Jurasic).

The Rundown

Nick suffers an appendicitis attack. An elderly bounty hunter moves into the 12th Precinct. A sugar addict causes a disturbance in a candy store when they skip past his number for service.

Subtle Culture

The episode opens with Nick complaining of an upset stomach. When Wojo asks if it was something he ate, Nick says, "I think the fish I ate last night. It didn't agree with me." Wojo says, "Spoiled." Nick replies, "No, cooked." This is one of the more subtle references to Nick's Japanese heritage.

A True Addiction

Noted character actor Michael Durrell plays Howard Altman, a professed sugar addict. The men treat him with a patronizing indulgence as he professes the evils of sugar and sugar addiction. Naturally, Dietrich sympathizes with him to a certain extent and even gives us all a brief history of sugar and how it came to be a refined and traded commodity. Today there have been countless academic papers and numerous books written about the ill effects of sugar on the mind and body.

File This under "Pain"

Barney loses his temper about a missing file and the disheveled state of the filing system. He yells at Nick only to discover that the file in question was buried under papers on his own desk. Later on, Barney insinuates that Nick is complaining of not feeling well as a way to avoid filing. This lack of faith only increases his guilt when Nick has to be carried out of the squad room on a gurney with appendicitis.

As they wait for the ambulance to arrive, Barney asks Nick if there's anyone he wants them to call. Nick replies, "Well, there's a three-horse parley at Belmont." When Barney explains that he meant relatives, Nick says no. When the medics finally arrive, Nick is concerned about explaining his filing system to Barney before they take him away. Just in case. Happily, Nick survives the operation and while coming out of the anesthetic was mumbling to the nurses, "Appendix comes before Armed Robbery."

Wanted: Dead or Alive

Abel Kleiner, a sweet, little old Jewish man comes in looking for wanted posters. He's new to the neighborhood and happens to be a bounty hunter. Retired with plenty of time on his hands, Mr. Kleiner claims, "Everybody's offering rewards: the FBI, the post office, the Kiwanis club. You know, I go up to Times Square, Central Park, on a good day you can spot maybe seven, eight-hundred dollars' worth of people."

Kleiner is portrayed by actor Jack Bernardi, the older brother of Herschel Bernardi who was best known for his stage work as Tevye in *Fiddler on the Roof* and voice work as Charlie the Tuna in a series of commercials for StarKist Tuna in the 1970s.

Dietrich Doesn't Know Everything

Dietrich makes a comment to Wojo about Mr. Kleiner being an unusual bounty hunter. Wojo fires back, "Ain't exactly Steve McQueen."

Dietrich: Why would he be?
Wojo: Steve McQueen. He used to be a bounty hunter on television.
Dietrich: Oh!
Wojo: Yeah. He was Josh Randall on *Wanted: Dead or Alive*.
Dietrich: I didn't know that.
Wojo: You're not the only esoteric person around here.

The funniest and most surprising aspect of that entire exchange is Wojo's use of the word "esoteric."

The Last Word

Mr. Kleiner speaks for us all when he tells Levitt, "You're a cute, crazy little person."

Season 4, Episode 15: "Rape."
Original Airdate: January 26, 1978.
Writer: Dennis Koenig.
Director: Noam Pitlik.
Cast of Characters: Steve Landesberg (Dietrich), Jack Soo (Yemana), Hal Linden (Barney), Max Gail (Wojo), Ron Glass (Harris), Michael Pataki (Marvin Lindsay), Joyce Jameson (Catherine Lindsay), William Bogert (Neil Korchak), Dick Balduzzi (Mr. Duggan), Linda Dano (Leslie Dornan), Harvey Gold (Ross).

The Rundown

A wife comes into the precinct and accuses her husband of rape. Dietrich and Harris differ in theory about a string of robberies they're investigating. Nick is excited about the prospect of the new OTB services available to him.

Define Rape

Hal Linden has discussed that it was quite common for the show's writers to scour the headlines of the day for stories they could use on *Barney*. "I remember when they found a woman in Seattle who accused her husband of rape," Linden told me. The truth, however, is a little murkier.

In researching the original case that may have served as an inspiration for this episode all I could find was the case of John and Greta Rideout of Oregon. Mrs. Rideout accused her husband in October of 1978 of rape and the court case was adjourned in December in favor of Mr. Rideout. The complications arise from the fact that this particular *Barney Miller* episode dealing with the wife accusing her husband of rape aired in January of 1978, at least nine months before the accusation or the trial was made public. The only possible explanation is that in 1977, Oregon passed a state law that permitted a wife to accuse her husband of rape. This was a strange and new concept in 1977 and quite possibly made the national news. The writers may have seen that news story and it planted a seed in their imagination. If so, it's then possible that this episode of *Barney Miller* may have given Mrs. Rideout the idea, and/or the courage, to accuse her husband of rape when their altercation occurred months later.

Mr. Rideout was cleared of all charges in 1978 but he was prosecuted for rape once again in 2016 relating to two separate accusations from two different women stemming from 2013. He was convicted on both charges and sentenced to two one-hundred-month sentences.

A number of online sources relating the incidents of the Rideout court case mention that two years after the case, a CBS made-for-TV movie aired, called *Rape and Marriage: The Rideout Case*, starring Linda Hamilton and Mickey Rourke. No sources could be found mentioning the *Barney Miller* episode of January 1978.

Uncomfortable

This is one of those episodes that won't hold up for everyone when viewed through a twenty-first-century lens. The accusation by Mrs. Lindsay that her husband raped her is treated in turn with humor, derision, and confusion. Barney describes it as a gray area that he's never before had to navigate. Dietrich says, "Actually, the husband has always been allowed the assertion of certain conjugal rights." Nevertheless, she makes an argument that seems very clear and very reasonable today when she says, "What's gray about it? It's black and white. I didn't want to and he made me."

A Whole Other Level

On top of the sexism involved in the approach to the accusation, there are further complications when the Assistant District Attorney (ADA) sent to the 12th to discuss the case with Mrs. Lindsay, is a woman. Mr. Lindsay's male attorney reacts with shock when he sees that the ADA is a woman!

Finally, in the end the ADA wants to make a test case out of this but ultimately, the storyline ends up being about a woman who wants a little more consideration and respect from her husband. It's more about a wife feeling neglected and disrespected than a woman genuinely feeling she has been raped. This outcome trivializes the seriousness of the subject matter. Ultimately, while it may have been a little bit of a step forward in terms of pushing the envelope of subject matter, the writers basically fail to see it through.

Many sitcoms of the 1970s became so enamored with their messages that they often forgot to retain their humor. In this case, they kept the humor but failed to resolve a serious issue with a solution worthy of the gravity of the situation.

A Very Controversial Episode

In addition to the controversial subject of marital rape, this episode also includes a subplot of Sgt. Harris, a black man, hitting on the ADA, a white woman. At the end of the episode, the ADA does indeed invite Harris to lunch. It seems like nothing today but that was pretty progressive television in 1978.

Another Way to Save

In this episode we learn that Nick the gambler gives up his bookie and is directing all future bets to the new state-sponsored Off Track Betting parlor. He figures a portion of the fees taken from OTB will go to pay his salary. Therefore, Yemana looks at OTB as kind of a Payroll Savings Plan.

Who Are They?

In this episode there is a calendar hanging on the wall near the airshaft to the right of the cage. The calendar comes from Liebowitz Delicatessen. This particular deli has never been mentioned in any show. We've heard of Tannenbaum's Fine Liquors and Delicatessen, Grossman's Delicatessen, even a place called Sid's, but never Liebowitz's. All we can assume is that the men of the 12th liked their calendars but not their pastrami.

Season 4, Episode 16: "Eviction—Part 1."
Original Airdate: February 2, 1978.
Writers: Tony Sheehan and Tom Reeder (teleplay). Tom Reeder (story).
Director: Noam Pitlik.
Cast of Characters: Jack Soo (Yemana), Ron Glass (Harris), Max Gail (Wojo), Hal Linden (Barney), Steve Landesberg (Dietrich), Ron Carey (Levitt), James Gregory (Inspector Luger), Rosanna DeSoto [as Rosana Soto] (Elena Elezando), Dave Madden (Clayton Walsh), Felipe Turich (Jorge Rodriguez), Donna Baccala (Jennifer DiLucca).

The Rundown

The men of the 12th Precinct are given the unpleasant duty of evicting the residents of the Manchester Hotel that is being razed to put up condominiums. The tenants refuse to leave their home until the city finds other accommodations for them. An attractive young woman picked up for shoplifting is suffering from amnesia. Inspector Luger is struggling to decide where to go on his long overdue vacation.

Come on, Get Happy

Dave Madden makes his one and only appearance on *Barney Miller* as Clayton Walsh, the man working for Drexler-Boz, the corporation that is tearing down the Manchester Hotel. To be precise, he's in one *Barney Miller* storyline but two episodes since this is a two-part episode.

Madden enjoyed two full decades of TV success with regular or recurring roles on shows like *Camp Runamuck* (1965–1966), *Laugh-In*, and *Alice*. However, the role for which he is best remembered by most Baby Boomers is that of Reuben Kinkaid, the band manager of the fictional *Partridge Family* during the four-season run of that sitcom on ABC from 1970 to 1974. Madden died in 2014 at the age of eighty-two.

Dereliction of Duty

Barney is relieved of command and put on modified assignment when he refuses to forcibly remove the protesting tenants from their apartments/rooms.

Naturally, Barney wants to try to find a humane solution to the problem but the department has different ideas. When Luger comes to inform Barney he's being temporarily relieved of command, he has to pass Barney's badge and gun on to the next in command. Barney turns and says, "That's Nick." Nick responds with the simple but effective, "Oh my God."

Where to Go

Luger hasn't taken a vacation in almost thirty years and the department insists he deplete his backlog of days. His last vacation was 1949 and after rambling on to Barney for a while he decides to just stick around the big city. He notes, "There are a lot of shows he still hasn't caught because he's never had the time."

In one of the few inside jokes of its type for a *Miller* script, Luger asks Nick Yemana, "Hey Nick, Is the *Flower Drum Song* still running?" On the surface it seems to be just another racially insensitive remark from the ol' Inspector as he assumes because Nick is Japanese he'll know whether a Broadway show based on Asian culture is still running. However, the inside joke stems from the fact that Jack Soo played Frankie Wing in the original 1958 cast of *Flower Drum Song* on Broadway. After a year, he replaced Larry Blyden in the larger role of Sammy Fong and then reprised the role of Fong in the 1961 film based upon the hit show.

Lost and Found

Finally, there's the amnesiac shoplifter who can't remember her name or where she's from. She's dressed conservatively and has a very wholesome attractiveness about her. Barney is concerned that Dietrich may be attracted to her and he warns his officer that real life isn't a Mickey Spillane novel. Dietrich responds, "She's just another case to me, . . . with your average sensational gams."

Season 4, Episode 17:	"Eviction—Part 2."
Original Airdate:	February 9, 1978.
Writers:	Reinhold Weege and Tom Reeder.
Director:	Noam Pitlik.
Cast of Characters:	Jack Soo (Yemana), Max Gail (Wojo), Hal Linden (Barney), Steve Landesberg (Dietrich), Ron Glass (Harris), James Gregory (Inspector Luger), Ron Carey (Levitt), Bruce Kirby (Lt. Rossmore), Rosanna DeSoto [as Rosana Soto] (Elena Ele-

zando), Dave Madden (Clayton Walsh), Felipe Turich (Jorge Rodriguez), Donna Baccala (Sister Jennifer DiLucca), John Calvin (Lt. Vogel).

The Rundown

The 12th gets an indifferent new commanding officer in Barney's absence. Dietrich grows more attached to his amnesiac. Barney has to go before the review board to defend his actions (or lack thereof) regarding the barricaded tenants of the Manchester Hotel.

First Offender

Bruce Kirby makes his first of three *Barney Miller* appearances in "Eviction—Part Two" as Lt. Rossmore of Manhattan South. Kirby's long résumé of character work on stage, screen, and television included many police officers and/or detectives in shows such as *Kojak*, *Hunter* (1984-1991), *Columbo* (1971-2003), and *Holmes and YoYo* (1976-1977). In fact, his work on screen as a police officer goes all the way back to 1961 and a recurring role on *Car 54, Where Are You?*

Spoiler Alert

In the coat pocket of his amnesia victim, Dietrich found a ticket with Harrisburg, Pennsylvania listed on it. He sends out bulletins to all the towns within a certain radius of Harrisburg and does indeed get a positive ID. When he tells her that her name is Jennifer DiLucca, the fog begins to lift. She's initially happy until she realizes that she may be a nun. Dietrich responds, "I wasn't going to mention it if you didn't."

The Solomon of the 12th

Since Barney is the one person who wants to resolve the eviction crisis by peaceful means, the residents of the Manchester Hotel are willing to talk and negotiate only with him. He pleads with them to give up before someone gets hurt. They maintain their refusal to leave without a place to go together as a community.

When he returns to the precinct, Barney encounters a drunken Mr. Walsh (Dave Madden). Barney tells Walsh, "You've been drinking," and Walsh responds, "Oh yeah . . . for years. I'm very good at it." Barney suggests that his company has plenty of empty properties where they might be able to transfer the tenants. Walsh hits him with the unvarnished truth, "Drexler-Boz is a very big corporation. We're interested in the development of real estate. Not the petty problems of human beings." When Barney says, "That is a singularly stinking attitude," Walsh immediately replies with "Why do you think I drink?"

Season 4, Episode 18: "Wojo's Problem."
Original Airdate: February 23, 1978.
Writer: Tony Sheehan.
Director: Maxwell Gail.
Cast of Characters: Hal Linden (Barney), Max Gail (Wojo), Ron Glass (Harris), Jack Soo (Yemana), Steve Landesberg (Dietrich), Stanley Brock (Bruno Bender), Ray Girardin (Vince Licori), Henry Slate (Louis Frankel), Mari Gorman (Officer Rosslyn Licori).

The Rundown

Everyone's favorite gun nut Bruno Bender returns to the 12th when his sporting goods store is robbed. Officer Roz Licori is assigned to the squad as a replacement for Chano Amenguale. A very determined curmudgeon in a wheelchair attempts to rob a local market. Oh, and Wojo has a "problem."

Wojo's True Dilemma

On the surface, it appears that Wojo is having a slight performance problem in bed. However, when Barney brings him into the office for a heart to heart, Wojo confesses that the real problem is his relationship with women in general. They just won't leave him alone! One wants to move in with him, another wants him to move in with her. Apparently, Wojo's biggest problem is that he's just a chick magnet.

The Future Mrs. Bender

This episode marks the first of a three-episode-arc for Mari Gorman as Office Roz Licori. According to the storyline, Barney had put in a request two years earlier to replace Chano and the department finally sent his replacement in the form of Licori. Of course, maybe Barney actually forgot to inform the department of Chano's exit because we, the audience, were certainly never informed.

Unfortunately for Roz Licori the 12th Precinct was just not a place that retained female officers for very long. She worked in only three episodes near the end of the fourth season before she was transferred. However, once Danny Arnold liked an actor/actress, he always found a way to bring them back. Mari Gorman returned in Season Eight as none other than Bruno Bender's wife, Naomi.

A Clean Slate

Henry Slate makes his one and only *Barney Miller* appearance as Louis Frankel, a wheelchair-bound stick up artist. Slate was one of the famous Slate Brothers, a comedy/dance team from the 1930s and 1940s whose signature style was a combination of the Nicholas Brothers and the Ritz Brothers. Despite their energy and ingenuity, they never made a big name for themselves in front of the cameras but performed successfully on stages around the country for twenty years. In later years, the brothers owned and managed a nightclub that employed at different times the likes of Lenny Bruce and Don Rickles.

Henry eventually left the team and struck out on his own. He was able to score a consistent number of small character parts on film and television from the early 1950s through the early 1980s. He can be found in a half dozen Disney films of the 1970s, including *The Strongest Man in the World* (1975) and *No Deposit, No Return* (1976). He may be best remembered for his role as the leader of "Bobby Fleet and his Band with a Beat" on *The Andy Griffith Show*.

Just the Facts

This was the first of five episodes directed by Max Gail.

Season 4, Episode 19:	"Quo Vadis?"
Original Airdate:	March 2, 1978.
Writers:	Tony Sheehan (teleplay). Douglas Wyman and Tony Sheehan (story).
Director:	Alex March.
Cast of Characters:	Max Gail (Wojo), Ron Glass (Harris), Ron Carey (Levitt), Hal Linden (Barney), Barbara Barrie (Elizabeth Miller), John Dullaghan (Milt Loftus), Ivy Bethune (Miss Jacobs), John O'Leary (Mr. Levant).

The Rundown

A surly woman comes in complaining about a smut shop on Christopher Street that turns out to be an art gallery displaying paintings of nude women in the window. One of the detectives is on vacation so Officer Levitt gets his first chance at plainclothes duty. Due to the manpower shortage, Barney goes out on a call with Dietrich and gets shot.

Everyone's a Critic

Ivy Bethune appears as Miss Jacobs, an older woman who demands that an art gallery be shut down. When they explain to her that they can't shut down a legitimate gallery for displaying paintings, she goes to the gallery and throws liquid shoe polish on a nude painting that offends her.

In a career that spanned well over sixty years, Bethune appeared in guest roles on dozens of TV shows like *Perry Mason*, *General Hospital* (1963–present), and *That Girl* before finally landing a regular role on the short-lived *Father Murphy* (1981–1983) starring Merlin Olsen and produced by Michael Landon. She is one of a dozen actors/actresses featured in the 2011 documentary, *Troupers*, that looks at twelve actors actively working into their eighties and nineties. Ms. Bethune died on July 19, 2019, at 101 years of age.

A Union Unravels

This is the first episode where we start to see genuine strain on the Miller marriage caused by Barney's job. In the early years, Liz's unhappiness with Barney's job was always expressed with a little humor or a smile. She never liked his job but she also knew she wasn't going to change him.

When the show was created it was going to be about the push and pull of a policeman's life at the station and at home. The focus quickly shifted to the station house and thereby left little for Barbara Barrie to do. While she will be referred to for many years to come, this is actually the second to last time we'll see her on screen.

Birds of a Feather

John Dullaghan shows up in his last one and done appearance as a robber named Milt Loftus. Next time we see him will be in Season Five's "Open House" as Ray Brewer, and as that character he will turn up in a total of six episodes adding up to an impressive total of ten appearances on the program for the actor.

In this episode he plays a professional thief who empathizes with Barney as his marital problems begin to play out in front of the entire squad room while Loftus is in the cage. Loftus tells the Captain, "My wife walked out on me two years ago." Barney corrects Loftus, saying his wife hasn't "walked out." Loftus continues, "Suddenly, one day she says, 'Milt, I can't handle it anymore.' And when we got married she knew what I was!" Barney tells Loftus he's not interested in discussing his personal life in public. Loftus completely ignores him, saying, "I mean I told her right up front what it'd be like. The lousy hours, late evenings, temporary separations . . . and she agreed! Right? Well, didn't your wife agree?" Barney thinks this over and realizes that maybe he and Loftus *do* have something in common before he says, "Yeah!"

Later in the episode as Loftus is being transferred, Liz returns to the squad room. Loftus sees her and says, "Hey lady, give him a break. You knew what you were getting into when you married him." When she asks rather indignantly, "Who are you?" he looks at her and says, "Just a friend of Barney's."

Roll Call

According to Wojo's opening remark, they have a detective on vacation. That detective is apparently Nick Yemana because he is absent from this entire episode. In truth, Jack Soo had been diagnosed with cancer. He would be absent from the last five episodes of this season before returning for seven of the first eight episodes of Season Five prior to his untimely death in January of 1979.

Season 4, Episode 20:	"Hostage."
Original Airdate:	March 23, 1978.
Writers:	Reinhold Weege (teleplay). Chris Hayward and Reinhold Weege (story).
Director:	Hal Linden.
Cast of Characters:	Ron Glass (Harris), Max Gail (Wojo), Hal Linden (Barney), Steve Landesberg (Dietrich), Oliver Clark (Vern Bidell), Don Calfa (Leon Bidell), Alix Elias (Louise Helman), Earle Towne (Oscar Leeds), Mari Gorman (Rosslyn Licori), Sammy (A grotesque piece of lumber).

The Rundown

Harris brings in a habitual criminal for armed robbery who fears that another conviction will put him in prison for life. The man's fear yields a disastrous escape plan. A ventriloquist and his dummy are arrested for harassing a woman on the street and Sgt. Roz Licori is struggling to fit in with her new squad.

A Great Pair

Two of the funniest actors of the 1970s have to be Oliver Clark and Don Calfa. Both of these men worked in countless TV programs and films as well as making repeated visits to the *Barney Miller* squad room. They specialized in playing eccentric characters and are at their hilarious best in this episode about a poorly planned, and even more poorly executed, escape attempt.

When Oliver Clark was interviewed for this book he didn't remember this particular episode but he fondly recalled working with "Crazy Don" Calfa.

Manpower Report

Leon (Calfa) Bidell calls his brother Vern (Clark) and convinces him to help him escape. At gunpoint, they stuff all the officers and civilians in the squad room into very close quarters in the cage. Barney attempts to convince Leon that he'll never get away with the escape because there are 170 uniformed officers in the building. Levitt corrects him saying there are only 157: six in court, seven out with the flu.

Ya Big Dummy!

Oscar Leeds (played by Earle Towne) is arrested for a 1052—Public Nuisance/Disturbing the Peace after his ventriloquist's dummy said vile and disgusting things to Miss Helman (played by Alix Elias). The ventriloquist disassociates himself from his dummy, Sammy, assigning a certain level of autonomy to the puppet that Dietrich recognizes as a classic case of schizophrenia.

Dietrich encourages Mr. Leeds that once he starts to accept the fact that the dummy isn't real, he can break free from his power. In the end, Sammy "dies" and Mr. Leeds is free. Or is he?

For the Record

Roz introduces a flower into the squad room, a pink carnation on Nick's desk, which causes quite a stir. Inspector Luger is dropping in without any stated reason and Barney is wearing his favorite tie, a blue, green, and silver striped cravat.

Wood Chips

This episode is ripe with humor directed toward Mr. Leeds's ventriloquist's dummy, Sammy:

Miss Helman: You're a sick piece of wood.
Luger: What's with the dummy, Barney? Escape from a lumber yard?
Vern: That's a dummy in there. Why didn't I notice that before? We're holding a dummy prisoner!

Season 4, Episode 21: "Evaluation."
Original Airdate: May 4, 1978.
Writer: Larry Balmagia.
Director: Noam Pitlik.
Cast of Characters: Max Gail (Wojo), Steve Landesberg (Dietrich), Hal Linden (Barney), Ron Glass (Harris), Ron Carey (Levitt), Kay Medford (Irene Schuman), Richard Libertini (Mr. 1223 / Ira Grubb), Eugene Elman (Eddie Shuman), Garn Stephens (Susan Schuman-Edwards), Larry Block (Russell Shuman), Mari Gorman (Officer Rosslyn Licori).

The Rundown

Harris brings in a man who caused a disturbance in the bank after he tried to open a checking account under the name "1223." The boys investigate a disturbance at the Garden of Earthly Delights, a local porno shop.

Ira Grubb, Numerologist

Grubb, played by the inimitable Richard Libertini, lives at 322 Lexington, The Marquis Hotel. He picked it for the address. The numbers add up to seven, "that's the number of beauty, rhythm, harmony, co-existence with my environment, co-existence with the entire galaxy, . . . and there's a great little coffee shop."

This is Richard Libertini's first *Barney Miller* appearance. He will make two more appearances on the show in the next two seasons. He was a much sought-after comedic actor for over forty years. He started his long career as a musician, performed with the famed Second City troupe in Chicago, and appeared in dozens of films and television programs. He is best remembered for his portrayal of the rather eccentric South American dictator, General Garcia, in the 1979 film *The In-Laws* with Peter Falk and Alan Arkin.

Ma & Pa Porno

The owners of the porno shop that is being targeted by vandals are a cute old Jewish couple. When Barney inquires how they got involved in such an endeavor Mrs. Schuman, played by the wonderful Kay Medford, replies, "Survival, sir. If you don't go with the times, you don't survive." As Medford delivers this line, you can see Steve Landesberg behind her trying to control his laughter. The couple used to own a nice little grocery until an A&P moved into the neighborhood and drove them out.

The vandals turn out to be the Schuman's son and daughter who are embarrassed by their parents' business. Russell Schuman, played by Larry Block, says, "How long do you think we were going to stand around and watch you eke out a living selling smut and filth?" Mrs. Schuman tries to explain their attitude to her concerned children, "We're merchants. We've been merchants all our lives. We used to sell tomatoes and bread, now we sell magazines." It's about the work and a sense of identity and purpose more than what they're selling.

Lady in the Squad Room or the Accidental Voyeur

Wojo walks into bathroom while Roz is in there and sees a little too much. She's embarrassed. He's embarrassed. This is why we can't have ladies in the squad room.

Just the Facts

- Mrs. Schumann recognizes Levitt. Draw your own conclusions.

Evaluations

Barney is filling out performance evaluations for the men and women of the 12th and they're all anxious to see what he's written. Eventually, Barney hands out all the evaluations and says, "Read them, discuss them, you may copy them if you wish." They all silently read what he's given them. He asks rather sarcastically if they approve and all sheepishly respond that they're happy. Barney walks into his office and closes the door.

Wojo: I don't know what he meant by "aggressively zealous."
Roz: I don't think I'm that "methodical."
Harris: Anybody else get "flashy efficiency?"

Season 4, Episode 22: "The Sighting."
Original Airdate: May 11, 1978.
Writers: Tony Sheehan (teleplay). Reinhold Weege and Tony Sheehan (story).
Director: Alex March.
Cast of Characters: Ron Carey (Levitt), Steve Landesberg (Dietrich), Ron Glass (Harris), Hal Linden (Barney), Max Gail (Wojo), Doris Roberts (Harriet Brauer), Peter Hobbs (Philip Brauer), Jack Bannon (Captain William Donnelly).

The Rundown

Wojo is convinced he's seen a UFO over Staten Island. A woman wants her husband arrested because he's selling off the couple's assets to buy gold.

Danny's Folly

According to Hal Linden this was another "paranoid with proof" scenario in Danny's mind because there was a lot of talk in the financial world of the weakening of currency. Danny Arnold himself bought gold for fear of a monetary collapse. He encouraged Hal Linden and others to buy some as well.

Harris is mesmerized by the collection of Mr. Brauer's gold. Dietrich explains to him the mystical and dangerous hold that gold has had on people through the ages while Harris just stares longingly at the precious material, ignoring Dietrich's subtle warnings. Finally, Harris looks at Dietrich and says, "Looks like he got it all. Looks like he didn't leave none for nobody else. That's what it looks like."

Harris is so taken by Mr. Brauer's mania and his collection of gold that he gives Mr. Brauer a personal check for $225 and in return Brauer gives him a Mexican gold five-peso piece, an ounce and a quarter pure gold.

I Got It

When Levitt struggles to bring the material evidence, a.k.a. Mr. Brauer's gold, into the squad room, the scene calls to mind a schtick that Ron Carey employed the year before in the Mel Brooks feature, *High Anxiety* (1977). In the film Carey plays Brophy the limousine driver who always seems to be picking up objects too heavy for him to handle. Each time he does it, he says, "I got it. I got it. I got it. (pauses and then drops the object to the floor) I don't got it."

Close Encounters

This episode premiered roughly five months after *Close Encounters of the Third Kind* came out. Wojo calls the US Air Force to report his sighting. He learns from Captain Donnelly, played by actor Jack Bannon, that there are approximately twenty-five hundred sightings of UFO's every year that tend to be classified under four basic types of sightings: 1) man-made objects, 2) no explanation, 3) hoaxes, 4) reports that are discounted as made by people determined to be mentally unstable.

It's later discovered that half a dozen other people in NJ saw the same thing and reported sightings of a similar type as Wojo. In the end, the Air Force claims the National Weather Service had an atmospheric observation craft over the Staten Island area during the time in question, a.k.a., a weather balloon. Wojo doesn't buy it.

Man of Mystery

Dietrich chimes in saying, "You know, more and more people are becoming convinced that there is other intelligent life in the universe. And they recognize the possibility that these creatures may have already made exploratory journeys here. Some also believe that these aliens have already entered our society and at this very moment are living among us." (Dietrich flashes Barney and Wojo a mischievous smile.)

Harris: I just wrote off a desk appearance ticket and gave him that spiel, you know, the one you always give about uh, keeping one's perspective.
Barney: Well, I'm glad you felt free to use it.
Harris: Well Barn, I mean, that must be in Public Domain by now.

Season 4, Episode 23: "Inauguration."
Original Airdate: May 18, 1978.
Writers: Reinhold Weege and Carol Gary.
Director: Alex March.

Cast of Characters: Hal Linden (Barney), Steve Landesberg (Dietrich), Ron Carey (Levitt), Max Gail (Wojo), Ron Glass (Harris), Philip Sterling (Noel Cadey), Basil Hoffman (Allen Korbel), Florence Halop (Evelyn Hawley), Dino Natali (Officer Zatelli).

The Rundown

The men of the 12th are investigating all threats to the mayor as the city prepares for his inauguration. Dietrich and Levitt bring in a cranky old lady who likes writing threatening letters. Harris accepts a job offer to be part of the mayor's staff and quickly regrets his decision. Wojo brings in a man who's high on marijuana that he claims was prescribed by his doctor while another man is brought in proclaiming to be the People's Mayor.

Prophetic Prescription

As we enter the third decade of the twenty-first century, it is quite common for marijuana to be prescribed for a wide variety of illnesses. However, in 1978, the thought of prescribing an illegal drug for legitimate medical reasons seemed crazy to Wojo. Dietrich's explanation that the Federal Government had sanctioned the use of marijuana in glaucoma treatments resulted in a "raspberry response" from Wojo.

Poison Pen—Socialist Grandma

Florence Halop makes her third *Barney Miller* appearance (out of an eventual six) as the spirited Mrs. Hawley. Halop was one of the funniest and most memorable character actresses of the time with her squatty build, trademark waddle, and froggy voice, reminiscent of her brother, and former Dead End Kid, Billy Halop.

This and her previous episode, "Bus Stop," were both written with the contributions of Reinhold Weege. Seven years later, Weege had his own hit situation comedy, *Night Court*. Following the second season of *Night Court*, Weege hired Halop as the wisecracking bailiff following Selma Diamond's untimely death from lung cancer at the age of sixty-four. Halop was equally funny in the role but she lasted only one season before also succumbing to lung cancer at the age of sixty-three.

The Famous Harris Euphemisms

Anybody can call it "an ambulance from Bellevue" but in the imagination and words of Det. Harris we get: the cookie truck, the Twinkie mobile, the Disoriented Express, and the Hotel Silly.

Belated Inauguration

This episode was broadcast on May 18, 1978, almost five months after Ed Koch's actual inauguration as Mayor of New York that took place on January 1, 1978. It's possible the show could have been shot around that time and saved but knowing what we do about how Danny Arnold's production team worked, that seems improbable. I could find no suggestion, information, or confirmation of Danny Arnold ever shooting an episode and then letting it sit for months prior to broadcast. It's more likely that they needed one more episode to fill the season's order and reached back to an older story idea as inspiration for an episode.

One More Time

Levitt is even more high-strung than usual as he gets his first extended assignment to plain clothes. The new plaid jacket he buys for the occasion is something you'd expect to see on a Damon Runyon character in *Guys and Dolls*. With Levitt working upstairs, we get our first introduction to Officer Zatelli who will play a prominent role in a Season Five storyline.

Levitt's bump up to the detective squad is due to Yemana's continued absence. Nevertheless, Barney reminds Levitt, "Even with Harris on duty with the Mayor's office and Yemana out, it's still temporary. Could be just a few days."

We were initially led to believe Nick was on vacation but his absence has now stretched on too long to make that claim. Jack Soo was, in fact, diagnosed with cancer near the end of the Fourth Season but he wasn't ready to quit. He would appear in nine more episodes at the start of Season Five before making his final exit from the 12th.

Fifth Season

Two unhappy events would plague the *Barney Miller* production in 1979. On January 11, 1979, the wonderful Jack Soo died at the age of sixty-one from complications due to esophageal cancer. For an explanation of how his death was handled within the context of the show, please see the Episode Guide's entry for the last episode of this season.

As the season neared the end, Danny Arnold who had been struggling with some health problems himself, notified writer and associate producer Tony Sheehan that he would be leaving the show for an extended period of time because he was being scheduled for quadruple bypass heart surgery. Sheehan spent the next two seasons as *Barney Miller's* showrunner.

Even with all the turmoil behind the scenes and in front of the camera, the show finished the season as the fifteenth-highest watched program, tied with the *ABC Sunday Night Movie*.

Season 5, Episode 1: "Kidnapping." This episode appeared on September 14, 1978, as a special, hour-long season premiere. Therefore, it appears correctly as one episode in the Shout! Factory box set. However, it was split into two separate episodes in syndication and listed as such on IMDb. Therefore, even though they are listed on the DVDs as one episode, they are split into two separate episodes here as episode 1 and episode 1B for the 1978–1979 season. What that means historically is that there were twenty-two episodes in Season Five but twenty-three half hours produced and seen in syndication.

Original Airdate: September 14, 1978.
Writers: Danny Arnold, Reinhold Weege, and Tony Sheehan.
Director: Noam Pitlik.
Cast of Characters: Steve Landesberg (Dietrich), Ron Glass (Harris), Jack Soo (Yemana), Hal Linden (Barney), Max Gail (Wojo), James Gregory (Inspector Luger), Beverly Sanders (Lorraine Siegel), Todd Susman (Andrew Siegel), Barrie Youngfellow (Marsha Dixon), John O'Connell (Philip Martin, FBI), Ralph Manza (Eddie Blake), Stefan Gierasch (Andrew Glanzman), Fred Sadoff (Robert Joseph Wilmore).

The Rundown

Wojo brings in a friendly prostitute and her client, a Southern gentleman, who refuses to admit his complicity in the crime. Mr. Siegel of Siegel's Department

Store gets kidnapped and his children must make some crucial decisions in his absence. The FBI agent who's brought in on the case is less than helpful.

Memories of a Lifetime

The kidnapping not only leads Inspector Luger to remembering his days in the department during the Lindbergh kidnapping but also brings out his penchant for recalling gory details of his glorious past on the force. Barney tries to squelch Luger's detailed descriptions so as not to alarm the victim's children.

> **Inspector Luger:** Then there was the time they put the snatch on Zero Zacchetti. Remember how they sent him back? Mason jars.

Better Than a Singles Bar

Beverly Sanders makes her only *Barney Miller* appearance as Lorraine Siegel in this hour-long episode. During the tense hours of waiting for her father's safe return she takes notice of Sergeant Harris's physique and wonders if he's ever modeled before? While she's ogling Harris, her brother is striking up a friendship with Barrie Youngfellow's Marsha Dixon, the happy-go-lucky neighborhood prostitute. Marsha gives Andrew Siegel, played by Todd Susman, the understanding, encouragement, and confidence that he never received from his family.

Game Day

Dietrich beats Harris in a game of Backgammon with sixty-four dollars on the line. When Harris writes Dietrich a check for the money before he goes out on his next call Dietrich tells him that's not necessary. He can wait. Harris reminds him, "Every time a cop goes out there's always a chance that he won't come back." Dietrich says, "So?" Harris tells him, "Well, it's not that I enjoy paying you the sixty-four dollars but I ain't owing nobody nothing for eternity."

As for Nick, he doesn't play backgammon but he does have a home version of Beat the Clock.

The Last Word

Barney comes out of his office and asks Nick, who has just returned from a riot at Siegel's Department Store, "What's it like out there?" Nick responds, "Uh, lots of yelling, screaming, stomping . . . actually pretty normal for this time of day."

Season 5, Episode 1B: "Kidnapping: Part 2."
Original Airdate: September 14, 1978.
Writers: Danny Arnold, Reinhold Weege, and Tony Sheehan.
Director: Noam Pitlik.
Cast of Characters: Hal Linden (Barney), Max Gail (Wojo), Ron Glass (Harris), Jack Soo (Yemana), Steve Landesberg (Dietrich), Ron Carey (Levitt), James Gregory (Inspector Luger), Beverly Sanders (Lorraine Siegel), Todd Susman (Andrew Siegel), Barrie Youngfellow (Marsha Dixon), John O'Connell (Philip Martin, FBI), Ralph Manza (Eddie Blake), Stefan Gierasch (Andrew Glanzman), Fred Sadoff (Robert Joseph Wilmore), Harold J. Stone (Mr. Siegel).

Precursor to a Revolting Revolution

Stefan Gierasch as Mr. Glanzman is brought in for pushing an old lady to the ground and thereby facing a charge of assault. He's dragged into the station unrepentant and complaining about being targeted and made to feel guilty because he's white, male, and middle class. "I pay taxes! I paid until it hurts and now I'm taking my fair share!" He then points at Harris and says, "I thought he was a looter!"

Glanzman continues to dig himself deeper into a hole as he says to Harris, "I've got nothing against you people either. If a guy works hard, saves his money, I'm on his side. For thirty years they've been gauging us—sucking the blood out of the middle class to pay for the poor people's food stamps and the rich people's loopholes!" Well, at least he acknowledged the "rich people's loopholes."

It should also be noted that Lt. Paul Glanzman was a NYC police officer who served as the show's technical advisor.

Kidnapper's Demands

The ransom demand comes in for $200,000 and as Inspector Luger observes, "That's $150,000 more than Bruno wanted," referring to Bruno Hauptmann, the man convicted and executed in the kidnapping of the Lindbergh baby in 1936.

But I Love Ya!!

In the heat of the moment, the normally meek and indecisive Andrew stands up to his sister and decides that they will pay the ransom and he calls the bank for the $200,000.

Stalwart character actor Harold J. Stone portrays the kidnapped Mr. Siegel. When we meet Mr. Siegel following his release, we immediately understand Andrew's lack of self-confidence. The father is upset to learn how much his son paid the kidnappers for his safe return, "My God, are you crazy? I'm sixty-one years old, I've had two bypasses, I've got a pig's valve right here (pointing to heart)—at tops I'm worth $50,000!" The chemistry between Susman, Stone, and Sanders works to paint a portrait of a loving, if dysfunctional, family.

Harold J. Stone was, in fact, sixty-five years old at the time this episode was filmed and lived another twenty-seven years, dying in 2005 at the age of ninety-two.

He's Definitely Got a Type

As always, Wojo has a contentious relationship with a lady of the evening, in this case Marsha Dixon, played by Barrie Youngfellow. He's rude and sarcastic to her but she just keeps smiling. When she's free to go, he insults her again and then apologizes, promising to call her a cab to take her home. Instead he asks Barney if he could spare him for a few minutes. When Barney tells him it's no problem, Wojo suggests it might be an hour, or two hours until Barney finally tells him to just take off early. Wojo heads out the door and says, "See you tomorrow . . . I might be late." Just as in Season One's, "The Courtesans," the message of where Wojo is going and what he's planning to do with his night off is crystal clear.

Conditions must have loosened up during the intervening three years in the network's standards and practices department because neither Hal Linden nor Max Gail have any memories of there being any controversy over this liaison with a prostitute like there was the first time. It's also not the last relationship Wojo will have with a prostitute or former prostitute.

Ominous Foreboding

As well written and well acted as this story is, it's nevertheless a sad two-parter to look back on as the deterioration in actor Jack Soo's health is now clearly evident. He looks drained and he moves and speaks and acts without the energy he once had.

Season 5, Episode 2: "The Search."
Original Airdate: September 21, 1978.
Writers: Bob Colleary and Tony Sheehan (teleplay). Bob Colleary (story).
Director: Noam Pitlik.
Cast of Characters: Hal Linden (Barney), Max Gail (Wojo), Jack Soo (Yemana), Steve Landesberg (Dietrich), Ron Glass (Harris), Jenny O'Hara (Teresa Schnable), Bruce Kirby (Franklin Claymore), Arny Freeman (Milton Holly / Mr. Science).

The Rundown

Harris must finally take his turn at mugging detail in the park. Unfortunately, the duty requires that he shave off his beloved moustache. A young woman comes into the station looking for her missing father and the host of a kid's TV science show flips out on the air.

The Human Condition

Barney Miller's greatest strength was its ability to always reflect the human condition at its best *and* at its worst. The show was consistently successful in mixing pathos with laugh out loud funny moments. This particular episode is one of the best examples of that mixture of humor and poignancy.

Actress Jenny O'Hara portrays Teresa Schnable, a twenty-eight-year-old woman who claims to be looking for her missing father. In reality, she was orphaned at birth and has spent years tracking down the man she believes to be her father but now that she's found him, he won't see her. It's a painful story not just because of the talents displayed by the two marvelous actors involved but because it seems so plausible.

O'Hara plays it with such sincere desperation that you can't help but root for this woman. Bruce Kirby is his usual brilliant self as Franklin Claymore, the man Miss Schnable believes to be her father. He just wants to be left alone. In the end, we're not given the usual, "all's well that ends well" sitcom happy ending where all the loose ends are tied up but instead, a human connection is made that is even more satisfying in its truth, simplicity, and potential.

Be Careful, He Bites

Harris finally relents to Barney's orders and shaves off his moustache. When he emerges from the bathroom, the change is transformational. He tells Barney that he's now happy to have shaved it off. That said, his words indicate otherwise as he pointedly says to the mustachioed Barney, "I mean, actually, what is the function of a moustache anyway? It's really just a masculine affectation. It's kind of silly when you stop and think about it. I mean it's just a stupid clump of hair sitting over your mouth—a meaningless, superficial demand for attention."

Ironically, remember that Harris shows up in the epilogue of the second pilot, "Ramon" in a dress with his moustache *still on* but Barney must have changed the requirements.

Explosion in the Lab

Wojo was absent from the room when Mr. Science, played by the wonderful Arny Freeman, was brought into custody. As he's being released, Wojo recognizes him and gets all excited. He tells the kid show's host, "I never missed your show. You were the only guy on television who ever sounded like he meant what he was saying. And I didn't just watch. I did the experiments. Yeah, the baking soda in the motors, the ant farm, I had an ant farm!" The obviously pleased old gentleman smiles and says, "I hope you learned something." Wojo assures him, "Sure! I watched your show every Sunday for five years." "Why did you stop?" Hawley asks. "Oh well, I had to," replies Wojo, "I joined the Marines." Mr. Science triumphantly exclaims, "Now that's a kid!"

That's No Lady, That's Harris

The boys are stunned at how good Harris looks as a woman.

He says to Nick, "Go ahead, Nick. Get all your clever little comments out of your system." Nick's only reply is, "You look lovely." Barney and Wojo back up his review of Harris's appearance.

Harris responds, "I want to look good but not better!"

Season 5, Episode 3: "Dog Days."
Original Airdate: September 28, 1978.
Writer: Reinhold Weege.
Director: Noam Pitlik.

Cast of Characters:	Hal Linden (Barney), Jack Soo (Yemana), Ron Glass (Harris), Max Gail (Wojo), Steve Landesberg (Dietrich), Rosalind Cash (Carolyn Slade), Joseph V. Perry (Joseph Lasorda), John Lawlor (Morris the dogcatcher, a.k.a. Humane Technician).

The Rundown

Harris is smitten with an attractive woman who comes in to report a missing husband. We learn that Barney and Liz are taking a little time apart. Wojo gets bitten by a dog and fears he may have to endure a series of rabies shots.

Repeat Offender

Joseph V. Perry shows up as Joseph Lasorda in his third out of four *Barney Miller* appearances. He's been arrested for dog fighting and is being held until they can find his dog that bit Wojo.

Perry was an extremely active character actor on TV during the 1960s and 1970s showing up in such shows as *Wanted: Dead or Alive* (1958–1961), *The Untouchables* (1959–1963), *and I Dream of Jeannie* (1965–1970). He made four or more appearances on many long-running shows like *Gunsmoke, That Girl, Bewitched, The Partridge Family,* and *Mannix*. However, it wasn't until the very end of his career that he finally landed a recurring role on a hit show as Nemo, the owner of the local pizzeria, on the popular CBS sitcom, *Everybody Loves Raymond*. He was in seven different episodes of the Ray Romano sitcom through the first four seasons of the show's nine-year run. Sadly, Perry died in the middle of the show's fourth season at the age of sixty-nine due to complications from diabetes.

Memories of Mr. Kopechne

In this episode, Nick gets spooked when Mr. Lasorda's dog Max walks into the squad room barking and snarling and showing his teeth. Nick's voice ascends an octave or two as we see that same cautious fear that Nick displayed in the Season Three episode, "The Werewolf," when faced with a man who believed he was a werewolf. When Lasorda won't cooperate and call off the dog, Nick wisely pretends he's letting the man out of the cell and then pushes the perp back into the cage and joins him with key in hand.

It's yet another reflection of the intelligence and reality of this show as it differs from the previous police sitcoms like *Car 54* and *The Andy Griffith Show*. In *TAGS*, Barney Fife would often lock himself in a jail cell by accident thereby looking like a buffoon. It was definitely funny but he also wasn't the kind of guy you'd want to see patrolling your streets. In *Barney Miller*, we know Nick to be a gambler, slightly lazy, and someone with a rather dry and sometimes biting wit, but he's no fool. When it comes down to the nitty gritty, he doesn't panic and he makes the intelligent move.

Goodbye (She Quietly She Says)

This is the second episode where the marital troubles of Barney and his wife, Liz, are discussed. From what we can gather, Liz has gone away for a few days to think things through. At the end of the episode, Barney is talking to Liz over the phone and as they're hanging up he pauses with a pained look on his face and says, "I do too," leading us to believe that Liz has said, "I love you" to him. The pain on his face shows us all we need to know. The hurt is real. These two people still love one another but it appears as though they have reached the end of their road together.

Like all storylines or emotions on *Barney Miller*, nothing is ever allowed to get out of control or take over the show. Everything that happens in the *Barney Miller* universe is a piece of the whole.

The Last Word

Nick tells Barney that his grandfather had a saying about marriage, "Marriage is like a horse with a broken leg. You can shoot it but that don't fix the leg."

Season 5, Episode 4: "The Baby Broker."
Original Airdate: October 5, 1978.
Writer: Tony Sheehan.
Director: Noam Pitlik.
Cast of Characters: Jack Soo (Yemana), Ron Glass (Harris), Steve Landesberg (Dietrich), Hal Linden (Barney), Ron Carey (Levitt), Max Gail (Wojo), Ivor Francis (Professor Henry McDowell), Phoebe Dorin (Harriet Adelman), Fredric Cook (Harold Adelman), Michael Durrell (Philip Kubrick), Gisela Getty as "Martine Getty" (Ana Schlesinger).

The Rundown

Wojo brings in a German-speaking young woman and a couple that was dragging her off a bus against her will. Turns out that the couple had made a "legal" agreement to buy/adopt the young woman's baby as soon as it was born. Harris and Dietrich bring in a man who was making lewd suggestions to a woman in the park.

Have Baby, Will Travel

The Adelmans are desperate to have a baby but cannot get pregnant. Michael Durrell plays a rather sleazy lawyer who sets up a sorority house full of women so he can then sell/arrange adoptions for their babies. The ethics of this operation, if not officially illegal, are certainly questionable.

Dietrich informs the couple of the new experiments that are taking place in the field of In Vitro Fertilization or what at the time were called "test tube babies." Mrs. Adelman perks up with hope at the idea that she might be able to carry her own child. Mr. Adelman is less than thrilled with the idea of his wife being fertilized by an outside donor. This obstetrical advice from Dietrich is almost exactly the same as what he told Mr. and Mrs. Hamel in "The Bank" (S. 4/Ep. 12). In both cases, the wives are relieved to learn this new information but their husbands are not.

The 12th Makes for Strange Bedfellows

Gisela (aka Martine) Getty portrays Ana Schlesinger in this episode. She was the wife of John Paul Getty III, the grandson of oil tycoon J. Paul Getty who in 1966 was named the World's Richest Private Citizen by the Guinness Book of World Records with an estimated worth of $1.2 billion.

In July of 1973, John Paul Getty III was kidnapped in Rome and held for ransom for six months by captors who eventually cut off his ear to illustrate their intentions. His grandfather eventually paid the ransom after negotiating the amount down from $17 million to $3.2 million. Word is that Grandpa paid $2.2 million and Daddy paid $1 million that was actually loaned to him by Grandpa at 4% interest. This story was the basis for the 2017 film, *All the Money in the World*.

Gisela and Getty III were married nine months after his release. They eventually divorced but remained close until Getty's death at the age of fifty-four in 2011.

Dangerous Research

Ivor Francis, in his second *Barney Miller* appearance, plays Professor Henry McDowell, PhD, an academic writing a dictionary of the complete compilation of obscenity and profanity in the English Language. He was approaching people in the park to research their reaction to certain vulgarisms. He's been researching for ten years but is only up to the letter "S."

His case is reminiscent of Prof. Betram Potts, a character from the 1941 film *Ball of Fire* starring Gary Cooper about a professor and seven colleagues who are working on a dictionary of slang words and phrases. In Potts's case, his work got him in trouble with criminals as opposed to the law. The screenplay was by Charles Brackett and Billy Wilder.

Speaking of Lifts

When Wojo enters the squad room with Mr. and Mrs. Adelman and Anna, he appears to be wearing some funky lift type shoes of the '70s. They look to be a brand called Famolare named after the second-generation shoe manufacturer who designed them, Joe Famolare. It was created to be a comfortable design to aid movement.

Different Tie

One of the great consistencies about *Barney Miller* is the wardrobe. Guys would wear suits more than once with the possible exception of Harris whose vast wardrobe was an important point of pride for him. For example, Barney had this green/blue striped tie that he wore quite often. In this episode, Barney surprises us with a new blue and red paisley tie. Naturally, the new blue and red paisley will eventually be seen more than once as well.

This type of sartorial realism is unusual in television. For example, a few years before *Barney Miller*, Danny Arnold worked as a producer on the show *That Girl* (1966–1971) with Marlo Thomas. Through the years TV viewers wondered exactly how Anne Marie, a struggling actress, was able to not only live in her own one-bedroom apartment in Midtown Manhattan but also afford a wardrobe of clothes fit for a wealthy fashion model. The answer was that in reality she couldn't have but *That Girl* didn't concern itself with that aspect of reality. *Barney Miller* did.

Season 5, Episode 5: "Accusation."
Original Airdate: October 12, 1978.

Writers:	Wally Dalton and Shelley Zellman.
Director:	Max Gail.
Cast of Characters:	Max Gail (Wojo), Steve Landesberg (Dietrich), Hal Linden (Barney), Jack Soo (Yemana), Ron Glass (Harris), Miriam Byrd-Nethery (Doris Whitaker), Michael Tucci (Rubin), Eugene Elman (Rabbi Joseph Greenblatt), Ruth Warshawsky (Ruthie Greenblatt), George Murdock (Lt. Ben Scanlon).

The Rundown

A woman reports young people breaking into mailboxes. In the course of making her report to Dietrich she develops a little crush on him. Unfortunately, the crush does not end well. Nick and Harris investigate a rabbi who is running a gambling casino out of his temple for charity.

All the Lonely People

Miss Whitaker, played by Miriam Byrd-Nethery, is a very lonely person. She is taken with the kindness and humor of Sergeant Dietrich and mistakenly interprets his professional courtesy as an overture to romance. When she makes subtle advances and he does not respond, she accuses him of lewd and lascivious behavior. This instigates a visit from Lt. Scanlon of Internal Affairs.

In the end, Dietrich does the opposite of what an attorney would have advised when he apologizes to Miss Whitaker. His apology is essentially for *not* making advances towards her! She admits to him that her pride was hurt and she ultimately rescinds her complaint against the innocent officer. Naturally, this does not sit well with Scanlon.

What a Character

George Murdock's interpretation of Lt. Ben Scanlon is one of the most memorable of all the oddball characters that passed through the 12th Precinct over eight seasons. The relish with which he does his job is always entertaining and in this episode his over the top antics seem to amuse both Captain Miller and Hal Linden more than usual.

Job Fulfillment

Never have we seen Nick as happy in his work as he is cataloguing all the gambling paraphernalia seized from Rabbi Greenblatt, played by Eugene Elman in his last of three *Barney Miller* appearances. In addition to the cards, dice, chips, and one slot machine that were brought in, we learn that there are ten more slot machines back at his makeshift casino.

As Nick and Harris are leaving to answer the initial call, Nick turns to Harris and asks him if he has any money he could borrow? When Harris gives him a decisive "No," Nick exclaims, "Thank God!"

Solitary Confinement

The saga of Barney and Liz's breakup continues but quietly. In this episode we learn that Barney is no longer living at home. He has taken up residence at the Greenwich Hotel, Room 320.

Season 5, Episode 6: "The Prisoner."
Original Airdate: October 19, 1978.
Writers: Reinhold Weege, Wally Dalton, and Shelley Zellman.
Director: Noam Pitlik.
Cast of Characters: Hal Linden (Barney), Ron Glass (Harris), Steve Landesberg (Dietrich), Max Gail (Wojo), James Gregory (Inspector Luger), Ron Carey (Levitt), Jeff Corey (Ralph Timmons), Peggy Pope (Frances Newbound), Bruce Glover (Fred Denton), Henry Jones (Father Clement).

The Rundown

Harris and Dietrich are working on a string of cat burglaries that seem oddly familiar to Harris. Wojo arrests an ex-con for possession of a firearm. Barney faces some interdepartmental counseling from a priest.

The Exact M.O.

Harris is pleased with himself when he determines that the man he believes to be committing the burglaries is indeed a past offender, a thief by the name of Henry Newbound. Unfortunately, as Dietrich is anxious to point out, he's been dead for two years. When they take a call about a burglary in progress they rush out to discover that, in a way, both men are correct. Newbound is indeed dead but his wife isn't. His widow, played ever so sweetly by Peggy Pope, grew bored sitting around the apartment and needed something to do with her time so she picked up where her departed husband had left off.

Old Habits Die Hard

Wojo brings in an ex-con for carrying a weapon. It turns out the man wants to be sent back to prison. After thirty years in the slammer, he no longer knows how to function in society. The world has passed him by.

Well-known character actor and acting teacher Jeff Corey plays Ralph Timmons, the ex-con. Corey is one of the many who were blacklisted from Hollywood during the 1950s due to the Red Scare and the rantings of publicity seeking politicians like Martin Dies and Joe McCarthy. When he found himself out of work for refusing to name names, Corey used the money from his GI Bill to go back to school and take courses in Speech Therapy. He began giving speech classes in his garage. Those sessions soon turned into acting classes. By the time he was able to re-enter the industry in front of the cameras he had gained a reputation as one of the premiere acting coaches in Hollywood. He appeared in dozens of films from 1938 to 1951 and even more following his return to the screen (big and small) in 1960. Throughout his long career he appeared in such iconic films as *My Friend Flicka* (1943), *True Grit* (1969), and *Little Big Man* (1970) as well as the TV shows *Perry Mason*, *Bonanza*, and *Night Court* (1984-1992).

Boy, Do You Have the Wrong Guy

The recognizable Henry Jones plays Father Clement, a police priest who is sent to question and counsel Barney about his marital problems. Unfortunately, during their conversation he discovers that Barney is not a Catholic. Barney is clearly uncomfortable with the interaction but he's got to accept the bureaucratic oversight.

Jones was a seasoned actor whose work dates back to the very beginnings of television. He followed up a successful career on the New York stage with a screen career of almost half a century, appearing on such TV classics as *The Twilight Zone*, *Alfred Hitchcock Presents* (1955–1962), *Gunsmoke* (1955-1975), and dozens more. He was equally popular on the big screen with memorable turns in *The Bad Seed* (1956), *Vertigo* (1958), and *Support Your Local Sheriff* (1969). He was active into his eighties and died in 1999 at the age of eighty-six.

The Last Word

Barney, Wojo, and Nick are discussing who they could talk to and confide in when they were young and looking for guidance. Dietrich volunteers the following about his mysterious childhood.

> **Dietrich:** I was an only child. Both my parents worked and I didn't have any friends. The only thing I had to talk to was my teddy bear. And he stuttered.

Season 5, Episode 7: "Loan Shark."
Original Airdate: November 2, 1978.
Writers: Tony Sheehan (teleplay). Judith Anne Nielsen, Richard William Beban, and Bob Colleary (story).
Director: Noam Pitlik.
Cast of Characters: Max Gail (Wojo), Jack Soo (Yemana), Steve Landesberg (Dietrich), Ron Glass (Harris), Hal Linden (Barney), Boris Aplon (Leo Fallon), Mario Roccuzzo (George Willis), Lewis Charles (Nicolas Dellarosa), Larry B. Scott (Leland Turner).

The Rundown

Nick is feeling unappreciated as he marks twenty years in the NYPD and is treated as nothing more than a glorified clerk. A tattoo artist and his client file assault charges against one another. Harris follows the trail of a loan shark and discovers the guilty party is a teenaged kid.

How Times Change

In this episode, Wojo says to the tattoo artist, "I told you, tattooing is illegal in New York City." This is an amazingly out-of-date concept considering how ubiquitous tattoos now are in American culture. Interestingly, Wojo, the ex-Marine, finds tattoos and the idea of someone burning a picture onto your body to be disgusting. Dietrich says to Barney in his own inimitable way, "Strange custom tattooing. Some people consider it an atavistic reversion to an earlier, primitive state."

Ultimately, Barney reveals that he has a tattoo that he got on V.E. day. It's under his left arm—the initials V.E. with a little rose under it.

Maternal Instincts

Mario Roccuzzo makes his first of six *Barney Miller* appearances as George Willis, the man who gets cold feet halfway through getting his tattoo. He paid for "Mother" but only got as far as "Moth" before he decided he didn't want anymore. Unfortunately, when Dietrich describes in gruesome detail the way to get the "Moth" removed, he decides to go ahead and get the "-er" to complete his original vision. There was no laser removal of tattoos in 1978. The procedure included some painful surgery.

Just a Little Respect

Nick's twentieth anniversary on the force passes without anyone noticing or marking the occasion. The next day Nick is feeling unappreciated and lets his feelings be known as he walks out of the squad room to an early and long lunch.

When Nick returns he and Barney talk it out in his office. Nick reveals his anger when he gets into Barney's office saying, "So this is it, huh?" Barney asks, "This is what?" Nick replies, "The office." Incredulously, Barney answers, "C'mon, you've been here before." Nick responds, "Just briefly, not like Wojo and Harris—they spend the better part of their day here." And, of course, he's right. Through the years Barney had many talks with Wojo, Harris, Luger, and even Fish in his office. Rarely have we seen Dietrich or Nick in there.

Barney apologizes for missing his anniversary and Nick points out that he's missing the point. It wasn't about the anniversary as much as his feeling unappreciated. When Barney says he depends on him for a thousand little things, Nick responds, "yeah, coffee, filing, spring cleaning . . ." Barney admits that's true but says he also depends on him for "your experience, your sense of humor that gets us through the day, your composure . . ."

Their heartfelt conversation ends as follows:

Nick: You know I wasn't coming back here today?
Barney: Why did you?
Nick: Mostly because I felt a sort of special obligation to you on account of all the time we worked together and the high regard I have for you.
Barney: Thank you.
Nick: And besides, Disco Danny blew it in the stretch.

Just the Facts

- The horse in the third race, on which Nick places his bet, is called Disco Danny. It's hard to imagine the name "Disco Danny" was just a coincidence with creator Danny Arnold's interest in horse racing. Nick put "twenty dollars right on his nose to commemorate the twenty years that I served on this force."
- Actor Mario Roccuzzo was a story contributor to this episode.
- Harris's salary is $23,000 per year.
- If this was Nick Yemana's twentieth anniversary on the force, he must have been in his late thirties to early forties when he became a cop. Jack Soo was sixty-one in this episode. Even if he were playing a character five or six years younger, he'd still have been in his mid-thirties when he became a cop so the question is, what did he do before that?

The Last Word

Wojo tells Nick, "You know, uh, sometimes people work together for a long time and they never ever say how they really feel. So uh, so I want you to know that I feel really lucky to be working with you. I mean it. I learn a lot from you."

This is Nick's second to last appearance on the show. Everyone knew he was sick. One must wonder if what they were saying in the script wasn't written in to reflect exactly how the actors, writers and production staff felt about Jack Soo as well.

Season 5, Episode 8:	"The Vandal."
Original Airdate:	November 9, 1978.
Writers:	Dennis Koenig and Tony Sheehan.
Director:	Noam Pitlik.
Cast of Characters:	Jack Soo (Yemana), Hal Linden (Barney), Max Gail (Wojo), Steve Landesberg (Dietrich), Ron Glass (Harris), Jay Gerber (Lloyd Edelson), Howard Honig (Lawrence Snepp), Christopher Lloyd (Arnold Scully).

The Rundown

Someone trashes and vandalizes the squad room and Barney's office. They also spray-paint a message on the hallway wall, "Miller is a dirty . . ."— but we can't see the rest of the phrase from the viewpoint of the camera. Wojo and Dietrich bring in two men who were fighting in a coffee shop over the new TV season.

Meta, Man, Meta

Merriam-Webster defines "meta" as, "showing or suggesting an explicit awareness of itself or oneself . . . clearly self-referential." In that regard, this is definitely a "meta episode" on a number of levels. A substantial portion of the program is a debate between Jay Gerber as Lloyd Edelson and Howard Honig as Lawrence Snepp not only as to the worthiness of television but decrying certain styles of television that were very much under scrutiny at the time.

> **Mr. Snepp:** I think we've got some very exciting programs this season!
> **Mr. Adelson:** Boobs and behinds, bouncing and jiggling! Meanwhile, my kid, he can't even read a menu!

This exchange clearly refers to "jiggle TV" or "T & A TV" which ABC popularized with the introduction of shows such as *Charlie's Angels* and *Battle of the Network Stars*, both of which premiered in 1976.

As stylish as it was to berate the inanity of television in the late 1970s, it all seems even more prophetic today. At one point, Mr. Adelson's complains, "Nobody reads a book anymore, nobody talks to anyone anymore. They just sit and stare at that idiot box." It sounds very similar to our modern society's concerns about smart phones, social media, and the Internet.

In keeping with the "meta" theme, we have the exchange between Mr. Snepp, the TV executive, and Wojo when Mr. Snepp learns that Wojo watches very little TV besides sports and news.

> **Mr. Snepp:** What about drama, comedy?
> **Wojo:** (derisively) Just ain't real. You know, it's just a bunch of actors saying words that some other guy wrote for him.

Homage

At one point, Mr. Snepp snaps and stands on the bars of the cell and screams, "I'm mad as hell and I'm not gonna take it anymore!" When Wojo asks him what he's doing, he looks at Wojo and says, "Don't you go to the movies either?" If you're as culturally removed as Wojo, may I suggest the Oscar-winning film, *Network* (1976)?

Ice Cold Revenge

If revenge is indeed a dish best served cold than Mr. Scully served up a real frozen dinner for Barney. Christopher Lloyd (*Taxi*, *Back to the Future*) plays Arnold Scully, the man who trashes the squad room and Barney's office as a reprisal for a citation Barney wrote out to him for littering seventeen years prior.

Scully: I bet you didn't think you'd be seeing me again?
Barney: I don't think I've ever seen you before.
Mr. Scully: You saying you aren't B. Miller, badge number 233451 . . . who issued a citation to me for throwing down a lousy half of a hot dog on the sidewalk on May 13, 1961?
Barney: 1961? (Barney chuckles) I'm afraid I don't remember.
Scully: I do. I told you how I had an appointment but you just kept on writing out the ticket. I told you it was for a real important job but he just kept me there, giving me this spiel about being patient and keeping my perspective.
Nick: Even then, huh?

Mr. Scully blames Barney for the unfortunate trajectory his life took after that fateful day.

Damage Assessment

Terrible shows listed by Mr. Edelson: *My Mother the Car* (1965–1966) (NBC), *Me and the Chimp* (1972) (CBS), *The San Pedro Beach Bums* (1977) (ABC), *The Chicago Teddy Bears* (1971) (CBS), *On the Rocks* (1975–1976) (ABC).

Items destroyed during the vandalism attack: Wojo's nameplate was busted in half, Harris's alpaca sweater was torn to shreds, and Nick's chair leg was broken.

Final Words

At the end of the episode, Barney asks Nick to start reorganizing the files. Nick looks at him and asks, "Why me?" then points to the perp and says, "He did it!" Exasperated, Barney snaps, "Just get at it, will ya?" Nick sarcastically responds, "Yes sir." Barney inquires, "Something else you'd like to say?" At this point, Nick looks at the message on the wall, "Miller is a . . ." and says, "I have nothing to add."

A poignantly perfect last line for the episode as these are the last words of dialogue we shall ever hear from Sergeant Nick Yemana. Jack Soo never appeared in another *Barney Miller* episode. He died of cancer on January 11, 1979.

Season 5, Episode 9: "The Harris Incident."
Original Airdate: November 30, 1978
Writers: Wally Dalton, Shelley Zellman, and Reinhold Weege.
Director: Noam Pitlik.
Cast of Characters: Hal Linden (Barney), Steve Landesberg (Dietrich), Max Gail (Wojo), Ron Glass (Harris), Ron Carey (Levitt), Michael Lombard (Sanford Whitney), Ed Peck (Patrolman Frank Slater), Rick Wain (Patrolman Walt Darvic), Marilyn Chris (Ruth Whitney).

The Rundown

Wojo brings in a beggar who he feels is too healthy to be begging. Uniformed police take a shot at Harris as he is apprehending a prisoner.

Stock Analyst, Beggar, What's the Difference?

Michael Lombard makes his first of four appearances in *the Barney Miller* universe as a former stock analyst who's lost his job and turns to begging when he accidentally discovers how easy it is to do. As far as he's concerned, he's performing a public service by helping the ethically challenged, guilt-ridden stockbrokers feel good about themselves by allowing them to give him money. In Mr. Whitney's own words, "I'm making a contribution, for God's sakes!"

Simple Logic

Dietrich: Begging, it's the world's oldest profession.
Wojo: I thought that was prostitution.
Dietrich: Well, somebody had to ask for it.

A Man, a Friend, a Partner

This was an important episode in the history of the series. *Barney Miller* never shied away from racial issues but it was not as constant a subject for source material as it was on a show like *All in the Family*. In this episode, Ron Harris arrests a criminal in the middle of a robbery. He then gets mistaken *as* a criminal by uniformed cops merely because they saw a black man on the scene with a gun. He identified himself as a police officer but was not immediately believed and they take a shot at him. As they explained what happened to Barney, the younger of the two officers in a slip of the tongue blurts out, "We saw him and just thought he was another . . ." At this point, Harris yells out, "Hold that thought!"

Collaborative Squad

Hal Linden was quick to bring this episode up when asked about what kind of input the actors were able to have in the development of their characters. I'll let Linden tell the story about the pivotal scene of this episode:

> Danny wrote a scene, basically, where Harris comes back and says "Listen, I'm sorry. I just got a little too hot under the collar," and basically apologized. And we read the scene, we stage it, and we're almost ready to shoot it when Ron Glass slaps the paper down on the desk and he says, "What the hell am I apologizing for? Why should I apologize? I was the one shot at." [*sic*] Silence. I know my reaction was not shock but, *you know, he's right, he's right. Why should he apologize for losing his temper?* I didn't apologize for ameliorating a situation that I should have pointed out as unjust.'
> And we all sat down. Then Danny said, now this is maybe one o'clock in the morning, this is with cameramen standing around . . . he's paying for golden time, double-double, who knows what it was costing him? And he just sat down and he looked at Ron and he said, "What would you say?"

Linden says they all sat around and talked it out. What would each of them say to one another? In the end, Harris does not apologize but true to the *Barney Miller* style of no easy answers, the situation is ended with everyone acknowledging that this probably won't be the last time something like this happens and they'll need to handle and talk out each situation as it comes along.

Linden said:

> It didn't have gravitas, it didn't have a brilliant right answer for all the problems. It just acknowledged the problem. That was what we accomplished. We acknowledged that there was a problem and that we all are going to have to face it and find out how to deal with it.
>
> But my point is that this scene was written right around the table, based on how four actors felt, from the point of view of their characters,

of course, 'cause they knew their characters—and that's how the scene was created and that's how it was shot.

I'm not sure if that happened all the time but it seems clear from interviews done with cast and crew that Danny Arnold was almost always willing to take creative suggestions. Then he would take those comments and go up to his office alone, or with the writers, and put it together on the page.

Regardless of the exact details, what's most impressive is Danny Arnold's ability to avoid wrapping every issue up in a neat little package at the end of a given episode. As we know, life doesn't work that way but for many years in the sitcom world, all the problems introduced in the episode had to be resolved in roughly twenty-five minutes. Danny Arnold did not allow himself or his show to be limited by those traditional conventions.

The Last Word

Harris: It's been a bad day.
Miller: There may be more.
Harris: There *will* be more.
Miller: We can handle it.
Harris: Thank you.

There's also a beautiful little moment when Levitt sends Harris a look of respect and compassion. Nice that he was included in the discussion.

Season 5, Episode 10: "The Radical."
Original Airdate: December 7, 1978.
Writers: Tony Sheehan (teleplay). Lee H. Grant (story).
Director: Noam Pitlik.
Cast of Characters: Steve Landesberg (Dietrich), Hal Linden (Barney), James Gregory (Inspector Frank Luger), Corey Fischer (Jonathan Dodd/Gerald Morris), Stuart Pankin (Anthony Moreau), Craig Richard Nelson (Arnold Moraz), Sam Ingraffia (Ambulance attendant).

The Rundown

Wojo arrests a shoplifter not realizing that the suspect is a 1960s radical wanted by the FBI. Harris and Dietrich bring in a burglar with a weight problem. Inspector Luger has what appears to be a heart attack.

Alias

Corey Fischer plays Gerald Morris, a man arrested for shoplifting at Cotterman's Market. (Must have been a brother to the Cotterman who ran the liquor store?) Morris is incredulous that they don't know who he is. He explains that Morris is not his real name despite what Wojo took from his driver's license. Morris explains, "I have thirty different licenses. I have Gerald Morris, Morris Philips, Philip Morris, *Helen Hayes*!" He finally reveals that he is Jonathan Dodd. The name still means nothing to the officers and he finally has to tell them that the FBI and the US Marshall have been looking for him for nine years. It turns out he was a 1960s radical who made a name for himself protesting the Vietnam War.

In acting circles, Fischer made a name for himself by appearing in Robert Altman's first three feature films of the 1970s: *MASH*, *Brewster McCloud*, and *McCabe & Mrs. Miller*. In 1978, he founded the Traveling Jewish Theatre with two other actors. The theater troupe became a favorite of San Francisco theatergoers and lasted for well over three decades.

To Protest or Not to Protest

The arrival of Mr. Dodd fuels some heated debate in the detective squad room. We know that Wojo is a Vietnam Vet but we learn in this episode that prior to joining the Coast Guard, Harris was actually protesting the war. Wojo is angry but Dietrich explains that there were many who protested the war aggressively but peacefully and lawfully. Harris tells Dietrich he came out against the war in 1966. Dietrich says he came out against the war in 1957 when Eisenhower first sent military advisors over to train South Vietnamese personnel. When Harris tries to figure out how old Dietrich would have been in 1957, Dietrich says, "I was fourteen. I got a scout badge for international affairs."

First Time Offender

Versatile character actor Stuart Pankin makes the first of two appearances in this episode as a corpulent burglar. He is hypersensitive about his weight and assumes all look upon him as a subject of disgust. His characterization is somewhat ironic in that his size in the episode doesn't seem so huge these days when obesity is a common problem in America.

The Ol' Inspector

As inappropriate as Inspector Luger can sometimes be, it should be noted that like Barney, he almost always defends the men under him and tries to protect them. He may be part of the "management level" of the NYPD but he is always very loyal to his officers. In this episode, he seems bored and just stops by to give the men a little morale boost. After suffering his attack, he's wheeled out on a gurney but stops the attendants before they take him away to tell the boys, "I've been a very lucky man to have the opportunity to serve and work with what I consider to be one of the finest group of police officers ever assembled in the history of the NYPD." He then looks behind him and spots Levitt with a heartwarming look on his face. Luger gives him a wink and says, "You too, Levine."

For the Record

- Inspector Luger mentions how hot it is for October but the episode aired in December.
- Barney mentions to Inspector Luger that Nick is at the D.A.'s office for a while. Sadly, we now know better.

Season 5, Episode 11: "Toys."
Original Airdate: December 14, 1978.
Writers: Wally Dalton, Shelley Zellman, and Tony Sheehan (teleplay). Wally Dalton and Shelley Zellman (story).
Director: Noam Pitlik.
Cast of Characters: Hal Linden (Barney), Max Gail (Wojo), Ron Glass (Harris), Ron Carey (Levitt), Steve Landesberg (Dietrich), Barbara Barrie (Elizabeth Miller), Sydney Lassick (Arnold Cummings), Gregory V. Karliss (Clyde Perry), Walter Janovitz (Stefan Metterling), Zachary Berger (Nathan Berman).

The Rundown

Barney is in an unusually good mood because Liz is coming in to discuss their mutual finances. Levitt brings in a claustrophobic man who tried to hold up a liquor store. Harris and Dietrich arrest a man who's robbed a toy factory.

Bookkeeping

Liz comes to the station to work on the family checkbook. She and Barney also discuss the upcoming holidays and the cabin in Vermont that they've rented for fifteen years at Christmastime. They both agree, unenthusiastically, that they should cancel their reservation this year.

Later, Liz comes back and tells Barney when she got home she found some more checks. "It took me a long time but I found some," she says. She tells Barney that she still wants to rent their Christmas cabin in Vermont. Barney does too. Barney and Liz share a tender moment and it's obvious that despite their problems, they still love one another.

Boxed In

Sidney Lassick is wonderful as Arnold Cummings, a man who held up a liquor store. As he tried to escape the clerk tackled him and locked him in a closet until the police arrived. When released from the closet he was whimpering and scratching at the door due to his acute claustrophobia. Later in the episode, he will lose his cool again when the confines of the cage become too much for him.

This is Lassick's first of two *Barney Miller* roles. He is best known for his portrayal of Charlie Cheswick in the feature film, *One Flew Over the Cuckoo's Nest* (1975). With his high, scratchy voice, Lassick was often cast as very high-strung nervous characters.

Christmas Caper

One toy manufacturer sends a thief to rob another toy manufacturer of his most recent toy technology. It turns out the business isn't easy for anyone these days as the two rivals end up commiserating with one another over the fickle tastes of their customers.

Walter Janovitz plays Stefan Metterling, owner of the Perfecto Toy Company. This is the second of five *Barney Miller* roles for Janovitz. He appeared previously in the famous "Hash" episode from Season Three.

Zachery Berger appears as the rival toymaker in his first appearance on the program. He will show up one more time in Season Seven as the mysterious owner of a novelty shop in one of the series most powerful episodes.

The Last Word

Stefan Metterling: Let me tell you all about the toy business. It's all thieves and cutthroats.

Dietrich: I thought it was mostly elves.

Season 5, Episode 12: "The Indian."
Original Airdate: January 4, 1979.
Writers: Reinhold Weege (teleplay). Judith Anne Nielsen, Richard William Beban, and Reinhold Weege (story).
Director: Noam Pitlik.
Cast of Characters: Max Gail (Wojo), Steve Landesberg (Dietrich), Ron Glass (Harris), Hal Linden (Barney), Ron Carey (Levitt), Charles White Eagle (George Ten Fingers), Alix Elias (Maggie DuBois), Phil Leeds (Horace Chandler), Richard Stahl (Philip Owens), Dino Natali (Officer Zatelli).

Rundown

A man with a shoe fetish robs a woman of her shoes at a bus stop. Wojo develops a relationship with an American Indian he's arrested for trespassing in a restricted area of Central Park. Levitt is growing impatient and disgruntled with his lack of progress to the detective ranks.

Bureau of Indian Affairs

Max Gail has a long and cherished relationship with the American Indian movement. This is the first of two story ideas around Indigenous people and their history that he was able to get included in the *Barney Miller* series. The second one actually propels the final storyline of the series.

In this episode George Ten Fingers, played by a man named George White Eagle, has gone to Central Park to die. At one point, he says to Wojo, "When you speak, there's fire in your eyes and thunder in your voice." That's about the best description you'll ever hear of Stan Wojciehowicz.

Wojo calls in the Bureau of Indian Affairs to answer some questions without consulting Barney. As usually happens the individual from the outside agency, in this case the indispensable Richard Stahl as Philip Owens, is perturbed to have been called in for a situation involving one solitary individual. In fairness to Mr. Owens, Wojo did tell the bureau that there might be some sort of treaty involved in order to get them to respond. To quote Mr. Owens, "I deal with entire Indian nations, not people!" Conversely, in the 12th Precinct, individual people are treated with the dignity and respect of entire nations.

In the end, Wojo is supposed to bring Mr. Ten Fingers to Bellevue but instead he takes him back to the park. When Barney starts to get angry, Wojo blurts out, "He's dead, Barn. I uh, I stayed with him a while and we talked, and then we just sat and he died." Ultimately, Wojo feels good about the experience because it's what the old man wanted.

The depth of feeling established between Wojo and George Ten Fingers in this short twenty-five-minute episode is quite touching. Max Gail really shows off his acting chops in this simple but beautiful storyline.

Step on It!

Phil Leeds makes his fourth of seven appearances here as Horace Chandler, a man with a fetish for shoes. As Harris is filling out the arrest report he asks if Chandler was married? He tells him he's divorced and Harris says, "Sorry." Mr. Chandler says, "Hey, listen it was the best thing that could have happened. She was always on my back. Yelling at me, screaming, she had the temperament of a bull . . . and the feet of a brontosaurus."

No Apology Necessary

Levitt is resigned to the fact that his temporary assignments to plain clothes will lead nowhere. "It's just accepting the fact that these little jaunts up here to the world of plain clothes are about as transient as life itself." Barney is somewhat stunned. "Why Levitt, that's almost existential." A concerned Levitt asks, "Should I apologize for that, sir?"

> **Wojo:** You can point to every item in the Sears catalog and somebody, somewhere, wants to sleep with it.

Season 5, Episode 13: "Voice Analyzer."
Original Airdate: January 11, 1979.
Writers: Reinhold Weege and James Bonnett (teleplay). James Bonnett (story).
Director: Noam Pitlik.
Cast of Characters: Ron Glass (Harris), Max Gail (Wojo), Hal Linden (Barney), Steve Landesberg (Dietrich), Ron Carey (Levitt), Allan Rich (Mr. Ramsen), Philip Roth (Mr. Sanders), Barry Pearl (Mario Pellegrini), George Murdock (Lt. Ben Scanlon).

The Rundown

A furrier comes in to report that a man stole his vehicle filled with $20,000 worth of furs. Following a series of articles in the paper about detectives taking bribes, Lt. Scanlon shows up at the 12th to question the men, using a lie detector machine.

Beating the System

The origins of the polygraph, or "lie detector" test, go back to the 1920s. The machines measure various physiological factors in an individual when they're being interrogated. However, other factors such as an anxiety disorder in the participant can and will affect the outcome of such interrogations.

Harris does fine and says all you have to do is remain calm. This is a problem for Wojo who is naturally high-strung. Combine that with the fact that Lt. Scanlon always knew how to push Wojo's buttons and it spells disaster for our young Polish hero. Dietrich helps out their case when he tells the machine that he was born "long, long ago in a galaxy far, far away," [a reference to the then-recent *Star Wars* movie] and the machine reads that he is telling the truth. Finally, Captain Miller gets Scanlon to accidentally admit his prejudices toward the squad into the machine and the witch hunt ends for the day. Scanlon, however, will continue his attempts to bring down the men of the 12th for as long as they're around.

A Regular John Dillinger

Barry Pearl plays fur thief Mario Pellegrini while Allan Rich portrays the less than ethical furrier, Mr. Ramsen. This is another one of those ideal casting jobs that we see so often on the show. Pearl is very funny as a streetwise punk, a self-professed anti-social who is proud of his résumé. When he gets caught because of running a red light, he tells Barney, "Hey, I got convictions on my record like burglary, dealing drugs, assault with a deadly weapon, you expect me to obey the rules of the road?"

This is Allan Rich's first of three appearances on the show. His characters will be marked by his apoplectic reactions to the situations he's in. No one could play indignant or exasperated better than the talented Mr. Rich. When the perp points out that the furs are junk, Barney tells Ramsen that, "for some strange reason the word 'fraud' seems to pop into my head." At that suggestion, Pellegrini pops up out of his seat and says, "White collar crime makes me sick!" Harris turns to Pellegrini and says, "Down, Dillinger."

Rich got his first professional job in the theatre when hired by Milton Berle and Clifford Hayman for the play *I'll Take the High Road* in 1943. Rich got good notices, the play did not. Nevertheless, he was hooked and continued to work wherever and whenever he could. By the time he was nineteen, he toured the Pacific Theater with the USO to entertain the troops. He contracted a serious form of bacillary and amoebic dysentery and was sent home to the states after he lost eighty pounds. The postwar years were tough and his big break finally came in 1951 with the Broadway show *Darkness at Noon*. His role was small but he played opposite Claude Rains on Broadway and was then given a larger role opposite Edward G. Robinson in the road company.

He was blacklisted in the 1950s when he was mentioned in *Red Channels*, a slanderous publication written by an ex-FBI agent and a right-wing TV producer. A man of conscience, Rich had been a member of the Theater Action Committee to Free Willie Magee, a black man who'd been falsely accused of rape. The publishers of *Red Channels* looked at the committee as a subversive organization and blacklisted anyone who was part of it. Rich would say that he never understood how or why he was thought to be a communist but when he saw the company he was in (Arthur Miller, Leonard Bernstein, Pete Seeger) he wore it like a badge of honor. Danny Arnold made a habit of hiring blacklisted actors through the years.

Allan Rich made a major comeback in *Serpico* (1973) and never looked back. He worked steadily for another forty years after that film.

Missed Opportunity

This is Barry Pearl's one and only appearance in a *Barney Miller* episode. The actor, who became best known for his portrayal of Doody in the movie version of *Grease* (1975), was thrilled when he landed a guest spot on the Danny Arnold sitcom. In the end, it was a more disappointing experience than he'd originally anticipated because of an unforeseen circumstance beyond his control. Pearl wrote me that, ". . . At the age of eleven, I moved, overnight, from Pennsylvania to New York to take over the role of Randolph McAfee in *Bye Bye Birdie* on Broadway. I went on to do the national tour of the show and then in the summer of '62, I did the show in Vegas at the Riviera Hotel.

"While there I saw Jack [Soo] in *Flower Drum Song*. I was so impressed with his work. For some reason he just really stuck out to me. And I'll never forget how he used to wiggle his fingers when he was just standing still onstage. I had asked someone why he would do such a thing. I was told that it was part of his timing. That always stuck with me.

"Fade out fade in to forty years ago, I landed a guest star role on *Barney Miller* in an episode entitled, 'Voice Analyzer.' I was so looking forward to the first day of rehearsal where I would get to meet one of my idols, Jack Soo. When I got there, I came to learn that he had been hospitalized for esophageal cancer. It made very me sad.

"Ironically the night that my episode aired was the night that Jack passed away, January 11, 1979."

Inside Wojo's Mind

It's not easy being Wojo. When Barney asks him if there was anything on his mind that might be bothering him, something that could affect the result of the lie detector tests, Wojo tells him nothing more than usual. Just the stuff he normally thinks about such as "What am I going to have for lunch, how's my mother getting along, whether or not we're going to have a nuclear war."

The Last Word

Wojo: You can take your machine and stick it up your internal affairs.

Season 5, Episode 14: "The Spy."
Original Airdate: January 18, 1979.
Writer: Tony Sheehan.
Director: Noam Pitlik.
Cast of Characters: Hal Linden (Barney), Ron Glass (Harris), Max Gail (Wojo), Steve Landesberg (Dietrich), Ron Carey (Levitt), Philip Sterling (Mitchell Warner), Stanley Brock (Bruno Bender), Estelle Omens (Felice Douglas), Flip Reade (Leslie Phillips).

The Rundown

A pedestrian woman is the victim of a flasher. A disgruntled and paranoid ex-spy gets arrested for disorderly conduct after causing a disturbance at the Unemployment Office. Bruno Bender gets brought in with a mime who was blocking the entrance to his store.

Just the Facts
- Bruno Bender's taste in comedy: The Three Stooges and The Ritz Brothers.

A Deeply Troubled Man

Character actor Philip Sterling makes his third of six appearances here as Mitchell Warner, an ex-CIA operative. In his many appearances on the show, he specialized in deeply troubled men. People who had difficulty handling the stress of their daily lives and subsequently lose their grip on reality. Twenty-two years with "The Company" made Mr. Warner paranoid of all around him until he finally believes that the entire 12th Precinct is just an elaborate ruse by the CIA to set him up.

The Humanity

Once again, the heart of so many great *Barney Miller* stories is the humanity of the characters. In those few minutes of time when he is convinced that everyone is a CIA operative conspiring against him, Mr. Warner is rude to Ms. Douglas, the middle-aged victim of the flasher. He all but calls her a dog and she is visibly hurt. Once he's regained his senses and has given up the gun he used to hold them all hostage, he sincerely apologizes to Ms. Douglas for what he said and tells her he enjoyed talking to her. Her reply to his apology is, "I was flattered to think that anyone thought I was someone other than myself." It's an incredibly sad and insightful look into this quiet lady's self-image. However, there is a moment between them and when she learns that he's going to Bellevue, she asks Barney what the address is for the hospital, leading us to conclude that she will visit Mr. Warner there.

Estelle Owens plays the character of Felice Douglas in her first of two *Barney Miller* guest spots. She is probably best remembered for her role as Edna, one of the bank employees, in *Dog Day Afternoon* (1975).

Back on the Horse

The first time Mr. Warner is being led out of the squad room, he overpowers Levitt and takes his gun from him. The second time, when he's being transferred to Bellevue, Barney turns to Levitt once again, showing him that he still has confidence in him. When Wojo volunteers to go with him, Barney says no and he calls Levitt "a good cop." It's a nice moment for Levitt and Captain Miller in that it's a compliment Levitt didn't have to coax out of him.

Season 5, Episode 15:	"Wojo's Girl." This episode appeared on January 25, 1979, as a special, hour-long episode. Therefore, it appears correctly as one episode in the Shout! Factory box set. However, it was split into two separate episodes in syndication and listed as such on IMDB. Therefore, even though they are listed on the DVDs as one episode, they are split into two separate episodes here as episode 15 and episode 15B for the 1978–1979 season. What that means historically is that there were twenty-two episodes in Season Five but twenty-three half-hours produced and seen in syndication.
Original Airdate:	January 25, 1979.
Writers:	Tony Sheehan and Danny Arnold.
Director:	Noam Pitlik.
Cast of Characters:	Ron Glass (Harris), Hal Linden (Barney), Max Gail (Wojo), Steve Landesberg (Dietrich), Darlene Parks (Nancy), Lewis Arquette (Nells Finney), Philip Bruns (Frank Mallory), Michael Conrad (Col. Charles Dundee), Peter Hobbs (Philip Brauer), Doris Roberts (Harriet Brauer).

The Rundown

Wojo is having difficulty deciding whether he should move in with his new girlfriend or not. An old customer returns to the 12th Precinct to complain about her husband and his involvement with a mercenary group. A travel agent and his disgruntled customer come to fisticuffs over a refund for a nightmarish trip.

Gun Control

It seems safe to say that Danny Arnold was on the right side of history in terms of the national debate over gun control. Years before it was a daily point of contention on the nightly news, the officers of the 12th Precinct made clear the necessity of gun control and regulation.

In this episode, we are introduced to a mercenary recruiter who revels in war and guns. Harris mentions to Barney that Col. Dundee, played by character actor Michael Conrad, has quite a stash of weapons. Dundee responds with the answer of too many gun enthusiasts: "I've got a right to secure my place of business." A reasonable claim to be sure but when Harris describes the "weapons of defense" he found at Dundee's office, the list includes thirty-six assorted small arms, fourteen heavy caliber, semi and automatic weapons, fifty-six pieces of assorted pyrotechnics, two flame throwers, and an M-12 anti-tank gun.

Midlife Crisis

Philip Brauer, played brilliantly as always by Peter Hobbs, is going through a difficult time of life. He's fifty years old and he's desperate to feel necessary. He tells his wife, "I want to participate [as a mercenary]. I can do something. I can affect something." His wife Harriet, portrayed by four-time *Barney Miller* player Doris Roberts, convinces him that *she* needs him.

Twenty-Eight Days of Horror

Philip Bruns, as weary traveler Frank Mallory, makes his second of four visits to the 12th Precinct. In this one, he tussles with his least favorite travel agent, Nells Finney, played by Lewis Arquette. Finney sent Mr. Mallory and his wife on a less than ideal twenty-eight-day tour of Europe where everything seems to have gone wrong. In the end, Finney gets fed up with Mallory's complaints, revealing that the travel agent himself has never gone anywhere. "I'm stuck in a cold, filthy city in a box of an office."

Eventually, they both agree to drop charges against one another and that compels Dietrich to point out what the rest of us are thinking.

> **Dietrich:** That's an interesting tactic you use.
> **Barney:** What's that?
> **Dietrich:** Whenever we have assault cases, you always put the two combatants in the cell together. Give them the opportunity to reconcile.
> **Barney:** Thank you.
> **Dietrich:** Or beat the hell out of each other again.

Speaking of Self-Awareness

We learn that Wojo's new girlfriend was a call girl. Seeking the advice of his surrogate father, Barney, Wojo tells him, "I always seem to get hooked up with fallen women. Remember Wentworth?" Barney shouts, "She was a cop!" To which Wojo replies, "Yeah, but she reminded me of a hooker." Barney raises his eyebrows on that bit of information.

Finally, Wojo comes to a perceptive realization: "It's like I need to think that they need saving and I'm the only guy in the world that can do it." The fans of the show could have told him that a long time ago. Not to delve too far into the psychology of it all but it sort of makes you wonder what his mom was like.

Just the Facts

- Lewis Arquette, who plays Finney the travel agent, is the father of actors Rosanna, Patricia, and David Arquette. He was also the son of actor Cliff Arquette, who's best remembered for his characterization of "Charley Weaver" on *The Hollywood Squares*.
- Michael Conrad makes his only *Barney Miller* appearance in this episode. Conrad's career in television went back to the mid-1950s. Two years after this appearance, he landed the role of a lifetime as Sgt. Phil Esterhaus on the NBC police drama, *Hill Street Blues* (1981–1987). Conrad won two Emmys for Outstanding Supporting Actor in a Drama Series for *Hill Street* but sadly, died of cancer ten episodes into the show's fourth season. He was fifty-eight years of age.

Season 5, Episode 15B: "Wojo's Girl."
Original Airdate: January 25, 1979.
Writers: Tony Sheehan and Danny Arnold.
Director: Noam Pitlik.
Cast of Characters: Darlene Parks (Nancy). CREDIT ONLY: Lewis Arquette (Nells Finney), Philip Bruns (Frank Mallory), Michael Conrad (Col. Charles Dundee), Peter Hobbs (Philip Brauer), Doris Roberts (Harriet Brauer).

The Rundown

This episode was written and run as a pilot for a potential spinoff revolving around Wojo's character.

Hard to Watch

This episode may very well be the weakest link in the eight-season run of the series. It's actually painful to watch. I don't really think anyone's heart was in it.

Danny Arnold always had his hand in a variety of pilots but during the run of *Barney Miller*, his focus was always on making *Barney Miller* the best it could be.

Throughout this episode Wojo is uncomfortable and ill at ease and although the character was supposed to act that way in order to portray the angst he was going through to make a commitment, the end result is that it just makes the viewer uncomfortable as well. Everything Nancy does bothers Wojo. Even when she dresses in a seductive nightgown to lure him to bed, where we've been led to believe they do get along well, he opts to stay up and watch a basketball game and a Charlie Chan movie.

All that can be said for this effort to spin Wojo off into his own show is that happily it failed. According to Gail, the network wanted Danny Arnold to write this spinoff and Max Gail was hesitant from the start. Gail and Arnold contributed ideas but, in the end,, they never really hit on anything that Gail thought was all that funny. He also realized he was in a good show already and had seen Abe Vigoda strike out on his own and fail so there was no real impetus for him to jump ship. Gail let Arnold know how he felt so that prior to actually going ahead with the spinoff idea, Arnold had to promise Gail that he'd write a letter saying if the network wanted to pick up the pilot, Max Gail was free to turn it down. When all was said and done, there was no need for the letter. The pilot generated little interest.

To what end?

What did we learn for our trouble in this less than humorous episode? Wojo likes hockey, Nancy's favorite color is turquoise, and Wojo's apartment is nearly as dingy as the precinct house.

Nancy

According to Harriet Helberg, who served as the Casting Director for Season Five, Shelley Long was among the young women who auditioned for the role of Nancy in "Wojo's Girl." Helberg thought she was quite good but can't exactly remember why they went instead with Darlene Parks. Max Gail said that he remembers Stockard Channing auditioning but although he thought she would be a good choice, the producers didn't think she was right for the part. Max Gail didn't think Parks did much of anything after *Barney Miller* and IMDb, although not always reliable, backs up that supposition. While both Shelley Long and Stockard Channing went on to long and productive careers, Darlene Parks faded into obscurity.

Season 5, Episode 16: "Middle Age."
Original Airdate: February 1, 1979.
Writers: Wally Dalton and Shelley Zellman (story). Reinhold Weege and Danny Arnold (teleplay).
Director: Noam Pitlik.
Cast of Characters: Ron Glass (Harris), Hal Linden (Barney), Max Gail (Wojo), Steve Landesberg (Dietrich), Richard Libertini (Richard Perito), Raleigh Bond (Herbie Glass), Kres Mersky (Mrs. Perito), Nehemiah Persoff (Yacov Berger).

The Rundown

A Hasidic diamond merchant is robbed on the streets of New York. Wojo brings in a man who endangers people in the park with his javelin throwing and Dietrich is throwing a party.

Dead End

This is a strange episode. After the disappointment of "Wojo's Girl" one is looking to laugh out loud again with the men of the 12th and their eccentric visitors but this one falls short. There's Dietrich's party that we know we'll never see. There are the diamond thefts that provide the great actor Nehemiah Persoff the chance to play with a traditional Jewish characterization but we learn next to nothing about the thief. He steals because he would never be able to afford diamonds on his salary. As Barney wisely points out, "You're not alone, buster." Otherwise, the diamonds are introduced as yet another option for the investment-minded Sgt. Harris. Finally, Mr. Perito, played by the wonderful Richard Libertini, is a man with a dream. As he and his wife are leaving, she tells him to either give up his dream to compete in the Olympics or else she will divorce him. She walks out, he looks back at the men in the squad room and leaves. That's it. No remark, no joke, no nothing. Dead end.

This isn't a bad episode like the second half of "Wojo's Girl," it's just an anemic one. You should pardon the pun but it just doesn't sparkle.

Four Eyes Are Better Than None

Much is made of Barney's new reading glasses and how that must mean he's getting old. In an attempt to use the observation for flattery, Harris tells Barney that the glasses make him look more distinguished, reflective. In fact, he realizes he looks just like Walter Pidgeon. Barney, however, is not too flattered when he realizes that "the man must be eighty years old by now." Point in fact, Walter Pidgeon was eighty-one when this episode premiered.

Dietrich's Party Games

Dietrich gives details to one of the party games he's planning for his get-together. "As each guest comes in they draw from a hat the name of a fourteenth-century philosopher and assume his character. Then by quoting various thoughts and phrases during the course of a normal conversation each guest tries to guess the other's identity." Dietrich asks Levitt, "You ever play that?" Levitt replies, "I play Yahtzee."

Season 5, Episode 17:	"The Counterfeiter."
Original Airdate:	February 8, 1979.
Writers:	Frank Dungan, Jeff Stein, and Reinhold Weege.
Director:	Max Gail.
Cast of Characters:	Hal Linden (Barney), Max Gail (Wojo), Steve Landesberg (Dietrich), Ron Glass (Harris), James Gregory (Inspector Luger), Ron Carey (Levitt), J. Pat O'Malley (Walt Hathaway), Jack Riley (Robert Lovell), George Pentecost (Dr. Rene Boudreau), Al Ruscio (Mr. Becker), Susan Davis (Lisa Lovell).

The Rundown

Wojo attempts to make sense of Nick's filing system. Someone is passing small denominations of counterfeit money to local merchants. The inspector returns to the precinct for the first time since his heart attack. Wojo and Levitt bring in yet another pair of mutual assault combatants.

It's Only Skin Deep

Jack Riley plays Robert Lovell, a man who attacks the plastic surgeon who performed surgery on his wife. Wojo asks Lovell if his wife consented to the surgery. His reply is, "That woman will sign anything, petitions to ban the bomb, stop pollution, save the baby seals! It's depraved isn't it?"

This is Riley's second and last appearance on *Barney Miller*. By the time Riley made this appearance, *The Bob Newhart Show* (1972–1978) had finished its six-year run on rival CBS. He would continue to be one of the busiest and well-respected comic actors in the business showing up in numerous Mel Brooks movies, in TV guest spots on *One Day at A Time*, *Diff'rent Strokes*, and *Night Court* as well providing the voice of Stu Pickles on the popular and long-running children's animated series, *Rugrats*.

Seems Like Old Times

Harris's warm feeling towards Walt Hathaway, the local counterfeiter, calls to mind his similar response to Roscoe Lee Browne as Charles Evan Jeffers in the Season One episode, "Escape Artist."

In this episode another legendary character actor, J. Pat O'Malley, plays the charming felon. He has engraved some magnificent one-dollar plates. Unfortunately, one of the shopkeepers grew suspicious when he tried to pass a phony five-dollar bill. When Barney checks it out, he says, "Looks pretty good to me." Harris recommends he "Check Abe's jacket" and it's only then he realizes it resembles a leisure suit. Walt explains his eyes aren't what they used to be when he originally made the one-dollar plates in 1963! He's been printing the singles ever since but "only as [he] needed it."

He received his training in engraving during World War II, making the metal plates for military script. Harris is clearly taken with Walt as "one of the most interesting, colorful, informative people I have ever met." All of a sudden, it hits him, "My most unforgettable character—*Reader's Digest*!" Once again, Harris has reduced an emotional life experience into a potential writing assignment.

Harris, however, is not altogether without feeling. He asks Barney if they really have to prosecute the old gentleman? Walt tries to ease Harris's concern, telling him, "I found I couldn't live on a small disability pension from the Army so those just helped out. Well, now I don't have to worry about it." [Walt is looking at the bright side of being fed and housed in prison] Doesn't say much for military pensions.

Is Honesty Really the Best Policy?

Al Ruscio makes his second of five appearances in this episode as Mr. Becker, the shopkeeper who spotted the phony bill. Unfortunately, he learns after he turns in his counterfeit money that he doesn't get reimbursed with the genuine article. "You know, they never tell you about these little things in Civics class," he says. "All they ever tell you is you should vote in every election and that everybody is entitled to a little justice." Harris gives him a short legal lesson from a great barrister.

> **Harris:** "There is no justice, in or out of court," Clarence Darrow.
> **Dietrich:** "But, upholding the law is everybody's business," Dick Tracy, Crime Stopper's Textbook.

As Jeff Stein remembered it, the Dick Tracy joke was the first contribution he and Frank Dungan ever got in to a *Barney Miller* script.

For the Record

The file on Prostitution is empty. Nick had them filed according to specialty, "C" for Call Girls, "S" for Streetwalkers, "M" for Massagers, and "T" for Twins.

> **Season 5, Episode 18:** "Open House."
> **Original Airdate:** February 15, 1979.
> **Writers:** Wally Dalton, Shelley Zellman, and Tony Sheehan.
> **Director:** Noam Pitlik.
> **Cast of Characters:** Max Gail (Wojo), Steve Landesberg (Dietrich), Ron Glass (Harris), Ron Carey (Levitt), Hal Linden (Barney), Allan Miller (Dr. Gregory Bickman), John Dullaghan (Ray Brewer), Carmen Filpi (Bum), David Fresco (Monty, a bum), Christopher Lloyd (Vincent Carew).

The Rundown

The 12th Precinct hosts an Open House to cultivate police/community relations that leads to our introduction to Ray the Bum. Barney is moving out of the Greenwich Hotel and back into his apartment with Liz. A psychiatrist tries to better understand his arsonist patient.

Quite a Crowd

No one seems too excited about the Open House with the possible exception of Levitt who's put in charge of the refreshments and "lays out a little buffet for the guests" that includes cocktail wieners, saltines, chips, horseradish dip, a bowl of Cheetos, etc. Apparently, the community wasn't all that interested either because the only patrons that came in were, in the parlance of the day—bums. Today we would call them homeless people.

However, the Open House provides us with our introduction to actor John Dullaghan's character Ray Brewer, a man who will be part of the *Barney Miller* universe for the remainder of the series. Ray is impressed with Levitt's buffet and comes back with two more bums/friends to enjoy the feast. Ray describes them to Barney as "two of your biggest supporters." The visitors are soon stuffing the food into their pockets.

Together Again

Barney lets the men know that he is moving back in with Liz. They are all overjoyed. Unfortunately, the manager of the hotel doesn't care and refuses to return the remainder of the rent for the month that Barney paid in advance. When the manager reveals his plans to rent the room, thereby getting paid twice for the same space/time, Barney has an epiphany. Before Ray and his group of homeless friends depart, he gives them his key to Room Forty-Five and invites them to use the room, with his compliments, for the remainder of the month. Dietrich tells Barney, "I admire you, Captain. It isn't very often a person has the chance to do something for his fellow human beings and stick it to a hotel at the same time."

Doctor/Patient Privilege

Wojo and Dietrich find a man suspiciously observing a fire set by an arsonist. It turns out the man is a psychiatrist, Dr. Gregory Bickman, played by Allan Miller, who is treating the man responsible for setting a half dozen fires. When Wojo asks for his name, the doctor tells him that due to doctor/patient privilege, he can't divulge his name. When Wojo points out that someone could have been hurt, the doctor tries to reassure them, "Believe me, the man is conscientious which is a result of excessive mothering."

When a second fire gets set in the same day and two men are almost killed, Barney applies the pressure and Bickman gives up the name—"Vincent Carew, Morris Hotel." As soon as he identifies his patient, he is wracked by guilt.

The Last Word

Christopher Lloyd is his usual brilliant self in his portrayal of the arsonist. Carew tells Wojo, "I stopped wetting the bed in '66." Wojo tells him, "Nobody cares!" Carew replies, "Maybe not now."

Season 5, Episode 19: "Identity."
Original Airdate: March 1, 1979.
Writer: Tom Reeder.
Director: Noam Pitlik.
Cast of Characters: Ron Carey (Levitt), Hal Linden (Barney), Max Gail (Wojo), Ron Glass (Harris), Steve Landesberg (Dietrich), Don Calfa (Calvin J. Kendall), David Clennon (Justice Department Counsel Chester Monahan), Jack Somack (Mr. Cotterman), Kip King (Nicholas Baskin).

The Rundown

Mr. Cotterman finally catches a robber but isn't allowed to keep him. An air traffic controller flips out and pulls a gun on a crowded subway. Harris is upset at the fact that Dietrich saved his life.

Mistaken Identity

Played by Don Calfa, Mr. Cotterman's most recent thief, Mr. Kendall, is not what he appears to be. In 1975 Kendall testified against some very powerful and dangerous people. They were all convicted. After testifying, his life was in danger so he was given a new identity. Monahan, the Justice Department counsel played by David Clennon says, "We found that keeping him alive provides an incentive to the others."

Out of Uniform

Barney asks Levitt to work with the detectives on short notice and Levitt gets upset because he's in uniform as opposed to being in plain clothes. He volunteers to rush home and change but Barney tells him he doesn't have time. Not one to be easily deterred, Levitt goes out on his lunch hour and rents a tuxedo.

The Troubles Begin

Kip King plays overworked air traffic controller Nicholas Baskin. The poor guy is having a bit of a breakdown due to the high-pressured nature of his job. The men send him to Bellevue to get the proper care. Unfortunately, assuming he got back on his feet and returned to work, unemployment was not far off. On

August 3, 1981, nearly 13,000 air traffic controllers went on strike asking for a raise in salary and a shorter workweek. Their reasonable demands were instead met by a wholesale firing from the new President of the United States, Ronald Reagan.

A Debt

When Harris and Dietrich responded to the disturbance call regarding Mr. Baskin, Dietrich knocked a gun out of Mr. Baskin's hand just as he was about to shoot Harris. Now, Harris can't stand the idea that he might be in debt to Dietrich and tries to repay him with two fifth row orchestra seats to the Philharmonic, an "in" at Studio 54, three vacation days, etc. He tells Dietrich, "Anything, anything you want, just ask." Dietrich asks, "Can I call you Ron?" Harris immediately says, "No" (wags his finger). Ultimately, Dietrich will refer to Harris as Ron more than once before the series ends.

Billings, Montana

Barney asks Kendall if they've ever met before? Kendall tells him not unless he's spent some time up around Billings, Montana. Barney confirms he has not. Kendall tells him, "Don't feel bad. It's kinda like Cleveland, with sheep."

Season 5, Episode 20:	"Computer Crime."
Original Airdate:	March 15, 1979.
Writers:	Dennis Koenig and Calvin Kelly (story). Calvin Kelly (written).
Director:	Maxwell Gail.
Cast of Characters:	Ron Glass (Harris), Max Gail (Wojo), Hal Linden (Barney), Steve Landesberg (Dietrich), Ron Carey (Levitt), Mabel King (Mother Zilla), Barry Gordon (Stanley Fine), Rod Colbin (Michael Harvey), Roger Aaron Brown (Dr. Anthony Keeling).

The Rundown

An employee of a brokerage firm breaks in after hours and is caught with a briefcase full of rare stamps. Harris and Wojo bring in a professional man and the Jamaican woman he believes has put a curse on him.

Times They Are-a-Changing

In the absence of Nick Yemana's character, Dietrich seems to get more material from which to draw numerous laughs. His vast storehouse of knowledge is no longer the only trick in his bag as his increasingly sarcastic deadpan attitude accounts for continuous guffaws.

The Best Policy

Barry Gordon guests as Stanley Fine, a seemingly meek computer programmer who's caught with a briefcase full of rare stamps. It turns out he embezzled over half a million dollars from the firm where he works and converted the cash into the valuable stamps.

Barney is aghast when he learns that the firm is not going to press charges. They cannot afford the publicity. Fine's boss Mr. Harvey, played by *Barney Miller* favorite Rod Colbin, explains the reality of the situation to Barney. "Captain, we're a brokerage firm. People trust us with their money. Now, what kind of confidence would you have in a firm that would allow itself to be ripped off for half a million dollars by some $15,000 a year proletariat."

Memory Loss

The show opens with Harris answering the phone. His conversation starts, "No ma'am, I'm sorry. We can't arrest your husband for going out in one of your dresses." However, that's not exactly true. Wojo actually did exactly that in "The Vigilante" (S. 1/Ep.9), when he arrested Gabe Dell for merely being out in public in a dress.

It's Not Nice to Fool with Mother Zilla

Mabel King makes her only visit to the 12th as Mother Zilla, a Jamaican woman of extraordinary powers. She has put a curse on a Jamaican doctor and they are brought in for causing a disturbance. Harris is offended by the black doctor's belief in voodoo and the supernatural. He feels it demeans the race and makes them seem foolish.

Mabel King played Mabel Thomas on the first two seasons of *What's Happening!!* The show ran for three seasons on ABC and was, at various times, the lead in to *Barney Miller*. Her next role after Mother Zilla was as Navin Johnson's (Steve Martin) mother in the feature film, *The Jerk* (1979).

Just the Facts

- Obeah: a system of belief among blacks, chiefly of the British West Indies, that is characterized by the use of magic ritual to ward off misfortune or to cause harm.

Season 5, Episode 21: "Graveyard Shift."
Original Airdate: May 10, 1979.
Writer: Tony Sheehan.
Director: Noam Pitlik.
Cast of Characters: Ron Glass (Harris), Hal Linden (Barney), Max Gail (Wojo), Steve Landesberg (Dietrich), James Gregory (Inspector Luger), Lee Kessler (Natalie Blier), Raymond Singer (Philip Bart), Paul L. Smith (Leon Stipanich).

The Rundown

A tourist from Youngstown, OH, loses her luggage at airport, has a cabby bring her into New York by way of Connecticut and then gets robbed outside of her hotel. A man who believes he's being visited by a demon while he sleeps attempts to get amphetamines with a forged prescription. The 12th has a bomb scare while Harris decides to dictate a new book to be called, *Precinct Diary*.

Bomb Threat

Someone has called in a bomb threat to the 12th Precinct. Initially Barney evacuates the building and calls in the bomb squad. They check the building and assure Barney there is no bomb. Therefore, when the bomber calls back later, Barney makes the decision to stay in the building. When the bomber calls back to ask why they didn't evacuate a second time, they trace his call and bring him in.

Leon Stepanich, "the bomber," played by Paul L. Smith, turns out to be their next-door neighbor. He made the threats in the hope that the precinct would move. "All day long, hookers and deviants in front of my house," he tells the men. "All night long, sirens howling, people screaming, shouting. And all you people are always in a hurry." He also says he's been robbed seven times in the fifteen years he'd been there. When Barney tries "we're kind of busy up here" as an excuse, Leon replies, "Busy? Too busy to say good morning when you walk by with a *New York Times* under your arm? Too busy for a little friendly conversation? 'What's happening? How's it going? Anything new, Leon?' Too busy to be human beings?"

Once again, the foundation of the story and the underlying inspiration is the humanity of the situation. Are we too busy to be human beings? These were the kind of questions *Barney Miller* asked on a regular basis.

Just Saying

When Leon asks, "Too busy to say good morning when you walk by with a *New York Times* under your arm?" This question could be seen as a direct reference to Barney in the shot that we see in the opening credits of every show.

What the Brochures Leave Out

Lee Kessler plays innocent Natalie Blier from Youngstown, Ohio, whose first foray in the Big Apple starts off on a disastrous note. She admits to Barney and Harris that, "You know, I'd watch all those 'I Love New York' commercials back in Youngstown, you know, the ones with the Broadway actors, singing and dancing and everything was so exciting, colorful."

Barney: They're very appealing, yes.
Blier: They never mention the people with knives.
Harris: Well, they only have a minute!

Just the Facts

- At the top of the show, Dietrich and Wojo are rehashing the Super Bowl even though this show premiered on May 10, 1979. For the record, Super XIII between the Pittsburgh Steelers and the Dallas Cowboys was played on January 21, 1979. The Steelers won 35–31.
- Succubus: certain demonic spirits from the Middle Ages. Webster's definition is a little more specific: a demon assuming female form to have sexual intercourse with men in their sleep.

Popular Opinion

According to Harris, "Humor is a very important part of police work." Tony Sheehan, Danny Arnold's sons, David and Dannel, and a variety of articles of the time, confirm that numerous police officers cited the humor within the

12th Precinct's squad room as having that ring of truth to it that made the program a favorite of real-life law enforcement. Many officers said a certain gallows humor was necessary to ease the tension and get through the day.

The Last Word

Barney: I'm sure that getting robbed at knifepoint and spending half the night up here wasn't exactly what you had in mind.
Ms. Blier: It was better than seeing *Annie*.

Just as an aside, *Annie* was the first Broadway musical I ever saw in September of 1979. Personally, I thought it was wonderful.

Season 5, Episode 22:	"Jack Soo—A Retrospective."
Original Airdate:	May 17, 1979.
Writers:	Improvised.
Director:	Noam Pitlik.
Cast of Characters:	Just the regular cast. Guests only in retrospective clips from earlier episodes.

The Rundown

This episode was, in its way, the most unique in the run of the show. There is no narrative story. Instead it is just as the title suggests, a retrospective. A collection of clips of Jack Soo's work from earlier episodes tied together with the sincere and heartfelt memories of his fellow cast members.

A Road Not Taken

There was a discussion of exactly how to handle Soo's death within the storyline of the show. Linden suggested that they do an episode where the staff finds out Nick has died and the characters all process his death on the show. Linden thought that Barney's character could tell the men that Nick had been in the hospital but didn't want Barney to tell anyone. In the end, Danny Arnold did not want to profit from, or exploit in any way, Soo's death and instead chose to do a clip show honoring their friend. All the actors appeared on set but as themselves, not their characters, to salute their departed cast mate.

Hal Linden told me that Arnold informed the cast, "What we're gonna do is a clip show in honor of Jack showing all the wonderful things he did and I would appreciate it if each of you would prepare what you would like to say about Jack. I'm not gonna write anything for you."

It seems unlikely that Arnold or the writers didn't contribute anything to the writing and structure of the episode. All the actors said something different about Soo and their combined stories gave a balanced portrait of their friend. They may have contributed their memories and feelings but almost certainly had it smoothly put together by Arnold or the writers.

From the Heart and Off the Cuff

James Gregory: Nick Yemana was more than just a maker of bad coffee. He had a unique attitude and presence that gave scenes a special quality. He had an ability to take in stride even the most bizarre of situations and the most abrasive of people. But mostly he was able to see the humor in things and was never hesitant to say so.

Hal Linden: Jack Soo was born Goro Suzuki and along with many other Japanese Americans spent a good deal of World War II in detention camps on the West Coast. It was an indignity he never forgot but rather than retreating into bitterness, he faced the world with humor and he imbued Nick Yemana with a sense of humor about his ancestry and his heritage but also a sense of dignity and pride.

Steve Landesberg: Jack and I were like little kids together. We would never get through a scene without breaking up and whenever there was something deadly serious going on, I would be sitting at my desk giggling and I'd look over here [Yemana's desk] and Jack's entire body would be shaking, he'd just be shaking with laughter. He was my friend and I'll miss him.

Max Gail: You could go through all of those people [his fellow actors and production staff] and all the people who encountered Jack away from the studio in real life and not find anyone that he hadn't touched in some way, at some time, because his love for humanity and people was stronger than his anger at the things people had done to him. And that's why he was able to give us the gift of Yemana.

Hal Linden: No one actor in a show is indispensable and *Barney Miller* will continue without Jack. But it will be different. There will be times when in the middle of a crisis Nick should make a joke, but will not, or exasperate Barney, but will not. He'll be missed.

Sixth Season

The entire dynamic of the show begins to make a permanent shift in Season Six. Nick Yemana is gone and so is Danny Arnold. Reinhold Weege also left for a new deal with Warner Brothers that would allow him to write and produce his own show. From one season to the next, *Barney Miller* lost two of its three main writing talents and one of the show's most popular characters. It was a devastating, but amazingly not fatal, blow.

Early in the season, a variety of writers are utilized but by midseason most, if not all, the heavy lifting is being done by Tony Sheehan and his two proteges, Frank Dungan and Jeff Stein. The season's scripts deal with everything from homosexuality to slavery with the focus remaining on keeping all scripts funny no matter how serious the subject matter. It seems impossible to make a show about modern slavery funny in any way but somehow they succeeded in doing so without minimalizing the seriousness of the subject matter. Nevertheless, the quality of writing for this type of show can last only so long in the hands of two or three people alone. We'll begin to notice the strain of the challenge more in Season Seven.

Harris adopts a new fashion statement this season of wearing his sportscoats with the collars up and festooned by a variety of scarves around the heightened collars.

This season also has Noam Pitlik listed as Producer along with Tony Sheehan while Frank Dungan and Jeff Stein are given credit as Story Editors.

Season 6, Episode 1: "Inquisition."
Original Airdate: September 13, 1979.
Writers: Tony Sheehan (teleplay). Jim Tisdale and Calvin Kelly (story).
Director: Noam Pitlik.
Cast of Characters: Steve Landesberg (Dietrich), Ron Glass (Harris), Ron Carey (Levitt), Max Gail (Wojo), Hal Linden (Barney), Dino Natali (Officer Zatelli), Norman

Bartold (Jack Corwin), Peter Jurasik (George Alsop), David Darlow (burglar), George Murdock (Lt. Scanlon).

The Rundown

It's Dietrich's third anniversary at the 12th. A man attacks the "Muzak" machine in Siegel's Department Store. An anonymous letter brings Lt. Scanlon into the precinct searching for a homosexual cop.

Paranoids with Proof

For me this is the quintessential "paranoid with proof" episode. Peter Jurasik as George Alsop tries to explain to Barney why he had to destroy the inane music being piped into the department store. He tells Barney, "They are trying to take control of our minds!" He even lists some specific "mind numbing, syrupy melodies: 'The Sound of Music,' 'Mona Lisa,'" to which Harris adds, "'Whistle While You Work!'"

Harris produces an article that Alsop was carrying in his pocket about companies like Muzak and Automated Moods putting subliminal messages under the music. Mr. Alsop tells Barney, "They have been playing 'You Light Up My Life' for the last two years!"

Barney replies, "Cruel, I agree, but that does not justify your actions."

You Can Never Be Too Careful

On the Shout! Factory set of *Barney Miller* DVDs, the name Muzak has been muted on the soundtrack. You can read Harris's lips the first time he says Muzak but you don't hear the name. What's interesting is that the writers/producers must have been somewhat concerned about the company's reaction at the time because the company whose equipment was destroyed by Mr. Alsop wasn't actually owned by Muzak but by a competitor, Automated Moods, Inc.

Keep It Out of Court

Norman Bartold, in his second of five *Barney Miller* guest shots, is Jack Corwin of Automated Moods, Inc. The muting of the forbidden word actually eliminates one of the jokes when Harris refers to Mr. Corwin as "the Muzak Man."

The Loyal Leader of Men, All Men

In the privacy of Barney's office, Lt. Scanlon reads the anonymous letter from a homosexual cop and Barney doesn't blink. He immediately reminds Scanlon that, "Municipal policy guarantees equal opportunity to everyone regardless of sexual preference." Barney's personality is always consistent. He never betrays any particular political views to his men or the audience. As long as his men do their jobs and respect the rights and privacy of others, that's good enough for him.

Honest Barney

Scanlon: You know, we've never been very fond of each other but I uh, hey c'mon, I've gained a grudging respect for you. I mean as a cop and as a person. I'd just kinda maybe like to feel that the feeling is mutual.
Barney: It's not.
Scanlon: I was only kidding.

Confide in the Barn

Officer Zatelli comes in to deliver Barney's mail and quickly divulges that he is the homosexual cop. Barney's first reaction is to ask, "Why me?" Zatelli says, "I had to trust somebody. I mean Levitt is always speaking of you in the highest terms. Fair, honest, compassionate, a little picayune."

Barney doesn't care one way or another about the man's sexual preferences but he didn't really want the burden of having to keep Zatelli's secret. He uses the old Reverse Psychology on Zatelli when he suggests that maybe being gay and a cop is an insurmountable problem, "Maybe you're just unfit to be a policeman." Zatelli insists, "I'm a good cop, sir!"

Barney knows what a good cop Zatelli is but he wants him to be proud enough to let everyone else know that he's a good cop, homosexual or not. It's an easy piece of advice for a non-gay man to give to a gay man but not so easy to do, especially in 1979. While their ABC neighbor, *Soap* (1977–1981) gets all the credit for presenting revolutionary gay characters on network television in the 1970s, the truth is that *Barney Miller's* writers handled this situation multiple times and always with the success of achieving both sensitivity and laughs around the situation—not an easy order to fill.

Season 6, Episode 2: "The Photographer."
Original Airdate: September 20, 1979.

Writer:	Bob Colleary.
Director:	Noam Pitlik.
Cast of Characters:	Hal Linden (Barney), Steve Landesberg (Dietrich), Ron Carey (Levitt), Ron Glass (Harris), Max Gail (Wojo), Kenneth Tigar (Jesus Christ), Phil Leeds (Gilbert Letier), Sal Viscuso (Joseph Beatty), Anita Dangler (Louise Myers).

The Rundown

Levitt brings in a man who tried to sell him a bag full of pills that Levitt believes to be uppers. Harris helps a woman who has come in to complain about a man posing as a photographer who robbed her. Finally, Wojo brings in a man for assault and disorderly conduct who just seems to be asking for trouble.

Another Pontius Pilate

Wojo's "belligerent" collar finally admits to being Jesus Christ. This angers Wojo even more and his first reaction is to call him, "a real fruitcake." And yet, there is no doubting the man's own belief that he actually is Jesus Christ. As the episode plays out, the perp's calm demeanor, ever-present smile, and obvious sincerity lead Wojo and a few others to wonder if it's not, in fact, possible that he could be who he says he is?

Jesus is played by *Barney Miller* favorite Ken Tigar, who is probably best remembered for his role as Stefan Kopechne in the Season Three episode, "Werewolf." In his last appearance, still two seasons away, Kopechne will return as a man possessed by a demon. Personally, as much as I love the Kopechne character, this portrayal is just as strong. First of all, it's beautifully underplayed and nuanced and leads us to the question that if you believed in Jesus, and if he was going to come back, how exactly would we be certain this guy wasn't him? His performance and the responses from the people he meets is another example of the basic core of truth that is always running through this show. Many years ago when I was in college, I took a screenwriting class and I have always remembered one of the lessons taught us by our teacher, "The story doesn't have to be true or real but it does have to be believable." No matter what the situation, *Barney Miller* was always believable.

Peddling for Eternity

Sal Viscuso plays accused drug dealer Joseph Beatty in his third of four *Barney Miller* appearances. One more conviction could put him away for life. When Jesus is put into the cell with him, Beatty mocks him and asks him where his friends are? When Jesus admits the disciples are all dead and he might need some new help, Beatty tells him he'd help him out but he's probably not going to be available for about forty years unless Jesus can perform a miracle to help him out. When Jesus agrees, Beatty laughs and tells Wojo all about it.

In the end, the circumstances "miraculously" change for Mr. Beatty and when they take Jesus away to Bellevue, Beatty follows!

Tour de Force

Ken Tigar has vivid memories of what he remembers as his favorite Barney Miller role:

> The problem is that everybody has got a personal relationship to Jesus. Whether you're religious or not, whether you're a Christian or not, everybody knows who Jesus is. I realized that I had to relate to everybody that was going to watch the show, be it an atheist, a Christian, a Jew, a Muslim, everybody ... and be their Jesus for them. And I thought, there's only one way to do this and that is to become Jesus. Whatever that means. So I stopped eating. I fasted for four days. I started meditating constantly. I started reading the Bible. That four days was one of the most intense acting experiences of my life and when we shot it on the fifth day, ... when I came in it was as true as I've ever gotten. It was my very favorite thing that I have ever done.

Next Door Neighbors

Sal Viscuso spent two seasons as Father Timothy Flotsky on the sitcom *Soap*. The two shows actually shot on adjacent sound stages. According to Viscuso, "You came out one door and went right into the other door. *Barney* to the right, *Soap* to the left." However, the atmosphere on the two sets was decidedly different. Viscuso recalls Steve Landesberg visiting the *Soap* set and observing, "It felt like we were walking into East Berlin." The environment on the *Soap* soundstage was much more tense. As an example, Viscuso told me, "Paul [Junger Witt] had a pet tarantula in a glass container in his office."

Handsome Devil

Robbery victim Louise Myers, played by Anita Dangler, is having trouble finding her assailant in the mug books. They're all too ugly. According to

Ms. Myers, her robber was handsome and charming, he had a certain allure about him. She describes him as sensuous. Therefore, imagine everyone's surprise when they catch the thief and it's Phil Leeds. Leeds was a brilliantly funny actor but Cary Grant he was not! Casting director Lori Openden said to me, "Oh my God, nobody was uglier than Phil Leeds."

Just the Facts

- Wojo takes a thirteen-page statement from Jesus which he describes to Barney as "Wojo's Epistle to the Manhattanites."
- Wojo hasn't been to Mass in three years.

The Last Word

Jesus (to Wojo): You people have been much nicer than last time.

Season 6, Episode 3: "Vacation."
Original Airdate: September 27, 1979.
Writers: Frank Dungan and Jeff Stein.
Director: Noam Pitlik.
Cast of Characters: Ron Carey (Levitt), Max Gail (Wojo), Hal Linden (Barney), Ron Glass (Harris), Steve Landesberg (Dietrich), Bruce Kirby (Frank Rossman), Ben Slack (Leo Rossman), Jack Bernardi (Mr. Gilman).

The Rundown

Barney posts a vacation chart so that the men can avoid problems later in the year. Two brothers fight over one kidney. An anonymous source is calling in false alarms that lead to concerns about a potential ambush.

Pick a Day, Any Day

Barney is a little miffed at the problems the vacation schedule caused in the previous year. In order to avoid a recurrence of stress, he wants the guys to choose their times now to avoid conflicts later on.

Naturally, Harris and Dietrich's plans conflict with one another but Dietrich claimed the dates before Harris and he can't change his plans. His reserved time is for the annual Wolfgang Goethe Festival. Each year Goethe aficionados from all over the world come to Pennsylvania Dutch Country for ten days of lectures, discussions, and workshops on his writings concluding with a performance of Goethe's *Faust* in the original German (and all the pretzels you can eat). Harris has booked reservations at an exclusive Jackson Hole Ski Resort.

A Familiar Suspect

Bruce Kirby makes his final of three appearances on *Barney Miller* as Frank Rossman, a man unwilling to donate his kidney to his younger brother. He brings his usual trenchant comic attitude to his part and thereby makes a small role memorable.

Ben Slack plays Kirby's brother in the episode in his only turn on *Barney Miller*. His other TV appearances included *Cagney & Lacey* (1981–1988), *The Wonder Years* (1988–1993), and *The Practice* (1997–2004).

Just Browsing

The adorable Jack Bernardi makes his second and final *Miller* guest shot as Mr. Gilman. It turns out elderly Mr. Gilman was shopping around for a new, safer neighborhood in which to live so he was testing the response time of local emergency services. In addition to the police, he was calling in false alarms to fire departments, paramedic units, and a couple of pizza joints on Bleeker Street. Mr. Gilman explains, "Shop around, that's what Bess Myerson says."

In 1945, Bess Myerson became the first Jewish Miss America. In 1969, Mayor John Lindsay appointed Myerson the first Commissioner of the NYC Department of Consumer Affairs in 1969. In the years after *Barney Miller* went off the air Myerson, now a member of the Koch Administration, was entangled in a bribery and conspiracy case that forced her to resign her government position.

Season 6, Episode 4:	"The Brother."
Original Airdate:	October 4, 1979.
Writers:	Wally Dalton and Shelley Zellman.
Director:	Noam Pitlik.
Cast of Characters:	Ron Carey (Levitt), Ron Glass (Harris), Hal Linden (Barney), Steve Landesberg (Dietrich), Max Gail (Wojo), John Christy Ewing (Brother Thomas Kelvin), Gary Imhoff (Joseph Hutton), Elise Caitlin (Ms. Strauss), James Gregory (Inspector Luger).

The Rundown

A religious Brother is concerned about the disappearance of one of his officiates. Inspector Luger comes into the precinct with some sad news. Dietrich has mugging duty.

Seems a Little Late

Wojo gets upset at Barney for constantly coming out of his office and "taking over." Wojo tells Barney, "If you're gonna keep coming out and jumping in there and showing us how to do it, we're never gonna get to learn to be good cops ourselves. Ya gotta back off, Barn! Give us a crack at it!"

This is a rare occurrence in the *Barney Miller* universe that a storyline seems so out of place. There have been many sitcoms through the years that reach a point where they run out of ideas and end up introducing a storyline that doesn't seem to fit in with a show's current time frame. *Barney Miller* rarely made that mistake but that seems to be the case with this particular storyline. Wojo's outburst seems out of place after a hundred episodes and five years on the air.

The End of Ol' Brownie

Inspector Luger comes in with the news that the last of his old partners, Brownie, has died in the nursing home in Vermont. Referencing his three former partners, Foster, Kleiner, and Brownie, Luger says, "Three down, one to go." Barney tells the inspector not to be so negative. Luger informs Barney that he's in his will. "It ain't a fortune but it's nothin' to be sneezed at neither, Barney. You know because you got my insurance, you got my pension benefits, some Studebaker stock."

Miss Dietrich

Dietrich comes out dressed as a woman for his mugging detail and the men are stunned by how he looks. He has no idea that he's not quite as alluring as he may have hoped.

> **Luger:** What the hell was that?
> **Wojo:** Dietrich pulled mugging duty. You gonna let him go out like that, Barney? In broad daylight?
> **Luger:** The muggers will laugh him right out of the park.

Harris: Barney, he looks worse than Fish.
Barney: Let's not get brutal about it.

I must agree with Barney. He hardly looks worse than Fish did. And what's Wojo commenting about? He looked awful when he had the assignment. Again, this storyline is funny but it's forced. The truth is the only one who ever looked good as a woman was Harris.

Nevertheless, Barney brings Dietrich into his office alone to break the news to him that he looks nothing like a woman and will have to pull him from the duty. He goes so far as to tell him he looks ludicrous. Dietrich replies, "Well, maybe I'm over accessorized."

Turn the Other Cheek

Brother Kelvin, played by John Christy Ewing, is very thin-skinned about people calling him "Father." He's not a priest! He blows up at Harris and says, "Sure, they get all the glamour stuff—saying mass, hearing confessions, running bingo. I want to tell you something, that's not the whole enchilada!"

The Last Word

Brother Kelvin: I'm cloistered, I'm not stupid.

Season 6, Episode 5: "The Slave."
Original Airdate: October 18, 1979.
Writers: Frank Dungan and Jeff Stein.
Director: Noam Pitlik.
Cast of Characters: Ron Glass (Harris), Hal Linden (Barney), Max Gail (Wojo), Steve Landesberg (Dietrich), Manu Tupou (Philip Azari), Sumant (William Nu), Peg Shirley (Arlene Kenton), Stanley Kamel (Lance Parks), James Gregory (Inspector Luger).

The Rundown

Wojo nearly causes an international incident when he brings in a man and woman who were in a traffic accident and discovers that the man is the property of a Burmese diplomat. Inspector Luger buries an old friend.

Not Your Average Fender Bender

As Wojo takes Mr. Nu's statement, he assumes that Nu, played by an actor named Sumant, is the employee of the Burmese diplomat Philip Azzari played by Manu Topou. Nu, however, informs Wojo that he doesn't require payment because he belongs to Mr. Azzari.

They soon discover that Mr. Nu is involved in a case of debt bondage that, as Harris explains, is an ancient form of loansharking. Harris naturally wants to run out and haul Azzari in but as Barney points out, they're dealing with the case of a foreign national. He correctly assumes that Mr. Azzari will claim Diplomatic Immunity.

Man, Just Try and Free Some People

Wojo and Harris fervently take up the cause of Mr. Nu and try to convince him he doesn't belong to anyone. They tell him that anything would be better than his current situation but he answers, in very practical terms, "I eat. I know many who don't." Exasperated, Harris finally says, "I'm talking about having some control over your life." Nu asks, "And that's what freedom will give me?"

Wojo by the Book

Azzari claims Diplomatic Immunity on all charges and Barney is about to release him when Wojo informs Azzari that he's not insured for the traffic accident that began the whole debate. Azzari says it's not required, as a diplomat, to have insurance. However, Wojo has been reading one of those long-winded manuals that none of us ever read and has discovered The Diplomatic Relations Act. It passed the previous year (1978) and in it the President set liability insurance requirements for each delegation relating to risk arising from the operation of any vehicle in the United States.

Barney Miller, Psychologist

As the episode unfolds, Mr. Nu finds his own voice and decides that he would like to try freedom. Barney convinces Azzari that "from a pragmatic point of view, there's nothing worse than a servant who's tasted freedom." Azzari forgives the debt and Mr. Nu has won his freedom. When the men tell Nu he is free to go, he innocently asks, "Where?"

Just Another Example

This episode is just another example of the brilliance of this show and the intelligence and sophistication of the writing. A man should be free. That is an idea that can have no intelligent, compassionate dissenters. And yet, we are shown that many questions cannot be resolved with a simple yes or no. There are often layers of complexity that must be addressed. "Layers of complexity" is an idea that is more or less foreign to sitcoms. Nevertheless, the 12th Precinct encounters it on a regular basis. Yes, Mr. Nu deserves to be free but in his case, as he so poignantly points out, he's never known another life. Where does he go now? What does he do? Luckily, he lets the men off the hook by saying he has some friends in town and he does not regret his decision. Even so, the whole storyline has made us contemplate some very basic questions of humanity not often stirred up in the average thirty-minute sitcom.

Alas, Dear Brownie

Inspector Luger comes in and tells Barney, "Just buried Brownie. Missed a lovely service. The old inspector gave a nice little eulogy, then the padre mumbled something in Latin and then the organ played 'I'll Take Manhattan.' Brownie's favorite."

As always, the two men retreat to Barney's office and Luger reveals that the department is calling him in for a career conference. He assumes they're looking for a way to force him into early retirement. He tries to think of other things he could do in his retirement like opening a liquor store or starting a worm ranch but he breaks down as he tells Barney he's a cop, first and always.

Barney: Inspector, a man of your vast expertise and long experience in criminal investigation should put that to use when you retire! Do something where you can pass than knowledge on to others. Teach others what you've learned.

Never Say Never

At the time, James Gregory was actually working on another ABC sitcom entitled *Detective School* in which he played a PI named Nick Hannigan who ran a school for would-be investigators. Three episodes were shown on ABC during the summer of 1979 and then, seemingly renewed, ten more episodes aired between September and November of 1979 before it disappeared forever. This most likely explains Gregory's three-month absence from the 12th Precinct between October 1979 and January 1980.

Just the Facts

- Harris has completed the book he began last year, *Precinct Diary*, and has sent the manuscript out to some of the better publishers. Barney wishes him good luck and he tells Barney he's bracing for a bidding war. *Precinct Diary* will become *Blood on the Badge*.

Season 6, Episode 6: "Strip Joint."
Original Airdate: November 1, 1979.
Writers: Jaie Brashar, Frank Dungan, and Jeff Stein.
Director: Noam Pitlik.
Cast of Characters: Steve Landesberg (Dietrich), Ron Carey (Levitt), Hal Linden (Barney), Ron Glass (Harris), Max Gail (Wojo), James Cromwell (Neil Spencer), Todd Susman (Edward Yakel), Diana Canova (Stephanie Wolf), Rosanna DeSoto [as Rosana Soto] (Teresa Tasco), Walter Janowitz (Ivan Kessler).

The Rundown

Wojo brings in a man who jumped into a public fountain to prevent self-combustion. A bookstore owner complains about a topless bar in his neighborhood while Dietrich becomes enamored with one of the employees of the bar.

Doubting Barney

Todd Susman makes his second of three *Barney Miller* appearances as Edward Yakel, a human combustible. When he tells the officers he could go up in smoke at any moment, Dietrich says, "Sounds like SHC, Spontaneous Human Combustion." Barney wants none of it, saying, "Dietrich. I wish you wouldn't encourage these people." Dietrich once again comes to the aid of this week's "paranoid with proof" when he explains that "Nobody knows why or how it happens but it seems that under the proper conditions, and with no certain reason, certain people are not only capable of going up in flames but also projecting tremendous amounts of fire and heat telekinetically."

A Hot Mess

Wojo, like Barney, initially thinks Yakel is a case for Bellevue but Yakel tells him, "I've been evicted five times in two years because my apartment caught fire. Is that in my head? I take the subway, somebody's *Times* goes up in smoke. I walk into a department store, the sprinkler systems turns on. What do you call that?"

Wojo says, "Coincidence?"

At one point, Yakel complains of "burning up" and moments later a trash can goes up in flames. Barney tries to come up with logical reasons for the fire but no one's buying it. He and Wojo agree to let Yakel go with a D.A.P. (desk appearance ticket). To quote Barney quoting Shakespeare in an earlier episode, "there are more things in heaven and earth . . ."

Same Old, Same Old

Susman is terrific in this episode. He's a perfect actor for the *Barney Miller* universe because he possesses a wonderfully understated sense of instability. He certainly elicits your sympathy for his problem but you still can't help but laugh when he mentions his bed of mud.

His scene in the second half of the show with another *Barney Miller* favorite, Rosanna DeSoto, is charming, sensuous, and hilarious all at the same time. Ms. Tasco is turned on by Susman's combustibility. This was DeSoto's final of three *Miller* guest shots and these performances make you wish both actors had done more.

Bop and Grope

Harris and Dietrich bring in Walter Janovitz as Mr. Kessler of Kessler's New and Used Books and two dancers from the Club Aphrodite, a topless bar that Kessler wants to have shut down. The two members of "The Bolshoi Bump and Grind," as Harris calls them, are Stephanie Wolf, played by Diana Canova, and Teresa Tasco, played by Rosanna DeSoto. Dietrich, immediately smitten with Ms. Wolf, volunteers to take her statement. He learns that she is a student working on her Master's in Cultural Anthropology at Columbia. Dietrich shows off his intellectual prowess as he says, "Borneo tribesman. When a young eligible lady wants to encourage a prospective suitor she invites him to lay his head on her lap while she very delicately plucks his eyebrow hairs with a pair of ritualistic brass tweezers." She's impressed and says, "Right." He then takes off his glasses and pointing to his eyebrows asks, "You think these need a trim?"

Off the Clock

Off the set at the time of this taping, Steve Landesberg and Diana Canova were, in fact, a couple. They lived together for four years before separating. Canova told me, "I was crazy about him [Landesberg]. To be around that all the time . . . I felt I was incredibly lucky. We parted as friends but, you know, it's . . . hard when you split. But, in the meantime, it was great being around that whole gang [the cast and crews of *Barney Miller* and *Soap*]. It was such a wonderful time." At the time, Canova was also a regular on the ABC sitcom, *Soap*.

The Last Word

Stephanie Wolf: You know, there are many places where nudity and the exhibition of the female body are not only considered respectable but are even revered.

Dietrich: My place, for one.

Season 6, Episode 7: "The Bird."
Original Airdate: November 8, 1979.
Writers: Judith Nielsen, Richard W. Beban, Frank Dungan, and Jeff Stein (story). Frank Dungan and Jeff Stein (teleplay).
Director: Noam Pitlik.
Cast of Characters: Hal Linden (Barney), Steve Landesberg (Dietrich), Max Gail (Wojo), Ron Glass (Harris), Michael Lombard (Walter Elkins), Miriam Byrd Nethery (Myrna Dunbar), Martin Garner (Samuel Tragash).

The Rundown

Wojo buys a bird. Harris announces his book will be published. A volunteer on a Suicide Hotline snaps and contemplates jumping off a ledge.

On the Edge

Character actor Michael Lombard visits the 12th as suicide hotline worker Walter Elkins, who the men of the 12th save from jumping off a building. As poor Walter remembers it, "The last straw was the lady, she calls every day, the same junk! 'Life is pointless, the world is sick, people are better off dead.' I finally realized—she's right!"

Later, that same woman comes down to the precinct to visit him. Myrna Dunbar, or as Walter calls her, "Schizo Myrna," is played by the decidedly unusual Miriam Byrd Nethery in her second of four visits to the 12th Precinct. Myrna is trying to comfort Walter and winds up depressing him again. She explains, "I don't mean to depress people. It's just a gift."

Myrna continues to try to cheer up Walter by telling him, "Sometimes I call even if I'm not depressed. Just to talk to you." When Walter tells her, "They're taking me to Bellevue," she immediately responds with, "Oh, they have a very nice brunch there."

In the end, Myrna gives Walter her phone number in case he ever needs to talk. Once again, the writers paint an uplifting scene of human kindness tinged with humor and absent any maudlin sermonizing.

Giving Him the Bird

Passing the pet store on the way to work Wojo decides to buy a parrot in the window. Unfortunately, the bird dies within a few hours of his purchase. Wojo is naturally upset and angry. He calls the pet shop and they tell him they're sorry but no refunds. In the course of the conversation, it is revealed that Wojo's a cop. Soon the pet shop owner arrives with the full $225 Wojo paid for the bird. He's terrified that unless he returns Wojo's money, he'll be a target of police harassment.

This attitude makes Wojo (and Barney) even angrier. Assuring him that they're not making threats but just want to be treated like everyone else, the pet shop owner takes back the money and walks out, leaving Wojo more dumbfounded than before.

Blood on the Badge

This is the episode where we learn that the title of Harris's soon to be published book, *Precinct Diary*, has been changed to the racier, *Blood on the Badge*. Everything is moving smoothly on the publication with one minor detail. All the detectives need to sign release forms since they're all characters in the book. Interestingly, Wojo is the first to sign. Dietrich balks and refuses to sign while Barney wants to read the manuscript first.

This is just the beginning of the friction that Harris's book will cause within the squad. The more successful it becomes, the more carried away with the glamorous life Harris will become. He tells Dietrich in this episode, "Hey look man, sometimes I get so wrapped up in myself and my own goals that I, . . . I tend to just, you know, forget about other people's needs and expectations." This statement will prove to be a prophetic one.

Respect for Authority

In the book, Harris has described Barney's style as a "unique mixture of compassion, logic and perspective, ladled out in liberal and occasionally ponderous portions."

Just the Facts

- Harris dedicated the book to Captain Miller. "Written with all the admiration befitting a respected superior and a truly good friend."
- The storyline of Wojo's parrot is almost certainly inspired by Monty Python's "Dead Parrot Sketch," first performed on British television in 1969. The sketch, as performed by Michael Palin and John Cleese, is a classic piece of material.

The Last Word

"Purpose is our nexus. The common thread that binds our lives as one." You know who said that? Harris, in *Blood on the Badge*. Just ask him and he'll tell you.

Season 6, Episode 8: "The Desk,"
Original Airdate: November 22, 1979.
Writers: Frank Dungan and Jeff Stein.
Director: Noam Pitlik.
Cast of Characters: Ron Glass (Harris), Steve Landesberg (Dietrich), Max Gail (Wojo), Hal Linden (Barney), Ron Carey (Levitt), Jeff Corey (Caleb Webber), Alex Henteloff (Arnold Ripner), Fred Sadoff (Dr. Milton Prentice), Don Calfa (Gilbert Lesco).

The Rundown

Wojo brings in "a real fried banana" who tried to stick up a liquor store with a toy gun. An Amish man is the victim of a mugging. Ambulance chaser Arnold Ripner offers his services pro bono!

A Once-Great Criminal

Don Calfa made seven appearances on *Barney Miller* as seven different characters. Gilbert Lesco may be his tour de force. Wojo arrests him for robbery even though Lesco used a toy ray gun in the commission of the crime. Once at the station, Wojo discovers that Lesco lives in a halfway house for mental patients. Wojo tells Barney, "Sort of a Waldorf Hysteria." When Barney shoots him a disapproving look he replies, "Well Harris does it."

Barney questions Lesco and discovers he's had an operation called an amygdalotomy. Resident in-house expert on everything, Dietrich, blurts out, "Look out!" and Barney and Wojo turn to Dietrich for an explanation. Dietrich tells them, "It's not pretty. Amygdalotomy is a recent neurological technique. It's a more sophisticated version of a lobotomy."

When Lesco's doctor (played by Fred Sadoff) shows up at the precinct he asks why Mr. Lesco is being held. When Barney tells him he was arrested for robbery the doctor laughs and says, "Oh, no, Captain, he doesn't do that anymore." Gilbert's lawyer, the honorable Arnold Ripner, yells, "You mean he doesn't get away with it anymore!"

No Clarence Darrow

It seems only fitting that Lesco's attorney turns out to be Arnold Ripner, the recurring ambulance chaser played over the length of the series by Alex Henteloff. The lawyer is outraged at the current condition of his once larcenous client saying, "When I knew this man he was a vicious, productive criminal. Now he can hardly put two words together."

After arguing with Lesco's doctor, Arnold reveals that he's so upset at what's been done to his client, he will happily sue the doctor for free without any motivation of monetary or material gain. As everyone is leaving, Barney says, "Thanks Arnold, for whatever you were doing here." Then he goes too far and tells the lawyer that his actions could almost be described as noble. Arnold looks at him and warns him a comment like that could be viewed as slander.

Not in the Bible

Jeff Corey makes his second and last *Miller* appearance as an Amish mugging victim, Caleb Webber, who is not shy about expressing his disdain for modern society. Harris is stunned by just how out of step Mr. Webber is. As he's trying to fill out Webber's report complaint he discovers that he does not have a phone number, a social security number, or a driver's license. Webber explains that none of those things are in the Bible and in the society from which he hails, "if it ain't in the Bible, it ain't in your life."

A New Life

Following Ripner's threat of legal action against Dr. Prentice, the doctor asks Gilbert if he's unhappy the way he is now? Gilbert tells him no. However, he admits, "I'm not happy either. I'm not anything. Mostly I'm just . . . here."

Lesco is, however, intrigued by Mr. Webber's tales of being a farmer and we get the distinct feeling, as they leave together, that Webber may have found a new convert for his way of life.

Season 6, Episode 9:	"The Judge."
Original Airdate:	December 6, 1979.
Writers:	Frank Dungan, Jeff Stein, and Tony Sheehan.
Director:	Noam Pitlik.
Cast of Characters:	Ron Glass (Harris), Hal Linden (Barney), Steve Landesberg (Dietrich), Max Gail (Wojo), Ron Carey (Levitt), Peggy Pope (Lois Marcum), Philip Sterling (Judge Philip Paul Gibson).

The Rundown

A woman comes into the squad room wanting to report a disturbance, a rape, and a shooting. She's witnessed this crime spree all through her "one small window." Wojo has to testify in court and ends up having to arrest the judge. The loss of Yemana's desk leaves a void.

Time Marches On

In this ninth episode of Season Six, the first season with no more Nick Yemana, two guys from supply come and haul away Nick's old desk. They called ahead to inform Barney but he forgot to warn the guys. They walk in one morning and the desk is gone, leaving a huge physical void in the room just as Nick Yemana's death has left a void within the squad.

Harris sees the new office geography as a way to put a little space between he and Dietrich. He suggests they spread the remaining desks out around the room. However, when Levitt comes up for mail call he sees it as a sign that he has no future in the detective squad. He is so disgusted that he prepares to put in for a transfer. When Barney realizes the implication, he calls supply and orders them to bring the same desk back to the detective's squad room.

Barney: All I can say is, that no matter what happens in the future this desk is going to be here for you to use.
Levitt: Thank you. (Levitt smiles.)
Barney: Now, that's not intended as a firm commitment or any kind of guarantee.
Levitt: Can I at least take it as an empty promise?
Barney: Fine.

Another World

Peggy Pope plays concerned neighbor Lois Marcum, who believes her neighbors are involved in drugs, organized crime, and prostitution. She tells the detectives, "Rick Edwards, he's a friend of mine, they sent him to prison for embezzlement. He only did it to get the money to pay the doctors for his mother's cornea transplant. She's going blind. Of course, she's not his *real* mother, he was abandoned as an infant. That's why he gets those terrible headaches. Of course, it isn't all bad. He does have those two lovely illegitimate children."

When Harris and Dietrich check out her story they discover that she lives in a windowless basement apartment. However, they do find a whole stash of soap opera magazines. The "crime spree" she's witnessing on a daily basis is on her favorite soap opera, *Endless Tomorrows*. When they report their findings Harris asks Barn, "Should I call *General Hospital*?"

No, You're Out of Order!

Philip Sterling returns, this time as Judge Gibson. Wojo was waiting outside his courtroom when he heard yelling. He ran in and found the judge beating up on an attorney with his gavel. According to Gibson, "He [the attorney] was wearing a turtleneck. People in my courtroom wear ties. We are not Studio 54."

The judge is fed up. There's no respect anymore for his position. "We used to be gods," he says. "Revered. Held in awe. Now one bad ruling, one little joke about rape and they're all over you!"

When the judge is bailed out by the District Attorney, he won't leave. The judge gets angrier and angrier until he breaks down to the point of tears. Sadly, he's simply a man who's gone over the edge.

The Last Word

Miss Marcum: I can't help watching. I find it so repulsive yet compelling.

Twenty years before it became popular, Miss Marcum inadvertently provides the explanation that will be used by fans of reality television for years to come.

Season 6, Episode 10: "The DNA Story."
Original Airdate: December 13, 1979.
Writers: Rich Reinhart and Jaie Brashar (story). Rich Reinhart (teleplay).
Director: Noam Pitlik.
Cast of Characters: Ron Glass (Harris), Hal Linden (Barney), Steve Landesberg (Dietrich), Max Gail (Wojo), Ron Carey (Levitt), Jack Kruschen (Rudolph Kamen), Stefan Gierasch (Dr. Joseph Burlson), Raymond Singer (Dr. Eric Rubin), A Martinez (Claudio Ortez), Kay Medford (Mrs. Mitzi Kamen).

The Rundown

A woman reports her husband as missing although he's not exactly missing. Someone breaks into a laboratory and steals some dangerously valuable cultures.

One of Your Boys

Yet another Danny Arnold favorite, Stefan Gierasch, shows up in this episode as Dr. Joseph Burlson who, along with his colleague Dr. Eric Rubin, played by Raymond Singer, runs an experimental lab. Their facility was robbed but we don't know exactly what was stolen. As Wojo makes out the report, Dr. Rubin whispers to Burlson, "We are dealing with mutant strains. How do we know this isn't infectious or even deadly?" Wojo looks up from the typewriter and asks, "What's that?" Dr. Burlson quickly distracts him with, "Nothing. Just talking shop, Sgt. Wojciehowicz. How about that pope? One of your boys, huh?"

This is another timestamp of the era as Burlson is referring to Pope John Paul II whose given name was Karl Wojtyla. He was a Polish Cardinal who became the first non-Italian pope in over four hundred years when he was elected to the papacy on October 16, 1978.

A Brave New World

The list of items stolen from their lab included an autoclave, a centrifuge, a digital thermometer, and a container of assorted cultures. The cultures taken were of a combinant DNA. According to Dr. Rubin, "We take the DNA from a living organism and we combine it with the DNA from another organism, thereby creating an entirely new living substance. Now this particle recombinant form has just been developed and we can't guarantee that it might not be virulent or even pestilent!" The danger lies in the fact that, "the DNA was spliced from a polyomavirus into a strain of Escherichia coli."

According to pubmed.gov, polyomaviruses are small, non-enveloped DNA viruses, which are widespread in nature. The Escherichia coli is what we now all know as E. coli, which the cdc.gov site tells us are bacteria found in the environment, foods, and intestines of people and animals. So the next time some vegetable or meat product disappears off your supermarket shelf due to an E. coli scare, you'll know these two guys are probably the ones to blame!

No Big Deal

Fearful of jeopardizing his future funding, Burlson downplays the danger, saying, "There is a small, very small, chance of contamination . . . or epidemic."

He tells Captain Miller, "If we can unlock the genetic puzzle of DNA, we could eliminate birth defects, genetic diseases, increase intelligence, weed out all the negative traits and characteristics, and create a whole new superior race of . . . really nice people." A terrific piece of dialogue that not only explains and touts the once-respected idea of eugenics but, with the tag line "really nice people," sarcastically hints at the fact that the predilection of Nazis for eugenics soured the world on its practice, at least temporarily, back in the postwar period.

Call Me Mitzi

Kay Medford turns up as Mitzi Kamen, a woman who believes her husband has been replaced by someone, or something, else. Harris says, "Did you check the basement for pods?" She looks at him very seriously and says, "That's the first thing I did." [A reference to the 1956 film *Invasion of the Body Snatchers* and its 1978 remake.]

When Mitzi's husband, played by Jack Kruschen, comes to the squad room Mitzi runs to hide in the bathroom. We learn that Mr. Kamen felt he wasn't "satisfying" her and so he went out and bought some self-help books. He says, "I was only trying to please you. I'm sorry. I'll never do that again."

Harris joins Mitzi inside the bathroom to talk and she reveals the real crux of the problem to him. She asks her new friend, "Why do people have to change, get old? Why can't things stay, the way they were. Ron, sometimes I get so scared I don't know what I'm going to do."

Harris: Look, everybody feels that way sometimes.
Mitzi: You sure?
Harris: Hey, look, none of us knows what's going to happen to him or her and that's pretty scary. But there's one thing you do know, you don't have to go through it alone.

Once again a delicate subject matter is handled with sensitivity, humor, and poignancy without ever slipping into the trap of melodrama.

Too many sitcoms of the 1970s and 1980s, almost all of which were shot in front of a live studio audience, ended up becoming overly sentimental when they would tackle sensitive subject matters. You knew such an episode was coming when the network advertised it with the line, "Next week, on a very special—insert name of show here—." The writing of those shows would often sink to the level of sophomoric morality tales with scripts more suited toward children's educational TV of the period rather than a primetime, adult situation comedy.

Just the Facts

- Mitzi takes Diazapam (used to treat anxiety, alcohol withdrawal, and seizures) and advises Harris, "Forget brand names, buy generic. You will save plenty of money." A prophetic declaration considering just how bad prescription drug prices would get!
- This is the only episode in which we get to see the inside of the infamous 12th Precinct detective's bathroom.

Season 6, Episode 11: The Dentist.
Original Airdate: December 27, 1979.
Writers: Frank Dungan and Jeff Stein.
Director: Noam Pitlik.
Cast of Characters: Steve Landesberg (Dietrich), Ron Glass (Harris), Hal Linden (Barney), Max Gail (Wojo), Jenny

O'Hara (Sgt. Holly Scofield), Arthur Malet (Henry Creighton), Estelle Omens (Evelyn Swafford), Oliver Clark (Dr. Richard P. Gesslin, DDS).

The Rundown

A woman reports her dentist taking advantage of her while she was under the gas and a "musician" is arrested for disorderly conduct and disturbing the peace.

All Business

Jenny O'Hara appears as Sgt. Holly Scofield, a policewoman who is all business. She's been sent over from Manhattan South to go undercover and visit the handsy dentist to see if he makes a move on her. She gives Barney her credentials, "Seven years on the force, three in plain clothes, various commendations. Two cavities and an impacted wisdom tooth."

Introduced as brusque, guarded, and almost rude, when she returns from seeing the dentist she is a different person due to the nitrous oxide she received at her appointment. She is now tipsy, decidedly unguarded, and even a little flirtatious. Barney brings her into his office to rest but she insists she's fine and reports that the dentist did not make any untoward advances.

An Attractive Target

When she learns that the doctor made a move on another woman after she left she breaks down crying, quite upset that he didn't find her attractive enough to molest. When she finally confronts the dentist, played by Oliver Clark in his fourth of six appearances, she wants answers.

Dr. Gesslin:	Hey, I really find you quite appealing. I like you very much.
Scofield:	Well you certainly have a funny way of showing it.
Dr. Gesslin:	The thing is, I never touch a woman on the first appointment.
Scofield:	Oh really?
Dr. Gesslin:	I deal with a very classy clientele. I respect that. But I was going to have you back for a follow up.
Scofield:	You had your chance, pervert.

A Musical Artist

In his first visit to the 12th Precinct, Arthur Malet plays Henry Creighton, a man who makes music with his hands. Harris is not a fan, describing Mr. Creighton's art as "annoying, crass, obscene noises." The said "music" derives from squeezing air through your hands and making a sound closely connected with flatulent tones. Historically, these were thought of as obscene noises made by immature schoolboys to disrupt the classroom. However, in the 1970s a gentleman named Jim Twomey got a taste of fame through multiple appearances on *The Tonight Show Starring Johnny Carson* "playing his hands." Twomey used the word "manualist" to describe his musical practice although the term manualism was initially coined in the nineteenth century to describe the method of using sign language to educate the deaf in American schools. Watching this episode, you may wonder if Malet was providing his own music or if it was dubbed in. The answer lies in the episode's credits, "Manualist and Technical Advisor, John Twomey." It was Twomey himself who made the music we thought was coming from Mr. Creighton's magical hands.

A Protégé

Harris and Barney are both disturbed by Mr. Creighton's music but Wojo is able to recognize how some people might appreciate it. Sensing this, Creighton tells Wojo, "You've got the perfect hands for it. Large palm area, thick meaty fingers, you're probably a baritone." He begins to give Wojo instruction on how to make the sound.

As he's leaving he reminds Wojo, "Now don't forget everything I've shown you. And remember to practice every day, every day, every day, every day and take care of those hands. Wear gloves when it's cold, a little baby oil at night, and, uh, . . . no sex." Dietrich looks at Wojo and deadpans, "Tough choice."

> **Season 6, Episode 12:** People's Court.
> **Original Airdate:** January 3, 1980.
> **Writers:** Frank Dungan and Jeff Stein.
> **Director:** Noam Pitlik.
> **Cast of Characters:** Ron Glass (Harris), Steve Landesberg (Dietrich), Hal Linden (Barney), Max Gail (Wojo), Ron Carey (Levitt), Stanley Brock (Bruno Bender), Howard

Honig (Donald Ganz), Michael Tucci (Danny Rizzo), Rod Colbin (Charles Bogert), Helen Verbit (Stella Neimier), Ralph Manza (Leon Roth), Judson Morgan (Philip Lukeather).

The Rundown

A census taker forces his way into an apartment to get his information. A local community court goes rogue and Barney must figure out a way to buy his apartment that is going condo.

Just Wait . . .

Howard Honig is Donald Ganz, a census taker who was getting no cooperation from residents until he finally snaps and pushes his way into an apartment to try to count heads. He pleads his case to Dietrich, saying, "If people would only realize! An accurate census is important for everyone. It determines political representation, allocation of federal funds. It's even used in targeting vital programs." The erudite Sgt. Dietrich empathizes with Ganz, telling him, "I know. It's just that today people are becoming more and more hostile, and even paranoid, about any kind of government intrusion. Even when it's for legitimate and beneficial purposes."

Ganz: You know, you are the first civilian I've ever spoken to who really appreciates our problem.
Dietrich: Okay, in here, Mr. Ganz.
Ganz: Look, . . . call me Don. And you are?
Dietrich: Nice try.

Mr. Ganz's problem is, in a way, a double shot of Danny Arnold's "paranoids with proof" theory. His concerns about the census are true but so is Dietrich's explanation of people's fear of their government. If anything, this type of paranoia is even more rampant today than it was then.

Prophetic Words

Barney has lived in his apartment for fifteen years and now it's being turned into condominiums. The asking price is $137,000. He doesn't have it. Barney loses his temper on the phone and prophetically says to the new owners, "For

God's sakes, can't you see where this is going? If it keeps up like this we'll have all the rich people living in Manhattan, all the poor people living in the Bronx, the society will be even more isolated and alienated than it is now . . ."

Who knew just how prophetic Barney's words were going to be? This is a real problem that cities around America are confronting right now in the twenty-first century. The gap between rich and poor at all levels of society has been particularly felt in the real estate markets with Barney's dire predictions becoming the norm rather than the exception.

The People's Court

Bruno Bender leads the tenants of an apartment complex to form a court of vigilante justice. They arrest a thief on the premises, try him for robbery, find him guilty, and lock him up in a cage in the basement.

Wojo tells Barney, "You should see this operation. I mean they got a jail in the basement, they got a rec room turned into a court room with a jury box and a bench, an American flag, picture of Nixon." Bender says, "He's coming back, Miller. Ya see him at the ballgame with Gene Autry? He looks sensational!"

Just the Facts

- This episode marks the first time we hear the term, "BOB," for *Blood on the Badge*. According to Harris, "That's what they're calling it on the cocktail circuit."

Season 6, Episode 13: Vanished: Part 1.
Original Airdate: January 10, 1980.
Writers: Tony Sheehan, Frank Dungan, and Jeff Stein.
Director: Noam Pitlik.
Cast of Characters: Steve Landesberg (Dietrich), Max Gail (Wojo), Ron Glass (Harris), Hal Linden (Barney), Ron Carey (Levitt), Elaine Giftos (Laura Kiergo), John Dullaghan (Ray Brewer).

The Rundown

Residents of one of the local homeless missions are disappearing in the middle of the night. A woman is arrested for an unusual type of solicitation. Inspector Luger gets busted down to Captain and assigned to the 12th.

Crossword Caper

Barney comes out of his office to ask Dietrich for some help with the newspaper's crossword puzzle. He's stuck on "Seventeen Down, occupation on the floss, six letters." Dietrich eventually figures out that it's "Miller," as in George Eliot's (Mary Ann Evans) novel, *Mill on the Floss* (1860). As he's leaving to answer a call he asks Barney, "You need any help with 'Blank' Google?" The reference is to the legendary comic strip character, Barney Google.

A Friend of the 12th

John Dullaghan makes his second appearance as Ray Brewer in "Vanished, Part 1 and Part 2." From the moment we meet Ray Brewer in "Open House" (S. 5/Ep. 20), you realize that he's not your average bum. He genuinely likes people and wants to be part of the group. It never occurs to him that his lack of a home or a job might make him a less than natural member of the 12th Precinct's circle of friends. His affection for them and his presumption that they would only naturally feel the same way about him is part of his charm.

Ray tells Harris that his friends keep disappearing from the mission every night. When Ray asks, "What's our next move? Going undercover?" Barney thinks it's a good idea and Harris gets the plum assignment.

An Offer Few Would Refuse

In her only *Barney Miller* storyline, Elaine Giftos appears as Laura Kiergo, a woman who was in a bar looking for a man to sire her child. Despite Kiergo's lack of professional status, the bar owner is still pressing charges for solicitation, trespassing, and disorderly conduct as she caused something of a riot in the bar. She explains to Barney, "I want to have a baby, it's just that I'm not particularly interested in having a husband." Barney wonders, "Who's pressing charges?" Wojo tells him, "The owner. He's the only one she didn't ask."

The Return of the Ol' Inspector

"Ta-da! Inspector Luger's back and the 12th Precinct's got him." With those words, James Gregory as Inspector Frank Luger returns to the 12th after an absence of seven episodes. He was last seen in episode five, "The Slave," broadcast on October 18, 1979. The career conference the inspector mentioned in "The Slave" has now taken place and the department is indeed trying to force him into retirement. They essentially told him he could retire as an Inspector or stay around but with a demotion to Captain.

Luger: They tried to pull the same trick on Kleiner a couple of years back. They tried to squeeze him out too.
Barney: What happened?
Luger: Nothing. Two weeks later he was gunned down on 13th Street. They dropped it after that.

A Sucker for a Song

It's safe to say that Inspector Frank Luger was the most musical member of Barney's law enforcement fraternity. You never knew when Luger might break into song as he does near the end of this episode.

Barney: Listen, everything's going to work out just fine, I'm sure.
Luger: Yeah. I been a cop for thirty-four years, Barney. I helped build this department, I helped make it run, . . . I helped, what's that, (begins to sing) *Once I built a railroad, made it run, . . .*

The song he recalls is "Brother, Can You Spare a Dime?" (1930), written by E. Y. Harburg and Jay Gorney. The Depression-era anthem was written in 1930 and featured in the 1932 musical revue *Americana*. Bing Crosby's 1932 recording of the song rose to number one on the charts.

The Last Word

When Inspector Luger sees Harris dressed as "a vagrant" he is naturally surprised. Luger says, "Hey Hare, what happened to our Dapper Dan? Our resident Beau Bridges?" [He means Beau Brummell.]

Season 6, Episode 14: Vanished: Part 2.
Original Airdate: January 17, 1980.
Writers: Tony Sheehan, Frank Dungan, and Jeff Stein.
Director: Noam Pitlik.
Cast of Characters: Hal Linden (Barney), James Gregory (Inspector Luger), Ron Carey (Levitt), Max Gail (Wojo), Steve Landesberg (Dietrich), Ron Glass (Harris), Elaine Giftos (Laura Kiergo), John Dullaghan (Ray Brewer), David Fresco (Monty), Ralph Olivia (Bum), Leonard Frey (Alfred Royce).

The Rundown

A man robs a market and its patrons to raise money for his Presidential campaign. Harris is kidnapped with a host of other residents of the mission he was staking out.

The People's Choice?

Leonard Frey appears in his second and last *Barney Miller* episode as a character named Alfred Royce, an independent thinker and candidate for President of the United States. Unfortunately, as a virtual unknown he needs help with campaign funds and so he turns to armed robbery for the seed money. He used a snub-nosed .38 in the commission of the crime and tells Barney, "Do you know how easy it was to get this? Gun control is going to be among my first priorities as President!"

Ramblin' Ron

Harris eventually calls into the precinct informing Wojo he's in North Carolina. When he returns to the 12th he reports to Barney, "It was basically a shanghai operation. Two guys came into the mission about 11 p.m. and offered me and a couple of other bums a bottle of gin if we'd take a ride with them. Next morning we pull up to a peanut farm on the Carolina border. Anyway, I picked about half a bushel and then I decided to make some arrests."

Devoted Citizen

Ray Brewer is the one who reports Harris missing. He hangs around the precinct all day wanting to help. He answers phones, directs traffic. Ray is a guy who thinks of himself as a part of the 12th Precinct even though he's not a cop.

Barney: I'm sure you have better things to do.
Ray: Not recently. I had a dentist appointment in '68. Missed it.

Office Pet

The inspector is less than a stellar worker. He takes his time, reads the paper, has his snacks, and still ends up going into Barney's office to sit on his couch and chew the fat, pawning his work off onto Levitt and Dietrich. The first call he takes is a report of a robbery. He barks at the caller, "Slow down! I'm not a

Kelly Girl!" He still hasn't completed his one arrest report when Barney blows up.

Kelly Services is an American office staffing company. Back in less enlightened times, the temps you'd hire from the company were called "Kelly girls."

Fond Farewell

As they leave, the boys in the squad room all make a point of saying goodnight to *Inspector* Luger, using his old title as a sign of respect instead of his new diminished title of Captain. When Levitt says goodnight, Luger says, "Goodnight, Levitt." He's been calling him Levine throughout the episode so using his real name is a mutual sign of respect that he'll do only one other time in the series.

Season 6, Episode 15:	"The Child Stealers."
Original Airdate:	January 24, 1980.
Writers:	Frank Dungan (written by) and Jeff Stein (written by).
Director:	Noam Pitlik.
Cast of Characters:	Ron Glass (Harris), Max Gail (Wojo), Ron Carey (Levitt), Hal Linden (Barney), Steve Landesberg (Dietrich), Richard Libertini (Adam Boyer), Jack De Leon (Marty Morrison), Ray Stewart (Darryl Driscoll), Dino Natali (Officer Zatelli), Joanna Miles (Eleanor Driscoll).

The Rundown

Marty's friend, Darryl Driscoll, abducts his own son because his wife refuses to abide by the custody agreement. Wojo and Harris are called out to talk down a jumper from the Washington Arch. Officer Zatelli accidentally "comes out."

Kids!

Jack DeLeon, as Marty Morrison, and Ray Stewart, as his friend Mr. Driscoll, come in to complain that Driscoll's ex-wife isn't complying with their custody agreement. This is the episode where Mr. Driscoll gets a little more "butched up," presumably to meet network requests. Ray Stewart couldn't remember if it was a network directive or not but he did appreciate the opportunity to expand upon his character. Marty says to Captain Miller, "My, you've certainly done some lovely things with this room since the last time . . ." Driscoll interrupts him saying, "Could we stop perpetuating the stereotype for a moment and get on with this?"

Disgusted by Miller's inability to help, Driscoll abducts his own son and the 12th Precinct is forced to get involved. Mrs. Driscoll, played by actress Joanna Miles, comes down to the precinct to sign the complaint against her ex-husband.

> **Mrs. Driscoll:** Look, Captain, I'm not out to put him in jail. I just want him to be kept away from Jason. You can understand that.
> **Barney:** Not entirely, no.
> **Mrs. Driscoll:** Look, you are a policeman. You deal with these, uh, people all the time. I mean you know how they are. The things that they do, right?
> **Zatelli:** I'm gay!

Partially Open

Prior to this episode, only Captain Miller knew of Officer Zatelli's lifestyle outside the precinct. In this episode, he blurts out his secret in defense of Mr. Driscoll, thereby exposing his secret to his fellow officers at the 12th. However, the real trouble begins next season in Zatelli's final episode, "Movie: Part 1" when Scanlon of Internal Affairs learns the truth.

History's Man of Mystery

This is the wonderful episode with Richard Libertini as a time traveler named Adam Boyer from the year 2037. He claims to be a Cultural Historian at Columbia University, "I specialize in the latter 1900s. I just came back to gather some additional data on the prevailing social attitudes, mores, you know, this type of thing."

> **Barney:** You realize we don't believe a word you're saying.
> **Boyer:** Of course, that's why I can tell you.

The Cost of Success

Harris is complaining that he can't spend and invest the money he's making from his book fast enough. Harris, the author, is slowly and subtly separating himself from his peers in the squad room.

As for Mr. Boyer, there's no record of him. His name doesn't check out, prints don't check out. When he overhears Harris's conversation with his broker, he tells the avid investor, "Gold [was] replaced as the world standard by another commodity—Zinc." Initially, Harris laughs this bit of information off as the ramblings of a lunatic. Ultimately, however, Harris calls his broker back and we hear him tell the man, "Zinc going for 37.5¢ a pound? Yeah well, look I might be willing to spring for a coupla tons."

To be clear, if Harris bought two tons of zinc using the prices of January 24, 1980, it would have cost him about $1,500 and that investment would have been worth roughly $4,680 as of February 2021. The same purchase of gold in 1980 would have cost him $38 million and would translate into a current value of $116 million. The percentage increase is roughly the same so Mr. Boyer's suggestion was actually a pretty solid one.

Waste Not, Want Not

As happens more than once in the series, Harris displays his exasperation at having wasted his time typing up a report regarding the Driscolls only to have to crumple it up and throw it out when she decides not to press charges. Barney had a way of getting mutual complainants to drop charges so all the men/woman of the 12th had to throw away reports at one time or another.

Man of Mystery

There were a few occasions in the course of the series when we are led to speculate about Arthur Dietrich. Is he a mere mortal, is he an alien, or is he a figment of our imagination? This exchange is my favorite. As our time traveler Mr. Boyer is leaving, he spots the nameplate, "A. Dietrich." He enquires about the full name and is excited and impressed to meet *the* Arthur Dietrich. He addresses Dietrich, saying, "Could I shake your hand? What an honor this is, sir." Then turns to the men and says, "You're all very privileged." He walks out and Dietrich turns back towards his colleagues and says, "Hey! I couldn'ta done it without youse."

Season 6, Episode 16: "Guns."
Original Airdate: January 31, 1980.
Writers: Rich Reinhart, Tony Sheehan, Frank Dungan, and Jeff Stein.
Director: Noam Pitlik.

Cast of Characters:	Hal Linden (Barney), Ron Glass (Harris), Steve Landesberg (Dietrich), James Gregory (Inspector Luger), Max Gail (Wojo), Jack Dodson (Mr. Vogel), Madison Arnold (Joseph Osborne), David Paymer (Felix Morrissey), Mario Roccuzzo (Vincent Turso).

The Rundown

A young man tries to hold up a drugstore with a 100-year-old dueling pistol. His arrest leads the men to a prolific but unlicensed gun collector. A man pushed to the brink by bureaucratic red tape gets arrested for stealing his own TV set and the men of the 12th are struggling to adapt to the style of their newest officer, *Captain* Frank Luger.

Verboten

Jack Dodson appears as Mr. Vogel, a gun collector with a little secret. It was *his* 1850 double action pepperbox that David Paymer, as Felix Morrissey, bought to use in his robbery attempt. It turns out Mr. Vogel had his entire collection stolen but neglected to report the theft. Barney asks, "Is it just possible, Mr. Vogel, that included in that collection are some illegal firearms?" Vogel smiles and says, "Heh, heh, heh, I see you've guessed my little secret."

Dietrich answers a phone call, "Barney! Bank holdup. Guy's got a bazooka." Barney looks at Vogel who quietly says, "That's probably mine."

History Lover

Before he leaves, Vogel feels compelled to explain his fascination with guns to Barney. "You see, guns are America," Vogel says. "The history of the gun is the history of this country. From the pilgrim's blunderbuss to the Winchester, the Colt, why even the snub-nosed .38 you carry." Barney responds sarcastically, "Quite a cavalcade."

Vogel:	Culminating with the ultimate gun, the atomic bomb. The one that may make all other guns obsolete.
Barney:	Unfortunately, you'll have to do without that one in your collection.
Vogel:	(Chuckles) Yes, I guess so. (Walks away with a quizzical look.)
Dietrich:	I'll keep the file open.

Let's hope Mr. Vogel never meets James Thayer from S. 4/Ep. 11, "Atomic Bomb."

Hard to Keep It Straight

The men of the 12th are struggling with the new detective on the squad, Captain Frank Luger. Harris complains to Barney about Luger "telling those same old morbid stories—how they gunned down Foster, how they blew up Kleiner."

Barney: They gunned down Kleiner. They blew up Foster.
Harris: Whatever, Barn. The man is not fun to be with!

It Can Happen Anywhere

Madison Arnold as Joseph Osborne gets arrested for stealing his own television set out of the police warehouse. The poor guy is frustrated because he got robbed over a year ago and although the police recovered his set shortly after the robbery, he's still waiting to get it back. He explains the whole tortuous runaround through red tape hell to Barney, concluding with, "Then they tell me they have to hold it in case the guy who took it puts in a claim. It's diabolical!"

When Dietrich runs the serial number, it's discovered that Mr. Osborne didn't actually steal his own TV but another identical model. Therefore, he not only got arrested but when Dietrich finally does find his actual set, the nightmare begins anew because, as Dietrich explains, "We gotta hold this for your trial . . . because of the way your defense is set up, the similarities, the TV, etc., well, you understand. Don't worry. We'll take care of this. We'll get it to you in good shape as soon as the trial is over."

This is the type of storyline that *Barney Miller* carried off so brilliantly. It shines a light on the ludicrous aspects of a bureaucratic machine that may, in fact, be responsible for pushing people over the edge into eccentric and antisocial behavior. It's a sociological spin on the question of what comes first, the chicken or the egg?

All's Well That Ends Well

At the end of the episode, Barney receives a call from the Commissioner's Office informing him that Captain Luger is being reinstated as Inspector Luger. The news is met with elation from the men of the 12th, maybe a little too much from the Inspector's point of view.

Season 6, Episode 17: "Uniform Days."
Original Airdate: February 7, 1980.
Writers: Judith Anne Nielsen and Richard Beban (written by).
Director: Noam Pitlik.
Cast of Characters: Ron Carey (Levitt), Max Gail (Wojo), Hal Linden (Barney), Steve Landesberg (Dietrich), Ron Glass (Harris), Stuart Pankin (Alex Fleischer), Leonard Stone (William MacDonald), Michael Alaimo (Michael Farentino).

The Rundown

One day a year, plainclothes officers are required to wear their full uniform. All the detectives show up in their dress blues except Harris. Dietrich is busy tracking down a robbery suspect from 1973. He has until midnight to bring in the culprit. Wojo and Harris go out on a disturbance call on Delancey Street and bring in a delinquent postman.

The Original Pilfering Postman

Stuart Pankin takes on his second *Barney Miller* guest assignment as the negligent postman, Alex Fleischer. Historically speaking, the role of Fleischer the postman who isn't delivering the mail to his customers actually precedes the character of Newman, another mailman who "fails to deliver" on *Seinfeld* by twelve years.

Leonard Stone also returns to the 12th as William MacDonald, postal branch supervisor and Fleischer's boss. Stone is his usual overwhelmed self but this time with a sense of humor, as in "postal humor," as in "I zipped right over here," "let me know where they forward him," etc. As MacDonald leaves, Barney says, "I'll keep you posted."

Priority Mail

Wojo is disgusted by Fleischer's lack of a sense of duty. He tells him, "You probably caused a lot of hardship for a lot of people." Fleischer assures him that's not true, "I gave people all the stuff they really needed, Social Security checks, utility bills, *TV Guide*."

Snappy Dressers

Levitt explains: "Regulation 312/B—Requires all plain clothes officers to be in uniform once a year to insure a full uniform capability in the event of civil disorder or natural disaster." He then adds, "Also gives the guys downstairs a few laughs."

When Harris shows up in plain clothes Barney is rightfully upset. Harris says he may have gotten rid of his uniform when he updated his wardrobe. He tells Barney he'll have it next year. Barney tells him he will have it by 6 p.m. that evening.

Harris is having an identity crisis. The success of "BOB," his best-selling book, *Blood on the Badge*, is overwhelming his life. "I am juggling a lot of things right now! I mean Barn, it's just hard for me to, uh, to deal with these marginal duties."

The "marginal duties" quote sets Barney off and he tells Harris he's sick of hearing about BOB. He tells him, ". . . you're going to have to make your mind up what you want to be! I cannot afford a cop who only dabbles in police work." After Harris storms out, Wojo suggests to Barney that perhaps he blew up at Harris because the uniform makes people feel flushed with power. Personally I always agreed with Barney that he "didn't say anything that didn't need to be said." The fact is a policeman not focused on his duties is not only a poor public servant but also a potential danger to his fellow officers.

Eventually, Harris comes back with the uniform and he and Barney negotiate something of a truce. In the great *Barney Miller* tradition, this is one of those cases where the situation isn't resolved as much as the participants come to an agreement that there actually is an issue that they must continue to acknowledge and work at in good faith. In other words, much like in real life, there are no easy answers.

Just the Facts

- Barney makes rare use of Yiddish with the word, "mishegoss."
- Harris ends up liking how he looks in his uniform. He comments, "uniforms are kind of in right now, you know with The Village People and all." This is a dated reference to the popular disco singing group of the time who enjoyed hits like *YMCA* and *In the Navy*. When Barney doesn't understand the reference, Harris compares them to the Modernaires, a singing group of the 1940s.

Season 6, Episode 18:	"Dietrich's Arrest—Part 1."
Original Airdate:	February 28, 1980.
Writers:	Frank Dungan, Jeff Stein, and Tony Sheehan.
Director:	Noam Pitlik.
Cast of Characters:	Hal Linden (Barney), Steve Landesberg (Dietrich), Ron Carey (Levitt), Ron Glass (Harris), Max Gail (Wojo), George Murdock (Lt. Ben Scanlon), Candice Azzara (Audrey McManus), Peter Hobbs (Roy McManus).

The Rundown

Dietrich attends a big Anti-Nuclear Rally and gets arrested with a host of other participants. A lottery winner gets arrested for throwing his money out of a window and causing a riot. Barney is struggling to figure out how to stay in his apartment as it turns condo.

Multiple Personality

Many actors played multiple parts on *Barney Miller* during its eight years on the air. Peter Hobbs, who shows up in this episode as a Roy McManus, first appeared on *Barney* in "Strike: Part 1" (S. 3/Ep. 21) as Charlie Prevette. In Seasons Four and Five, he created and recurred as the character Philip Brauer with Doris Roberts playing his wife, Harriet. Okay, no big deal. However, after he does his turn in this episode as Mr. McManus, he will return one more time next season as Philip Brauer. Many actors played multiple characters over the years but few ever played character one, character two, character three and then returned one last time as character two again.

A Yutz in Every Crowd

In this story, McManus created a riot outside the Greenwich Hotel when he started throwing loose cash out of a fifth-floor window. It seems Mr. McManus won $1 million in the New York State Lottery and ever since, he's been inundated with requests from charities and individuals alike. The sob stories and pressure proved too much to handle for him. As he sees it, "A ten-million to one shot and I'm the yutz who gets nailed!"

Barney: Very sorry. Those things happen.
McManus: Aw sure, that's big talk from a poor person.

How I Stopped Worrying and Learned to Love...

Lt. Scanlon stops by and gets wind of Dietrich's plans to attend an antinuclear rally even though it's against department policy. Scanlon cites Regulation 104-1, Paragraph 5, limiting the political activity of a police officer be it on public or private time. When Miller questions the application of said regulation in this specific instance, Scanlon tells him, "Miller, all I know is on one side you've got a bunch of 'no nuke kooks' and on the other side you've got a bunch of 'pro-nuke kooks' and that makes it political!" When Miller sarcastically compliments Scanlon on his grasp of our political system, Scanlon replies with an unintentional, self-indictment, "Miller . . . a cop is supposed to be above all those things . . . He don't work for no Democrats, he don't work for no Republicans. He doesn't stand for anything. He doesn't stand against anything. A New York cop stands for nothing! At least I know, I don't."

When the nuclear demonstration turns into a melee, numerous protesters are arrested for unlawful assembly and failure to disperse. Dietrich, not wanting to take advantage of his position, insists on being arrested with them.

Time Stamp

When Wojo tells McManus that he thinks he could do something more positive with the money than throw it out the window, McManus says, "Yeah? You mean like give it to some charity, huh?"

Wojo: Well, yeah! Yeah, you could do that.
McManus: Which one? I've been hit up by all of them; the heart people, the lung people, the whale people, my Chrysler dealer . . .

At the time, the Chrysler Corporation was on the brink of bankruptcy. They were bailed out by the government in January of 1980 in a move that ultimately saved the company and made a celebrity out of Chrysler President Lee Iacocca.

Season 6, Episode 19:	"Dietrich's Arrest—Part 2."
Original Airdate:	March 6, 1980.
Writers:	Frank Dungan, Jeff Stein, and Tony Sheehan.
Director:	Noam Pitlik.
Cast of Characters:	Ron Glass (Harris), Steve Landesberg (Dietrich), Max Gail (Wojo), Hal Linden (Barney), Ron

Carey (Levitt), James Gregory (Inspector Luger), Allan Miller (Nelson Haskell), George Murdock (Lt. Ben Scanlon), Kay Medford (Lila Wakeman).

The Rundown

Dietrich is arrested as part of an anti-nuclear demonstration. One of the men arrested from the demonstration instigates a riot among the anti-nuclear protesters inside the precinct. Barney and the boys meet the cleaning lady they never knew they had.

Double Duty

It was a busy night of network television for Allan Miller who plays Mr. Haskell, the nuclear engineer pleading his case that nuclear power is perfectly safe. He appeared in this episode of *Barney Miller* as well as the episode of *Soap* that immediately followed it on the network. The first year, 1978–1979, both shows finished in the top twenty. In 1979–1980, *Barney Miller* finished in the top twenty with *Soap* in the top thirty. The following season, 1980–1981, *Soap* was moved to Wednesday night at 9:30 p.m. behind *Taxi* and it fell out of the top thirty and went off the air for good in April of 1981.

Keep It Clean

Barney and the audience are surprised to discover that the 12th actually has a cleaning lady. He asks her, "Are you new here?" When she tells him "Only four years," he's shocked. He tells her, "Funny, I don't remember ever seeing you before." She replies, "Well, I keep a low profile," and he remarks, "Yeah, we've noticed." She doesn't appreciate his remark but by the looks of the squad room it's entirely reasonable to think this is her first time there.

We soon learn, however, that Mrs. Wakeman knows more about the men of the 12th than they know about her. She read Harris's *Blood on the Badge* in its first incarnation by pulling the manuscript out of the trash. She knows about Barney trying to secure a loan to buy his apartment. When Luger sees her, he refers to her as "Hazel" to which she replies, "Another comedian." *Hazel* was a sitcom starring Shirley Booth that ran from 1961-1966.

Sadly, this was Medford's third and last appearance on *Barney Miller*. She died five weeks after this episode aired of cervical cancer at the age of sixty. She was a brilliantly accomplished comedienne who should have had years of character parts ahead of her.

Keep Pitching

Naturally, no one is more pleased with Dietrich's arrest than Lt. Scanlon. He wants to paint Dietrich as "a rogue cop." As always, he's dying for the opportunity to expose the 12th as a cesspool of corruption. He tells Barney, "You know, uh, Captain, I can't help thinking if you'd only exercised your authority and ordered him not to go, this whole senseless tragedy could have been avoided and I wouldn't be here now . . . having all this fun."

Well, at least he's honest about how much joy his job brings him.

Season 6, Episode 20:	"The Architect."
Original Airdate:	March 27, 1980.
Writers:	Jim Tisdale and Calvin Kelly (story). Tony Sheehan, Frank Dungan, and Jeff Stein.
Director:	Noam Pitlik.
Cast of Characters:	Ron Carey (Levitt), Hal Linden (Barney), Ron Glass (Harris), Steve Landesberg (Dietrich), Max Gail (Wojo), Paul Lieber (Gunman), Norman Bartold (Bob Schuyler), Chu Chu Maleve (Gunman), Jesse Aragon (Joseph Vella), David Clennon (Howard Speer).

The Rundown

Dietrich has been put on restricted duty due to his arrest at the nuclear power demonstration and Harris is headed to Jackson Hole, Wyoming, for a ski trip. An architect threatens to blow up a building he was hired to design and two crooks attempt to hold the detectives hostage with little success.

Quite a Statement

David Clennon returns to the 12th Precinct, this time as Howard Speer, an architect. When asked why he was spraying graffiti on his own building, he says, "Not that building. Mine had terraces and skylights, form and substance! That's no more than a sterile lump of glass and metal!" According to Speer, his building was "real, genuine. Not like that Cortland across the street."

Dietrich picks up on the fact that Speer keeps asking the time. He also tells Barney, "When he first came in he said a few things that sounded familiar. Just now he mentioned Cortland. Cortland was the name of the building in *The Fountainhead*, a novel by Ayn Rand."

Barney: Oh yeah. Remember Patricia Neal wore that gown with the fur on the . . .

Dietrich: Yeah, yeah, remember Gary Cooper plays the architect who blows up his own building?

When they ask Speer if there's a bomb in the building he confirms their suspicions telling them, "Several. TNT charges with quartz timers." Speer won't divulge anything other than the bombs are set to go off at 2 p.m. Speer says, "I'm sorry but these people have to be made to understand. A man's ideas, the creations of his own mind, belong to him. They can't be bought or traded or bastardized to serve somebody else's interest. [This sounds very much like it could be Danny Arnold talking to network executives and censors]

Dietrich counts down to two o'clock when the bomb is supposed to go off and nothing happens. Barney starts to say, "Very funny, Mr.—," when we hear the explosion. Ironically, just before the bomb goes off we get a quick glimpse of a "boom" mike in the shot as Barney walks towards the cage.

Command Performance

Chu Chu Maleve makes his first appearance since the show's two pilots. In most interviews Hal Linden has said that only he and Abe Vigoda were in both pilots. That's not entirely true. He and Vigoda were the only two holdovers for the makeup of the detective squad but Anne Wyndam as Rachel Miller, Michael Tessier as Davey Miller and Mike Moore as Stanley Mankowitz all appeared in both pilots, as did Chu Chu Maleve who played the hostage-taking drug addict in both pilots as well.

Here, he and Paul Lieber appear as gunmen trying to break a friend out of jail. Unfortunately, their friend has already been transferred to the tombs. "Hey! Nobody told us!" Lieber and Maleve are very funny as two small time hoods upset at the lack of attention they receive because of the hoopla around the bomb scare. Lieber's character tells Barney, "It's tough for a new gang to get started, what with the Mafia and all. This would bring us a little prestige."

Lieber will return during the next season in a three-episode arc as Det. Eric Dorsey thereby making him yet another detective who played a criminal first.

A Rare Compliment

Speer: You know this room is a marvelous room. Real wood frames. Lathe and plaster walls. It's got strength and character. You people are very lucky. [We haven't heard too many nice things said about the building over the years]

Among My Souvenirs

Harris asks Barney if there's anything he'd like from Jackson, Wyoming? Barney says he'd like one of those string ties with the turquoise on top (a Bolo). Naturally, Harris questions the request but says, Okay, it's your neck."

Season 6, Episode 21: "The Inventor."
Original Airdate: May 1, 1980.
Writers: Frank Dungan, Jeff Stein, and Tony Sheehan.
Director: Noam Pitlik.
Cast of Characters: Hal Linden (Barney), Steve Landesberg (Dietrich), Ron Glass (Harris), Max Gail (Wojo), Ben Piazza (John Essex), Arny Freeman (Herbert Emory), Dan Frazer (Dr. Matthew Kramer).

The Rundown

Harris is complaining about all the taxes he has to pay now that his successful book has pushed him into a higher tax bracket. A scientist gets arrested for trying to steal his own ideas out of his company's safe. Wojo can't remember the details of a robbery and reluctantly agrees to hypnotism. Barney proudly wears a custom-made bolo tie that Harris brought back for him from Wyoming as a joke.

The Corners of Your Mind

Dan Frazier makes his one and only visit to the 12th as Dr. Matthew Kramer, a psychologist who uses hypnosis in his work. He's been called in to hypnotize Wojo in the hopes he will recall details of a crime, specifically the name he heard one thief call the other in an attempted robbery.

Frazier was a busy character player whose work dates back to the early days of television. He appeared in dozens of shows like *The Phil Silvers Show [Bilko]* (1955-1959), *Route 66* (1960–1964), and *The F.B.I.*(1965-1974), most often as doctors or authority figures of some kind. He's best remembered for his portrayal of Capt. Frank McNeil, the officer in charge of keeping Lt. Theo Kojak in check on Telly Savalas's popular CBS police drama, *Kojak*.

A hypnotized Wojo reveals some hidden feelings, saying, "I always feel like Barney needs to talk down to my level, make some kind of allowances for me, not, not like, uh, well like Dietrich, Dietrich doesn't patronize ya. He talks to ya. Like you can understand what he's talking about. A lot of the time I don't but that's just because Dietrich's a smart person. I mean I think Dietrich's got more brains that the rest of us put together."

Dietrich: I gotta sit here and take this garbage?

Farm Fresh

There are two pop culture references in this episode having to do with poultry. Wojo is reluctant to submit to hypnosis. Dietrich tells him, "Hypnosis can be used very effectively. Taps the subconscious. Helps to locate facts or images that seem to have been lost or forgotten."

Wojo: Yeah, or make a guy act like a chicken.
Dietrich: Yeah, I love that stuff.
Wojo: Harris? Think I oughta get hypnotized?
Harris (shrugs) We can use the eggs.

Harris's comment references Woody Allen's *Annie Hall* (1977) where Allen concludes the movie with the narration, "And I thought of that old joke: this guy goes to a psychiatrist and says, 'Doc, my brother's crazy; he thinks he's a chicken.' And the doctor says, 'Well, why don't you turn him in?' The guy says, 'I would, but I need the eggs.'"

Once the psychologist has Wojo under hypnosis he says, "All right. Sergeant, I want you to return with me now . . ." Before he can say anymore, Wojo shouts, "Hi-Yo Silver!" This reference is to the opening narration of the *Lone Ranger* radio program that ran on various networks from 1933–1956. The opening narration read, "Nowhere in the pages of history can one find a greater champion of justice. Return with us now to those thrilling days of yesteryear. From out of the past come the thundering hoof beats of the great horse Silver. The Lone Ranger rides again!"

Build a Better Battery

Arny Freeman returns to the 12th, this time as inventor Herbert Emory who was hired by a company called PowerRite Electronics to build a better battery.

Unfortunately, he built the perfect battery. Now the company wants to squash his idea because of the damage it would do to future sales.

Ben Piazza plays John Essex, the sleazy lawyer for PowerRite Electronics, in his first of three *Barney Miller* appearances. He tries to paint Emory as a crackpot but his real goal is to get back the plans for the battery. When Barney informs him that they're evidence he quickly decides the company won't press charges.

Emory reminds the lawyer that he still has all the knowledge in his head. Essex is so sure he won't find anyone to bankroll him that he expresses no concern. However, when Essex tells Barney, "The only thing it's good for is somebody else's tax shelter," that gets Harris's attention.

Season 6, Episode 22: "Fog."
Original Airdate: May 8, 1980.
Writers: Mark Brull (story). Frank Dungan, Jeff Stein, and Tony Sheehan (teleplay).
Director: Noam Pitlik.
Cast of Characters: Steve Landesberg (Dietrich), Max Gail (Wojo), Ron Glass (Harris), Ron Carey (Levitt), Hal Linden (Barney), Sydney Lassick (Victor Karsh), J. J. Barry (Fred Bauer), Robert Levine (Howard Kimbro), William Dillard (Edward Jennings / Fast Eddie).

The Rundown

Levitt arrests a street musician for disorderly conduct and disturbing the peace. A distraught man is arrested for taking a sledgehammer to the microwave dishes on top of the phone company building. Barney is upset at being passed over once again for Deputy Inspector.

Try, Try Again

Barney has been passed over once again for promotion to Deputy Inspector. He confides to Wojo that, "They gave it to Maddox." He admits his disappointment and says, "Of course, it doesn't hurt to be assigned to narcotics. Get to make all those flashy busts, get your picture in the paper. TV interviews."

Wojo and Barney have always had a father-son type of dynamic. Barney is Wojo's counselor; he calms him down when he upset and boosts him up when he's ready to throw in the towel. Now, and as the series moves forward, Wojo helps and supports Barney. He consistently tries to get Barney to open up and share his feelings, which is against Barney's basic nature. It makes for a complex relationship that is often both poignant and humorous.

Netted Another One

Harris and Dietrich bring in Victor Karsh who was arrested on top of the phone company building while smashing numerous satellite dishes. Sydney Lassick plays Karsh in his second and last *Barney Miller* role. Once again, he seems like a raving lunatic but he is, in fact, this week's "paranoid with proof." As the PWP often do, Mr. Karsh has newspaper articles to back up his claims.

> **Harris:** You see Barn, Mr. Karsh lives on the top floor in the building right next door [to the phone company].
> **Karsh:** Don't you know what those microwaves are doing to us? They're attacking our nervous system, destroying our senses, boiling our blood.
> **Barney:** These things happen.

Barney's mood inspires his unusually cold and patronizing response. Incredibly, forty years after the broadcast of this episode, we're still trying to determine the extent to which this type of radio frequency radiation affects our bodies. The innovation of cell phones and other handheld devices has only created increased concern and study.

Unusual Circumstances

Both Levitt and Harris catch Barney sitting in his office in the dark. The men are concerned and go into his office to try to cheer him up. Barney admits that he doesn't really feel that bad if he never makes Deputy Inspector and that's the problem.

> **Barney:** It's getting harder and harder to keep a sense of purpose around here. I mean we bring people in, we ship'em out. Nothing changes.

This is a common frustration that is expressed numerous times in the series, particularly in the later seasons.

Just the Facts
- Barney reveals to the men that he had his own group of "Foster, Kleiner, and Brownie" when he started out on the force. Their names were Baxter and Crewson.

Playing the Blues
William Dillard plays Edward Jennings, a trumpet-playing street musician arrested for disorderly conduct and disturbing the peace. He went a little crazy and assaulted a string quartet from Julliard because they were on his corner. Before they take him away to the tombs, however, they let him play his horn one last time. His version of "I Can't Get Started" finally draws Barney out of his office.

Seventh Season

Season Seven gets off on the wrong foot when one of the precinct's (and thereby, one the show's) dearest friends gets murdered. It is, in the opinion of the author, a total miscalculation of the audience's willingness to indulge such an abruptly violent storyline. We've been surrounded by violence and the talk of violence throughout the series but there was never an inkling that such a fate could befall an established character. Not only does it set a darker tone but it also seems to initiate some awkwardly quick and even lazy endings to storylines. In the "Homicide" storyline that opens the season, we are literally stunned by the death of a recurring character and yet the following scene not only doesn't resolve the event in any way but also doesn't even discuss it. In fact, the character's murder will never be mentioned again.

Frank Dungan and Jeff Stein are listed as story editors once again this year, primarily because they are the entire writing staff working under Tony Sheehan. They will use occasional scripts from outside writers but the only regular writers assigned to the show are Dungan and Stein. Like Season Six, this season was also produced without the creative writing input of Danny Arnold. As talented as Dungan, Stein, and Sheehan are—their legacy with this show alone is a testament to their skills—the absence of Danny Arnold begins to show. The show begins to lose something of its soul. *Barney Miller* was special because it was a program that always considered "the human condition" in everything it did or attempted to do. It feels like that emphasis and awareness wanes in this seventh season.

To be fair to the writers, the program also suffers from the fact that the producers were never able to fill the emotional void left behind by the passing of Jack Soo/Nick Yemana. His character was a dependable figure that held all the various personalities together. Once Yemana was absent from the squad room, something was lost that was never fully regained.

Season 7, Episode 1: "Homicide—Part 1."
Original Airdate: October 30, 1980.
Writers: Frank Dungan and Jeff Stein.
Director: Noam Pitlik.
Cast of Characters: Ron Glass (Harris), Max Gail (Wojo), Hal Linden (Barney), Steve Landesberg (Dietrich), Ron Carey (Levitt), Jack Dodson (Henry St. Martin), Harold J. Stone (Steven Haddad), Jack Somack (Mr. Cotterman), Tricia O'Neill (Alex Kramer), Al Ruscio (Leonard Roth) Marjorie Bennett (Mrs. Stratton), Johnny Silver (Kingman), Allyn Ann McLerie (Harriet Shulton), James Gregory (Inspector Luger).

The Rundown

The episode opens with more rumors about department closings. Inspector Luger arrives with the news that the department is reorganizing and the 12th Precinct's responsibilities will soon change. Two neighboring merchants are in a feud exacerbated by their individual backgrounds as an Arab and a Jew.

Meta-TV Deduction

As Mr. Haddad and Mr. Cotterman are throwing insults back and forth at each other in the cage, one comment in particular sparks a completely off-topic but interesting discussion.

Haddad:	Your Zionist hoodlums stole our homeland.
Cotterman:	Zionist hoodlums? Where'd you pick that up, Lynn Redgrave?
Haddad:	That's Vanessa, stupid. Lynn is the one in the hospital show.
Cotterman:	(Suddenly interested) What hospital show?
Haddad:	You know, the one with the guy who used to be on M*A*S*H.

Cotterman:	Oh yeah, why isn't he on Trapper John?
Haddad:	How do I know? Ask the guy from Bonanza!
Cotterman:	You ask him, what am I, your slave?
Haddad:	You were once!

Reference number one: the term "Zionist hoodlums" was used by Vanessa Redgrave at the 1978 Academy Award ceremonies. In 1977, Redgrave funded and narrated a documentary film entitled *The Palestinian* (1977) about Palestinians and the activities of the PLO (Palestine Liberation Organization). That same year, she co-starred in the film *Julia* where she played a woman killed by the Nazis during World War II. When nominated for Best Supporting Actress for her role in *Julia*, she was criticized, picketed, and hung in effigy by members of the Jewish Defense League. When she won the award, she thanked the Academy for their courage in refusing to be "intimidated by the threats of a small bunch of Zionist hoodlums," thus the term used by Haddad and the comment made by Cotterman. However, Cotterman mixed up Vanessa Redgrave with her actress sister, Lynn Redgrave.

Reference number two: At the time, there was a television show on CBS entitled *House Calls* based on the 1978 movie of the same name set in a hospital. The television show starred Wayne Rogers and Lynn Redgrave. Prior to *House Calls*, Rogers had co-starred in the TV version of *M*A*S*H* as Dr. "Trapper John" McIntyre.

Reference number three: At the very same time, there was yet another show on CBS entitled *Trapper John, M.D.* (1979–1986) that was supposed to rejoin the life of "Trapper John" McIntyre thirty odd years after the Korean War. However, many TV fans of the day (including myself) wondered why instead of using the same actor, Wayne Rogers, to recreate his earlier television role, they cast Pernell Roberts, who looked and sounded absolutely nothing like Wayne Rogers. To further add to the confusion and explain Mr. Cotterman's confusion, up to that time Roberts was best known for his role as Adam Cartwright, the oldest son of Ben Cartwright on the long-running NBC western, *Bonanza*. In one of the more regrettable decisions in TV history, Roberts left *Bonanza* in 1965 after six seasons with the show. It went on to run for another eight seasons.

Specialty Squads?

Luger arrives with the news that the department is doing away with individual neighborhood precincts and creating specialty squads. Much to the chagrin of the detectives, he tells his men that he has secured the plum assignment of Homicide for his good ol' 1-2.

First of all, in the last episode of Season Six Barney laments losing the Deputy Inspector job to Maddox who had the advantage of working in Narcotics where they get to make a lot of flashy arrests. This tells us that a separate Narcotics Division already existed. Plus, every other movie and television program we've ever watched has big city police forces in it with squads for Homicide, Vice, Narcotics, etc. so how is this something new or unusual? And finally, it's totally impossible that a squad the size of the 12th could handle homicides for a city the size of New York.

Deep Thoughts

Their new role as a homicide squad has the men thinking some deep, dark thoughts.

Wojo: Life is really just marking time until it's over. Sittin' around waiting for something to happen.
Dietrich: Is Mike Douglas on tonight?

As a point of interest, Steve Landesberg made at least a dozen different appearances on *The Mike Douglas Show* in the 1970s and 1980s, including a week-long stint as a guest co-host in May of 1980.

Just the Facts

- For some reason, Inspector Luger calls Levitt "Carol" in this episode instead of his usual "Levine." What's that about? [Carol instead of Carl?]

Season 7, Episode 2: "Homicide—Part 2."
Original Airdate: November 6, 1980.
Writers: Frank Dungan and Jeff Stein.
Director: Noam Pitlik.
Cast of Characters: Hal Linden (Barney), Max Gail (Wojo), Steve Landesberg (Dietrich), Jack Dodson (Henry St. Martin), Harold J. Stone (Steven Haddad), Jack Somack (Mr. Cotterman), Tricia O'Neill (Alex Kramer), Michael Alaimo (Vincent Sykes), Ben Piazza (David Shulton), Allyn Ann McLerie (Harriet Shulton) James Gregory (Inspector Luger).

The Rundown

The 12th's role as a homicide unit takes a decidedly personal turn when a friend gets murdered. Barney has to decide whether or not to recommend the inspector for a job for which he is clearly not qualified.

Who's Afraid of Harriet Shulton?

Allyn Ann McLerie plays a naive housewife who meets a man in a bar and hires him to kill her husband. Later, she decides she doesn't want him to go through with it so she reports the potential crime and its whereabouts to the 12th.

Ben Piazza is terrific as the husband. When the men find Mr. Shulton and bring him in to inform him of his wife's plan, he calmly says to her, "Harriet, I've been reviewing this little assassination attempt of yours and frankly I'm shocked. I don't mean to sound negative but I can only conclude that something's gone woefully wrong in our relationship."

Take a Number

Mr. Cotterman, the 12th's most loyal customer over the years, comes in to report that a brick he thought was thrown through his window by his neighbor Mr. Haddad was actually the work of two young punks in the neighborhood trying to shake him down for protection money. Unfortunately, Barney has to break the news to him that they can't help him anymore. They only answer homicide calls now. Mr. Cotterman is dumbfounded.

Mr. Cotterman:	But Captain, . . . couldn't you make an exception for a regular customer?
Barney:	I'm afraid not. Look, for extortion you have to go over to the 14th Precinct.
Wojo:	No, Barn, that's prostitution. He's got to go over to the 10th on twentieth.
Barney:	Oh right, the 10th over on twentieth.

Sober Reality

Later in the episode Mr. Haddad bursts into the 12th to tell them that Cotterman is dead. Haddad explains, "Two punks shot him. The ones who were shaking him down for protection. He told me he told you." Barney asks, "What about the 10th, where the hell were they?"

Haddad: He never went down. He said, 'I'll take care of it myself.' He said, 'I don't like to deal with strangers.' They put a gun to his head and they, they killed him like it was nothing.
Wojo: Well, I guess we can handle it now.
Haddad: He deserved better . . . from both of us.

At the end of the episode, we learn that the 12th is restored to their normal duties but it's never explained why.

Rough Cut

As a fan, I always felt that the second half hour of the special one-hour "Wojo's Girl" was the least funny episode in the history of the program. That said, "Homicide: Part 2" was the episode in which I felt the most betrayed as a viewer. The magic of *Barney Miller* was that even when dealing with important issues like atomic bombs, gun control, or corporate deceit, they never failed to stay true to their comedic roots. In "Homicide: Part 2," the writers lose their way and write a gratuitous script for what seems like no other reason than to have a sensationalized way to open a season. Aside from Marty Morrison, Leon Roth, Ray Brewer, or Bruno Bender, there was no other customer of the 12th Precinct to whom we felt closer than Mr. Cotterman. He, or a similar character representing what eventually became the Cotterman character, had been with us since Season One.

I was somewhat surprised at Tony Sheehan's reaction when I told him how angry and betrayed I felt by this episode. He had obviously heard the same complaint from other fans through the years but said they [the writers] thought people would see humor in the irony of the situation—the fact that they couldn't help him until after he was dead. Sheehan expressed surprise that no one seemed to have a problem with the man who kills his barber.

The writing talents of Tony Sheehan, Frank Dungan, and Jeff Stein are undeniable but I am fascinated that they could be so off the mark at understanding the backlash to this storyline. Cotterman was a friend, a character we'd known for years. The guy who kills his barber is a stranger to us as is his barber.

Just the Facts

- When Harris answers the phone, he still answers, "12th Precinct, Harris." Why wouldn't he answer "Homicide, Harris?"

- The barber killer has also killed his wife but the police don't know that yet.
- Levitt is a hero, again. He pushed Mr. Shulton out of the line of fire.

Season 7, Episode 3: "The Delegate."
Original Airdate: November 13, 1980.
Writer: Jim Tisdale.
Director: Noam Pitlik.
Cast of Characters: Hal Linden (Barney), Ron Glass (Harris), Steve Landesberg (Dietrich), Max Gail (Wojo), Ron Carey (Levitt), Bonnie Bartlett (Ellen Milford), Don Sherman (Mr. Turner), Tom Henschel (Edmund Lasky), Bob Dishy (Richard Milford), Phil Leeds (Louis Nash).

The Rundown

A new but wizened officer gives Levitt some competition in the clerical arena of precinct work. Wojo and Dietrich bring in a Pennsylvania delegate to the 1976 Democratic Convention who's been on a four-year bender. There's a serial robber on the loose who works on a very regular schedule.

The Big City

Bob Dishy is his usual brilliant self as Richard Milford, the long-lost convention delegate. He tells Wojo that after the convention was over he realized that he'd never been in the big city alone so he decided to stay in New York for a few days. He pauses momentarily and says, "Well, then after the first year went by I realized I couldn't go home again unless I had a rather compelling explanation."

It's interesting to note how accepting Wojo is of Mr. Milford and his transgressions. He is far less judgmental and disgusted than he would have been under similar circumstances a couple of years earlier. Is he more tolerant or just broken?

Is That a Problem?

Phil Leeds plays Louis Nash, the newest and most efficient member of the 12th Precinct. Levitt, threatened by this senior-citizen dynamo, looks into his records and discovers he's not a real cop. When Barney confronts him, it turns out he's a retired C.P.A. who read about police layoffs and staff shortages and wanted to help. He had a friend who worked at a uniform company and the rest was easy. No one ever questioned his presence because they appreciated the help!

The comedy in this segment relies on Barney trying to explain to Nash that he's broken the law. Nash can't understand why the force wouldn't want his help whether he's a real cop or not.

Praise Indeed

Officer Nash tells Harris, "For my money, you're a much better writer than that Joseph Wambaugh." Harris replies rather curtly, "So why bring him up?" Wambaugh, the former LAPD officer turned best-selling novelist, author of *The Blue Knight*, was on record as being a fan of *Barney Miller*.

Overachiever

Harris tracks a thief who strikes at very specific times and days of the week. When they finally catch him, it's revealed that he's a prisoner who is let go three times a week on a work release program. He's supposed to be attending classes at City College for computer programming and ethics.

Barney: Obviously, you missed a few sessions.
Thief: Yeah, well, it's tough juggling school and a career.

Season 7, Episode 4: "Dorsey."
Original Airdate: November 27, 1980.
Writer: Tony Sheehan.
Director: Noam Pitlik.
Cast of Characters: Hal Linden (Barney), Ron Carey (Levitt), Max Gail (Wojo), Ron Glass (Harris), Steve Landesberg (Dietrich), Darrell Zwerling (Bill Adelson), Andrew Bloch (Edward Devoe), Cal Gibson (Mr. King), Michael Lombard (Kenneth Pryor), Paul Lieber (Det. Sgt. Eric Dorsey).

The Rundown

The 12th gets a new, albeit wary, member of the squad. A happy drug addict begins to go through withdrawal while awaiting transfer. A man attending a stop smoking clinic snaps and causes a disturbance.

New Recruit

Paul Lieber joins the squad for a three-episode arc as Det. Sgt. Eric Dorsey. Technically speaking, he becomes the fifth criminal to become a member of the precinct. In the previous season, he appeared in "The Architect" as one of the guys trying to break his buddy out of jail. Steve Landesberg and Ron Carey both appeared as criminals prior to their being cast as members of the squad. Actress Mari Gorman also appeared first as Roberta Kerlin, a Connecticut housewife attempting prostitution to get her husband's attention. She later came on in her own three-episode arc as Detective Rosslyn Licori. Jenny O'Hara was brought in for trespassing at the Continental Baths while attempting to talk with the man she thought was her father. In her second and last episode, she portrays Sgt. Holly Scofield, a female detective brought in to try to trap a handsy dentist.

As with most transfers of officers who come to the 12th, their assignments add up to little more than temporary duty. In this case, Dorsey arrives with a big chip on his shoulder and the assumption that his fellow cops are on the take. This is interesting because as honest as we know the men of the 12th to be, this clearly indicates that Dorsey has come from other precincts where that has not been the case.

Once again, we must remember that *Barney Miller* came to television just a year or two after the film *Serpico* (1973) about a clean cop trying to survive in a corrupt system. Unfortunately, as serious as these claims are, particularly from someone you're going to work with and need to trust every day, the issue was resolved too quickly and simplistically in this episode. The men assure Dorsey that they're honest cops. He apologizes, says he believes them and soon after, it's made clear that he does not believe them. They go through the same talk, turn down a bribe in front of him and all of a sudden, he believes them again. It doesn't ring true.

A Different Time

This episode tackles addictions to both heroin and over-the-counter cigarettes. While the effects of withdrawal are shown to be anything but fun, the fact is that many people today might not find either subject too amusing. Cigarettes have helped kill millions of people from cancer and other sicknesses while the opioid crisis rages on in America as serious as it's ever been.

Darrell Zwerling plays Bill Adelson, the administrator of a clinic designed to help people stop smoking, the New York Institute for Smoking Modification, Inc. Mr. Pryor, played by veteran character actor Michael Lombard, takes umbrage at some of the methods used in the clinic which includes zapping patients with thirty volts every time they take a puff on a cigarette.

Harris, the enthusiastic smoker in the group commiserates with Mr. Pryor and has some sadistic fun of his own when Mr. Adelson comes down to press charges by subtly blowing smoke in his face. Finally, Adelson says to Harris, "Sergeant, what you do in private is none of my business, but when your smoke invades my breathing space, I have to ask you to stop."

Within the context of the show, Adelson was made to look like the goofy one. Today, it seems only natural that the rights of non-smokers be upheld but it took a while.

Season 7, Episode 5: "Agent Orange."
Original Airdate: December 11, 1980.
Writer: Tony Sheehan.
Director: Noam Pitlik.
Cast of Characters: Hal Linden (Barney), Max Gail (Wojo), Steve Landesberg (Dietrich), Ron Glass (Harris), Michael Currie (John Fulton), Louis Giambalvo (Gerald Serrano), Robert Phalen (Capt. Ronald Dupre), Lyman Ward (Len Macready), Joe Regalbuto (Peter Rankin), Doris Roberts (Doris Brauer), Peter Hobbs (Philip Brauer), Paul Lieber (Det. Sgt. Eric Dorsey).

The Rundown

Wojo discovers new implications concerning his time in Vietnam when a war vet gets arrested for attempted robbery and blames his health problems on the toxins in Agent Orange. The battling Brauers return to the 12th to debate the benefits and/or detriments of nudism.

The Bickersons Return

Mrs. Brauer is upset that the new owner has turned her apartment building into a "clothing optional" residence. Mr. Brauer on the other hand has embraced the newer, freer lifestyle so Mrs. Brauer has him locked up. When actor Michael Currie arrives as the owner of the building, Barney tells him Mrs. Brauer is entitled "not to be offended." He's let off with a misdemeanor citation for creating a public nuisance and an admonition by

Harris to "keep your pants on," at least in all areas of the building that are open to public view.

Mrs. Brauer gets the last laugh when she threatens to go nude in the squad room and Mr. Brauer panics. Nevertheless, the threat did turn him on a little and they leave together happy, as always, for the time being.

Close to Home

Gerald Serrano, played by actor Louis Giambalvo, attempts to rob a liquor store claiming that he has to rob in order to recreate the excitement he experienced as a pilot in Vietnam. Dietrich volunteers the newfound studies surrounding something called Vietnam Syndrome. According to Dietrich, "It's a recently diagnosed disorder of some vets who because of their exposure to violence and danger in Vietnam seem to have a psychological need for it in civilian life." Interestingly, in the years following the end of *Barney Miller*, the term "Vietnam Syndrome" would take on an entirely different meaning. In the 1990s and beyond, it came to mean a reluctance and/or fear to commit American military power and engagement anywhere in the world unless it's absolutely necessary to protect the national interests of the country. Of course, it hasn't prevented the government from doing so but at least we named it.

Don't Call Us, We'll Call You

Serranno mentions that he has a rash in the back of his neck from the dioxin in Agent Orange, as well as numbness, tingling, liver damage, abdominal tumors. When he informs Wojo that he too was most likely exposed to Agent Orange, Wojo calls in the VA, the USAF, and Thresher Chemical Company, the manufacturers of the chemical in question.

This is an emotional issue for Wojo and yet when he's initially conferring with Lyman Ward as the VA's Len Macready, Joe Regalbuto as the chemical company's Peter Rankin, and Robert Phalen as Capt. Ronald Dupre of the USAF, he seems to be having a difficult time staying awake. Anecdotal evidence concerning *Barney Miller's* shooting schedules suggests this was another late-night shoot and Max Gail was exhausted. Either that or he was method acting the boredom inspired by the corporate mumbo-jumbo being fed to him by Mr. Rankin.

Wojo ultimately gets quite animated when he finally blows up and tells the group that he was in Vietnam as well as Serranno. In an impassioned plea,

Wojo says, "I don't care anymore whose fault it is or who did what or who's suing who. Mr. Serranno and me would like to know what the stuff did! And what it's going to do. Right?" He turns to Serranno who sheepishly looks back at him and says, "I just wanted a lawyer."

In the end, Ultimately, we're given the classic *Barney Miller* unresolved ending, the anti-sitcom ending, wherein the men Wojo has called together admit to him that they can't answer his questions because they just don't know the extent of damage done by the Agent Orange. They admit there are numerous studies still to be conducted but until they're all complete, they have no concrete answers to give him.

The Last Word

Len Macready: Do you people do this often? (calling high level agencies regarding local precinct arrests).
Wojo: I do.

Season 7, Episode 6: "Call Girl."
Original Airdate: December 18, 1980.
Writers: Frank Dungan and Jeff Stein.
Director: Noam Pitlik.
Cast of Characters: Ron Glass (Harris), Steve Landesberg (Dietrich), Max Gail (Wojo), Hal Linden (Barney), Arnold Malet (Malcolm Gower), Sarina Grant (Lenore DuBois), Tasha Zemrus (Rhonda Halek), Paul Kent (Ray Athens), Nancy Bleier (Christine Scott), Paul Lieber (Det. Sgt. Eric Dorsey).

The Rundown

Dietrich has decided to give up sex for a year or two to increase his productivity. Harris and Dorsey bring in a trio of prostitutes who inadvertently tempt Dietrich's new life plan. One of the call girls turns out to have a high-ranking client list and another is only fifteen years old.

The New Celibacy

In August of 1980, *The Washington Post* ran a story about "The New Celibacy." We know it was a common practice for the *Barney Miller* writers to scan the newspapers for story ideas. There's no way a comedy writer was going to be able to pass up an idea like this one. Dietrich comes in early one morning and hands Barney a load of paperwork that should have taken him weeks to complete. He tells Barney he's given up sex for a while to increase his productivity and clear his brain. It works until Harris brings in attractive prostitutes and Dietrich is forced to interact with them.

It should be noted this same idea was later used in the *Seinfeld* episode, "The Abstinence," where George Costanza gives up sex and soon becomes a borderline genius. The joke being that without the idea of sex and how to get it clouding his thinking, George's focus becomes laser sharp.

Timeless Sentiment

Nancy Bleier plays a call girl named Christine Scott with a very valuable "phone book" of clients. Following her arrest, Barney is inundated with calls from judges, businessmen, and politicians. Her beauty and fragrance capture Dietrich's attention while her connections and stock tips entice Harris. By the end of the episode, Barney is at his wit's end as he answers one last phone call from a concerned party.

> **Barney:** If you and your highly placed friends would spend half the energy trying to serve the public as you do trying to cover up your extra-curricular activities this city, the whole damn country for that matter, would be in a hell of a lot better shape!

In the years since this episode aired, there are volumes of stories that have been written about the extracurricular activities of our politicians and men of power, proving that some things never go out of style.

Bombs Away!

Dorsey mentions his love for the video game, "Missile Command," and tries to explain it to Wojo. Unfortunately, Wojo can't get past the premise of trying to save cities from nuclear attacks and tells Dorsey, "Well, it just seems to me that the whole idea of getting your kicks playing around with nuclear holocausts is kinda warped."

In the years since this episode aired, the debate about the harmful effects of violent video games has been an ongoing one. Today there are literally hundreds of new games in this area with new, intensely disturbing, graphics.

Season 7, Episode 7: "Resignation."
Original Airdate: January 8, 1981.
Writers: Frank Dungan and Jeff Stein.
Director: Noam Pitlik.
Cast of Characters: Max Gail (Wojo), Ron Glass (Harris), Hal Linden (Barney), Steve Landesberg (Dietrich), Ron Carey (Levitt), Steve Franken (Edward Novak), Peter Elbling (Jordan Heath), Mario Roccuzzo (Ira Russo), Allan Rich (Leonard, the theater producer).

The Rundown

Dietrich returns fire on a robbery suspect and then faces a moral crisis concerning his future. A man tries to turn himself in for a crime he committed out of state. An actor and a playwright come to blows over the interpretation of a play.

A Crooked Victim?

Mario Roccuzzo is terrific as Ira Russo, a man racked with guilt for stealing $1,300 from a group of nuns running an orphanage for Indian kids in the Arizona desert. According to Russo, "They hired me, they trusted me. Two days before Christmas I stole their bank accounts and their bus. Spent it on liquor and prostitutes." So why then do we feel sorry for him?

The Arizona authorities don't think it's worth their time or trouble to pay to have him sent back but if he wants to pay his own way, they'll be happy to prosecute him. This is one of those bureaucratic scenarios that sounds so ridiculous it could actually be true. Shining the light on bureaucratic inefficiency was a *Barney Miller* specialty.

The Show Must Go On

An altercation ensues between an actor, played by Peter Elbling, and a playwright, played by Steve Franken. Wojo and Harris are forced to march on stage to break it up. Both Elbling and Franken make their second and final appearances on *Barney Miller* with this episode and both are very funny as the stereotypical actor trying to find his motivation and the playwright trying to protect his words. The characterizations are nothing new but the depictions are solidly funny. The most enjoyable of all comes from veteran character actor Allan Rich as Leonard, the producer of the play. His apoplectic portrayal is the cherry on top of this show biz sundae as he screams at his actor and playwright, "We are doing a play! Not *Hamlet*!"

Second Thoughts

When Dietrich has to return fire on a robbery suspect hitting him in his buttocks, he returns to the station and turns in his resignation claiming his morals and integrity won't allow him to have the power of life and death over his fellow man.

When Wojo asks why he became a cop in the first place, Dietrich tries to make a joke saying, "Stood in the wrong line." Barney reacts to his flippancy by reminding Dietrich that he apparently stood in quite a few wrong lines as they review his earlier decisions to start and quickly abandon law school, medical school, teaching, acting, etc.

> **Barney:** Seems to me you've had a continuing difficulty committing to anything.
> **Dietrich:** Yeah, so?
> **Wojo:** So maybe the high moral code and integrity are really just an intellectual smokescreen to rationalize away the fact that you're quitting again.
> **Dietrich:** When'd you get so smart?

This showdown scene is the centerpiece of the episode so it's a shame it doesn't work. It's reasonable and even commendable to want to have characters grow throughout a series but the turnaround in Season Seven in the makeup of Wojo's character lacks credibility. Wojo's deep psychological diagnosis of Dietrich's attempt to flee a tough situation has Dietrich asking what we're all thinking, "When'd you get so smart?" Wojo's comment, in addition to an uncharacteristically strange conversation with Harris at the beginning of the episode about their lack of communication, seems forced and out-of-place. Ultimately, I like the growth of the Wojciehowicz character over the course of the series. I just think the writers seem unable to figure out how to make the transition more gradual and natural, particularly in this episode.

For that matter, Dietrich has undoubtedly been in other life-and-death situations as a cop so why, all of a sudden, does he have this crisis? Tough transitions for a twenty-five-minute story.

The Last Word

After the boys have their consultation with Dietrich, Leonard the producer comes over and asks, "Is the performance of *Detective Story* over now?"

The line is funny in and of itself but considering that the program was based, in part, on the play and movie *Detective Story*, it takes on extra meaning. [Now *that's* Meta!]

Season 7, Episode 8: "Field Associate."
Original Airdate: January 15, 1981.
Writer: Jordan Moffet.
Director: Noam Pitlik.
Cast of Characters: Ron Carey (Levitt), Hal Linden (Barney), Steve Landesberg (Dietrich), Ron Glass (Harris), Max Gail (Wojo), Jeffrey Tambor (William Klein), Florence Halop (Karen Golden), Ned Glass (Stanley Golden).

The Rundown

Dietrich and Harris bring in an elderly second story man. There's a mole in the precinct leaking information to Internal Affairs. A man breaks up the offices of the Trilateral Commission.

The Mole

Wojo thinks Levitt is the Field Associate leaking information to the brass downtown. Barney eventually breaks down and asks Levitt, who admits it's true with the explanation that if he didn't do it, the department would have chosen someone else who may not have been so willing to overlook major transgressions and focus on the picayune stuff.

Wojo is not buying it and Barney has to physically restrain him from going after Levitt. When Wojo asks him how the men are supposed to continue working with him, Levitt suggests they never did. "Has it ever occurred to any of you that I wouldn't have been doing this if I'd gotten one ounce of respect from you guys? But all I got was 'Hi there, Li'l Levitt, File this, L'il Levitt, See ya later, Li'l Levitt.'"

Harris: Well, I only meant that in the, uh, diminutive sense.
Levitt: You never treated me as anything but a joke!

When Barney sheepishly admits, "Levitt, I'm partially responsible for that," Levitt agrees with Barney saying, "Maybe I'd have had a little credibility with them if you stopped yanking me up and down like a yo-yo. One day I'm in uniform, then plain clothes . . . for God's sakes, sir, make up your mind!"

> **Levitt:** Look, I know there's supposed to be a bond, a trust between cops . . . and I broke that trust. I owe everyone here an apology for doing that. I just hope you understand why I did it and you give me another chance to prove myself.

This is a poorly handled scene. First Levitt says he took the assignment to protect them but then he says he wouldn't have done it if they'd treated him as a part of the team. Then he apologizes for breaking "a trust" that, in reality, would have probably never been restored. I think the exhaustion and stress on the writers is starting to show here. The bulk of the work being on primarily three writers leads to quick and easy resolutions. It's just not up to *Barney Miller* standards.

Hopeless Romantic

An elderly lifetime criminal reveals that he's dying of cancer and only has a few months to live. Veteran character actor Ned Glass makes his second and final *Barney Miller* appearance as Stanley Golden, a man whose colorful history intrigues Harris. Our dapper sergeant bubbles with enthusiasm as he relays to Barney Mr. Golden's record of "115 arrests, fourteen grand jury indictments, [and] twenty-three felony convictions dating back to 1933." Even more impressive, Mr. Golden worked for Lucky Luciano and Bugsy Siegel.

Harris is a little miffed when Barney assumes that his interest in Mr. Golden is for material for another book. When Harris tells Barney that the thought never occurred to him, Barney is flustered.

> **Harris:** Well maybe it's because I just like him. You know, relating to him, one human being to another.
> **Barney:** Yeah, well, I just, never saw you do that before.
> **Harris:** Thank you, Barney.

Since I've been critical of the writing this season, I should give credit where credit is due on this plot concerning Harris and Mr. Golden. It's not only a touching story but it's consistent with the history of the show. Harris has a track record of adopting certain criminals such as Roscoe Lee Browne in S. 1/Ep. 11, "Escape Artist," and J. Pat O'Malley in S. 5/Ep. 19, "The Counterfeiter." On the other hand, considering the development of Harris's personality since his book was published, it's also reasonable that everyone thought Harris was taking an interest in Golden for the book and movie rights.

The dynamic between Harris and Golden is the best of *Barney Miller* because, once again, it's about a human connection. Your heart breaks when Golden reveals that he has no other friends beside Harris. For one afternoon, Harris makes him feel connected to the world again.

Season 7, Episode 9: "Movie—Part 1."
Original Airdate: January 22, 1981.
Writers: Frank Dungan and Jeff Stein.
Director: Noam Pitlik.
Cast of Characters: Max Gail (Wojo), Steve Landesberg (Dietrich), Ron Carey (Levitt), Ron Glass (Harris), Hal Linden (Barney), Dino Natali (Officer Zatelli), Dennis Howard (Jed Brickman), Arny Freeman (Philip Helm) George Murdock (Lt. Ben Scanlon).

The Rundown

Harris is given the assignment of making a pornographic film in order to infiltrate the industry. Scanlon comes to the 12th on a fishing expedition and catches a whopper. A radio reporter attacks a pretty boy television personality when he steals his interview subject.

Style vs. Substance

Philip Helm is a qualified, veteran reporter with WLX All News Radio 1610. He's also short, balding, and mature. When a young reporter from the local TV Action News team steals an interview subject from him, Helm retaliates and attacks the TV hotshot. Arny Freeman, in his last of six different characterizations, is hilarious as Helm.

This prescient subject matter would be more fully explored six years later in the James L. Brooks film, *Broadcast News* (1987), about two reporters at a television network: one who's informed and qualified and the other who's handsome and comfortable in front of a camera.

Closet Opened

Under grilling about a different matter, Wojo blows Zatelli's cover in front of Lt. Scanlon. To sum up the gaffe in the words of Officer Levitt, "I was the Field Associate and I'm disgusted."

Naturally, Scanlon uses the revelation to threaten Miller's position and put pressure on Zatelli to resign. As we would expect, Barney defends Zatelli's rights and position and Zatelli tells Scanlon he will not resign.

Wojo apologizes to Zatelli, saying, "I was on the spot and you were the first gay guy I knew." Zatelli is incredibly gracious telling Wojo, "Look, I didn't plan on this thing coming out this way. But, then again, I probably wouldn't have had enough guts to do it on my own, so I just want to say thanks for doing it for me." Wojo sheepishly replies, "Glad I could help."

In the end, it turns out Wojo really did help Zatelli when we learn he's been transferred to a better position as an Administrative Assistant in the Chief Inspector's office. He tells the squad, "I think I have someone at the top who's a paisan." Levitt asks, "Italian?" Zatelli says, "Yeah, that too."

As Zatelli says goodbye and leaves the squad room for the final time, Wojo says to Barney and Harris, "I thought I ruined him."

Barney: Apparently not. This could be the best thing that ever happened to his career.
Levitt: I'm gay! (They all turn to look at him) It's worth a shot.

This is a magnificently progressive ending to this storyline. It may be ahead of the actual progress in the real workplace, particularly police forces, but it's a great message to be sending in a very transitional and tumultuous time for the gay community in America.

Another Heaven's Gate?

Harris is assigned to make a simple pornographic film, or in the words of Barney, "a modest little skin flick . . . to get a better idea of how they operate." Harris proceeds as if he doesn't hear Barney, showing him his designs that include four different settings. When Barney complains, Harris replies with, "They didn't bother Cimino until he'd gone over $40 million."

The comment refers to director Michael Cimino's 1980 Western epic, *Heaven's Gate*. At the time it was heralded as one of the biggest box office bombs in movie history with a price tag of $44 million and a domestic gross of less than $5 million. In the decades since, there's been a positive critical reappraisal of the film.

Just the Facts

- Harris names his fictional production company Starry Night Productions.
- Harris's stock footage requirements: the Manhattan skyline, day and night, assorted street scenes, Times Square, a fireworks display, a volcano, possibly Mt. St. Helens? And if they can get it, that old Puffed Wheat commercial with the cannon.

Season 7, Episode 10: "Movie—Part 2."
Original Airdate: January 29, 1981.
Writers: Frank Dungan and Jeff Stein.
Director: Noam Pitlik.
Cast of Characters: Ron Glass (Harris), Steve Landesberg (Dietrich), Hal Linden (Barney), Jay Gerber (Howard Fuller), Ralph Manza (Leon Roth), J. J. Barry (Arthur Duncan), Norman Bartold (Carl Bernie), James Gregory (Inspector Frank Luger).

The Rundown

A mugger is targeting handicapped victims. A fundraiser elicits donations at knifepoint. Inspector Luger is unhappy in his new job and Harris premieres his long-awaited pornographic film for the men of the 12th.

A Sight for Sore Eyes

Barney notices Mr. Roth at Dietrich's desk "feeling his way" through the mug books. When Barney asks Dietrich why, Dietrich answers matter-of-factly, "He got mugged."

Barney: The man is blind!
Dietrich: You tell him.

Ralph Manza's Mr. Roth is one of the outstanding characters in the *Barney Miller* universe and one that must have been great fun to write. His appearance in the series-ending episode no doubt reveals the love that the writers and producers also had for the character.

When Barney tells Mr. Roth they don't have an eyewitness to the mugging, Roth cites himself. Barney says that they were hoping for a physical description and Roth says, "He smelled short."

Never Forget a Face

Inspector Luger has never been particularly good with names (i.e., Levine for Levitt) but he's even less concerned with the victims and criminals who are in the squad room whenever he arrives. On this visit he says hello to everyone and then spots Mr. Roth sitting at Nick's old desk and addresses him as "Mr. Shearing," referring to the famous blind jazz pianist, George Shearing.

Author, Author

Harris's modest little porno flick was originally budgeted at slightly less than $3,000. In eight weeks' time he's spent in excess of $22,000. His answer is, "But just wait 'til you see it, it looks like I spent $50,000!"

Finally, the big moment arrives to preview the film for the men of the 12th. Those in attendance include Barney, Dietrich, Wojo, Levitt, Inspector Luger, Mr. Roth, and Mr. Fuller (in the cage). During the running of the film, Levitt and Wojo leave to answer a "robbery in progress" call and in the course of the film, Mr. Bernie and Arthur Duncan will join the audience. At one point Norman Bartold's Mr. Bernie asks, "Who wrote this?" When Harris answers in the affirmative, Bernie shoots back, "Why?"

The film is much longer than expected and the patrons begin to get bored; Dietrich yawns, Luger starts paging through the phone book. When they finally reach the climax—of the movie, that is—everyone is more than satisfied with the result. Well, almost everyone.

Everyone's A Critic

Wojo: Pretty good Harris. (Barney gives him a look) What I saw of it.
Mr. Roth: Same here.
Dietrich: I give it three smiles.
Luger: Great. You got stuff in there that would gag a maggot.

Barney tells him, "No, it wasn't quite what I expected. But I can see what you tried to do. However, it was a bit verbose, the choice of music was questionable, wouldn't hurt to lose about a half an hour in the editing room."

Introduction of a Slimeball

This episode marks the first appearance of Arthur Duncan, a felon portrayed by J. J. Barry. Barry had appeared in three previous episodes as different characters but from this episode on, he will play Duncan in four different episodes over the final two seasons.

Whenever I hear this character's name, all I can think of is Lawrence Welk's token black entertainer on his long-running television show, Arthur Duncan, a very talented tap dancer. Could it be that writers Frank Dungan and Jeff Stein were Welk fans?

The Last Word

As Harris begins to roll film, Mr. Roth yells out, "Let's see a little skin up there, a little skin!"

Season 7, Episode 11:	"The Psychic."
Original Airdate:	February 5, 1981.
Writers:	Tony Sheehan, Frank Dungan, and Jeff Stein.
Director:	Noam Pitlik.
Cast of Characters:	Ron Glass (Harris), Hal Linden (Barney), Steve Landesberg (Dietrich), Ron Carey (Levitt), Max Gail (Wojo), Ken Tigar (Philip Pollock), Fred Sadoff (Ronald Hanna), Rod Colbin (Roger Joyce), Larry Hankin (Earl Kelso), Robert Burgos (John Gittes), James Gregory (Inspector Frank Luger).

The Rundown

A psychic is charged with assault and battery trying to stop a purse-snatching before it happens. Dietrich and Levitt bring in a grammarian for ripping down a subway ad for Aunt Sally's Pickles. Inspector Luger recruits Barney's aid in writing reports.

Should Have Seen That Coming

Ken Tigar returns in another tale of paranormal activities but this time, instead of being harassed by a ghost or turning into a werewolf, he's Philip Pollock, a man with the gift of precognition. Walking the streets of Manhattan, he "sees" that a man is going to snatch a woman's purse so he jumps the man and pins him to the ground. When the two men are brought into the precinct everyone is dubious of Pollock's claim of being psychic.

However, Wojo checks Pollock for priors and finds that he's clean but the man he attacked, the man he claimed was going to snatch the lady's purse, Mr. Kelso, played by Larry Hankin, has thirteen previous arrests, nine of them for purse-snatching.

Inside Joke?

At the start of the show, Barney announces that PAL (Police Athletic League), is staging its annual benefit variety show. Harris asks Barney, "Back in college didn't you used to do a little singing?" Barney's response is, "Me? No." This is a little "inside joke" because Hal Linden played the reeds and doubled on vocals when he started out in show biz in the big bands of the late 1940s and early 1950s. He does, in fact, have a very fine singing voice that he displayed on numerous network variety shows in the 1970s and 1980s.

Grammar Police

Fred Sadoff is Prof. Ronald Hanna, a Professor of Linguistics and English at NYU, who rips down a sign on the subway because of its ungrammatical content that reads, "Aunt Sally says, 'My pickles are the tongue teasingest, the lip-smackingest, and the crun-crun-crunchiest.'"

Hanna tells Barney that, "The English language is one of the most beautiful and expressive of all tongues but it's being corrupted and debased by its chronic misuse. Manufactured lingo like that, dull-witted cliches, redundancies, mindless phraseology." Ridiculous advertising campaigns and slogans had been around for decades by the time this episode aired but Hanna also notes that, "The manipulation of language is one of the primary methods used by those in power to confuse and divert the public. A false statement isn't a lie, it's simply no longer operative. War becomes pacification, and bombing? The vertical deployment of anti-personnel devices."

Comedian and social commentator George Carlin also addressed this issue with a track called "Euphemisms" from his 1990 album, *Parental Advisory: Explicit Lyrics*. Carlin was a comedian who was fascinated by the English language and used it to his advantage in many brilliantly conceived comedy routines.

If anything, "alternative facts," have become even more of a problem in the twenty-first century.

Season 7, Episode 12: "Stormy Weather."
Original Airdate: February 12, 1981."

Writer:	Nat Mauldin.
Director:	Noam Pitlik.
Cast of Characters:	Hal Linden (Barney), Ron Glass (Harris), Max Gail (Wojo), Steve Landesberg (Dietrich), Ron Carey (Levitt), Robert Costanzo (Ed Foronjy), Seymour S. Bernstein (Attorney Lucas), Peter Wolf (Tiano), Phyllis Frelich (Madeline Schaefer).

The Rundown

Harris is at work with a bad case of the flu because of a manpower shortage. Wojo and Dietrich bring in a deaf prostitute and are surprised to find an interpreter within their own precinct. Wojo jumps into the river in pursuit of a suspect.

Help Is in Short Supply

When Wojo and Dietrich bring in Madeline Schaefer, a deaf prostitute played by Phyllis Frelich, it's clear that they are going to have a difficult time booking her. Levitt enters and seeing their struggle immediately starts signing to the suspect. We learn that Levitt is fluent with sign language because he has a deaf sister.

Phyllis Frelich was a trailblazing deaf actress on Broadway and in Hollywood. She was the oldest of nine children, all with hearing loss, and attended Gallaudet University. She originated the lead role in the Broadway production of *Children of a Lesser God* and her performance earned her a nomination for the Drama Desk Award as well as the 1980 Tony Award for "Best Actress in a Play." Following her Broadway success she appeared on television in shows such as *Spenser: For Hire* (1985–1988), *L.A. Law* (1986–1994), and *ER* (1994–2009). She died in 2014 at the age of seventy.

Nice Guys Finish Last

Wojo and Harris discover Ed Foronjy, played by Robert Costanzo, breaking into a warehouse near the docks. Wojo chases him down to the end of the pier when Foronjy jumps in the water.

> **Ed Foronjy:** I figured only a real hot dog would come in after me.
> **Wojo:** So I did. The next thing I knew, he's swimming out into the river.

Ed: I got family in Jersey.

Wojo cramps up and starts to go under yelling for help. That's when Foronjy comes to his rescue and pulls him to shore. Wojo says, "He got me up on the pier, brought me around . . . then I arrested him."

As a criminal, Mr. Foronjy is at a disadvantage. He's a nice guy. He works as a volunteer on a crisis hotline and as a Big Brother. He tells Wojo, "I don't know what's wrong with me. I mean other guys I know who are making it big in crime, they're vicious, they're ruthless, they'd shoot you just as soon as look at you. But not me! Last week I went to hold up a liquor store in Queens, who's running it? Vietnamese refugees. I wound up giving them twenty bucks to help the boat people. I mean I don't know what my problem is!"

Unsolicited Endorsement

When Ms. Schaefer's lawyer arrives he, too, is deaf. Levitt assists him in speaking with Barney. He also helps Dietrich make out the police report with Ms. Schaefer. When she makes her bail, her lawyer thanks Barney for his cooperation and, through Levitt's interpretation, "I also want to add that Officer Levitt's assistance was invaluable."

At the end, Barney stops Levitt and simply says, "Thank you." Levitt just gives him the ASL sign for, "It was nothing."

Just the Facts

- Dietrich is attracted to the prostitute and asks her out to dinner at a Chinese restaurant named Charlie Woo's on Third Avenue. However, in another episode Dietrich claims the MSG in Chinese food gives him headaches.

Season 7, Episode 13: "The Librarian."
Original Airdate: February 19, 1981.
Writers: Frank Dungan, Jeff Stein, and Tony Sheehan.
Director: Noam Pitlik.
Cast of Characters: Max Gail (Wojo), Ron Glass (Harris), Steve Landesberg (Dietrich), Hal Linden (Barney), Allan Miller (Williams Collins, Justice Dept.), Titos Vandis (Stefan Beruit), Miriam Byrd-Nethery (Louise Austin), Zachary Berger (Werner "Bob" Zlinka), James Gallery (Neil Pomerantz).

The Rundown

Wojo wonders why a merchant is reluctant to pursue the case of a brick thrown through his store window. A librarian has a breakdown and shoots a gun off in the library.

What About Bob?

Zachary Berger returns for his second and final *Barney Miller* appearance in this emotionally charged episode. His name is Werner Zlinka but he tells everyone to call him "Bob." He owns a joke and novelty shop but his playful persona covers up the fact that he is a former Nazi of the Third Reich. There aren't enough hand buzzers in the world that can put a humorous spin on that one.

Walking to work, Wojo spots Zlinka sweeping broken glass and notices a swastika and graffiti spray-painted on the man's store and brings him in to fill out a report. Dietrich soon apprehends the culprit, a Stefan Beirut, played by Tito Vandis in his third and final guest spot on the show. It turns out Mr. Beirut is a gypsy and a survivor of a World War II Nazi concentration camp. He accuses Zlinka of being a war criminal.

Beruit: He was at Birkenau.

Dietrich: That's the concentration camp in Poland built to handle the overflow from Auschwitz. There was a special section for gypsies.

Beirut: I was brought there in 1943 with my father and brothers. A thousand other gypsies were there already. Those who were strong enough were put into work details—we dug canals, we hauled stones from a rock quarry. Fourteen hours a day in the cold and snow. In October, there were 1,100 men and women in the work groups. By spring of 1944, fifteen of us were left. Zlinka was in charge of our detail. I escaped a month later while I was being transferred to another camp.

All the men are shaken by this revelation. Wojo and Harris call the Justice Department as well as Poland. When Allan Miller shows up as William Collins of the Justice Department he tells Barney they need solid proof. Collins stresses, "It's been thirty-five to forty years since these incidents took place. Memory, perceptions, become distorted. Most importantly, we need corroboration otherwise it is just one man's word against a gypsy's."

Collins' wording suggests that even in 1981 the prejudice against the gypsy background still existed. It may not be malevolent or even intentional but it's there.

Harris rushes in with evidence from the American Embassy in Warsaw. The Polish Government Archive have camp records from Birkenau including a staff roster that lists a Sgt. Zlinka, W., who was stationed there through August of 1944 when the final liquidation of the camp was ordered and "approximately four thousand gypsies were gassed."

Wojo gets in Zlinka's face. He's angry and emotional and says, "There must be some explanation, some reason why you did what you did."

Zlinka: I'm an old man who would just like to be left alone.
Wojo: Well, you won't be! Ya gotta say somethin'!

Zlinka turns away in silence.

Throughout the series, Wojo and Harris always seemed to make special connections with various members of the senior community. In this episode we have two old men, one a victim and one a perpetrator of unimaginable horrors against humanity.

When Barney tells Zlinka that he's free to go, Harris protests. Collins tells him it's not a criminal matter until he returns to his native country. Harris is outraged. Collins asks Zlinka if he can give him a lift. It's a small sign of humanity towards a man who doesn't deserve it.

Overdue for a Rest

The secondary plot involves Miriam Byrd Nethery's portrayal of Miss Louise Austin, the assistant librarian at the Sixth Avenue branch who, when pushed over the edge by the rudeness and indifference of the patrons, pulls out a twenty-two automatic and fires off a shot. Miss Austin explains, "They were chattering. Noise is the only thing these people understand."

It's My Party

Harris is having a party for his new socially elite friends and hasn't invited the guys from the 12th. After a day in the trenches trying to win justice for victims of unspeakable war crimes, he changes his plans and asks his friends if they're free to attend. It's a spark of community after a day of revisiting the legacy of man's inhumanity to man.

Season 7, Episode 14: "Rachel."
Original Airdate: February 26, 1981.
Writers: Frank Dungan, Jeff Stein, and Tony Sheehan.
Director: Homer Powell.
Cast of Characters: Hal Linden (Barney), Ron Glass (Harris), Ron Carey (Levitt), Steve Landesberg (Dietrich), Max Gail (Wojo), Anne Wyndham (Rachel Miller), Alex Henteloff (Arnold Ripner), Stanley Brock (Bruno Bender), Chu Chu Maleve (Joseph Rubio).

The Rundown

Captain Miller's daughter Rachel visits the precinct. A local merchant sets a booby trap for would-be robbers. Shyster lawyer Arnold Ripner discovers information that will lead to the downfall of one of New York's finest.

Daddy's Little Girl

Barney's daughter Rachel, recently graduated from Hobart, comes to the precinct to invite her father to dinner. He can't go but Wojo volunteers to take his place. Unfortunately, Barney is uncomfortable with this arrangement and tells Wojo he'd rather he didn't date his daughter. Ultimately, Barney has to confess that it's not Wojo he objects to but Wojo's track record of dating and bedding a large variety of women.

Wojo makes Barney face the fact that after four years away at college and a summer in Europe, it's more than likely Rachel isn't "the little girl" that Barney wants to believe she still is.

It's interesting that Barney could even think his daughter might still be a virgin since he let her move into her own apartment when she was seventeen for "privacy" in the first season episode, "The Courtesans" (S. 1/Ep. 5).

Just Trying to Help

Bruno Bender is arrested for reckless endangerment. He set up a crossbow behind the back door of his store so if somebody came in the door they'd get an arrow through the head. Bruno explains, "Just trying to save you guys some paperwork!" Luckily, due to the shortness of the robber, no one was hurt—this time.

Arnold Ripner, the 12th's regular ambulance chasing lawyer, rushes to the station to grab himself a client in the short thief, Joseph Rubio, played by Chu

Chu Maleve. Unfortunately, while there, Ripner notices Barney's copy of *Blood on the Badge*. When he asks Barney what it's about, he tells the barrister, "Sort of a day-to-day journal about the squad room." You can already see the dollar signs in Ripner's eyes when he asks, "You mean, sort of a real-life account of happenings in this office, people who come in here?"

No Silver Screen Fame Now

Ripner returns and serves Harris with papers of his pending legal action for liable, defamation of character, unlawful use and usurpation of likeness seeking punitive and substantive damages in the amount of $5 million." Harris's immediate reply to Arnold is "You are out of the movie!"

Harris tries to laugh off Arnold's attempt to cash in on his book, telling him, "In the first place, it hasn't been established that the character in question is even you." Unfortunately, it's impossible to argue with Ripner's logic when he tells Harris, "The character in question has been referred to as, quote, 'a shyster attorney, a parasitic lowlife, and a bespectacled cretin.' Who else could it be? I've already underlined a dozen passages describing despicable and unscrupulous behavior that my own mother would recognize!"

Season 7, Episode 15:	"Contempt: Part 1."
Original Airdate:	March 12, 1981.
Writers:	Tony Sheehan, Frank Dungan, and Jeff Stein.
Director:	Noam Pitlik.
Cast of Characters:	Ron Glass (Harris), Max Gail (Wojo), Steve Landesberg (Dietrich), Hal Linden (Barney), Ron Carey (Levitt), Maggie Brown (Lt. Melinda Holly, Salvation Army), John Dullaghan (Ray Brewer), Dale Robinette (Matt Hagan), Larry Gelman (Sidney Bouton), Jack Murdock (Officer Perelli), Roy Andrews (Guard), William Windom (Cellmate—voice only).

The Rundown

Barney goes to jail for Contempt of Court. Ray Brewer has become a member of the Salvation Army. A man is denied a table in a restaurant for aesthetic reasons.

This Whole Court Is out of Order!

Barney has to testify in court in the Gorman Case, an $8 million cocaine bust the squad made that came from a tip from one of Barney's sources. Who knew he even had sources?

Barney returns from court and he's been cited for contempt for refusing to name his source. He told the judge that "revealing the man's identity was tantamount to signing his death warrant." The judge said Barney was jeopardizing a very important case based on some misguided code of ethics. The bottom line is Barney's going to jail.

Not That Easy to Get In

Levitt brings Barney a care package for jail including magazines, nonpareils, cigarettes, and soap-on-a-rope. Ray's advice to Barney is, "Tell them you keep kosher. You'll eat better."

We watch as Barney suffers the indignity of a strip search before he enters the jail. It's difficult for us to watch as we all know and recognize Barney to be anything but a criminal. His cell is dark and all we see of his cellmate are feet hanging off the top bunk. The voice is that of Danny Arnold's old friend, William Windom.

He's in the Army Now

John Dullaghan returns as Ray Brewer, one of the 12th's biggest fans. He's turned his life around and joined the Salvation Army. No matter what Ray's troubles or history, it was always obvious he had a good heart. In the previous season's two-part episode, "Vanished," it was clear that he wanted to belong to a group bigger than himself. This new career not only uses that good heart in the service of a charitable cause but gains him a new circle of friends, a new family if you will, that actually serves part of his old family, in terms of the homeless and the needy.

Ray's shares his story with Barney, "I was at a real low point, even for me. You know, sleeping in doorways, giving blood three to four times a week, picking through trash cans for half-eaten hot dogs. Then something incredible happened. I was going down an alley jiggling doorknobs . . . and I found one that wasn't locked." Barney guesses that it was a church but no, Ray corrects him, "Liquor store. And there I was, all alone at a booze buffet. And I went for it. Red wine. White wine and that blue stuff that goes great with any dish. Apricot brandy, Kahlua, Drambuie, I drank whiskey out of an Elvis decanter!

"But for some reason, I felt empty. Then at one point or another, I must have blacked out because when I came to a coupla weeks later, I was on the subway! I was driving it! That's when I realized that my life lacked direction."

The blue stuff that goes great with any dish was Blue Nun, an affordable German white wine very popular in America in the 1970s and popularized by a series of radio ads by the husband-and-wife comedy team of Jerry Stiller and Anne Meara.

An Army Matter

Ray's trip to the precinct is precipitated by a robbery at the Salvation Army Center. However, when his boss, the attractive young Lt. Melinda Holley, played by actress Maggie Brown, learns he's reported the crime to the police, she doesn't want to pursue it, telling Wojo, "You see Sergeant, our policy is to deal with problems like this internally. We're in the business of helping people that do this." Wojo asks, "If you can't catch them how can you help them?"

She makes out a report listing the items stolen from various locations that includes an entire rack of pool cues from the Community Center." When Wojo expresses surprise at the pool cues, Lt. Holley tells him, "We're allowed to have fun as long as it doesn't include, alcohol, tobacco and drugs." Wojo smiles and asks, "Aren't you leaving one out?" She asks, "What'd you have in mind, a weekend in Havana?" He says no and wonders why she'd say such a thing? The reference is to Frank Loesser's and Abe Burrows' classic Broadway show, *Guys and Dolls*, where a gambler makes a bet that he can get a lovely but repressed female Salvation Army member to go to Havana with him.

Beautiful People

The hilarious Larry Gelman is featured as Sidney Boughton, a man denied a table at a fancy restaurant because he didn't quite measure up to their minimum standard for aesthetic appearance (or as he says, "I'm ugly"). He naturally takes offense and when Harris and Dietrich arrive, he has the maître d' in a headlock.

The owner insists on pressing charges. It seems Le Bon Mot (the good word) prides itself on its beautiful people clientele. If you're not attractive, you don't get in. Boughton looks to Barney, "All I wanted was an omelet and a glass of iced tea. Look, I admit that I'm no Gavin MacLeod but I don't think that I deserve to starve." The restaurant owner tells Boughton, "You left marks on a perfectly good waiter. I had to let him go."

Season 7, Episode 16:	"Contempt: Part 2."
Original Airdate:	March 19, 1981.
Writers:	Frank Dungan and Jeff Stein.
Director:	Noam Pitlik.
Cast of Characters:	Hal Linden (Barney), Steve Landesberg (Dietrich), Ron Glass (Harris), Max Gail (Wojo), Ron Carey (Levitt), Maggie Brown (Lt. Melinda Holly, Salvation Army), John Dullaghan (Ray Brewer), J. J. Barry (Arthur Duncan), Jack Murdock (Officer Perelli), William Windom (Cellmate—voice only).

The Rundown

Barney does a stretch in the pen. Wojo works with Ray and his commanding officer to try to find the person who's robbing various Salvation Army sites.

The Cake Is in the Mail

The gang visits Barney after his first night in jail. Barney notices a yellow ribbon on Levitt's lapel. When he asks Levitt about it, he responds, "I had one left over. I figured, what the hell, you're worth it. Have a good day one, sir." Levitt is referring to the recently ended Iran Hostage Crisis where fifty-two Americans were held against their will in Iran for 444 days from November 4, 1979, until January 20, 1981. To show support for the hostages, Americans wore yellow ribbons and displayed them in their yards as a reference to the number one hit song "Tie A Yellow Ribbon Round the Old Oak Tree," recorded in 1973 by Tony Orlando and Dawn. In the song a returning prisoner or prisoner of war (it is unclear which) writes his sweetheart and tells her that he's coming home and if she still wants him then she should "tie a yellow ribbon round the old oak tree." When his bus pulls up the tree is festooned with a hundred yellow ribbons.

Tough Time

Barney is losing his patience "doing time" and when Ray comes to visit, he lashes out saying, "I just wish somebody would explain to me why a man who's committed over twenty years of his life to what he knows is right, deserves to wind up in a rathole like this." The anger that builds in Barney in this episode is indicative of the frustration he feels the longer he's on the job. Throughout the course of the series he will, at times, question whether the work they do really makes a difference. This exasperation seems to grow as the years go by.

He's let out that afternoon because, according to Barney, "I guess the judge figured that between the two of us we were doing a fine job of destroying each other's careers so he postponed the trial a couple of weeks—he's going to try and work out some sort of compromise."

Just the Facts

- Barney's cellmate claims to have been on the October 8, 1943, cover of *Life Magazine*. In reality, there was no edition of *Life* on that date. The actual editions of the magazine were October 4 and October 11, 1943.
- The October 4, 1943 cover photo was of Anthony Biddle, an American Diplomat, while Mrs. John Cross was on the Oct 11, 1943 cover sporting a Half-Hat.
- The Salvation Army robber turns out to be Arthur Duncan, the same man who was previously arrested for assaulting and robbing the handicapped. Classy guy.

Season 7, Episode 17:	"The Doll."
Original Airdate:	March 26, 1981.
Writers:	Jordan Moffet and Nat Mauldin (story). Tony Sheehan (teleplay).
Director:	Noam Pitlik.
Cast of Characters:	Steve Landesberg (Dietrich), Max Gail (Wojo), Ron Carey (Levitt), Ron Glass (Harris), Hal Linden (Barney), Oliver Clark (Eugene Corbett), Dee Croxton (Christine Lawson), Philip Bruns (Elvin Swift), A. Martinez (Joseph Montoya), James Gregory (Inspector Luger).

The Rundown

A distraught woman comes into the squad room to report a rather odd kidnapping. A man gets swindled with a fake ticket on the Space Shuttle. Inspector Luger asks Barney's advice on how to spend his fortune.

Quite a Doll

A lady comes in to report the kidnapping of a doll named Victoria Ellen that is worth about $5,000. Following the instructions on a ransom note, they soon capture an all-too-trusting thief named Joseph Montoya, played by the talented A Martinez. He tried to fence the doll but everywhere he took it, they made fun of him. He tells Harris, "the whole time I had her up in my room, you know, making up the ransom note. She kept staring at me with those little beady eyes . . . like she was human." Harris consoles him, saying, "Man, look, don't worry about it. You don't have to see her again until she testifies at the trial."

Heeeeeere's Vicki!!

Levitt needs to bring the doll to the property room but Barney is absent-mindedly cradling "the evidence" in his arms. Levitt asks, "Sir, can I take Miss Vicki now?"

The "Miss Vicki" reference calls to mind one of the most famous weddings in television history, that of pop singer Tiny Tim (born Herbert Butros Khaury) and his bride Miss Vicki (Victoria Budinger) who were married on *The Tonight Show Starring Johnny Carson* on December 17, 1969, in front of an audience of millions. It became an iconic moment in *Tonight Show* history as well as of the 1960s.

Opticians in Space!

The wonderful Oliver Clark returns to the 12th as Eugene Corbett, arrested for creating a disturbance at the Goddard Institute for Space Studies. He was trying to confirm his reservation on the Space Shuttle and shows them the ticket he bought from a man outside the planetarium for $500. Barney reads the ticket aloud, "NASA Champagne Shuttle, departing Cape Canaveral, Florida, 10 a.m. April 7, 1981, returning Edwards Air Force Base, April 8, 1981." Barney has to break the news to him that he's been defrauded.

Phil Bruns shows up as Elvin Swift, Space Shuttle relations. NASA is running short on money and Mr. Corbett broke a shuttle model that costs $75. When Corbett volunteers to pay for the model, Swift agrees not to press charges. Corbett hints he'll pay just about anything to go on the shuttle. Swift says, "We'll certainly take your money but I'm afraid that no passenger flights are as yet scheduled although they are envisioned by the end of this decade." (Passenger flights never happened, no doubt influenced by the Space Shuttle

Disaster of January 1986.) Swift tells him they're looking for mission specialists. When Corbett says he's just an optician, Swift says they're sending up a space telescope in 1984 and they're looking for opticians. If he qualifies with the right agencies, it's possible.

Quite a Rainy-Day Fund

Luger is going over his assets and since Barney is his sole heir he asks him what he should do with the money between now and his imminent departure. Barney tells him, "Inspector, all I can say is don't save it for me." Then Luger tells him he has $233,000.

Barney: I beg your pardon?
Luger: Yeah. Yeah, that's what I'm stuck with Barney. And you think I oughta do something crazy with it, huh?
Barney: Well, within reason.

Remember, this was $233,400 in 1981. That would be over $650,000 today. We don't want to call Inspector Luger cheap but "twenty years in that dingy one room apartment, one hot plate, eating in greasy spoons . . ." In fact when his Dumont broke down he wouldn't even buy a new TV.

The Last Word

Dietrich went to see the Three Stooges at the Gramercy. Levitt expresses his surprise. He didn't think Dietrich would go in for that kind of stuff. "Are you kidding? They're my favorites. I think they're one of the most underrated comedy teams of the thirties and forties. Surrealistic use of violence and mayhem, the almost Chekhovian interplay between Curly and Moe . . ."

Levitt: I like the ones with Shemp.
Dietrich: I don't think we have anything further to say to each other.

The Curly vs. Shemp debate is one that has gone on for years among Three Stooges aficionados. Personally, I like them both. I think the reason many don't like Shemp is he looks too much like his brother, Moe. Curly's lack of hair made the difference between the two more distinct.

Season 7, Episode 18: "Lady and the Bomb."
Original Airdate: April 9, 1981.

Writer:	Lee H. Grant.
Director:	Noam Pitlik.
Cast of Characters:	Ron Glass (Harris), Steve Landesberg (Dietrich), Ron Carey (Levitt), Hal Linden (Barney), Max Gail (Wojo), Peggy Pope (Doris Carlisle), James Murtaugh (Ron Giles), Judson Morgan (Frederick Houston), Ben Freedman (Milton Corshak), Howard Mann (Lou Carlisle), and special guest star, Abe Vigoda (Detective Fish).

The Rundown

Harris goes to court for the decision in his trial with Arnold Ripner over *Blood on the Badge*. Bored to death by retirement, Phil Fish returns to the 12th after an absence of more than three years. A woman complains that the hospital where her husband works is storing atomic medical waste that is affecting "his performance." Two elderly gentlemen assault one another over a game of chess they play through the mails.

Bomb Squad

Peggy Pope, in her fourth visit to the 12th Precinct, plays Doris Carlisle. She's afraid the nuclear medical waste being stored in the hospital where her husband works is sapping his strength and making him unable to perform in bed. She has gone through all the proper channels but no one is willing to address her concerns. The police are her last chance. When they can't help either, she produces a homemade bomb. This was long before the Internet so she went to one of those radical bookstores in the Village and bought a manual called *Recipes for the Revolution*.

Rookies and Veterans

James Murtaugh makes his first *Barney Miller* appearance as Ron Giles, a hospital administrator. Actor Judson Morgan appears in this episode as Frederick Houston in his third of four appearances. Morgan had appeared two times previously as Philip Lukeather before this role as the postal chess player Houston. He returns one final time to say good-bye to the gang in the series' final episode as their old pal, Mr. Lukeather.

Bad Day in Court

Harris returns from court a defeated man. He is oblivious to the bomb/hostage situation taking place, explaining the court awarded Ripner $320,000 in damages. When Levitt points Mrs. Carlisle out to Harris and says she's got a bomb and is threatening to set it off, Harris replies, "Fine."

Nothing Like Experience

Just like Fish's other post-retirement visit to the squad room (S. 4/Ep. 5 "Burial"), he helps the boys resolve an issue with a suspect through his unique perspective as the senior citizen of the group. Fish weaves his magic by explaining to Mrs. Carlisle that a man doesn't need to be exposed to radioactive waste to lose his abilities or desire to perform. When she asks what caused Fish's "lack of energy," he tells her, "I don't know. It just happened. People change. The years take their toll. It's all just a part of nature's rich pageantry."

The Last Word

This is Phil Fish/Abe Vigoda's last appearance on *Barney Miller*. As Fish leaves, Barney thanks him for his help and says, "Give my love to Bernice." Fish turns around, looks at Barney in the way that only Fish can and says, "Haven't you been listening?"

Season 7, Episode 19:	"Riot."
Original Airdate:	April 30, 1981.
Writers:	Greg Giangregorio (story). Frank Duncan and Jeff Stein (teleplay).
Director:	Noam Pitlik.
Cast of Characters:	Max Gail (Wojo), Hal Linden (Barney), Ron Glass (Harris), Ron Carey (Levitt), Steve Landesberg (Dietrich), Nehemiah Persoff (Yacov Berger), Howard Platt (Bill Nelson), Susan Tolsky (Wendy Nelson), Pat McNamara (Roland Kent), Victor Brandt (Mugger), James Gregory (Inspector Luger).

The Rundown

Harris appeals the $320,000 judgment awarded to Ripner in his defamation suit. The local Hasidic community feels the police are not doing enough to protect them from harassment. A survivalist couple takes up residence in the New York City sewers.

Old Friend

Nehemiah Persoff returns as Mr. Berger, the Hasidic diamond dealer (see S. 5/Ep. 18). He tells Barney, "A fine Jewish man is lying in a hospital room with three cracked ribs and a broken arm because you people failed to respond." He warns them that the Hasidic Community is upset. They are tired of being the easy target of criminals.

Soon a group of about two hundred Hasidic Jews are gathering outside the precinct. Inspector Luger says, "I'll just go down and straighten them out." Barney tries to dissuade him but the ol' inspector isn't having it. Soon, Dietrich answers a call from the front desk—the Hasidim are rioting.

A Riot Squad

The situation downstairs is wholesale destruction. A couple of cops need stitches and fifteen Hasidim are sent to the hospital. Luger returns to the squad room with his clothes torn to shreds. Barney asks what happened. Luger tells him, "I don't know, Barney. I walked out on the step and I says, 'This is Inspector Luger, NYPD, I want you to know we're working on your problem. In the meantime, why don't you all go home and take a shave.' Next thing I know, I wind up as a welcome mat."

Mr. Berger returns and Barney is disgusted and feels that the concerns of the Hasidic community did not justify a riot. When Berger says, "A drowning man will grab even the point of a sword," Barney, in a rare moment of losing his cool with a constituent says, "With all due respect Mr. Berger, you can stick that in your hat!"

Here Come the Nelsons

Bill and Wendy Nelson, played by Howard Platt and Susan Tolsky, are survivalists living in the steam tunnels of the subway with food and supplies to last six months. Mr. Nelson tells Barney, "It's over. This society is on the verge of collapse, Captain." They tell Barney they're going to be prepared as Dietrich produces their stash of two twenty-two caliber rifles, pellet guns, an assortment of knives, a bayonet, and a slingshot. The sewer residence is temporary. According to Mrs. Nelson, "We have our eye on a lovely old National Guard Armory in Maine."

The NRA Ideal

Pat McNamara is Roland Kent, owner of Armageddon Supply and Minimart where the Nelsons purchased all their weapons and supplies. Kent tells Barney, "one of the very keys to survival is the procurement of undocumented firearms . . . social collapse is just a step away and then martial law. You leave a trail of paperwork, soon you'll have the gun confiscation squad kicking in your door, violating your rights, violating your wife, leaving you defenseless."

Barney, repulsed and exhausted says, "No, maybe you're right Mr. Kent. Maybe it is all coming apart. You've got people of law and faith behaving like animals, cops who can't even make a dent in crime. We've got Ozzie and Harriet living in a sewer. Maybe it is all over. But I'll tell you something, crawling into a hole with a machine gun and a year's supply of powdered eggs may be survival but it sure as hell ain't living. And personally, if society is going, I just as soon go with it because I do not relish starting all over again with people like you."

Where's My Ball

In the melee of the office Wojo wonders where his signed baseball is? At the very end of the episode, he tells Barney he's been cleaning up and still can't find his ball. Harris says, "I think Luger took it." What, again? See "The Social Worker" (S. 2/Ep. 2).

The Last Word

Berger: Who knows? Maybe something good will come out of all of this?
Barney: Maybe, but I seriously doubt it.
Berger: That's good. Too much hope can drive you crazy.

Season 7, Episode 20: "The Vests."
Original Airdate: May 7, 1981.
Writer: Nat Mauldin.
Director: Noam Pitlik.
Cast of Characters: Ron Carey (Levitt), Hal Linden (Barney), Ron Glass (Harris), Max Gail (Wojo), Don Calfa (Arthur Thompson), Alice Hirson (Dorothy St. Clair), Warren Munson (John Norvis), James Gregory (Inspector Luger).

The Rundown

The squad is issued new bulletproof vests. An inventor causes a disturbance at a company that claims to be helping him market his product. A released mental patient has a standoff with the police.

A Sobering Thought

Barney is trying out the bulletproof vest and Wojo asks him, "C'mon, tell the truth. What do you think?" Barney replies, "There's definitely a feeling of security. Then again, it's a constant reminder of what it's there to prevent. What scares me is that a little thing like this can be the difference between living and dying."

Wojo: Well, I been thinking about it and you know what occurred to me? The contract to make them went to the lowest bidder.

Barney: That's very profound.

Thanks, But No Thanks

In the end, Wojo chooses not to use his vest because he doesn't like the fact that they make him feel invincible. He tells the Captain, "Barn, I don't know about anybody else, okay, but when I put that thing on, I feel, like some kind of super cop. If I start feeling like I can't get hurt then I forget that maybe I can hurt somebody else."

In the end, Barney lets the men make their own decision and all of them decide against keeping their vests. We're not completely sure how Barney feels about this but Luger seems to approve, "So, you decided to live dangerously, huh? Bully for you! It's the way to go! Why, if you put on those things, it's just the same as admitting to all that scum and killers out in the street that you're scared of them! That you'd rather hide behind some sissy little apron instead of going down like a real cop!" Luger's statement has Dietrich rethinking his decision.

A Sunny Idea

Barney Miller favorite Don Calfa returns in this episode as an inventor named Arthur Thompson. He's arrested for destruction of private property at Inventrex, a company that charges a fee to market and develop ideas like Thompson's invention of tan alert, a machine that warns you of potential sunburn. This was the weakest storyline and character that Calfa was given in his seven appearances on the show.

Call Me Blanche

The men come back from a standoff with an older woman named Dorothy St. Clair played by Alice Hirson. The landlord was pressuring her for non-payment of rent but she "didn't realize it was such a serious infraction" because "I've only been paying rent for such a short time." Dietrich informs Barney that, "Until recently, Miss St. Clair was a resident of the East Side Psychiatric Center. She was released as part of a program to integrate patients back into the community." Miss St. Clair quips, "I believe it's called dumping."

When Harris offers her coffee or tea she asks for tea and tells him, "You know, Sergeant, I have always been dependent on the kindness of strangers." When he asks, "Didn't Blanche DuBois say that?" She responds, "Not to me."

Season 7, Episode 21:	"The Rainmaker."
Original Airdate:	May 14, 1981.
Writers:	Paul Hunter (story), Frank Dungan (story), and Jeff Stein (story). Frank Dungan (teleplay) and Jeff Stein (teleplay).
Director:	Noam Pitlik.
Cast of Characters:	Ron Glass (Harris), Hal Linden (Barney), Max Gail (Wojo), Steve Landesberg (Dietrich), Ron Carey (Levitt), J. Pat O'Malley (Walter Dooley), Leonard Stone (Ernest Lun) Beatrice Colen (Lilian Hamilton), Bruce MacVittie (Gerald Clayton).

The Rundown

A lack of rain combined with a quickly drying reservoir is causing concern in the city. A rainmaker starts a fire in the park and a foreigner from the Far North gets mugged.

Does He Dance?

The men get called to the scene of a bonfire in the middle of Washington Square Park. They think it could be arson until they discover it's just lovable Walter Dooley, played by the inimitable J. Pat O'Malley, singing over the flames and dangling a chicken. He's a rainmaker who claims he was hired by the city to end the drought.

Mr. Lum of the Water Department, played by everyone's favorite harried bureaucrat Leonard Stone, arrives at the 12th and is naturally embarrassed. He doesn't want anyone to know he hired Dooley. He tells Barney, "When this Dooley character came along and was spouting off about how he could make it rain, well, I suppose, somebody in the office must have figured, why not give it a shot?"

Barney: That would be you.
Lum: Could have been. Captain, I mean, if it ever leaks to the press that some drip from the Water Department hired a rainmaker at the taxpayer's expense well, now, that could prove to be very embarrassing to everybody involved.
Barney: That would be you.
Lum: You keep saying that!

Stranger in a Strange Land

Lilian Hamilton, native of Canada, is this week's mugging victim but she's the one who feels guilty. She realizes that as a foreigner, she was an obvious target. She spots her robber in the mug books and the men bring him in. Bruce MacVittie as the assailant Gerald Clayton complains, "That Canadian junk might look pretty, just try and spend it. The guy wouldn't even take fifty dollars worth for a lousy cup of coffee and danish. Then, he throws it in my face. Calls me a deserter." Clayton proudly says, "I was in jail during that war!" He's referring to the fact that many American draft-age men fled to Canada during the Vietnam War to avoid participation in what they felt was an unjust war.

Singin' in the Rain

When it starts to rain, Mr. Dooley has a big grin on his face. A wet Mr. Lum comes running in with Mr. Dooley's water-soaked bail ticket, "I did it! I gotta get back to the department. When I tell them where this rain came from, they aren't going to believe it." Barney says, "You're probably right." Mr. Lum's face drops.

Vice Is Nice

In one of the stranger storylines we've seen, there is an opening posted in the Vice Squad and everybody applies. When they discover the unintentional plan for wholesale desertion Wojo wonders why they all want to leave. Barney is hurt but won't show it and suggests, "This is not exactly the time or place for this kind of discussion."

Harris replies, "Aw, c'mon, Barn. I mean it's not just you. It's all of us. Barney, we've all had our moments together, some, damn good ones. But there just don't seem to be a whole lot left."

That's when Barney snaps and says, "What the hell difference does it make to me? I mean, one of you may leave, eventually all of you are going to leave and I'm gonna be stuck right here!" He reconsiders what he's said and apologizes, telling them they don't owe him anything, "It's just that I been watching you guys for a lot of years. It's going to be hard to let go."

It seems like the ennui of the entire squad comes on rather suddenly. However, it should be noted that Danny Arnold initially considered ending the show following this Seventh Season. Was this his way of setting up a proper ending?

Season 7, Episode 22: "Liquidation."
Original Airdate: May 21, 1981.
Writers: Frank Dungan (written by) and Jeff Stein (written by).
Director: Noam Pitlik.
Cast of Characters: Ron Glass (Harris), Hal Linden (Barney), Max Gail (Wojo), Ron Carey (Levitt), Steve Landesberg (Dietrich), Walter Olkewicz (Walter Cushing), James Cromwell (Jason Parrish), Martin Garner (Martin Golden).

The Rundown

Harris goes to court to appeal Ripner's original judgment against him. One man learns to make his daily routine pay dividends while another sings to overcome his fear of social interaction.

Take It Easement

Martin Garner plays Martin Golden, a man arrested for trespassing, destruction of private property, and aggravated assault. Golden cut through a construction site to get to his newsstand. When the workers tried to stop him, he took a swing at them. Golden says, "For twenty years I had a perfectly vacant lot to walk across. And now, boom. In one day as if it fell from the sky, I got a bunch of roughnecks putting up a building." When Dietrich suggests he change his route he says, "I can't walk down that street. The hookers won't leave me alone. They love to harass me. 'Hey stud, want to party? Looking for a good time?' Tell me, Sergeant, do I look like I'm looking for a good time?" Dietrich, "Not to me."

James Cromwell is Jason Parrish, legal counsel for Liberty Bell Development Corporation, a multinational investment syndicate made up of French, West German, and Kuwaiti interests. Dietrich gets the lawyer's attention when he tells him that Mr. Golden's use of the property to get to his place of business for the past twenty years has created an easement, meaning he has the right to have the building moved, redesigned, or taken down. Cromwell then gets his bosses on the phone to explain the problem to them in English, French and German.

With his clients still on the phone, Parrish says, "My clients have decided not to proceed against Mr. Golden. Assuming, of course, Mr. Golden agrees not to proceed against us, okay?" Mr. Golden slyly says, "Oh, that's very generous of you but I prefer that the building come down." In the end, Mr. Golden does some fancy horse-trading and gets a new indoor newsstand, an all-expense paid trip to Europe, and a female companion to accompany him.

I Love to Singa

Walter Olkewicz plays Walter Cushing, a man involved in a type of therapy that teaches you to lose your inhibitions by singing in public. They picked him up in the housewares department at Siegel's. He approached the lady doing a yogurt demonstration and went into a chorus of *Hey Good Lookin', What You Got Cookin'?* He started driving people away so the manager asked him to stop but he just kept singing. Cushing points out that, "In the movies when people used to start singing everybody would join in. In real life they just look at you like you're crazy."

Breakdown

The episode is entitled "Liquidation" but it could have just as easily been called "Breakdown" because that's basically what happens to Harris after he loses the appeal to Ripner. The judgement against Harris for $320,000 essentially bankrupts him. He has to liquidate all his assets, leaving him with nothing after having ridden the wave of fame and fortune in the wake of his first published novel.

Harris returns from court drunk. Barney leads him to the inner office to sleep it off. He wakes up and looks like hell. Barney asks him, "How's it going Harris?" His reply is, "You are looking at one mad N*gg*r." Barney is obviously taken aback by the statement and so are we. It wasn't unusual to hear that word on Norman Lear vehicles like *All in the Family* or *Good Times* in the 1970s but this was the only time that word was ever used on *Barney Miller*.

Harris puts his head down on his desk in abject defeat and starts crying. Cue Mr. Cushing in the cage as he starts singing, "Next time you're found with your chin on the ground there's a lot to be learned, so look around. Just what makes that little ol' ant thinks he'll move a rubber tree plant . . ." It's a perfect example of the magic of *Barney Miller*. Some of the more acclaimed sitcoms of the 1970s might easily have ended this episode with Harris in tears. In the *Barney Miller* universe, however, no matter how serious the situation (with the possible exception of episodes related to Nazis), there is still a way to deal with it through humor. As Mr. Cushing pushes through singing the entire "High Hopes" song, Harris reaches for where his gun was before Barney took it away from him.

Eighth Season

This is the final season of the show. Arnold was going to end the show after Season Seven but his arch-nemesis, Ted Flicker, claimed he was doing that to hurt Flicker's bottom line. If we look at Danny Arnold's history and the personal picture that's been painted of him by those who knew him best, it's doubtful that Flicker's threats are the actual reason he pushed on through an eighth season. It could also be he wanted to put his personal imprint on one last season. Tony Sheehan left the show once Danny returned, but Danny asked him to come back and help out with the three-part series finale. It was a very different type of season because Dungan and Stein, who'd written most of the episodes in Season Seven, were Tony Sheehan's proteges, not Danny Arnold's. That is most likely the reason there are more freelancers who return to contribute to that show's final season. In a related issue, it's also worth noting that the credits for Season Eight no longer list Dungan and Stein's names as story editors. Instead they are now producers.

I think you can see and feel a difference in Season Eight due to Danny's return, particularly from Season Seven. There is more of a focus on the awareness that "we're all stuck in this rat race together" that permeates the proceedings. Barney and the men show that any assistance, understanding, and empathy we can extend to one another can only help the situation.

Season 8, Episode 1: "Paternity."
Original Airdate: October 29, 1981.
Writer: Nat Mauldin (written by).
Director: Danny Arnold.
Cast of Characters: Ron Glass (Harris), Hal Linden (Barney), Steve Landesberg (Dietrich), Max Gail (Wojo), Ron Carey (Levitt), Stefan Gierasch (Victor Lupton), Rebecca Holden (Wendy McWilliams), Dana Gladstone (Arthur Frane), Pierrino Mascarino (Joseph Banning).

The Rundown

A beauty pageant contestant gets mugged. Wojo gets hit with a paternity suit and a man disrupts a movie theater protesting the gratuitous violence of the films being shown.

Smile and Stay Positive

Rebecca Holden appears as Wendy McWilliams, a contestant in the Miss New York State Thruway beauty pageant. She finished fourth runner-up because, as Harris correctly guessed, she dropped her baton.

Come to Papa

Wojo gets hit with a paternity suit but the mother's name, Maureen Elizabeth Ballantine, doesn't ring any bells for him. Wojo asks Barney, "So, you have any idea who she is?" Later, he recalls that he met her in a beauty parlor. "It was snowing real hard and I just went inside to get warm and I saw Maureen giving some old lady a manicure, you know, so, the next thing I know, she's got a kid." Apparently, someone forgot to give Wojo "the talk."

Wojo's blood test reveals that he's sterile which means he's not the father of Ms. Ballantine's child. It also leaves him less than secure in his own manhood.

Everyone's a Critic

The highlight of the episode is Dana Gladstone as Arthur Frane, a moviegoer who snaps at his local theater, enters the projection booth, knocks out the projectionist, and starts cutting up the film and throwing it into the audience like confetti. This was Gladstone's only appearance on *Barney Miller*, which is a shame because he is hilarious as the distraught Mr. Frane.

The name of the offensive film is *Arbor Day* about some cute little cub scouts on a camping trip to plant trees. He describes the horror, "and they're singing their songs and they're planting trees and before you know it, somebody starts killing them off. One kid takes a sapling right through the brain."

Dietrich: Park Ranger, right?
Frane: They trusted that man!

He then describes in graphic detail how the audience changed through the course of the film. They began "behaving as a pack of jackals in a slaughterhouse!" Barney tries to calm Frane down and finally he tells Barney, "If that widescreen horror and carnage isn't stopped then somebody is really going to snap and do something crazy." Barney looks at him and says, "Like you." Frane's reply, "See?"

Hard to Please

Barney Miller favorite Stefan Gierasch makes his final appearance as Victor Lupton, owner and manager of the Tivoli Theater, where Mr. Frane had his breakdown. Lupton was left with "an unconscious projectionist, a ruined print, [and] two hundred animals stampeding through my lobby demanding a refund." When Mr. Frane complains that the movie was "pandering to the dankest recesses of the human mind," Lupton says, "It was almost over!"

Frane berates Lupton, telling him to run some good movies. Lupton yells, "Where were you when I played *Dodsworth*, *Paths of Glory*, *African Queen*? You weren't in my theater! Nobody was in my theater until I started playing trash like, *Arbor Day*, *Hotel Hacksaw*, *Mermaids from Hell*!"

Lupton allows Frane to work off the $600 for the print replacement cost as an usher in this theater. When Lupton says, "I can probably find a print of *Stella Dallas* in the basement," Frane complains about that film as well. Lupton asks, "Listen you, how would you like to sit through a George Brent Comedy Film Festival?"

Season 8, Episode 2: "Advancement."
Original Airdate: November 5, 1981.
Writers: Frank Dungan and Jeff Stein.

Director:	Danny Arnold.
Cast of Characters:	Ron Glass (Harris), Hal Linden (Barney), Max Gail (Wojo), Steve Landesberg (Dietrich), Martin Garner (Ira Buckman), Howard Honig (Mr. Yager), Anna Berger (Miriam Buckman), Mario Roccuzzo (Ed Brotsky), Philip Simms (Anthony Shapper), James Gregory (Inspector Luger).

The Rundown

A new business owner gets robbed on the day of his grand opening. Harris may have a deal in the works to write a gruesome new paperback. A couple come to the precinct claiming their lives are in danger from a man who wants to kill them.

A Natural Salesman

Regular guest player Mario Roccuzzo is Ed Brodsky from Ed's House of Mugs. He gets robbed before he officially opens his store on the first day of business. Brodsky finds his assailant in the mug books just as Harris is running off to a lunch meeting with a potential new publisher. Barney stops him, saying, "Listen Harris, for two years, I put up with cocktail parties, autograph sessions, late lunches and it's not going to happen again! Understood?"

They arrest robber Anthony Shapper, played by Philip Simms, and book him. When Harris tells Barney's he's running Shapper to the tombs and then going home, Barney says, "I'm going to get Wojo to do that, maybe we can—" Harris says, "Talk?" He laughs in his face and says, "Good night," and walks out of Barney's office. This is a grudge that will carry over into the next episode.

Take a Number

Martin Garner and Anna Berger play the Buckmans, owners of a deli who are being threatened by a Mr. Yager because Mr. Buckman forgot to send in the lottery numbers from Mr. Yager's winning ticket. Howard Honig as Yager hasn't worked in eight months. The numbers he played every week came from the zip code of his mom's sanitarium in Plattsburgh. He dreamed of hitting it big so he could get his mother out of that snake pit. They find Yager robbing the Buckman's deli. Instead of pressing charges, the Buckmans want to give him enough money to get his mother out of Plattsburgh and send her to

Miami, at least for the winter. He breaks into tears because they're being so nice to him! All three actors are terrific in this standout scene of the episode. Yager doesn't want the money but Ira begs him. He finally agrees to take the money but only because of his mom. Miriam says, "What a wonderful son."

A Long Way to Tipperary

Luger comes in to tell Barney that, "As of 25 May, year of our Lord 19 and 82, in accordance with the official policies of the NYPD, Inspector Frank D. Luger will cease to exist." Interesting because just last season he said his retirement date was 1984 but now he's being forcibly retired. Luger's vision for his future is bleak, "sitting on some lousy park bench, pigeons flying around peckin' at my hat, snotty little kids running around spittin' at me."

His biggest concern is that he has no one by his side to help him face retirement. "After all," he tells Barney, "I mean ol' Foster, Kleiner, Brownie, right now they're nothin' but worm mush. And you? You'll be stuck in this lousy little office for another twenty years or so. Fish? Fish never returns my phone calls." Now *this* is quite a revelation. He's been calling Phil Fish to no avail? Who knew?

Oddities

Thankfully, this is the last episode in which we're subjected to the really pretentious Ron Harris. Soon, his humility and humanity return for good but not before we hear this odd utterance from him.

"I left it in the W.C." W.C. being short for Water Closet, a term originating in England for bathroom. He has *never* used that term before.

The Last Word

Barney starts writing Luger's first letter to a potential mail order bride and as he writes the salutation he looks to the heavens and says, "Compassion. I really needed it." It's the character's perfect self-realized commentary on his role in life and in the series.

Season 8, Episode 3: "The Car."
Original Airdate: November 12, 1981.
Writer: Nat Mauldin.
Director: Bruce Bilson.

Cast of Characters: Ron Glass (Harris), Hal Linden (Barney), Max Gail (Wojo), Steve Landesberg (Dietrich), Ron Carey (Levitt), Joe Regalbuto (Officer Earl Slatic, Sanitation Police), Pat McNamara (Burt Boskin), Larry Gelman (Joseph Hilyer), Alice Backes (Miss Louise Shawcross).

The Rundown

Purely by accident, Wojo stumbles onto a car thief twenty-five years after he committed his crime. A sanitation officer has difficulty accepting the limits of his position. Levitt performs his duties heroically and Harris makes a shocking confession.

All in a Day's Work

Levitt takes a call to chase some kids away from equipment at a construction site on Amsterdam. The routine call turns into a heroic moment for Levitt when he rescues a young boy hanging onto a broken scaffold on the side of a building. In the course of saving the kid, Levitt loses his grip and falls, making a perfect three-point landing on another scaffold one floor below."

When Dietrich returns with Levitt, he's got a foam collar around his neck and his arm is in a sling. Levitt plays down the injuries but Dietrich says, "He's got a fractured wrist, a very decent neck sprain, [and] the doctor said he should be off his feet for the next two weeks." Barney tells him they're proud of him and to go home and rest. When Barney says he's going to put him up for a medal of valor, Levitt deadpans, "Sir, you must be toying with me."

Showroom Condition

Larry Gelman as Mr. Hilyer is arrested for spraying a group of Japanese tourists with glass cleaner for smudging his car. He also took a swing at Wojo because, "He looked like a chrome smudger."

The car in question, a 1957 DeSoto Fireflite, was stolen by Mr. Hilyer on October 6, 1957. Introduced in 1955, the car was produced for six years until Chrysler discontinued the entire DeSoto line of cars in November of 1960.

Wojo finds the owner, a mild-mannered spinster named Louise Shawcross played by Alice Backes, who filed the stolen car report in 1957. Hilyer introduces himself to Miss Shawcross, and she says, "I must say, Joseph, you've taken very good care of the car."

Hilyer: Sure. I've devoted half my life to it.
Shawcross: You must love the DeSoto very much.
Hilyer: Are you kidding? We haven't been apart for one day all these years. You know, if this didn't happen, I was going to surprise her next month with a set of classic plates. You know, for our twenty-fifth anniversary.

Larry Gelman was in a total of four *Miller* episodes and was hilariously funny in every one. A ubiquitous comic character actor, he appeared on dozens of TV shows of the 1970s and 1980s including recurring roles on *The Odd Couple*, *The Bob Newhart Show*, *Maude*, and *Eight Is Enough* (1977-1981).

Isn't This Standard?

Wojo says he checked with the DA for fun and the statute of limitations on the car theft was up eighteen years ago. Wait, what? Why would he have to check? He's a police officer. Shouldn't he know the statute of limitations on car theft? This may explain why Wojo had to take the sergeant's exam five times before passing it.

A Comrade in Arms

A young and very funny Joe Regalbuto guests as Officer Slatic of the Sanitation Police. He's brought in for prodding a man with his nightstick forcing him to crawl around on the ground and pick up cigarette butts and candy wrappers. "I identified myself as a Sanitation Officer and he laughed at me and just kept walking." That's when Officer Slatic fired two warning shots into the air. "You don't make a mess on my beat and just walk away!"

Writer's Block

At the start of the episode, Harris is sulking over the missed meeting from the previous episode but when he gets another call from his agent he tells Wojo he can't take it. Barney insists that Harris go to the meeting. He says, "*I'll* cover for you!" That's when Harris reveals the truth, "I can't! I can't write anymore. This whole thing was a joke."

Later he explains to his co-workers that, "What it really comes down to is that I haven't been able to write a thing since *Blood on the Badge*. I mean, I tried, I really have. I sit, I stare at my typewriter and uh, nothing happens." He then tells Barney that, in truth, he really appreciated Barney not letting him go to those meetings about the new book.

Season 8, Episode 4:	"Possession."
Original Airdate:	November 19, 1981.
Writers:	Tom Reeder and Roland Kibbee.
Director:	Bruce Bilson.
Cast of Characters:	Ron Carey (Levitt), Steve Landesberg (Dietrich), Hal Linden (Barney), Ron Glass (Harris), Max Gail (Wojo), Allan Miller (Father Clement), Kenneth Tigar (Stefan Kopechne), Susan Peretz (Norma Griswold), Phil Rubenstein (Roy Griswold).

The Rundown

An old friend returns to the 12th but brings along a rather devilish associate. A wife assaults her husband for trying to make her into something she's not.

The Return of Stefan Kopechne

On the way to work Wojo catches a man throwing a garbage can through a store window. Turns out to be our old friend, Stefan Kopechne, the man who previously visited the 12th convinced he was a werewolf. He's now possessed by a demon named Belial. Ken Tigar reprises the role of Kopechne in his sixth, and final, *Barney Miller* appearance.

Who Dat?

According to the Dead Sea Scrolls, Belial was the King of Evil. In Hebrew it means "worthless" and later came to represent the devil. Kopechne wants to be exorcised by a priest rather than go to Bellevue. Barney doesn't want to hear it until Dietrich informs him that satanic possession was recently used in a Connecticut murder case as a defense. When Kopechne starts smashing his head against the bars of the cage, bouncing up and down and hangs upside down against the bars of the cell, Barney is spooked and relents to calling in a priest.

Bless Me, Father

Allan Miller arrives as Father Clement in his last of four *Barney Miller* roles. Kopechne's demon begins mocking the priest until he snaps and attacks

Kopechne. Father Clement now feels he's failed as a priest because he allowed himself to be provoked to attack a man in need. His guilt is assuaged when Kopechne, temporarily out of the control of the demon, sees him and having no memory of what just happened asks for the good father's help. The scene ends with Father Clement agreeing to accompany him to Bellevue.

Ken Tigar said they used a small trampoline for the jumping up and down and he slipped his feet through the bars above to hang upside down.

In a Tight Spot

Susan Peretz and Phil Rubenstein are the Griswolds. Mr. Griswold is a widower and Mrs. Griswold is his second wife. Unfortunately, Mr. Griswold is having a difficult time letting go of the memory of his first wife. He talks about her, compares his new wife to her, and when his new wife asks for a coffee mug he buys her one with the name Cynthia on it. Unfortunately, her name is Norma. Cynthia was his first wife's name. Norma knocks him upside the head with the mug inflicting a gash worthy of a few stitches and an arrest for spousal abuse.

There is no storybook ending for these two, just more *Barney Miller* realism. Mr. Griswold chooses not to press charges against his wife but she leaves acknowledging her need to get used to rejection.

Father Paul?

When the police priest shows up Dietrich tells Wojo that he once considered studying for the priesthood himself but he couldn't stand being celibate. Wojo asks him, "Well, how do you know? You don't have to be until after you're ordained."

>**Dietrich:** I practiced.
>**Wojo:** For how long.
>**Dietrich:** Three and a half, no, four hours.

It seems both Dietrich and Wojo completely forgot about Father Paul from The Church of the Street. (S. 2/Ep. 1.)

The Last Word

>**Norma:** (to Roy) Let's face it, Roy, you cannot have two women at the same time.
>**Harris:** Not if you want to be sharp the next day.

Season 8, Episode 5: "Stress Analyzer."
Original Airdate: November 26, 1981.
Writer: Nat Mauldin.
Director: Bruce Bilson.
Cast of Characters: Hal Linden (Barney), Steve Landesberg (Dietrich), Ron Glass (Harris), James Cromwell (Dr. Edmund Danworth), James Murtaugh (Peace Corps Recruiter Vincent Bondell), Phil Leeds (Brent LaMear), Florence Halop (Wanda LaMear), Ann Morgan Guilbert (Ms. Swallock), Rod Colbin (William Jessup), James Gregory (Inspector Luger).

The Rundown

A doctor, studying the stress level of police officers, hooks Dietrich up to a stress monitor and gives the squad quite a scare. A Peace Corps recruiter busts up a NYU job fair and a woman comes in to complain about the lady across the alley trying to steal her husband.

National Service

James Murtaugh returns to the precinct in the meatiest of his three *Barney Miller* roles as Vincent Bondell, a frustrated Peace Corps recruiter. The 1980s had begun and Ronald Reagan was creating a policy of taking from the poor to give to the rich. In a few more years Gordon Gekko would espouse the "Greed is good" ethics of the decade in the film *Wall Street* (1987). The changing times are frustrating to a guy like Bondell who believes in public service. At the job fair, all the young recruits are flocking to the high-paying employers and ignoring his Peace Corps pitch. Bondell finally snaps and tears apart the Xerox booth. According to Harris, when he and Wojo arrived, "Mr. Bondell had the Xerox recruiter in a headlock trying to get a photocopy of his face."

Sexy Housekeeping

Florence Halop returns to the 12th, this time as Mrs. Wanda LaMear who fears her husband is having an affair with the mystery woman across the alley. The men answer a call about a disturbance in LaMear's apartment building and arrive to find that "Mrs. LaMear was chasing the mystery woman, Miss Swallock, around the apartment, blasting everything in sight with one of those high-pressure fire hoses you get in the hallway."

Ann Morgan Guilbert makes her one and only *Barney Miller* appearance as Ms. Swallock, "the flashy blonde." To Baby Boomers Guilbert was most famous for her role as Millie Helper, the nosy but sweet next-door neighbor to Rob and Laura Petrie on *The Dick Van Dyke Show*. To a later generation, she's probably more recognizable as Yetta Rosenberg on the TV series, *The Nanny* (1993–1999). Guilbert died in 2016 at the age of eighty-seven.

Stress and Strain

Dietrich partakes in a program to study the stressful aspects of a police officer's daily routine. James Cromwell is Dr. Edmund Danworth, a cardiologist who works for the department and runs the study. He attaches electrodes to Dietrich that will track his pulse, blood pressure, and nerve impulses on a monitor in the squad room. When Dietrich goes out on the call to the LaMear's apartment, his signals get erratic and then stop suddenly. Concerned they ask Danworth what it all means and he hints Dietrich may be dead. Barney is horrified, calls dispatch and learns, "They have reports of people running out of the building screaming, windows being blown out of the fifth floor . . ."

Turns out Mrs. LaMear was blasting the fire hose at Miss Swallock when she hit Dietrich and the intensity of the water disconnected his electrodes. In the end, Mr. LaMear pays for the damages to Miss Swallock's apartment and she drops all charges. By the way, the sexy Mr. LaMear turns out to be none other than loveable, frog-faced Phil Leeds.

Why the Hostility?

Once Dietrich returns safely with the water-soaked equipment that was monitoring his vital signs, Dr. Danforth packs up his gear and prepares to leave. He says to Barney, "Anyway, I just wanted to apologize for making things kind of hectic around here. Sort of defeated the whole purpose of the program, doesn't it?" Barney tersely says, "Goodbye, doctor." Barney's hostility towards the doctor is strange. The guy was just doing his job and Dietrich had volunteered for the program. In the last couple of seasons, Barney could be much more prickly than he was in the early years of the program, and often without a great deal of provocation.

Season 8, Episode 6: "Games."
Original Airdate: December 10, 1981.
Writer: Jordan Moffet.

Director:	Gennaro Montanino.
Cast of Characters:	Max Gail (Wojo), Hal Linden (Barney), Steve Landesberg (Dietrich), Ron Glass (Harris), Philip Sterling (Frank Rilling, FBI), Carol Rossen (Sgt. Lake), Sarah Kennedy (Spec. Alice Grant), John O'Leary (Leo Hadden, KGB), Vernon Weddle (Lawrence Oaks), Trinidad Silva (Puente), Warren Munson (James Seinbeck).

The Rundown

Wojo arrests a most unlikely hooker and a low-level thief stumbles onto a potential sale of computer chips to be used for weapons systems.

Help for Mother

The adorable Sarah Kennedy as Specialist Alice Grant of the US Army is brought in for soliciting. Her service pay isn't enough to cover her rent and help pay for her mother's nursing home so she needed extra money.

Sarah Kennedy worked a little over a decade as an actress, scoring her first big break as a regular on the final season of the NBC comedy/variety show, *Rowan & Martin's Laugh-In*. She went on to appear in shows such as *Love, American Style*, *Barnaby Jones* (1973-1980), and *Laverne & Shirley*. It would appear that *Barney Miller* was her last major television appearance.

Carol Rossen plays her superior, Sgt. Lake, who comes to the precinct to pick her up. Rossen appeared in numerous episodes of the 1961 drama *The Lawless Years* (1959–1961) starring James Gregory. Unfortunately, as Inspector Luger doesn't appear in this episode, Rossen and her old co-star miss out on the opportunity for an onscreen reunion.

Frank & Leo, Ralph & Sam

A young thief is caught attempting to rob a warehouse. One of the stolen items is a box that Dietrich (of course) recognizes as $15–$20,000-worth of microprocessor chips that were headed for Wolinski Importing Company, Gdansk, Poland. Dietrich is suspicious of the end use for such chips and Barney tells him to call the FBI.

John O'Leary guests as Leo Hadden, owner of Delancy Exports while Philip Sterling plays FBI man Frank Rilling in his fifth *Barney Miller* role. Leo and Frank greet one another warmly as old friends and we learn that Hadden is actually a KGB agent. Rilling and Hadden have been friendly adversaries for years. The situation is wonderfully reminiscent of the classic Warner Brothers cartoons that featured Sam the Sheepdog and Ralph Wolf, a dead ringer for Wile E. Coyote with very subtle differences. The two walk to work every morning and chat amiably until they reach the meadow, where they both punch in at a time clock attached to a tree. Once the morning whistle blows. Ralph attempts to steal the sheep that Sam is guarding and Sam invariably stops him and beats the hell out of him for his effort. At the end of the day, the whistle blows and they walk home together as chums. For reference, see *Steal Wool* (1957).

Hadden claims the chips are to be used for video games but Dietrich and Rilling are suspicious. If the chips are going for military purposes, they can't be exported. If they are going to be used for electronic games, they can because, according to the law, "Non-reprogrammable chips can be exported if they're used in amusement devices." However, as Dietrich points out, "there's no such thing as non-reprogrammable chips if you can afford to reprogram them."

In the end, Leo our KGB agent is free to go but his chips are not. FBI Frank claims he's going to retire soon so they bid a fond farewell to one another. It's only after Leo leaves that Frank reveals to Barney that he'll never stop pursuing Leo.

A Sad Case

Trinidad Silva plays Puente, the guy who opens up the whole FBI/KGB incident when he attempts to rob the warehouse where the chips were stored. Silva was a familiar presence in 1970s and 1980s television appearing on shows such as *Baretta*, *The White Shadow* (1978–1981), and *Lou Grant* (1977–1982), as well as playing recurring character Jesus Martinez on *Hill Street Blues* from 1981–1987. Sadly, Silva was killed by a drunk driver during the filming of his final film, *UHF* (1989). He was only thirty-eight years old at the time.

Season 8, Episode 7: "Homeless."
Original Airdate: December 17, 1981.
Writers: Jordan Moffet, Frank Dungan, and Jeff Stein.
Director: Lee Lochhead.
Cast of Characters: Ron Glass (Harris), Ron Carey (Levitt), Max Gail (Wojo), Steve Landesberg (Dietrich), Hal Linden

(Barney), Stanley Brock (Bruno Bender), Ben Piazza (Arthur Minch), Don Calfa (Edward Pratken), David Clennon (Howard Weckler), Mari Gorman (Naomi Bender), Walter Janowitz (Sam Belinkoff), Zane Busby (Linda), Paul Stolarsky (Joseph Kellog).

The Rundown

A homeless man is arrested for camping out in a sporting goods store. A greeting card writer is angry at getting fired by Santa Claus at the office Christmas party.

No Room at the Inn

It's Christmas Eve in the city and an arrest brings the homeless crisis right into the squad room of the 12th Precinct. Don Calfa makes his seventh and final *Barney Miller* showing as Eddie Pratken, a homeless man who sneaks into Bruno Bender's sporting goods store at night to sleep. One morning Bender (Stanley Brock) discovers him in the store and attacks him with a cattle prod.

Wojo learns Pratken has a job in a diner where his boss says he's an honest, hard-working person. He and about fifty other people got thrown out of the $25-a-week hotel that was their home. Now they're all out on the street with no affordable place to live. Wojo calls the city's Human Resources Administration and they send Howard Weckler, played by actor David Clennon, who tells Barney that this homeless group are "just victims of J51—the city's new tax abatement program . . . to revitalize old neighborhoods. With hefty tax incentives in hand, real estate developers started buying up dilapidated properties . . . then gut them, refurbish them, and turn them into contemporary condominiums at 250 grand a pop." Mr. Weckler is talking about the gentrification process that succeeded in driving out the majority of middle-class citizens from the cultural centers of their respective cities.

He's Married?

To add to the mayhem, the men of the 12th are shocked to discover that Bruno Bender has a wife. When she tells Harris, "I'm looking for my husband, Bruno Bender." His response is, "Oh, I'm so sorry," to which she replies, somewhat puzzled, "Everyone says that."

When she approaches Bruno in the cage, he's surprised to see her and responds furiously to the news that she closed the store to come down and bail him out. As he yells at her she flinches, suggesting previous spousal abuse. Amazingly, the audience (or rather the laugh track) is laughing at this bit of business. Needless to say, few would find such a suggestion humorous today. In fact, both Hal Linden and Mari Gorman, who portrayed Naomi Bender, expressed their surprise and shock looking back on that aspect of the episode.

A Christmas Miracle

Bruno's frozen heart melts just like the Grinch's as from the cage he recognizes Eddie's sincerity and his friend Linda's (Zane Busby) good intentions. Not having witnessed Bruno's transformation as we did, Barney is shocked when Bruno tells him he's decided not to press charges. The entire squad room is shocked when he announces Eddie is coming home with him, saying, "Why not? I mean the little lady's gonna be spending half the night in the kitchen anyway and I got my choo-choo set up in the den so why don't you and Princess Grace (meaning Linda) here head on over?"

Corporate Scrooge

Paul Stolarsky is Joseph Kellogg in his only *Barney Miller* appearance as a greeting card writer who gets fired on Christmas Eve. When the boys arrived at the Loving Touch Greeting Card annual Christmas party, Kellogg was decking the halls by submerging Kris Kringle's head in the punch bowl. Kellogg was standing in line waiting for Santa to give him his Christmas bonus when the fat slob handed him a sympathy card with a pink slip in it. Ben Piazza plays the heartless boss, Arthur Minch. Not only does his Scrooge's heart *not* melt but he's relishing the sadistic firing that he conceived. He signs the complaint against Kellogg and walks out of the squad room as one of those rare people Barney is unable to sway with his humanism.

The Last Word

When Levitt asks Mr. Kellogg if he'd like to step into the squad room he says, "Why not, I'm a has-been. Where else am I going to go?" Harris says, "*Love Boat*?" and laughs. Interesting to note that *Love Boat* (1977-1987) was an ABC program just like *Barney Miller*. It's also a well-known fact that Danny Arnold didn't allow network executives on the set. No scripted show today would be allowed to practice such self-deprecating humor aimed at its own network. By the way, Captain Miller (Hal Linden), Sgt. Phil Fish (Abe Vigoda), and Inspector Luger (James Gregory) all "sailed" on *The Love Boat* at one time or another.

In another bit of inside network humor, the episode ends with a shot outside the squad room's window with the lights of their little Christmas tree shining through. In voiceover we hear the men saying "Good night" to one another in the tradition of the CBS drama *The Waltons* that had run concurrently or as a lead-in to *Barney Miller* on a different network (CBS) from 1975–1981.

Season 8, Episode 8: "The Tontine."
Original Airdate: January 7, 1982.
Writers: Dick Wesson and Nat Mauldin (story). Nat Mauldin (teleplay).
Director: Homer Powell.
Cast of Characters: Steve Landesberg (Dietrich), Hal Linden (Barney), Ron Glass (Harris), Max Gail (Wojo), Ivor Francis (Henry Mercurio), Ian Wolfe (Joseph Spidoni), Jay Robinson (Horace Sharp), Dennis Lipscomb (Lawrence Prine), Lou Cutell (Mr. Roselle), Jane Dulo (Mrs. Edna Sligman), Joseph V. Perry (Mr. Marken), Sam Ingraffia (Ambulance attendant).

The Rundown

A CPR instructor throws food at customers in a department store to get their attention. A man tries to jump to his death for the benefit of his cousin. Levitt rounds up the witnesses of his heroic venture.

Tough Way to Earn a Buck

Two cousins are the last remaining members of a legal contract called a tontine. It's a form of insurance where all members of a family or group put in a certain amount of money and the last person standing collects the dough. In this case, the last two are elderly gentlemen who, because of their fondness for one another, decide that one should commit suicide so the other can enjoy the money while he's still able.

Mr. Mercurio, played by Ivor Francis, and Mr. Spidoni, played by Ian Wolfe, believe that they have $3,000 coming to them. However, the law firm overseeing the agreement informs them that it's actually worth $700,000. They tell the lawyer, "That's not our tontine. We only put in $200 bucks a piece."

Mr. Sharp, the lawyer played by Jay Robinson, tells them, "Well, we didn't just sew up the money in a mattress, fellas."

Miscasting

Spidoni, Mercurio, Uncle Dominic, Uncle Carmine—It's fascinating to note that according to the names, we should be dealing with Italians and/or Sicilians. As a member of that ethnic group, I feel I have the right to say that neither of these gentlemen look or seem remotely Mediterranean in background. In fact, you couldn't get more English-looking players if you were casting Shakespeare's *Henry IV*.

Familiar Face

Legendary character actor Ian Wolfe plays Joseph Spidoni in this, his second and final *Barney Miller* appearance. Wolfe was a steady presence in films and television from the mid-1930s right on through his last acting job at the age of ninety-three in the feature film, *Dick Tracy* (1990). He appeared in hundreds of parts in a career that covered stage, screen, and television but he was most often cast as a butler, a judge, or a doctor. Unlike most actors, as he grew older and more wizened his opportunities seemed to increase and he became a beloved and familiar presence, particularly on television. Wolfe appeared in dozens of classic TV shows including *Playhouse 90* (1956–1961), *The Twilight Zone*, *Perry Mason*, *All in the Family*, *The Mary Tyler Moore Show*, and many more. On the big screen, Wolfe was in the cast of an amazing fourteen feature films that were nominated for the Academy Award for Best Picture.

Strange Bedfellows

Dennis Lipscomb makes his only appearance as Lawrence Prine, a CPR instructor trying to teach people this life-saving skill from his booth in Siegel's Department Store. Unfortunately, high-strung Mr. Prine suffers a breakdown in Siegel's. Among his troubles is an unhealthy relationship with Vicki, his CPR dummy. He may be a little unhinged but he does end up saving Mr. Spidoni's life when the older man has a mild heart attack in the squad room.

Two-Way Player

Dick Wesson was credited with writing the story for this episode along with Nat Mauldin. Wesson was a popular character actor in films and on television in the 1950s with a costarring role in the TV series *The People's Choice* (1955–1958) starring Jackie Cooper.

The Last Word

Harris is going to bring Mr. Prine and "Vicki" to Bellevue. We're used to Harris's euphemistic names for the hospital but in this episode, he retains the spirit of his humor by tossing in a bit of a change-up when he tells Barney, "Uh Barn, I'm gonna run Steve & Eydie over to Manhattan South."

For you young kids, Steve (Lawrence) and Eydie (Gorme) were singers who enjoyed a long and successful partnership on TV, recordings, and in nightclubs, as well as a fifty-five-year marriage.

Season 8, Episode 9:	"Examination Day."
Original Airdate:	January 14, 1982.
Writer:	Jordan Moffet.
Director:	Gennaro Montanino.
Cast of Characters:	Max Gail (Wojo), Steve Landesberg (Dietrich), Ron Glass (Harris), Hal Linden (Barney), Ron Carey (Levitt), Jack Kruschen (Benjamin Diamond), Lyman Ward (Harv Jetter), Louis Giambalvo (Warren Shippel), James Gregory (Inspector Frank Luger).

The Rundown

The uniformed officers are taking the sergeant's exam so all plainclothes officers are in uniform. Inspector Luger comes back to the 12th to don his old patrolman's blues and hit the streets. A neighborhood butcher's reputation is impugned by a local TV personality.

Patronizingly Encouraging

Levitt checks in with the detectives before he heads off to take his sergeant's exam and they all wish him good luck including Harris who says, "Go get'em, Little Levitt." It's an interesting exchange because they all know Levitt doesn't really appreciate that nickname and yet Harris is quite sincere in his good wishes for his colleague so it seems an odd juxtaposition of messages.

He's No Pat O'Brien Either!

Luger, who must also don the patrolman blues on Examination Day, opts to do his stint at the 12th, "among people where I can gripe about it." Soon he's sent out on a call with Harris. When they return, Luger addresses their collar as a vermin and maggot. Harris surreptitiously slips into Barney's office to tell him about Luger's style on the street, that of your basic, old-fashioned police brutality.

When Barney questions Luger about his conduct, the Inspector defends his actions by telling Barney, "When I was at the 9-3 over in Brooklyn, we used to lean on those lousy little punks all the time." He fails to grasp that was over thirty years ago and the times have changed. When Luger uses some deflective sarcasm Barney blows up at him and says he violated the prisoner's civil rights.

Luger: Ahhh, don't give me that legalese bunk, will ya.
Barney: IT IS NOT BUNK, DAMMIT. IT'S THE LAW! AND WE, OF ALL PEOPLE, HAVE TO UPHOLD IT! No matter what your personal opinion happens to be.

Luger tells him that although he's got a lot of respect for Barney he believes, "It's bleeding hearts like you, Barney, that cause all these problems in the first place. It's just that I think that a real cop doesn't always have to go by the book."

Barney: Oh, I'll go along with you there.
Luger: Oh, will you?
Barney: If I went by the book, I'd have you up in front of Internal Affairs.

We've never seen Barney this tough with the inspector. Luger has driven Barney crazy on numerous occasions but Barney almost always indulges him and treats him with the respect due an elder. In this case, the integrity of the job is too important for him to let Luger's actions slide. However, as he suggests, he does *not* report Luger to Internal Affairs so there was obviously a limit to how far he'd go in disciplining Luger.

When Luger leaves at the end of the day Barney tells him, "Look, I know in the heat of the moment back there we said some things to each other which were not exactly pleasant. I just want you to know that If I came down hard on you, it's only because I guess we come down the hardest on people we care the most about." Luger replies, "Thanks Barn, me too."

What's important in that exchange is not only that their father–son dynamic has been restored but that Barney does not apologize. He explains why he was upset but he doesn't say he was wrong for getting so angry, thereby sustaining the integrity of his position.

Here's Your Salami

The wonderful Jack Kruschen appears as kosher butcher Benjamin Diamond whose business and reputation is being threatened by a self-serving TV reporter named Jetter, played by Lyman Ward, who claims Diamond tried to pass off non-kosher meat to his customers. Diamond is visibly upset, telling Dietrich, "Who knew? They told me they had a rabbi. For a religious Jew this is a calamity. A Kosher butcher's reputation is based on trust." Dietrich eventually makes Mr. Diamond feel a little better when he tells the old guy that he believes him.

When Barney fails in getting the reporter to drop the charges (Mr. Diamond hit him with a salami) Dietrich says, "Hey, I'll bet *20/20* would love to hear a story about how channel twenty-seven ruined a little butcher's life." [*20/20* was a popular investigative show on ABC at the time.] Jetter immediately drops the charges and Mr. Diamond is not only free to go but Jetter promises not to run the story.

In a Pinch

Second time this season that Dietrich gets his cheek pinched. First Luger does it in "Stress Analyzer" and now Mr. Diamond. He pinches Dietrich's cheek and says, "Ooh, you are a mensch!" A mensch is a Yiddish term for a good man.

Rewriting History

In this episode, Barney teases Wojo about taking the sergeant's exam three times. However, according to "Bus Stop" (S. 3/Ep. 4) and "Copy Cat" (S. 4/Ep. 6), it's quite clear that Wojo took the sergeant's exam five times before passing, not three.

Season 8, Episode 10: "The Clown."
Original Airdate: January 21, 1982.
Writer: Sam Simon.
Director: Alan Bergmann.
Cast of Characters: Ron Glass (Harris), Steve Landesberg (Dietrich), Max Gail (Wojo), Hal Linden (Barney), Walter Olkewicz (William Krebs a.k.a. Bingo the Clown), Howard Platt (Andrew Landry), Philip Bruns

(Gordon Kaiser), J. J. Barry (Arthur Duncan), Michael Tucci (Gilbert Doyle), Michael Alaimo (Vincent Royer), Jed Mills (Edward Crenshaw).

The Rundown

Harris and Levitt break up an out of control recruiting party while Wojo and Dietrich collar some convicts trashing an all-night cafeteria after being secretly released from Riker's Island. In a busy night of crime, there's also a thief targeting street performers within the precinct.

Bingo Is His Name-O

Mr. William Krebs, stage name Bingo (Walter Olkewicz), is a street clown. He was knocked off his unicycle and robbed of his "thank you basket" containing almost fifty bucks. Bingo is the latest street performer targeted within the precinct in the last two weeks, including a mime, a juggler, and a couple of one-man bands.

We learn that Krebs left his wife and three kids to become, "Bingo, a clown who brings joy and laughter to a world hungry for both." So let me see if I understand this correctly, you're devoted to bringing joy to the world but you deserted your wife and children? I remember seeing this episode as a kid and thinking what a jerk Bingo was.

Speaking of jerks, it is ultimately revealed that Bingo was a victim of the 12th's favorite criminal with a theme, J. J. Barry's Arthur Duncan. Prior to this robbery, he's been arrested for ripping off Salvation Army centers and mugging the handicapped.

A Cultured Cop

Levitt comes in for Midnight Mail Call, sees the clown and says, "I like your opera." He's referring to Leoncavallo's 1892 opera entitled *Pagliacci* that translated into English literally means "Clowns."

It's My Party

Harris and Levitt haul in Andrew Landry, played by *Barney Miller* favorite Howard Platt, for disturbing the peace, destruction of private property, and solicitation of prostitution. Landry is in town recruiting police officers for the town of Mesa City, New Mexico. He reserved a hospitality suite in the hotel and "was hosting a stag film while assorted trollops served cocktails to the guests and the food fight just raged on in the master bedroom." "I hope you realize you have ruined my party," Landry tells Harris who immediately shoots back, "Oh, that's okay. You can cry if you want to." When Landry says, "You would cry too if it happened to you" they both laugh as Landry says, "I've got the album." Barney who's standing behind them says, "What album?" They just look at him blankly and move on.

In later years, the writers picked up the habit, especially when Harris is involved, of demonstrating that Barney is either out of touch with current trends or much older than the men who work for him. In reality, in 1981, "It's My Party" couldn't exactly have been considered hip so it's a rather odd attempt at alluding to Barney's "squareness." "It's My Party" was released by Lesley Gore in 1963, eighteen years before this episode aired. It was the first number one record for her and a producer named Quincy Jones.

Barney Snaps Again

A rough night pushes Barney over the edge and he tells the men to let everyone go. "All we're doing up here is spinning our wheels! Pretending that what we do means something and it means nothing! I think we should all just pack up and get out of here—leave this stinkin' city to go to hell in a handbasket because, let's face it, we're in the way!"

This is not the first time that Barney has snapped at the seeming futility of their efforts. This episode calls to mind similar outbursts by Barney in the episodes, "Rain" (S. 2/Ep. 11), and "Riot" (S. 7/Ep. 19).

A Bright Future

The writer for this episode is a very young Sam Simon. He went on to write multiple episodes of *Taxi* (1978–1983), *Cheers* (1982–1993), and *It's Garry Shandling's Show* (1986–1990) before gaining fame and fortune as one of the creators, writers, and producers of *The Simpsons* (1989–) until his untimely death from cancer in 2015. He was fifty-nine years old.

The Last Word

Michael Alaimo as Vincent Royer, tells his life story to Bingo the clown, "So then around '65 I couldn't make up my mind whether I wanted to go straight into med school or work in a hospital first, get some practical experience. So I robbed a shoe store and bought drugs."

>   **Season 8, Episode 11:** "Chinatown: Part 1."
>   **Original Airdate:** February 4, 1982.
>   **Writers:** Frank Dungan and Jeff Stein.
>   **Director:** Danny Arnold.
>   **Cast of Characters:** Ron Glass (Harris), Ron Carey (Levitt), Steve Landesberg (Dietrich), Hal Linden (Barney), Max Gail (Wojo), Joanna Barnes (Miss Caroline Fitzjames), Fred Sadoff (Alfred Walker, IRS), Leonard Stone (Sidney M. Botnik), Chao-Li Chi (Victor Ling), George Murdock (Lt. Ben Scanlon).

The Rundown

Harris and Dietrich have come to an impasse in an important case involving gang killings in Chinatown. Wojo attempts to help a wealthy mugging victim while a restaurant owner gets arrested for robbing his own establishment.

Wrong Side of Town

The wealthy and attractive Miss Caroline Fitzjames, played by Joanna Barnes, was exiting her furriers when a thief ripped a $40,000 brooch off her neck. Miss Fitzjames is a widow. When Wojo asks, "What do you do for a living?" Fitzjames replies, "I've been amply provided for." No longer hiding his judgmental reaction, he asks, "I've always been a little curious about what people like you do with all your free time?" Offended by his rudeness, she quietly and matter-of-factly says, "Mostly, we sleep around."

Mind Your Own Business

Harris and Levitt answer a break-in call at a restaurant. They return with Mr. Sidney Botnik played by Leonard Stone in his fifth and final *Barney Miller*. Botnik was ransacking a restaurant that actually belongs, or rather belonged, to him until the IRS padlocked the establishment due to non-payment of taxes. He'd worked out a payment plan with the IRS but he missed a couple of payments.

Fred Sadoff arrives as the heartless IRS man, Alfred Walker. He tells Barney that any attempted rescue of seized property on Botnik's part is a felony. Botnik yells from the cage that they should arrest Walker. "He's trying to ruin my life." Walker answers, "That's my job."

Barney tells Walker, "according to Mr. Botnick there was no prior notification of action, no warrant to enter the premises, no court order to close it down. I don't know, the whole thing sounds blatantly unconstitutional." Walker simply states, "We're the IRS. We can do that."

Forget It, Jake

Harris and Dietrich are working on a murder case that took place at the Jade Palace restaurant in Chinatown. However, maybe they should just forget it. After all, it *is* Chinatown. The only witness to the murder is a waiter who refuses to cooperate for fear of reprisal. Mr. Ling, played by an actor named Chao-Li Chi, has worked in Chinatown for forty-three years.

Pressure from the Mayor's office forces the DA to have the court designate Mr. Ling a material witness. Until he cooperates, Harris and Dietrich will keep him in protective custody at the Greenwich Hotel. Harris is aghast, Dietrich is nonplussed, and Levitt is thrilled, sensing that with two detectives out on assignment, he'll get the call upstairs—and he does.

As they leave Wojo tells them to watch out for themselves, "Some of those Tong gangs would just as soon slit your throat as look at you." When Harris responds, "At least there's a bright side," you just know a good time is going to be had by all.

A Creepy New Side

Lieutenant Scanlon drops by to give Wojo a hard time about his paternity suit and is immediately attracted to Wojo's mugging victim, Miss Fitzjames. So much so that he gets tongue-tied and his inability to speak in front of her only makes him creepier. Needless to say, she is not in the least bit interested.

Just the Facts

- Dietrich books Harris, Mr. Ling, and himself into the Greenwich Hotel under the name The Smith Brothers, as in the popular brand of cough drops that date back to the 1850s.

R-E-S-P-E-C-T

Harris says, "C'mon, L'il Levitt, got a call." When Levitt mimics Harris patronizing, Harris actually gets a little miffed and says, "I think I'm going to ignore that." What's he snippy about? He's the one who continues to disrespect Levitt with the "L'il Levitt" moniker.

Season 8, Episode 12: "Chinatown: Part 2."
Original Airdate: February 11, 1982.
Writers: Frank Dungan and Jeff Stein.
Director: Danny Arnold.
Cast of Characters: Ron Glass (Harris), Steve Landesberg (Dietrich), Hal Linden (Barney), Max Gail (Wojo), Ron Carey (Levitt), Joanna Barnes (Miss Carolyn Fitzjames), Chao-Li Chi (Victor Ling), Peter Pan (Mr. Chao), Phil Diskin (Gillis), George Murdock (Lt. Ben Scanlon).

The Rundown

Harris and Dietrich drive each other crazy as they try to convince a witness to testify during an extended stay at a rundown hotel. The tables turn as a woman threatens to make a formal complaint against Lt. Scanlon.

Lt. Stalker

Miss Fitzjames returns to report that Lt. Scanlon has been calling her on the phone, dropping by her apartment at odd hours to discuss her case and then inviting her to breakfast, lunch, dinner, whatever's appropriate for the time. Barney and Wojo are shocked. When she asks Barney, "He does belong to you doesn't he," Wojo says with a smile, "He does now."

Miller tells Scanlon that Miss Fitzjames is filing a formal complaint against him for harassment. Scanlon is surprised, embarrassed, and hurt. He pours his heart out to Miller that "she's a special kind of woman," but Barney must tell him he's making her nervous and uncomfortable. Scanlon tries to blame Barney, saying, "You must really hate my guts." He then descends into a rant about how they all hate him in that office. "I promise you this," Scanlon says, "That's the last you'll ever see of my charm, my gentleness, my caring and all the rest of that good stuff."

Nice Guys Infuriate Him!

Right before he leaves, Barney tells Scanlon, "Look . . . I know we've had our differences in the past, I just want you to know that anything that was said in that room will stay in that room." Scanlon stares at Barney and says, "God, how I despise you!" It absolutely drives him crazy that Miller is such a genuinely nice guy.

Barney the Realist

In the end, the campout at the Greenwich is for naught as Mr. Ling assures them he will never testify because if he did . . . he would not survive. Barney calls off the assignment. From the one-sided phone call we hear between Barney and the D.A. it's obvious the D.A. disagrees with Barney's decision. So much so that he has the cook at the Jade Palace picked up and brought in for questioning, starting the whole treadmill again!

Ring a Ding Ming

At one point in the hotel room, Harris says to Dietrich, "It's your turn to watch Ming the Merciless." The reference dates back to the *Flash Gordon* comic strip started in 1934 and subsequent manifestations of the character in film and television. Ming the Merciless is Flash Gordon's arch-nemesis.

The Last Word

Miss Fitzjames says to Wojo about her complaint against Scanlon, "You know, I really don't enjoy doing this." Wojo's reply is, "Maybe you're not trying hard enough."

Season 8, Episode 13:	"Hunger Strike."
Original Airdate:	February 18, 1982.
Writers:	Stephen Neighher and Tony Sheehan (story). Tony Sheehan (teleplay).
Director:	Tony Sheehan.
Cast of Characters:	Steve Landesberg (Dietrich), Ron Glass (Harris), Ron Carey (Levitt), Max Gail (Wojo), Hal Linden (Barney), Larry Gelman (Philip Bishop), Nora Meerbaum (Miss Smith), Stanley Kamel (Dr. Michael Packer), Ion Teodorescu (Joseph Obrockian).

The Rundown

Dietrich diagnoses an escaped mental patient who has taken some flowers from a local florist's shop. A man threatens an indefinite hunger strike until certain world issues are addressed. Barney is reluctant to make another attempt at the position of Deputy Inspector.

Reruns

The individual making an impassioned, if albeit fruitless, attempt to change the world by threatening suicide, blowing up the precinct, and/or staging a hunger strike is a familiar storyline in the course of the series. However, in the case of *Barney Miller*, the repetition makes sense. The one part of a policeman's job that *Barney Miller* was never afraid to show us was the boredom, the drudgery, the repetition, the futility of a small squad of men and women battling the sins and vices of a civilization that has been suffering from the same problems for centuries. In other programs, the repetition of storylines might fall flat. Here, it makes complete sense.

Starve Yourself for Peace

Larry Gelman shows up in his fourth and final episode as Mr. Philip Bishop, arrested for trespassing and creating a public nuisance after chaining himself to the fence in Washington Square to bring attention to his hunger strike. Among his demands, "I want to put a halt to the nuclear buildup in Europe. I want the Camp David Agreement put back on track. And I want my cleaning deposit back!" Apparently, he kept his apartment spotlessly clean and now all of a sudden his landlord is telling him his deposit is non-refundable.

Bishop is obviously hungry but when Wojo offers him a donut, he says, "I'll eat when Europe is nuclear free." Wojo, worried about Mr. Bishop not eating until one of his demands is met, convinces the man's landlord to refund his cleaning deposit. Bishop was hoping for more but it is a start. Unfortunately, now that he can eat again without losing face, the donuts are gone and Dietrich is not anxious to share his lunch with him.

Say What?

Dietrich picks up a woman on Lexington who walked out of a flower shop with a bouquet. He's unable to understand what she's saying but according to her bracelet, she's a resident of the Eastside Psychiatric Center. We will learn that Miss Smith, a difficult role played with aplomb by Nora Meerbaum, has been institutionalized for twenty years. When the doctor from Eastside arrives, played by Stanley Kamel, he tells Barney that what she does is called verbigeration, the repeating of senseless phrases. He claims she suffers from hebephrenic schizophrenia. Dietrich is skeptical.

Dietrich goes to Columbia University and discusses the case with a linguistics expert who sends him to a deli where many Eastern Slavic dialects are spoken. When Dietrich plays a tape of Miss Smith "talking," one gentleman recognizes her "gibberish" as a type of Macedonian dialect spoken when he was a child. Dietrich brings him back to the squad room and the man successfully communicates with Miss Smith. When he accompanies Miss Smith and Dr. Packer back to Eastside, the two new friends are wearing broad smiles on their faces while the doctor is wearing humble pie on his.

Try, Try Again

Levitt comes in to post the bulletin with the list of promotion candidates for Deputy Inspector, Spring, 1982, one of whom is Barney. Everyone is confused when Barney announces, "I've decided to remove my name from consideration for Deputy Inspector." As his faith in his career purpose continues to founder, he's "decided I'm not going to let them jerk me around anymore . . . what is the point of putting myself through it all over again?" The men, taking a page from Barney's psychological playbook, eventually convince him that he owes it to all of them to try to move up so that they can also eventually move up as well.

Season 8, Episode 14: "The Arrival."
Original Airdate: February 25, 1982.
Writer: Jordan Moffet.
Director: Lee Lochhead.
Cast of Characters: Ron Glass (Harris), Max Gail (Wojo), Hal Linden (Barney), Steve Landesberg (Dietrich), Andrew Bloch (Vincent Brysom), Alan Oppenheimer (William Deats), Carina Afable (Perlita Avilar), Mario Roccuzzo (Norman Deluca), James Gregory (Inspector Frank Luger).

The Rundown

A humanitarian pays for his inherent kindness. A member of MENSA rejects his intellectual group. The ol' inspector's mail-order bride arrives and he begins to get cold feet.

Filly from Manilly

Carina Afable plays Perlita Avilar, Luger's mail-order bride from the Philippines. Afable worked in the film and television industry in the Philippines until martial law was imposed in 1972. At the time, she would come back and forth to the U.S. to shoot an occasional commercial. Writer Jeff Stein remembered, "We wanted to hire [her] but she lived in the Philippines and Danny goes absolutely nuts! He says, 'Do you know what a first class ticket costs for this? It's got to be $18,000 - $20,000.' And we said, 'We don't think so, Danny. We don't think it's as bad as that.' Danny says, 'Well, hold on. I'll call Donna.' Now Danny's wife, Donna, was a travel agent. She owned a travel agency. So he calls Donna and we're sitting there. 'I'm going to show you - Donna, first class from Manila to L.A., how much?' We listened and waited. [Danny yells], 'What do *you* know!' He gets off the phone and says, 'My wife the travel agent.'"

Let's Not Get Physical

Luger is shaken when he walks into the squad room and spots Miss Avilar. He immediately retreats to Barney's office and admits to Barney that he applied for a sweetheart visa and in a weak moment signed some immigration papers. Now he's scared out of his wits. Barney tells him "that woman just traveled 10,000 miles on the basis of your proposal!"

Eventually, Luger apologizes for his behavior. He's embarrassed. She's "a little young, not too tall, and healthier than [he] had planned." He finally admits he's lonely and she says, "Me too." They decide to go out to dinner but he tells her after they eat he can't promise her any "dancing." Wink, wink.

Nice Guys Finish Last

Mario Roccuzzo is nice guy Norman Deluca. He was on his way to the Jewish Home and Hospital for the Aged for his weekly volunteering when he spots a woman lying face down on the sidewalk. As he goes to her aid, she grabs him in a headlock, and starts biting his ear while two accomplices go through his pockets, kick him in the ribs, and leave him behind.

Harris: God, I'm really sorry.
Deluca: Oh no, no, no, that's okay. I mean, better me than someone less fortunate.

There's nothing inherently funny about this story. In fact, it's a scenario that's been used all too often in the real world in the years since *Barney Miller* to lure Good Samaritans into criminal traps. The humor in the story comes from Roccuzzo and his portrayal of this annoyingly nice guy. The character is so obsequious that you eventually want to sock him in the mouth yourself!

Displaced Person

Vincent Brysom seems like an ordinary street punk except he has a genius IQ. He's arrested for ransacking the offices of MENSA of which he's a member. Nevertheless, Brysom, played by Andrew Bloch, can't stand the organization or the type of people it attracts like William Dietz, played by Allan Oppenheimer, whose first words out of his mouth are, "I'm William Dietz, MENSA." Wojo's reply is, "Stanley Wojciehowicz, moron."

Missing in Action

A lady calls in to report that the Waltons are missing. Harris says, "I think the mother's a nurse now." He's referring to a 1981–1982 show called *Nurse*, starring Michael Learned, the actress who portrayed the mother, Olivia Walton, on the long-running CBS drama, *The Waltons* (1972–1981). Both *Barney Miller* and *The Waltons* were Thursday night staples on American television throughout the 1970s, *Barney* on ABC and *The Waltons* on CBS. In fact, from January 1975 through 1977, the two programs were directly opposite one another in the TV listings until *Barney* was moved to a later time slot.

Just the Facts

- Wojo spends the episode playing with the hottest toy of the day, Rubik's Cube, a 3D puzzle/toy invented in 1974 and licensed to the Ideal Toy Company in 1980. By the time this episode aired, it was an international craze and sold in the hundreds of millions.

Season 8, Episode 15: "Obituary."
Original Airdate: March 11, 1982.

Writer:	Nat Mauldin.
Director:	Gennaro Montanino.
Cast of Characters:	Hal Linden (Barney), Ron Carey (Levitt), Ron Glass (Harris), Steve Landesberg (Dietrich), Max Gail (Wojo), Richard Stahl (Herb Lund), Will Seltzer (Andrew P. Jessel), Phil Diskin (Louis Beilin), Barney Martin (Wendell Bergendahl), Peggy Pope (Ruth Bergendahl).

The Rundown

It's Barney's birthday and he's not anxious to celebrate the passage of time. A man steals chicken from a government warehouse and exposes a bureaucratic quagmire. A man attacks a young reporter who wrote and published his obituary.

Dead to Rights

In a storyline reminiscent of "Discovery" (S. 2/Ep. 8), wherein the department mistakenly lists Fish as deceased, a young cub reporter runs an obituary of a Wendell Bergendahl but Mr. Bergendahl, played by Barney Martin, isn't dead yet and takes offense to the reporter's gaffe. Actor Will Seltzer is Andrew P. Jessel, the reporter inspired to his vocation after reading *All the President's Men*. He's now frustrated by the fact that his duties are nowhere near as exciting as the Woodward/Bernstein yarn.

Peggy Pope shows up at the precinct as the "dead man's" wife. As it turns out, she's looking for another Wendell Bergendahl, her ex-husband, who ran off with the neighbor's foreign exchange student three years ago. She got a divorce and was granted alimony and his life insurance but hasn't been able to collect on either.

The Bergendahl in the cage strikes up a conversation with "Mrs. Bergendahl." He's a lonely man who's led a rather mundane life. She's a lonely woman who's been taken advantage of by a heartless man. The cad's potential death has united two kindred spirits looking for kindness.

Before she leaves, Ruth asks Wendell what he did to end up behind bars. He tells her, "I hit somebody." The sadder-but-wiser Mrs. Bergendahl asks, "A woman?" When he tells her no, she gives him a little smile and her number, 555-4349.

Why'd He Cross the Road?

This week's "paranoid with proof" is the man who steals chicken from a government warehouse claiming he's exercising his rights as a citizen since the stuff is just sitting there going to waste. Wojo discovers he's right. The government leased the place six months ago and the food is sitting there while people go hungry.

When Wojo calls the Department of Agriculture they send Herb Lund (Richard Stahl), yet another overworked bureaucrat. Lund reluctantly explains the fundamentals of supply side economics and the purchase of surplus food to maintain stable wholesale prices. Barney is satisfied. Wojo is not.

Lund agrees with what Wojo says but his hands are tied. That's when Jessel challenges him by suggesting that for all the time he's wasted in the precinct explaining, "a few dozen hungry kids could have had something to eat, or don't you think about things like that?"

> **Lund:** Yes, I think about things like that! What, you don't think I have feelings? You think I don't get frustrated? You don't think there [are] days I'd like to pitch the book of regulations out the window?
> **Wojo:** Then why don'tcha?
> **Lund:** Because, that would be, heroic. I'd like to be a hero, it'd be nice to be a hero, 'Herb Lund—Hero.' I'm not a hero, all right?

It's a poignant scene about one small man who feels powerless against the system that controls him. He can't give away the food to just anybody. They need forms and that would take endless hours so the food sits in the warehouse. Rotting. Perhaps like the future of humanity.

A Reluctant Hero

When Jessel threatens to write an expose about the wasted food, Lund panics. Jessel assures Lund he'll be an anonymous source but Lund says, "That's not the point, the point is I have a responsibility to the system! To the people! We have guidelines to adhere to! We have precepts! We have rules! (Quiets to a whisper) We have . . . peanut butter in New Jersey." Jessel speaks excitedly to his editor on the phone, "Wait! They got peanut butter!"

Change of Pace

When Levitt brings the mail he refers to Harris and Dietrich as Ron and Art. Dietrich was the only one who ever referred to Levitt as Carl with any regularity.

Season 8, Episode 16:	"Inquiry."
Original Airdate:	March 26, 1982.
Writers:	Frank Dungan and Jeff Stein.
Director:	Gennaro Montanino.
Cast of Characters:	Steve Landesberg (Dietrich), Hal Linden (Barney), Ron Glass (Harris), Ron Carey (Levitt), Max Gail (Wojo), Bonnie Bartlett (Emily Loftis), Norman Bartold (Gordon Wendell), Barry Gordon (David Fingler), Sal Viscuso (Victor Renaldi), Joe Mantell (Raymond Waymond), Allan Rich (Edward Meyers), Michael Lombard (Joseph M. Loftis).

The Rundown

A man gets mugged on the street and then mugs someone else to get train fare home. A couple are involved in a disturbance at a local private school. Wojo is forced to shoot a man in a holdup and is subjected to the new department procedure following such an incident.

A Man Alone

Allan Rich shows up in his third and final *Barney Miller*, this time as Edward Meyers of Paramus, New Jersey. He was mugged, losing both his wallet and his wristwatch to the thief. After appealing to the humanity of his fellow New Yorkers and being summarily dismissed or ignored, he mugged a woman to try to get train fare back to Jersey. According to Mr. Meyers, his freezer plant business is in the toilet, his wife ran off to Orlando with a Cuban named Raoul, and "life is sludge."

That's My Boy

Wainwright Private Academy for Boys is the most prestigious nursery school in the city. Unfortunately, Master Jeffrey Loftis, not yet four years old, did not measure up to the high standards of the exclusive school. When his parents, played by Bonnie Bartlett and Michael Lombard, approach the Head of Admission to protest the slight against their son, harsh words are exchanged and a scuffle ensues. The idea of parents worrying about the trajectory of their child's academic and professional future based upon pre-school qualifications is rather common nowadays. The storyline has been repeated numerous times in film and on television but in 1982 it was still a pretty novel idea as Barney's reaction to their anxiety displays.

Following Procedure . . . Almost

Wojo and Levitt go out on a robbery call and encounter gunfire from the assailant. Wojo responds and hits the perp in the shoulder. Everyone is okay but while Wojo brings the suspect to the hospital, Levitt returns to the precinct and tells Barney that, "I gathered complete and comprehensive statements from all witnesses thereby fulfilling my obligation towards the department's new and stricter guidelines regarding the duty related discharge of an officer's firearm." We soon learn he fulfilled all but one of the new guidelines. He did not read his partner his Miranda rights. When Wojo returns he's overwhelmed with attorneys and the news that this shooting, as harmless as it seems, is under new, stricter guidelines.

Two lawyers converge on the 12th. Joe Mantell as the gung-ho Officer Raymond Waymond, a cop and a lawyer who represents the department, and Barry Gordon as David Fingler, there to represent Wojo on behalf of the Sergeant's Benevolent Association. When Wojo returns with the suspect, Victor Renaldi portrayed by Sal Viscuso, Renaldi is still higher than a kite. The lawyers and Wojo adjourn to Barney's office for questioning and statements. It's clear that Wojo acted accordingly but between the immediacy with which this inquiry was thrust upon him and the intensity of Raymond Waymond, Wojo gets fed up and storms out of the office.

Unrealistically Realistic TV Cop Show

When you consider the number of times television cops discharged their guns during the decades of the 1970s and 1980s without anyone ever blinking an eye, this episode is highly unusual. There were a few serious police dramas that produced special episodes where a cop was forced to kill someone and it was treated with an attempted sensitivity towards the officers and their feelings. In fact, *Barney Miller* itself had an episode just like that at the end of Season One, "The Hero." In this case, we have a shooting where no one was killed and there are no serious questions or suspicions about the circumstances but they still show us the mundane procedures that are, and must be, a part of any law enforcement agency. This is yet another reason why real-life law enforcement had such respect and affection for this program.

And Now, the End Is Near

This episode includes the final *Barney Miller* appearances of six renowned character actors, all of whom visited the 12th on multiple occasions through the years: Bonnie Bartlett, Norman Bartold, Barry Gordon, Michael Lombard, Allan Rich, and Sal Viscuso.

Season 8, Episode 17: "Old Love."
Original Airdate: April 2, 1982.
Writer: Phillip Jayson Lasker.
Director: Hal Linden.
Cast of Characters: Hal Linden (Barney), Ron Carey (Levitt), Steve Landesberg (Dietrich), Max Gail (Wojo), Ron Glass (Harris), Audrey Christie (Mrs. Kroner), Sharon Spelman (Cynthia Reese Barrow), Wynn Irwin (Mr. Felch), Mitch Kreindel (Irwin Kroner), Ben Hammer (Harold Lipkin), Mario Roccuzzo (Norman DeLuca).

The Rundown

Nice guy Norman Deluca returns after both assaulting and saving a man's life at the same time. Wojo arrests a former child star while Dietrich receives a visit from a long-lost love.

Don't Get Corky with Me

Wojo arrests Irwin Kroner, an actor played by Mitch Kreindel when he assaults his agent. Kroner explains, "I didn't mean to hit him. I only wanted him to phone this producer about a part for me. But he vacillated so I insistently offered him the phone and I chipped his tooth. And cut his lip. And his eye."

Audrey Christie plays the overbearing stage mother of Kroner. She won't talk to him through the bars so Wojo lets her into the cage. Emphasizing his talent, she tells her son, "the whole world cried when you cried." He stops her and puts it in perspective, saying, "Ma, I cried after the director told me you got hit by a streetcar and that you died in the ambulance on the way to the hospital and I was never gonna see you again. Then he stuck me with a pin."

Character actor Ben Hammer plays Kroner's agent Harold Lipkin. This was Hammer's only appearance on Barney Miller but he was a busy actor, performing on Broadway and television throughout the '60s, '70s, and '80s.

Connections

Philip Jayson Lasker notches his only *Barney Miller* writer credit with this episode. However, four years later, he earns a creator credit along with Chris Hayward and Danny Arnold for *Joe Bash* (1986). In 1990 and 1991 he was nominated for an Emmy as a producer on *The Golden Girls*.

It's worth noting that Lasker wrote a play that premiered in 2018 called *Beginner's Luck* about a young man in his twenties dealing with the loss of fame following his childhood acting career. Hmmm, sounds familiar.

Nice Guys Make Me Sick

Dietrich and Levitt answer a call about an altercation in the park. Mario Roccuzzo returns as Norman Deluca, a character we were introduced to just three episodes ago. This time he performed the Heimlich maneuver on an unsuspecting choking victim who assumed he was being attacked. In the course of saving the man's life, he also broke his ribs.

Wynn Irwin comes in as the angry and dull-witted Mr. Felch who is anxious to press charges against Deluca. Barney asks, "Mr. Felch, have you ever heard of the Heimlich maneuver?" Felch's response is, "Sure. The Krauts pulled it in '43." Barney can't reason with him and sadly tells Mr. Deluca that Sgt. Harris is going to have to book him. As Harris writes up the complaint, Felch says to Deluca, "Let me get this straight, you're saying that you saw me in trouble, so you came over for no reason, with nothing in it for you, and saved my life?"

Deluca: Yes.
Mr. Felch: You're sick!

Naturally, Felch doesn't sign the complaint. He starts to leave. He gives one last look at Deluca with that beatific smile on his face and says, "What's happening to people?"

Tossed Salad

Sharon Spelman appears as Cynthia Reese Barrow, an old flame of Dietrich's. Suddenly Arthur Dietrich, know-it-all nerd, turns into a cool, suave Cary

Grant. Their hello kiss is a long, full-lipped trip down memory lane. They last saw one another at the Columbia riots, fourteen years ago.

She's now happily married to some guy named Eddie who presumably Dietrich knows. She just came up on an impulse. He says, "Sure. We're just two old friends." He asks her out to lunch and after lunch they say their good-byes and she asks, "May I give Eddie your best?" Dietrich smiles and says, "I think he's already got it."

Spelman was a familiar face on television during the 1970s and 1980s. She's no doubt best remembered for her recurring role on the short-lived but fun Garry Marshall sitcom *Angie* starring Donna Pescow and Robert Hays.

Season 8, Episode 18:	"Altercation."
Original Airdate:	April 9, 1982.
Writer:	Tony Sheehan.
Director:	Alan Bergmann.
Cast of Characters:	Max Gail (Wojo), Ron Glass (Harris), Steve Landesberg (Dietrich), Hal Linden (Barney), Ron Carey (Levitt), Alex Henteloff (Arnold Ripner), Todd Sussman (Neil Hackett), Myriam Byrd-Nethery (Beverly Wakefield), Rod Colbin (Lawrence Wheeler), Robert Pastorelli (Edward Guthrie).

The Rundown

Dietrich brings in a mysterious woman who's had her purse stolen. Wojo and Harris arrest a Wall Street drug addict. Arnold Ripner returns to the 12th Precinct and stirs up trouble.

Miss Stalker, I Mean, Wakefield

The odd but always effective Myriam Byrd-Nethery returns for her final *Barney* appearance as purse-snatching victim Miss Wakefield. She tells Barney, "It's really my own fault. I shouldn't have been walking alone in such a dangerous neighborhood." He asks her where it happened and Dietrich says, "Out front."

Wojo catches the thief who upon seeing Barney says, "Hey! You're the guy in the purse." It turns out, Miss Wakefield carries newspaper clippings about Barney in her purse. She says, "You don't remember me, do you? I'm the lady you helped on Lexington Avenue in 1966. Some boys were bothering me, teasing me about my mini-skirt and you came up and told them to leave the lady alone." Barney has no idea who she is but looks at her and says, "Yes, of course!" She admits that she's kept a scrapbook of his career with interest and pride ever since but apologetically says she can stop intruding on his life and keeping track of his accomplishments. Barney tells her, "No that's all right. I appreciate the interest."

As she leaves, she says, "You know, I sent David a check for his bar mitzvah." Barney chuckles nervously and says, "I'm afraid I don't recall getting it." She tells him, "You cashed it."

Rock Solid, i.e., Stoned

An extremely stoned Neil Hackett is arrested for trying to sell Wojo and Harris a lid of grass. He tells Barney, "Hey look, I'm not a pusher. I only sell what I don't use myself which as you can see is not a lot lately."

The inimitable Todd Susman is stockbroker Neil Hackett in his last of three *Barney Miller* episodes while Rod Colbin is present as Lawrence Wheeler, Hackett's boss, in what will be Colbin's last of seven episodes. When he sees Hackett in the cage, Wheeler asks Levitt, "What's the matter with him?" Levitt responds, "I believe he's stoned out of his head."

Wheeler: Stoned? He's our best broker!
Levitt: He seems to have closed a little higher today.

The Return of Arnold Ripner

Arnold Ripner returns to try to bleed more money from Harris. He heard about Harris's new book deal and threatens to reopen the lawsuit to try to prove that Harris withheld knowledge of future earnings. Harris loses his cool and ends up hitting him in the mouth.

Barney pulls Harris into his office for a private chat and is really upset. Harris tells him, "Take it easy, Barney. I mean, I'm the one who punched Ripner and I'm the one who has to pay the price. I'm the one who goes on modified duty and I'm the one who goes up on charges."

Barney: And I'm the one who's up for Deputy Inspector!
Harris: But enough of me.

This is another peek into just how much Barney is thinking about this promotion. All of this is building to the end of the series that is now only a few episodes away.

Harris returns to the squad room to share his animosity with Ripner and learns that our favorite shyster didn't make any money from the original lawsuit. According to Ripner, his attorneys got all the money from the lawsuit while he "got the bric-a-brac." The bric-a-brac being Harris's art collection that Ripner mentioned was hanging on his wall.

He tells Harris, "What do you think I'm doing around here scrounging around for clients?" Harris laughs. Finally, he has his sweet revenge. Arnold rethinks his plan to sue again but needing to save his dignity, he demands an apology from Harris and $1,000. No way he's getting $1,000 but Harris finally apologizes saying, "Uhhhhh, look, I'm sorry I hit you Arnold. No one has the right to use physical violence against another human being and I give you my word that it will probably never happen again." Arnold finds that satisfactory.

Reprise

Barney's on the phone with Liz and says, "The boy's not seventeen years old yet for God's sake. All of a sudden he needs his own apartment? Didn't we just go through this with Rachel?" His daughter's identical request came in "The Courtesans" (S. 1/Ep. 5) broadcast on February 20, 1975. He never should have set the precedent.

Season 8, Episode 19:	"Bones."
Original Airdate:	April 30, 1982.
Writers:	Lee H. Grant, Jordan Moffet, and Nat Mauldin (story). Jordan Moffett and Nat Mauldin (teleplay).
Director:	Maxwell Gail.
Cast of Characters:	Hal Linden (Barney), Steve Landesberg (Dietrich), Ron Glass (Harris), Max Gail (Wojo), Howard Platt (Gordon Lynch), Ivor Francis (Dr. Otto Traven), Mark Banks (James Long), Luis Avalos (Jorge Jesus Maria Sanchez), Panchito Gomez (Gilbert Pedrosa).

The Rundown

A mugger makes the mistake of robbing a scoutmaster. An American Indian is happily arrested for burglary and disturbing the peace. Wojo makes a significant but costly discovery.

Old Bones

Mark Banks plays American Indian James Long. Banks was the brother of Dennis Banks, a controversial American Indian activist who founded the American Indian Movement in 1968.

Long is taken into custody for holding a sit-in in front of a Native American exhibit to protest a museum's recent discovery and excavation of bones from the Catskill Mountains. He stole the bones from the lab and then blocked entrance to the exhibit in an attempt to get some publicity for his cause. He's trying "to preserve the cultural and traditional integrity of the Mohawk nation." He tells Wojo, "You know, you people have ruined this land. You wasted our animals, our forests, fouled up the air, polluted the rivers. You keep that up and Manhattan's going to be worth even less than you paid for it."

Max Gail was an activist for American Indian civil and political rights. In Season Five, *Barney Miller* presented an episode entitled, "The Indian." Prior to the Eighth Season, Gail had asked for and been promised another storyline about Indigenous cultures. As they neared the end and Arnold announced that he had an idea for the series-ending trilogy, Gail suggested perhaps a four-part ending that could include the original inhabitants of New York City. Gail had an idea that used three Indian characters of different generations and backgrounds, in part to show the diversity of their culture. He knew he couldn't write it but at least wanted to be included in the construction of the story with Dungan and Stein. In the end, it was Arnold who took one of Gails characters and condensed his idea into this storyline with Mark Banks as the young Native American activist squaring off against the archeologist.

The Absent-Minded Professor

Ivor Francis plays Dr. Otto Traven, the museum archeologist, who comes to retrieve his bone specimens. Long sees him and shouts, "Desecrator, violator of sacred soil!" Traven asks innocently, "Have we met?"

Traven has no hard feelings towards Long. As an archeologist, he's just doing his job. Long asks, "If you're so interested in Indians, why don't you try talking to a couple live ones?" The professor explains, "I'm not an anthropologist."

In the end, Barney tries to talk Dr. Traven out of pressing charges and he's leaning in that direction until Long begs him *not* to drop the charges. Long wants to go to court so he can draw more attention to his cause. Dr. Traven agrees to sign the complaint to help Mr. Long.

I Didn't Know That

At one point, Long says, "Who do you think inspired the Articles of Confederation and the Constitution? Washington, Jefferson? Forget it! The Iroquois, man!" Both Dr. Traven and Barney are surprised to learn this. Dietrich, of course, confirms the veracity of this claim.

Short People Got Nobody

There is no water at the 12th so popular 1970s character actor Luis Avalos arrives on the scene as Jorge Jesus Maria Sanchez, the maintenance man who's been called in to address the problem. (Beckman must have retired) They need to break down a wall in the basement to get to a pipe and he needs help. Barney volunteers Levitt. A short time later, Levitt returns to the squad room soaked in water and covered in mud. Barney thinks it's amusing, Levitt does not. Wojo passes Levitt in the hallway and asks Barney what happened. When Barney tells him he sent Levitt into the basement to help with the plumbing issue, Wojo says, "He's a cop, Barn!" Soon Wojo heads to the basement to help Sanchez as well.

When Sanchez returns to inform Barney the issue has been resolved, he praises both "the Big Guy," a.k.a. Wojo, and Levitt who he says in Spanish "has the heart of a lion." As a fellow "little guy," Sanchez understands Levitt's struggle for respect.

Avalos's masterfully funny portrayal reminds us of Danny Arnold's penchant for Hispanic dialect humor. There was something about the mixture of anger and accent that poked Arnold's funny bone. As for Avalos, he was simply one of the best and brightest character actors from the late 1970s to the turn of the century.

Just the Facts

- Wojo knows the Miranda rights in at least three languages. English, Spanish, and Polish.
- Howard Platt makes his fifth and final appearance as an enthusiastic scoutmaster named Gordon Lynch who was mugged by a young crook but was able to overtake and hold him until the police arrived.

Be Wary of Hidden Treasures

When Wojo finds an old rifle in the basement the doctor is intrigued and wants to take it to do some research on it. Wojo agrees, having no idea of the implications. The discovery of that gun will lead to the end of the 12th Precinct as we know it.

Season 8, Episode 20:	"Landmark: Part 1."
Original Airdate:	May 6, 1982.
Writer:	Tony Sheehan.
Director:	Tony Sheehan.
Cast of Characters:	Ron Glass (Harris), Steve Landesberg (Dietrich), Hal Linden (Barney), Philip Sterling (Howard Spangler), James Gallery (Christopher Galt), Susan Tolsky (Victoria Hoffline), Al Ruscio (Jack Norrell), Keith Langsdale (Mr. Dozier), Pepe Serna (Julio Rodriguez).

The Rundown

Harris lands a big advance for a new book. A businessman has been changed forever by his time in captivity as a hostage. A preservationist and a building developer walk into an old building—sounds like a joke but it spells the end of the 12th.

Here We Go Again

Happily, it turns out Harris did have another book in him. The promise of a big cash advance from his new publisher has him reinvesting in the stock market. At the same time, he's taking a statement from the unemployed Mr. Dozier, played by Keith Langsdale, who was robbed at knifepoint of $170. Dozier tries to guilt Harris into reimbursing him the money out of the "famous author's" upcoming advance to pay for bartending school. In the end, Harris puts his cards on the table with Mr. Dozier, "Look I could give you the $170 and I really wouldn't miss it. But I'm not going to. You see, it just wouldn't be right. There are certain boundaries we just don't cross. I mean there are people who come in here every day in trouble, wanting things, you know? I mean people more despondent and more desperate than you! And I promise you, I have never lifted a finger to help them either!"

As much as we're tempted to think, "Gee, he really could have given him the money," the fact is that Harris is correct. He deals with hundreds of victims every year. He can't personally help them all. Honestly, Dozier was even more annoying than Norman Deluca!

Sizing It All Up

Susan Tolsky is Victoria Hoffline, a museum curator contacted by Dr. Traven about the antique gun Wojo discovered in the previous episode. Hoffline learns the gun belonged to Teddy Roosevelt and says that Barney's office may have been Teddy's office when he was the head of the NYC Police Department from 1895 to 1897. According to Hoffline, the building was department headquarters. Interesting since those of us paying close attention know that according to the building's original *Barney Miller* superintendent Mr. Beckman, "there was a big scandal when the building was built in 1932," see "Rain" (S. 2/Ep. 11).

Next to visit is Al Ruscio as developer Jack Norrell. He's considering buying the place if the building gets landmark status because, as he explains, "Anybody who buys it and puts it back in its original condition gets a twenty-five percent tax credit. This place would make great dental offices, you know, 1890s style."

It's a perfect bit of *Barney Miller* irony that this building which was always a wreck and brought the men of the 12th nothing but grief, a building with only occasional running water, a leaking roof, termites, rats, and cockroaches, in the end becomes a hot commodity.

Not Again

Philip Sterling is Howard Spangler, a recently released hostage but, as he says, "Oh no, [not] one of the fabulous fifty-two." The reference was to the recently released fifty-two American hostages held in Iran from 1979–1981. Spangler, held hostage for eighteen months in South America, is clearly suffering from Post-Traumatic Stress Disorder.

The taking of a tragic situation and finding humor in it was another *Barney Miller* specialty. The young executive, Christopher Galt played by James Gallery, who took Spangler's job while he was in captivity, comes to bail him out.

> **Galt:** Look Howard, we all know that you've been through a rather harrowing experience and our only concern is your well-being and getting you back up to snuff. But I must tell you that some of your recent actions have been a bit disconcerting.
> **Spangler:** What are you talking about?
> **Galt:** Well, this memo for example that you sent to the Sales Department yesterday. "From the desk of Howard Spangler to the Imperialist Pigs who sit on the backs of the workers."

In the end, Spangler wants to go back to the country where he'd been held hostage. Turns out his kidnappers won the revolution and are now in charge of the country. He feels as though he contributed to the cause and has been cheated out of the spoils of victory. Few character actors who came through the 12th could break your heart the way Philip Sterling could.

Just the Facts

- We're used to Inspector Luger crooning tunes in the squad room but in this episode it's Mr. Spangler who can be heard singing "Swinging on a Star" (1944) in his cell. When he gets to the end of his chorus, he finishes it in Spanish, leading us to assume that this was a song appreciated by his captors.

Season 8, Episode 21:	Landmark: Part 2."
Original Airdate:	May 13, 1982.
Writers:	Frank Dungan and Jeff Stein.
Director:	Danny Arnold.
Cast of Characters:	Max Gail (Wojo), Ron Glass (Harris), Hal Linden (Barney), Steve Landesberg (Dietrich), Al Ruscio (Jack Norrell), Robert Costanzo (Prof. Vincent Thorndyke), Florence Halop (Wilma Kestner), Helen Verbit (Estelle Bobis), James Murtaugh (Joseph Saxon), Carina Afable (Perlita Avilar), James Gregory (Inspector Frank Luger).

The Rundown

The building has officially been sold to real estate developer Jack Norrell. Wojo and Dietrich bring in two little old ladies who try to pass bad checks and credit cards.

Professor Rip-Off

Florence Halop's Wilma Kestner and Helen Verbit's Estelle Bobus take a course from Professor Vincent Thorndyke, played by Robert Costanzo. The course is called, "Rip-Offs, the System and You." They're arrested for trying to use a phony credit card they purchased from Professor Thorndyke. They tell Wojo, "We didn't want to steal but we couldn't make ends meet any other way." The idea of certain criminals as the victims of trying economic circumstances who are not inherently bad people is a familiar one on *Barney Miller*. It's a subtle but effective use of empathy to reveal the human condition and the inequities of our society.

Thorndyke runs the Econo Institute of Mercantile Management out of some bar with courses that include "False IDs, Theory and Application" and "Check Kiting: Does It Work?" Thorndyke claims, "I'm just educating and enlightening people." However, Dietrich returns from Thorndyke's office with a container filled with assorted credit cards, blank birth certificates, driver's licenses, car registrations, and hall passes.

Teacher's Pets

He claims not to know the ladies who fingered him. Nevertheless, they still feel a little guilty. When Mrs. Bobus apologizes to Thorndyke from the cell, he suddenly recognizes the women, "Hey, wait a minute. Bobus and Kestner, right?"

Bobus: Right.
Thorndyke: You know the check the two of you gave me for tuition? It bounced.
Kestner: We thought you'd be pleased.

Goodbye Building

Al Ruscio returns as Jack Norrell to inform the men he's bought the building. They'll have thirty days before they have to leave. This announcement leaves the squad room thick with tension as the men ponder their fate. By the end of the day, Barney snaps, "C'mon, it's just a building! And a damn lousy one at that! I mean we sweat like pigs in the summertime, we freeze our tails off in the winter, I got a bathroom that's an embarrassment, the roof leaks—you really want my opinion? We should have been out of here years ago! All right, it's been home. We've done some damn fine work here. But what would be so terrible if we moved into some nicer quarters, someplace with electric typewriters, with a bathroom that's a bathroom . . . and a window that actually looks out on something. The point is, what's the difference where we work, as long as we're working together?"

It's not obvious at the time but Miller's speech includes some ominous foreboding. After they all leave, we see that even Barney doesn't believe the speech he just delivered.

Frank and His Filly from Manilly

Inspector Luger's mail order bride Perlita wants to know where their relationship is going. Luger tries to avoid discussing love, marriage, or anything else with her. Eventually, they retreat to Barney's office and Luger stumbles to the point, "We can't avoid the vast differences in our ages. If we got married, you'd probably want to move right in with me, right? And then you're young, attractive, and vital, no, it just doesn't make any sense." She doesn't exactly understand what he's trying to say until Luger finally blurts it out, "I'm saying that I want to marry ya! What do you think I'm saying?"

They come out and announce to the men that they're engaged. Everyone congratulates the couple and while the ol' inspector is happy, he's also still a little scared. He says, "See all you guys when I get back from my honeymoon ... *if* I get back."

Aliases

In this episode, Florence Halop's Wilma Kestner and Helen Verbit's Estelle Bobus are twice compared to famous female entertainers or characters of the past. At one point, Wojo tells Barney, "I finished processing the Cherry Sisters." The Cherry Sisters were a vaudeville act that many, including George Burns, thought to be the worst in the business. Their infamous act dates to the 1890s.

Later in the episode Dietrich asks Barney, "What do we do with Lucy and Ethel?" Lucy Riccardo and Ethel Mertz were neighbors on television's classic *I Love Lucy* (1951–1957).

Here's a question: how would Wojo know about an obscure vaudeville act like the Cherry Sisters? Dietrich might know about them but Wojo? I doubt it. On the other hand, Wojo would definitely have been familiar with Lucy and Ethel.

Season 8, Episode 22:	"Landmark: Part 3."
Original Airdate:	May 20, 1982.
Writers:	Tony Sheehan, Frank Dungan, and Jeff Stein.
Director:	Danny Arnold.
Cast of Characters:	Max Gail (Wojo), Hal Linden (Barney), Ron Glass (Harris), Steve Landesberg (Dietrich), Ron Carey (Levitt), J. J. Barry (Arthur Duncan), Earl Boen (Warren Gimble), Stanley Brock (Bruno Bender), Oliver Clark (Carl Ebling), Jack De

Leon (Marty Morrison), John Dullaghan (Ray Brewer), Mari Gorman (Naomi Bender), Walter Janowitz (Sam Belinkoff), Ralph Manza (Mr. Roth), Judson Morgan (Phillip Lukeather), F. William Parker (Wallace Lowell), Ray Stewart (Darryl Driscoll), Meshach Taylor (Melvin Jackson), Carina Afable (Perlita Avilar), George Murdock (Lt. Ben Scanlon), James Gregory (Inspector Frank Luger).

The Rundown

Someone's been stealing manhole covers right off the city streets. A scientist steals his own discovery from a pharmaceutical company who refuses to put it to good use. The men of the 12th Precinct are forced to say goodbye to their workplace, their community, and one another.

Opening Salvo

Wojo: A lot of stuff piles up in seven and a half years.
Barney: A lot of memories too.

Never Had a Chance

There are three actors in the final episode making their first and last *Barney Miller* appearance: Earl Boen, F. William Parker, and Meshach Taylor. Their stories, concerned with the crimes of the week, are incidental in this episode. In fact, never before have crimes been so quickly resolved in an episode of the show than they are here. This episode is all about endings, goodbyes, and even some new beginnings.

Marching Orders

As the hours wind down, Luger comes in for one final visit. He enters the squad room singing, "The Boy [Girl] from Ipanema." When Barney tells him that they didn't expect to see him back from his honeymoon so soon, Luger says, "Oh, well I wasn't about to miss the last gasp of the ol' 1-2." Barney receives a call from downtown and takes it in his office. When he returns, he's received their orders for their next assignment.

Wojo: Okay, where we going?
Barney: Dietrich, 34th Precinct, Washington Heights; Harris, 107th Precinct, Flushing Meadows; Wojciehowicz, Roosevelt Island, Canine Corps; Levitt, 73rd Precinct, Brooklyn.
Dietrich: So much for carpooling.

Wojo is understandably upset. He thought, or maybe was just hoping against hope, that they'd all be transferred en masse to a new location. So did we.

We Can Only Wonder

When Harris returns from a call, he's given his new orders for Flushing Meadows and he tells Barney he'll quit. Barney looks at him very seriously and tells him, "If that's the way you feel then that's what I think you should do." It leaves open the question, whatever became of Ron Harris? Did he actually stay on the force or did he become the next Joseph Wambaugh?

The Gang's All Here!

Sixteen guest stars populate the series finale. Of those sixteen actors and actresses, all but three of them had previously appeared on the program. Of those thirteen, twelve were recurring characters. Oliver Clark had been in five previous episodes but never as the character in this episode, Carl Elbing.

A group of 12th Precinct regulars come down to say goodbye and thank you. Bruno Bender donates a bowling trophy to give to Barney that they've inscribed to him and all the men. It's a nice scene in that it shows that the men and woman of the 12th were always there for their community just as these actors built a community for us, the viewers.

Poetry

In a brushstroke of poetic justice, Lt. Scanlon accidentally ends up being the one to inform Barney that he's been made Deputy Inspector. You almost feel sorry for Scanlon that not only does he never get any dirt on the men of the 12th but in the end, he's a messenger of happy news for his arch-nemesis, now Deputy Inspector Barney Miller. You don't really feel sorry for him but almost.

One Last Salute

Luger is crying as he relives some of them golden moments from years gone by. "You know Barney, it seems just like yesterday that I was sittin' here, me and Foster, Kleiner, Old Brownie, . . . oh God, Barney, (weeping) I don't want to be married. I can't keep up!"

Before Luger leaves, he gives Barney a copy of the official orders for him and all the men. He then hands a paper to Levitt and says, "And that's for you, Levine." Levitt gets angry and corrects Luger for the last time, telling him, "It's Levitt. Officer Carl E. Levitt!" The ol' inspector wags his finger at his underling and says, "Correction, Sgt. Carl E. Levitt. You report to Captain Murtaugh, Detective Squad, 73rd Precinct." After everyone congratulates the new detective, Luger bids farewell to the squad saying, "Gentlemen, I salute you."

The Long Goodbye

After the crowd and Luger have left the building, it comes down to just the detective squad and Levitt. They invite Barney to come with them and we're given the impression they're going out together for a drink. He bows out, saying he has a few things to finish up but it seems he doesn't want to prolong the pain of saying goodbye. Initially, the men casually say goodbye as if they'll see each other soon but they end up walking back into the room to try it again.

Harris: Police officers get transferred all the time. It's no big deal. But I think it's been different with us. Something really special happened here.

Dietrich: You guys made me feel like I was part of something. And I love you guys.

Wojo: We're not getting split up. I mean we're going to different places and we may not see each other again but I think each of us got something special from each other and we're going to nurture it and carry it with us for the rest of our lives. [This is a particularly telling bit of dialogue because each and every character was created from a part of Danny Arnold's personality.]

When they leave, Barney shakes Harris's and Dietrich's hand. Wojo and he embrace. Levitt, at a loss for words, puts his head on Barney's chest and Barney embraces him. As he walks slowly to his office, he passes the empty desks and we see clips of his memories of Chano, Fish, Wentworth, and, of course, Nick. A subtle and classy touch.

The show ends in the same way *The Mary Tyler Moore Show* ended five years earlier as Barney simply moves his peg on the board to show he's "out," shuts off the light, closes the door, and leaves.

Superimposed over the darkened squad room are the words "Goodbye and thank you from all of us at the Ol' One Two."

Last Thoughts

As for the ending, I think it is solid and well done. As an eighteen-year-old when the series ended, I did not like the fact that they were all being separated. After all, I started watching the show with my dad seven years earlier and his death following Season Two left me alone to watch the remainder of the series. I wasn't ready for the gang at the ol' 1-2 to go away but looking back now, Danny Arnold did the right thing. Too many shows carry on too long and end up tarnishing their own legacy. Arnold's decision was gutsy at the time and proved to be a prescient one. Season Seven had probably been the weakest season of the series run and Season Eight recaptured some of the earlier magic. The finale gave us all we could hope for in a final bow: the return of old friends and no feelings left unexpressed.

They make it clear that they'll try to stay in touch but that people drift apart. The work, the squad, the 12th Precinct, is what made them a family and kept them together for over seven years. The intimation that they probably won't stay connected is just that final perfect touch of reality from Danny Arnold and everyone who made *Barney Miller* one of the greatest shows in the history of television.

Epilogue

What makes a classic TV show a classic? It helps to start with a unique idea but it's not really necessary. It can be a story that's been told a hundred times before. What it needs to be special is the spin you put on it, the style and the manner in which the familiar tale is told.

Great stars are important but not necessary. A star can get a show started and might keep a network interested long enough to allow the show to gain traction with the public but if an actor isn't right for the character, he/she could be the biggest star in the world and it wouldn't matter. What's important are the right actors in the right roles. *Barney Miller* didn't really enter the TV wars with any big stars but what it did have were actors who all had experience on the stage in legitimate theater. They had acting skills and likable personalities. In television, acting prowess is wonderful but likability is king.

Finally, great writing is probably the most important single aspect of an enduringly successful television show. A funny script may be successful in the present but a great script will be successful in the future as well. Great writing is timeless. *Barney Miller* was silly, funny, and smart. The writing of the show was always layered and true. The writers never talked down to the audience. The intelligence of this show was something special but it's not the only reason it's a classic. This show was filled with humanity and heart. As long as there are human beings around to watch it, *Barney Miller* will resonate because it focused on the humanity of our shared struggle, about our differences as well as our similarities. Compassion and integrity formed the foundation of everything that went on in that squad room.

I knew all of that, more or less, before I began to write this book. What I learned during the writing of this book was slightly different. The creators and writers and artists involved in the production are only part of what creates the legacy of a classic program such as this. The people who are really in charge of the legacy are the audience. We the people decide what makes a classic and why. This realization had been dawning on me for a few years when it all became crystal clear the day I listened to the DVD commentary tracks over the "Landmark" trilogy that finishes the program. Tony Sheehan, Frank Dungan, and Jeff Stein provided the commentary and indeed provided some interesting and entertaining trivia for a fan of the program like me. However, I also felt by listening to their commentary that I knew more about these characters and this show than they did and they wrote a large number of the episodes. For those three talented men, *Barney Miller* had been a job. It had been a part of their career path. For me as a fan, it was something much different.

Look, I understand that these are just stories, just TV shows, just movies, just songs, just a silly game, whatever the case may be. However, for every person the world over, popular culture is a part of, as well as a reflection of, who we are as human beings. Classical music was once the pop music of its day. Viewing a painting by Cézanne or Da Vinci was like going to see a movie. These works are a part of us. This show was just one show, albeit a special one, in a career full of jobs for people like Danny Arnold, Hal Linden, Max Gail, and all the rest of the talented artists behind *Barney Miller* but to me, the show was an important part of my youth. It was a show that connected me to my dad and one that I remembered fondly into adulthood. I became emotionally involved with this television community.

As a twelve-year-old kid whose father had just died and who didn't always fit in with the cool kids, *Barney Miller* was a comforting presence in my life. It was a refuge. Wojo, Dietrich, Harris, Nick, Fish—these guys were all my friends. Thursday night was my night at the 12th. It was something to look forward to and something I could count on.

Unlike Peggy Pope's character in "The Judge" (S. 6/Ep. 9) who believes the characters she watches on her soap opera are real people, I knew these were just actors. I knew I couldn't go down to Greenwich Village and search for Barney and the boys. I knew it was art or craft or whatever you feel comfortable labeling it. I knew all of that, but it didn't alter the comfort and enjoyment I derived from it.

Truth be told, I think it was more than just a job for those who worked on it as well because while it was one of many jobs for almost all of them, the people who made it recognized it was something special. As I learned, the reason the show was so special was because the personalities who put it together week in and week out were and are incredibly special people.

Finally, I must admit one conceit. I am proud that from here forward, I'll be known as the guy who "wrote the book" on *Barney Miller*. I consider it a great privilege. It is one of the very best sitcoms in the history of the medium. It's been out of the primetime lineup for forty years and yet it's still relevant, still a prescient observation of the human condition and, most important, it's still incredibly funny.

Acknowledgments

First and foremost, I must thank Ben Ohmart. I'm grateful that he was a fan of this great show and for his encouragement and infinite patience. Thanks also to Stone Wallace, Senthil Kumar, and Brian Pearce.

Huge and heartfelt thanks to Hal Linden and Max Gail. Both of these gentlemen have been incredibly generous with their time. Hal seems to me to be indefatigable and indestructible. He can still weave his magic on stage and in front of the cameras and I hope he continues to do so for many years to come.

Max Gail is one of the kindest and truly caring men with whom I've ever come into contact. You know how Wojo showed that deep well of love, concern, and passion for the bag lady, the Indian who wanted to die in Central Park, and the Vietnam vet with Agent Orange exposure? Well, that's Max Gail. He truly cares for his fellow humans.

Outside of Danny Arnold's family, Tony Sheehan is the only other person with whom I spoke who spent as much time with the show's creator as did Hal and Max. Tony Sheehan contributed to the show as a writer, story editor, producer, as well as the showrunner for Seasons Six and Seven. He, too, was incredibly generous with his time and his insights. I was honored when he told me I was only the third interview he'd given in a forty-five-year career.

I have a special respect for Tom Reeder, Frank Dungan, Jeff Stein, Ron Friedman, Shelley Zellman, and all those who contributed to the magnificent writing of this show. My conversations with them were wonderfully entertaining storytelling sessions. A special thank you to Shelley Zellman for her gift of an original copy of a *Barney Miller* script. I treasure it.

Sal Viscuso encouraged and even nagged me to start writing this book. It was through his assistance that I was able to first make contact with Max Gail. Once Sal Viscuso believes in you, you've got the greatest cheerleader there is in the world. Thank you, my friend.

There are photos in the book with Max Gail and Hal Linden at a fan convention in New Jersey in 2019. The day I sent the picture to my kids, my daughter wrote back and said, "What would your ten-year-old self say if he could see these pictures?" It was a trenchant observation. The truth is, I was thrilled by every interview I landed for this book. To talk with these artists who had given me so much happiness throughout my life with their work was a gift. I thank them all: Barbara Barrie, Diana Canova, Oliver Clark, David Clennon, James Cromwell, Rosanna DeSoto, Peter Elbling, Alex Elias, June Gable, Mari Gorman, Alex Henteloff, Milt Kogan, Paul Lieber, A Martinez, Joanna Miles, Allan Miller, James Murtaugh, Dino Natali, Jenny O'Hara, Stuart Pankin, Joe Regalbuto, Lavelle Roby, and Ray Stewart.

Prior to working on this book, I was honored and lucky to interview Candice Azzara, the late Lou Cutell, and the aforementioned Sal Viscuso, all of whom shared *Barney Miller* memories with me. Millie grazie mi paesani.

The very first *Barney Miller* actor I ever met also deserves a special shout out and that is Kenneth Tigar. I met Ken ten years ago when he came through Rochester, New York, to star in *On Golden Pond* at the Geva Theatre. I went to see the production because it was starring *Barney Miller*'s Mr. Kopechne but my wife and I were blown away by the brilliance of his performance. I thank him for his encouragement, his kindness, and the photos he was generous enough to share.

Special thanks to TV legend and personal hero, Bill Persky. As a writer for *The Dick Van Dyke Show* in the early 1960s, he and his partner Sam Denoff set the standard for great sitcom writers. Persky delighted me with stories of his friend Danny Arnold and his early writing experiences. The opportunity to speak with him was a dream come true for me.

Thanks to Bruce Bilson, one of the most prolific TV sitcom directors in the history of the medium for his time and memories.

Profound thanks to members of the production staff, all of whom were extremely helpful, including Shirley Alberti, Susan Beavers, Harriet Helberg, Perry Krauss, and Lori Openden.

I was honored to have the cooperation of Danny Arnold's family in this endeavor. My deep gratitude goes out to the late Donna Arnold and her sons David and Dannel Arnold who, along with Danny, made up the four Ds of Four D Productions. A very special thank you for sharing of some of the terrific photos in this book as well.

In that same vein, I must thank Sharon Carey, Nancy Ross Landesberg, Elizabeth Landesberg, John Kirby, Michael Druxman, and Jackie O'Neill for their kindness and willingness in sharing their memories with me.

My appreciation goes out to Bob Claster who provided me with an unabridged copy of his extensive interview with Danny Arnold from 1987. Thanks to Peter Manera Manse for the contribution of his behind-the-scenes *Barney Miller* photographs. Special thanks as well to Jodie Mann, Barry Pearl, Tom Leopold, and Frank Santopadre.

My gratitude to Michael Simmons and Dr. Joseph Tempesta - both read parts or all of the manuscript and offered sage advice. I met Michael through the inimitable Max Gail and Dr. Tempesta was one of the greatest teachers I have ever had. Since my days as his student, he has been a dear and cherished friend.

On a more personal level, there are two people without whom this book would never have come to fruition. First is the man who was telling me to "write the book on Barney Miller" long before I ever seriously entertained such a thought, my valued friend Tim Madigan. Our shared love of trivial pop culture is what began our friendship over twenty years ago. In addition to his encouragement, he also read the manuscript and contributed numerous helpful suggestions and finally, pestered me to "finish it already!"

The other angel of this product is my dear friend, Jane Best. Her surname could not be more perfectly suited to her. She has provided tireless and indescribable assistance in getting this book completed. She is, quite simply, "the best."

Thanks to Chris Hawes, Rob Linton, Chuck Ingersoll, and Bob DeRosa for numerous little acts of assistance that helped move this project along. A special thank you to my son Nick for constantly helping his dad with technical issues that I had no patience for.

For all types of aid, encouragement, support, and love, I thank my siblings, Joe, Bob, and Suzanne and my uncles, Art and Bob Agnello and Tony Murabito. Thanks to those special friends who have encouraged my dreams for many years including but certainly not limited to Deb Koen, Jane Margolis, Thom Marini, Joe Morelle, and Scott Schindler.

Love and gratitude to my three children, Jennie, Frank, and Nick, who have provided my wife and myself with love, humor, and endless reasons to be proud. Finally, thanks to the one person other than myself who deserves the most credit for this book, my wife MaryBeth. She has believed in me throughout our decades together usually more than I believed in myself. Without her, none of this could have been accomplished. She has my undying love, respect, and gratitude.

Partial List of Sources

Books

Bedell, Sally. *Up the Tube, Prime-Time TV and the Silverman Years.* New York: The Viking Press, 1981.

Berman, A. S. *SOAP: The Unauthorized Inside Story of the Sitcom that Broke ALL the Rules.* BearManor Media, 2013.

Cowan, Geoffrey. *See No Evil: The Backstage Battle Over Sex and Violence in Television.* New York: A Touchstone Book published by Simon & Schuster, 1978.

Habeeb, Bill, and Dan Harrison. *Inside Mayberry: "The Andy Griffith Show" Handbook.* New York: HarperPerennial, A Division of HarperCollins Publishers, 1994.

Pegg, Robert. *Comical Co-Stars of Television: From Ed Norton to Kramer.* Jefferson, NC and London: McFarland & Company, Inc., Publishers, 2002.

Pope, Peggy. *atta girl: Tales from a Life in the Trenches of Show Business.* Bloomington: iUniverse, Inc., 2011.

Rich, Allan. *A Leap From the Method: An Organic Approach to Acting.* Bloomington, IN: AuthorHouse, 2007.

Magazines

Burke, Tom. "Jack Soo of *Barney Miller*." *TV Guide*, July 16, 1977, pp. 22–26.

Carroll, Margaret. "'Barney Miller': a caring for character." *Chicago Tribune TV Week*, May 4–10, 1980, p. 7.

Hano, Arnold. "*Barney Miller*'s Hal Linden." *TV Guide*, July 19, 1975, pp. 22–26.

"Jack Soo of 'Valentine's Day.'" *TV Guide*, March 27, 1965, pp. 10–12.

Knoedelseder, William K., Jr. "James Gregory of *Barney Miller*." *TV Guide*, October 25, 1980, pp. 27–30.

Pesta, Ben. "Ron Carey of *Barney Miller*." *TV Guide*, May 23, 1981, pp. 21–24.
Russell, Dick. "Steve Landesberg of *Barney Miller*." *TV Guide*, November 26, 1977, pp. 29–32.
———. "Why Is *Barney Miller* Successful?" *TV Guide*, July 7, 1979, pp. 18–21.
Torgerson, Ellen. "Ron Glass of *Barney Miller*." *TV Guide*, September 23, 1978, pp. 36–38.
Whitney, Dwight. "Abe Vigoda of *Barney Miller*." *TV Guide*, February 7, 1976, pp. 22–26.
Windeler, Robert. "Over the Tube: For 19 Years, Linda Lavin Took It In Showbiz; Now As 'Alice,' She's Dishing It Out." *People Weekly*, April 24, 1978, pp. 84–89.
Yuknes, Lt. John J. "A Real Life Barney Miller." *TV Guide*, March 21, 1981, pp. 41–44.

Interviews

Alberti, Shirley. Telephone interview. January 28, 2019.
Arnold, Dannel. Telephone interview. October 12, 2016.
Arnold, David. Telephone interview. October 3, 2016.
Arnold, Donna. Telephone interview. October 6, 2016.
Azzara, Candice. Telephone interview. October 15, 2012.
Barrie, Barbara. Telephone interview. June 11, 2020.
Beavers, Susan. Telephone interview. August 23, 2020.
Bilson, Bruce. Telephone interview. April 6, 2017.
Burstein, Mike. Telephone interview. December 10, 2019.
Canova, Diana. Telephone interview. July 26, 2016.
Carey, Sharon. Telephone interview. February 6, 2017.
Clark, Oliver. Telephone interview. February 7, 2019.
Clennon, David. Telephone interview. April 3, 2017.
Cromwell, James. Telephone interview. October 12, 2016.
DeSoto, Rosanna. Telephone interview. October 16, 2020.
Druxman, Michael. Telephone interview. October 5, 2020.
Dungan, Frank. Telephone interview. April 20, 2020.
Elbling, Peter. Telephone interview. July 20, 2016.
Elias, Alix. Telephone interview. April 3, 2018.
Friedman, Ron. Telephone interview. March 5, 2020.
Fuchs, Carol Vigoda. Telephone interview. September 26, 2020.
Gable, June. Telephone interview. August 4, 2016.

Gail, Max. Telephone interviews. July 8, 15, August 3, September 14, 2016., and January 23, April 13, 2020.
Gorman, Mari. Telephone interview. August 15, 2016.
Hall, Richard. Telephone interview. October 9, 2020.
Helberg, Harriet. Telephone interview. March 22, 2019.
Henteloff, Alex. Telephone interview. July 30, 2020.
Kirby, John. Telephone interviews. June 22, July 20, 2020.
Kogan, Milt. Telephone interview. January 17, 2017.
Krauss, Perry. Telephone interview. January 4, 2017.
Landesberg, E. B. and Nancy. Telephone interview. April 24, 2020.
Lieber, Paul. Telephone interview. April 25, 2017.
Linden, Hal. Telephone interviews. August 16 and 22, 2016.
Manse, Peter Manera. Telephone interview. April 23, 2020.
Mark, Geoffrey. Telephone interview. August 11, 2020.
Martinez, A. Telephone interview. August 12, 2020.
Miles, Joanna. Telephone interview. April 11, 2018.
Miller, Allan. Telephone interview. August 10, 2016.
Murtaugh, James. Telephone interview. March 19, 2018.
Natali, Dino. Telephone interviews. April 14, August 10, 2020
O'Hara, Jenny. Telephone interview. January 25, 2017.
Openden, Lori. Telephone interview. June 22, 2020.
Pankin, Stuart. Telephone interview. March 28, 2018.
Reeder, Tom. Telephone interview. September 22, 2016.
Regalbuto, Joe. Telephone interview. February 14, 2017.
Roby, Lavelle. Telephone interview. August 10, 2016.
Sheehan, Tony. Telephone interviews. November 20, 2017, and April 5, 2020.
Stein, Jeff. Telephone interview. April 22, 2020.
Stewart, Ray. Telephone interview. December 13, 2016.
Zellman, Shelley. Telephone interview. September 19, 2016.

About the Author

Otto Bruno Jr. has loved film, television, music, and baseball for as long as his memory serves. As the youngest of four children, his siblings have reminded him for over half a century that he was able to get away with more than they ever did but the only special privilege he ever really cared about was staying up late to watch more television.

Losing his father at an early age, the comfort, company, and inspiration of film and TV grew in importance. When he was told he could study Film and Television at college, he assumed it would be a dream come true. It was not. Ithaca College was and is a great school for film production, but Bruno was mechanically and technologically inept. He would have been better served majoring in film history and criticism because that's where his true interests were. As a result, he has spent the last forty years doing that on his own, one book, one documentary, and one interview at a time.

In the last twenty years, his energies have been directed toward writing and teaching about the pop culture he loves. He has also been a producer and host of various radio programs on the publicly supported Jazz 90.1 FM radio in Rochester, New York, since 2000. He has been a contributing writer of reviews and monthly profiles on Italian American film, television, music, and baseball stars for *Fra Noi* in Chicago, Illinois for over twenty years.

He's been happily married for over thirty years and he and his wife have produced three wonderful humans.

Index

Numbers in **bold** indicate photographs

79 Park Avenue 56

A.E.S. Hudson Street 17, 55, 66, 90, 92, 126, 131, **168**, **169**, **170**, 266, 279, 296, 302
Adelman, Sybil 102, 209
Adventures of Dudley Do-Right, The 89
"Agent Orange" 6, 83, 134, 153, 469-471
Alberti, Shirley 21, 27, 86, 276
Albrecht, Howard 85, 218
Alice 116, 125, 132, 212-213, 218, 355
All in the Family 5, 7, 59, 117, 124, 143, 145, 216, 240, 244, 247, 258, 323, 324, 388, 504, 520
Andy Griffith Show, The 3-4, 7, 9-10, 84, 107, 250, 324, 359, 376
"Andy on Trial" 10
Ann in Blue 16
Arnold, Dannel 12, 18, 20, 26, 29, 37, 38, 54, 412
Arnold, Danny ix, x-xi, 3, 4, 5, 6, 7, 8, 11-18, 19-23, 26-39, 42, 44, 48, 52, 53-54, 55, 56-57, 58-60, 64, 66, 68, 71, 75, 76-77, 79, 81, 82, 84-87, 88-89, 90-93, 94-95, 96-97, 98, 100, 101-102, 104, 110, 111, 112, 113, 115, 117, 118, 119, 123, 125, 126, 131, 133, 135, 137, 139, 140, 141, 142, 146, 150, 152-153, **186**, **193**, **194**, **195**, **196**, **197**, **200**, 201, 202, 203, 204, 205, 206, 207, 209, 210-211, 212, 214, 216, 218, 219, 221, 223, 225, 227, 229, 230, 231, 232, 233, 234, 236, 238, 242, 244, 246, 250, 251, 252, 253, 254, 256, 258, 259, 260, 261, 262, 263, 264, 266, 270, 274, 276, 277, 278, 279, 281, 282, 283, 284, 286, 288, 293, 294, 295, 296, 298, 299, 300, 302, 306, 307, 309, 314, 318, 319, 320, 321-322, 323, 324, 326, 327, 330, 331, 332, 333, 336, 338, 339, 345, 359, 365, 368, 369, 371, 378, 384, 388-389, 396, 399, 401-402, 403, 412, 413, 415, 434, 439, 455, 460, 489, 502, 504, 505, 507, 518, 526, 528, 532, 539, 544, 547, 549, 552, 553, 555, 557
Arnold, David 11-12, 13, 15, 18, 20, 31, 34, 37, 38, 412
Arnold, Donna 11, 14, 18, 20, 31, 37-38, 71, 532
Arsenic and Old Lace 57, 246

"Arsonist, The" 93, 145, 240-242
Asher, William 15
Azzara, Candice 120-121, 234, 235, 288, 289, 451

Baer, Richard 85, 214
Bari, Len **170**
Barrie, Barbara 76-77, 101, 117, 149, 151, **158**, 202, 227, 233, 359, 360, 391
Barry, J. J. **168**, 229, 342, 343, 458, 479, 480-481, 491, 524, 524, 549
Bartold, Norman **168**, 334, 336, 416, 454, 479, 480, 536, 538
Beavers, Susan 28, 36, 55, 57, 253
Beckman, Henry 148, 225, 226
Bedell, Sally 19-20, 21
Belack, Doris 55, 254, 256
Bell, Joseph N. 14
Bells Are Ringing 42, 43
Bernhardi, Lee 40, 244, 256, 264, 266, 291, 320, 348
Bewitched xi, 14-15, 40, 85, 242, 375
Bilson, Bruce 33, 39, 40, 262, 298, 302, 307, 311, 313, 508, 511
"Bird, The" **177**, 428-430
Birney, David 122
Bishop, Joey 63, 270
"Blizzard" **186**, 336-338
Bridges, Todd **170**, 227-228
Brock, Stanley 140-141, 251, 252, 269-270, 326, 358, 397, 438, 487, 517, 549
Brooks, Mel 3, 75, 139, 237, 250, 283, 346, 405
"Brother, The" 120, 421-423
"Burial" **172**, 332-334, 496
Burns, Allan 90

Caddy, The 13, 299
Caesar, Sid 3
Caesar's Hour 3

Calfa, Don 141, **164**, 320, 321-322, 334, 335-336, 361, 362, 408, 430, 431, 498, 499-500, 517
Campus Cops 98
Canova, Diana 71, 121-122, **165**, 335, 349, 427, 428
Car 54, Where Are You? 3-4, 7, 10, 265, 297, 357
Carelly, Jayne Soo 62
Carey, Ron 17, 69, 70, 72, 74-76, 81, 139, **162**, **183**, **188**, **198**, 270, 279, 280, 286, 287, 289, 304, 307, 310, 315, 322, 324, 329, 330, 343, 350, 355, 356, 359, 363, 365-366, 367, 376, 380, 387, 391, 393, 394, 397, 406, 408, 409, 415, 418, 420, 421, 426, 430, 432, 438, 440, 442, 444, 449, 451, 453, 454, 458, 461, 466, 467, 468, 473, 475, 477, 481, 483, 487, 488, 491, 492, 495, 496, 498, 500, 502, 505, 509, 511, 516, 526, 528, 529, 534, 536, 538, 540, 549
Carey, Sharon 74, 76
Carsey, Marcy 30
Cassisi, John 79, **170**, 296, 320
Charles, Lewis **197**, 336, 337, 382
"Child Stealers, The" **163**, 444-446
Clark, Oliver 122-123, 234, 298, 361, 362, 437, 492, 493, 449
Claster, Bob 12-13, 14, 16, 17, 22, 32, 35
Clennon, David 123-124, 313, 314, 318, 319, 408, 454, 517
Coburn, James 18
Colleary, Bob **191**, 373, 382, 418
Comedy Company, The 56
Corey, Jeff 110, 115, 380, 381, 430, 431-432
"Courtesans, The" 25, 30, 209-212, 372, 487, 542
Cromwell, James 36, 124-125, 320, 426, 502, 503, 513, 514

Crosby, Bing 62, 306, 442
Cutell, Lou 120, 125-126, **186**, 336, 338, 519

Dalton, Abby 147, 151
Dalton, Wally 87, 100, 379, 380, 387, 391, 403, 406, 421
Darin, Bobby 71
Davis, Jerry 85, 209
Dean Martin Presents: The Bobby Darin Amusement Company 71
Dean Martin Roast 56
DeLeon, Jack 136, 141-142, **163**, 203, 221, 244, 284, 285, 286, 318, 444
Denoff, Sam 15, 74, 101, 139, 216, 558
DeSoto, Rosanna 126, 131, 209, 355, 426, 427
Detective School 68, 425-426
Detective Story 23-26, 475
Dibie, George Spiro 51, 152, 258, 276
"Dietrich's Arrest" **178**, 451-454
DiMaggio, Joe 62
"Discovery" 96, 244-246, 534
"Doomsday" 71, 229-231, 255
Druxman, Michael 56-58
Dullaghan, John 142-143, 262-263, 317, 335, 359, 360-361, 407, 440, 441, 442, 488, 489, 491, 550
Dungan, Frank 27, 29, 30, 31, 69, 87-89, 90, 92, 93, 95, 97-98, 99, 105-106, 114, 152-153, **192**, 235, 404, 415, 420, 423, 426, 428, 430, 432, 436, 438, 440, 442, 444, 446, 451, 452, 454, 458, 460, 461, 465, 471, 473, 477, 479, 481, 484, 487, 488, 491, 500, 502, 504, 506, 516, 526, 528, 536, 543, 547, 549, 555, 557

Einstein, Albert 3
Eisner, Michael 8
"Election, The" **161**, 291-293

Elliott, Jack 151
Even This I Get to Experience 91
"Experience" 127, 203-204, 205, 232

Fantastiks, The 45
Farina, Dennis 103, 106
"Fear of Flying" 94, 266-269
Ferguson, Allyn 151
"Fire 77" 139, 311-313
Firefly 60
Fish 17, 40, 53, 54, 55-57, 78, 90, **170**, 227-228, 255, 256, 282, 298, 325
Fish & Bernice 55
Flicker, Theodore J. 7, 16-17, 18-22, 32, 37, 39, 84, 88, 89, 97, 201, 202, 279, 504
Flippen, Ruth Brooks 101
Flower Drum Song, The 62, 63-64, 306, 356, 396-397
Fortune Cookie, The 40, 127
Foy III, Eddie 31
Frank, Charles **161**, 271, 273
French Connection, The 16, 72, 103, 104, 106
Frey, Leonard **166**, 223, 224, 442, 443
Friedman, Ron 28, 85-86, 89, 97, 204, 222

Gable, June 100, 101, 112-113, 114, 298, 299, 307
Gail, Max ix, 11, 17, 20, 21, 27, 32, 39, 46-50, 51, 54, 60, 70, 72, 79, 106, 111-112, 117, 129, 140, 142, 143, 144, 146, 150, 152, **157**, **180**, **183**, **186**, **187**, **190**, **198**, **199**, 202, 203, 204, 206, 209, 212, 214, 218, 221, 223, 225, 227, 229, 231, 234, 236, 238, 239, 240, 242, 244, 246, 251, 254, 257, 259, 262, 264, 266, 268, 269, 271, 274, 277, 278, 281, 282, 284, 286, 288, 290, 291, 293, 296, 300, 302, 304, 307, 308, 310,

311, 313, 315, 317, 318, 320, 322, 324, 326, 327, 329, 331, 332, 334, 336, 338, 340, 342, 344, 346, 348, 350, 352, 355, 356, 358, 359, 361, 363, 365, 367, 369, 371, 372, 373, 375, 376, 379, 380, 382, 384, 387, 391, 393, 393, 394, 397, 399, 402, 403, 404, 406, 408, 409, 411, 414, 415, 418, 420, 421, 423, 426, 428, 430, 432, 434, 436, 438, 440, 442, 444, 447, 449, 451, 452, 454, 456, 458, 461, 463, 466, 467, 469, 470, 471, 473, 475, 477, 481, 483, 484, 487, 488, 491, 492, 495, 496, 498, 500, 502, 505, 507, 509, 511, 515, 516, 519, 521, 523, 526, 528, 529, 531, 534, 536, 538, 540, 542, 543, 547, 549, 555

Garner, Martin **177**, 274, 275, 310, 311, 428, 502-503, 507

Garrett, Lila 85, 101, 206

Gelbart, Larry 92-93

Gierasch, Stefan 133, 300, 301-302, 369, 371, 434, 505, 506

Gilbert, Joanne 14

Glanzman, Lieutenant Paul 104, 371

Glass, Ron 27, 49, 58-61, 72, 135, **157**, **183**, **186**, **194**, **198**, 202, 204, 209, 221, 223, 225, 227, 229, 231, 234, 236, 238, 240, 244, 246, 249, 251, 253-254, 259, 262, 264, 266, 269, 271, 274, 278, 282, 284, 286, 288, 291, 293, 296, 298, 302, 304, 307, 308, 310, 311, 313, 315, 317, 318, 320, 322, 324, 326, 327, 329, 331, 332, 334, 336, 338, 340, 342, 344, 346, 348, 350, 352, 355, 356, 358, 359, 361, 363, 365, 367, 369, 371, 373, 375, 376, 379, 380, 382, 384, 387, 388, 391, 393, 394, 397, 399, 403, 404, 406, 408, 409, 411, 415, 418, 420, 421, 423, 426, 428, 430,

432, 434, 436, 438, 440, 442, 444, 447, 449, 451, 452, 454, 456, 458, 461, 466, 467, 469, 471, 473, 475, 476, 477, 479, 481, 483, 484, 487, 488, 491, 492, 495, 496, 498, 500, 502, 505, 507, 509, 511, 513, 515, 516, 519, 521, 523, 526, 528, 529, 531, 534, 536, 538, 540, 542, 545, 547, 549

Godfather, The 16, 51, 52

"Goodbye, Mr. Fish" 56, 95, 140, 256, 325, 326-329

Gordon, Barry **170**, 409, 410, 536, 537, 538

Gordon, Steve 85, 203, 204

Gorman, Mari 38, 101, 113-114, 329, 330-331, 358-359, 361, 363, 468, 517, 518, 550

"Graft" 8, 101, 206-209

"Graveyard Shift" 119-120, 411-413

Gregory, James 60, 67-69, 80, **156**, **162**, **183**, **198**, 227, 231, 257, 259, 277, 282, 284, 285, 286, 291, 302, 310, 311, 322, 324, 325, 327, 329, 348, 355, 356, 369, 371, 380, 389, 404, 411, 414, 421, 423, 425-426, 441-442, 447, 453, 461, 463, 479, 481, 492, 496, 498, 507, 513, 515, 519, 521, 531, 547, 550

Grosso, Sonny 72, 106

Haid, Charles 48, 147, 150-151

"Hair" 78, 225-227, 256, 273

Hano, Arnold 43

"Happy New Year" 101, 253, 262-264

Hayward, Chris 85, 86-87, 89-90, 93, 96, 204, 206, 209, 214, 216, 218, 221, 223, 225, 227, 229, 231, 234, 236, 238, 242, 244, 246, 251, 254, 256, 259, 262, 264, 274, 277, 278, 282, 288, 296, 298, 307, 361, 539

Helberg, Harriet 28, 86, 94, 111, 402

Henry, Buck 18
Henteloff, Alex 127, **186**, **195**, 203, 231, 232, 270, 298, 336, 337, 430, 431, 487, 540
Hepburn, Katharine 129-130
Hiken, Nat 10, 91, 297
Holliday, Judy 43
Hoover, J. Edgar 18

I Love Lucy 107, 549
"Identity" **164**, **165**, **166**, 408-409
"Inquisition" **164**, 415-417

Joe Bash 17, 37, 90, 118, 126, 333, 539
"Judge, The" **160**, 432-434, 555
Jurasik, Peter **194**, 346, 416
Just for Laughs 16, 22

Kajiwara, Sachi 62
Kaye, Sammy 43
Kibbee, Roland 85, 90-92, 97, 110, 214, 305, 310, 318, 511
"Kidnapping" 137, 144, 309, 369-373
King, Kip **166**, **190**, 340, 408
Kingsley, Sidney 23
Kirby, Bruce 127-128, 356, 357, 373, 420, 421
Kogan, Milt 114-115, 203, 214, 215, 221, 234, 235, 236, 287
Krauss, Perry 21, 28
Kruschen, Jack **172**, 332, 333, 434, 435, 521, 523
Kushnick, Helen 99

Landesberg, Elizabeth 60, 72, 73
Landesberg, Nancy Ross 29, 32, 60, 70, 71-72, 73
Landesberg, Steve 17, 29, 32, 55, 60, 62, 69-73, 75, 80-81, 98, 99, 106, **160**, **175**, **181**, **183**, **190**, **198**, 229, 231, 254, 255, 256, 270, 281-282, 288, 291, 300, 310, 311, 317, 318, 322, 324, 326, 327, 329, 330, 331, 332, 334, 336, 338, 340, 342, 344, 346, 348, 350, 352, 355, 356, 358, 361, 363, 364, 365, 367, 369, 371, 373, 375, 376, 379, 380, 382, 384, 387, 389, 391, 393, 394, 397, 399, 403, 404, 406, 408, 409, 411, 414, 415, 418, 419, 420, 421, 423, 426, 428, 428, 430, 432, 434, 436, 438, 440, 442, 444, 447, 449, 451, 452, 454, 456, 458, 461, 463, 463, 466, 467, 468, 469, 471, 473, 475, 477, 479, 481, 483, 484, 487, 488, 491, 492, 495, 496, 500, 502, 505, 507, 509, 511, 513, 515, 516, 519, 521, 523, 526, 528, 529, 531, 534, 536, 538, 540, 542, 545, 547, 549
Larroquette, John 96
Lavin, Linda 101, 112, 114, 115-116, **161**, 213, 216, 217-218, 238, 239, 242, 269, 271, 299
Lawless Years, The 68, 515
Lear, Norman 7, 13, 59, 91, 114, 124, 145, 210, 262, 273, 504
Leeds, Howard 85, 223
Leeds, Phil 110, 143-144, 251, 252, 320, 321, 335, 344, 393, 394, 418, 420, 466-467, 513, 514
Lembeck, Michael 112, 225-226, 273
Leonard, Sheldon xi, 15
Levin, David 60
Levine, Emily 55, 70, 254, 255-256
Levine, Ken 85, 305
Lewis, Jerry 13, 36, 207, 252, 299
"Life and Times of Barney Miller, The" 7-8, 16-17, 19, 20, 21, 23, 34, 44, 147-148, 149, 151, 207, 226, 247
Linden, Hal viii, 7, 11, 13, 17, 19, 20-21, 23, 27, 29, 30, 31, 32, 39, 42-46, 49, 52, 54, 60, 62, 79, 81, 82, 106, 118, 128, 141, 147, 150, 151, 152, **155**, **157**, **183**, **186**, **189**,

193, **198**, **199**, 202, 203, 204, 206, 210-211, 212, 214, 215, 216, 218, 221, 223, 225, 227, 229, 231, 234, 236, 238, 240, 242, 244, 246, 249, 251, 254, 257, 259, 260, 261, 262, 264, 265, 266, 268, 269, 271, 274, 275-276, 277, 278, 281, 282, 284, 286, 288, 291, 293, 295, 296, 298, 300, 302, 304, 306, 307, 308, 310, 311, 313, 315, 317, 318, 320, 322, 324, 326, 327, 329, 331, 332, 334, 336, 338, 340, 342, 344, 346, 348, 350, 352, 353, 355, 356, 358, 359, 361, 363, 365, 367, 369, 371, 372, 373, 375, 376, 379, 380, 382, 384, 387, 388-389, 391, 393, 394, 397, 399, 403, 404, 406, 408, 409, 411, 413-415, 418, 420, 421, 423, 426, 428, 430, 432, 434, 436, 438, 440, 442, 444, 447, 449, 451, 452, 454, 455, 456, 458, 461, 463, 466, 467, 469, 471, 473, 475, 477, 479, 481, 482, 483, 484, 487, 488, 491, 492, 495, 496, 498, 500, 502, 505, 507, 509, 511, 513, 515, 516, 518, 519, 521, 523, 526, 528, 529, 531, 534, 536, 538, 540, 542, 545, 547, 549, 555

M*A*S*H 5, 7, 64, 85, 92, 123, 124, 127, 137, 139, 219, 247, 267, 289, 305, 324, 346, 461, 462
Maharis, George **156**
Manchurian Candidate, The 68, **156**
Manza, Ralph 131, 144, 259, 260, 308-309, 369, 371, 439, 479, 550
March, Alex 40, 318, 359, 365, 366
Mark, Geoffrey 72
Marshall, Garry 114, 540
Martinez, A 128-129, 434, 492, 493
Mary Tyler Moore Show, The 7, 15, 77, 92, 216, 324, 520, 553

"Massage Parlor" 138, **161**, 271-274, 295
Mauldin, Nat 87, 483, 492, 498, 505, 508, 513, 519, 520, 534, 542
Meyer, Russ 135
Miles, Joanna 129-130, **163**, 444, 445
Miller, Allan 130-131, **168**, 406, 407, 453, 484, 485, 511
Miller, Denise 79, **170**, 282, 283, 296, 320
Miller, Detective Lucas 105
Moffet, Jordan 87, 475, 492, 514, 516, 521, 531, 542
"Mole, The" 75, 278-281, 287, 343
Monk 156
Monster and the Ape, The 12
Montgomery, Elizabeth 14, 15
"Movie" **168**, **185**, 445, 477-481
Mr. Belvedere 41, 69, 93, 98, 114
Mr. Inside/Mr. Outside 44, **155**
"Ms. Cop" 116, 216-218, 313
Munsters, The 90
Murdock, George 26, 112, 116-117, **185**, 269, 270, 320, 321, 338, 379, 394, 416, 451, 453, 477, 526, 528, 550
Murtaugh, James 131-132, 495, 513, 547
My Mother the Car 90, 386
My World and Welcome to It xi, 15-16, 32, 207, 216, 230

Natali, Dino 54, 117-118, **164**, **185**, 367, 393, 415, 444, 477
Natoli, Sarah **170**
Nielsen, Judith Anne 102, 382, 393, 428, 449
Night Court 33, 95-96, 117, 123, 127, 134, 138, 141, 143, 266, 323, 367, 381, 405
Nightcap 2-3
NYPD Blue 105, 132

O'Hara, Jenny 132-133, 373, 437, 468
O'Neill, Dick 112, 118-119, 206, 236
O'Neill, Jackie 112, 118-119
Odd Couple, The 5, 7, 40, 60, 64, 143, 205, 213, 219, 244, 248, 305, 324, 510
On a Clear Day You Can See Forever 44
On the Road & Other Places 73
One Flew Over the Cuckoo's Nest 47, 48, 392
Openden, Lori 32, 39, 53, 420
Oppenheimer, Robert 3

Pankin, Stuart 133-134, 389, 390, 449
Papillon 65, 95
Parks, Darlene **171**, 399, 401, 402
Paul Sand in Friends and Lovers 71
Pegg, Robert 67, 68
"People's Court, The" **162**, 438-440
Persky, Bill 15, 29, 31-32, 74, 101, 216
"Photographer, The" **167, 169**, 417-420
Pincus, Irv 14
Pitlik, Noam 21, 39, 40-41, 88, 119, 203, 204, 206, 209, 216, 218, 221, 223, 227, 229, 231, 234, 236, 238, 240, 242, 246, 249, 251, 254, 259, 269, 274, 281, 282, 286, 288, 293, 300, 304, 308, 310, 313, 315, 316, 344, 346, 350, 352, 355, 356, 363, 369, 371, 373, 374, 376, 380, 382, 384, 387, 389, 391, 393, 394, 397, 399, 401, 403, 406, 408, 411, 413, 415, 418, 420, 421, 423, 426, 428, 430, 432, 434, 436, 438, 440, 442, 444, 446, 449, 451, 452, 454, 456, 458, 461, 463, 466, 467, 469, 471, 473, 475, 477, 479, 481, 483, 484, 488, 491, 492, 495, 496, 498, 500, 502
Pope, Peggy 38-39, 322, 324, 325, 380, 381, 432, 433, 495, 534, 555

"Possession" 97, 293, 511-512
Powell, Homer 39, 487, 519
President's Analyst, The 18, 279
Presley, Elvis 18, 490
"Protection" 144, 259-262, 309

"Quarantine" 119, 284-288

"Radical, The" 119, 389-391
"Ramon" 149-151, **154**, 202-203, 226, 230, 374
Real McCoys, The xi, 14, 252
Rebel in Town 13
Reeder, Tom 19, 31, 57, 85, 86-87, 96-97, 104, 110, **191**, 244, 259, 264, 269, 291, 304, 305, 313, 338, 344, 345, 355, 356, 408, 511
Regalbuto, Joe 134-135, 469, 470, 509, 510
Reilly, Charles Nelson 122, 213
Reiner, Carl 3, 4, 40, 121, 139, 216
Rich, John 20, 212, 214
Ritz, The 112, 113, 299
Robertson, Stu 86
Roby, Lavelle 135-136, 209, 329
Rocky and His Friends 89
Ross, Jerry 85, 225, 288, 315
Rothschilds, The 42, 44, 82
Ruditsky, Barney 68

Sanford and Son 7, 40, 59, 65, 142, 145, 313
Scheiner, Elliot 122
"Search, The" **184**, 373-374
Segal, Andy 8
Serpico 26, 104, 225, 273, 330, 396, 468
Seven-Ups, The 103, 104, 106
Shavelson, Mel xi, 15, 16, 221
Sheehan, Tony 12, 17, 19, 20, 21, 27, 28, 29, 30, 31, 32, 33, 40-41, 45, 51, 79, 85-88, 89, 91-94, 95, 97, 98,

101, 114, 137, 139, **193**, 214, 240, 249, 251, 256, 271, 274, 276, 277, 284, 286, 288, 293, 300, 302, 308, 311, 313, 315, 318, 320, 324, 331, 334, 336, 342, 346, 350, 355, 358, 359, 365, 369, 371, 373, 376, 382, 384, 389, 391, 397, 399, 401, 406, 411, 412, 415, 432, 440, 442, 446, 451, 452, 454, 456, 458, 460, 465, 467, 469, 481, 484, 487, 488, 492, 504, 529, 540, 545, 549, 555, 557
Sierra, Gregory 55, 65-66, 79, 92, 101, 112, 131, **157**, **169**, 202, 203, 204, 206, 209, 214, 216, 218, 221, 223, 225, 227, 229, 231, 234, 236, 238, 240, 242, 244, 246, 249, 251, 254, 257, 259, 262, 264, 266, 269, 271, 274, 277, 278, 279, 299
"Sighting, The" 28, 365-366
Sister Kate 93-94, 98
"Slave, The" 120, **167**, 423-426, 441
Smith, Queenie **168**, 242, 243-244, 293
"Snow Job" 54, 204-206, 240, 300
Soap 66, 71, 117, 120, 121, 122, 127, 131, 139, 142, 144, 243, 285, 289, 312, 323, 335, 349, 417, 419, 428, 453
"Social Worker, The" **158**, 231-234, 498
Somack, Jack 144-145, **165**, 213, 240, 241, 259, 326, 408, 461, 463
Somers, Brett **161**, 212, 213, 291
Soo, Jack 13, 17, 27, 61-64, 79, 101, 150, **156**, **157**, **179**, **186**, **190**, **197**, **198**, 202, 203, 204, 206, 209, 214, 216, 221, 223, 225, 227, 229, 234, 244, 246, 249, 251, 254, 257, 259, 262, 266, 269, 271, 274, 277, 278, 282, 284, 286, 288, 290, 291, 293, 294, 296, 297, 298, 300, 304, 306, 307, 308, 310, 311, 313, 315, 317,

318, 320, 322, 324, 327, 329, 330, 331, 332, 334, 336, 338, 340, 342, 344, 346, 348, 350, 352, 355, 356, 358, 361, 368-369, 371, 372-373, 375, 376, 379, 382, 384, 387, 397, 413-415, 461
Spinout 18
"Stakeout, The" 21, 78, 212-214, 256
Stanley, Florence 55, 57, 77-78, **170**, 212, 225, 256, 296, 313, 320, 327, 329
Stein, Jeff 27, 29, 69, 87-88, 89, 91, 93, 94, 95-96, 98, 99, 114, **192**, 235, 404, 406, 415, 420, 423, 426, 428, 430, 432, 436, 438, 440, 442, 444, 446, 451, 452, 454, 456, 458, 460, 461, 463, 465, 471, 473, 477, 479, 481, 484, 487, 488, 491, 496, 500, 502, 504, 506, 516, 526, 528, 532, 536, 543, 547, 549, 555, 557
Steinberg, Norman 16
Sterling, Philip 145-146, 244, 367, 397, 398, 432, 433, 515, 545, 546, 547
Stewart, Ray 39, 131, 136-137, 142, **163**, 244, 284, 285, 286, 444-445, 550
"Strip Joint" **165**, 426-428
Sumant **167**, 423, 424
Susman, Todd 137, 369, 370, 371, 372, 426, 427, 541
Suva, Jim 114-115
Swift, David 39, 329, 340, 342

Takei, George 63
Tardan, Dennis 8
Tennessee Ernie Ford Show, The 14, 85, 91
That Girl xi, 15, 74, 85, 101, 142, 207, 216, 244, 360, 375, 378
Thomas, Marlo 15, 378
Thurber, James 15-16, 230

Tigar, Ken 138, **169**, **187**, **198**, 271, 272, 293, 294, 295, 348, 349, 418, 419, 481, 511, 512
"Toys" **184**, 391-393
Troublemaker, The 18
Tucci, Michael **162**, 304, 379, 439, 524

"Uniform Days" **176**, 449-450

"Vanished" **166**, 440-444, 489
Vigoda, Abe 17, 27-28, 44, 51-58, 79, 101, 106, 118, 147, **157**, **170**, 202, 203, 204, 206, 209, 212, 214, 216, 218, 221, 223, 225, 227, 229, 231, 234, 235, 236, 238, 240, 242, 244-245, 246, 249, 251, 254, 257, 259, 262, 264, 265-266, 269, 271, 274, 279, 282, 284, 286, 290, 293, 296, 298, 300, 302, 304, 307, 308, 310, 311, 313, 315, 320, 321, 325, 327, 328, 328-329, 332, 402, 455, 495, 496, 519
Vinciguerra, Thomas 105
Viscuso, Sal 75, 120, 137, 139-140, **167**, **169**, 288, 289, 311, 312, 335, 418, 419, 536, 537, 538

Wackiest Ship in the Army, The xi, 13, 14-15, 216, 299
Walden, Robert 47-48
Walker, Jimmie 70, 73, 97, 99, 261-262
Wambaugh, Joseph 105, 223, 467, 551

War Between Men and Women, The 14, 16, 221
Ward, Jay 89-90
Warden, Jack 15
Weege, Reinhold 27, 28, 32, 33, 86, 87, 92, 93, 94-96, 98, 99, 117, 141, **193**, 266, 278, 288, 293, 296, 298, 300, 302, 305, 307, 310, 313, 316, 318, 322, 324, 326, 327, 338, 340, 344, 345, 348, 356, 361, 365, 366, 367, 369, 371, 374, 380, 387, 393, 394, 403, 404, 415
Weeks, Christopher *see* DeLeon, Jack
Weinstein, Sol 85, 218
"Werewolf, The" 95, 138, **187**, 244, 272, 282, 293-296, 375, 418
Werner, Tom 30
Westheimer, Dr. Ruth 72
Wilson, Demond 60
Windom, William 15, 229, 230-231, 488, 489, 491
"Wojo's Girl" **171**, 399-402, 403, 465

Yarmy, Dick 72
"You Dirty Rat" 150, 246-248
You Don't Know Jack: The Jack Soo Story 62, 63
Your Show of Shows 3
Yuknes, Lt. John J. 104

Zellman, Shelley 86, 87, 100, 102, 379, 380, 387, 391, 403, 406, 421

www.ingramcontent.com/pod-product-compliance
Lightning Source LLC
Chambersburg PA
CBHW080719300426
44114CB00019B/2423